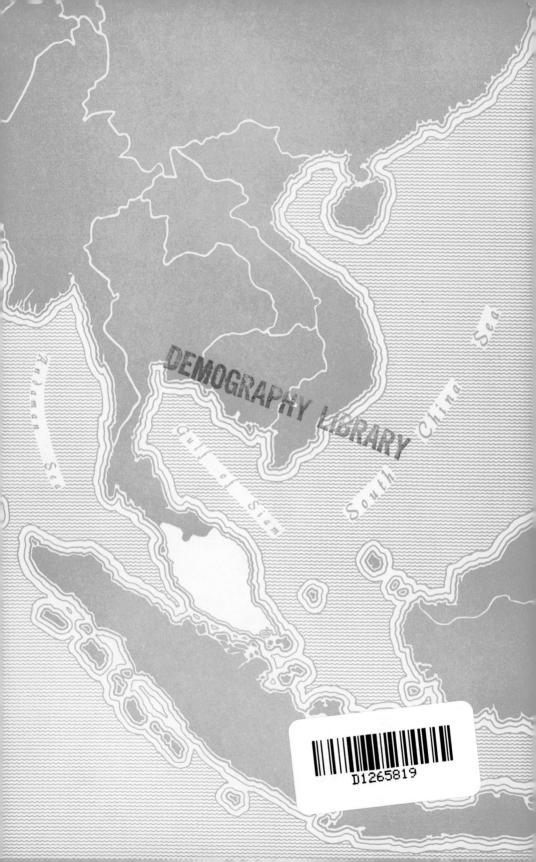

DEMOGRAPHY LIBRARY

Andaman Sea

South China Sea

Gulf of Siam

D1265819

THE ECONOMIC DEVELOPMENT OF *Malaya*

*Report of a Mission organized by the
International Bank for Reconstruction and Development
at the request of The Governments of
the Federation of Malaya, the Crown Colony
of Singapore and the United Kingdom*

THE ECONOMIC DEVELOPMENT

OF MALAYA

PUBLISHED FOR The International Bank for Reconstruction and Development
BY The Johns Hopkins Press, Baltimore

© 1955, The Johns Hopkins Press

Distributed in Great Britain by
Geoffrey Cumberlege: Oxford University Press, London

Printed in U. S. A. by the William Byrd Press, Richmond

Library of Congress Catalog Card No. 55–12042

Second Printing, 1960

THE MISSION

Sir Louis Chick, **K.B.E.,** Chief of Mission
    Francantonio Biaggi, Adviser on Power
    John Franklin Booth, Agricultural Economist
        Isidore S. Falk, Adviser on Social Services
    William M. Gilmartin, Economist
    Erich R. Hondelink, Adviser on Transport and Communications
        E. H. Jacoby, Adviser on Land Tenure
        Bruno Lincke, Adviser on Industry
        G. C. Monture, Adviser on Mineral Resources
    Carl Adolph Murray, Adviser on Public Finance
    John F. V. Phillips, Adviser on Agriculture
        Trevor Swan, Economist
        A. M. Thomson, Adviser on Agricultural Marketing

        Ann Friedman, Secretary

This is the report of a mission to Malaya, organized by the International Bank for Reconstruction and Development at the request of the Governments of the Federation of Malaya, the Crown Colony of Singapore and the United Kingdom.

The task of the mission, as agreed upon by the three Governments and the Bank, was to assess the resources available for future development, to consider how these resources might best contribute to the economic and social development of Malaya, and to make recommendations for practical measures to further such development. Since this was a general survey mission, it addressed itself primarily to broad issues of development policy and general lines of priority investment, rather than to details of particular development problems and issues and of individual investment projects.

The mission consisted of thirteen members. Four of the members, specialists in agriculture and related fields, were nominated by the Food and Agriculture Organization of the United Nations. Eight members (including the Chief of Mission, one of the general economists and the advisers on public finance, mineral resources, transport and communications, industry, power and social services) were recruited by the Bank from outside its staff. One member (a general economist) is a regular member of the staff of the Bank.

The mission arrived in Malaya in January 1954 and remained until May. Members traveled widely and conferred extensively with government officials and private individuals in both the Federation and Singapore. The mission then reassembled in Washington to prepare its report. While the report was being written, close contact was maintained by correspondence with the Governments of the Federation and Singapore. As drafts of findings and proposed recommendations concerning the individual sectors of the economy, the various fields of social services, and the prospective availability and allocation of financial resources were completed, they were submitted informally to both governments for comments. Various international agencies were also given an opportunity to comment on the portions of the report relating to their particular fields of interest, and the Executive Directors and management of the Bank were also invited to comment generally on the report. While all comments were given careful consideration, the entire report and the recommendations it contains are to be regarded as the sole responsibility of the mission. In transmitting the report to the High Commissioner for the Federation of Malaya and to the Governor of the Crown Colony of Singapore in June 1955, the President of the Bank pointed out that the Executive Directors and the management customarily do not review recommendations of missions in detail, and that the report represented the views of the mission rather than positive recommendations of the Bank itself. He added, however, that the Bank believed that the findings and conclusions of the mission deserved most careful consideration and discussion.

The report is in five parts. Part I contains a general introduction to the economy of Malaya and a discussion of the problems and prospects of Malaya's development. It also sets forth the broad outlines of a proposed public development program, discussed in more detail in subsequent parts. Part II deals with sectors of the economy which are themselves productive or closely associated with productive activity. Part III is devoted to the various fields of the social services, including education. Part IV presents the mission's proposed public investment program for 1955–59, based upon its appraisal of the public financial resources which may be expected to be available for development during that period. It also contains the mission's recommendations for certain organizational and institutional measures to facilitate execution of the development program. Part V consists of twelve Technical Reports (on agriculture and forestry, irrigation and drainage and river conservancy, land tenure, fisheries, mining, power, transport and communications, industrial development, education, public health, social welfare and currency and banking), and a Statistical Appendix.

The mission wishes to express its appreciation for the wholehearted cooperation and warm hospitality extended to it by Malayan leaders, government officials and members of the business community. In particular, the mission acknowledges the invaluable assistance of its Liaison Officer, Mr. Richard West, and of the other officials in the Federation and Singapore with whom it was most closely associated, including Mr. T. M. Hart, Director of Commerce and Industry, Singapore, and Mr. A. J. D. C. Loch, Controller, Economic Division of the Treasury, Federation of Malaya. The mission also wishes to thank Ruth Hill Falk for her valuable contribution to the portion of the report relating to education.

CONTENTS

LIST OF TABLES

Part V

MAPS AND FIGURES

Maps

Figures

EXCHANGE RATES

$$1 \text{ Malayan } \$ = 2\text{s. } 4\text{d. sterling}$$
$$= \$0.33 \text{ U.S.}$$
$$1 \text{ £ sterling} = \$8.57 \text{ Malayan}$$
$$1 \text{ U.S. } \$ = \$3.06 \text{ Malayan}$$
$$1 \text{ million Malayan } \$ = \text{£}116{,}667 \text{ sterling}$$
$$= \$326{,}667 \text{ U.S.}$$

All figures in the report given in dollars refer to Malayan dollars unless otherwise expressly stated.

PART **I** *GENERAL*

CHAPTER 1 *INTRODUCTION TO MALAYA*

1 GEOGRAPHY AND CLIMATE[1]

Malaya, comprising the Federation of Malaya and the Colony of Singapore, lies to the south of Thailand in the long narrow peninsula which reaches out southward from the southeastern corner of Asia to near the equator. Singapore Island, at the peninsula's southern tip, is joined to the mainland by a causeway across the Straits of Johore. To the west, across the narrow Straits of Malacca, lies the large island of Sumatra which, together with smaller islands lying within 10 miles of Singapore, form part of the Republic of Indonesia.

The Federation, with an area of approximately 51,000 square miles, is slightly larger than England without Wales, or the State of New York. About one-quarter of its area has an elevation of more than 1,000 feet and rather more than one-sixth is above 1,500 feet. Nearly four-fifths is covered by dense jungle.

Singapore Island, with adjacent islets, has an area of only 225 square miles.

The Federation's coast line extends for over 1,000 miles. Along the west coast, wide plains only slightly above sea level and consisting in many places of mangrove swamps and mud flats extend inland almost to the foot of the mountain ranges. On the east, the coast for the most part is flat, palm-lined beach, offering no natural harbors. Topographically, the northern half of the country is split by a series of low mountain ranges, which have their greatest development in the north central area, where some of the peaks reach an elevation of over 6,000 feet. Southward the mountains diminish in altitude but the characteristic of steep, jungle-covered hillsides rising abruptly from the coastal plains or narrow valleys persists.

The main mountain range runs approximately parallel to and about 50 miles from the west coast and forms a continuous watershed from the Thailand border to Malacca. Most of the rivers to the west side of this

[1] Much of the descriptive material in this Chapter has been included for the benefit of readers unfamiliar with Malaya.

watershed thus have comparatively short courses. Gradients in the upper reaches are very steep, many of the rivers dropping over 4,000 feet in less than 15 miles before emerging into the coastal plain. The easterly flowing rivers are longer and have flatter gradients in their upper reaches. In nearly all parts of the country the drainage assumes a trellis-like pattern, the hill slopes being cut by small transverse streams or gullies.

Malaya's climate is equatorial, its characteristic features being uniform and fairly high temperatures throughout the year, abundant rainfall and high humidity. The seasons are marked by the incidence of rainfall rather than by changes in temperature. Over most of the country, rainfall is heaviest during the months of October to December or January and lightest in February or July. In total it varies substantially from year to year and place to place but averages around 100 inches annually. With the exception of a few spots in the mountain ranges, the east coast has the highest rainfall, with averages of over 120 inches. In other parts of the country, the averages lie between 80 and 120 inches, being somewhat lower in the northwestern and southwestern regions than elsewhere.

II POLITICAL DEVELOPMENT AND MACHINERY OF GOVERNMENT

At the time of the Japanese occupation at the beginning of 1942, the Straits Settlements of Singapore, the island of Penang (with Province Wellesley on the mainland) and Malacca were administered as a Crown Colony, while the nine Malay States were protectorates under treaties made with Great Britain between 1874 and 1914. The treaties provided for the appointment of a British Resident or Adviser in each State whose advice had to be followed except in matters concerning Malay religion and custom. The Governor of the Straits Settlements was High Commissioner for the Malay States. The four central States of Perak, Selangor, Negri Sembilan and Pahang were constituted a federation in 1895, with a largely centralized government: a Federal Council, appointed by the High Commissioner, had most of the legislative power. A measure of decentralization was introduced in 1932 by returning to the States some of the legislative power as well as the control of some departments, but the States remained dependent upon block grants voted by the Federal Council. The other five States (Johore, Trengganu, Kelantan, Kedah and Perlis), while administered with the aid and advice of British officials, remained unfederated, each a separate political entity.

In 1945, after the Japanese occupation, this political and constitutional structure was profoundly altered. The Rulers of the Malay States agreed to a transfer of sovereignty to the British Crown, and a unitary state, the Malayan Union, was created, embracing the former Federated and Unfederated Malay States and the Settlements of Penang and Malacca. Singapore remained outside the Union as a Crown Colony. The Malayan Union's constitution created a common citizenship not restricted to Malays but open to all—Malays, Chinese, Indians and others—who could claim to belong to the country by reason of birth or a specified period of residence.

The new constitution evoked the resentment and hostility of the Malays, who feared that a common citizenship and a unitary form of government would undermine their old political status. The upshot was the revesting in the Rulers of the power and jurisdiction they had enjoyed before the Japanese occupation and the formation, under the protection of Great Britain, of a federation comprising the same territories as the Malayan Union, in which there would be a common federal citizenship for all persons qualified by birth or residence. The Federation came into being on February 1, 1948.

The Agreement establishing the Federation, made between the British Crown and the Rulers of the Malay States, expresses the desire of all parties for progress towards eventual self-government and provides for a Federal Government comprising a High Commissioner, a Federal Executive Council to aid and advise the High Commissioner, and a Federal Legislative Council with a membership of 75. All members of the latter, other than three *ex officio* members and 11 representatives of the State and Settlement Councils, are appointed by the High Commissioner; many are, however, the nominees of organizations representative of special interests, such as labor, mining, agriculture and commerce. The Executive Council includes, as a step towards full ministerial responsibility, unofficial members of the Legislative Council who have responsibility for various Federal subjects and departments. Each State has a State Executive Council to aid and advise the Ruler, and an appointed legislative body styled a Council of State. Each of the two Settlements has a Settlement Council with legislative powers similar to those of the Councils of State.

In addition, the Federation Agreement set up a Conference of Rulers to provide a formal opportunity for discussion and consultation between the

Rulers and the High Commissioner. The Agreement specifically requires the Conference to be consulted on immigration policy and provides that the Conference may, if it wishes, discuss proposals concerning salary scales of the Federal officials and the creation or major reorganization of a Federal department. A standing Committee of the Conference gives the Rulers' assent to legislation passed by the Federal Legislature. Their assent, as well as that of the High Commissioner, is required by the Agreement.

The constitutional division of powers between the Federal Government and the State and Settlement Governments is unlike the division found in federal systems elsewhere, in which federal and regional governments are coordinate and each is independent in its own sphere. Indeed, the preamble to the Agreement proclaims the intention to form a federation "with a strong central government," and accordingly the list of matters with respect to which the Federal Government is empowered to legislate is extremely comprehensive; the area in which the State and Settlement Governments may legislate is very small indeed, though it includes, in the case of the States, the important subjects of the Malay religion and custom. But while virtually the whole of the legislative power—and therefore the policy-making power—is vested in the Federal Government, the Agreement requires that laws made by the Federal Legislature in many of the most important fields of government shall confer the executive authority on the State and Settlement Governments "except insofar as matters of policy common to any two or more of the States and Settlements are involved." In this way it was sought to achieve another of the main objectives of the framers of the Agreement: the maintenance of the individuality of each of the States and Settlements.

We comment later on this compromise between a unitary system and a federal system as it affects economic development.

The other tier of government in the Federation comprises the Municipalities of George Town (Penang), Malacca and Kuala Lumpur and a medley of town councils, town boards, rural boards and local councils. The development of responsible local government has come slowly, and only in the last few years has it received a stimulus. Present policy aims at a structure of municipalities for the largest towns, town councils for the smaller towns and a network of local councils. All will have a majority of elected members; their authority will range from the responsibility of the municipalities for all local government services to the very limited responsibilities of local councils in the less advanced areas. In pursuance of this policy, the wholly nominated town boards are being replaced gradually by town councils, and a large number of local councils have been established. Steps are also being taken to give greater financial autonomy to town councils and town boards.

Singapore has a much simpler political and constitutional structure. Founded in 1819, it was administered first by the East India Company and then by the Government of India until 1867, when it passed to the control of the Colonial Office and, with Penang and Malacca, became the Crown Colony of the Straits Settlements.[2] In 1946 it was constituted as a separate Colony, and Penang and Malacca became part of the Malayan Union. The Order in Council constituting the Colony provides for a Governor, an Executive Council and a Legislative Council. Nine of the Legislative Council's 25 members are elected by the public and three by the Chambers of Commerce. Members of the Legislative Council elect two of their number for appointment to the Executive Council.

Local government functions are discharged in the urban area by a City Council which is for the most part an elective body, and, to a much more limited extent, by the Rural Board in the rural area and adjacent islands.

Both the Federation and the Colony are on the eve of important constitutional changes.[3] In both, the legislatures are to be enlarged and altered in character by popular election of a majority of the membership. In the Federation, the Federal Executive Council will continue to be advisory to the High Commissioner but the appointment of its members (other than the official members and representatives of the State and Settlement Councils) will be made only after consultation with the members of the Legislative Council commanding the major support among the elected members. In Singapore, however, the Executive Council is to give way to a Council of Ministers which, subject to the Governor's reserve powers, will assume full responsibility for policy in all matters except external affairs, internal security and defense. At the outset, the Council is to consist of three official members and six members appointed from among the elected members of the Legislative Assembly after consultation with the leader of the largest party (or coalition) in the Assembly.[4] The Council will have collective responsibility for its decisions.

[2] The Straits Settlements also included Labuan, now part of North Borneo.

[3] Since this was written, the constitutional changes have come into effect in Singapore.

[4] The Constitutional Commission envisaged the possibility that one of the four nominated unofficial members of the Assembly might be appointed a Minister on the advice of the leader.

A further change of considerable significance is to be made in local government: an elected Singapore City and Island Council is to replace the present City Council and the Rural Board and is to be responsible for all local government functions on an island-wide basis. The geographical area of jurisdiction of the Colony Government and of the City and Island Council will therefore be coterminous.[5] The City and Island Council will be free from financial control by the Colony Government, except that the raising of public loans will continue to be subject to the government's approval.

A number of public agencies perform a variety of functions in both the Federation and the Colony. In the Federation, the Malayan Railway Administration[6] operates the railway and provides port or harbor facilities at Port Swettenham, Prai and a number of minor ports; the Central Electricity Board operates and develops public power supplies; the Penang Harbour Board[7] provides port facilities at Penang and maintains a ferry service to the mainland; the Rural and Industrial Development Authority (RIDA) is charged with the task of promoting economic development in the rural areas, in which the bulk of the Malay population lives, and assisting the rural population to improve its living standards by providing better essential services and amenities; the Housing Trust has broad responsibilities to meet housing needs; the Petaling Jaya Authority is responsible for the development of a satellite town to Kuala Lumpur, and the Rubber Industry (Replanting) Board supervises the replanting of rubber smallholdings and makes grants towards the cost of such replanting.

In Singapore, the Harbour Board owns and operates the ocean harbor proper (as distinct from the roadstead) and the Singapore Improvement Trust is the government's agent for all matters concerning housing, town planning, and land use.

In addition, the War Damage Commission assesses claims for war damage and settles them on behalf of the two governments and the British Government; and the Commissioners of Currency, Malaya and British Borneo, are the sole issuing authority for notes and coins for use as currency in the Federation, Singapore, Sarawak, North Borneo and Brunei.

British officials predominate in the higher levels of the civil service but

[5] Except that the Council will have no responsibilities in Christmas Island and the Cocos-Keeling Islands in the Indian Ocean.

[6] The Railway Administration, though a department of the Federal Government, is an entirely separate accounting unit.

[7] The Board is shortly to be merged into a Penang Port Authority which will also operate the port installations at Prai on the mainland.

in both the Federation and Singapore the civil services are being Malayanized as rapidly as qualified persons become available.

iii THE PEOPLE

The Federation has a plural society in which Malaysians[8] and Chinese are the two main racial and religious groups and Indians and Pakistanis form a substantial minority. A very much smaller minority includes other Asians, Europeans (mainly British), Eurasians, etc. Singapore's population is overwhelmingly Chinese.

Both the Federation and Singapore have high birth rates and low death rates and the very rapid rates of population growth are among the highest in the world.

Table 1 indicates the composition of Malaya's population in mid-1953.

TABLE 1   Estimated Population of Malaya, Mid-1953

(Millions)

	Malaysians	Chinese	Indians and Pakistanis	All others	Total
Federation	2.80	2.15	.67	.08	5.70
(% of total)	(49)	(38)	(12)	(1)	(100)
Singapore	.14	.86	.08	.04	1.12
(% of total)	(12)	(77)	(8)	(3)	(100)
	2.94	3.01	.75	.12	6.82
(% of total)	(43)	(44)	(11)	(2)	(100)

SOURCE: Registrar of Statistics.

On the basis of these estimates, the over-all density of population in the Federation is 113 persons per square mile. This figure, however, has little significance since a large part of the Federation's surface is covered by dense tropical jungle. If account is taken only of the area of alienated land and Crown or State land not under forest—in 1952, 13,183 square miles out of a total area of 50,690 square miles—the over-all density then becomes 433 persons per square mile.

Singapore Island, a bustling city with suburban and rural fringes and

[8] Indigenous Malays and immigrant Indonesians of similar stock.

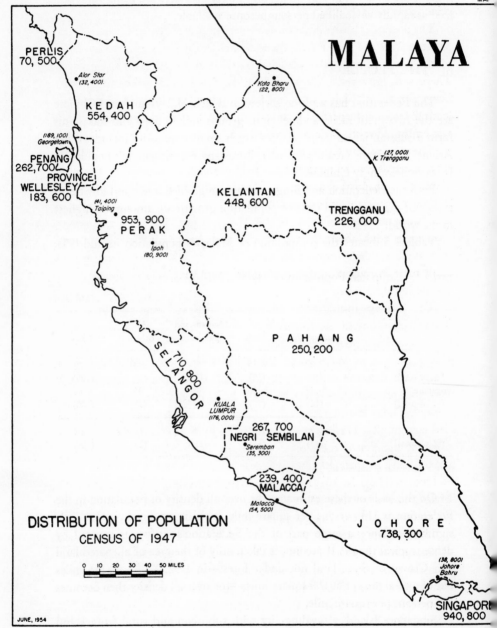

MALAYA

PERLIS
70, 500.

Alor Star
(32, 400).

Kota Bharu
(22, 800)

KEDAH
554, 400

(189, 100)
Georgetown

(27, 000)
K. Trengganu

PENANG
262, 700.

PROVINCE
WELLESLEY
183, 600

KELANTAN
448, 600

TRENGGANU
226, 000

(41, 400)
Taiping

953, 900
PERAK

Ipoh
(80, 900)

PAHANG
250, 200

710, 800
SELANGOR

KUALA
LUMPUR
(176, 000)

267, 700
NEGRI SEMBILAN

Seremban
(35, 300)

239, 400
MALACCA

Malacca
(54, 500)

JOHORE
738, 300

DISTRIBUTION OF POPULATION
CENSUS OF 1947

0 10 20 30 40 50 MILES

(38, 800)
Johore
Bahru

SINGAPORE
940, 800

JUNE, 1954

a population of close on one million, has an average density of about 5,000 persons per square mile.

The ancestors of the present Malay race migrated from Northern China between 2500 and 1500 B.C. Some remained in the peninsula, mainly in the coastal plains in the north, while others went on to the Indonesian islands. There was, however, a return flow in medieval and modern times when many persons of Malay stock left Sumatra, Java and other Indonesian islands to settle in the peninsula, mainly in the south and the southwest. Islam was embraced in the 15th century and today almost all Malays are Muslims.

There were few Chinese in Malaya at the beginning of the 19th century. Thereafter, the opportunities and peaceful conditions in the Settlements of Singapore, Penang and Malacca attracted Chinese immigrants in ever-increasing numbers and the influx was further swollen when peace and order were established in the Malay States. Chinese immigration reached its peak about the turn of the century but continued on a large scale until the depression of the early '30s. A quota was then imposed on adult male immigration, followed some years later by a similar quota on female immigration.

The Chinese immigrants—laborers, artisans and cultivators—went to Malaya largely with the intention of making money and then returning to China. Many, however, remained as settlers. In 1931 less than one-third of the Chinese in Malaya had been born in the country and there were nearly two Chinese males to one Chinese female; sixteen years later, in 1947, that proportion was nearly doubled and the sex ratio was much more normal. Today the majority of the Chinese in Malaya are probably a settled community. Having come from many parts of China, they speak the different dialects of their places of origin. Many have learned Kuo Yu (Mandarin) as their common Chinese language, and it is taught in the Chinese schools. In the Federation, large numbers have learned some Malay; in the towns and in Singapore, many have also learned English which serves as the *lingua franca* for all races.

Indian immigration on a significant scale began with the establishment of plantations during the second half of the last century and grew quickly with the expansion of the rubber industry during the first two decades of this century. In the years before the war, Indian immigration differed from Chinese immigration in two respects: first, until 1938 (when the Indian Government banned the emigration of unskilled labor to Malaya) it was assisted immigration, financed by a levy on employers of Indian labor, whereas Chinese immigration was for the most part unsponsored; secondly, Indian immigrants had less tendency than the Chinese to settle in Malaya. The Indian and Pakistani element of the population decreased between the censuses of 1931 and 1947 but now numbers just over three-quarters of a million or about 150,000 more than in 1947.

While the Federation's population is preponderantly rural, the urban element varies considerably with the three main racial groups. The 1947 census classified only 11% of the Malaysians as urban, that is, living in towns and villages with a population of more than 1,000, whereas 43% of the Chinese were so classified. The urban element of the Indian and Pakistani population was put at 34%.

Tables 2 and 3 show the percentage occupational grouping of gainfully occupied persons in the Federation and Singapore, according to the 1947 census.

TABLE 2 Percentage Occupational Grouping
of Gainfully Occupied Persons, 1947, Federation

	Malaysians	Chinese	Indians, Pakistanis and others	All gainfully occupied persons
Agriculture				
Rubber cultivation	20.0	23.4	47.1	25.9
Padi cultivation	48.4	6.2	2.7	24.7
Other agricultural occupations . . .	6.7	16.8	8.0	10.7
	75.1	46.4	57.8	61.3
Fishing	4.8	2.5	.2	3.1
Mining and quarrying	.5	4.3	1.4	2.1
Manufacturing, etc.	5.1	12.9	4.0	7.8
Transport and communications	3.0	3.3	5.6	3.6
Commercial and financial	3.0	14.4	7.3	8.0
Public administration and defense				
(not otherwise classified)	1.8	.1	1.4	1.1
Professional occupations	1.6	1.8	2.7	1.8
Personal service	1.1	7.5	5.6	4.3
Clerical, etc. occupations	.8	2.9	2.7	2.0
Other and indeterminate occupations .	3.2	3.9	11.3	4.9
	100.0	100.0	100.0	100.0

SOURCE: Report on the 1947 Census of Population.

TABLE 3 Percentage Occupational Grouping
of Gainfully Occupied Persons, 1947, Singapore

	Malaysians	Chinese	Indians, Pakistanis and others	All gainfully occupied persons
Agriculture				
Rubber cultivation	1.4	.7	.2	.7
Padi cultivation	—	—	—	—
Other agricultural occupations . . .	6.6	7.6	1.5	6.6
	8.0	8.3	1.7	7.3
Fishing	4.2	1.2	—	1.3
Mining and quarrying	—	.3	—	.3
Manufacturing, etc.	11.5	21.4	14.2	19.2
Transport and communications	31.3	11.8	15.2	14.6
Commercial and financial	3.5	20.3	15.8	17.7
Public administration and defense				
(not otherwise classified)	10.1	.3	4.3	2.0
Professional occupations	1.8	2.4	5.2	2.8
Personal service	5.1	14.6	7.1	12.3
Clerical, etc. occupations	3.7	8.2	10.8	8.1
Other and indeterminate occupations .	20.8	11.2	25.7	14.4
	100.0	100.0	100.0	100.0

SOURCE: Report on the 1947 Census of Population.

IV THE ECONOMY

The population and economic life of Malaya are concentrated largely in the coastal areas and hinterlands on the western side of the peninsula and in Singapore. Settlement on the east coast is limited to a few scattered pockets and about three-fifths of the entire territory of Malaya is virtually uninhabited.

The economy of western Malaya and Singapore is fairly advanced by Asian standards, with reasonably well-developed systems of roads, railways, ports, coastal transport, communication services, power facilities and other social capital installations. The per capita level of national income, estimated in 1953 at about $800 (equivalent to almost £ 95 or more than U. S. $250), is the highest in the Far East.

Achievement of these economic standards has been possible mainly because of a favorable ratio of population to resources, a natural environment particularly suited to rubber cultivation, rich and abundant deposits of tin and an advantageous location as an entrepot center. On these bases, Malaya has built an active economy concentrated to a large extent on the production of rubber and tin for export, on the output of a variety of foodstuffs and secondary manufactures mainly for domestic consumption, and on commercial and financial services for the domestic markets and for the large entrepot trade with most of Southeast Asia. The role of foreign capital and enterprise (particularly European and Chinese) and of foreign labor (particularly Chinese and Indian) has been of special significance in the economic development of Malaya and accounts for the heterogeneous character of the population.

Malaya is now the world's largest producer of tin and is second only to Indonesia in the output of natural rubber. The extent to which the economy is specialized on these two commodities may be indicated by the fact that in 1953 their export value represented about 85% of all domestic exports, and accounted directly for about a fifth of the national income. Of the two, rubber is of much the greater importance to the economy; it occupies about 65% of the entire cultivated area of Malaya and contributes about 60% of domestic export earnings. A measure of the significance of the entrepot trade, concentrated largely in Singapore, is the fact that the value of goods handled is approximately as large as the total value of domestic exports and imports for domestic consumption.

The degree of specialization in the Malayan economy on rubber, tin and trading operations should not, however, obscure the importance of other lines of economic activity which contribute in total far more to the national income than do the rubber and tin industries directly. (See Table 1 on p. 21.

Agriculture

The dominant position of agriculture (including rubber cultivation) in the Malayan economy is indicated in these national income figures and in the occupational grouping of the population in the Federation shown in Table 2.

Rubber, as noted, occupies well over half the cultivated area and, because of the suitability of the environment, ease of cultivation, an relative income advantages it is not only the principal crop produced on agricultural estates but is also by far the most important crop in terms of land cultivated by peasant smallholders. Of the total rubber area of about 3.7 million acres, about two million is included in estates and about 1.7 million in smallholdings, the great majority of which are less than 10 acres.

Next in importance to rubber in terms of area is rice cultivation. Rice is grown on almost 850,000 acres or about 15% of the total cultivated area. It is entirely a smallholder's crop and, while concentrated in the so-called "rice bowl" areas of Perlis, Kedah, Province Wellesley, Kelantan and Trengganu, is also important in the agriculture of most other States. Rice yields are relatively high by Southeast Asian standards and production has shown a substantial increase since prewar years. Malaya, nevertheless, depends on imports for about half its total rice requirements.

The other most important commercial crops are coconuts, grown on about 485,000 acres by both estates and smallholders, and oil palm, which occupies about 100,000 acres and is almost exclusively an estate crop.

In addition to these major crops, Malaya produces a variety of fruits, vegetables and other foodcrops, spices and many additional miscellaneous agricultural commodities. Over 350,000 acres are devoted to these minor crops, consisting in the main of a large number of small peasant holdings. Much of this produce is grown in what are essentially village (kampong) gardens cultivated for subsistence purposes and often as a supplement to income from such major crops as rubber, rice and coconuts. Specialized commercial cultivation is, however, also important, especially of fresh vegetables and fruits, including pineapples for the canning industry, and tea, mainly for domestic consumption.

In spite of the importance of agriculture in the economy, Malaya is far short of self-sufficiency in foodstuffs due to the relative advantages of and degree of specialization in rubber, the limitations of soil and terrain for many food crops and the large proportion of employment outside the agricultural sector. Imports of foodstuffs, including rice, accounted for more than half the imports for domestic consumption in 1949 and for over 40% in 1953.

Other Primary Industries

Production of tin is Malaya's most important primary industry outside the agricultural sector. The only other metallic minerals of substantial commercial significance are iron ore and, to a lesser extent, bauxite, gold, ilmenite, columbite and tungsten. Known fuel deposits are limited to small deposits of coal of the sub-bituminous variety—only one of which is at present being exploited—and to peat, whose possible utilization for power generation is now being investigated.

Other primary industries of major importance are fishing and forestry. The fishing industry extends along most of Malaya's coastline and is an important contributor to the food supply and to employment in both the Federation and Singapore. The forestry industry supplies Malaya's domestic requirements and a small amount of timber for export. In spite of the very large forest area of Malaya, however, only a very small part is commercially exploited, mainly because of low average qualities and difficulties of access.

Secondary Industry

The development of manufacturing in Malaya is fairly advanced by Asian standards and is exceeded in the Orient probably only by Japan, India and Hong Kong. It accounts for almost 10% of gainful employment in the Federation and Singapore and, among the various sectors of the economy, only agriculture makes a larger contribution to national output. The typical Malayan industry is, however, quite small and there is a very wide variation in technical standards.

Most industrial activity is concentrated in lines associated with primary producing and trading activities or in fields where there are particular advantages of location in serving the domestic market. In addition to handicraft production for the domestic market, the principal lines of industrial activity are the processing of rubber, tin and foodstuffs; the manufacture of food preparations, drinks and tobacco; engineering works; and the production of a variety of miscellaneous consumer goods of which the rubber goods, furniture and printing trades are the most important.

Economic Specialization and Instability

While contributing to Malaya's relatively advantageous economic standards, specialization in rubber, tin, entrepot commerce and related economic activity has at the same time created a considerable element of instability in Malaya's economic structure. This arises out of the fluctuating fortunes of rubber and tin in world markets and the ups and downs of entrepot trading, which follow the swings in trade and changing trade and exchange policies of other Southeast Asian countries. As a consequence, Malaya's imports and other foreign payments, public finances, cost-price relationships and general economic activity have alternated between periods of marked buoyancy and difficult downward adjustment in response to external influences. Nevertheless, with the margin for adjustment provided by the relatively favorable economic position of the people, Malaya has been able to weather periods of adverse markets for its principal exports, especially in the early 1920's and again in the 1930's, without serious internal repercussions.

There are, in addition, longer-run economic uncertainties associated with the specialized character of the economy due especially, in the case of rubber, to the competition which has arisen with the development of the synthetic rubber industry and, in the case of tin, to the long-run technological economies in world tin utilization. These uncertainties arise at a particularly critical period in Malaya's economic development when an unusually rapid rate of population growth places special emphasis on the need for a steady and substantial pace of economic expansion.

v THE "EMERGENCY"

For almost seven years Malaya has been plagued by armed internal insurrection, commonly referred to as the "emergency." It began in June 1948, following the shift in tactics of the Malayan Communist Party from a so-called "moderate" line of agitation through penetration of labor and other organizations to outright guerilla warfare operating from and within the protective cover of the Malayan jungle.

For a time terrorist violence interfered with the normal functioning of the Federation's economy as planters and others were murdered, villagers were terrorized, rubber trees were slashed and transport lines. and supply stocks were raided. However, prompt and effective countermeasures by the governments, strongly supported by British forces, confined terrorist operations to localized incidents and prevented any consolidation of Communist gains. While raids, ambushes and terrorism have continued, the number of such incidents has steadily and greatly diminished and casualties, captures and surrenders of terrorists have increased. At present the emergency constitutes only a minor disruptive influence on day-to-day economic activity.

Nevertheless, Communist terrorism continues as a serious menace and a heavy drain on the resources of Malaya. Indications are that through recruitment, terrorist numbers have been more or less maintained, in spite of casualties. They manage to survive within the shelter of the dense jungle and are held in check only by a large and effective armed force and a vigilant control over possible sources of supply. In noting that "the offensive capacity of the armed terrorist organization has been drastically reduced," the most recent Annual Report of the Federation of Malaya also states that "the hard core of the enemy remains at large in the deep jungle: ambushes will continue to be laid and murders committed by Communist bands intent on terrorising the population and thus obtaining food, money and supplies; and the Communists will no doubt continue to attempt the penetration of trades unions, political organisations and youth groups."[9]

For the time being, the emergency constitutes a drag on further private and public economic development. It has necessitated the resettlement of more than half a million persons as a means of preventing supplies from flowing to the terrorists and limits the possibilities for settlement of new agricultural areas. It hampers and increases the cost of mineral exploration, and the necessity for protection adds to the expense of operating much of the agricultural estate areas. Resource surveys by the government are similarly handicapped. Perhaps the most serious obstacle which the emergency has thrown in the path of economic development is the heavy and continuing financial burden it has imposed on the Federation Government in addition to the much larger expenditure met directly by the United Kingdom for British forces maintained in Malaya.

[9] *Federation of Malaya Annual Report 1953*, Government Press, 1954.

CHAPTER 2 *MALAYAN DEVELOPMENT—PROBLEMS AND PROSPECTS*

I THE POSTWAR STRUCTURE AND TRENDS OF THE ECONOMY

Malaya emerged from World War II with its economy inevitably disrupted by three and a half years of occupation and by destruction during the hostilities which preceded it; unemployment and destitution were widespread and a major task of reconstructing and rehabilitating mines, estates and other productive facilities lay ahead.

The subsequent rapid restoration and recovery of the economy were a striking achievement and a tribute to the energy, efficiency and cooperative effort of private enterprise, labor and, initially, the British Military Administration, later, the reconstituted civil governments of the two territories. By 1947 and 1948 the foundations of the economy had in large measure been restored; rubber and rice production exceeded the prewar output; tin production was nearly back to the average of the 1930's; shipping was again at about prewar levels; and the effects of the war on production and commerce generally were rapidly disappearing. Despite the outbreak of the "emergency" in 1948, and the economic and financial problems which it has created (referred to in Chapter 1), economic recovery continued and by 1950 Malaya was able to turn from its preoccupation with reconstruction to the problems of further economic expansion.[1]

In Chapter 1 we noted the importance in Malaya's past economic growth of the production of primary raw materials for export and of a thriving entrepot commerce, both of which were developed mainly by foreign capital. Largely through these and related economic activities, together with an expanding agricultural output for domestic consumption, Malaya's economic growth over the past 50 years or more has considerably outdistanced the growth of population. Employment opportunities increased faster than did the labor force through natural population increase alone,

[1] A Draft Development Plan for the Federation was published in June 1950.

making necessary a periodic inflow of immigrant workers. And while the economy's dependence on world markets subjected it to wide fluctuations, adjustments to these fluctuations were eased by the migratory character of a considerable part of the labor supply, which moved into and out of Malaya with changes in levels of economic activity.

Raw material exports, agricultural output for domestic consumption and the entrepot trade will certainly continue to be among the mainstays of the economy. But the pattern and problems of economic expansion in the years ahead are likely to differ markedly from those of the past.

By Asian standards, the Malayan economy has reached a relatively advanced stage, not only in the level of per capita income, but also in structure: it is a more varied and complex economy than is characteristic of most underdeveloped countries. Power, transport, communications and other basic facilities are reasonably well developed; a considerable foundation of secondary industry has been established; there is a substantial nucleus of skills and enterprise; standards of public administration are high; and institutional patterns and habits of commerce and finance are correspondingly advanced. Industrial, commercial, professional and governmental activities outside the fields of primary industry now probably account for nearly half the national income; they, as well as primary raw material and food production, can be expected to continue to expand. Accordingly, further economic development will undoubtedly follow a broader and more varied pattern than prevailed until fairly recent times.

Recent Trends in National Income

In the period since the immediate postwar reconstruction years, the broad picture of economic activity in Malaya has been dominated by an upswing to high prosperity followed by a decline, corresponding to world market conditions following the outbreak of the Korean war in mid-1950. The mission's estimates, shown in Table 1 below, indicate that Malaya's gross national product, valued at current market prices, more than doubled between 1949 and 1951 and by 1953 had dropped back to a level about 60% above that of 1949.

During the post-Korea boom, the economy was subject to strong inflationary pressures and the money supply, price levels and wage rates rose sharply. By the end of 1953, when the effects of the boom period had largely subsided, the money supply was still about 80% larger, while domestic prices were probably on the average 25-30% higher, than in 1949.

TABLE 1   Gross National Product by Origin

(Million $)

	1949	1950	1951	1952	1953
Rubber	420	1,400	2,025	1,080	715
Mining	250	295	480	440	325
Other agriculture and forestry .	840	1,030	1,380	1,355	1,430
All other activities	1,825	2,355	3,260	3,100	2,925
Gross national income	3,335	5,080	7,145	5,975	5,395
Indirect taxes	215	265	375	375	385
Gross national product (at market prices)	3,550	5,345	7,520	6,350	5,780

NOTE: Estimates prepared by the mission, based in large measure on data furnished by the Registrar of Statistics, Singapore. For various classifications of the national income and expenditure and explanatory notes see the Statistical Appendix, Table 14, in Part V.

Much of the increase between 1949 and 1953 in the gross national product, measured in current prices, was thus the result of a higher price level. While data are lacking for an accurate adjustment of the gross national product for price changes, the available indices of export prices and cost of living would suggest that over the period 1949-53 there was a gain, in real terms, of something approaching 20%.

We have already remarked on the importance of the contribution of activities elsewhere than in the primary industries. It is also significant that much of the recent expansion in real output has been entirely outside the primary producing fields. The volume of tin production in 1953 was only slightly higher than in 1949, while that of rubber was actually lower. On the other hand, the output of a number of commodities within the field of primary industry did increase substantially, notably rice, copra, tea, pineapple, forestry products, fish, iron ore and various minor minerals. But taking primary industry as a whole, it seems clear that the 1953 volume of output was not as much above that of 1949 as was the real output of goods and services of the economy as a whole.

Much of the real gain outside the primary producing sectors may be explained by the very large increase in government activities, especially those associated with the emergency, and by the expansion in social services and in government-owned power, telecommunications, transport and other quasi-commercial services. There was also a large rise in both government and private construction and a greater volume of trading in imports for domestic consumption and for entrepot commerce.

But it also seems clear that secondary industry (and manufacturing, professional and commercial services generally) contributed substantially to the growth in real income. Statistical information is inadequate for an accurate measure of recent trends of physical output in secondary industry. But material examined by the mission[2] pointed to considerable advances in a variety of lines of industrial production, much of it in small-scale establishments in both the Federation and Singapore.

The Balance of Payments

Exports of domestic produce, almost entirely raw materials and foodstuffs, constitute over a third of the gross national product. Imports for domestic consumption are mainly rice and other foodstuffs, textiles and other consumer manufactures, petroleum products, manufactured equipment and industrial raw materials. Almost a third of gross domestic expenditure goes in imports.

Two aspects of this pattern of trade and its magnitude in relation to the national income are of particular relevance to the development problem of Malaya.

The first is the relatively large and highly fluctuating character of export earnings, which makes it necessary for Malaya to maintain a much higher reserve of sterling balances than would be required were the international payments structure more stable. Under the present currency system, which requires the currency issue to be backed to at least 100% in sterling, fluctuations in export earnings tend to be reflected at once in corresponding movements in internal liquidity and consequently in patterns of spending, including spending on imported goods and services. Balance of payments deficits are in this way corrected without a persistent or serious

---

[2] Data of the Labour Departments on industrial employment, figures of electric power consumption, information on installed horsepower of manufacturing equipment, dates on which active industrial enterprises were established and lists of new industries which have begun operations over the last several years.

drain on sterling balances and it is not possible for an "exchange" problem to arise.[3] But even with an independent monetary authority, whose establishment we recommend elsewhere,[4] a high level of sterling reserves will also have to be maintained and in formulating monetary policy, balance of payments considerations will have to be kept predominantly in mind.

TABLE 2 Merchandise Trade of Malaya, 1949–53

(Million $)

	1949	1950	1951	1952	1953
Exports of domestic produce					
Rubber	558	1522	2279	1277	898
Tin	241	412	506	470	351
Coconut products	49	74	85	48	58
Palm oil & kernels	42	37	45	49	37
All others	53	84	136	129	142
Total	943	2129	3051	1973	1486
Re-exports	779	1887	3025	1946	1534
Total exports	1722	4016	6076	3919	3020
Imports for domestic consumption					
Rice	200	177	222	213	277
Other foodstuffs	315	388	538	566	516
Drink & tobacco	63	74	106	114	101
Petroleum products	78	77	120	171	170
Textiles	169	221	355	211	135
Vehicles, machinery, metals, etc.	181	219	432	458	337
All others	185	293	539	442	328
Total	1191	1449	2312	2175	1864
Imports for re-export	660	1466	2443	1698	1374
Total imports	1851	2915	4755	3873	3238
Merchandise trade balance	−129	+1101	+1321	+46	−218

NOTE: The figures include the trade of both the Federation and Singapore, exclusive of trade between the two territories. For explanation of the basis for division between domestic and entrepot trade see Chapter 6, p. 119.
SOURCE: Registrar of Malayan Statistics, Singapore.

The second aspect is the high proportion of gross domestic expenditure spent on imports. Income generated through deficit fiscal policies or the

[3] See Technical Report 12.
[4] Chapter 9, p. 217.

creation of commercial bank credit can be expected to lead quickly to an increased demand for imports. The margin for financing development through budget deficits or liberal credit policies without creating balance of payments difficulties is consequently very narrow.

The major categories of Malaya's trade and the wide trade fluctuations of recent years, reflecting on the export side principally price changes in the course of the post-Korea cycle, are shown in Table 2.

A similar division between domestic and entrepot trade is not available for 1954. However, total trade in 1954, including the entrepot trade, was approximately balanced, with exports at $3,139 million and imports at $3,109 million.

In its nontrade transactions abroad, Malaya usually has substantial external payments, arising from transfers of earnings on foreign investments and from overseas remittances. These generally fluctuate with the fortunes of rubber and tin; they are highest when export earnings are high. There is no reliable basis for more than very rough estimates of the size of payments abroad in respect of profits, dividends and personal remittances in recent years but it is clear that they continue as fairly large items in the balance of payments. At the same time, as shown in Table 2, Malaya's merchandise accounts have been approximately in balance, except in 1950 and 1951 when the rapid rise in export values far outdistanced imports. There were trade deficits in the postwar period up to 1949 and again in 1953, while in 1952 the export surplus was quite small. This maintenance of payments abroad in respect of profits, dividends and family remittances, along with an approximately even or trade deficit position, has been offset in the balance of payments in recent years by large sterling receipts arising from expenditures of British forces in Malaya. There have in addition been sterling receipts from some public borrowing abroad, and from grant and loan assistance from the United Kingdom. In 1953, however, there was a net reduction in Malaya's sterling balances.

In Table 3, which shows the mission's estimate of Malaya's recent balance of payments position, the figures for net current invisible transactions are only rough approximations. In estimating transfers of profits and dividends, no deduction is made for that part of foreign income reinvested in Malaya. These reinvested earnings are included under the heading "Private capital inflow, errors and omissions." Family remittances are allowed for more or less on a token basis. Other transactions included in the invisibles figure are expenditures in Malaya by the armed forces of the United Kingdom, United Kingdom grants-in-aid and miscellaneous transactions mainly on government account.

TABLE 3   Estimates of Malaya's Balance of Payments, 1949–53[1]

(Million $)

	1949	1950	1951	1952	1953
A. Current Account					
1. Domestic exports and imports for domestic consumption	−248	+680	+739	−202	−378
2. Re-exports and imports for re-export	+119	+421	+582	+248	+160
Net merchandise account	−129	+1101	+1321	+46	−218
3. Net invisible transactions	+7	−417	−607	−151	−26
Balance on Current Account .	−122	+684	+714	−105	−244
B. Capital Account (net inflow shown as +, net outflow −)					
1. New public loans raised abroad . .	+68	+5	+14	+10	+13
2. U.K. war damage grant and loan .	—	—	+34	+68	+89
3. Other official liabilities.	—	+17	—	+38	−39
4. Sterling balances of government authorities, currency board and banks (increase as −, decrease as +)	−51	−561	−697	−26	+116
Total of identifiable items . .	+17	−539	−649	+90	+179
5. Private capital inflow, errors, and omissions	+105	−145	−65	+15	+65
Balance on Capital Account .	+122	−684	−714	+105	+244

[1] These estimates are presented in somewhat greater detail and with explanatory notes in the Statistical Appendix, Table 7, in Part V.

With regard to the balance of payments outlook for the next few years, we have assumed in our estimates of public financial resources during 1955-59 (see Chapter 8) that export earnings from rubber and tin will be somewhat below recent levels, due in the case of rubber mainly to the possibility of lower prices and in the case of tin mainly to the prospect of curtailed output under the proposed International Tin Agreement. We would not, however, expect an abrupt corresponding adjustment in imports and other payments, in view of the accumulated public and private savings remaining from the boom period of 1950 and 1951, reflected in the large sterling balances held by the governments, the banks and the currency board. These balances amounted to $2,121 million at the end of 1953 and probably were not reduced significantly in 1954. They are large in relation to Malaya's imports, amounting to the equivalent of more than one year's supply of imports for domestic consumption at recent rates. Even with some decline in export earnings, the accumulated sterling balances, and the liquidity in the economy which they represent, allow some latitude for public and private expenditures for current and investment purposes in excess of current income and, consequently, for some deficits in international transactions.

II PROBLEMS OF DEVELOPMENT

In the previous discussion we have noted the large contributions to the national income not only from export production but also from a wide variety of other economic activities within and outside the fields of primary production. To assure satisfactory rates of further expansion and development, it is essential that both the export sector and a broad range of activities serving domestic economic requirements continue to contribute to a rising national output. Because of the structure and stage of development of the Malayan economy this diversified progress is to be expected. The question is, however, whether development can keep pace with population growth. This poses a number of difficult problems for Malaya. These are discussed elsewhere in the report; the most significant may be summarized briefly here.

The Population Problem

The problem of perhaps the greatest significance for the future standard of living of Malaya is the rate of population growth. It is not feasible here to discuss in detail the structural characteristics and growth patterns of the population but we can mention the following factors which have contributed to the very rapid rate of population growth, now among the world's highest: a steady trend in recent years toward a more "settled" and less transient population; more normal sex ratios, instead of the long-prevailing high proportion of males to females; a large concentration of population in the younger age groups; high birth rates and greatly reduced death rates. And at the same time, migration, a traditional adjustment to prevailing levels of economic activity, has ceased to be of significance.

Since 1947, births per 1,000 population have ranged between 42 and 44 in the Federation and between 46 and 49 in Singapore; deaths per 1,000 population declined between 1947 and 1953 from 19 to 12 in the Federation and from 13 to 10 in Singapore. As a result, current rates of natural population growth exceed 3% a year in the Federation and 3.5% in Singapore, as shown in Table 4.

TABLE 4   Recent Annual Rates of Natural Population Growth

(Per 1,000 of population)

	Federation			Singapore		
	Births	Deaths	Increase	Births	Deaths	Increase
1947.	43	19	24	46	13	33
1950.	42	16	26	46	12	34
1951.	44	15	29	46	12	34
1952.	44	14	30	48	11	36[1]
1953.	44	12	32	49	10	38[1]

[1] Apparent inaccuracy is due to rounding.

Projections of population trends are of course reliable only to the extent that the assumptions concerning birth and death on which they are based prove to be correct. Nonetheless, it is a major consideration in the longer-run economic outlook for Malaya that the "youthful" composition of the present population (with well over 50% of the female population of 19 years of age or less) and the recent birth and death rates suggest the possibility that Malaya's population may double within the next 25 years. And because of the present age pattern and the increasingly settled character of the population, the available labor force may well increase at an even faster rate.[5]

Financial Resources

The availability of financial resources presents one of the most difficult problems affecting the pace of Malaya's development, especially in the public sector of the economy.

[5] In contrast are the fairly recent labor supply trends as indicated in the census figures of 1931 and 1947, in which the male population of working age (15-54) was at about the same level, due primarily to alterations in age structure in the course of population growth and as a result of migration.

The nature and difficulty of this problem are discussed in Chapter 8. Essentially it is one of mounting government expenditure requirements in a period in which revenue, which is closely related to trends of Malayan trade, is not likely to rise correspondingly. Recurrent government outlays have risen substantially in recent years in the Federation due particularly to the heavy financial burden of the emergency, and in both territories to mounting requirements and insistent demands for steady expansion of education and other social services.

Our estimates, allowing for some decline in earnings from exports of rubber and tin during the next few years, suggest that in the Federation the cost of meeting what we consider priority investment and recurrent expenditures, including those necessitated by the emergency, may well prove too great to be financed from domestic sources, even if taxation is increased and government balances are further reduced. It seems reasonable to assume, however, that the Federation will continue to receive some measure of assistance from the United Kingdom Government in the financing of priority expenditures. Singapore's ability to meet public financial requirements from domestic resources appears greater, but the priority economic and social development needs can probably be financed only if, as in the Federation, additional taxes are levied and present balances are drawn upon. It may also be possible to use existing currency reserves for investment purposes under the revised monetary arrangements; we believe, however, the scope for prudent investment financing from this source to be small and we have not made allowance for it in our estimates of resources available for government investment.

In the field of private finance, Malaya is well served with banking facilities provided by both foreign and Malayan banking institutions. The predominance of bank deposits in the total money supply attests to the extensive development of banking habits. As would be expected, however, bank credit is largely concentrated in short-term lending, mainly for activities associated with foreign and domestic trade. Arrangements for medium- and long-term credit are inadequately developed and poorly organized; long-term private investment is financed in large measure either through reinvestment of earnings to expand existing enterprises or through personal or family contacts with noninstitutional sources of capital.

Malaya must now depend on domestic saving to finance private investment to a degree in marked contrast to the traditional pattern of substantial inflows of new private foreign capital; the latter are now of reduced significance. Existing foreign investment remains of major importance to the Malayan economy; so does local reinvestment of earnings from this source. It is most important to maintain an investment climate which will induce foreign capital to remain in Malaya and to reinvest its earnings there, and which will attract new foreign investment. But for various reasons, including constitutional developments within Malaya and political uncertainties in Southeast Asia generally, Malaya is not likely, for some time at least, to be able to count, as in the past, on a large inflow of new private capital from abroad: dependence on domestic savings to provide capital for the private sector of the economy will undoubtedly be much greater than used to be necessary.

As a result of the post-Korea prosperity, the volume of liquid private savings is still substantial and it seemed to us that expansion of private economic activity was not being seriously retarded by lack of capital. The situation may change, however, as accumulated savings decline.

Our estimates suggest that the rates of saving are not particularly high in relation to national income except in periods of unusual prosperity. Public and private consumption in the recent years of prosperity reached levels inconsistent with any substantial increase in the rate of saving in the near future, especially if income from rubber and tin should decline. The inadequacy of institutional arrangements affects the availability of capital, and the fluctuating character of the economy contributes to the marked preference for reasonably liquid short-term, as distinct from longer-term, investment; this adds to the difficulty and cost of obtaining long-term financing.

Our principal recommendations in the field of currency and credit are for the establishment of a Central Bank of Malaya, to take the place of the currency board as the monetary authority for the two territories, and for early consideration of the establishment of specialized lending facilities for industry and agriculture.

The Major Exports

In Chapter 1 we referred to the main problems confronting Malaya's major exports. They arise, in the case of tin, from technological economies in its use and the effect of such economies on trends of world consumption. In the case of rubber, they stem from the competition of the recently developed synthetic rubber industry. Given the uncertain market outlook for tin, any substantial expansion of tin production seems unlikely in the near future. It is nevertheless important that Malaya's tin industry maintain at least its present relative position as the world's largest single supplier. This cannot be accomplished without resolving difficult problems and issues of policy relating to prospecting and development of new deposits on a scale adequate to compensate for the depletion of old ones. The burden of taxation carried by the industry is also a difficult issue.

The problems of the tin industry are of less critical significance to the economy as a whole, however, than those of the rubber industry, because rubber contributes far more than tin to the national output. Whether Malayan rubber production can maintain a satisfactory competitive position vis a vis synthetic rubber is a question of overriding importance for Malaya's economic future. In our view, it can, provided the industry, with the co-operation of the government, makes a determined effort to strengthen the competitive position of Malayan rubber by replanting with trees yielding more at lower unit costs. We consider this to be the country's highest and most urgent development priority. If a replanting program can be successfully carried out, Malayan rubber production is likely to expand very substantially.

Agricultural Production

The possibilities for expanded agricultural production, in rice and a variety of other products as well as in rubber, appear promising; but a quickening of the pace of such development presents difficult problems.

The most significant of these are the inadequacy of the knowledge and evaluation of unutilized agricultural potentialities; hindrances to the improvement of cultivation practices and to settlement and development of new lands, imposed by tradition, habit and inertia; and the adverse effects on incentives to improve and expand agriculture created by unsatisfactory credit and marketing arrangements, unfavorable developments in land tenure relationships, and, in the case of rice, by falling world price levels which may tend to stabilize at much lower levels than in recent years. These and other specific problems are discussed subsequently.

If there is to be a more rapid and diversified realization of Malaya's agricultural potentialities, the present admittedly substantial governmental effort in research and experimentation must be strengthened and land development programs continued. These measures must be supplemented by

land-use and soil surveys, pilot projects and improvements in the availability of agricultural data in order to add to the knowledge of Malayan
agriculture and its development potentialities; by much broader and more
effective extension services; and by measures and policies to increase agricultural incentives.

We appreciate the stubborn nature of some of these problems. Yet
special efforts must be made to solve them, because of the importance of
the contribution of the agricultural resources to the expansion of the
economy.

Secondary Industry

Malaya must, and undoubtedly will, continue to broaden its base of
secondary manufacturing to supplement the contribution to additional
employment and income likely to be made by primary production.

Malaya is not well endowed with the raw material requirements for
an extensively industrialized economy. Nonetheless, manufacturing, in
terms of contribution to national output, comes close to rivaling the agricultural sector. Since much of the manufacturing is spread over a wide
variety of small and relatively simple industrial operations, its development
is unspectacular and its importance tends often to be overlooked. But it is
these individually small advances over a wide range of industries, rather
than the establishment of large mass-producing units along "Westernized"
lines, which in the aggregate can be expected to go on making a major
contribution to economic expansion. Our expectation of continuing industrial growth is founded on the fact that Malaya possesses a much higher
degree of enterprise, business experience and skills than most Asian countries, established habits and disciplines conducive to manufacturing operations, and a domestic market benefiting from income and consumption
levels which are high by Asian standards.

But the industrial field poses difficult problems, too. While large in
relation to population, the domestic market is small by standards of modern
industrial output. Against the relatively high incomes must be set the wage
levels, likewise high by Asian standards. And industrial development, so
far closely associated with primary production and trade or with special
advantages of location, must henceforth to an increasing extent enter fields
of foreign competition.

Industrial development must depend primarily on private initiative, enterprise and capital. Nevertheless, we believe it can be facilitated in both the Federation and Singapore if the governments adopt measures to improve further the climate for private industrial enterprise and help to reduce some of the problems involved in extending manufacturing operations. The most obvious contribution government can make is to expand overhead facilities such as power, transport and communications, and these are major items in the program of government investment we propose. But Malaya's particular circumstances suggest other ways in which government can be of assistance.

Techniques and organizations appropriate to the problems of Malayan industrialization are considered subsequently. The basic need, in our view, is for increased organizational and technical efficiency within a continuing pattern of essentially small-scale operations. Government assistance can make an important contribution to this need by expanding vocational training facilities, assisting in technical and market research, providing suitable sites and other services for new industries, improving industrial credit arrangements, and, in appropriate cases, adopting policies of protection within the Federation.[6]

Federal-State Relationships in the Federation

The Federation has a problem arising out of the nature of the federal system. There are often inherent difficulties in such a system in coordinating the investment activities and policies of the federal government with those of the several regional governments in the various fields affecting economic development. Fortunately, this need not necessarily be true in the Federation of Malaya, where the Federation Agreement gives the Federal Government much broader legislative powers than is usual in such cases. Indeed, the Federal Government has the legislative authority—and therefore the policy-making power—in all major fields of government activity. Moreover, the financial arrangements between the Federal and the State and Settlement Governments prescribed by the Agreement give the Federal Government a negative power of control over the distribution of. State and Settlement expenditure among the various activities financed from State and Settlement revenues, including the lump sum Federal grant. These powers of direction and control have, however, been used very sparingly. Policy with respect to many of the most important mat-

[6] See Chapter 6 and Technical Report 8.

ters—land use, agriculture, forestry, animal husbandry, education and medical and health services—has in practice largely been decided by the State and Settlement Governments. It has been their decision whether to alienate land for new planting of rubber or tin mining, whether the politically popular social services rather than the economic services should be expanded, and so forth, and their decisions presumably have been reached in the light of their respective interests.

It must be recognized that policies so arrived at are not necessarily best for the Federation as a whole. If the Federation is to husband its resources, if it is to be able successfully to meet the challenge of its fast-growing population, development must be more closely planned at the center and the execution of approved plans must be more closely controlled. This does not require reducing the powers conferred on the States and Settlements by the Federation Agreement; it means rather the fuller exercise by the Federal Government of its powers and responsibilities. We later recommend various measures designed to secure closer Federal control over formulation and execution of policy while at the same time giving a greater measure of financial independence and responsibility to the States and Settlements.

III RECOMMENDED LINES OF PUBLIC INVESTMENT

Our conclusions and recommendations regarding public development expenditures are discussed in detail in the following chapters. It may be convenient at this point, however, to indicate our views on the broad lines of priority investment by the Governments of the Federation and Singapore.

We have necessarily directed our attention to government effort and investment. We emphasize, however, the private enterprise character of the Malayan economy. Taking into account Malaya's stage of development and the availability of private enterprise, capital, skills and experience, it can be expected that private investment and the resulting additional output will continue to make the major contribution to further expansion of the economy. Essentially, our recommendations for government action and investment are for the fostering and assistance of private development: facilitating private exploitation of natural resources, agricultural as well as mineral; expanding transport, communications, power and other overhead facilities serving private enterprise; providing additional education, health and other social services; and adopting policies conducive to investment and expansion in the private sectors of the economy.

The public investment programs which we recommend for the Federation and Singapore do not represent significant departures from the recent patterns of public investment in both territories, either in amount or character.

In each territory government capital outlays have risen substantially during the last several years, reflecting the very great governmental contribution during that period to Malaya's economic and social development. And while our assessment of the public finance outlook does not indicate that the level of public investment can rise within the next few years much beyond the point already reached, it does suggest that it can be sustained at the level which has already been reached, probably equivalent to 4-5% of national income.

The broad lines of priority in our proposed allocation of public investment resources are also similar to the present pattern. This is particularly so in Singapore, where the heaviest public investment requirements are now and are likely to continue to be for public utilities and other quasi-commercial services and facilities, for housing and for the social services generally. In the Federation, the principal difference between the past and the proposed investment programs is a somewhat greater emphasis on agriculture in the latter.

The Federation

For the Federation, we have proposed a public investment program of $775 million over the years 1955-59.

The nature of Malaya's known pattern of natural resources suggests that agriculture is one of the fields in which governmental assistance can be most productive. Accordingly, of the total of our recommended investment program, about 25% is allocated to various phases of agricultural development. In terms of public capital outlays, the two largest items of proposed expenditure are for assistance in the planting of high-yielding rubber by both estates and smallholders, and for irrigation and drainage works to improve already cultivated areas devoted mainly to rice and to open up new lands for rice and other crops. Other measures of special importance, although calling for smaller expenditure, cover land-use surveys to add to Malaya's knowledge of its agricultural resource potentialities, expansion of cocoa production and an increase in oil palm output, rehabilitation of coconut areas, and the expansion of governmental services such as extension programs, research and experimentation, marketing services and training of technical staff.

The expansion of these services will contribute to an improvement in methods and production, and to an increase in the yields and acreage of most of Malaya's crops. We also emphasize the need to improve land tenure and agricultural credit arrangements, and we urge further encouragement of the cooperative movement among cultivators. Finally, we recommend, in view of the recent sharp drop in world rice prices, that consideration be given to the support of domestic padi and rice prices not only for the benefit of Malaya's many rice cultivators but of the economy as a whole.

In forestry, it is difficult on the basis of present information to foresee either a large or rapid expansion in the output of forest products. With advances in knowledge, however, Malayan forests may become a much more important productive asset: the forest area is large and growing conditions are very favorable. We therefore recommend an increase in expenditures on forest protection and reafforestation for conservation and maintenance, and possible expansion of the relative size of the forests' contribution to long-run national output.

In fisheries, the most promising lines for increasing production and improving the lot of fishermen generally appear to be in motorized fishing craft, better catching techniques, and the improvement of harbor and handling facilities. Any substantial progress in these directions, particularly in the introduction of modern fishing units, is likely to take considerable time; while we have recommended relatively modest public expenditure in 1955-59, we would expect a steady upward trend in both public and private investment in the fishing industry over a longer period.

We have recommended the greatest government investment in basic services, including transport, communications and power. While these services are reasonably well developed, they must go on expanding to keep pace with the growth of the economy. Over 20% of our program is for transport and communications. The largest single item is for roads, although our figure for trunk road improvements and extensions is considerably smaller than has been officially proposed. We also recommend that particular attention be given to feeder roads serving existing and new agricultural areas, and in this connection we believe that a considerable contribution can be made by programs of village "aided self-help" in road construction and maintenance. The next largest item is for port development and improvement, principally for facilities to handle the increased traffic at Port Swettenham; most of the balance is for ferry and lighterage facilities at Penang. The postwar reconstruction of Malaya's railway network is virtually complete, and standards of efficiency and service are high despite operational problems created by the emergency. Proposed expenditure is chiefly for a contemplated change-over from steam to diesel locomotives, further rehabilitation of rolling stock and improvement and extension of yards and shops, which we support. Standards of postal and telecommunications services in Malaya are also relatively high; the principal investment requirement is for an extension of telephone facilities. The improvement of civil aviation facilities calls for relatively small expenditure.

Expansion of power facilities to keep ahead of consumption requirements is another major item in the recommended investment program, to which about 11% has been allocated. Substantial progress in this direction has been made with the recent construction of the Connaught Bridge Station, the second stage of which is scheduled to begin operation in 1955. Most of the proposed additional expenditure in the 1955-59 period is for further expansion and extension of the capacity and network of the government-owned Central Electricity Board. We also support expenditures on additions to and modernization of power facilities for Penang and nearby mainland areas.

Much of the remainder, and a very large part, of our recommended public investment expenditure in the Federation falls within the broad category of social services. There is a strong and insistent public demand for more educational and medical and health facilities, and we believe that further extension and improvement of these services should be supported. At the same time we urge greater attention to the limitations of finance and personnel upon this expansion. We would also stress our view that the beneficiaries of these services should be required to relieve Federal finances of part of the cost through larger contributions at State and local levels. The increases in expenditures which we recommend assume that larger contributions will be made and will represent an increasing share of the necessary financing. We have also proposed modest additions in government contributions to social welfare activities, a substantial outlay for improved sewerage and water supply facilities, and a considerable contribution to official housing, to private housing for low income groups through loans and subsidies, and to the re-siting of unsatisfactorily located "new villages."

In the minerals field, the principal short-run prospect for increased production is in iron ore, but this is a fairly small component of total mineral output. In the tin industry, as we have already remarked, world market conditions make it likely that production will fall somewhat, rather than rise, over the next few years. It is only in the longer run that appreciably higher levels of output may possibly be realized. There is, however, a serious problem of locating and developing new ore bodies as old deposits are worked out. Our main recommendations are for geological surveys so that more can be known of mineral possibilities, and for government policies more hospitable to private prospecting and development of tin and other mineral resources.

Singapore

For Singapore, we have recommended public investment of about $610 million in the 1955-59 period. As is to be expected in a large and growing metropolitan area, much of the capital requirement is for the expansion and improvement of capacity to provide essential services, including electricity, gas, water, sewerage, telecommunications, streets and roads, and market and abattoir facilities. Proposed expenditures for these purposes, for an extension of port facilities and for the new airport now nearing completion, together with miscellaneous capital outlays mostly for administrative and official housing purposes, account for over half of the recommended investment expenditures.

The rest is for what may be broadly classified as social services, including public construction of low cost rental housing by the Singapore Improvement Trust. These are usually major items in the capital budget of any important city; they are particularly prominent in Singapore's public capital requirements because of the congestion and associated social problems which already exist in the city, and the high rate of population growth. The existing and prospective need for governmental intervention in the housing problem is particularly great, and the recommended expenditure for rental housing for the lower income groups is the largest single item in the proposed investment program. A measure of Singapore's education requirements in the immediate future is the prospect that the primary school-age population may increase by as much as 50% in the next five or six years, during which the major impact of the high postwar birth rates and reduced infant and child mortality rates will be felt. Thereafter, in the early 1960's, more moderate rates of increase in the school-age population are to be expected. We estimate capital requirements for public schools in Singapore during 1955-59 at about $55 million[7] and a doubling of annually recurrent expenditures on education in the same period. We strongly support the establishment of the Singapore Polytechnic Institute to meet the urgent need for vocational training. In view of the size and trend of Singapore's population, substantial increases in recurrent and capital expenditures on medical, health and welfare services are necessary.

IV PROSPECTS

For obvious reasons, we cannot attempt to forecast the rates of expansion for the Malayan economy as a whole. Even in sectors in which the extent of development opportunities can be evaluated, wide differences in the rates of expansion seem likely.

For example, new rubber trees require about seven years to reach maturity, so that the proposed replanting programs which we support will not increase production in the next five years. On the contrary, there will be some decline in the short run as old trees are taken out to be replaced with new high-yielding varieties. But with satisfactory rates of replanting, production can be expected to increase rapidly beginning in the early 1960's; estimates of a rise of 50% in output by the early 1970's and the maintenance of further substantial rates of increase thereafter seem reasonable, both in terms of productive potentialities and market prospects. Similarly, in the case of cocoa, oil palm, coconuts, pineapple and a number of other crops, and the expansion of kampong cultivation generally, while large advances are probable in the longer run, immediate gains may be smaller if, as we recommend, effort and expenditure are concentrated on improving the basis for a subsequent expansion. On the other hand, for rice acreage and production and in the cultivation of fruits and vegetables and livestock, steady long- and short-run gains are probable. Current programs to improve and extend the rice area, mainly through irrigation, would affect

[7] Compared with capital outlays of only about $10 million in 1949-53.

some 270,000 acres in the 1955-59 period and it seems reasonable to expect that subsequent rates of gain will be comparable. Meanwhile, research and experimentation and more active extension services in wider use of fertilizer and improved varieties and in fostering better techniques generally should result in an increase in yields of rice and other crops on presently and newly cultivated lands.

We have indicated that expansion prospects in the minerals and forestry fields appear less promising. Some rise in tin production is, however, possible in the longer run, and the proposed geological and mineral surveys may indicate greater possibilities than are now apparent for other minerals. In forestry, we would expect the output of forest products, largely for domestic purposes, at least to keep pace with the growth of the economy as a whole; it might expand at a faster rate in both domestic and export markets if current research and experimentation should show new commercial potentialities such as the manufacture of wood pulp and fiber board production.

With regard to the promising outlook for expansion of Malaya's fish production, the major rates of gain are more likely to come in the 1960's than in the next five years; extensive conversion to mechanized operations is essential and, moreover, processing and distribution facilities must be developed to handle the increased output.

In the field of basic services for the economy, substantial and steady advances are to be expected in both the Federation and Singapore in the provision of electric power, telecommunications and other utility services and in the capacity of rail, road, water and air transport facilities. Some of these improvements will contribute directly to a higher national output and all will facilitate faster expansion in a wide variety of private agricultural, industrial and other activities.

In industry, we would expect a continuing growth of manufacturing activity in the Federation and Singapore, mainly following the pattern of an expansion of small- and medium-scale enterprise over a very wide front but possibly also in a few lines of larger-scale manufacturing. How large and how rapid this expansion is likely to be is, of course, impossible to predict but we believe it can be accelerated by the governmental measures and policies we recommend.

The wide field of commercial, financial, professional and craft services to the domestic market will grow with the economy and contribute to an expanded national output. Although the entrepot trade of Singapore, as well as Penang, can be expected to have its ups and downs with economic and political developments in Southeast Asia, we believe that it rests on solid and permanent foundations of valuable commercial, financial and processing services. The strengthening of sterling should further contribute to the entrepot trade, which in the past has suffered to some extent from free-market exchange rate advantages in neighboring areas. Short of serious political disturbances in Southeast Asia, we are optimistic about a rising trend of entrepot activities, in which we include the processing and manufacture of imported materials for export, consistent with the prospective economic advances in South and Southeast Asia generally.

By and large, then, we are favorably impressed with Malaya's economic potentialities and prospects for expansion. There remains, nevertheless, the crucial question whether the rates of economic progress and additions to employment opportunities can move ahead of or even keep up with the pace at which the population and the labor force are growing.

Our estimates suggest that in recent years employment and the output of goods and services have at least kept up with, and perhaps have exceeded, this pace. But this has been a period of special circumstances due both to the prosperity fostered by the post-Korea boom, and to the very large rise in employment and income generated in the government sector, mainly by measures to combat the emergency, and by the rapid expansion in social and other governmental services. We have noted that rates of investment and saving in the economy do not appear to be particularly high in relation to national income; our estimates indicate that gross investment has recently been about 10% of gross national product and gross savings somewhat less.[8]

Experience in other countries suggests that these rates of investment and saving may not be able consistently to sustain the rates of growth in the real output of the economy achieved during the period 1949-53. Thus, while there is promise of a large, continuing and varied expansion in the economies of the Federation and Singapore, it is difficult to predict with the same assurance that the expansion will be sufficient to provide both adequate employment opportunities and an improved standard of living if the population maintains its present rate of growth.

It would be possible to be much more sanguine about the outlook for long-run advancement in standards of living and economic well-being if

[8] See estimates of public and private investment and savings in the Statistical Appendix, Table 13, in Part V.

the high birth rates of both the Federation and Singapore were likely to fall. We recognize, of course, the strong cultural and practical obstacles, common to many countries, to a wider acceptance of the principle and practice of family planning and family limitation. Possibly, these obstacles may be less formidable in Malaya than in some other countries. It is often ignorance and misunderstanding, or the desire for a large family as a form of old-age insurance, which stands in the way of any change in a pattern of high birth rates. In Malaya, these factors may not prove to be as important as in other areas which are less literate, poorer and economically more insecure.

Nevertheless, the adoption of family planning and its practical reflection in a lower birth rate will at best be gradual developments. This makes a prompt beginning the more important. We strongly urge that public and private efforts in this direction be given sympathetic government support and assistance in both the Federation and Singapore in the long-run interest of the Malayan people and their welfare.

PART **II** *THE PRODUCTIVE SECTORS*

INTRODUCTION

In Part I we described in general terms the nature and stage of development of the Malayan economy, emphasizing especially the need for and the problems involved in maintaining a rate of growth in employment and productivity commensurate with the rapid growth of the population and the labor force.

In this part we turn from the general to the particular and examine the needs in the various sectors of the economy. For each of these sectors we make a number of recommendations concerning projects or policies, indicating briefly the reasons for each. More extended discussion will be found in the corresponding Technical Reports.

We think it appropriate to begin with a comment on our objectives and the period to which our recommendations relate.

For technical and other details and the cost estimates of particular projects, we have relied to a considerable extent upon the departments and agencies of the Federation and Singapore. We have thought that our efforts would be of greatest use to the governments if they were directed, not to working out or reviewing the details of individual projects, but rather toward drawing together the plans of the various departments and agencies and fitting them, modified as seemed to us desirable, into a development program which appears reasonable in relation to prospective resources. Accordingly, we have concerned ourselves principally with (1) the availability of resources for development and the scale of total public investment consistent with those resources, (2) the general lines of development which in our judgment should have first priority, given the limitations on public investment, and (3) the policies and organizational patterns which appear likely to facilitate execution of the proposed development program.

When the mission was in Malaya, the two governments were themselves giving consideration to a program for the period 1955-59. We have therefore limited our recommendations to what seems possible of accomplishment within that period; we have not thought it practicable or profitable to attempt to forecast the availability of resources thereafter.

After the mission left Malaya, and while this report was being prepared, the departments and agencies of the Federation and Singapore made specific commitments for development expenditure in 1955. Since complete details of these commitments were not available to us when we were formulating our conclusions in the latter part of 1954, the program we have recommended not only overlaps a period for which commitments have already been made but may to some extent propose expenditures different in scope and amount from those actually made or to be made during 1955. The variations are not, however, likely to be great or significant, since a continuing exchange of views with the governments during the preparation of the report has kept us informed of the general outline of official planning for 1955. Moreover, our concern having been with a five-year program as a whole, the assignment of particular projects and expenditures to a particular year has been to a considerable extent arbitrary; it has been done principally to reveal more clearly the nature of the development financing problem discussed in Chapter 8.

At the risk of stating the obvious, we point out that it is not the purpose of this report to present a detailed blueprint of a development program for adoption by the two territories; it is rather to outline proposals to assist the governments in framing policy and in making their own determination as to what their public investment objectives should be during the next few years. We must also emphasize that our recommendations are necessarily made in the light of present prospects. They need to be reviewed periodically and revised as may be dictated by the inevitable changes in the variety of circumstances relevant to public investment decisions.

CHAPTER 3

AGRICULTURE, FORESTRY AND FISHERIES

---

1 AGRICULTURE

For the foreseeable future it seems clear that the agricultural resources of the Federation offer one of the largest potentials, among the various sectors of the economy, for increased output and employment. Some estimates have placed the area of unused but potentially productive land at almost 50% of present cultivated acreage. These estimates are, of course, little more than guesswork in the absence of any systematic survey of Malaya's agricultural resources. However, in view of the large unoccupied areas of potentially cultivable land and the possibilities for improved utilization of land now under cultivation, there seems little doubt that to anticipate a 50% increase in total agricultural output would in the long run be very conservative.

Such long run prospects are hardly comforting, however, when weighed against Malaya's very high rates of population growth and the uncertainties of the Malayan rubber industry.

The problem of the rubber industry is simply that about three-quarters of the rubber area is still planted to trees of an advanced age with poor and declining yields and uncertain competitive prospects in relation to the synthetic rubber industry. Malaya is, therefore, faced with the possibility of a steady deterioration in its most important industry at a time when a rapid expansion of national output is essential to keep pace with the unusually high rate of population growth.

Because of the uncertainties surrounding the future of natural rubber and of the instability of the Malayan economy, arising from its heavy dependence on the fluctuating fortunes of rubber in world markets, there has been considerable interest in greater diversification of agriculture. Certainly there are physical and economic potentialities for a continuing and substantial increase in the production of a variety of other crops. The mission is convinced, however, that none of these crops, or any combination of them, promises possibilities for expansion on a scale and at a rate which

47

could compensate for a major decline in rubber production. We believe, therefore, that within the agricultural sector the highest development priority should be given to maintaining the position of the rubber industry in the Malayan economy. Fortunately, varieties of rubber trees are now available which will produce two to three times as much latex as ordinary rubber trees at greatly reduced unit costs. However, replacement of low-yielding trees with these improved varieties requires a substantial invest-ment and means a loss of income for about seven years while the new trees are reaching maturity.

A   RUBBER

Prospects

Cost data from a representative cross-section of rubber estates indicate that the production of high-yielding rubber on well-managed estates could continue to compete profitably with synthetic rubber even if prices of the latter were to fall well below present levels. Smallholdings on high-yielding rubber cultivated mainly with family labor or on a crop-sharing basis would be even less vulnerable to lower synthetic rubber prices. And it seems clear that high-yielding rubber trees, once they reach bearing age, promise a return greater than that of any other crop for which the vast majority of smallholdings would be suitable.

Nor is it likely that the additional output to be expected from practicable rates of new planting and replanting would lead to excessive supplies in relation to prospective world demand. A United States agency, the President's Materials Policy Commission (Paley Commission), has fore-cast a rise in world rubber consumption outside the Communist area to about twice the present level by about the mid-1970's. On the other hand, the Rubber Growers' Association in London has estimated future Malayan production at about 50% above present levels by the early 1970's. This estimate is based on present acreage and assumes estate replanting with high-yielding rubber at a rate of 60,000 acres a year and a higher average rate for smallholders. In the mission's view, this appears to be a reasonable and feasible objective.

The Paley Commission estimates may be unduly optimistic and they hardly provide an assured basis for present policies. Nevertheless, the out-look for future world rubber consumption appears sufficiently favorable to make it unlikely that replanting and new planting at rates which seem possible of achievement would lead to over-production by Malaya. Indeed, unless there is in prospect an increase in natural rubber production through substantial planting of high-yielding trees within the next few years, rising world demand may well stimulate a considerable further development of synthetic rubber capacity to the long-run detriment of the natural rubber industry.

Investment by efficient estates and smallholdings in high-yielding rubber thus appears to be justified by what seem to be reasonable expectations of future markets and by the increase in output to be realized at reduced unit costs. From the standpoint of the Malayan economy, the encouragement of replanting and new planting of high-yielding rubber would be justified even if the risks were much greater than they now appear, in view of the critical importance of rubber to Malaya, the uncertain future competitive position of ordinary rubber trees, and the absence of other lines of production which might compensate for a major deterioration in the rubber industry. Such a deterioration could only mean something near eventual disaster for the Malayan economy.

Replanting

At present about two-thirds of the total estate acreage of about 2 million acres and nearly all smallholdings (about 1.7 million acres) are still in ordinary low-yielding trees. The government's present program aims at the replanting of a total of 500,000 acres by smallholders during the seven-year period 1953-59; financial assistance is provided through a 4½ cents per pound cess levied on exports of smallholders' rubber, distributed for approved replanting at the rate until recently of $400 per acre, now $500.

The imperative need for steady replacement of low-yielding trees with high-yielding varieties has been emphasized recently by an independent Mission of Enquiry into the Rubber Industry of Malaya.[1] This Mission (hereinafter referred to as the Rubber Enquiry) made a very thorough and careful examination of the industry and we have been greatly assisted in our task by its report. We refer here only to those of its recommendations which we particularly wish to support or on which our wider terms of reference make it necessary for us to comment.

[1] *Report of a Mission of Enquiry into the Rubber Industry of Malaya*, Government of the Federation of Malaya, 1954.

The Rubber Enquiry endorsed the replanting program for smallholders, and for estate rubber stressed the necessity of a continuous replanting program, recommending a minimum annual replanting rate of 3% of present estate acreage, or about 60,000 acres; the 3% rate was based on a 30- to 35-year economic life of a rubber tree. It urged a more ambitious rate of replanting in the next two or three years, to make up for past inadequacies and to strengthen the competitive position of the industry as rapidly as possible. And it also proposed a method of providing financial relief to encourage replanting.

We share the Rubber Enquiry's view of the importance and urgency of enlarging the area planted to high-yielding rubber as rapidly as possible. Accordingly, we strongly support the recommendations that the small-holders' replanting scheme be continued and that a definite program of estate replanting be instituted. We must, however, emphasize the strain that would be imposed on the government by the financial assistance to the industry proposed by the Rubber Enquiry to facilitate the financing of replanting.

The Rubber Enquiry Proposal. Foreseeing little prospect in the near future of a significant inflow of new external capital into the Malayan rubber industry, the Rubber Enquiry pointed to the need to rely mainly on current earnings for replanting. As a means to this end it recommended that the portion of the present cess of 4½ cents on exports, known as the Schedule IV cess,[2] collected on estate rubber and now returned in full to estates, should instead be retained (as is the case with the portion collected on smallholders' exports) and be deposited in a replanting fund to the accounts of individual estates on the basis of their production.

Under this scheme, an estate would draw on its account to finance expenditures on approved replanting incurred subsequent to the imposition of the retainable cess. Withdrawals in excess of replanting expenditures would be allowed where the yield from the cess on the production of a particular estate is greater than the costs incurred in replanting at a satis-

---

[2] There is at present another replanting cess called the Schedule II cess which is levied on exports on a sliding scale when the price of rubber is above 60 cents a pound. The part collected on smallholder rubber is paid into the smallholder replanting fund while that collected on estate rubber is repaid to estates to the extent of replanting expenditure incurred since 1946. The rates of the cess are, however, quite low in relation to replanting costs and collections amount to no more than a small part of the financial requirements for satisfactory rates of replanting. The estate replanting cess as recommended by the Rubber Enquiry would replace this Schedule II cess.

factory rate. On the other hand, the Rubber Enquiry recommended the extension of long-term credit in cases where, because of low yields per acre, the return from the cess is inadequate to finance replanting at a satisfactory rate, or where further financing is needed for an approved program of accelerated replanting.

The Rubber Enquiry concluded that at the lower levels of rubber prices, a low-yielding estate could not both pay export duty on the present scale[3] and set aside an adequate amount for replanting. For this reason and also because of the general objections to export duties, it recommended that no duty be imposed on exports when rubber prices are 60 cents per pound or less, and that at prices above 60 cents there be a graduated export duty starting at levels of less than 10% of present rates, reaching about 50% of present rates at a rubber price of 69 cents and rising to about the level of present rates only at a price of 77 cents. Above 77 cents the recommended rates would increase much more steeply than do present rates. Within a rubber price range of 63 to 67 cents per pound the recommended duty rates would vary from 17% to 38% of present rates. The Rubber Enquiry also recommended an increase in the cess for rubber research from the present 0.5 cents per pound to 0.75 cents in order to expand research and advisory services to the industry.

We recognize the objections to the present schedule of export duty on rubber and agree that tax relief would increase the financial incentives of the industry and assist many estates to keep to a satisfactory rate of replanting at the lower levels of prices. But account must be taken of the fiscal importance of the rubber export duty in view of the very heavy financial burdens of the government and the difficulties of financing a reasonably satisfactory program of economic and social development. It cannot be assumed that a cut in the revenue from export duty could be

[3] The duty varies with the f.o.b. price per pound of rubber, as follows (duty and price in cents per pound):

Price	Duty
Under 60	5% ad valorem
60	3.00
65	3.75
70	4.50
75	5.375
80	6.125
90	7.675
100	9.25
150	17.00

made good by other new and additional taxation since, as discussed elsewhere, it is in any case essential that additional sources of revenue be tapped.

Our concern arises in connection with the proposed changes in the schedule of export duty in the lower ranges of rubber prices. At price levels of over 80 cents a pound, reached in the latter part of 1954, the proposed rates would be higher and more steeply graduated than existing ones. We agree with the principle that rates should be more steeply graduated when the price of natural rubber is substantially higher than present or likely synthetic prices. We believe that any wide divergence in favor of natural rubber which may occur from time to time as a result of changing demand conditions and consumption patterns is likely to be transitory, and that the impact on the general price and cost structure of the economy should be minimized through appropriate fiscal measures.

We believe it realistic to expect that over an extended period the price of natural rubber will tend on the average to move within a limited range of synthetic rubber prices. For purposes of financial calculations we have assumed an average Singapore export price for smoked sheet grade No. 1 of 75 cents per pound in 1955 and of 65 cents in the subsequent four years.

It is this low price of 65 cents per pound that we have in mind in the following comments on the Rubber Enquiry's recommendation respecting export duty. At this price the rate proposed would be little more than one-quarter of the present rate and the loss of revenue to the government would be $30 to $35 million a year, depending on the volume of exports. The government's existing and prospective commitments are such that a loss of revenue of this magnitude would have serious implications; consequently it is necessary to inquire whether the objective of a satisfactory replanting program cannot be achieved at less cost to the government if rubber prices fall to the 65 cents a pound level.

We start from the premise that in the Federation's present financial circumstances, the government's contribution towards the cost of a satisfactory replanting program should not go beyond what is necessary to supplement the contributions which can reasonably be expected from rubber producers themselves, and that it should take such form as will best ensure that the program will be carried out. These criteria are difficult to apply in practice since the financial and physical capacities and the inclination to replant are not uniform among elements of the industry; moreover, they vary with the price of rubber. Perhaps the most important relevant difference among estates is in their unit costs of production, due to a variety of reasons of which the most significant by far, as noted by the Rubber Enquiry, is variation in yields per acre. These in turn are largely attributable to the proportion of the mature area planted to high-yielding rubber.

In the circumstances it is probably impossible to devise an ideal scheme of assistance for replanting. The objective must, however, be a scheme which diverges from the ideal as little as possible. With this in mind we have considered the Rubber Enquiry's proposals regarding tax concessions and arrangements for financing replanting, for smallholders and for estates, in each of the groups into which the Rubber Enquiry divided them. For reasons set forth in detail in Technical Report 1, we have reached the following conclusions: (a) For smallholders, tax concessions are in themselves unlikely to have any significant influence on replanting. (b) For the great majority of "superior" estates ("superior" estates being those with over 30% of their area in high-yielding rubber, representing roughly one-half of the total estate area), the present schedule of export duty does not appear to be a decisive hindrance to replanting. (c) For the "poorer" estates (those with only about 10% or less of their area in high-yielding rubber, representing about 20% of the total estate acreage), the problem of rehabilitation is not likely to be solved by large tax concessions, even if linked with a compulsory replanting cess. (d) For the intermediate group of estates, those with between 10% and 30% of their area in high-yielding rubber, there appears to be a strong economic case for tax concessions or alternative forms of assistance which would supplement their own replanting expenditure by an amount sufficient to permit them to finance at least a 3%, and possibly for a time a higher, rate of replanting. But the estates in this group account for only about one-quarter of the estate area and for only 15% of the entire rubber area, including smallholders. In view of our conclusions with respect to the other 85% of the industry, we believe that the advantages to be gained in replanting under the Rubber Enquiry proposals would not be commensurate with the adverse effect on the government's financial position.

For several reasons, also set forth in the Technical Report, we do not support an alternative proposal of the Rubber Producers' Council, an association representing rubber growers. The principal disadvantage of that proposal is that the amounts which would be credited under it, when prices are low, to the accounts of estates in greatest need of assistance would be far from adequate to enable them to maintain a satisfactory rate of replanting.

A third suggested method of financial assistance to encourage replanting is that the government make a uniform grant per acre towards the cost of replanting a stipulated proportion of an estate's planted acreage within a prescribed period; rates of export duty would remain approximately as at present at the lower price levels. A proportionate contribution would also be made by the government towards the smallholders' replanting fund. This method, too, is open to objection, notably that if the grant is considered as an alternative to the reduction of export duty at the lower price levels, it favors the estates which have not pursued sound replanting policies at the expense of those which have. On the other hand, this proposal directly relates government assistance to areas actually replanted and avoids the disadvantages and complications of a replanting cess credited to the accounts of individual estates regardless of their financial circumstances, replanting policies and prospects for maintaining or achieving satisfactory rates of replanting.[4]

On balance we believe this proposal is preferable to either of the others, and we recommend its adoption; we have accordingly assumed it for the purpose of the forecasts and the capital expenditure program set forth in Chapter 8. We are aware that means of dealing with the replanting problem are being considered by the government and the Rubber Producers' Council and that some other method may be agreed upon in these discussions; in that event our figures would require adjustment.

In view of the financial burden which this proposal would impose on the government we suggest that the present schedule of export duty be retained at lower ranges of rubber prices, up to, say, about 75 cents, and that its progression should be substantially steeper in the higher ranges. The latter would be justified by the fact that the government contribution to replanting costs would be fixed, although the need for assistance would decline as prices increased, and by the advantages from the standpoint of general economic and financial stability. In revising the export duty schedule at higher price ranges, however, allowance should be made for the fact that wage rates of estate labor are linked to and also rise with rubber export prices.

----

[4] Under this proposal the present Schedule IV cess would continue to be collected on rubber exports and that part from rubber produced on estates would still be unconditionally refunded to estates in accordance with their production as at present.

With replanting costs of $800 an acre spread over a seven-year period, the annual cost of a seven-year program to replant 3% of the estate acreage each year—say 60,000 acres annually—would rise to a maximum of $48 million in the seventh year when the final expenditure necessary to bring to maturity the trees planted in the first year would be incurred. Assuming that the government grant were equal to half the replanting cost incurred each year, the government's contribution would increase from about $7 million in the first year to about $20 million in the fifth year and about $24 million by the seventh year. Thereafter it would decline to about $2 million in the thirteenth year when the trees planted in the seventh year will have reached maturity. We have assumed this scale of cost in our figures in Chapter 8. While the net cost to the government would be thus greater than under the Rubber Producers' Council's proposals, we believe that the scheme would be more effective. Moreover, the cost of the grants would be less over the 1955-59 period than the loss of revenue which would result from the reduction in the export duty, at a price of 65 cents a pound, to the extent recommended by the Rubber Enquiry.

An accelerated program of estate replanting at more than a 3% annual rate in the next five years would correspondingly increase the burden of the government. If, for example, 21% of the estate area were to be replanted in four rather than seven years, the amount of government grants in the first five years would be increased by about 60%. Nevertheless, we believe that the government should assume this additional burden to the extent that an accelerated replanting program proves feasible, even if it should mean spreading beyond 1955-59 some of the other items of the recommended investment program which are deemed to have a lower immediate priority. It may be noted, however, that in estimating the cost to the government of such a replanting program, we have assumed a replanting cost of $800 an acre. The actual cost may, as pointed out by the Rubber Enquiry, be considerably less; our estimates of the cost to government in an accelerated, as well as a 3%, program of replanting may therefore be considered maximum figures. There may also be limitations on the extent to which an accelerated program can be carried out, especially since such a large proportion of the backlog of neglected replanting is among the "poorer" estates, which have limited resources to contribute their own share of replanting expenditure and apparently little inclination to maintain even a 3% replanting rate. In this connection we believe consideration should be given to making the refund to estates of the Schedule IV cess, now automatic, conditional on the maintenance of some minimum standard of replanting.

Smallholdings. In Technical Report 1, we discuss the smallholders' replanting program in some detail. Here we wish to comment on only a few aspects of the program.

Because it is in the national economic interest to increase the high-yielding smallholder area, we believe there is a case for a further increase in the replanting allowance, recently raised from $400 to $500 per acre. Even with the increase, it is hard for most smallholders to make the requisite sacrifices (particularly losing income from the part of the holding occupied by immature trees), necessary to secure the long-run benefits of higher yielding trees.

If the allowance were increased, the smallholder replanting program could no longer be self-supporting on the basis of a 4½ cent cess, as was estimated to be approximately the case with a replanting grant of $400 per acre. It is, however, part of what we have called the third method of assisting estates to replant that the government should also contribute to the smallholders' replanting fund.

Assuming the cost of estate replanting to be $800 an acre, a government grant of half that amount, and an estate replanting program of say 420,000 acres over seven years or possibly less, the total cost to the government would be $168 million. Since smallholder rubber production is about 40% of the total, a proportionate government contribution to the smallholder replanting fund would be $112 million. This would allow a subsidy of about $200 per acre and would enable the total allowance per acre of replanting to be increased to an average of about $600 per acre for 500,000 acres.

However, instead of raising the allowance above the present level of $500 per acre, it may be preferable to use the added subsidy for financing additional services to assist smallholder replanting. We have in mind such things as providing fencing, specialized services for eradication and control of lalang, for tree poisoning on a more extensive scale, for transporting felled trees to points where they may be sold for firewood, etc.

On the basis of the established annual replanting targets and assuming that the increased allowance were to be distributed in annual installments in the proportions prevailing when the allowance was $400 an acre, the addition to estimated payments from the replanting fund, and consequently the amount of the government subsidy, may be estimated as increasing from about $7 million in 1955 to a maximum of about $16 million in 1959. We have included this schedule of subsidies for the smallholder program in our financial estimates for 1955-59.

So far measures to increase the smallholders' high-yielding area have emphasized replanting almost exclusively. As noted by the Rubber Enquiry, possibilities for new planting on unoccupied land have received comparatively little attention since the late 1930's. Instead, the alienation of additional land for rubber is being severely restricted by States and Settlements Governments as a matter of policy, mainly because of concern over the fluctuating and uncertain fortunes of rubber and a consequent interest in more diversified land use, especially for lands which might be suitable for food crops.

The Rubber Enquiry emphasized the advantages of new planting, as well as replanting, for better maintenance and more rapid increase in rubber output. It also pointed out that, given the large unsatisfied demand for additional rubber land, the alienation of land for new planting would be one of the most effective means of bringing fresh capital into the industry. New planting has other advantages, such as easier lalang control and, in some cases, the possibility of establishing a stand of high-yielding rubber while continuing to obtain an income from old trees on present holdings.

We agree that it would be desirable to liberalize land alienation policy for new rubber planting, which should not only be permitted but encouraged. We have noted that practicable possibilities for replanting in relation to prospective growth in world rubber consumption would appear to leave considerable room for new planting as well. And from the standpoint of agricultural development as a whole, the economic advantages of mature high-yielding rubber compare favorably with those of any other smallholder crop for which, on the basis of present information, a substantial expansion is practicable. Indeed, rubber is the only crop which is suitable for extensive cultivation in much of the large unoccupied area.[5]

We recognize, of course, that it is necessary to consider other possible uses of land before its alienation to rubber, e.g., where mining opportunities are indicated, where forest reserves have overriding priority in the interest of conservation, or where lands are more suitable for development in large unified projects than individual holdings.

[5] E. H. G. Dobby, "The Development of Malaya's Uplands," *The Development of Upland Areas in the Far East,* Vol. 2., Institute of Pacific Relations, 1951, pp. 17, 18.

These conflicting claims should, ideally, be evaluated in connection with a land-use program based on systematic land-use surveys. But completion of surveys on a comprehensive scale would require an extended period. To postpone reconsideration of land alienation policies until completion of the surveys would mean a prolonged delay which we consider inadvisable.

Pending such surveys, we believe that the importance of additional new planting is such that the suitability of unoccupied lands for rubber should receive special attention by local agricultural officials and the Small-holders Advisory Service of the Rubber Research Institute. The relative advantages of rubber and possible alternatives on particular sites can, of course, be decided only on the merits of each case, but in reaching such decisions the importance and high priority of rubber should, we believe, be emphasized as a matter of government policy. We would, however, stress the potential danger of serious soil erosion and the destruction of protective forest if land is indiscriminately alienated for rubber cultivation. We accordingly recommend that special consideration be given by the competent authorities to the potential deterioration of soils that might follow the development of a number of rubber smallholdings in any given locality.

As an encouragement to new planting we suggest that consideration be given to grants from the smallholders' replanting fund for new planting by a smallholder or his immediate family in cases where this is feasible and clearly preferable to replanting on the existing holding. Communications requirements for newly established rubber areas should be an important consideration in the planning of feeder road programs.

B   DEVELOPMENT OF OTHER LINES OF AGRICULTURE

While the rehabilitation of the rubber industry through a vigorous re-planting program will make a major contribution to the strengthening of the economy, the additional output from high-yielding rubber will not provide anything like a proportionate addition to long-run agricultural employment. Other potentialities in the agricultural sector should there-fore be developed as fast as possible to contribute to the demands on output and employment made by the growth in population.

Considerable research and some developmental and extension work have been devoted to most of the established Malayan crops and to a num-ber of new crop possibilities. The main emphasis of the Federation's agri-

cultural development policy and activity outside the field of rubber, however, has been on an expansion of rice production. This reflects an intense
and widespread interest in reducing as rapidly as possible the dependence
of the Federation on outside sources for about 40% of rice requirements.
It is not a serious exaggeration to say that agricultural development, other
than rubber production, has been conceived largely in terms of measures
which offer the greatest technical short-run possibilities for additional rice
output. As a consequence, funds and effort have been concentrated on the
improvement of existing rice areas, where results could be achieved more
readily than through the opening up of new lands. Insufficient attention
has been given to the relative advantages of expenditures and use of land
for other crops, and extensive preparation to meet Malaya's longer-run
need for expansion of the cultivated area has been subordinated to short-
run objectives. The preoccupation with a short-run increase in rice production is understandable in view of the severe shortages which Malaya
suffered during and immediately following the war, and of the high and,
until recently, steadily rising prices of imported rice in the postwar period.

Measures to increase rice production, especially the rice improvement
and development programs of the Agriculture and Drainage and Irrigation
Departments, have been a major factor in the postwar expansion in rice
output to about 25% above prewar levels. Further expansion of production
is bound to be an important element in any well-conceived program of
agricultural development. Taking into account possibilities for increasing
yields through irrigation and more active extension work in improving
varieties and techniques of cultivation, including more widespread use of
fertilizer; for expanding the area of double-cropping; and for developing
new lands for rice cultivation, it is reasonable to expect that the rates of
increase in output of the past two decades can be maintained or perhaps
exceeded over at least the next decade or two.

It must nevertheless be recognized that in view of Malaya's high ratio
of population to rice lands compared with other Southeast Asian countries
and its very high rate of population growth, anything approaching rice
self-sufficiency does not appear a practicable goal in the foreseeable future.
Furthermore, with world rice prices now declining and a possibility of
further decline, we think that greater attention should be given in the
future to the relative economic advantages of other crops.

The extremely limited agricultural development expenditure outside the
programs of the Drainage and Irrigation Department is indicated by the

fact that present Federal and State agricultural appropriations for administration, research (other than on rubber) and extension work represent only about 1% or 2% of the total budget—an amount less than that for public information services. This is the more serious in the light of official statistics indicating an absence of strong spontaneous growth factors among most of Malaya's minor crops. Acreage of all the principal classes of crops except rubber, rice and oil palm is now smaller than before the war. Finally, while improvement of existing rice areas is important, it is equally if not more important to prepare the basis for a considerable long-run expansion of the cultivated area, to provide employment for the growing population on a larger scale than is possible through improving already cultivated lands.

The change in emphasis which we have proposed will, however, require preliminary preparation through surveys, research, experimentation and extension activities. Proposals for increased activity along these lines are discussed subsequently. But they will require time and for this reason we recommend a gradual shift in emphasis rather than an abrupt change in or a curtailment of current agricultural development activity.

Lines of Immediate Activity

Drainage and Irrigation. The mission is impressed with the extent of the accomplishments of the Drainage and Irrigation Department. In the six years 1949-54, an estimated area of nearly 300,000 acres, mainly in rice, including about 40,000 acres of new land, has been improved through irrigation, and large additional areas in rice, rubber, coconut and other crops have been improved or protected through drainage works. Comparable results are expected in the 1955-59 period, again principally in existing rice areas. Under the pressure of national rice policy these projects have been carried out on the basis of broad and only approximate financial analyses; information is inadequate for an accurate and detailed evaluation of their net benefits in relation to cost, or of their economic advantage in relation to comparable expenditures on other crops or in other possible lines of public investment. As we point out later in this chapter, this limited attention to costs and benefits could lead to a misdirection of investment resources if rice development is pushed so far that returns on investment become unduly low. As nearly as could be determined from the available data, it would appear that by and large the proposed yearly expenditure on rice irrigation projects of the Drainage and Irrigation Department is undoubtedly justified by the anticipated gross additional output.

In view of this, of the important contributions which these Drainage and Irrigation Department projects can be expected to make to Malaya's agricultural development needs and of the limited preparatory work for a more broadly conceived agricultural development program, we believe it would be unwise to interrupt or delay the proposed DID program in order to give immediate attention to possibilities for increased emphasis on new land development and on crops other than rice. We do believe, however, that as a basis is established through surveys, research, experimentation and planning there should be a shift in emphasis in these directions. As far as new land development is concerned, considerable preliminary investigation has already been undertaken by the Agriculture and Drainage and Irrigation Departments in collaboration, in many cases, with the Survey Department, and the existing detailed surveys of the large Trans-Perak development proposal are a further step in this direction. But these surveys and investigations, too, have been oriented largely toward rice possibilities. We would urge that the relative economic advantages of other crops in these and other new areas be considered, that the relative merits of opening new land and of improving existing areas be more carefully weighed and that there be closer coordination among the Drainage and Irrigation, the Agriculture and other departments concerned in the selection, planning and execution of agricultural projects, including the colonization phase of new land development.

We mention especially the colonization phase because it is one of the most difficult aspects of the problem of new land development. We urge that closer consideration be given to it. We believe there is need for further investigation of the amount and nature of inducements necessary to overcome the reluctance of peasant cultivators to move from established to newly opened areas, and for more careful planning and closer coordination among the officials and departments concerned with colonization than has been the case in the past.

In our recommended program for 1955-59 we have allocated $55 million for capital costs of drainage, irrigation and river conservancy, and allowed for annually recurrent expenditures of the Drainage and Irrigation Departments of the Federal and State and Settlement Governments rising from $8.8 million in 1955 to $10.7 million in 1959 (compared with just under $8 million in the budget estimates for 1954). The capital figure is only slightly higher than the capital requirements as estimated by the Drainage and Irrigation Department for departmental projects proposed for 1955-1959. We believe that the Department's estimates are too low since they do not make provision, in the case of new land development, for payments to settlers by State and Settlement Governments, mainly for the work of land clearance, and for other costs outside the jurisdiction of the Department. Financing of some of the latter costs, such as roads, schools and dispensaries is, however, taken into account under other heads of our program. The total we have projected for capital expenditure should make it possible for the Department to make provision in its own five-year program for somewhat greater new land development than is at present contemplated. A substantially greater emphasis on such development is, however, likely to be practicable only in subsequent years, as the basis is established for extensive development of the Trans-Perak project and as further land-use survey work and other aspects of the planning for an extension of the cultivated area progress.

In Technical Report 2 on Irrigation and Drainage, we suggest some organizational changes, especially with regard to relationships between the Federal Drainage and Irrigation Department and corresponding departments in the States and Settlements.

Land-Use Investigations. In broadening the range of agricultural development objectives many desirable lines of possible development are apparent; if undertaken together, they would be far beyond Malaya's financial and technical capacities and could result only in an excessive dispersion of effort and a waste of personnel and resources. For the immediate future, therefore, the field should be limited to those objectives which seem most urgent and are within existing capacities.

But even in planning to meet a limited number of short-run objectives, a most serious handicap is the inadequacy of data on present agricultural patterns and unrealized agricultural potentialities. A comprehensive land-use survey is needed and we strongly recommend that a start be made on such a survey as soon as staff can be recruited.

Initially the land-use investigation should be directed toward what appear to be the most promising crop possibilities and those objectives of agricultural development which (besides rubber replanting and further improvements in present rice areas) appear of highest short-run priority.

The possibilities for opening new land to cultivation should be further evaluated. Available information suggests a considerable potential, including large sections on the eastern side of the peninsula (in many of which anti-malaria and other health measures will be necessary), some 760,000 acres of swamp jungle scattered through the west and southeast, and several hundred square miles in southern Johore. Rice potentialities within these areas are known in varying degree of detail as a result of Agriculture and Drainage and Irrigation Department investigations and, as already mentioned, a detailed survey is now under way on about 180,000 acres included in the proposed Trans-Perak irrigation project. Reconnaissance of other areas and other crop possibilities should be made as a guide both to individual settlement (as emergency conditions permit) and to the planning of new land development projects for more detailed examination and possible execution. Particular attention should be given to the extensive peat lands which offer promising possibilities for pineapple, other fruits and various vegetables and, where the peat overlay is thin, oil palm and coconuts. So far research and experimentation on the potentialities of peat soils for padi cultivation have not been encouraging, except possibly on the shallower soils; further investigation may, however, be more rewarding.

Special attention should be given to a survey of areas in which oil palm cultivation may be expanded, in view of the favorable conditions of cultivation in the Federation and of reasonably satisfactory long-term market prospects (although possibly prices may be somewhat below recent levels). Within such areas, detailed investigations should be made of possible sites for one or more smallholder pilot projects. Although elsewhere oil palm is grown predominantly by smallholders, it is almost exclusively an estate crop in Malaya; there is a widespread view that it is not suited to smallholdings. Small-scale cultivation should be possible in Malaya. This will require suitable and convenient processing facilities and a carefully organized and supervised system for collection and processing.

The survey of lands suitable for cocoa cultivation should be completed as soon as possible. This crop is now of little significance in Malaya but the extensive research and experimentation of the Agriculture Department have been most promising and indicate that cocoa cultivation can probably be greatly expanded in time. It has been estimated that there may be as much as 300,000 acres of suitable lands, mostly on the east side of the peninsula. Although experimental plantings have been undertaken only on an estate basis, cocoa is also suited to smallholder cultivation. It is suggested, therefore, that particular attention be given at the outset to the selection, among provisional locations already examined, of a site for a pilot small-holders' project. Steps should promptly be taken to recruit supervisory personnel so they may familiarize themselves with local conditions and problems of cocoa cultivation well before the project is begun. Meanwhile, experimentation should continue, emphasizing the problems of smallholder cultivation.

A survey should be made of areas now under coconut and of suitable new areas. This would serve as a basis for plans to check the current deterioration of the industry, by a replanting program in areas found to be favorable, the shifting of cultivation from unfavorable to more suitable localities, and, where feasible, by rehabilitating areas where replanting is inadvisable, through the encouragement of alternative crops.

Other tasks for the land-use survey team include the survey aspects of a coordinated approach, in cooperation with various departments, to such problems as determination of more productive uses for run-down rubber land; investigation of pasture potentialities in connection with an expansion of livestock raising; consideration of the shifting of forest reserves from lowland areas suitable for agriculture to upland areas; assistance in devising suitable techniques and programs to rehabilitate degraded mining lands; and investigation of ways to guide the natural expansion of kampong agriculture into favorable areas in a manner which will accelerate its development and improve its economic position. In the longer run these matters may become equally as important as the priority objectives listed above. We contemplate that the survey will continue well past the next five-year period, and that its emphasis will change as immediate objectives are reached and as new agricultural problems emerge.

Even the more immediate objectives will pose a task of major proportions; we believe that a special team is called for, one free from departmental duties and assisted by an aerial photographic survey.[6] The team should be responsible to the Head of the Secretariat of the proposed Economic Committee; its tasks, and the priorities to be given to them, should

[6] A well-balanced team would consist of an agriculturist (whose personal qualifications should fit him to be leader of the team), an ecologist, a pedologist, a cartographic draftsman/surveyor and an agricultural economist. Occasions may arise requiring a strengthening of the team; in that case we would hope that qualified departmental officers might be released to serve with the team for the necessary period, although consideration of some addition to the continuing membership of the team may later be desirable, depending on financial considerations and recruiting possibilities. See also Technical Report 1.

be prescribed by the Economic Committee after considering the views of the proposed Technical Advisory Committee on Development.[7] It should assemble, in collaboration with the Federal and State departments concerned, all relevant available data. The team should function as a survey and advisory group; actual project planning and execution should be done by the appropriate department.

As a rough estimate of the cost of the survey, we have allowed for an increase in annually recurrent expenditure to $250,000 and a capital outlay of $3.3 million during the period 1955-59.

Much of the actual project planning and execution following from these preliminary surveys will probably not be possible within the next five-year period. But with proper staffing and organization it should be possible to undertake some projects in the near future, in particular some increase in the rate of new land development, the pilot projects for smallholder cultivation of oil palm and cocoa and a start on an officially guided and supported program of replanting, shifting and crop substitution and coconut cultivation.

Research and Extension

It would seem almost unnecessary to emphasize the importance of research, experimentation and extension work in contributing to agricultural development, were it not that public expenditure on these services has been very small in relation to agriculture's role in the economy. Recognizing the difficult financial position of the government, the mission nevertheless believes that additional expenditure on these services is essential if agricultural output is to grow at a faster rate. Suggested directions for research and extension services, as well as proposals for staff and funds, are outlined in Technical Report 1 on Agriculture.

We suggest that research and extension priorities for specific commodities should be as follows:

Rubber. The very valuable work of the Rubber Research Institute should be expanded and its finances increased through a higher research cess, as recommended by the Rubber Enquiry. We also endorse the Enquiry's recommendation for rapid expansion of chemical work on latex, its products and possible derivatives. In this connection we would suggest ar-

[7] Concerning the proposed Economic Committee and Technical Advisory Committee, see pp. 217 and 220.

rangements for closer liaison on a technical level with the principal rubber manufacturers in the United Kingdom and the United States so that their particular requirements may guide research on the adaptability of natural rubber and on how it may be marketed to best advantage. In the extension field, guidance in new smallholder planting by the Smallholders Advisory Service should be given particular attention, with some addition to staff if necessary.

Rice. While average rice yields are already higher than in neighboring countries of Southeast Asia, yields per acre can be increased through wider dissemination of more productive and disease resistant strains; greater use of fertilizers; more effective utilization of water; and improvement in other techniques of field husbandry. In this connection we think that the program of fertilizer subsidies in Kelantan and Trengganu should be continued and, as justified by further experimentation, extended to other areas. We also suggest that consideration be given to a return to the subsidy rates of 1953, if the recent rate reduction should result in a substantial drop in the use of fertilizers.

An expansion of the extremely small area where double-cropping is now practiced should also be possible through wider use of early maturing varieties where seasonal and soil conditions permit. Progress in these directions will require not only continuing research but also more direct and frequent contact with rice cultivators. The government proposes to establish additional experimental facilities and to increase staff as necessary, in order to expand the work on padi breeding, fertilizer experiments, soils, pest control and relationships between soils and water. The results of this work can be disseminated only if personnel of the Field Branch of the Department of Agriculture, particularly at the more junior levels, is increased. We therefore urge the recruiting and training of a larger staff; the recent improvement in the terms of employment of Agricultural Assistants and Agricultural Subordinates is an important step in this direction.

Oil Palm. The high yields and promising prospects for expansion of oil palm warrant further intensive research on improving production methods. Special attention should be given to means for organizing and supervising smallholders' cultivation and the collecting, handling and processing of their crop, in conjunction with the pilot projects previously suggested. Closer cooperation in research between the Department of Agriculture and the private companies engaged in oil palm cultivation should also be arranged.

Coconut. Research and extension work on coconut has received little attention since the war due to shortage of staff and facilities. This situation has recently improved, but in view of the deterioration of the industry, it seems essential that additional attention be given, in conjunction with the surveys, to investigation of satisfactory alternative crops for coconut areas, improving varieties and cultivation practices and developing seedling supplies, and to the extension services involved in the program to replant or shift coconut areas and to rehabilitate present coconut lands unsuited to replanting, as previously suggested.

Cocoa. Emphasis should continue to be placed on cocoa research because of its newness and great promise. It is suggested that two qualified specialists be recruited as soon as practicable—one to concentrate on research problems raised by experimental cultivation and one, with practical experience in both the management and technical aspects of cocoa cultivation, to take charge of the proposed smallholders' pilot project.

Pineapple. Because of the pineapple's adaptability to the better types of Malaya's extensive peat and muck soils, continuing support should be given to the two pineapple experiment stations with a view to possible expansion of the canning industry.

Other Commodities. As funds and personnel permit, studies should also continue on other commodities which are discussed in Technical Report 1 on Agriculture: tea, coffee, tobacco, pepper, manila hemp, livestock and poultry and a variety of fruits and vegetables. Particular attention should be given to the economic and social basis of kampong agriculture and to extension activities for improving typical kampong crops and encouraging interest in such important food crops as groundnuts, soya bean, sweet potato and maize. We consider that the need for better extension services for kampong agriculture ranks in importance with that for rice cultivation, although we recognize that it presents special problems and difficulties. Accordingly, we recommend that the Food and Agriculture Organization or other agencies with experience in rural community development programs in other countries be asked to provide specialized guidance for this extension work.

Our specific recommendations for an enlarged extension service are presented in Technical Report 1 on Agriculture. We recognize the limitations of facilities for training agricultural field workers but believe that additional funds should be made available for this purpose. At present, agricultural training for subordinate staff is conducted by the Department of Agriculture at Serdang; there is a three-year course for Agricultural Assistants and a one-year course for Agricultural Subordinates. Consideration has also been given to the establishment of a Faculty of Agriculture in the Federation as a part of the University of Malaya.

While recognizing the importance and advantage of an agricultural faculty of university level, we believe this should be a long-term objective. Only a limited number of the requisite advanced agricultural specialists is available, the financial requirements are large, and there are many problems and difficulties in establishing a staff and facilities of appropriately high standard. A possible approach might be through steady expansion and improvement, under the direction of the University, of the present three-year course at Serdang with a University diploma given in recognition of satisfactory completion. At the same time, the Serdang one-year course, which is essentially a practical one, might be removed to another center where more students can be accommodated. As a rough estimate we have placed the capital cost of establishing a new one-year training center at $250,000 and the additional recurrent cost at about $25,000. We have made no attempt to estimate the additional financial requirements for improvement and expansion of facilities at Serdang but these would presumably be covered by the estimates of financing for the University of Malaya as a whole.

Rice Policy

Price. The government's policy of fixing minimum prices for padi, designed to assist the small padi cultivator, has been primarily of psychological benefit, while prices of imported rice were high and rising and domestic padi prices tended to stay above the fixed minimum. More recently, however, the world rice picture has changed markedly; the price of imported rice has taken a sharp downward course. Furthermore, trading in imported rice has now been returned to private channels, after several years as a government monopoly (except in certain grades of rice); domestic rice and padi prices have consequently become more sensitive to import prices. In the circumstances, the guaranteed price set for domestic padi when rice prices were high ($17 per picul of 133⅓ lbs. for the 1952-53 and 1953-54 crops) would have been far out of line with the more recent world price levels. Accordingly, for the 1954-55 crop it was reduced to $12 per picul. In the early part of the 1954-55 marketing season domestic padi prices were only slightly above the new guarantee level, in correspondence with prices of imported rice, and world market conditions indicated that import prices might drop still further.

These developments have made necessary the re-examination of the government's padi price policy. In view of the large element of uncertainty in the world market, it is most difficult to devise an appropriate long-run policy; measures adopted now should be reviewed as the world rice situation becomes more stable. It seems clear, however, that a guaranteed producer price for padi fixed at a figure above a level corresponding to internal and external market influences to be really effective would undoubtedly require a system of government purchases and sales at a loss. This would require the creation of a large purchasing organization and give rise to many administrative difficulties; moreover, the government's financial position does not warrant the assumption of such losses, unless the national economic interest clearly justified the diversion of funds from other requirements.

From the standpoint of the national economic interest, it is the mission's view that these funds could more effectively be employed to expand padi production through direct expenditure on drainage and irrigation programs, the opening and settlement of new lands, the subsidized distribution of fertilizer and better seed, and more effective extension services to improve the techniques of padi cultivation generally. For this reason and because of the considerable practical difficulties, we do not favor a policy of guaranteeing domestic padi prices at a fixed level out of line with external and internal market conditions and maintained regardless of domestic and foreign market developments.

At the same time, in view of the sagging world rice prices and the uncertain outlook in world rice markets, we believe there is a strong case for shielding Malayan padi production from the full impact of competition from imported rice. As has been noted, economic standards in Malaya are in general substantially higher than in the major rice exporting countries of Asia. And this is also true specifically in the case of the Malayan padi cultivator as compared with his counterpart in neighboring rice surplus areas, where government policy has been to stabilize padi prices far below comparable levels in Malaya. Consequently, to the extent that export prices move more closely into line with domestic padi prices in the surplus areas and to the extent that there is a corresponding downward movement in domestic padi prices in Malaya, the Malayan padi cultivator's economic position would become increasingly depressed relative to other elements of the Malayan community. While we question the necessity or advantage of large government outlays in guaranteeing a high fixed padi price as a means of fostering greater output, we nevertheless believe that there is a point beyond which the relative economic position of the padi cultivator cannot be allowed to deteriorate if there is not to be a loss of incentive to increase or even to maintain production.

It may be said that such an impairment of the cultivator's position is an unfortunate but natural development which on economic grounds should be allowed to take place. But this assumes that there are adequate alternative employment opportunities outside of padi cultivation and overlooks the prevalent under-employment in padi areas, the traditional limited occupational mobility among padi cultivators, and the need for a continuing expansion of padi production as one important practicable outlet for the rapidly growing labor force. The prospect of employment alternatives for the increasing population in the padi areas on a scale which would compensate for a declining or even a static padi industry is not promising. Diminishing production would undoubtedly mean a loss to the economy as a whole by way of reduced investment of labor and resources of padi cultivators in additional productive capacity, and an increasing waste of unutilized labor as under-employment in the padi areas grew and the unemployed population moved into urban communities. Moreover, it would cause downward pressure on wages and living standards in employment in other fields and increasing social problems in both rural and urban areas.

We therefore regard it as in the interest of the Malayan economy that the padi farmer be given some protection from the competition of rice produced under the much lower economic standards of neighboring surplus areas. This would maintain the incentives for an expanding output. Moreover, without such protection, other measures to expand rice production would undoubtedly lose much of their effectiveness. Until recently protection was provided by the scarcity conditions prevailing in world rice markets and reflected in the very high level of import prices. Now, however, this has been greatly reduced and it may be reduced still further.

We therefore recommend, as an alternative to a fixed government guarantee of padi prices, that consideration be given to imposing a moderate import duty on rice and to subsidizing domestic padi as long as import prices remain below a prescribed minimum. That minimum and the amount of the duty and subsidy payments themselves could be set only after further investigation of the economic conditions of the cultivator and on the basis of prevailing market circumstances. We are not in a position to make a specific recommendation on this point.

We do recommend, however, in the interest of rice consumers and the economy generally, that the retail price level for rice in Malaya should not be allowed to get far out of line with prices of imported rice. We therefore suggest that the specific duty be set anew each season within a maximum limit of 10% of the import price at the beginning of the particular season. We believe the amount of the subsidy payments should also be set anew each season and should be limited as nearly as possible to the revenues from the import tariff. While this would impose some penalty on rice consumers, even the maximum duty suggested would have relatively little impact at the retail level, and we believe it would be justified in the larger economic interests of the community as a whole.

This proposal presents obvious administrative problems and has certain other disadvantages. However, the only other practicable alternative with the advantage of administrative simplicity would appear to be an import duty sufficiently high to provide, in itself, adequate protection for domestic padi and rice, making a subsidy unnecessary. But this would put a heavier burden on rice consumers and the adverse impact on wages and prices generally would be greater. Therefore, unless the administrative costs, especially in manpower, involved in combining a moderate duty with subsidy payments should be found disproportionate to the benefit realized by the padi producer, we believe this to be preferable to a higher import duty.

The most difficult administrative problem would be to devise a method of paying the subsidy so that the benefit would be realized by the padi producer. To achieve this fully would undoubtedly require that the government purchase padi directly from the producer. We doubt, however, the advisability of attempting to create the requisite extensive governmental organization unless possible alternatives should prove quite unsatisfactory.

As a more immediately practicable alternative, we recommend the use of the subsidy to support the price of commercially marketed padi at the point where it is sold to the rice mills. In other words, it is suggested that the mills be enabled to pay more for padi than they otherwise could, by paying them a subsidy based on the volume of domestic padi milled and sold to regular commercial channels. This would still present difficult administrative problems if the subsidy is not merely to result in larger padi buyers' or millers' margins, although some increase in those margins would be unavoidable. But it should be less difficult to ensure that the subsidy serves its intended purpose of giving padi producers higher prices than appears to be the case at first sight, for although there are several hundred rice mills and a much larger number of padi buyers in the Federation, in practice 50 larger self-contained mills mill the bulk of the commercially marketed padi crop. And prices paid by padi buyers must in large measure reflect the prices paid by these mills, in view of competition among buyers. Five of the larger mills are government-owned and would provide a standard of mill prices for padi after making allowance for the subsidy. The real problem of effective administration would then be confined mainly to instituting a satisfactory system of reporting, inspection and supervision in the remaining 45 privately-owned larger mills, and this should be feasible.[8]

Production. Another aspect of rice policy, to which we have referred earlier, arises from the very strong pressure for a much greater effort to expand production, reflecting the fairly widespread view that the Federation should aim at self-sufficiency in rice. Often the proponents of this view have little regard for considerations of cost or for the fact that limited resources would be diverted from other lines of priority expenditure.

We have indicated that we regard improvement and extension of rice cultivation as an important development priority, to be encouraged both by substantial public investment and by offering incentives to cultivators. Large investments in padi development have been made and the inducements of low taxation, subsidized irrigation, and distribution of fertilizer and improved seed are already being offered. We have recommended such additional measures as an expanded extension service, more satisfactory tenancy and credit arrangements and, in view of the sharp drop in world rice prices, support of domestic padi prices.

[8] A plan for payment and supervision would presumably include arrangements for weekly or bi-weekly reporting by the mills on padi handled for commercial distribution, as the basis for the subsidy payments, and on prices paid; separate reporting by commercial rice dealers on the volume of rice purchased from individual mills; an inspection staff for checking and verification of mill reports; and a system for regular collection and dissemination by wireless of padi market information, including the current level of prices paid at government and other larger mills. The requisite special staff would be well justified in the interest of the padi cultivator and of the economy generally. Administration of the system should be financed from the revenue derived from the proposed import duty on rice.

Nevertheless, we must emphasize that rice development is only one of several important public investment priorities and we reiterate our conclusion that rice self-sufficiency is not a practicable goal for the Federation, not only for physical and technical reasons but for economic and financial reasons as well.

Even if self-sufficiency were technically feasible, it would call for enormous effort and expenditure. Taking account of present domestic rice production and consumption and rates of population growth, self-sufficiency over, say, the next decade would require a rise in production to well over twice the present level. And even on the basis of the most favorable assumptions with respect to the possibility of increasing average yields on presently cultivated areas, it would still be necessary almost to double the existing padi area. This could be accomplished only with a rate of land development which appears physically impracticable and which would also demand expenditure clearly prohibitive, except at the cost of seriously neglecting other essential public investment requirements.

There seems little question, then, that a practicable objective must fall considerably short of self-sufficiency. It remains to decide what would be an appropriate rate of expenditure on rice development, as one part of an investment program which must take account of many other competing claims on available public investment resources. There are no uniform criteria by which the relative merits of all these claims can be measured. Noneconomic considerations admittedly weigh heavily in determining expenditures for social and administrative services. In allocating available public investment resources among the productive sectors, however, the standard to be applied should be whether a satisfactory return from the investment can be expected in the form of additions to the national product; these additions may be direct or indirect, as where services necessary to the expansion of private economic activity are provided. In practice, it is difficult to say what minimum of increased output in relation to investment is necessary to justify a public investment project. But approximate standards can be established by proper calculation and comparison of cost-benefit relationships among various investment possibilities open to the government. In the case of rice development, for example, given Malaya's limited resources, it would obviously be unwise to carry investment to the point where the cost-benefit relationship becomes quite unfavorable compared to that of alternative public investment possibilities.

Unfortunately, under the pressure for large and rapid increases in rice production the attention to cost-benefit relationships of individual rice projects has been quite inadequate. Until these projects are more carefully analyzed it is not possible to determine how far investment in rice development should be carried at the expense of other investment requirements.

In calculating these cost-benefit relationships, we suggest that the cost figures cover all the private-and public cash outlays which would not otherwise be incurred, while the benefit estimates should be based on a realistic assessment of the additional output to be expected, not only in rice but in other produce as well. Properly to assess the actual economic benefit Malaya would receive from the additional rice output, output should be valued at prices corresponding to prospective prices of imported rice, rather than subsidized prices.

The largest public expenditures on rice development are for the irrigation projects of the Drainage and Irrigation Departments. Standards of economic justification for similar projects in other countries vary widely, ratios of investment to gross additional output running as high as five or six to one and sometimes higher. Where a high ratio is nevertheless regarded as satisfactory, it is usually because investment alternatives are limited and relatively unattractive. This is apparently not the case in Malaya. In smallholder rubber, for example, the ratio of cash investment (including loss of income to the smallholder during the maturing period of new trees) to the gross value of additional output when trees reach maturity appears to be only three or four to one.

The matter of cost-benefit relationships in rice development and in other lines of public investment requires the collection of much more extensive data and much more careful study before it will be possible to arrive at reasonable standards by which to determine the justifiable extent of investment in rice development projects. For the present, and as a very rough rule of thumb, we would suggest that for projects to develop new rice land the ratio of total public and private cash investment to gross annual benefits should not be higher than four, and preferably about three, to one. Where already cultivated rice land is to be irrigated, the additional output can usually be realized with little additional annually recurring expense to the cultivators or the government, except for costs of maintenance and depreciation of irrigation works. Gross and net benefit are consequently very nearly the same in such projects and reasonable cost-benefit standards should therefore allow for a higher ratio of investment to output, perhaps about six to one.

These yardsticks for economic evaluation of proposed investment in rice development are suggested only on the basis of what seems reasonable by comparison with other countries, and in view of the apparently favorable public investment opportunities in Malaya in nonagricultural fields as well as in agricultural fields other than rice. As indicated in Technical Report 2 on Irrigation and Drainage, it would appear, making allowance for the very inadequate data, that the great majority of the rice irrigation projects would meet these cost-benefit yardsticks.

On the other hand, taking into account the fact that estimates of acreage benefits are probably unduly favorable and that cost information is incomplete, available data suggest that some of the projects may be running fairly close to the margin of economic justification. In view of the very heavy pressure for steady expansion of expenditure on rice development, we urge much greater attention to the collection and analysis of cost-benefit data on individual rice projects for comparison with other investment opportunities; this will avoid misdirection and uneconomic use of the Federation's limited public investment resources. It is possible that such analysis will suggest standards for justification of rice projects quite different from those which have been suggested here.

Agricultural Production in Singapore

Singapore's agriculture and agricultural resources are of limited and decreasing relative significance in the island's economy. In relation to Singapore's population of over a million persons, the cultivated area is very small—only about 33,000 acres in 1953, most of which was in rubber and coconuts. Less than 10,000 acres were devoted to fruits, vegetables and other food crops (excluding coconuts). Consequently Singapore relies on imports from the Federation and elsewhere for the bulk of its foodstuffs, the only exceptions being pork and poultry products, mainly supplied from within the island, and fresh leafy vegetables, of which about half the supply is locally grown. The relative importance of local supplies is likely to continue to diminish as demand increases and land is taken over by the rapidly growing urban population.

Since 1940 the cultivated area has decreased by about 50%. Such a decline, and an increasing dependence on outside food supplies, is of course the normal pattern for a large and growing metropolitan area. As is also normal, more of the cultivated land has been devoted to intensive cultivation of food crops of high value per acre. This trend was accentuated by food shortages during and immediately following the war. The decline has been mainly in rubber acreage; the area in food crops has either been fairly stable or has increased. Between 1940 and 1953 the acreage planted to fruits, vegetables and other foodstuffs (excluding coconuts) increased from about 15% to 30% of the total cultivated area while rubber's share of this area dropped from about 75% to 50%.

While urban requirements will inevitably continue to absorb land in Singapore, it would seem advisable to foster the natural trend toward improvement and expansion of intensive high value crops, especially fruits and vegetables. This is the present emphasis of Singapore's agricultural policy and the mission can only endorse the lines of approach being followed by the government through the Commerce and Industry Department and its Agricultural Division.

Attention is being given to greater efficiency in fruit and vegetable cultivation. Experimentation with chemical fertilizers suggests their very great economic advantage over the commonly used prawn dust. These experiments should be continued and extended to additional localities because of their demonstrational value.

Substantial progress has been made in the control and reduction of disease among poultry and pigs, an integral part of most Chinese vegetable farms. This has contributed to a large increase in the pig and poultry population since the war.

Surveys have been conducted to determine the suitability for fruits and vegetables of island areas now uncultivated or devoted to less intensive farming. As a result, some thousand acres of Crown land are now being developed for settlement in two-to-three-acre holdings, and similar additional development is proposed. In general, however, the surveys indicate that economic possibilities in this direction are limited by unsatisfactory soils, the high cost of reclamation and high land values. The mission commends the careful attention that has been given to costs in spite of some apparent pressure to regard reducing dependence on outside food supplies as more important than cost considerations.

It would seem advisable to continue to rely mainly on private initiative for practicable extension of intensive cultivation. At the same time, government assistance can be provided through financially sound reclamation programs and through experimentation and extension services emphasizing improved management and cultivation practices. We believe it necessary to supplement the present limited knowledge of the island's agriculture, especially of crops other than rubber and coconut, through land-use and management surveys covering the number of individual holdings, size of holdings, kinds of production, yields, methods of cultivation and marketing, incomes realized, and the extent of family and hired labor. In planning for the further expansion of Singapore, provision should be made for agricultural land use, especially in the proposed "green belt" around the city, and in this connection we believe that land-use planning would be facilitated and guided by a soil-survey of the eastern part of the island, comparable to the soil-surveys already made in the western part.

In the longer run the more important opportunities for development of nearby sources of foodstuffs for Singapore are likely to be in Johore rather than on the island itself. But for the present a faster development of market gardening in Johore is hampered by terrorist activity, the necessity of concentrating cultivators in "new villages" and other aspects of the emergency. With more settled conditions, greater cooperation between Singapore and Johore in such developments should be encouraged from the standpoint not only of Singapore's food supplies but also as an avenue of emigration from the island.

C MARKETING AND CREDIT

General

Most of the inequities and inadequacies of prevailing systems of agricultural marketing, credit and land tenure in Asia are to be found in greater or lesser degree among the small cultivators of Malaya. Unfortunately, information as to their impact on the cultivators' economic position is scanty. Our impression is that by and large the small cultivator suffers less from inefficient and one-sided marketing arrangements, from usurious credit systems and from unsatisfactory tenure relationships in Malaya than in many other South Asian countries. But this is only an impression, and improvement in marketing and credit arrangements and in tenure conditions is obviously needed.

The principal problems arise from an absence of recognized standards or grades of quality, a lack of uniformity in weights and measures, poor transport and communications facilities in some rural areas, a lack of information on market conditions, and the presence of various factors which tend to reduce or eliminate competition among buyers. The most significant of the latter is buyer financing, a system in which the borrowing cultivator commits himself, well in advance of harvest, to sell his crop to the lending buyer at an established price.

Rubber smallholders appear to be less adversely affected by these factors than are other small cultivators. This may be attributed to (1) the absence of a seasonal pattern of credit requirements among rubber producers, making them less subject to the financial control which dealer-lenders exercise over producers of seasonal crops; (2) the terms of licensing of rubber dealers, which prohibit purchase of latex or rubber directly on the holding; (3) the relatively efficient organization of the entire rubber market; and (4) the wide and systematic dissemination of market information. These conditions contribute to greater competition among buyers of rubber than among buyers of other crops. Sample inquiries among rubber smallholders indicate that almost 60% regularly contact more than one buyer before selling their rubber. They also indicate that for given grades of smoked rubber sheet the price received by the smallholder is usually over 90% of the Singapore price (less export duty and cess). This, of course, does not allow for undergrading by dealers, made possible by the large subjective element in the grading of rubber sheet. It is impossible to give any indication of the scale on which undergrading is practiced but it appears to be the principal disadvantage of the present marketing system. The establishment of objective grading standards is a difficult and complex problem which is receiving the attention of the rubber trade. An increasing proportion of rubber is being marketed in the form of latex (16% of Federation rubber exports in 1954); this enables the smallholder to avoid grading problems. Such sales may now be made to some of the larger rubber companies and, in one case, through a cooperative society. Indications are, however, that these sales as yet represent only about 5% of the smallholder output.

Marketing and credit problems for producers of rice, coconuts and miscellaneous fruits, vegetables and other food crops appear more serious. Cultivators are confronted in varying degree, depending on the crop, with the same difficulties that beset rubber cultivators, as well as with unsatisfactory techniques in harvesting and preparation for sale, inadequate terminal market facilities and other factors which contribute to market disorganization, restrict competition and encourage unnecessary elements in the marketing chain. As far as rice is concerned, the shortcomings and suggested means of reducing or eliminating them are discussed in a recent report by the Food and Agriculture Organization, "The Marketing of Rice in the Federation of Malaya" (the author of which was a member of the mission). It was not possible for the mission to undertake a survey of the complex marketing problem sufficiently detailed to serve as the basis for a systematic plan to improve marketing of agricultural produce in general. We regard the problem as sufficiently important to warrant establishing a marketing division within the Department of Agriculture to undertake the necessary investigations (assisted by outside specialists if possible) and to establish and supervise practicable improvements and procedures.

Perhaps the most serious and difficult obstacle to improving the marketing of crops produced by small-scale cultivation is the pattern of agricultural credit customary among peasant farmers in much of Asia. The extensive reliance on dealers for such credit places the cultivator in an unsatisfactory competitive position in the marketing of his crop. In Malaya a high proportion of cultivators relies on dealer credit (inquiries in major rice areas suggest up to 80%). The most common form of credit arrangement among rice cultivators is the so-called padi *kuncha*[9] system in which the cultivator obtains credit from a padi dealer, in the course of the cultivation cycle, for which he pledges repayment in the form of an agreed quantity of padi at harvest time. The value of the pledged quantity is usually far higher than the credit obtained, the difference representing payment of interest at rates often running up to 100% or more. The dealers frequently act as agents for, or are financed by, rice millers who in turn may obtain their financing from commercial banks. Similar credit arrangements involving an advance pledge of the crop to a dealer are common among growers of coconut and other commercial crops produced by peasant cultivators.

The unfavorable terms of these arrangements are traditional and probably date back to periods in which cultivation was primarily for subsistence and cultivators borrowed mainly for special needs arising at times of crop failure, illness, weddings, funerals, etc. In a largely noncommercial agricultural environment the supply of credit for such purposes was undoubtedly scarce and the risks of default high. The justification for these terms has diminished with the progressive commercialization of cultivation and a

[9] The kuncha is a customary unit of volume measure equivalent in weight for padi to around 850 lbs. The terms of credit advances at various stages of the cultivation cycle are commonly expressed as the amount of credit for each kuncha of padi to be turned over to the creditor at harvest time.

consequent regularly recurring cycle of productive credit requirements.

Nevertheless, terms of this character continue to be imposed for the seasonal pattern of credit requirements as well as for irregular consumption purposes. One reason for this is that cultivators seldom distinguish clearly between the two types of credit needs and wish to ensure availability of credit for both purposes, usually from the same source. The more compelling reason, however, is undoubtedly that the cultivator usually has no alternative source which will meet his regular credit requirements on appropriate terms. And in the absence of such alternative facilities, dealers and shopkeepers continue to perform this essential service and are able through the terms of their financing to pass on to the cultivators much of the risk and to operate in a less efficient and more costly manner than would otherwise be possible.

The establishment of alternative arrangements to meet the recurring credit requirements of the small cultivators on reasonable terms and in accordance with commercial principles is, however, a most difficult and complex problem. The provision of such credit involves considerable risk and expense for a number of reasons. These include the administrative difficulty of assessing the creditworthiness of a large number of individual smallholders and of disbursing and collecting many small loans; the very low and fluctuating incomes of farmers; the uncertainty in some areas of land titles of owner-cultivators; the insecurity of tenure among tenant-cultivators; the general absence of developed commercial attitudes toward the use of credit; and the general lack of distinction between commercial credit requirements and credit desired for purely consumption purposes. In the circumstances, a satisfactory credit system requires an extensive organization to service and supervise a very large number of small loans and to foster the proper use of productive credit.

Thus, besides the problem of financing an adequate fund of agricultural credit there is the formidable organizational task, requiring a large and trained staff to maintain close contact with individual cultivators. The most promising line of approach to this problem for Malaya is to encourage marketing and credit cooperatives; these, being closely associated with the small producer, are in a position to assess his creditworthiness and to educate him in the proper use of credit. Growth of the cooperative movement in Malaya is encouraging and we strongly recommend that the work of the Cooperative Department in fostering its further development should receive full support. As yet, however, the movement plays only a minor role among the small cultivators and its development to a significant position in the financing and marketing of smallholder crops is likely to be gradual. Nevertheless, while for the present small-scale farming can be cooperatively financed to only a limited extent, it is not premature to establish a specialized organization for this purpose. We support the proposal to establish a cooperative bank at the apex of a pyramid of local cooperative credit associations and an intermediate association of existing cooperative banking unions. The interest which commercial banks have expressed in extending credit to such an organization is encouraging and additional credit for this purpose might also be obtained through the lending and rediscounting facilities of the proposed Central Bank of Malaya. Guarantee of the obligations of a central cooperative bank by the Federation Government should be considered as a means of facilitating its credit activities. At the same time we believe that the cooperative financing of the productive credit needs of small-scale agriculture should proceed within limits which are justified by the rate of growth of the cooperative movement and its capacity for sound and effective administration of such credits. In order to foster this growth we urge particular emphasis on the training of personnel to assume responsible positions at all levels, and especially the local levels, of the cooperative organization.

Marketing in Singapore

Considerable criticism has been directed toward the marketing of foodstuffs in Singapore, particularly toward the margin between retail prices and the prices received by producers. Several investigations of this problem have been made. While the mission did not itself undertake a detailed study, sample inquiries indicated that consumer prices for fresh produce were in most cases 50-100% higher than those received by producers. This is not an uncommon margin in the distribution of fresh fruits and vegetables. Whether it is justified in this case by necessary and desired transport and marketing services could be answered only by much more thorough and careful survey than we could make. It is apparent, however, that most of the margin is accounted for by the retail phase of distribution, attributable in part at least to the practice of house-to-house retailing by a large number of hawkers, each of whom handles a relatively small volume of produce. The fact that Singapore consumers want this service on a large scale not only adds to the expense of retail distribution of fruits and vegetables but also tends to reduce competition in the retail trade by linking consumers to only one or a few hawkers who serve their particular neighborhood. There is, however, a trend toward increased purchasing directly from retail centers where costs are undoubtedly lower per unit of produce handled.

Cost and inefficiency in distribution can also be reduced through improvement in marketing facilities, including a larger number of wholesale and retail markets, and better facilities, including refrigeration and cold storage, at existing and new markets. Investigation by the mission confirmed the views of officials and members of the produce trade that present markets are insufficient and unsatisfactory for a city the size of Singapore. This applies to marketing not only of fruits and vegetables but of fish, livestock and poultry products. There is also a need for the systematic collection of market information and its wide and regular dissemination.

Singapore's specific requirements for additional marketing facilities and services should be the subject of detailed studies. These studies and the establishment and supervision of the indicated facilities and services should be the function of a specialized marketing department of the City Council. It is therefore recommended that under the proposed consolidation of the present City Council and Rural Board there be created a separate Division of Marketing for this purpose and for bringing together the now scattered marketing responsibilities of government. Pending studies of requirements and costs of new market facilities, we have included in our program of capital expenditures for Singapore during 1955-59 a token figure of $5 million for this purpose.

D LAND TENURE [10]

1 Federation

Land Administration and Legislation. Property in all land in the States, not yet alienated, is vested in the Ruler. The Federal legislative power to ensure common policies in land matters and a common system of administration has not been exercised to any important extent; policy, as well as administration, has remained in the hands of the States and Settlements. The four former Federated Malay States have a common code, but each of the other five States has its own land law. There is, however, similarity in essen-

[10] See Technical Report 3.

tials, since the code served as a model for the State enactments and all adopted the Torrens system of registration.[11] The Settlements, on the other hand, register deeds, not titles, and, unlike the States, their land legislation has not been consolidated in a single enactment.

The standard of land administration varies from State to State and from district to district within a State but, in general, now falls short of what is necessary in a matter of such fundamental importance. This must be attributed largely to the emergency but partly, we believe, to insufficient supervision and direction of land office work. The emergency, so long as it lasts, will continue to hamper this work, but much can be done by way of closer supervision and inspection to improve the general standard. To this end, we recommend, first, the strengthening of the office of the Commissioner of Land, a Federal advisory agency, to permit more frequent visits to land offices and closer consultation with the senior Land Officers in the State and Settlement secretariats; this would also permit the office to implement or assist in implementing the mission's various recommendations concerning land legislation and land administration. Secondly, we recommend the appointment of a senior Land Officer in the secretariats of the three States which do not now have such a post; it should be his function to deal with land matters in the secretariat, under the State Secretary, to inspect land offices and to give training in land office subjects. Thirdly, we recommend the creation of a specialist cadre of senior Land Officers under the control of the Commissioner of Lands; from this cadre there would be no transfer to other branches of the administration. The officers would be appointed to the State and Settlement secretariats in the same way as doctors, engineers and the like are posted to State and Settlement departments by the Director of the corresponding Federal department.

There are very considerable arrears in title registration in the States of Kelantan, Perlis and Trengganu. The Federal Government is cooperating with the State Government of Kelantan in a drive to clear up these backlogs and similar action is contemplated for the other States. The mission attaches great importance to bringing registers up to date, not only in these three States but also in any district where arrears exist; it recommends that additional staff be provided where necessary. Registers which are out of date lose much of their value.

[11] A system under which the certificate of title establishes an indisputable right of ownership to the land registered.

We strongly endorse the plan to adopt title, rather than deed, registration in the two Settlements and recommend that the change be effected as promptly as possible.

Lastly, since uniformity in land legislation throughout the Federation is clearly desirable, we recommend the enactment, as soon as circumstances permit, of a Federal land code to take the place of the several State and Settlement laws. So that the maximum practicable uniformity may be achieved, "the necessary variations in any State or Settlement" to which the Federal legislature is required to have regard should be kept to the inescapable minimum.

Malay Reservations and Areas under Customary Tenure. Malays in the Federation are protected in the possession of their land by State and Settlement legislation which designates large areas as reservations or areas under customary tenure, and which prohibits the transfer, charge or lease to a non-Malay of any land held by a Malay within these areas. No land within the reservations may be alienated to non-Malays. The purpose is to protect Malay land ownership, rather than to exclude non-Malays from the reservations. Land held by non-Malays before the various enactments came into force may be retained by them and in most cases may be transferred to other non-Malays.

This protection of land ownership is of special importance to Malays in congested rural areas, where the economic independence of the cultivator is weakened by inadequately sized and fragmented holdings. Here cultivators are particularly vulnerable to the acquisition of their holdings by dealers, money lenders and investors in land. Since the stronger economic interests are largely non-Malay, the loss of land would undoubtedly be greater if transfer, lease or charge of Malay holdings to non-Malays were permitted. It is also reasonable that areas now within the reservations, which are suitably located and in definite prospect of settlement by Malays should continue to be so reserved as outlets to the pressure of population in already congested Malay areas.

On the other hand, the reservation of areas only sparsely settled and more distant from centers of congestion may impede their development: Malays are reluctant to move any considerable distance from their established communities, private Malay capital for investment is limited, and the restrictions on land ownership and use discourage investment of non-Malay capital in land development. For these areas within the Malay reservations which have development possibilities, we recommend a re-examination of the present policy concerning land use by non-Malays.

Education, agricultural extension, development of cooperatives and improved credit and marketing arrangements offer a positive approach to the problem of improving the economic situation of the Malays. Some steps are being taken along these lines. We recommend continued efforts. In the long run, these measures will both strengthen the Malays' economic position and increase their capacity to participate in and contribute to Malaya's development.

Subdivision, Fragmentation and Land Consolidation. The Muslim law of inheritance—which makes no distinction between real and personal property and prescribes elaborate and precise rules for distributing a deceased person's property—and population pressure in certain areas have combined to cause excessive subdivision and fragmentation of land. The extent to which the subdivision shown by the registers is reflected in physical subdivision of the land has not yet, however, been studied in detail.

Minute subdivision and fragmentation leads to uneconomic holdings, concealed unemployment, increased indebtedness, reduced productivity of land, abandonment of very small plots which thereupon become breeding grounds for pests and, in general, has a demoralizing effect on a rural community. The secular authorities are well aware of the need to check land subdivision and the religious authorities with whom the matter was discussed showed an understanding of the problem that impressed us. The difficulty is to find a generally acceptable solution.

Voluntary transfers between heirs cannot be relied on to reduce subdivision significantly. We believe that the only solution is by legislative restriction of subdivision, following the example of the State of Kelantan. The Kelantan Land Enactment (Section 37A) prohibits subdivision below an area equivalent to one-quarter of an acre. This limit is far too low but the Enactment is nonetheless important as a precedent. To be fully effective, the legislation should be supplemented by provision of credit facilities.

The mission recommends Federal legislation to restrict subdivision throughout the Federation. It should, however, be left to the State and Settlement Governments to determine the minimum permissible area, after taking into account crop, locality and presence or absence of irrigation.

To prevent the subdivision of land alienated in future we also recommend Federal legislation requiring that grants or leases of State land for smallholdings shall expressly prohibit subdivision, as well as transfer or lease to more than one person. Such provisions were included in the instruments of title issued for land in the Tanjong Karang scheme.

How to achieve consolidation of holdings already excessively subdivided is an extremely difficult problem. Voluntary exchanges should be encouraged, although they are unlikely to be of more than small assistance. Excessive subdivision can be effectively dealt with only if alternative livelihood is provided through the opening up of new areas for cultivation and the expansion of nonagricultural economic activity. In view of the rapid population growth and the limitations on financial resources, it is unlikely that the number of cultivators on already cultivated land can be significantly reduced. Projects for land development can relieve population pressure in other areas; in these cases land consolidation should be linked to the project, and an element of compulsion could be introduced. But such possibilities will be small in relation to the problem as a whole. As we see it, the most that can be done is to check further subdivision through the recommended legislation and by opening up new areas for cultivation.

Tenancy Security. While adequate land tenure investigations have not yet been made in the Federation, it is known that in some of the padi areas much of the land is cultivated under tenancy agreements. Inquiries made by or on behalf of the mission tended to support the estimates given to the Rice Production Committee that some 75% of padi land in Province Wellesley, and 70% and 50% in Kedah and Krian, respectively, is cultivated under such agreements. Tenancy also exists, though to a lesser degree, in the rubber areas of Johore and in some districts of Kelantan.

This is not objectionable if the tenant has security of tenure and a fair return for his labor and investment. But there is evidence that the owner-tenant relationship has deteriorated since the war; the practice of demanding "tea-money" (a form of premium) is spreading and the traditional rent in kind is in some cases being replaced by advance payment of rent in cash. The mission shares the misgivings expressed by the Rice Production Committee as to the effect of this deterioration on the economic position of the tenant and on agricultural production.[12] We therefore recommend that Federal legislation be enacted giving security of tenure to an efficient cultivator who pays his rent and observes the other terms of his tenancy agreement; the legislation should also confer the right to sub-

[12] Report of Rice Production Committee, Vol. 1, Federation of Malaya, 1953, p. 46.

stitute the customary payment in kind in cases where rent is required to be paid in cash in advance. At the same time, the landlord should have the right to terminate the tenancy upon, say, one year's notice, if he, his wife or his children intend to cultivate the land themselves.

To arbitrate disputes arising out of this legislation, we recommend the setting up of tenant security committees as outlined in Technical Report 3. Provision should be made for appeal from the committee's decisions. We suggest, as a first step, the appointment of committees in North Kedah, Province Wellesley and Krian.

New Villages. Since 1950 virtually the whole of the Chinese population living in scattered rural communities, generally without title to the land occupied, has been resettled in compact "new villages" where it can be protected from extortion and intimidation by terrorists. The resettlement was undertaken solely for security reasons, though it also served administrative ends. It was a remarkable achievement, involving the formation of some 550 villages, with a present population of around 570,000 persons, and the provision of basic services. The size of the operation, the speed with which it was carried out, and the considerable difficulties involved made it inevitable that some of the villages would be badly sited and would have no economic future. Their population will have to be resettled elsewhere. The mission was informed, however, that the majority of the new villages do in fact have prospects of development.

The success of the resettlement cannot be finally judged until the emergency is over: the test will then be the extent of the drift away from the new villages. If it is substantial and largely takes the direction of settlement in remote areas, a formidable land problem will arise, and further resettlement, involving large expenditures, might well become necessary. Clearly, everything possible should be done to prevent this: a community spirit must be awakened, better social services provided and opportunities for earning a livelihood made available where these are lacking. Although the authorities realize the need for these measures, a more imaginative policy is needed in one respect, the issuance of land titles to resettled persons.

The terms on which some States have offered land to resettled persons are in general less satisfactory than the terms usually offered by them and compare unfavorably with those offered in the Settlement of Malacca and those given to squatters in Kuala Lumpur who were resettled in the satellite town of Petaling Jaya.

Information regarding title applications by resettled persons is scanty;

we understand, however, that they have been disappointingly few. While this is due to several factors, there seems to be little doubt of the deterrent effect of the restricted period for leases and the cost involved. The importance of encouraging resettled persons to remain in those new villages with an economic future can hardly be over-emphasized; more favorable, even generous, terms would be helpful and we accordingly recommend that the terms now offered be reviewed to see if they can be made more attractive.

Field Survey of Various Aspects of Land Tenure. We have already referred to the lack of data on land subdivision and tenancy conditions. A census of padi growers in the principal rice-growing areas is being taken; it will also cover their production, costs, and consumption of padi. Research on tenure conditions in the Federation is also being undertaken. While these will provide some of the necessary data, more will be required before a government policy can be formulated. We accordingly recommend a systematic survey with the terms of reference outlined in Technical Report 3.

2   *Singapore*

Land administration is the responsibility of the Commissioner of Lands, whose office deals with land alienation and acquisition, the collection of land rent, registration of deeds and other routine land office work. The Commissioner's authority does not, however, extend to enforcement of the government's policy on land utilization. The Singapore Improvement Trust acts as agent for the government in matters relating to utilization of private land and as adviser to the Commissioner of Lands on questions of Crown land utilization.

A Diagnostic Survey Team under the Singapore Improvement Trust has been engaged since 1952 in preparing a master plan for the use of land in the Colony. To facilitate the plan's execution, a bill was submitted to the Legislative Council giving the government power to expropriate land for planning purposes and precluding inflated compensation to the owner. The bill met with strong opposition and was still pending at the time of the mission's visit.

One of the most important tasks in the field of land tenure confronting the Government of Singapore is the introduction of a title registration system. Complete and up-to-date survey records are now available and the government has received the report of an expert invited to study the legal and administrative problems. The mission shares his view that title registration should be introduced without delay. It also agrees that, in the case of Singapore, there would be advantages in modifying the strict application of the Torrens system of title registration by allowing a claim of title based on undisturbed physical possession for a prescribed period to prevail over the title of the registered owner or those claiming from him in certain well-defined circumstances. We further suggest consideration of the possibility of introducing an advanced system of title registration including registration of easements and ultimately government guarantee of the title.

The government is engaged in substituting 60-year agricultural leases for some 10,000 temporary occupation licensts granted to smallholders. The Food Production Committee has suggested that these leases include specific conditions designed to further the Committee's policy, but we think it would be preferable to give effect to the food production policy in some other way.

II FORESTRY[13]

The estimated value of Malaya's timber and other forest products produced in 1952 is almost $140 million and around $100 million for 1953. The area of commercially exploited forests, however, represents only a very small fraction of the total forest area, due to the low average quality of Malayan timber and the inaccessibility of a very large proportion of the forests. Most of the commercial extraction comes from elevations below 500 feet, mainly in the Lowland Dipterocarp forests. Only a few of the better qualities of timber are sold abroad. Exports represent only about 10% of the total volume of timber production; the remainder is used mainly for domestic construction or for firewood and charcoal.

Because of the low average quality, problems of conservation, cost and accessibility, and the competition in world markets from cheap coniferous timber, the prospects are not encouraging for large or rapid expansion in present lines of forestry production. Nor have investigations made so far been encouraging for the development of timber pulp or fiber board pro-

[13] See Technical Report 1.

duction or for the export of pulp wood, due to the very mixed character of the forests and the limited availability of satisfactory woods.[14]

However, if suitable pulp and fiber varieties which could be grown extensively under Malayan conditions were found, prospects for commercial forestry expansion would be much more favorable, since trees grow very rapidly in the Malayan climate. Experimentation on this problem is continuing and is to be expanded with completion of a laboratory for pulp and fiber board research. Some promise of satisfactory pulping properties has been found in a local fast-growing wood known as batai (*albizzia falcata*). But as yet there is no basis for expecting substantial expansion in this direction. Experimentation is also continuing on measures to improve, and increase the number of, Malayan timber varieties for commercial uses through durability testing, proper seasoning and preservative treatment. Commendable progress has already been made and these experiments should be continued along with the pulp and fiber board investigations.

The maintenance of a satisfactory rate of forest regeneration in relation to current rates of exploitation in the interests of conservation and long-run commercial operation presents a problem. Natural and artificial regeneration activities do not begin to keep up with felling. Formerly this was in part attributable to emergency conditions and shortages of labor, but now the principal limitation is financial. The Forestry Department estimates that expenditure of about $1.5 million a year on regeneration would be necessary to keep up with new fellings, whereas it has actually been spending only a little over $200,000.

While we recognize the importance of adequate reafforestation in Malaya's very long-run interest, we are also cognizant of the short-run considerations of financial stringency and urgently needed expenditure in a great many other directions. While this financial situation continues it will be difficult to carry out the kind of regeneration program which would be warranted in more favorable fiscal circumstances. Moreover, it is probable that some part of the present lowland forest reserve open to felling will eventually have to be given over to cultivation.[15] For these reasons,

[14] Cf. A. V. Thomas, "Prospects of Pulp Production in Malaya," *Malayan Forester*, 1950. Also E. H. G. Dobby, "The Development of Malaya's Uplands," *The Development of Upland Areas in the Far East*, Institute of Pacific Relations, 1951.

[15] This should be an important consideration in long-run land-use planning, although it seems likely that a comprehensive plan in this respect will have to be deferred pending solution of the more immediate and urgent land-use problems discussed elsewhere.

we do not advocate reafforestation at a pace commensurate with the rate of felling. It is inadvisable, on the other hand, to allow excessive neglect of Malaya's long-run forest interests. We therefore recommend that regeneration expenditures be increased to about $600,000 annually. We also recommend that, pending a satisfactory survey of possible alternative uses of land within the present forest reserves, the Forestry Department consult with the various other departments concerned with land-use, so that regeneration operations may be concentrated on lands with limited alternative economic possibilities or where reafforestation has high priority in the interests of soil and water control and conservation.

III FISHERIES[16]

The fisheries of Malaya contribute significantly to the national income;[17] they give employment to a large number of the working population, particularly Malaysians, and provide a major item of diet for people of all races and creeds. Measures to increase production, improve marketing and better the lot of fishermen accordingly deserve emphasis in the development program.

In the Federation, the Malayan Fisheries Department has drawn up a well-balanced program with those objectives. No single measure will do more to increase the supply of sea-water fish than further mechanization of fishing craft. Although considerable progress has already been achieved, in 1954 more than 80% of the craft were still propelled by oar, paddle or sail. Further mechanization is dependent upon capital and education. Capital must come largely from private and cooperative society investment, with RIDA[18] continuing to assist, but education must be provided by the Department. To fill this need, the Department has proposed a marine fisheries school, to offer instruction in mechanized fishing techniques, maintenance and repair of engines, simple navigation and fish handling.

Fresh water fish culture in padi fields, irrigation canals and drains and in ponds, often integrated with pig-rearing, poultry-keeping and vegetable production, is becoming increasingly important in the rural economy. To

[16] See Technical Report 4.
[17] The gross value of fish production in 1949 is probably not greatly below that of rice.
[18] Rural and Industrial Development Authority.

stimulate and guide this development, the Department has included in its program a fry and fish culture demonstration and training center, supplemented by a number of regional fry breeding and distributing centers. We endorse the first, on the understanding that it will be supplementary to the research institute referred to below, but are unable to judge whether all the proposed regional centers will actually be needed within the period covered by the program.

The current program makes provision for research. A marine fisheries research station at Singapore, financed from Colonial Development and Welfare funds, was expected to be in full operation by the end of 1954. Unfortunately, the rise in costs after plans had been made and the financing commitment accepted in 1948 has meant that the station will not be as well equipped as had been intended. In addition, a research institute to deal with problems of productivity in ponds, both of fresh water and brackish water, is expected to be established at Malacca early in 1955, also financed from Colonial Development and Welfare funds.

Lack of staff and facilities has hitherto precluded adequate attention to the preservation and processing of fish and to its distribution and marketing, except in Kelantan. We concur in the Department's view that these matters must be carefully investigated; efforts to increase production would be stultified if the increased catches could not be brought to the consumer as fresh or processed fish.

The mission recommends improvement of the approaches to a number of minor ports and the provision of additional facilities at ports used by fishing vessels; details are set forth in Technical Report 4.

The fisheries in waters adjacent to Singapore have been fully exploited and a recent notable development has been the fishing of more distant waters by mechanized craft. However, production is still only a fraction of Singapore's consumption and large quantities of fish are imported from the Federation and Indonesia.

The program for the Federation will contribute to an increase of Singapore's production. Singapore, as well as the Federation, will be served by the two research centers, and it will be able to send trainees to the Federation's marine fisheries school and the fry and fish culture demonstration and training center. In addition, it will benefit from the investigations into the preservation and processing of fish. When research and investigation have pointed the way, an increase in extension work in Singapore, with some small additions to staff, will be necessary.

The Colony Government is considering construction of modern landing facilities for fishing craft with an adjacent wholesale market on a site near Kallang. The project has not yet reached the detailed planning stage and no cost estimate is available. We support it and have included a token amount for it in our recommended program.

CHAPTER 4 *MINING AND POWER*

I MINING[1]

Tin is second only to rubber in commercial and financial significance in the Malayan economy. In 1953, the gross value of tin mined was more than 20% of the total value of Federation exports, while direct tax receipts from tin mining probably contributed 12-15% of the Federal Government's revenue. The value of other mineral products—chiefly iron ore, coal and quarried stone—was in all only about 10% that of tin.

For the last half-century, Malayan tin production has been practically stationary over the long run, although it has fluctuated widely from year to year. As new methods of mining were introduced and mechanization increased, employment in the industry fell sharply. In 1913 more than 200,000 workers were engaged in producing slightly less tin than was produced by about 40,000 in 1954, while over the same period the mechanical horsepower installed rose at least sixfold. About 50% of the output is now produced by European dredging companies, about 40% by gravel-pump mines (almost entirely Chinese), and the remaining 10% in hydraulic, open-cast, and underground mines (chiefly European-owned). European-owned mines account for about 60% of all production.

Expansion of tin production cannot be looked to as an important element in the future development of Malaya. On the contrary, the immediate problem is a threat of actual decline, arising from the economic circumstances facing the industry—its market prospects, and its exceptional tax burden—and from the difficulty of finding and acquiring suitable tin-bearing lands to replace worked-out mines.

A TIN MINING

Market Prospects

All tin produced in Malaya is exported, and represents a third or more of world production. The international tin market is extremely sensitive

[1] See Technical Report 5.

94

to changes in supply and demand. In the course of the Korean War, the price of tin more than doubled; by the second half of 1953, it had fallen back to £ 600 per ton, almost exactly the level which had prevailed in 1949 and the first half of 1950. As the price fell, many of the higher-cost gravel-pump mines ceased to operate and there was a substantial outflow of labor from that sector of the industry. But production by gravel-pump mines as a whole was maintained, and neither production nor employment by the dredges showed an appreciable fall, despite the fact that most of the boom increases in labor and other costs persisted through the period of price decline.

The tin market showed some improvement in 1954, and in spite of some weakness at the turn of 1954-55, prices were still well above 1953 lows. The improvement was made possible only by continued accumulation of tin in the United States strategic stockpile; this has, indeed, been a major factor in the market results since 1948. During 1949-53, world tin production averaged about 163,000 tons and consumption 134,000 tons—an average excess production of about 29,000 tons annually. In 1953, production and consumption were about 169,500 tons and 129,500 tons respectively—an excess of 40,000 tons.[2] The 1954 picture more closely resembled the 1949-53 average; during the first ten months of the year, production was at an annual rate of 165,000 tons and consumption at an annual rate of 136,000 tons, with a resulting surplus of 29,000 tons. However, strategic stockpiling may come to an end before long (the United States stockpile is already probably sufficient for several years' consumption) and thereafter the market would no longer be able to support excess production. Left to commercial forces, the price of tin would certainly fall far below recent levels. Under the proposed International Tin Agreement now awaiting ratification, this result should be prevented, first by the accumulation of a buffer stock of 25,000 tons, and then by limitation of net exports on the basis of percentage quotas established for the major producing countries. The aim will be to keep the price above a "floor" of £ 640 per ton (with a "ceiling", in the event of a tin shortage, of £ 880 per ton).[3]

Malaya's quota under the Agreement would be fixed initially at 36.61%

[2] Statistics 1949-53 are from the Statistical Bulletin of the International Tin Study Group, China and the U.S.S.R. excluded. Production is of tin-in-concentrates, and consumption is of tin metal.

[3] At the end of 1954 the Tin Agreement had not yet been ratified by the required proportion of the signatory countries and there were indications that a somewhat lower "ceiling" price would be proposed.

of the total net exports permitted from the producing countries. Production in recent years by countries outside the quota system has been about 10,000 tons.[4] Thus if total consumption were to remain at the 1954 level of about 136,000 tons (consumption from the export quotas at about 126,000 tons), and if all other producing countries were able to meet their quotas, Malaya could expect a quota of only about 46,000 tons, or 18-23% below its 1953 and 1954 production.[5] Even under very favorable circumstances, Malaya could hardly hope for a quota of more than 50,000 tons, once the restrictive provisions of the Agreement take effect—which, assuming the Agreement has by then come into force, is likely to be necessary within a few months after a United States decision to cease additions to the strategic stockpile.

Long-run prospects are more difficult to appraise. Demand has been seriously diminished by technological development which has reduced the need for tin in the manufacture of containers and in other uses. There is still a wide scope for the application of known economies, especially outside the United States. For example, the adoption everywhere of current U. S. processes and standards in the making of tin plate would, at recent consumption levels of tin plate, save more than 10,000 tons of tin, and U. S. industry sources are reported to expect further developments which in universal application would save another 10,000-20,000 tons. Whether this trend will be offset by new uses for tin and by the normal growth of world demand for industrial products requiring tin, it is impossible to foresee. The Paley Report[6] projects "free world" consumption at 193,000 tons by 1975.

The cost of additional output is likely to be much higher for some of Malaya's competitors than for Malaya. Thus Malaya should have an opportunity to increase its share of world consumption. To take full advantage of such an opportunity in any future quota negotiations, the Federation Government should keep itself closely informed on cost conditions in competing tin producing areas.

It appears, thus, that the short-run prospects—stock-piling apart—are for an agreed curtailment of Malaya's output within the next five years from the present 55,000-60,000 tons to something in the neighborhood of

[4] Again excluding China and the U.S.S.R.

[5] 56,000 tons in 1953; for 1954 (first 10 months) at the rate of 60,000 tons.

[6] *Resources for Freedom,* a Report to the President by the President's Materials Policy Commission, Vol. II, U. S. Government Printing Office, 1952.

45,000-50,000 tons. While, as we have said, longer-run prospects are more difficult to evaluate, for planning purposes we are inclined to think that a growth in export demand to around 65,000 tons during the decade or so after 1960 may reasonably be assumed. This figure might indeed require upward revision if further analyses should indicate that competing areas are likely to have difficulty in holding their present share of world consumption.

Burden of Taxation

Tin exported from the Federation is subject to a duty calculated by a formula which in practice results in the duty being 10-15% of the price of tin. The industry has been subject for over 50 years to a duty within this range of rates. In addition, from 1948 it has paid income tax (now 30%) on its profits, after allowances for the duty, depreciation of plant, machinery, etc., and for the writing-off of capital expenditure incurred in acquiring and developing the mine.

Much may be said, in principle, for the industry's claim that the advent of a modern system of income tax calls for a reduction in the rate of export duty. The duty falls heavily on mines which make little or no profit, discourages the full working-out of poorer ground, and deters production and investment in marginal mines. In the long run, the combination of export duty and income tax with low tin prices might conceivably be such a barrier to the attraction of new capital and reinvestment of the reserves of existing companies that the industry would gradually decline, even if its circumstances were otherwise profitable.

The arguments for tax concessions to the tin mining industry are, however, greatly weakened for the immediate future, since the market situation and the proposed International Tin Agreement will in any case almost certainly call for a considerable cut in tin production. Direct control of mine output must be envisaged, in addition to the restrictive effects of taxation, as a means of cutting production back to the quota limit. Arguments against the duty on equitable grounds remain valid, but in a general economic sense the effects of the duty must be regarded as less damaging if, after payment of duty, it is still profitable to mine as much tin as the market will take. It seems very probable that, with existing taxation, and even with the tin price at its "floor" under the proposed Agreement, this will be the situation for the next few years at least.

The claim for reduction of duty must, moreover, be considered against the background of the Federation's prospective revenues and expenditures. As shown elsewhere, the fiscal situation is difficult at present and in the circumstances the mission cannot recommend that the duty be reduced. It does, however, recommend consideration of the industry's claim if the Federation's financial position and prospects should improve and if direct restriction of production should prove unnecessary.

Availability and Acquisition of Mining Land

While in present circumstances it may be possible to take a fairly short-run view of the problem of taxation, it is not possible to do so in the case of the problem of establishing reserves of workable land to take the place of existing mines. Prospecting is eminently a forward-looking activity. It may take up to four or five years to prove and equip a dredging site; usually very large areas must be prospected before the best deposits are located; and if the long-run future of the price of tin is not bright, it is all the more important that high-grade ground be found and earmarked for mining, so that Malaya may continue to be a relatively low-cost producer.

The problem is urgent. For over 20 years prospecting has been severely restricted—first by controls associated with the international restriction schemes which began in 1931, then by the war and the Japanese occupation, next by the concentration of effort on postwar rehabilitation, and finally by the emergency, which in many regions still makes prospecting difficult or impossible. The consequences are now apparent in a deterioration of the average grade of ground worked, and in the fact that about 10% of the dredges are reportedly idle for lack of suitable ground.

Although basic geological mapping is incomplete, there is little doubt that substantial reserves of high-grade ground exist, to the west of the main range and also to the east, where the possibilities have been much less fully explored. The chief obstacle to prospecting—assuming that the difficulties of the emergency are progressively overcome—arise from a conflict between the interests of mining and the interests of agriculture and forestry. This conflict is inherent in alluvial mining in which the surface of the ground is stripped, waste soil (mostly sand and gravel, useless for agriculture) is excavated and disposed of, and large volumes of water are drained off with consequent problems of silting.

Secondary damage, outside the area actually mined, can usually be prevented by proper control schemes (e.g., regulating the amount of silt in water drained into rivers). The Mining Enactment now requires such control schemes; before they were instituted, tin mining understandably earned a bad name among the agricultural Malays. But in some instances, mining operations, such as those adjacent to an irrigation project, cannot help endangering surrounding areas, except at prohibitive cost. And in all cases the land actually used for mining is destroyed for purposes of cultivation, unless it can be rehabilitated after being worked out. The process of working-out itself usually takes many years, since mining leases ordinarily run for 21 years and may be renewed. After land has been dredged, the area is often reworked by gravel-pump mines.

The area leased for alluvial mining is only 0.7% of the whole area of Malaya (3.5% of the alienated area) but the ratio of mining land to cultivable areas is quite high in the principal mining States, and the scars left by mining in the past are very evident. The land underlaid by tin is usually suitable for agriculture and forestry.

The resulting conflict makes itself evident in two main ways:

1. Permits to prospect on State lands and subsequent mining leases are often granted only after long delay, and sometimes under conditions which make the proposition unattractive to the prospecting firm. The permits carry no legal right to a lease but the feeling that there is a moral obligation to grant a lease is an important factor in the hesitation of State Governments to issue the original permit. The prospector has no legal assurance that his investment will be protected by a subsequent lease, or any assurance that a rival undertaking will not be granted a lease in the area he has prospected.

2. The lessee is required to carry out certain measures (often expensive) for the rehabilitation of the area at termination of mining operations—resliming to certain depths, leveling and filling, etc. This is commendable in principle but does not usually result in restoring the land to a cultivable state. In fact, a good deal more research and experiment is necessary to determine what are effective rehabilitation measures; the type of land use which is contemplated may be relevant. Moreover, once the land reverts to the State the mine's responsibility ceases and protective work is neglected, followed by erosion and silting.

This is clearly unsatisfactory, not only for the mining industry but for the agricultural industries and the governments. In the mission's view, there is a strong presumption that it will be worthwhile from a national viewpoint to extract valuable mineral deposits, even though land is thereby made unavailable for agriculture for a long period, unless a particular mining location is such that serious secondary damage in surrounding agricultural areas can be expected. At the same time rehabilitation measures should be as effective as is reasonably possible. It should be feasible to make administrative arrangements consistent with these principles, which will avoid undue delay and unnecessary expense.

To this end we recommend that:

1. No land in areas designated as likely to be tin-bearing should be alienated for a purpose other than tin mining until due consideration has been given to the opinions of the Geological Survey and of the Mines Department as to its potential value as mining land; in the absence of compelling reasons to the contrary, mining should be given priority for land use. Areas on the eastern side of the main range of no potential mining value should be delimited as soon as possible and made available for settlement or other uses.

2. Each State Government should establish a Mines Committee composed of representatives of the departments concerned (Mines, Agriculture, Forestry, etc.) which should meet regularly to consider applications for prospecting permits and mining leases, and make prompt recommendations thereon to the Ruler-in-Council.

3. Prospecting permits should be granted to bona fide applicants after a minimum of investigation, and should be refused only when it is clear, on the recommendation of the Mines Committee, that any mining lease within the proposed prospecting area would be detrimental to the national interest. A prospecting permit should in itself carry no legal or moral right to a mining lease, but should give the holder priority over any other applicant for a lease in the prospected area within a prescribed period.

4. It should, however, be made known, as a matter of governmental policy, that a mining lease in standard form will be granted to any successful prospector who applies, except that if the Mines Committee so recommends, because of exceptional circumstances such as inevitability of secondary damage to an adjacent agricultural area, a lease will be refused, or issued subject to special conditions. The standard form of mining lease should contain only those provisions regarding land rehabilitation which are believed to be generally effective, and which can most efficiently be taken by the individual mine operator. Existing leases should be amended

to conform to this policy. All mining operations will of course continue to be subject to the Mining Enactment provisions for the control of silting, etc.

5. The State Government should prescribe measures for the rehabilitation of mining land, on the termination of a lease. These should be devised, wherever appropriate, in relation to a mining area as a whole, rather than for a single mine, and should take into account the future land use contemplated for that area.

6. The costs of rehabilitation measures should be met from a Mining Lands Rehabilitation Fund, to be financed by a small cess on all tin exported, and administered by the Federal Government in trust for the State Governments, whose shares would be proportionate to their tin output. A portion of the Fund should be retained by the Federal Government for research into mining land rehabilitation problems. The Federal Government should be empowered to make temporary advances, from any unused portion of the Fund, to a State Government which wishes to anticipate its share in the Fund in order to meet exceptional rehabilitation expenses.

B OTHER MINERAL RESOURCES

Tin mining in Malaya is associated with a number of minor by-products, including wolframite, scheelite, columbite, tantalite and ilmenite, some of which are produced in small quantities by independent mines as well. Iron ore, coal, quarried stone, gold and bauxite are other minerals being currently produced. Of these, only iron ore offers any considerable possibilities of development, and the production of coal (which is of low grade) has already been reduced by the competition of fuel oil. Since geological mapping and prospecting is very far from completely covering the country, it is always possible that commercial deposits of other minerals may be found, although the broad geological indications are not favorable.

C GOVERNMENT AGENCIES

The Mines Department and the Geological Survey, both under the Member for Natural Resources, are the Federal Government agencies directly concerned with the mining industry. It is of very great importance that their work should be intensified, particularly in gathering more information regarding the economic geology and potentialities of the known mining areas, and in research into ore-dressing and mining methods. Recommendations on these matters will be found in Technical Report 5.

II POWER [7]

1 Federation

Supply and Capacity. The production and distribution of electric power in the Federation is governed by the Electricity Ordinance, 1949. This Ordinance set up the Central Electricity Board (CEB) as an autonomous corporation to take over and operate the Federal Government's installations, to establish and operate any other electrical installations it deemed expedient, and "to promote and encourage the generation of energy with a view to the economic development of the Federation." The Board is also empowered to license electrical installations, public and private.

Public supplies of electricity are provided mainly by CEB, the Perak River Hydro-Electric Power Company, Ltd. (PRHE), and the Municipality of George Town in Penang. The main undertakings of CEB are in the State of Selangor; they also supply power to Negri Sembilan and Malacca. In addition, CEB operates a number of smaller stations throughout the country, and takes bulk supplies from PRHE and Singapore for distribution in certain centers of Perak and in Johore Bahru. Its own installed capacity is 84.5 MW, of which 15.7 MW is at 34 diesel stations. PRHE, in which the Federal Government is a substantial but minority shareholder, operates in the State of Perak under a concession which provides that CEB may take over the undertaking at an agreed price in 1976 or thereafter. With a subsidiary, it has an installed capacity of 84.5 MW, of which 27 MW is at the hydroelectric installation at Chenderoh. Penang has a steam station of 17 MW at Prai, which supplies Province Wellesley on the mainland as well as the island. Taking into account small public utilities, the total installed electric generating capacity of public suppliers in the Federation is 190 MW.

The total installed power capacity, including mechanical power units and private electrical installations is, however, much higher and can be put at the equivalent of 445 MW, roughly half electrical and half mechani-

[7] See Technical Report 6.

cal. The equivalent of some 150 MW is operated by mines and 105 MW by a large number of nonmining enterprises. The substantial proportion of installed capacity operated by the latter is due largely to the remoteness of a number of rubber estates and sawmills from public utility networks and the character of the load of large sawmills for which the smaller public utility diesel stations are unsuited. It is also due to some extent to the inability of the public utilities, particularly CEB and its predecessor, to meet the increased demand for power in the postwar years. Enterprises requiring power installed their own power sets rather than await supplies from public utilities.

The consumption of electrical power produced by public utilities and private installations in 1952-53[8] amounted to 650 million KWH. Production was approximately 780 million KWH or 137 KWH per capita.[9] Tin mining accounted for two-thirds of consumption, taking 90% of PRHE production and 43% of CEB production.

The high ratio of mechanical to electrical power and the preponderance (or, if mechanical power be taken into account, the near preponderance) of the tin mining industry as a consumer are the salient features of the pattern of power consumption in the Federation. The one is a challenge to the public utilities; the other points to the need for caution in expanding capacity, since long-term prospects for a significant increase in tin production cannot be assessed with confidence.

Future Requirements. Because of the tin mining industry's dominant role as a consumer of electric power and the uncertainty as to the level of future tin production, estimates of consumption for more than five years are too uncertain to justify commitments to expand capacity. Moreover, even the estimates for the five-year period should be reviewed periodically and development programs re-examined in the light of any substantial changes in consumption. We have accordingly not attempted to estimate consumption after 1957-58.[10] CEB has provided us with an estimate of its own sales in these years. We are inclined to think that its estimates for sales for tin mining may be optimistic, which makes it the more important that the estimate be kept under constant review. Accepting the CEB figure, however, and assuming only a modest increase in PRHE sales, the aggre-

---

[8] CEB Annual Report, 1952-53, p. 54. CEB's fiscal year runs from Sepetember 1 to August 31.

[9] This is exceeded in Asia only by Japan, Hong Kong and Singapore.

[10] Five years from 1952-53, the last year for which figures are available.

gate of public utilities' sales in 1957-58 can be put at around 822 million units. This compares with 550 million units sold in 1952-53.

The capacity needed to meet this demand must be considered system by system, since the various systems are not interconnected. PRHE's capacity will be adequate without further addition, but part of its plant will require renewal. The company has plans for such renewals and for extensions calling for expenditure of some $8 million but it is not yet prepared to commit itself to large expenditures. Penang proposes to install a new 20 MW station on the island by 1957 and to add a further 10 MW set to the station by 1960. When this set is commissioned, it is proposed to close down the old 17 MW station at Prai. The new and old stations, and later the new station alone, will provide an adequate margin of capacity. The supply for CEB's central network will be augmented by 40 MW when the second half of the Connaught Bridge station is commissioned in 1955 and, in addition, the Board has a project for a 20 MW (ultimately 40 MW) station at Malacca. With these additional units the central network will have sufficient capacity even after the obsolete Bungsar station of 26.5 MW is withdrawn from service. CEB should continue to take its supplies from the Pasir Panjang station in Singapore for Johore Bahru's requirements.

Penang's program for the period 1954 through 1960 is estimated to cost $25 million, the principal items being the new 30 MW station previously mentioned and extensions and improvements to transmission lines and networks. In view of the need to curtail the cost of the Federation's over-all development program and having regard to the fact that the new 20 MW station is likely to give sufficient capacity for a period beyond 1959, we have not made provision in our program for the proposed third 10 MW set.

CEB's program for 1953-54 through 1957-58 is provisionally estimated at $59 million in addition to $39 million remaining from the previous program. The main items in the new program are the 20 MW station at Malacca ($16.5 million), additional diesel generating plant and a small hydroelectric station ($3 million), and development of transmission lines and networks ($25 million). In connection with the last-mentioned item in the program we suggest that the proposed extensions to the 66 KV and 33 KV systems north of Kuala Lumpur, primarily to serve the tin mining industry, be installed only if there is reasonable assurance that the investment would be self-liquidating over the period of supply.

Looking further ahead, the Board has had under investigation for some time a hydroelectric station in the Cameron Highlands, with a wet season capacity of 114 MW, to be built in two stages. It would be linked to the present CEB and PRHE systems by a 132 KV line. In the dry season, capacity would be reduced to 80 MW. As envisaged at present, this development is not likely to be an economic proposition until the peak loads of the present systems increase very considerably. We recommend, however, that investigation of the project be continued and that it be planned for development in stages consistent with the quantities of power that can be economically used by the networks. Consideration will no doubt be given to the possibility of providing storage in order to reduce the additional thermal capacity required to meet peak loads during the dry season. The project concerns PRHE very closely and should be planned in consultation with it.

Of more immediate importance is investigation of the possibilities of small hydroelectric plants at sites sufficiently near the present or projected networks to be connected to them. Such plants are relatively inexpensive, present no complicated engineering problems and can be constructed in a short time; moreover, their full output could be absorbed immediately. Since they would be intended to take some of the peak load off thermal stations, their usefulness would be enhanced if water storage facilities were provided. The site of a medium-sized scheme has already been surveyed geologically. We recommend that the additional necessary surveys be pressed forward and that other possibilities, including the further utilization of the Ulu Langat catchment area, also be studied.

CEB proposes to acquire two private installations. While acquisition of these particular undertakings would have advantages, we take the view that the Board should in general concentrate its resources in the central area and be reluctant to disperse them by installing or taking over small stations in outlying areas. The Board should encourage private investment in small undertakings in areas not served by it.

Rates. It is CEB's long-term policy that its tariff rates should produce a surplus of net income after allowing for depreciation and the increased cost of replacing capital assets,[11] interest on loan capital and an appropriate dividend on the share capital. The surplus aimed at would be enough to build up reasonable reserves to strengthen the undertaking generally and to redeem loan capital over a long period or, alternatively, to provide funds for capital extensions without recourse to borrowing. For the present, the

[11] The amounts by which provision for depreciation based on cost is expected to fall short of the estimated future cost of replacement of capital assets.

Board has decided to appropriate annually (if net revenue after provision for depreciation permits) an amount equivalent to approximately 5% of the gross income from electricity sales for both the reserve for the increased cost of replacing capital assets and the other (general) reserves. Upon completion of the survey of the Board's capital assets it will be possible to assess, and provide separately for, the amounts needed over the years for the former.

The Board has loan obligations amounting to $69 million which are repayable within the next 10 years, including two loans of $35 million and $25 million from the Colonial Development Corporation. To provide in full for the redemption of these loans by the dates on which they become repayable would put a heavy strain on the Board and might well require tariff rates to be put at a higher level than would otherwise be necessary. Moreover, the greater part, if not the whole, of further capital expenditure would have to be financed by further borrowing. We accordingly recommend that an extension of the Colonial Development Corporation's loans be sought.

2 Singapore

Electricity. Electric power is supplied by the Electricity Department of the City Council from the St. James station and from a new station at Pasir Panjang, first brought into service at the end of 1952. Its present installed capacity of 50 MW is to be increased by further 25 MW stages until it reaches the ultimate maximum capacity of 150 MW in 1959. With one generator kept as a stand-by, the effective capacity of the station will then be 125 MW. The St. James station is to be withdrawn from service in 1956.

The Electricity Department's current program of capital expenditure from loan funds is estimated to cost $176 million up to the end of 1959; $69 million had been spent by the end of 1953. The principal items are the new power station, extensions to networks and purchase of appliances for hire.

The new station is likely to be able to meet demand until early in the 1960's. The Department is now considering rehabilitating the St. James station and installing in it either gas turbines or turbo-alternators. We support the study of this project but have made no provision for it in our program, as no substantial expenditure would be incurred before 1960.

Gas. The Gas Department of the City Council has a modest program totalling $4 million, in which the main items are a new water gas plant and a new gas holder. Rather more than $1 million was spent on the program up to the end of 1953. With these additions, the capacity of the gas works will be increased to 800 million cubic feet in 1956.

We do not subscribe to the view that gas will be ousted by electricity. The demand for gas has paralleled the demand for electricity, at a rate which suggests that it will catch up with capacity in 1957 or 1958. We accordingly recommend that expert consideration be given immediately to a further increase in capacity. A new site would have to be found, since there is no room for further extensions at the Kallang works.

Organization. The electricity and gas departments come under the purview of the City Council's Public Utilities Committee for policy matters and the Finance Committee for appropriations. Each Committee reports to the full Council.

The Special Commissioner appointed to report on local government in Singapore recommended "a separate body for the production and supply of electricity and gas for the whole island on the lines of the public corporations in Britain and with the same division of responsibility for policy and day-to-day management."[12] The Constitutional Commission subsequently reported, however, that "at present there is no need to transfer public utilities from one form of public ownership (municipal) to another and we therefore recommend that the utilities which are already under the City Council should, for the time being at any rate, be placed under the City and Island Council."[13] In our opinion, an autonomous statutory corporation responsible for both services would make for better coordination, greater continuity of policy and more flexible management than can be achieved while the two departments remain integral parts of the municipal machine and policy is decided by committees with frequently changing membership. Consumers' interests could be represented through the City and Island Council's nominees to the board of the corporation. We recognize that the immediate creation of such a corporation would be untimely, but we urge that earnest consideration be given to the matter, once the impending constitutional changes have become effective and the machinery of government has been adapted to them.

[12] Report on the Reform of Local Government by Dr. L. C. Hill, p. 65.
[13] Report of the Constitutional Commission, Singapore, 1954, p. 25.

CHAPTER 5 *TRANSPORT AND COMMUNICATIONS*[1]

Malaya's transport and communications systems are well developed. Singapore, one of the world's major ports and an important air junction, together with Port Swettenham and Penang, gives Malaya excellent overseas connections. An efficient state railway runs from Singapore through the western coastal plain to Prai (opposite Penang Island) and thence to the frontier. Short branches go to Port Swettenham and three minor ports on the west coast, while a long eastern branch line runs to the frontier from a point near the southern end of the central mountain range. Both the western and the eastern lines connect at the frontier with the State Railway of Thailand. A privately-owned company provides frequent air service, of a high standard of regularity and punctuality, between Singapore and eight main airports in the Federation, and a state-owned air service operated by the Malayan Railway Administration links a number of smaller centers to the main airports. The road network is dense in Singapore Island and in parts of the western coastal plain but thinner elsewhere, particularly to the east of the central range. A good trunk road stretches from the frontier to the Johore causeway, where it joins the Singapore road system. Another crosses the peninsula from Port Swettenham to Kuantan; improvements to the eastern half of this road are expected to be completed in 1955. The east coast has a parallel road for the greater part of its length, although the road is not yet of a high standard of construction and has a number of ferry crossings. Coastal shipping connects the three main ports with a number of minor ports on both coasts. The telecommunications system, which includes a teleprinter service between Singapore and some of the larger towns of the Federation, is efficient and well spread.

The framework of the transport and communications systems is thus nearly complete. But many extensions and improvements are required if the growing needs of the country are to be served efficiently. Our recommendations therefore include capital expenditure for this purpose of around $175 million in the Federation and about $90 million in Singapore during the five-year period.

[1] See Technical Report 7.

108

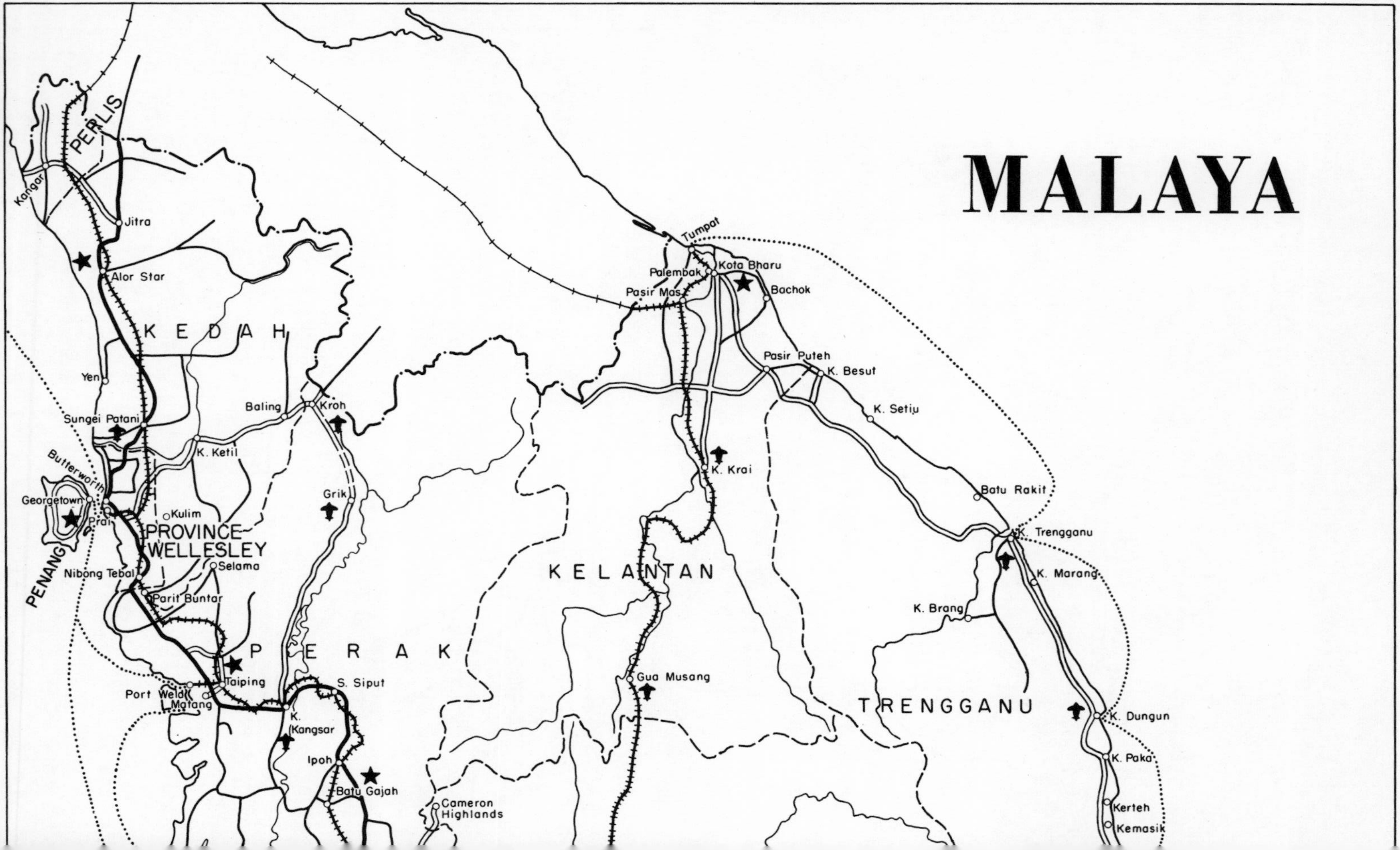

MAP 3

MALAYA

PERLIS

Kangar

Yen

Jitra

Alor Star

KEDAH

Sungei Patani

Butterworth

Georgetown

PENANG

PROVINCE WELLESLEY

Prai

Nibong Tebal

Parit Buntar

Port Weld

Matang

Taiping

Selama

Kulim

K. Ketil

Baling

Kroh

Grik

Port Patani

S. Siput

K. Kangsar

Ipoh

Batu Gajah

Cameron Highlands

PERAK

KELANTAN

Gua Musang

K. Krai

Tumpat

Kota Bharu

Bachok

Palembok

Pasir Mas

Pasir Puteh

K. Besut

K. Setiu

Batu Rakit

Trengganu

K. Brang

K. Marang

Morang

Dungun

K. Paka

Kerteh

Kemasik

TRENGGANU

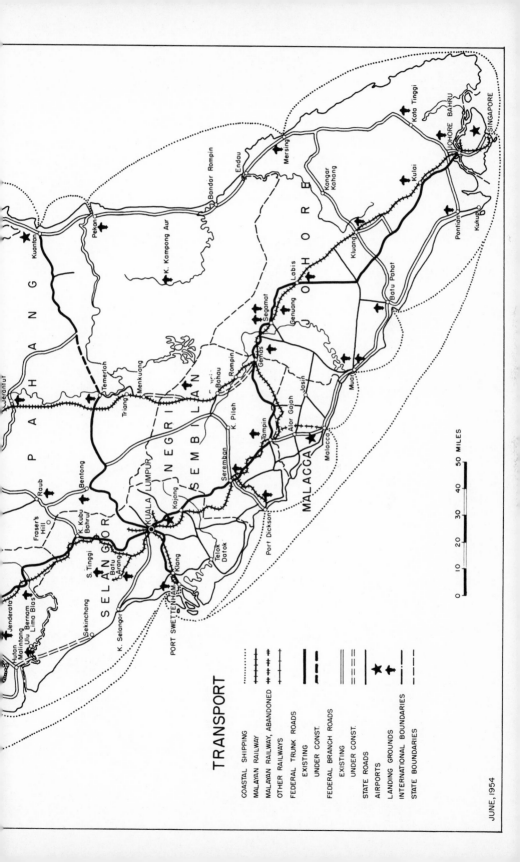

TRANSPORT

COASTAL SHIPPING	········
MALAYAN RAILWAY	┼┼┼┼
MALAYAN RAILWAY, ABANDONED	╫╫ ╫╫
OTHER RAILWAYS	┼┼┼
FEDERAL TRUNK ROADS	
EXISTING	▌
UNDER CONST.	▌ ▌
FEDERAL BRANCH ROADS	
EXISTING	═══
UNDER CONST.	═ ═ ═
STATE ROADS	
AIRPORTS	★
LANDING GROUNDS	├
INTERNATIONAL BOUNDARIES	·—·—·
STATE BOUNDARIES	— — —

JUNE, 1954

0 10 20 30 40 50 MILES

I TRANSPORT

A PORTS

The ports in Malaya have been the subject of several reports during the last four years.[2] The mission concurs generally in their recommendations. We suggest, however, an alternative way of providing the additional capacity required at Port Swettenham.

Singapore

Singapore's port facilities comprise the ocean harbor, owned and operated by the Singapore Harbour Board, a statutory corporation, the Outer and Inner Roads with a breakwater between them, and oil depots maintained and operated by oil companies on three adjacent islands. From 30,000 to 40,000 ships and craft, including some 5,000 ocean vessels, use the Roads annually.

The number and tonnage of ships using the Harbour Board's facilities have steadily increased since the war and in the last two years have been greater than in 1928-29, the best of the prewar years. The tonnage of general cargo handled by the Harbour Board rose to a peak of 4.1 million tons in 1951-52 but dropped to approximately 3.8 million tons in each of the following two years. Tonnage of fuel oil continued to increase and that of coal to decline.

The rise in the number of vessels and tonnage and the increasing overall length of modern vessels have taxed the capacity of the harbor's deepwater berths; congestion and delays have been avoided only by careful management. The Board is accordingly planning an extension known as the East Lagoon Scheme to add nine berths, totaling 5,600 ft. in length, in three stages of three berths each. The cost of the full scheme has been provisionally estimated at $40 million, half of which would be for the first stage, which would involve the heaviest construction work. While it cannot be said with certainty that the number and tonnage of vessels using the Board's facilities will remain at about the present level or will significantly increase or decrease, Singapore cannot risk losing some of its trade through

[2] Report on the Major Ports of Malaya, by D. F. Allen, May 1950; Report on the Minor Ports of Malaya, by D. F. Allen, October 1952; Report of the Federal Ports' Committee, April 1952; Supplementary Report of the Federal Ports' Committee, November 1952.

inability to provide the requisite harbor facilities. The mission therefore recommends that the planning of the East Lagoon Scheme be pressed forward and construction of the first stage undertaken within the next two or three years. The Harbour Board should be able to finance from its own resources the greater part, if not the whole, of that stage.

Port Swettenham

Although well situated in relation to the most developed area of the Federation, Port Swettenham is not ideally sited or designed; berthing and turning operations are difficult and the shore installations are cramped within a small area. Traffic has increased steadily. Tonnage of cargo handled, other than oil in bulk, is now 50% above its prewar peak of 600,000 in 1929. To meet the need for increased capacity, three additional berths are planned for the North Klang Straits, five miles seaward of the present port. The proposed site has the great advantage of deep water. On the other hand, the rail and road connections, which would have to be built across swampy ground and which would include a bridge across the Klang River, would be costly, and more equipment and a larger administrative and operational staff would be required in the aggregate than if the additional berths were to be built at the present site. The capital cost of the project was estimated in 1952 at $26 million; desirable improvements in the layout would probably raise it to nearly $30 million.

A feasible and probably less costly alternative both in capital and recurrent expenditure would be to construct the three additional berths at the present site, where there is room for them, and to rearrange the present layout of the port area to provide additional space for handling cargoes. Although dredging would be necessary to maintain a sufficient depth of water, this disadvantage is by no means decisive, and we recommend that the alternative be carefully studied and weighed against the North Klang Straits project before proceeding further with the latter.

Provision has been made in the recommended development program for only $20 million for the development of Port Swettenham on the assumption that the suggested alternative will be adopted.

Penang and Prai

Penang is a lighter port with good anchorages in deep sheltered water, a two-berth wharf, lighter basins and lighter landing stages. Prai is a railway port on the mainland opposite Penang in the mouth of the Prai River, with quays and other installations; it is badly silted up.

Penang's immediate requirements are improvements to the ferry service between the island and the mainland, and improved lighterage facilities. Projects for both have been prepared by consulting engineers.

The first calls for seven new double-ended ferry boats and a two-berth terminal at Penang, and single-berth terminals at Prai and Butterworth (on the mainland, north of the Prai River). The project is divided into three stages estimated to cost a total of $10 million. The mission's recommended program includes all the terminals and five of the seven ferry boats, leaving two to be provided at a later date. The project is sufficiently flexible to allow portions to be postponed if traffic fails to expand to the extent expected.

The projected improvement of facilities for lighter cargo movements, known as the Weld Quay Scheme, is estimated to cost approximately $3 million. The first phase is now under construction. One of the two remaining phases can be postponed until after 1959 without detriment to the port's needs and we have not included it in the recommended program.

The mission endorses the view of the Federal Ports Committee that substantial capital expenditure on deep-water berths would not be warranted now or in the near future. The need for measures to increase the depth of water alongside the quays at Prai should be re-examined, as the Committee suggested, within the next few years. The possibility of securing the extra depth by training works on the Prai River upstream of the port appears to merit investigation by consulting engineers.

Malacca and Minor Ports

Malacca, from which Malays, Portuguese and Dutch in turn once sought to command the Straits of Malacca and levy toll on shipping, and which in more recent times was a free port like Singapore and Penang, has seen its overseas trade dwindle until now it is no more than an occasional port of call for ocean vessels. Shipping and trading interests assert that some of the trade could be recaptured if the port facilities were greatly improved and if Malacca became a regular port of call for some of the Conference Lines steamers serving Malaya. While sympathetic, the mission cannot support either proposal; there is no room for a fourth ocean port on Malaya's west coast. We can go no further than to recommend that

Malacca be brought up to a standard permitting entrance of coastal vessels up to 150 ft. in length and 9 ft. 6 ins. in draught. We have noted with regret that the Shipping Freight Conference felt unable to agree to introduce certain ameliorative measures recommended by the Federal Ports Committee.[3]

Most of the minor ports are now less serviceable than they were before the war. We recommend that the Roads at the mouth of the Kelantan estuary, Kuala Trengganu, Dungun, Chukai and Kuantan on the east coast, and Port Weld, Telok Anson, Ulu Bernam, Port Dickson, Muar and Batu Pahat on the west coast, be improved to accommodate coastal vessels up to a length of 200 ft. and a draught of 9 ft. 6 ins. Dredging, improved lights and buoys in some cases, and regular maintenance of restored channels will be necessary. Additional dredging equipment will be required, for which appropriate provision has been made in the recommended program.

Minor ports used by fishing vessels and lacking the facilities they need should be provided with jetties for landing fish and loading gear and provisions, with adjacent space for the maintenance of nets and gear.

B RAILWAY

The Malayan Railway is just emerging from a period of reconstruction after the spoliation, damage and neglect it suffered during the Japanese occupation of Malaya. Terrorist attacks on stations, trains and telecommunications from 1948 onward hampered both reconstruction and operation but have now declined to the point where they no longer have a seriously adverse effect. Provided that terrorist activities are not again intensified, operating conditions should in the future be more favorable than at any time since the war.

The railway has reached a high standard in administration, operation and maintenance and serves Malaya's needs well. Extensions are not yet necessary: development in the eastern part of the country would have to proceed a great deal further before an east-west line would be justified.

We support the Railway Administration's investment program for the next few years and have made provision in our estimates of capital requirements for this to the extent of about $24 million during 1955-59.[4]

---

[3] See Technical Report 7.
[4] Exclusive of the cost of improvement of Port Swettenham.

This includes $6 million for the replacement of some steam locomotives by diesel locomotives. A number of the factors detailed in Technical Report 7 appear to favor diesel traction and we recommend that the matter be studied in detail with a view to drawing up a long-term program of substitution to a much greater extent than is provided in the railway program, should experience prove diesel traction to be more advantageous than steam.

We also recommend investigating the possibility of operating existing short branch lines by small passenger units, one unit per line, without signaling or staffing of intermediate stations.

C ROADS

Federation

The Federation has 6,200 miles of metalled roads, 2,200 of which are maintained by the Federal Public Works Department and the rest by the State and Settlement Public Works Departments. While the Federal roads are well surfaced and maintained, a large part of their mileage, and of State roads also, was built long before the days of fast and heavy motor traffic and is tortuous and somewhat too narrow. The standard of maintenance of State roads is variable, sometimes being influenced by the availability of sufficient funds. Over-all traffic density is not high, the ratio of registered motor vehicles to road miles being only 15:1.

A seven-year road program prepared by the Federal Public Works Department provides for expenditure of $145 million on trunk roads; of this amount $97.3 million is to be spent in 1955-59. It also contemplates expenditure of $60 million on other metalled roads in that period, of which $24 million is for new road construction, $25 million for road improvements and $11 million for roads to open up agricultural areas.

We agree that the trunk roads must be adapted to heavy, fast-moving traffic. But in view of the limited availability of funds, we think that this program unduly emphasizes improvements to the north-south trunk road and to the Port Swettenham-Kuala Lumpur section of the east-west trunk road. We believe that many of these could be postponed without serious detriment, particularly as the north-south road and the western section of the east-west road are paralleled by the railway. We therefore recommend that improvements be limited to sections liable to serious flood damage, to dangerous sections and to weak bridges, and that the work be so sched-uled as to permit its execution with staff already available. In our recom-mended program provision for trunk roads has accordingly been limited to $50 million.

As regards the program for other roads, we suggest that the proposed new roads from Gemas to Rompin and from Bahau to Menkuang be de-ferred, unless there are strong strategical reasons for their construction. Instead of $11 million for roads to open up potential agricultural areas, we have allowed a more or less token $5 million for links between existing roads and the perimeters of such new agricultural schemes as may be established. Within the areas to be developed, roads should be built as part of the schemes themselves.

Insufficient attention has, we believe, been given to the development of minor roads linking *kampongs* (villages) to the road network. Such roads have, indeed, been built and improved on the initiative of district officers and village headmen, and the Rural and Industrial Development Authority (RIDA) has done much to encourage their development by making grants to communities willing to contribute free or partly free labor. But a coordinated effort has been lacking. On social and economic grounds, we consider that a determined drive should now be made to de-velop these roads on the basis of a district-by-district survey. The possi-bilities will, of course, vary from State to State and the need will be less in areas with a dense network of main and secondary roads. We favor the RIDA method of aided self-help in the form of technical advice and grants of money or materials, or both. Where a local government authority exists, it would be appropriate to make it responsible for minor roads.

Singapore

Singapore Island has 400 miles of well-built roads, of which 225 miles are maintained by the Colony Public Works Department and 175 miles by the City Council's Civil Engineer Department. The standard of main-tenance is generally high.

The heaviest traffic naturally falls on the city roads, many of which are somewhat congested at times, due principally to the use of pedestrian sidewalks for other purposes, such as shop extensions and the parking of bicycles, and to the prevalence of open rain water drains. The covering of these drains and the construction and improvement of sidewalks are matters of high priority. The total cost of a comprehensive project would be some $3 million.

The road program for the Island as a whole includes in addition the following projects: construction of an esplanade road across the site of the present Kallang airport and a bridge across the Kallang River, and construction and realignment of road approaches, at an estimated cost of $13 million; widening of city streets and construction of roundabouts, for which we allowed $8 million over five years; and widening and extension of Island roads at a cost of about $4 million.

D ROAD TRANSPORT

Federation

The spectacular postwar growth of road transport brought with it many harmful practices. Eight years of control and guidance have, however, gone far toward creating a well-ordered system, and on the whole road transport operators now provide a good service. Some malpractices nevertheless persist, such as the misuse of limited carriers' and private carriers' licenses and the illegal acceptance by hire cars of bus traffic on scheduled routes. The enforcement staff of the Road Transport Department should be strengthened and the traffic police should be equipped to patrol the routes more extensively. Since other duties are becoming lighter, we believe that no over-all increase in the Department's staff is necessary. We have included $250,000 in our recommended program for vehicles for traffic police.

A road transport bill to consolidate and amend existing legislation was in draft at the time of the mission's visit. It would introduce a zoning system for haulers to restrict their range of operation, thus effectively preserving long-distance goods traffic for the railway or coastal shipping. We question whether, viewed broadly, this would be an improvement over the present system.

Singapore

Bus services within the city are provided by the Singapore Traction Company under an agreement with the government terminating in 1955 but renewable for a further period of seven years.

The agreement gives the government adequate powers of control. The company provides good and punctual services and its fares are reasonable. Consideration has been given to purchasing the company. But in view of the satisfactory service and level of fares, the magnitude of the purchase price and the demands that the development program will make on available financial resources, we think that extension of the agreement for another seven years is preferable to acquisition of the undertaking, whether by the government or the City and Island Council.

E CIVIL AVIATION

International air transport serving Malaya is centered on Singapore, although two foreign airlines call at Penang.

Internal air services are provided by Malayan Airways, a private company whose charter expires on April 30, 1957. Scheduled services are operated between Singapore and the main cities of the Federation, as well as to Indochina, Sumatra, Thailand, North Borneo and Sarawak, with 11 Dakota aircraft acquired second-hand between 1947 and 1952. The services are efficient and aircraft maintenance is of high standard. The company formerly operated five government-owned light aircraft on feeder services under an agreement which expired in July 1954. These are now operated by the Malayan Railway.

The company's fleet will have to be replaced, beginning in 1957, at a total cost of around $15 million. In view of the time it will take to obtain new aircraft and put them into service, a decision on the renewal of the company's charter should be made soon. We recommend that the charter be renewed, modified as may be appropriate, and conditioned on giving preference to applications from residents of Malaya in allotting any additional capital needed to finance the replacement of the fleet. In making this recommendation, we have in mind the excellent record of Malayan Airways' services, the limited financial resources available for development and the desirability of encouraging private capital in fields appropriate to it.

The feeder services should be maintained even at the cost of a subsidy. We recommend elsewhere that they should be used to a greater extent for the carriage of mail.

There are eight fully equipped airports in the Federation and 53 landing grounds, 15 of which are used on more or less regular schedules. The airport at Kuala Lumpur, the largest, has ample capacity for all internal air traffic likely to develop, but its difficult approaches make it unsuitable for the larger types of aircraft used in international flights. We advise against moving the airport, but recommend that plans be prepared for the improvement of approaches.

A five-year development program, requiring capital expenditures of not over $2 million, has been prepared by the Federation's Civil Aviation Department. We consider this program an appropriate basis for normal development.

A new airport in Singapore is under construction at Paya Lebar. The total cost to completion in 1956 is estimated to be $38 million. We recommend that an expert's advice be sought in designing the terminal facilities.

II COMMUNICATIONS

Postal Services

The postal services of the Federation and Singapore are combined in a pan-Malayan Postal Organization with headquarters at Kuala Lumpur. The number of communications handled has increased rapidly in recent years, especially in the Federation where it reached 150 million in 1953. Expansion of facilities has become necessary.

To this end a development program has been prepared for the Federation which would involve expenditure of approximately $7.5 million over five years. In our recommended program, however, we have spread the expenditure over a longer period because of financial limitations.

Telegraph and Telephone Services

Public telegraph and telephone services in the Federation and Singapore are operated by the pan-Malayan Department of Telecommunications, except for the local telephone service in Singapore. Security requirements have forced the pace of telecommunications development, with the result that these services are now of an exceptionally high standard.

The public telegraph service operates at a loss, the amount of which is expected to be reduced as new teleprinter apparatus and V.F.T. installations are brought into operation. The Department plans to spend $800,000 over the next five years on such equipment.

A development program for telephone services in the Federation, submitted by the Department, calls for capital expenditure of $42 million over five years to 1959. We recommend that expansion be more closely related to the growth of demand and that the program be spread over more than five years. Non-revenue-earning projects should be limited to essentials.

Singapore Telephone Service. The privately-owned Singapore local telephone service is being transferred to government ownership and is to be operated by an autonomous Singapore Telephone Board. Demand in Singapore is growing, requiring an expansion of facilities. We endorse the proposed development program, which provides for capital expenditure of $22 million over a five-year period. The government-owned Singapore trunk exchange, which is under the same management as the local service, will also shortly return to government management. It is inadequate even for present requirements, and construction of a new exchange at a cost of $720,000 has been planned; we recommend that it be begun forthwith. We strongly support the view that the trunk exchange should be administratively separate from the local service and be placed directly under the Department of Telecommunications. This arrangement would both reduce costs and ensure better coordination.

CHAPTER **6** *INDUSTRY AND ENTREPOT TRADE*

1 INDUSTRY[1]

Except for its deposits of iron ore, Malaya is relatively poorly endowed with the complex of basic raw materials usually associated with advanced industrial development. Convenient sources of cheap power are lacking and domestic supplies of fuel are very limited and of poor quality. Nevertheless, secondary industry employs about 10% of the working population and its relative importance in the economy is exceeded in very few other Asian countries.

This level of industrial development may be attributed to a sizeable enterprising element in the population and to the influence of rubber and tin production and a prosperous commerce in creating a demand for ancillary industrial services, in expanding the domestic market for manufactured goods and in generating savings available for industrial investment.

At the same time, however, the advantageous position of rubber, tin and other primary production and of trade has handicapped industrial growth through competition for labor and capital and the consequent establishment of wages and other costs at levels relatively high by Asian standards. As a result, industrial activity has tended to concentrate on lines which enjoy considerable natural protection from foreign competition: those closely associated with primary production and trade, operations which must be performed on the spot and industries sheltered by high transportation costs or other special advantages of location. Most of the industrial employment, other than handicrafts, is in the engineering trades, in the processing of agricultural, mining and forestry products, and in the manufacture of food preparations, beverages, tobacco, rubber goods, furniture, printed materials and building supplies.

The average industrial unit is very small by Western standards. This is especially true of the Federation, where nearly 40% of the "industrial" labor force consists of persons working on their own account and family workers; in Singapore the corresponding proportion is only 10%. Stand-

[1] See Technical Report 8.

ards of equipment and technique vary widely from plant to plant but in spite of this and of the typically small scale of operations a great many of the enterprises appear to be satisfactorily equipped and efficiently conducted.

It would be a mistake to judge industrial efficiency in Malaya by Western standards of size and equipment. In the local economic circumstances the most appropriate enterprise appears to be something between the large heavily capitalized Western pattern and the very labor-intensive pattern of poorer Asian countries. The former is precluded in Malaya by limitations of available capital, markets, organizational and technical skills and experience; the latter by wage and cost standards relatively high compared to those in many other countries of Asia.

The Role of Industry in Malaya's Economic Development

While there have been substantial postwar additions to Malaya's industrial capacity, statistical data are lacking for an accurate measure of actual recent rates of industrial growth. It would appear, however, that they have been no more than commensurate with the rates of increase in the working population. We have stressed the prospect for a very large increase in Malaya's labor force and the importance of a steady and substantial expansion in industrial employment opportunities if living standards are to be raised or even maintained. It is also clear, on the other hand, that these employment opportunities must be based on industrial activity sufficiently productive and profitable to warrant diverting from other possible uses the large amount of capital required per industrial worker, and to justify the wage levels on which Malaya's living standards are based.

Major technological or geological discoveries apart, the possibilities for the establishment of large new industrial enterprises seem limited. We have mentioned the comparative lack of basic raw materials for heavy industry except for iron ore, the domestic processing of which is handicapped by location, very heavy capital requirements, and the absence of metallurgical fuels and cheap power. Rubber normally gains in weight and bulk in the course of manufacture and its industrial possibilities are therefore largely confined to domestic and immediately neighboring markets. Tin is a very minor component in most of its industrial uses. Pulp and paper may one day become major industrial possibilities but at present

Malayan timbers appear to be generally unsuited for commercial pulping processes.

Malaya's industrial development in the future, as in the past, seems likely then to follow the pattern of individually small advances over a wide range of industries catering chiefly to the domestic and nearby markets. In this context the outlook is reasonably promising, as indicated in Technical Report 8 on Industrial Development.

The character of typical Malayan industry also seems likely to continue in some sort of intermediate position between East and West, generally avoiding the most highly mechanized and capital-expensive industries and processes on the one hand, and on the other avoiding the lavish use of labor, at the expense of equipment and training, which is possible in some other Asian countries.

But this is really only to state, not to solve, the problem of Malaya's industrial development, especially since it seems likely that, if satisfactory rates of progress are to be achieved, industrial activity will have to move increasingly into lines more directly and openly competitive with manufactured products from abroad.

Malaya is probably better able to meet this competition than much of the rest of Asia, by virtue of a considerable amount of enterprise, skill and industrial experience; reasonably satisfactory basic services for industry, such as power, transport and communications; a fairly substantial industrial base on which to build and to draw for assistance in further industrialization; and an adequate supply of savings, especially taking into account the large accumulations of fairly liquid funds remaining from the 1950-1951 boom.

These advantages are, however, only relative by Asian standards; substantial changes in the characteristic pattern of Malayan industry and in the industrial environment seem essential if competition from outside Malaya is to be met on a steadily expanding scale. The particular requirements in this direction appear to be:

1. A gradual swing away from the very small-scale "family" enterprise toward a more modern form of joint-equity organization. Such a form of business organization is advantageous in connection with mobilization of capital, accumulations of reserves, enlistment of specialized managerial and technical skills, adoption of up-to-date processes and continuity of organization and policy. This would not necessarily mean an increase in the scale of operations where small enterprises are properly equipped and

efficiently operated but it would facilitate expansion when desirable for greater efficiency.

2. Acceptance by managers and workers of the necessity for high and precise standards of quality, and recognition that modern principles of factory routine and performance can be applied to small-scale industrial establishments less mechanized than those of the West. This will require greater emphasis on training skilled and semi-skilled workers in modern factory techniques.

3. More systematic research of technical possibilities and potential markets as a basis for choice of industries, manufacturing methods and scale of establishment. Industrial research should not be left to individual firms or industries; a favorable opportunity for development at one point will often depend on parallel development elsewhere to make up an integrated pattern for the production and use of semi-finished manufactures, by-products, ancillary services, etc.

4. Establishment, as the need arises, of institutional arrangements to facilitate the raising of industrial capital and the provision of medium- and long-term industrial credit and to ameliorate to some extent the impact on the industrial sector of temporary but sharp fluctuations in the prices of tin and rubber.

The need to foster the development of secondary industry and improved industrial standards of organization and technique does not, of course, imply any less emphasis on the improvement and expansion of primary production and trade. These will for a long time provide the main support of Malayan living standards, domestic markets, accumulations of capital and foreign exchange earnings. Hence, measures to promote the success of primary production and trade are of the utmost importance for the development of secondary industries as well.

The primary responsibility for progress in the improvement of industrial organization and standards is, of course, that of private enterprise. In the Malayan economy, with its long history of individual initiative in commerce and industry, there is no question of government itself embarking on direct operation of manufacturing industries, nor do we consider that such a policy would be wise.[2] It was not, of course, within the mission's province to recommend action by private enterprise. Our recommendations are necessarily limited to government action.

[2] There are, however, five government-operated rice mills, and one plant for processing smallholders' rubber is operated by RIDA.

The Role of Government

We conceive of the role of the government in relation to manufacturing enterprise as twofold:

1. To provide adequate basic services: electric power, water supplies, transport and communications, etc. In these respects Malaya is relatively well equipped; the expansion of these services is discussed elsewhere.

2. To foster individual enterprise and to create a favorable climate for its development, through reinforcement and extension of measures already being undertaken by both governments. Specifically we have in mind the following:

(a) establishment of technological and market research services for secondary industry;

(b) emphasis on industrial and vocational needs in educational and training programs;

(c) active steps to interest overseas firms in Malayan industrial projects where their technical know-how may be important;

(d) improvement of facilities for the financing of sound industrial projects;

(e) close attention to the economic situation of secondary industries in determining fiscal, monetary and other policies;

(f) extension of official services to assist in the acquisition of factory sites and to help new enterprises overcome other initial problems; and

(g) use, in the Federation, of the tariff as a means of encouraging development, not to shelter inefficient or hopelessly high-cost industries but as an impetus to enterprises otherwise very near or only just over the margin of profitability or initially handicapped by temporary obstacles.

The two governments are aware of these possibilities and have taken action with respect to some of them. The remaining paragraphs of this section deal with possible further action. The question of tariff protection will be discussed at somewhat greater length than the other matters—not because we consider it the most important but because it often gives rise to misconceptions.

Protective Measures.[3] We must enter a caveat at the outset against any conception of tariff protection as a means of ensuring domestic production

---

[3] Our recommendations with respect to tariff policy do not apply to the free ports of Singapore and Penang, in which more than one-fifth of the total population lives. Physical and trading conditions in the two ports are such that it would be extremely difficult, with-

for the home market at prevailing wage levels regardless of the nature of foreign competition. Protective measures which merely excluded cheaper foreign products and forced Malayan purchasers to buy more costly home manufactures would result in an absorption of capital and resources which might better be employed in other lines. They would also tend to depress standards of living directly, by increasing living costs, and indirectly, by forcing up working costs to the disadvantage of export industries and trading activities.

The situations in which some degree of protection may be suitable and desirable may be summarized as follows:

1. Where a new industry has reasonable expectations at the outset of selling at prices little above those of foreign competitors and, within a few years, of reducing costs sufficiently to compete without protection, either because of its own growth and experience or because of gradual improvement in operating conditions as industrial development in general progresses;

2. Where local manufacturers can produce an equivalent article at a price competitive with imports but where protection is necessary to give investors confidence or to prevent the splitting of the market between home and foreign suppliers, thus making possible local production on a modern factory scale;

3. Where protection will give the local manufacturer an opportunity to overcome a superficial preference for the familiar imported product (in cases where it is clear that there is sufficient internal competition or official supervision to prevent exploitation of the consumer);

4. Where protection may be an important inducement to the establishment in Malaya of a foreign-owned industry which, while capable of serving the domestic market competitively, may be reluctant to make the investment if it may have to share the market with imports. Here again, the interest of the consumer should be carefully safeguarded; and

5. Where an industry is fairly close to the margin of profitability (i.e., its costs are such that it is nearly in a position to compete with foreign industries without protection), at an output sufficiently large for the domestic market, and where its competitive position could be reasonably

---

out serious adverse effects on entrepot trade, either to fence off "bonded" areas within which that trade could be conducted free of duty or to provide for refunds of duties upon re-export. If, however, these difficulties can be overcome, there would be some advantage in the integration of Penang in the Federation customs area.

assured, given time and opportunity to develop an additional regular market in neighboring areas. In this case a protected domestic market would, as it were, provide a safe "home base" from which to venture into unprotected markets further afield and to operate on a competitive scale in both the home and the external markets.

An important question in connection with Federation tariff policy is the position of manufacturers in Singapore and Penang in relation to the mainland markets. We have emphasized the essential economic unity of Malaya. We believe that manufacturers for whom Singapore or Penang is a convenient or desirable location should not be penalized in the mainland market, since this may deprive Malaya as a whole of industrial development which would otherwise take place. We therefore recommend that some way be found to relieve manufacturers in these ports from Federation customs duties on their mainland sales. We recognize that this would present certain administrative and financial problems but believe that these could be solved, perhaps by registering sales quotas in advance to ensure that only bona fide local manufactures were admitted free. There would also be some, if slight, effect on Federation revenues; possibly, in the case of Singapore, the two governments could agree on a reasonable scale of Colony Government contributions in lieu of Federation duties on Singapore manufactures.

Education and Training. Among the greatest obstacles to efficient factory operation are the inadequacy of publicly available training facilities, the absence of satisfactory systems of on-the-job apprenticeship within industry, and a lack of publicly recognized trade qualifications for skilled industrial workers. Here we wish only to urge greater attention to these requirements for satisfactory industrial progress. More detailed discussion of the problems and recommended measures for improvement are contained in Technical Reports 8 and 9.

Technological and Market Research. Only limited research effort has so far been devoted to problems directly bearing on Malaya's industrial future. The work on industrial uses of rubber, financed by a rubber cess, is carried out mainly in the United Kingdom and addresses itself primarily to the particular problems of the major rubber manufacturing industries in Europe and America. Other research of industrial relevance is confined largely to possible uses of forestry products. The scope for fairly quick rewards from industrial research is probably greater in Malaya than in most of the less developed countries, since Malaya possesses a considerable entrepreneurial class with the interest, initiative and capital to put research findings to practical use.

We therefore recommend a Malayan Institute of Industrial Research to investigate the technological and economic opportunities for industrial expansion. Such an organization, the details of which are set forth in Technical Report 8, should serve both the Federation and Singapore but should not, in our view, be established as part of the machinery of either government.

Industrial Finance. The mission found great difficulty in obtaining a satisfactory picture of the availability and character of sources of finance for industrial enterprise. This may be attributed to the very diverse and scattered elements which go to make up what may be called the Malayan money and capital markets and to the very limited degree of integration and organization among these elements. In general, it was our impression (supported indirectly by available data on the balance of payments, on public and private capital formation and on public finance) that rates of domestic saving in relation to national income are not particularly high, except under such boom conditions as prevailed in 1950 and 1951. At present there are, however, large and fairly liquid accumulations of savings retained from the high earnings of the boom period.

The more difficult and obscure part of the picture lies in the institutional pattern for the channeling of savings into productive investment. The commercial banking system is, of course, one source of short-term credit for reputable firms against the security of commodities or other good collateral. Its activity in the industrial field is, however, relatively limited. Insurance companies are probably another minor source of industrial funds, although we were unable to obtain any data on their significance in the domestic credit field (an important gap in official financial statistics which should be filled). Another source is Chinese and Indian money lending, which appears to be of considerable importance among the smaller-enterprises, usually at interest rates which are very high and which vary greatly according to the standing or circumstances of the borrower. Few new issues are made on the Singapore stock market.

The most characteristic form of industrial financing, especially medium- and long-term, appears to be through private transactions which take place within circles of varying degrees of intimacy, mainly among the Chinese community. Even here, however, the cases of large initial investment in industrial ventures are relatively few and there is apparently a strong and widespread preference for short-term or fairly liquid investments; this tends to put long-term capital at a higher premium than is usual in more highly organized and integrated capital markets. Consequently, the typical pattern of establishment of industry appears to be on a small "family" basis; subsequent expansion, insofar as it occurs on any appreciable scale, is financed mainly from profits.

Some finance for factory development in Singapore has also been provided by the Colonial Development Corporation—$622,000 in 1951, $505,000 in 1952 and $56,000 in 1953—and in the Federation RIDA has furnished a limited amount of credit to very small Malayan ventures. But, with these exceptions, there is no public source, nor is there a regular organized institutional channel, for new long-term industrial investment.

However, in view of the prevailing conception of industrial enterprise largely in terms of fairly small units, the present technical and managerial limitations on industrial investment in relatively large "lumps," the financial facilities available within various private circles of the community, and the savings accumulated in the past few years, the establishment of new institutional arrangements for industrial financing on a larger scale does not appear to be of immediate urgency. The number of applications for Colonial Development Corporation loans has apparently been small and it was not our impression that secondary industry is, in general, starved for capital.

Nevertheless, we are convinced that if Malaya is to make the most of industrial opportunities opened up through industrial and market research, technical training and other measures of encouragement, new institutional arrangements for industrial finance will become necessary. This need will be the greater and more urgent if the present degree of availability of industrial capital, sustained out of boom savings, should in fact prove to be a passing phase.

We believe, therefore, that early consideration should be given to the financial requirements for private industrial development and to the establishment of a separate organization to extend medium- and long-term financing to industry. This is discussed further in Chapter 9. Meanwhile, we believe that in appropriate cases and upon careful investigation the government should be prepared, if necessary, to back the financial needs of sound industrial projects with guarantees of back advances. In making this suggestion, we must stress that we have in mind that such guarantees would be given very sparingly.

Administrative Arrangements. Other aspects of the role of the government in fostering private industrial development are discussed in Technical Report 8. Both in the preceding discussion and in the Technical Report our considerations necessarily largely relate to principles of industrial policy rather than to the application of policy to particular cases. But the latter is probably the most difficult part of the problem and a continuing agency of government is needed to apply policy to individual cases as they arise. In Singapore this function is now performed by the Department of Commerce and Industry. There is no apparent need for organizational changes there, although some expansion in staff may become necessary as the part of government in fostering industrial development is expanded.

In the Federation, it is more difficult for the government to encourage private industry, mainly because of the scattered centers of industrial activity and of the detailed and complex task of sound and effective administration of tariff policy and its application to individual cases. Hence we believe that there should be a separate and specialized agency within the Federation Government to deal with these and the many other aspects of industrial promotion. For this purpose we recommend the establishment of a Division of Industrial Development under the Member for Economic Affairs; an indication of the possible activities of such a division is given in Technical Report 8.

II   ENTREPOT TRADE

Entrepot trade—broadly defined to include all goods that pass through Malayan hands from a foreign source to a foreign destination, even when they undergo some degree of processing on the way—is in terms of gross value about half of all the trade of Malaya. About 90% of this trade is conducted in Singapore, and very nearly all the remainder in Penang. From the point of view of Singapore and Penang, the entrepot business includes also the movement of goods to and from the Federation mainland; about three-quarters of Federation trade regularly passes through these two ports, Singapore having a somewhat larger share than Penang. But we are here concerned with the trade in which Singapore and Penang merchants act as intermediaries between foreign sellers and buyers.

This trade was important long before the tin and rubber industries were developed on the mainland. Its concentration in Singapore[4] had its origins partly in the facts of geography and partly in the accidents of history; its development owes much to the long partnership in the Straits Settlements, under peaceful administration, between Asian merchants—chiefly Chinese—and the manufacturing firms and merchant houses of Great Britain and the Continent.

The composition of the entrepot trade is evident from Table 1. The

TABLE 1 Malayan Entrepot Trade, 1949–53,
Singapore and the Federation

					(*Million dollars*)
	1949	1950	1951	1952	1953
A. Values of Entrepot Trade					
(1) *Rubber and tin* (import value)					
Rubber	123	612	1,249	497	308
Tin concentrates	31	60	68	47	38
Total	154	672	1,317	544	346
(2) *Other "Malayan" commodities* (import value)					
Copra	55	68	65	37	40
Pepper	20	33	37	38	50
Arecanuts	12	7	10	13	10
Sago and tapioca	5	4	8	7	6
Other "Malayan" commodities	25	35	33	30	31
Total	117	147	153	125	137
(3) *Other food, drink and tobacco* (export value)					
Rice	9	9	35	62	28
Fish (dried, salted, canned, etc.)	5	14	43	48	28
Raw coffee	10	21	12	7	10
Milk (condensed and powdered)	6	8	10	14	9
Other foodstuffs	40	64	127	97	68
Cigarettes, tobacco and drink	19	27	33	24	25
Total	89	143	260	252	168

[4] It is convenient in this section to speak usually of Singapore, as the main center of the entrepot trade, but many of our remarks should be taken to apply, with suitable modifications, to Penang also.

TABLE 1 (continued)

(*Million dollars*)

	1949	1950	1951	1952	1953
(4) *Petroleum products* (export value)					
Liquid fuel	51	60	60	92	87
Motor spirit	33	64	83	118	136
Gas oil and diesel oil	31	45	66	109	106
Other petroleum products	31	28	66	95	117
Total	146	197	275	414	446
(5) *Other manufactures, materials, etc.* (export value)					
Cotton piece-goods and other textile					
manufactures.	95	214	302	207	123
Vehicles, machinery, iron and steel, etc. . . .	43	62	104	142	113
Miscellaneous manufactures, materials, etc. . .	65	107	155	124	120
Total	203	383	561	473	356
Total (export or import value, as stated)	709	1,542	2,566	1,808	1,453
B. Estimated Value Added in Trade and Processing					
(1) Rubber and tin	47	316	424	112	61
(2) Other "Malayan" commodities	23	29	35	26	20
(3) Other food, drink and tobacco	12	22	40	40	25
(4) Petroleum products	7	13	9	17	15
(5) Other manufactures, materials, etc.	30	41	74	53	39
Total	119	421	582	248	160
C. Total Cost of Imports for Re-export					
[A − B(3), (4), (5)]	660	1,466	2,443	1,698	1,374
D. Total Value of Re-exports [A + B(1), (2)] . .	779	1,887	3,025	1,946	1,534

NOTES:
(a) These figures are based, with only minor adjustments, on an analysis of Malayan trade prepared by the Registrar of Malayan Statistics. Figures for 1947–50 were originally published in Benham: *The National Income of Malaya, 1947–49* (q.v. for details of the methods employed).
(b) In the above table, "Malayan" commodities in groups (1) and (2) are those of which Malaya has a net export. The declared value of imports is therefore taken to measure entrepot trade. The commodities in groups (3), (4) and (5) are those of which Malaya has a net import, hence the declared value of exports is taken to measure entrepot trade. (There are a few unimportant exceptions to this rule.)
(c) "Value added in trade and processing" has then been estimated by comparing unit export values with unit import values and from other data, giving the figures shown under B. These estimates are often uncertain. The figures for rubber (which make up nearly the whole of value added in group (1)) are particularly uncertain—there are serious doubts as to the accuracy of the declared value of rubber imports and also as to the representativeness of the price quotations which in this case have been used to estimate the value of the corresponding exports.
(d) To arrive at the total cost of imports for re-export, the estimated "value added" for groups (3), (4) and (5) is *deducted* from the total value shown under A. To arrive at the total value of re-exports, the estimated "value added" for groups (1) and (2) is *added* to the total value shown under A. The resulting figures are shown under C and D.
(e) Ships' stores and bunker fuel are included. Goods in transit are excluded.

Table also indicates the great vicissitudes which it has undergone in recent years. Movements in the volume of goods traded have not been as great as those shown by the money figures given in the Table, but they have generally been in the same direction and often very substantial. The major factor was of course the rubber boom of 1950 and 1951. High rubber prices induced a big increase in rubber production in Indonesia and other neighboring territories, especially of smallholders' rubber, most of which found its way to Singapore for processing and marketing; and the high prices also provided incomes out of which the people of these territories could buy the manufactures, materials and foodstuffs from all parts of the world which Malayan merchants offered. As prices fell in 1952 and 1953, production, incomes and demand fell with them, and at the same time some of the major entrepot markets and sources of supply were subjected to drastic official restrictions by Southeast Asian governments (notably Indonesia). These restrictions were aimed partly at overcoming balance of payments difficulties, but also partly at the deliberate substitution, for reasons of national policy, of direct trade for entrepot trade through Singapore.

Since the end of 1953 there have been signs of stabilization and, in some directions, of improvement, in trading conditions. Perhaps more significant for the future of the entrepot trade is the fact that even in 1953 the volume of trading, after allowing for price changes, seems on the whole to have been considerably above the levels of "good" years before the Japanese occupation, and also to have shown some important changes as compared with its prewar pattern. Statistics comparable with those of Table 1 are not available, and in any case price changes would make direct comparisons impossible, but there is sufficient evidence of changes in trade volumes to give the following picture of 1953 in relation to, say, the years 1938-40:

1. The trade in "Straits produce", which depends on bringing to Singapore the natural products of Southeast Asia and exporting them (after grading, processing, etc.) either to Western markets or to other neighboring territories, had on balance probably diminished. The volume of trade in rubber remained in 1953 considerably above pre-occupation levels (except for the single year 1940), chiefly because Indonesian small-holding production, although greatly below its postwar peak, was much higher than in any pre-occupation year. But the improvement in rubber was offset by the fact that 1953 trade in almost every other important

"Straits" commodity—e.g., tin, copra, arecanuts, pepper, rattans, jelutong, sawlogs, sago, rice, dried and salted fish—was substantially lower, in many cases only half or an even smaller fraction of its pre-occupation volume. Indeed, the trade in these commodities generally never recovered after the war, and in recent years has been fairly stable at the relatively low level which it had achieved by 1947-49. Late in 1953 and early in 1954 some substantial improvements in monthly trade volumes appeared, but it is not possible to say whether these will continue.

2. On the other hand, there has been a spectacular postwar increase in the volume of trade in "Western" manufactures, materials and foodstuffs brought to Singapore for distribution throughout neighboring territories and often farther afield. In spite of the decline from the extraordinary peak of 1951, the volume of cotton piece-goods and other textile manufactures traded in 1953 was still three or four times as great as in the pre-occupation years; the trade in machinery, vehicles, spare parts, galvanized iron etc., and in the wide range of miscellaneous manufactures was at an even higher relative level, and generally showed less tendency than the textile trade to lose the ground gained after the war; and the trade in condensed milk, canned fish, cigarettes, beverages and other provisions chiefly of "Western" origin was also in 1953 substantially above pre-occupation volumes. Towards the end of 1953 and in early 1954, trade in nearly all these items was running at a monthly volume considerably below the 1953 average, but in most cases there was a big margin still to spare above the pre-occupation average, and there were some indications of the beginnings of a recovery. There seems little doubt that Singapore's postwar entrepot gains in the distribution of goods from the outside world, even at their greatly reduced level of 1953 or 1954, have been more than sufficient to offset what was lost in the lower postwar volume of trading in "Straits produce" (other than rubber).

3. Finally, the entrepot movement of petroleum products has risen three- or four-fold above pre-occupation volume, and has gone on rising steadily during the postwar years—partly because Singapore is a major center for the blending and transshipment of the growing oil output of Sarawak and Sumatra, and partly because of the growth in bunker fuel requirements. The petroleum product trade is conducted almost entirely by the oil companies themselves, but the extensive shipping, handling and storage activities which it involves are an important source of income and employment in Singapore.

The two vital questions for the future of the entrepot trade are first, whether—from a strictly economic point of view—Singapore will be in a position to offer sufficient commercial advantages, in an economic environment offering sufficient opportunities, to justify the maintenance or expansion of its activities as an international trading center; and secondly, whether—taking politics into account—the position of a major international trading center will continue to be tenable in a Southeast Asia where nationalist and exclusionist attitudes in commerce may too often be linked with the concept of national independence.

The answer to both these questions involves, of course, the whole economic and political future of Southeast Asia, which we cannot be expected to predict. But if, as all must hope, that future leans towards economic progress and stable government, we see no reason for pessimism as to the prosperity of Singapore's entrepot trade.

In purely economic terms, there is no more reason to expect the displacement of Singapore as a major port and center of distribution and collection for much of Southeast Asia than there is to expect its displacement as the major port for the Malayan mainland. The extraordinarily long coastline and difficult terrain of most of the neighboring territories, and the frequent tendency for their development to concentrate in a series of disjointed coastal blocks, make a strong case for external lines of communication by sea; and this in turn implies at least a transshipment center to link the numerous small ports and landing-places with world shipping routes—a center for which, in respect of a very wide area, Singapore is both better placed and better equipped than any alternative port. The services, beyond transshipment, of the Singapore "middleman"—grading, processing, and packing local produce; providing access to organized markets and credit facilities; keeping a great variety of goods in stock; breaking up bulk shipments of goods from abroad into lots for local distribution—are all very real economic services, which someone must perform, and which are often most economically performed at the central point of transshipment.

The impact of national restrictions upon this essentially international pattern cannot be ignored. But it is not unreasonable to hope that national governments, especially as they grow in experience and become fully aware of the responsibilities of independence, will avoid at least the more extreme forms of exclusionism, realizing both the unnecessary costs they would impose upon their own peoples, and also the formidable administrative difficulties of making them effective. On the other hand, measures to restrict imports are sometimes entirely necessary in order to protect exchange reserves; measures to control the destination of exports may be equally justified to prevent illicit exchange profits; and trade may need to be regulated or supervised in a variety of other ways to ensure safeguards against commercial abuses or exchange control evasions. Purposes such as these have been at least a major element in most of the official obstacles that Singapore trade has had to face in Southeast Asia. From the point of view of Singapore, it is not easy to distinguish between one purpose and another (especially since the method of administering a policy may not always be well suited to its real or ostensible objective), nor is it the duty of Singapore authorities to police the exchange and trade controls of other governments. Nevertheless, we suggest that the Colony Government consider carefully whether there are more ways in which Singapore might be able to show practical sympathy with legitimate objects of exchange and trade controls operated by its neighbors, thereby helping to avoid unnecessarily burdensome administrative arrangements and also helping to encourage on their part a more reasonable attitude towards the genuine advantages which Singapore trade has to offer.

Given such an attitude, Singapore has little to fear and much to gain from satisfactory progress in economic development and in social and political institutions in neighboring countries. It is true that the development of processing capacity and manufacturing industries, and the spread of banking and other commercial facilities, can be expected to eat into the margins of Singapore's entrepot trade, but on the whole it has much more chance of gaining additional trade, as a result both of an increase in the supplies of Southeast Asian products and an expansion of the market for goods from abroad. It will not be surprising if the existing tendency for the latter type of trade to become relatively more important should continue into the future. In the long run, it may well be that some parts of what is now readily distinguishable as entrepot trade will become increasingly a matter of the import of raw and semi-finished materials for export as Singapore manufactures.

These, however, are not questions requiring official consideration or action now, except insofar as speculation about their outcome may influence plans and policies in other directions.

PART **III** *THE SOCIAL SECTORS*

CHAPTER 7 *THE SOCIAL SERVICES*[1]

The mission is concerned with standards of living as well as with productive resources, and has been mindful that economic planning involves the need to maintain an appropriate balance between expenditures for production and for social services.

When resources are limited, as they are in Malaya, an effort to plan for a higher level of living than might otherwise be attained demands restraint in current expenditures and even some temporary sacrifice of progress in well-being. This policy must, however, be pursued with moderation; planning for an increase in future productivity may be futile if the population is not equipped for the effort to build a stronger economy.

In Malaya many factors contribute to make unusually difficult the task of establishing a prudent balance between investment for future production on the one hand and current expenditure for human welfare on the other. The population is racially complex and heavily weighted with only partially Malayanized residents, and it is growing at an unprecedented pace—the gap between a persistent high birth rate and a declining death rate is 3-4% of population per annum. Malaya has only recently emerged from the wartime period of social and economic disruption. It is confronted with a newly awakened demand, widespread and insistent in all racial groups, for education to satisfy cultural aspirations and the need for vocational preparation. The necessity for large public expenditure to prevent malaria and other tropical diseases is never-ending; if uncontrolled, these diseases could wreck the best laid plans for economic development. The people of Malaya have learned the value of Western medicine, and in constantly increasing numbers they expect expansion of the long-established public medical services. The Federation must help its rapidly growing cities to become suitable places in which to live and work; Singapore's overcrowding requires a redistribution of population and a vast housing program. Social, economic and political situations are beyond question such that the governments must ensure the public provision of comprehensive social services which cannot be provided privately. Beyond a point,

[1] See Technical Reports 9, 10 and 11.

137

we cannot propose to substitute future economic advantage for present human need.

The Federation and Singapore are already spending substantial proportions of their public revenues for social services, yet are under strong pressure to apply much more for these functions. We have followed no single rule in deciding which expenditures should be expanded rapidly and which slowly. We have surveyed each major area of public service, attempted to assess performance and unmet need, and have developed our recommendations on the evidence before us—mindful of the over-all outlook and the competitive demands on resources. The financial results are summarized in Table 1 and shown in more detail in Tables 2 and 3,

TABLE 1 Public Expenditures for the Social Services

(Million $)

	Federation				Singapore			
	1949	1953	1954	1959	1949	1953	1954	1959
Annually recurrent expenditure	59	141	153	214	20	48	64	129
Capital expenditure . . .	3	18	12	16	1	5	22	19
Gross total	62	159	165	230	21	53	86	148
Revenue from services . .	3	4	6	15	4	7	7	12
Net total.	59	155	159	215	17	46	79	136

NOTE: Figures include education, public health and medical care, social welfare, labor and town planning; exclude housing, workmen's compensation, employees provident funds, grants to the University of Malaya, and miscellaneous services. (See Tables 2 and 3.)

pages 165 and 185. They show that despite the relatively large increases in public expenditures for the social services in the past five years, there should be similar increases in the next five years, in our judgment, to meet urgent needs and keep up with growth of population. The rising costs for which we have made allowance would result mainly from expansion and improvement of education and of public health and medical services.

If our recommendations are followed, net public expenditures for the social services in the Federation would rise from $27 per capita in 1954 to $31 in 1959. Annually recurrent and capital expenditures together are now 26% of revenues; they would equal 34% in 1959. Exclusive of capital items, they would increase from 24% of revenues in 1954 to 32% in 1959. While this proportion in 1954 is higher than the corresponding figures for some countries, it is about the same as, or lower than, those for other countries with lower or higher levels of national income. The increases in expenditures over the past five years or in the next five should not be taken to mean that these services are absorbing too large a share of gross national income or product. They accounted for only 2.5-3% in 1949 and about 4% in 1953, and, on the basis of our recommendations, would probably amount to only about 5% (more or less, depending on the attainments of the national economy) in 1959.[2]

In the case of Singapore, net public expenditures for the social services would increase from $68 per capita in 1954 to $103 per capita in 1959. The gross expenditures (annually recurrent and capital) which now equal 32% of total revenue would rise to 49% in 1959. These last figures, however, are heavily weighted with capital expenditures that will be unusually large in 1954-59 for schools, hospitals, etc.; if restricted to annually recurrent expenditures they are 23% of revenues for 1954 and 42% for 1959.[3] Measured against the total resources of Singapore's economy rather than revenues, these social services consumed 2% of gross national income or product in 1949, and about 3% in 1953 and may be expected to equal about 7-9% (more or less) in 1959. The proportionate rise in these figures is large but this is more a reflection of their low level in the past than of a high level five years hence. The mission believes that, by present perspectives, the recommended development of the social services will be within Singapore's economic capacity.

These conclusions represent the mission's assessment of needs with respect to the social services, and of over-all ability to pay for them, in the Federation and in Singapore. The recommended expansion of these services would add considerably to the costs of government. If the people decide they want the services, they will have to be prepared to pay the costs—whether through taxes, rates or fees of one kind or another or through contributions to social security funds.

[2] For the purposes of this analysis gross national income and gross national product (at market price) for Malaya as a whole (Table 14, Statistical Appendix, Part V) were divided between the Federation and Singapore in proportion to their respective total (ordinary) tax revenues. This gave, respectively, for gross national income $2,350 million and $985 million for 1949, and $3,777 million and $1,618 million for 1953; and for gross national product $2,502 million and $1,048 million for 1949, and $4,046 million and $1,734 million for 1953.

[3] The comparable social services cost about 33% of the income of local authorities in Great Britain (which has extensive national social services) and about 50% of the revenues of the large cities in the United States.

The details of our surveys in the main fields of social service are given in the Technical Reports. The considerations that have guided us and the major specific recommendations are summarized in the sections that follow.

I FEDERATION

A EDUCATION[4]

Of the social services directly reflected in the public budget, education is the largest and presents some of the most perplexing problems. It has become a primary activity of government, accounting for about one-sixth or one-seventh of total expenditures for civil functions. Yet various factors compound to make continuing expansion of the education program and still larger expenditure necessary. The school-age population is growing at an unprecedented rate and public demand for education is steadily mounting and insistent. Available facilities and teachers can provide for only a little more than half the children of primary school age and only one in 14 of those of secondary school age. Badly needed qualitative improvements would add to the costs. In addition, vocational education and training need expansion if they are to meet the requirements of industrial development.

The Federal, State and Settlement Governments have been keenly interested in expanding and improving education. They have been not only attentive to public demand but appreciative of the role that education can play in strengthening the economy and contributing to social and political development—helping to weld more or less disparate racial and linguistic groups into a unified Malayan nation. But government is now confronted by the hard fact that, apart from difficult technical problems involved in further rapid expansion of education, the finances of the program must be kept within the resources of the country, having regard for competing demands on the economy. Education expenditures, only $16 million in 1947,[5] rose to $95 million in 1953, were about $100 million in 1954 and could become $200 million within a few years—threatening

---

[4] See Technical Report 9.

[5] By the Federal, State and Settlement education departments only, exclusive of education expenditures by other official agencies.

Federal fiscal capacity or, if given absolute priority, compelling the neglect of other essential public functions.

The mission is deeply sympathetic with the desire to expand and improve education. But we must take account of the importance of ensuring that the costs do not become disproportionate to the resources of the economy. We have therefore sought a course of action that will give maximum acceleration to desirable developments in education compatible with the largest financial support which seems practicable.

Malaya's problems of education are unusually intricate because of the diversity of schools and the large backlog of children, adolescents and adults without the advantages of even elementary education or literacy.[6] The Federation's schools, classified according to the language of instruction, are Malay, Chinese and Indian (known as vernacular schools), and English. All types have primary schools, but only the English and Chinese offer secondary courses. They have diverse management and financing— there are schools maintained by government, nonprofit schools to which government gives financial aid, and private schools wholly dependent on their own resources. English schools are the only ones attended by children of all races.

There is little crossover from one type of primary school to another. The only formal bridge is between Malay and English schools—special classes in the latter give intensive training in English to enable selected Malay pupils to join the last primary classes. Almost no pupils go directly from the vernacular primary schools to the government or aided English secondary schools. The Chinese primary schools lead to the Chinese secondary schools. There are large variations in the qualifications of teachers and in the facilities for training them, and consequently in the level and quality of teaching.

General education policies and government aid are matters of intense and widespread concern to the people of Malaya, especially to the Malays and the Chinese. A pupil-year in Malay and Indian schools costs the government about $100, and in the English government and aided primary schools about $200, with fees only $2.50 a month. Aid to Chinese schools costs about $60 a pupil-year. The English secondary schools cost about $400 per pupil-year, and charge fees of $5.00 per month. In 1953, 37% of

---

[6] By the test of ability to read and write used in the 1947 census, 62% of the population 15 and over was illiterate (43% of the males and 83% of the females). The current rates are not known.

government education expenditures was for Malay schools and 38% for English schools; of the remaining 25%, 15% was for Chinese, 4% for Indian and 6% for "new village" (over 90% Chinese) schools. However, when account is taken of the numbers of each race in each type of school, especially in the English and new village schools, it is found that the amount spent from public funds for the education of each race is proportional to the racial distribution of the population (and presumably of the school-age population). On the one hand, this distribution of public expenditures is not clearly understood by the Chinese, who remember the many years when Chinese schools had little or no government aid and who think in terms of the current grant formula, which is less generous than aid for English schools. On the other, the Malays feel that the Chinese are getting their full share—and perhaps more—of the relatively expensive English education.

Directly after the war there were about 300,000 children in school. Under the impetus of an amazing change in attitude among all races and great pressure for places in school, the number has grown rapidly and now (1954) there are over 800,000 in the primary and secondary schools—of whom over 700,000 are in government and aided schools. The number of schools and teachers has had to increase at precipitate rates. Still, with 1.2 million children (20% of the total population) in the primary school ages 6+ to 12+ in 1954, there are now places in government and aided schools for only 56% (it was 58% in 1953);[7] and the primary school-age population, already growing at the rate of 60,000 a year, is expected to reach nearly 1.7 million (23.5%) by 1960.

Of the total primary school enrollment of 715,000 in 1953 in government, aided and nonaided schools, the largest numbers were in Malay and Chinese schools (338,000 and 236,000, respectively); 98,000 were in English and 43,000 in Indian schools. Large proportions of the pupils in vernacular

[7] About 17% of the places in primary schools (and about 9% in secondary schools) were occupied in 1953 by over-age children. Thus, government and aided primary school enrollment of children of primary school ages was about 48% in 1953 and was about 46% in 1954.

Estimates of school-age populations used throughout the report are based on data provided by the Department of Education. The estimates developed by the Registrar of Statistics are much lower (e.g., 927,000 instead of 1.141 million for children of primary school ages in 1953). If the lower estimates were used, school places would equal 71% (instead of 58%) for 1953, and enrollment of pupils of true primary age would be 59% (instead of 48%).

schools attend for only one to four years of vernacular schooling. Many of the schools offer less than the full six-year course.

The secondary schools, almost all of the academic type, have about 57,000 places—42,000 in English (34,000 in government and aided English) and 15,000 in Chinese schools, accommodating only about 8% of the primary enrollment and about 7% of the secondary age population.

Though some vocational training has been instituted recently, it still is available in only four post-primary technical schools and a school which teaches cabinetmaking, with total enrollments of about 700 in 1953, in a post-secondary Technical College (239 students), and in various full-time adult training classes (about 300 students) and part-time evening classes (about 1,000 students).

A principal factor limiting greater expansion of school enrollments is the number of trained teachers required and the limited capacity of the teacher-training facilities for both English and vernacular schools. Even if Malaya could provide unlimited financial support, expansion of education resources would be determined by the number of teachers that could be recruited and trained in a specified period, and all projections are bounded by this consideration.

As a result of the great expansion of education in Malaya since the war, the current provisions and enrollments compare favorably with those in many countries of Asia and other continents. Malaya's progress in education is neither the most nor the least notable among the non-selfgoverning territories or the less developed countries. It is highly commendable, however, in light of the difficulties created by the extremely rapid growth of child population and the complexities inherent in utilizing four types of primary and two types of secondary schools.

The Federation's long-range education policy, embodied in the Education Ordinance, 1952, is that primary schools for children aged 6+ to 12+ are to be national schools, free, and (eventually) compulsory, open to children of all races, with the medium of instruction either English or Malay at the option of the people of the area in which the school is situated. In English schools, Malay is to be taught to every pupil from the beginning of the third year and in Malay schools, English is to be taught to every pupil from the beginning of the first year. In all national schools, when the parents of 15 or more children of the same linguistic standard ask for it, facilities are also to be provided for the teaching of Tamil or

Chinese (Mandarin). Provision is also to be made for religious instruction, or, in the case of pupils whose parents have no religion, moral instruction. It has not been possible to develop national schools of the type specifically contemplated, but the Federation has been able to take some steps toward the pattern envisaged for the future.

Whether the objectives of the education program remain as expressed in the 1952 Ordinance or are amended in the course of time, the mission believes that the desirable next steps are clearly indicated by current needs and public demand.

We recommend a coordinated 10-point program,[8] in large measure an endorsement and encouragement of efforts and experiments already being made:[9]

1. Continued vigorous expansion of the education resources, aiming to keep pace with the growth of school age population and if possible increasing the percentage enrolled; and, in view of the acute shortage of English-medium schools, priority development of government English schools, locating them where need and demand are greatest;

2. Continued improvement of the quality of education in all types of schools, especially by raising the qualifications of the teachers and by providing adequate staff for inspection and supervision of schools;

3. Further strengthening and extending the teaching of languages: expanding and improving the teaching of English in vernacular schools; accelerating provision for the teaching of Malay in English, Chinese and Indian schools, and for the availability of Chinese and Indian language study in English and Malay schools; and encouraging the admission of children of all racial groups into all types of schools;

4. Enlarging the opportunities for transfer of pupils from vernacular to English schools by teaching more and better English in the primary and secondary vernacular schools; and, as interim measures, extending the scope of the special transitional classes in the English primary schools to include more Malays and to be available to the Chinese and Indian chil-

---

[8] The substance of some of these recommendations is contained in part or in whole in the White Paper on Education Policy (No. 67 of 1954) submitted by the Federal Government to the Legislative Council after a draft of our Technical Report had been made available to the government for review. Since the White Paper did not become available to the mission until after this chapter had been prepared, only a few details and comparisons are incorporated here.

[9] The sequence of the 10 points is intended to give an orderly picture of the program, not to indicate priorities among the several recommendations.

dren as well, and to make similar provision in the English secondary schools for Chinese middle school pupils who wish to complete their secondary education in the English schools;

5. Renewed efforts to reduce premature leaving in vernacular schools ("wastage"), through education of parents on the long-run value of keeping their children at school for at least four to six years, and by providing the upper primary classes in more schools and encouraging attendance at regional schools offering the upper classes;

6. Reduction of inequalities in the educational opportunities of children in different parts of the country—among the States and Settlements and between urban and rural areas;

7. Progressive adjustment of the scheme of government grants, working toward uniform treatment of all aided schools according to their levels of conformity to national standards;

8. Expansion of vocational preparation through accelerated development of nonacademic secondary schools (modern, commercial and technical), part-time adult classes, apprenticeship training, and establishing links with business establishments;

9. Greatest emphasis on expansion of teacher training, including temporary extension of part-time training, vigorous development of training colleges at home and abroad, experimentation with common training colleges to prepare teachers for English and vernacular schools, and maximum practical utilization of the University of Malaya and the prospective Nanyang University; and

10. Maximum practical expansion of part-time adult education, especially through aided voluntary associations, toward elimination of illiteracy within the next generation.

In addition, we recommend (a) expansion of professionally qualified staffs for administration and for research and development studies, and (b) with respect to review of current activities and development of new plans, use of consultative or advisory committees of private persons engaged in education services and informed on education problems and needs.

This program should strive to achieve by 1960 an increase in enrollments, in government and aided schools, from 73,000 to 200,000 in English primary schools, from 34,000 to 40,000 or more in English secondary schools, and from 594,000 to 766,000 in vernacular schools. If this could be achieved, primary school attendance of 966,000 in government and aided schools would maintain the 1954 level—56% of the estimated 1.695 million in the primary school-age population of 1960. The percentage should be higher if possible.[10] We are, however, inclined to believe these may prove to be unattainable goals for technical as well as financial reasons. But at least 50% of the increasing primary school population should be enrolled: 164,000 in 1959 and 169,500 in 1960 in English primary schools, and 656,000 in 1959 and 678,000 in 1960 in vernacular schools. In addition provision should be made through the advanced classes in secondary schools (Form VI) for 1,000 students preparing for institutions of higher learning in 1955 and in each year thereafter and for increase in this number to 1,500 or 2,000 if found necessary or desirable.

The mission has no reliable basis for estimating future enrollments in Chinese secondary courses.[11]

In view of the relatively small increase in English secondary enrollments proposed for 1954-60, we recommend preparation for substantial expansion in these schools (academic and nonacademic) after 1960, and experimentation with two-year intermediate education—with strong vocational bias—for children between the ages 12+ and 14+.

Except for expansion of the University of Malaya at Singapore and Kuala Lumpur (see p. 184), the mission does not recommend any enlargement of provisions for higher education in the next five years. We assume the Federation will continue to utilize the Technical College and the College of Agriculture, to support education at overseas universities and to benefit as much as may be practical from the Nanyang University now being developed at Singapore.

We estimate that a development program which would not permit primary school enrollments to fall below the minimum target of 50% by 1959-60 would result in gross expenditure (annually recurrent and capital) increasing from $102 million in 1954 to $145 million in 1959, and still increasing rapidly thereafter.[12] By present perspectives, such costs would

[10] The White Paper No. 67 of 1954 adopts the same goal—to maintain total primary school enrollment at the 1954 percentage—but provides only for not less than proportionate increase in English primary schools. Using lower estimates of school-age population (see footnote 7), it fixes as 1960 targets enrollment of 106,000 in English-medium national type schools and 682,000 in vernacular primary schools.

[11] See Technical Report 9.

[12] See Technical Report 9, Table 10. The White Paper No. 67 of 1954 includes estimates that rise to substantially the same figure ($143.5 million), and to $160 million in 1960 if special features of national schools are to be provided. It takes account of possible assistance

be beyond the resources of the Federal Government, and in our opinion it would not be sound for education mainly provided by the States and Settlements to be financed by the Federal Government alone. We therefore recommend that education functions be clearly divided between the Federal and the State and Settlement Governments and that all participate in financing the program.

The Federal Government should finance the education functions allocated to the Federal Department and continue to make grants, earmarked for this purpose (see p. 225), to the States and Settlements for functions allocated to them. To education grants beginning at the present level of State and Settlement expenditures should be added funds raised by the States and Settlements and, increasingly, by local authorities. By 1960, Federal grants should not exceed three-fourths and should subsequently decline to a lower proportion. We also recommend that the grants be adjusted among the several States and Settlements, taking account of their relative needs for Federal financial assistance as well as the prospective costs of their programs, and working toward the goal of uniform per capita grants after education opportunities have been brought to minimum national levels in all States and Settlements.

These Federal grants for education should be made, insofar as feasible, on a long-range predetermined pattern, enabling the Federal Government and the States and Settlements to make adequate substantive and financial plans and to adjust and strengthen their administrative agencies.

With the suggested pattern for grants, the Federal Government would be responsible for $117 million in 1959, the States and Settlements for $22 million, and fees for $6 million. The States and Settlements and their local authorities would have to provide increasing proportions of the rising costs thereafter.

On this basis, an expanding program of education may go forward. It cannot grow so rapidly or so well as to overcome all deficiencies in the present system, or bring education within reach of everyone in Malaya in a few years. No practical plan could do all this. But the program recommended here may provide a basis on which Malaya can live within its

---

under the Colonial Development and Welfare Act, the need for new local revenues for education, and the separation of Federal grants for education from the general Federal allocation to State and Settlement Governments. The last was recommended with respect to estimates for 1956 in White Paper No. 70 of 1954.

means while continuing toward its goal of a comprehensive system of education for all its people.

We appreciate that our estimates of Federal, State and Settlement fiscal capacity to support education may prove to be either too low or too high. If the former, the Federation may be able to proceed with expansion at rates higher than recommended and to gain on its unmet education needs in the next five years or in the years after 1959 or 1960. If, on the contrary, it develops that Federal fiscal capacity has been overestimated or if the States and Settlements should be unable to raise the share we have proposed, or both, the rate of increase in education expenditures would have to be reduced. The Federation would have to modify its development program and choose among various possibilities: reduced expenditure per pupil, more limited expansion of enrollments in English or vernacular schools or both, limitation of the provisions for secondary education or for primary education above the fourth or fifth year, increase in part-time education, etc.

B PUBLIC HEALTH AND MEDICAL CARE [13]

The health and medical services of the Federation have been eminently effective in achieving a relatively high level of health. Malaria has been brought under control in large parts of the country and various other endemic and epidemic diseases have been greatly reduced. As a result, Malaya, for centuries one of the unhealthiest places in the tropics, is now one of the healthiest and its death rates compare favorably with those of many countries in sub-tropical climates. The successful expansion of tin mining, rubber planting and agriculture generally, of industry and commerce—the increase in productivity and the wealth of modern Malaya— became possible as the conquest of tropical disease progressed.

Development of health services has been affected by alternating cycles of boom and depression, but there was progress decade after decade except for a bad setback during the Japanese occupation (1942-45), when the public health deteriorated badly. Local output of professional staff dried up, food was inadequate, anti-malaria work was neglected and health services generally were meagre or nonexistent. At the end of the occupation, health conditions were discouraging. Intestinal infections were

13 See Technical Report 10.

almost universal, yaws, smallpox, cholera, tropical typhus and beri-beri were common, malaria was widespread, tuberculosis was rampant and malnutrition was extensive on the rubber estates and among the children everywhere.

Most of the wartime damage was repaired in a few years through vigorous attack by the medical authorities. By 1949 health conditions were better than they had been in 1941, except for the apparently new prevalence of tuberculosis and the damaged health of young children, which continue to present serious problems to Malaya. Between 1947 and 1953, the crude death rate declined from 19 to 12 (deaths per 1,000), the infant mortality rate from 102 to 83 (infant deaths per 1,000 live births), and the maternal death rate from seven to less than five (maternal deaths per 1,000 births). All races shared in these gains.

Under the terms of the Federation Agreement, the Federal Government has an over-all responsibility for public health, sanitation, medical institutions, etc., and the States and Settlements have most of the executive authority. In practice, however, the functions are divided between the Federal and State Governments but are financed almost entirely by Federal funds provided through the lump-sum grants to the States. Together the governments operate more or less comprehensive public health programs and, in addition, national medical services which are largely free to all residents. These resources are supplemented by private practitioners, hospitals, clinics and nonprofit agencies.

The public health services are unevenly developed, so that malaria and some other endemic diseases are effectively controlled in the cities and towns and on many of the larger agricultural estates and mines but range variously from controlled to rampant prevalence in rural areas. Personal health services are provided through an extensive network of hospitals, outpatient departments, and fixed and mobile clinics and dispensaries.

The hospitals of Malaya provide over three beds per 1,000 persons,[14] with more than two-thirds in governmental institutions. This suggests a sufficient national supply, but the average conceals wide variations among the States. The supply of physicians—nearly one-half in the government services—averages 1 per 9,200 persons for the Federation, with heavy concentrations in the larger urban places. Rural medical services are largely

[14] Exclusive of specialized Federal institutions for tuberculosis, leprosy and mental diseases, with an aggregate of 8,300 beds (1.4 per 1,000 persons).

underdeveloped and complicated by the emergency resettlement of 10% of the population. There is acute shortage in nearly all categories of professional personnel.

Since the number of hospital beds decreased in the postwar years, the number of in-patients has not kept pace with population growth and steadily increasing demand in all racial groups for Western medicine. Many hospitals are overcrowded and have to maintain waiting lists. Some of the facilities are relatively modern and well equipped; others are dilapidated, ill equipped, unsanitary and uneconomic.

All government hospitals serve ambulatory patients through out-patient departments, most of them small, understaffed and badly overcrowded during clinic sessions. In addition, there are fixed and mobile dispensaries. All races call on these services more or less equally in proportion to population.

Public expenditures for public health and medical services increased from $18 million in 1947 to $55 million in 1954—from less than $4 to more than $9 per capita. With very uneven development of facilities in the States and Settlements, expenditures in 1953 ranged from $14 per capita in Negri Sembilan to about $3.50 in Kelantan.

Our survey indicates that, in the main, recent developments have proceeded on sound lines but that resources for service are insufficient and, as the population grows and larger proportions request Western medicine, they will become increasingly inadequate unless there is considerable expansion.

In view of the Federation's financial stringency, the mission recommends a comprehensive reconsideration of public health and medical plans. New plans for expansion of resources should give the strongest practical emphasis to preventive and out-patient services, to lighten the future medical load and minimize increase in costs. Among the main objectives should be improvement and extension of services where they are least adequate, balancing urban demands and rural needs, and working toward equalization of access to basic health services throughout the Federation.

To these ends, administrative arrangements should be improved by clarifying allocation of responsibilities between the Federal and State Governments. In addition, the governmental medical services should be organized into a network of six hospital regions, centering on Penang, Ipoh, Kuala Lumpur, Malacca, Johore Bahru and an East Coast town

(Kuantan, Kuala Trengganu or Kota Bharu). In each region, the central general hospital should be operated by the Federal Department,[15] the other governmental hospitals, clinics and dispensaries by the States and Settlements. Each central hospital should provide general and specialized services for local and referred patients, visiting staff for the secondary facilities, and training, survey and research services for the region.

Technical Report 10 presents detailed recommendations for improvement of public health and personal medical services. Here we would emphasize nine points to which we assign high priority:

1. Recruitment and training of needed professional and sub-professional staff, emphasizing as far as practical domestic recruitment and training in Malaya and at the University in Singapore, and utilizing overseas resources for specialists and other categories in which shortages are especially acute;

2. Improvement of existing hospitals by expansion of staff, partial reconstruction and modernization where necessary, and enlargement of out-patient departments—building new hospitals only where increased in-patient capacity is most acutely needed or replacement most urgent;

3. Expansion of independent facilities for ambulatory care, referring to the hospitals only those patients who need in-patient care or highly specialized or unusual services;

4. Vigorous development of the network of rural health centers throughout the Federation;

5. Improvement of nutrition, by completing the surveys undertaken by the Institute for Medical Research; educational activities to encourage wider use of enriched rice and a more varied diet; increased emphasis in the health centers on diet and nutrition, and supplementary feeding of school children; and through collateral programs that support development of the fishing industry and expansion of the fish supply, and encouragement of vegetable-growing on a family as well as a commercial basis;

6. Continued attack on malaria where it is still highly prevalent, on venereal diseases, yaws, intestinal infections and infestations, and other widely prevalent debilitating diseases;

7. A comprehensive campaign to bring tuberculosis—one of the most serious diseases in Malaya—under control, through surveys, development

---

[15] The Federal Medical Department now operates the two general hospitals in the Settlements.

of settlements for patients not requiring acute hospital care, maximum practical release of general hospital beds occupied by chronic and non-treatable cases, expansion of out-patient care and of BCG vaccination on a controlled experimental basis, and strengthening of other preventive services;[16]

8. Continued strong support of research, to maintain a constant quest for new and improved methods of prevention and treatment of disease; and

9. Large-scale expansion of health education, to be conducted through the medical, education and other departments, the information services and the voluntary agencies interested in health progress.

The Technical Report presents a development program at two levels, one comprehensive and the other somewhat more limited. Though the larger program is desirable and should be undertaken if possible, in view of the financial outlook we recommend only the lesser program and its schedule of priority capital projects. It includes (for the six years 1955-60) capital funds for a new hospital, nurses' hostel and training school in Kuala Lumpur, new facilities for central medical stores and manufactory, 25 rural health centers (including a training center), seven new tuberculosis clinics, and funds for miscellaneous secondary projects to improve, extend and modernize hospitals, clinics, etc.; and annually recurrent funds sufficient to carry out the recommended increase of staff and expansion and improvement of services throughout the Federation. This would involve gross total costs (annually recurrent and capital) rising from $55 million in 1954 to $74 million in 1959. Even this may be possible only if charges for in-patient hospital care are raised and more generally applied so as to reduce net costs, and we have assumed an increase of income from this source from $3 million in 1954 to $9 million in 1959.

In view of the steeply rising expenditures for health and medical services—in the next five years and subsequently—the health and medical program would soon be beyond the resources of the Federal Government. We therefore recommend that it become directly a joint Federal-State undertaking, with the same pattern of cost-sharing that we have proposed for education.

[16] The control of tuberculosis also involves two related measures: development of a program of treatment allowances for the tuberculous and their dependents, preferably by the Malayan Association for the Prevention of Tuberculosis and the Social and Welfare Lotteries Board, and maximum practical support of a housing program, especially in urban areas, to reduce spread of the disease resulting from unsanitary and overcrowded living.

The Federal Government should finance the activities of the Federal medical department, including general planning and direction, all recruitment and training activities, and operation of all central regional hospitals, special institutions for tuberculosis, leprosy and mental diseases, and other national services and facilities.

In addition, the Federal Government should indicate its intention to provide specific and limited grants to the States earmarked for medical and health purposes (see p. 225). We suggest the following pattern for these grants: in 1955 they should equal about $40 million; they should decrease between 1955 and 1959 so as to be about $30 million in 1960, financing not more than three-fourths of the activities to be administered by the States; and they should not be increased thereafter except as necessary to remain one-half of State expenditures for Federally approved programs. We recommend that the remainder of State expenditures, less income from fees and charges collected in State-administered hospitals and facilities, should derive from the revenues of the States and of local authorities whose development should be encouraged.

We estimate that on this pattern States (and local authorities) would have to provide additional funds amounting to $1 million in 1956 rising to $3 million in 1959, and increasing amounts thereafter depending on the further expansion of the program.

Insofar as applicable, the practices, procedures and cost-sharing requirements with respect to these Federal grants should be the same as for education.

C SOCIAL WELFARE [17]

Under the Federation Agreement social welfare is wholly a Federal responsibility. However, by administrative action the responsibilities for certain social welfare activities were in 1951 transferred to or left to be developed by State and Settlement Governments; in particular the provision of noninstitutional (home or "outdoor") relief ceased in practice to be a Federal responsibility. State and Settlement social welfare officers nevertheless still continue to be required to act as the Federal Government's agents for some Federal activities, although those officers are not directly responsible to the Federal Government.

There are sharp differences of opinion throughout the Federation about

[17] See Technical Report 11.

the social welfare services which have developed since the war. At least three focal points of dispute can be identified: The first centers on public assistance—whether it should be expanded or contracted, be made more or less adequate, be more of the institutional or the home type. The second concerns the roles of official and voluntary agencies—whether one function or another, and how much of what needs to be done, should be a responsibility of the one, the other, or both. The third arises from a conflict between Federal and State perspectives on the scope and level of official services. Solutions for these problems are not easily devised, nor can they be determined merely by reference to principles or practices accepted in other countries; unusual local situations must be taken into account.

Our survey indicates that the need for relief or public assistance, which was overwhelming directly after the war and then declined, is again rising; at the same time there is a slowly growing realization of the pressing need for other and more constructive social welfare services. Most of the voluntary welfare agencies have only small active memberships and very limited and uncertain financial resources so that they can meet only fractions of these needs. Less than a dozen of these agencies have been able to look for substantial assistance from Federal Government subventions or from grants by the official Social and Welfare Lotteries Board. No voluntary agencies, with the possible recent exception of the Boys' and Girls' Clubs, have been able to undertake major or extensive programs that would substantially substitute for governmental service and expenditure or make them unnecessary. Moreover, in the absence of arrangements for development of agreements between official and voluntary agencies on fields of interest and activity, and for joint planning and coordination of programs, potentially complementary relations are confused or even competitive.

The situation has been further complicated by proposals to abolish the State welfare departments and revert to a wholly Federal program; to abolish the Federal Department and assign its functions to the States; and to disperse the present Federal functions among several departments.

It is therefore not surprising that our survey finds many social welfare needs inadequately served or totally unmet and the public services of uneven quality and effectiveness.

We believe that the Federal Government should formulate a statutory policy as to the scope and objectives of social welfare services, indicating its intention to support and encourage both official and voluntary activities, and clearly allocating functions to the Federal and State departments.[18]

Our survey suggests that the official social welfare program should provide for at least the following eight major classes of service:

1. Public assistance for needy or destitute persons (institutional and outdoor);

2. Youth services (surveys of needs, training of leaders, encouragement of club organizing activities, etc.);

3. Children's services (prevention of dependency, protection, operation of homes, etc.);

4. Services for the blind (maintenance, education, training, workshops);

5. Probation and "approved" school services (training of staff, administration of approved and camp schools, remand homes, probation hostels);

6. "Emergency" services for detainees and other persons;

7. Staff training; and

8. Surveys, research and program planning.

In each of these services full consideration should be given to the extent and to the ways in which a greater degree of effective voluntary effort can be encouraged by the government through the establishment of permanent liaisons at all levels, through cooperation and practical assistance in the field, and through direct and indirect subventions.

In addition, as availability of funds and personnel permits, the welfare departments should also provide a variety of other services directly or in cooperation with other departments—services concerned with community development, resettlement, family welfare and advice, school feeding, crippled or handicapped persons, lepers and tuberculous persons and their dependents, mental deviates, etc.

As far as practical the operation of official welfare services should be decentralized and administration should be close to the locality. The Federal Department should be permanently responsible only for those functions which are inherently developmental or either multi-state or national.

Of the eight main services listed above only public assistance is substantially developed and operating in all the States and Settlements. It is therefore the only one which can be transferred from the Federal Depart-

---

[18] There is no general guide on policy now though there are ordinances dealing with special sectors (e.g., women and girls' protection, children and young persons, married women and children's maintenance, adoptions, etc.).

ment to the States at this time. Since outdoor relief is already lodged with the States, we believe the transfer to them of the old persons' homes should be effected as soon as practicable.[19] However, the allocation of public assistance to the States should be conditioned on the requirement that operations—now grossly inadequate in both institutional and outdoor assistance—meet Federal standards applicable throughout the Federation and be subject to Federal inspection. The standards should include careful investigation of applications for assistance, adequacy of aid by reference to the difference between needs and resources, and periodic review of cases receiving aid.

Services for youth, children, the blind and persons on probation are now scarcely more than pilot experiments or demonstrations in selected areas. They should be encouraged and fostered in the Federal department during the next few years; and they should be transferred to the States in stages—as each class of service becomes prepared for decentralized administration by sufficient extension to provide, upon transfer, the nucleus of an operating program in each State.

Responsibility for services concerned with the emergency, training of staff, performance of surveys, research and program planning, and the granting of Federal subventions to national voluntary agencies should remain permanently Federal.

Since all of the official social welfare services are inadequate despite the commendable efforts of social welfare officers working with meager resources, we recommend a modest increase in financial provisions to support activities at Federal and State levels. Public assistance needs more trained staff, more thorough investigation of applicants, more adequate institutional provisions and home relief—with maximum practical shift from the former to the latter, and more occupational and rehabilitation services. Institutional and outdoor relief for aged, blind, disabled and other groups need to be supplemented by special allowances for the tuberculous and their dependents; since this should preferably be operated by the Malayan Association for the Prevention of Tuberculosis and be financed by the Social and Welfare Lotteries Board (see footnote 16), we do not include funds for this program in our estimates here though recognizing that such government provision should be made if the recommended development cannot proceed adequately through the voluntary agency. (See

[19] Except the Home at Serdang (for alien destitutes and other transient cases and an institutional training center).

Technical Report 10.) The services which prevent destitution and strengthen community resources also need more trained staff and, in addition, development of widespread participation by voluntary agencies and the public; we would especially encourage the development of these services and the use of increasing proportions of the social welfare budgets for them.

We also recommend the establishment of (a) a permanent committee to coordinate related activities of the Department of Social Welfare and other agencies of the government (medical, education, labor, information, police, etc.); (b) effective coordination between the Department and the Social and Welfare Lotteries Board, with respect to financial support from the latter for voluntary agencies; and (c) an advisory body to the Department of Social Welfare on the coordination of voluntary and official social welfare services, with membership representing the voluntary social welfare agencies, other interested public groups and the government departments.

We estimate that Federal appropriations for Federal and State social welfare activities (annually recurrent, capital expenditures and subventions) should be expected to increase from $5.6 million in 1954 to about $8 million in 1959, exclusive of funds that may be needed for a program of tuberculosis treatment allowances.

D LABOR

The public services on behalf of labor are concerned with the protection and well-being of gainfully employed persons and their dependents, some aspects of the productivity of workers, and the maintenance and development of sound and orderly employment relations. The Department of Labour has broad and highly diverse duties which it carries out through a network of 16 field offices. This is a wholly Federal undertaking, without direct participation by the States. Various other departments are engaged in this field (e.g., Trade Union Adviser, Medical, Education). A new Federal labor code is being prepared to give an up-to-date base and direction to labor standards and services. Commendable related services (concerning safety in places of employment, certification of engineers, inspection of machinery, prevention of accidents, etc.) are provided by the Machinery Department, administering the Machinery Ordinance, 1953.

Conditions of work in Malaya are generally good by criteria applicable to an Asian economy; there is very little of the worst that might be expected and there is a sprinkling of the best to be found in agricultural, commercial or industrial enterprise. But standards for conditions of work and grades of workers are incomplete, inspections extend to only about one-third of the places of employment, and compliance with requirements of the labor code[20] is less than it can and should be, despite the commendable efforts of the authorities and the cooperation of many progressive and socially-minded employers. The inadequacy of the budget and staff resources of the Department of Labour is a serious handicap. Since only relatively small additional amounts would be needed to improve substantially the opportunities for more effective service, we have no difficulty in recommending a financial solution here. The results may be expected to more than repay the costs—in well-being and productivity and in social and political returns; the country now pays more for what it does not do.

Before the war, the labor force of Malaya had a long tradition of extreme mobility, the immigrant Chinese and Indians having been ready and able to move with the opportunities of the labor market and to adapt themselves to change of work. Extensive special arrangements provided for the foreign and domestic recruitment of labor for the estates and mines, and there was no large need for general public employment offices to match the requirements of employers seeking labor and workers seeking hire. But since the war, conditions have changed; immigration is substantially closed, the labor force is more stable and less mobile, urbanization introduces new elements of rigidity, and industrial development creates additional demands for a skilled labor force and its effective use. The labor exchanges must now play a more important role. The central exchange in Kuala Lumpur and the first branch in Penang were opened in 1953 and five more were established in the early months of 1954. We recommend that the total network of 16 contemplated by the Department be completed as soon as practical so that they may be ready as needed. They should also become useful directly in periodic compilation of essential information on employment, unemployment and available skills; in consultation with the Department of Education and the schools, they

[20] With respect to: hours of work; weekly holidays; employment of children, young persons and women; conditions of living and housing; and provision of medical care and amenities of living for agricultural estate and mining labor.

should serve as centers for advisory services to youths leaving school and needing guidance in training and employment, and to others seeking development of skills and upgrading in jobs.

It is widely agreed that the general statistical services of the Department need strengthening. The mission can testify from its own experience to the insufficiency of data on the labor force, the labor market, employment establishments, conditions of work, wages, employment, costs of living, etc. Both government and private enterprise are handicapped for lack of comprehensive current data. The Department has given thought to needs and to ways of meeting them. We recommend it be encouraged to fill as many gaps as possible, utilizing the aid of experts from the United Kingdom and international agencies.

The productivity of the labor force is a vital element in the outlook for the economy and the level of living it will be able to provide Malaya's rapidly growing population. We therefore have great concern for the contributions which the labor program can make through three measures within its field, supplementing the education and training facilities provided or to be developed by the Department of Education: (1) apprentice training in suitable centers and in the workshops of approved firms; (2) a comprehensive program of training within industry for semi-skilled and skilled workers and for supervisors; and (3) provision for the training and retraining of handicapped and disabled workers, and their placement in suitable jobs. We recommend that the first two of these measures be accorded high priority in government's plans for industrial development.

The cultivation of sound industrial relations must continue to receive the vigorous attention of the Labour and Trade Union Adviser's Departments. Trade unionism received a bad setback following the period of communist infiltration and domination after the war. Employees—especially manual workers—are still reluctant to join unions, and largely for this reason labor organizations are unable to make their proper contribution to good management-labor relations. We recommend redoubled efforts by these two Departments to extend education on labor relations and trade unionism, and to encourage the development of unions and increase of membership. These activities, of course, should continue to be supplemented by the Labour Department's services in investigating disputes and aiding in their settlement.

In our financial estimates we have recommended increases in the appropriations for the Department of Labour—from $2.2 million in 1954 to $3.7 million in 1959—so that it will be able to carry out the program we have suggested.

E SOCIAL SECURITY

Malaya now has two major schemes of social security, workmen's compensation and a provident fund, both operating reasonably well.

Workmen's compensation was greatly improved by an ordinance enacted in 1952 and brought into force in 1953. It is applicable throughout the Federation, superseding more limited Federal and State laws. It broadened coverage to embrace nearly all civilian workers (except domestic servants and family workers) earning $400 per month or less, increased the statutory benefits which the employer is required to pay in case of work accident or injury, simplified the administration of awards and settlements, and authorized the government to order an employer to insure against his liabilities. These changes represent good progress.

We recommend the consideration of further improvement in workmen's compensation. In the event of serious work accidents or injuries, employer liability can be extremely costly and even catastrophic for all but large firms. It may be wise and timely to substitute compulsory insurance. We also recommend that the adequacy of work accident reporting and of benefits be surveyed. Such a study should attempt to determine objectively the degree of compliance with the scheme, whether the half-monthly payments prescribed by the ordinance in temporary disability cases (two-thirds of wages or $50, whichever is less) are adequate in relation to wage levels and cost of living, and to what extent the prescribed lump-sum payments in permanent disability and fatal cases do in fact give economic security to disabled workmen and to dependents of those who are killed in work accidents.

The Employees Provident Fund, enacted in 1951, came into force July 1, 1952, and completed its first full year in 1953.[21] It is administered by a

[21] The scheme covers employees 16 and over earning not more than $400 per month. Covered employers are required to transmit graduated contributions payable by themselves and their employees, averaging about 5% of monthly earnings from each. Coverage extends to: estates with over 25 acres; employers of 10 or more employees in mines, factories and shops with manual labor, transportation, etc.; shops, restaurants, theatres and offices with five or more; registered school teachers and government employees. The contributions plus interest at not less than 2½% compounded annually are credited to the employee and may

Board (six each from government, employers and employees), with the Commissioner of Labour responsible for inspection and enforcement of employer reporting and payment of contributions. The finances of the Fund are guaranteed by the government. There were about 400,000 contributors a month in late 1953; by May 31, 1954 an aggregate of nearly 700,000 had been registered. Annual employer-employee contributions to the Fund are about $60 million a year. Withdrawals are still very small and the scheme will have a surplus of income over outgo for many years.

Our survey indicates that, despite initial misgivings in many quarters, the program has been working quite well. It is based on compulsory individual savings, not insurance, and provides only lump-sum rather than assured pension payments. These characteristics supposedly made its introduction acceptable. We have no doubt that it is a great improvement over voluntary personal savings as an instrument of social security for wage earners and their families, and that it has improved the economic status of young parents and of children by promising to relieve the young family of the burden of the aged. Moreover, it retains savings within the country, contributes to the stability of the resident population and gives immigrants a new stake in the institutions of the government.

Widespread acceptance of the Provident Fund leads us to suggest consideration of changes which we think would strengthen its social security functions while retaining its self-sustaining characteristics:

1. The present maximum of $400 a month might became a limit on the amount of earnings that are subject to contributions rather than a limit on the amount determining whether or not an individual is covered. This would extend and stabilize coverage and would simplify employer reporting.

2. The specifications might permit, if not require, annuity payments or periodic fractional repayments of the accumulations instead of lump-sum withdrawals. Such limited periodic payments would assure continuing income to beneficiaries and would protect them against improvident or hazardous use of their savings.

---

be withdrawn in lump sum by his survivors, or by him at age 55 upon becoming permanently incapacitated for employment, ceasing to be an employee or leaving the country permanently. In the latter two contingencies, the withdrawal excludes the employer contribution if less than 60 contributions have been paid. Exemption of employees (and their employer) is permitted if they are covered by a pre-existing employer fund as advantageous to the employees as the Government Fund, and if they are covered by a new fund provided that it is more advantageous to the employee than the Government Fund.

3. The general pattern of the Fund might be revised so as to provide group insurance protection as well as compulsory individual savings. It could then pay insurance benefits sufficient in most cases to meet subsistence needs with respect to persons who reach retirement age, become disabled or die before having been covered long enough to make many contributions or accumulate substantial savings. Such benefits might have to be limited to persons who meet at least minimum requirements as to duration of coverage and amount of contribution. Incorporation of the group insurance principle could probably be made acceptable if accompanied by provisions that guarantee return of at least employee contributions plus interest through periodic benefits and lump-sum payments.

4. Income protection might be strengthened by relating insurance benefits to family composition, and the social purposes might be best served if these benefits are bounded by minima and maxima.

F   HOUSING AND TOWN PLANNING

The most acute housing problems in the Federation are urban. The populations of the cities and towns have been increasing more rapidly than their housing could absorb. More than 50% of the urban residents live in shop houses, and as the population increases, density rises—in some places to appalling heights. In one area of Kuala Lumpur it was recently found to be 1,800 persons per acre. In Penang, Ipoh, Kota Bharu, and in some parts of Malacca—to mention only a few observed in the course of our survey—overcrowding and slum living have gone to such extremes that they impede the orderly development of commerce and industry, create health and other hazards and increase the costs of community life. Overcrowded housing is probably now the largest single factor contributing to make tuberculosis one of the most serious diseases of Malaya.

In rural areas, housing conditions are very uneven on the agricultural estates and mines and in the villages. The Labour Department has done much to ensure observance of at least minimum standards for the housing of laborers on estates and mines. It should be able to do more with the augmented resources we have recommended and with the cooperation of employers. RIDA has begun to give attention to the development of villages, particularly to increase the range of community facilities. It has also undertaken a number of rural housing and village improvement projects and intends to extend these activities as far as its funds permit.

The Federation has a Town Planning Department, but its functions are minimal and advisory and its resources (an office and small staff in Kuala Lumpur) are insufficient to deal with more than a small fraction of the current problem. Only the municipalities of Kuala Lumpur and Penang have planning staffs of their own. For the rest of the Federation, the planning and design of housing are fragmentary, and State and local controls have not kept up with the needs of rapidly growing urban areas.

The mission believes that there should be a comprehensive policy of town and regional planning throughout the Federation, made definitive through new legislation. As one step toward implementing such a policy, we recommend that the Town Planning Department be expanded so it can begin a general survey of housing conditions and needs, and be equipped to give advice on town planning matters, including slum clearance, major housing projects, etc. In our estimates we have included annually recurrent funds for the Department rising from $200,000 in 1954 to $500,000 in 1959 (in addition to $500,000 of capital funds for facilities to be built in 1956-59), to permit establishment of regional offices (e.g., in Penang, Ipoh, Johore Bahru and Kota Bharu) and to provide for consultant services in all parts of the Federation.

The construction of houses, which has lagged far behind needs, now has a new stimulus through the activities of the Housing Trust. It is charged with broad responsibilities to meet housing needs—whether by promoting and encouraging housing activities, preparing housing and land development schemes, developing sites, constructing and selling or letting housing, shops and flats, making loans, etc. Its resources include loans of $10 million by the Federation and authority to borrow additional sums for capital expenditures. By limiting initial projects to development and construction for outright sale, its present loan capital functions as a revolving fund. Purchases from the Trust have to be financed by personal resources or by loans from banks, cooperatives, etc. and from the Federal and Colonial Building Society, a quasi-public corporation established in 1950 to promote home ownership, which has $20 million available for long-term lending on housing in the Federation ($10 million from the Federal Government and an equal amount from the Colonial Development Corporation).

Though organized in 1951, the Housing Trust was not staffed for effective operation until 1953. In that year it utilized about $1 million of its available capital resources for pilot projects. It was gaining momentum in 1954. Its target is 500 houses for sale in 1955, and, if effective demand appears, 1,000 in 1956 and 1,500 in 1957—the latter figures being as high as, or higher than, can be financed with the capital already authorized. Since at least 10,000-20,000 dwelling units a year may be needed merely to keep pace with urban population growth, apart from rehousing, the Trust's targets are equivalent to very small fractions of the total need. Unless private construction takes a sharp upward turn the government program will have to be greatly increased. In addition, slum clearance and low-cost rehousing urgently needed in Penang, Kuala Lumpur, Kota Bharu and elsewhere may have to be aided by Federal loans and by Federal and/or local subsidy.[22]

The mission believes it has been sound for the Housing Trust to acquire its first experience with housing constructed for outright sale, and that the Trust should continue to adapt its plans to its survey findings, which ascertain the kinds of housing wanted and the financial resources of the groups desiring housing and able and willing to purchase it. However, we also believe the Trust will have to enter the more difficult field of constructing low-cost subsidized rental housing to meet the needs of low income families. We therefore recommend not only a more vigorous program of constructing houses for sale to middle and lower income groups, but also prompt preparatory studies of rental housing needs and projects —taking fullest advantage of the experience gained in this field by the Singapore Improvement Trust.

Our estimates include only the $20 million of loan funds to finance the Housing Trust and the Federal and Colonial Building Society. The larger capital needs of more comprehensive housing programs should be carefully considered and given as high priority as will be permitted by the financial outlook summarized elsewhere in this report.

---

[22] An important beginning has been made toward dealing with the housing problem in Kuala Lumpur through the development of Petaling Jaya, conceived by the Town Planner and the first satellite town in the Federation. It is a 3,000 acre layout located six miles from the overcrowded and rapidly growing capital city of Kuala Lumpur, on the main road and railway line to Port Swettenham. It is designed to be a self-sufficient community of 80,000 persons, with its own housing, industry, shops, government buildings, schools, etc., with special provisions for persons displaced from overcrowded areas of the city. Its resources include an initial grant of $3.1 million and a loan of $8 million from the Federal Government. It is developing rapidly now as a project of the Selangor State Government.

TABLE 2 Summary of Public Expenditures for Specified Social Services, Federation

(Million $)

Social services	Expenditures (or income)							(Est.)	Recommendations				
	1947	1948	1949	1950	1951	1952	1953	1954	1955	1956	1957	1958	1959
Education[1]													
Annually recurrent	15.8	28.9	30.1	32.1	50.4	57.5	83.5	92.3	97.0	105.0	115.0	125.0	134.0
Capital	0.2	0.3	2.1	1.7	4.5	6.5	11.7	9.3	10.0	11.0	11.0	11.0	11.0
Gross total	16.0	29.2	32.2	33.8	54.9	64.0	95.2	101.6	107.0	116.0	126.0	136.0	145.0
Less income (fees, etc.)	0.5	0.6	1.2	0.7	0.8	1.0	1.2	2.6	4.0	4.0	5.0	5.0	6.0
Net total	15.5	28.6	31.0	33.1	54.1	63.0	94.0	99.0	103.0	112.0	121.0	131.0	139.0
Public health and medical care[2]													
Annually recurrent	17.9	21.7	25.8	25.8	34.2	43.8	51.2	53.0	57.1	59.5	62.6	65.9	68.9
Capital	0.3	0.3	0.6	0.7	2.0	2.1	5.5	2.3	4.6	8.2	9.8	9.6	4.8
Gross total	18.2	22.0	26.4	26.5	36.2	45.9	56.7	55.3	61.7	67.7	72.4	75.5	73.7
Less income (fees, charges, etc.)	n.a.	1.4	1.7	1.7	2.2	2.7	2.9	3.0	5.0	6.0	7.0	8.0	9.0
Net total	n.a.	20.6	24.7	24.8	34.0	43.2	53.8	52.3	56.7	61.7	65.4	67.5	64.7
Social welfare[3]													
Annually recurrent	1.1	1.6	2.7	2.9	3.5	3.9	4.5	5.1	5.8	6.2	6.3	6.6	7.0
Capital	0.5	0.8	0.3	0.2	0.4	1.0	0.8	0.5	0.8	0.7	0.6	0.5	0.5
Total	1.6	2.4	3.1	3.1	3.9	4.9	5.3	5.6	6.6	6.9	6.9	7.1	7.5
Labor[4]													
Annually recurrent	n.a.	0.7	0.7	1.0	1.2	1.5	1.7	2.2	2.5	2.8	3.1	3.4	3.7
Capital	n.a.	0.0+	0.0+	0.0+	0.0+	0.0+	0.0+	0.0+	—	—	—	—	—
Total	n.a.	0.7	0.7	1.0	1.2	1.5	1.7	2.2	2.5	2.8	3.1	3.4	3.7
Town planning[5]													
Annually recurrent	0.1	0.1	0.1	0.1	0.1	0.2	0.2	0.2	0.3	0.4	0.5	0.5	0.5
Capital	—	—	—	—	—	—	—	—	—	0.1	0.2	0.1	0.1
Total	0.1	0.1	0.1	0.1	0.1	0.2	0.2	0.2	0.3	0.5	0.7	0.6	0.6
Total[6]													
Annually recurrent	34.9	53.0	59.4	61.9	89.4	106.9	141.1	152.8	162.7	173.9	187.5	201.4	214.1
Capital	1.0	1.4	3.1	2.6	6.9	9.6	18.0	12.1	15.4	20.0	21.6	21.2	16.4
Gross total	35.9	54.4	62.5	64.5	96.3	116.5	159.1	164.9	178.1	193.9	209.1	222.6	230.5
Less income (fees, charges, etc.)	n.a.	2.0	2.9	2.4	3.0	3.7	4.1	5.6	9.0	10.0	12.0	13.0	15.0
Net total	n.a.	52.4	59.6	62.1	93.3	112.8	155.0	159.3	169.1	183.9	197.1	209.6	215.5

[1] Includes Federal and State/Settlement Departments of Education. Excludes education activities of other government agencies, and grants to the University of Malaya.

[2] Includes Federal and State/Settlement Medical Departments. Excludes expenditures by Public Works Department on anti-mosquito activities and water supplies, by municipalities, and by estates and mines.

[3] Includes Federal and State/Settlement Departments of Social Welfare, and subventions to private agencies.

[4] Includes Department of Labour only.

[5] Includes Town Planner's Department only. Excludes Housing Trust, and Federal and Colonial Building Society (see Chapter 8, Table 5).

[6] See footnotes 1–5 above. Excludes Trade Union Adviser Department; Cooperative Department; Information Service; Employees Provident Fund; and current expenditure and accruing liabilities for pensions.

We would call attention to the need for coordination of town planning and housing activities and suggest that consideration be given at an appropriate time to their administrative integration.

II SINGAPORE

A EDUCATION[23]

Before the war, Singapore had limited public provision for education. About one-half the children were at school, with less than half of these in schools operated or financially aided by the government. One-half to two-thirds of the adult population was illiterate, largely due to the immigration of illiterate adults. During the war, education all but ceased.

After the war, an intense demand for public education emerged, with special emphasis on learning to speak, read and write in English as an open sesame to economic opportunity. At the same time, the Colony recognized an urgent need to expand public education to foster civic loyalty and responsibility and to meet the needs of economic rehabilitation and development. In 1949-50 the government adopted comprehensive plans directed toward universal free primary education and expansion of academic and technical secondary education and adult literacy. This was done despite an unprecedented rate of increase in the child population due to the high postwar birth rate and rapidly declining infant and child mortality.

In 1947 Singapore had 81,000 children in registered primary schools; now (1954) 158,500 are enrolled. Indeed, the primary schools have 13,500 more places than the 145,000 children estimated as being in the age group of 7 to 12, with many places occupied by over-age children who had not had opportunity to complete primary schooling before. In 1947 there were 5,900 pupils in registered secondary schools; now there are 21,900. These notable achievements have been made possible by great efforts on the part of education and public works authorities, the readiness of the Colony to provide increasing funds for new government schools and by grants in aid to many nongovernment private schools. Gross public expenditures for education, which were only $4 million in 1947, were estimated to be

23 See Technical Report 9.

about $38 million in 1954—an increase from $4 to $32 per person in the population.[24]

The rapid expansions of the recent past are only prologue, because Singapore's school age population has only just begun to receive the formidable impact of the postwar high birth rates and low death rates. The primary school age population decreased between 1950 and 1952 but began to increase in 1953 and 1954. In the next five or six years the increase is likely to be about 18,000 a year (about 9% of the primary school age population); thereafter it will continue to grow, though at a slower rate. To keep pace, the Colony would have to build an average of 18 new schools a year and, to staff them for two sessions a day, recruit more than 600 teachers annually.

The mission appreciates that Singapore must make every effort to meet these impending primary school needs, continuing—as the Colony proposed in a recent White Paper—to provide a place in school for every child. It must also expand academic secondary education to about 35,000 places by 1960 to meet the needs not only for teachers but also for other professions, the public services and general cultural demands. Though aware that these first priorities may tax the resources of the education authorities and the building industry, the mission believes that maximum practical provisions beyond those presently contemplated should also be made for:

1. Eventual expansion of primary education from six to eight years, with enrollment of children from age six to the employment age of 14; and, in the interim, experimentation with two-year intermediate schools or classes for pupils who may profit from further education with a vocational bias—so that the young children of this urban community will be at school and being prepared for future employment, and will not be either at loose ends or prematurely employed;

2. Expansion of nonacademic secondary education (technical, commercial and "modern"), to prepare Singapore's children of secondary school ages for proficiency and productivity in their future employments and to provide opportunity for increasing numbers to prepare for higher education in specialized fields; and

3. Adult education—to broaden part-time vocational adult education,

[24] More recent information indicates that actual expenditures may have been only $31 million in 1954 (annually recurrent $25 million and capital expenditures $6 million)—$26 per capita.

supplementing part- and full-time adult education, to become available through the Singapore Polytechnic and its affiliate resources scheduled to be developed in the next year or two; and to develop a vigorous program of part-time adult education in order to wipe out illiteracy within the next generation.

Adequate development of Singapore's education system is unusually difficult because of the racial complexity of the population, multilingualism, and the desire of each group to preserve its own heritage while participating in the evolution of a common culture and society. Like the Federation, Singapore has four types of primary schools, according to the language of instruction (English, Chinese, Malay and Indian), and English and Chinese secondary schools. Government maintains the Malay schools and its own English schools, and aids other English, Chinese and Indian schools. Quality of instruction varies greatly among the several types of schools, reflecting differences in the resources for teacher-training and in the qualifications of the teachers. Major steps are being taken to improve quality where it is especially weak, but much more needs to be done.

The mission is convinced that all practical steps should be taken through the schools to further the Colony's policy of bilingualism, developing the use of English as a common language among the people and in their commerce and industry, while also providing for the multiple lingual and cultural interests of the several racial groups in the population. This is the sound course for the development of an education system with coordinated relations between the primary and post-primary schools, leading to higher education and vocational preparation in institutions which utilize English as a medium of instruction.[25] To these ends the mission recommends that:

1. All practical efforts should continue to be made to extend and improve the teaching of English in government and aided schools;

2. Sufficient special classes should be provided in English primary schools to meet the needs of qualified pupils whose parents want them to transfer from vernacular to English schools;

3. Plans for new government schools should continue to include provisions encouraging the teaching of English in accordance with the wishes

---

[25] The University of Malaya teaches in English; the new Singapore Polytechnic will teach in English; and it is reported that the prospective Nanyang (Chinese) University intends to lean heavily on instruction in English.

of parents and the bilingual policy which has been adopted by the government;

4. Additional aid should be given Chinese schools, by application of the same standards and schedules of financial aid as apply to aided English schools, to encourage and assist improvement of bilingual education.

With respect to the Malay schools, we recommend special studies to reassess the relative values—to the Malays and to the Colony—of their bilingual pattern (which now provides for initial instruction in the home language and subsequent introduction of English) as against the pattern of the English schools. With respect to the Indian schools, we recommend that their place in the education system be reviewed especially in view of the very small numbers enrolled, the difficulty of staffing them with qualified teachers and the general preference of Indian families for enrollment of their children in English schools.[26]

The mission fully supports the Department of Education in emphasizing the importance it assigns to expansion and strengthening of teacher recruitment and training—the key to successful prosecution of the education program. The eventual objective is to have teacher-training-college graduates for all primary (and intermediate) teaching posts, and university graduates with Diplomas in Education for higher teaching levels. In the interim, with a period of crisis ahead, the Department of Education should utilize all resources at its command, including temporary extension of part-time normal training; expeditious completion of new facilities for the present Teachers' Training College and fullest possible staffing, recruiting to the faculty from overseas if necessary; development of a second college as rapidly as practical; more extensive use of teacher-training resources overseas; special provision for the training of teachers of non-academic subjects, and overseas recruitment; largest practical use of the training resources of the University of Malaya; utilization of qualified teachers who may be prepared by the prospective Nanyang University; and maximum practical use of part-time day and evening teachers.

We do not underestimate the difficulties in developing an adequate teaching staff, but in view of the importance of this aspect of the program, we urge new studies and explorations to find ways of meeting the problems that have to be met in the critical years 1955-60, with maximum preservation of qualitative standards and avoidance of any steps that

[26] See Technical Report 9.

might impair the professional attitude and spirit of dedication among the teachers in Singapore's schools.

Singapore's provisions for higher education at the University of Malaya, the post-secondary institutions of the Federation and the overseas universities appear to be adequate, especially in light of the scheduled expansion of the University of Malaya and the planned development of Nanyang University.

To help ensure a sound developmental program, the mission recommends that the staff of the Education Department be enlarged to adequate size for the functions of over-all administration, improved and increased school supervision and inspection, and for research and program planning. Vocational training should be coordinated among governmental and non-governmental agencies.

The mission believes that a comprehensive and adequate system of education—even broader in scope and larger in dimensions than that envisaged in the Colony's present program[27]—is vital to the development of Singapore. The financial support of such a system should not be stinted, though the costs will be large. The mission suggests that Singapore be prepared for gross education expenditures[28] that will increase from $38 million in 1954 to about $76 million in 1959.[29] Singapore should also expect still higher education costs after 1959 as the population continues to grow.

B   PUBLIC HEALTH AND MEDICAL CARE[30]

Singapore is a vigorous and healthy metropolis, made possible by the conquest of tropical disease. But its job of health protection is never done. Long ago Singapore learned the value of its public health and medical program, without which its population could not have increased and its commerce and industry could not have prospered. That lesson still determines its policy.

Singapore's recent health progress is especially remarkable in light of its early growth by immigration of hundreds of thousands who brought with them infections and infestations, ignorance of sanitation and hygiene, and indifference and even hostility toward efforts to control disease. Near

27 White Paper No. 25 of 1954.
28 Exclusive of grants to the University of Malaya.
29 Including the Singapore Polytechnic. See also footnote 24.
30 See Technical Report 10.

the end of the 19th century, when the Settlement had about 200,000 inhabitants, the death rate still exceeded the birth rate. Thereafter the newly devised methods of modern medicine and public health were applied to such good effect that by 1922-23 birth and death rates were equal and Singapore began to grow by natural increase of population as well as immigration. Health progress continued, except for almost catastrophic deterioration during the Japanese occupation in 1942-45.

After the war, sanitary controls were quickly restored and the course of health improvement was resumed. With a rapid change in attitude toward medical care, increasing proportions of all races began not only to accept but to demand Western medicine. Attendance at public clinics and admission to maternity and other hospitals grew by leaps and bounds. Some health problems were lightened by the virtual end of immigration. But the rise of the birth rate to unprecedented levels and the continued decline of the death rate brought a natural increase of population of 3-4% a year. This led to overcrowding, and substituted new health problems for old.[31]

Singapore's health progress was achieved by developing not only an effective program of public health services but also an extensive system of public medical care. The historic pattern persists. In addition to maintaining comprehensive public health measures, "It is the aim of the Government to provide necessary medical care at prices within reach of all citizens. In a large majority of cases this means free treatment."[32] Services are furnished through the Colony Medical Department, the City Council Health Department and the Rural Board. These public services are supplemented by private practitioners and by the hospitals and other facilities of voluntary agencies.

Except for an acute shortage of certain specialists and nurses, health and medical personnel is reasonably adequate for the present population.

The public health services are broad in scope, including registration of vital statistics and notifiable diseases; supervision of water supply and

[31] Singapore's birth rate reached 49 (births per 1,000 persons) in 1953, one of the highest in the world. In the same year it had 10 deaths per 1,000 persons, a crude rate at the level achieved only in the most progressive countries. Infant mortality, generally a sensitive index of public health, declined from 265 (infant deaths per 1,000 live births) in 1920 and 140 in 1940 to 67 in 1953. In 1920-53, the infant mortality rates fell from 80-90 to 25-30 in the United Kingdom and United States, from 165 to 55 in Japan and from 184 to about 115 in India.

[32] Annual Report, Colony of Singapore, 1953, p. 99.

of sewage and refuse disposal; port health and quarantine services; sanitation and control of malaria (there have been no indigenous cases of this disease for some years); vaccination against smallpox (there were no domestic cases in 1953); efforts to control leprosy (whose actual prevalence remains unknown); immunization against diphtheria; services to control venereal diseases; extensive attack on tuberculosis (the most serious communicable disease in the Colony); hospital, clinic and health center services for maternity, infancy and child welfare; protection of food supply; research; and recruitment and training of personnel.

The hospitals have about 2,200 beds (2 per 1,000 persons), three-fourths provided by government, with 800 in The (Colony) General Hospital.[33] These are supplemented by beds in institutions for patients with tuberculosis, leprosy and mental diseases; and by out-patient departments in hospitals, dispensaries and rural centers, and a large clinic operated by the Royal Singapore Anti-Tuberculosis Association (SATA).

Since the war, the demands on the government hospitals have greatly increased; though there were in 1953 only 24% more beds than in 1938, in-patients have more than doubled and out-patient attendances have increased more than ten-fold. Overcrowding of facilities has become chronic and—with continued rapid growth of population and increasing demand for Western medicine—resources are constantly taxed and strained.

Public expenditures for health and medical services, which were (gross) $10 million in 1947, had increased to $25.5 million in 1953, and may be about $39 million in 1954—an increase in seven years from $11 to $33 per capita. With allowance for fees, hospital charges and other income, the net governmental expenditures have grown from about $9 million to $36 million—from about $7 to $28 per capita.[34]

A Ten-Year Medical Plan was adopted in 1948 by the Colony; it proposed to make up current deficiencies and to anticipate future needs. However, only partial steps were taken until 1951-52, when a real beginning was made toward doubling the physical facilities. The Plan contemplated capital projects costing $49 million; of this, $35 million still remains for 1955-60. The City Council's capital program involves $4 mil-

[33] However, only about 1,460 of these beds (1.2 per 1,000 persons) are now available for acute general cases.

[34] Information furnished after our study was completed indicates that actual expenditures in 1954 were somewhat less than the revised estimates for that year used in our Technical Report.

lion (of which $2.9 million is for cemeteries, markets and abattoirs). Gross annual expenditures (recurrent and capital) for both would be expected to increase from about $39 million (or somewhat less) in 1954 to about $45-46 million in 1959 and 1960.

Upon completing the programs by 1959-60, Singapore will have rounded out its facilities, acquired substantially modern and up-to-date plant and equipment with nearly twice the present capacity for hospital in-patients,[35] and increased its clinic resources considerably. It is uncertain, however, that either the hospitals or clinics will be sufficient. If an increasing proportion of Singapore's present population accepts and demands hospital care on the Western pattern, the Colony will need at least 3,600-6,000 beds in general and special hospitals, and possibly more.[36] And it will need still more as population continues to increase. For example, with present patterns, even a doubling of maternity beds may be grossly insufficient if most of the births are going to occur in hospitals, especially if the birth rate remains at its present high level, if housing conditions are not substantially improved and the average hospital stay for maternity cases cannot be kept at its present low figure of three to four days. The provision of 600 beds in district or cottage hospitals scheduled for 1958-60 will quite certainly be too little and too late for local service in the expanding suburban and rural areas. Nor will these deficiencies be met by such increases in out-patient services as may be made possible by scheduled expansions of hospital out-patient departments and independent clinics.

As against 2.3 beds per thousand which Singapore may have in 1960, it may need at least five per thousand persons in the population expected for that year (1.354 million).

The proposed expansion of specialized facilities may also be insufficient for mental disease and leprosy and quite certainly will be inadequate for tuberculosis. Singapore now needs many times as many beds for tuberculosis as it has, and will need more for its expanding population if the disease is not checked or other measures are not undertaken. Thus, completion of the present programs may still find Singapore confronted with large and urgent unmet health and medical needs.

The mission therefore recommends that, in addition to carrying out its

[35] Beds in general and special governmental hospitals would increase from 1,660 in 1954 to 3,080 in 1960; and the ratio to (increasing) population would rise from 1.4 to 2.3 per 1,000 persons.

[36] For explanation of the wide range in the estimate, see Technical Report 10.

basically sound programs as rapidly as possible to overcome arrears, Singapore should undertake an expanded schedule, with increased emphasis on preventive activities in order to reduce the future burden of disease and disability and of recurrent costs for care of the sick. The mission recommends the following specific measures:[37]

1. Maximum practical restriction of the expensive primary hospitals to cases needing specialized care, and use of secondary and less expensive in- and out-patient facilities for other cases, with referral of selected cases to the primary hospitals;

2. Construction and staffing, earlier than scheduled, of district or cottage hospitals and of independent clinics and health centers for services to ambulatory patients;

3. Experimental development of special institutions or hospital-connected facilities for chronic, convalescent and recovery patients in order to reduce costs and the demands on limited staff by relieving the blockage of beds intended for acute cases;

4. Expansion of specific preventive services (e.g., school health, medical and dental services; periodic vaccination against smallpox; immunization against diphtheria; sanitary control of food prepared for public sale, and examination and licensing of food handlers in public eating places or operating as hawkers; sanitary and hygienic control of places of employment, and initial and periodic examination of gainfully employed children and young persons; and prevention of venereal disease);

5. A new and comprehensive campaign against tuberculosis, with the collaboration of SATA and other voluntary agencies, and with technical aid from international agencies—including initial and periodic surveys; development of settlements for nonacute patients who do not require hospital care; expansion of out-patient and domiciliary care and of BCG vaccination on a controlled experimental basis; health education of cases and contacts; and vocational rehabilitation of discharged cases;

6. Strengthening of the program against leprosy—by accelerating the development of new out-patient clinics and staff quarters; provision for education, training and rehabilitation of selected resident and out-patient cases; inauguration of a treatment-allowance scheme for dependents, to encourage cases to come forward early in the course of disease and to remain under treatment; and consideration of plans for a self-supporting

[37] Details are given in Technical Report 10.

settlement for discharged cases that cannot re-enter general community life;

7. Preparation for further expansion of mental disease institutions; provision of out-patient treatment for mental cases (at The General Hospital or elsewhere); and development of plans for mental hygiene clinics, mental hygiene educational activities in the community and an institution for mental defectives;

8. Priority for recruitment and training of professional and sub-professional staff—including support of expanding medical, dental and pharmacy schools in the University of Malaya; further development of nurse and midwife training facilities; training of dental nurses for service in hospital out-patient departments, independent clinics, health centers, schools and other public institutions, utilizing the Federation's education and training experience at Penang; and recruitment overseas; and

9. Large-scale expansion of health education of the public, with the aid of other departments and agencies of the government and of the voluntary agencies interested in health progress.

In the interest of maximum effectiveness, efficiency and economy, consideration should be given to integration in the highest degree practical of all health and medical functions now administered by the three official agencies. However, if complete unification will not be attainable under the new Constitution and these functions are to be divided between the Colony Government and the City and Island Council, both island-wide in jurisdiction, we recommend that all personal health and medical services (concerned with prevention, diagnosis, treatment and rehabilitation) be assigned to the Government and all environmental services to the Council —so that at least each group of activities may have the advantages of integration.

We also recommend as rapid extension as may be practicable of three collateral programs essential to health progress: (1) enlargement of the water supplies and fluoridation of the water to prevent dental disease; (2) extension of sewerage; and (3) housing for medium and low income families.

We believe that Singapore should assure the availability of funds to carry out the comprehensive program we recommend, expecting gross expenditures to increase from $39 million in 1954[38] to $51 million in 1959,

[38] See footnote 34.

and to increase thereafter concurrently with growth of population. We do not advise any fundamentally new policy with respect to fees though we do recommend, as desirable and justified, substantial increases in charges for hospital in-patients. If it develops that Singapore cannot afford these prospective costs out of general revenues, the program should not be reduced but consideration should be given to seeking additional revenue by partial financing of hospital or other personal medical services through a program of contributory social insurance.

C SOCIAL WELFARE [39]

Singapore has a long history of voluntary social welfare services. Many organizations have been active for decades, especially among the Chinese, in helping to meet family and individual needs. In 1946, however, voluntary agencies were unable to cope with more than a fraction of the urgent needs precipitated by the war and the Japanese occupation. Government had to assume new responsibilities and formed the Department of Social Welfare. Its first important tasks concerned mass relief of destitution and dislocation. After these were done, the Department began the orderly development of comprehensive welfare services. Its activities are now broad and diverse and include:

1. Public assistance—money payments to needy or destitute people (aged persons, widows and orphans, permanently or temporarily disabled, sick (including advanced tuberculous), or unemployed; those receiving tuberculosis treatment and likely to become self-supporting; and cases having miscellaneous unmet needs);

2. Residential institutions (for juvenile delinquents; orphaned, destitute and homeless children needing or seeking protected residence; and for aged persons);

3. Social centers (for day-care; creches; education and recreation of children; adult education; youth organizations; and for community development purposes);

4. Court probation services (for juveniles and adults);

5. Care and protection of women and children (suppression of brothels; prevention of prostitution and trafficking in women and children; taking into custody and protection of young girls; care and protection of destitute, neglected or ill-treated children; supervision of foster children);

[39] See Technical Report 11.

6. Counselling services (legal advisory services for the poor; counselling on marriage, domestic relations and disputes; guidance on adoption procedures);

7. Youth welfare services (technical and financial aid for recreational, educational and other youth activities of voluntary agencies);

8. Staff training and development (in-service training; education, in collaboration with the University of Malaya and overseas institutions); and

9. Social research (social survey of Singapore; studies of special social and economic groups, etc.).

The Department aims to keep government informed on the social needs of the community and to provide services that are not met by other government departments or by private agencies. Thus it is primarily concerned with residual needs. This is a sound position, especially since the Department is functioning in a community which has a vast amount of poverty and a large proportion of its population in a socially unsettled state, and which is still largely without adequate survey or assessment of social needs.

There has been much concern over the rising cost of public assistance. Expenditures for direct relief of needy persons were $0.2-0.3 million a year in 1946-47; in 1953 they accounted for $3.7 million of the total departmental expenditures of $5.7 million.[40] The average monthly case load of 3,600 in 1946, the first year after the war, declined to a minimum of 2,200 in 1949 and then increased to 8,100 in 1953.[41] Two points should be noted in evaluating the recent upward trend: in 1953, public assistance was being paid to about 5% of Singapore's families—a relatively small proportion in light of the socio-economic characteristics of the population and a downturn in the economy—and much of the increase in caseload and expenditures is an investment in an apparently successful program of contributing to the control of tuberculosis and reducing future burdens of dependency.

Our study indicates that, whether or not there are declines in the economy, Singapore should expect considerable further increase in public assistance costs—from about $5 million in 1954 to more than twice this amount in 1959. Various considerations point in this direction: flat monthly assistance payments are admittedly inadequate in many or most cases; the

[40] About 15% of the relief cases and nearly one-third of the total assistance payments came under the special tuberculosis treatment allowance program started in 1949. Public assistance expenditures exceeded $5 million in 1954.

[41] Average payments in 1953 were $30 per month for 6,835 assistance cases, and $82 per month for 1,253 tuberculosis treatment allowance cases.

old-age case load will be under strong pressure to climb for another decade before the prospective provident fund furnishes an offset; tuberculosis treatment allowances will expand if a vigorous campaign is undertaken against this disease as we recommend elsewhere;[42] and a similar program should be initiated for lepers and their dependents.[43]

It seems to us that the whole public assistance program should be given a new clear mandate and should be placed on a firm statutory base, which it lacks at present. Flat assistance payments should be replaced by amounts determined by the difference between needs and resources, after careful investigation of cases by a staff of adequate size.

We are concerned that public assistance should not become a heavy burden on the general revenues of future years. We therefore recommend that, as soon as practical after the plans for the central provident fund have been implemented, careful consideration should be given to development of a comprehensive contributory program providing insurance benefits for the aged and disabled and for widows and orphans.

Residential institutions for adults and for juvenile delinquents, creches, and hostels for boys and girls requiring public provision or protection need some improvement or extension. We provide for this in our financial estimates.

We strongly recommend development of the services which are not merely relief or palliatives but serve to prevent social breakdown and contribute to community development, especially community centers and youth welfare and recreational activities. These undertakings should be planned in cooperation with the Department of Education and voluntary agencies. Staff recruitment and training programs for these services should be vigorously pursued.

Since social welfare activities are still in a developmental state, government should continue to give technical and financial aid to voluntary agencies. However, it should encourage them to seek broad public support so that they can become independent of government financial aid and by their activities reduce the need for government services.

Planning and administration of social welfare and many other public services are handicapped by lack of reliable statistical information on levels and conditions of living, budgets and costs of living, status and resources of the aged and other special groups in the population. We therefore

[42] See p. 174 and Technical Report 10.
[43] See p. 174.

recommend that surveys of living conditions and similar inquiries now in a planning and pilot-study stage be carried forward.

Our studies indicate that the financial provisions for the government's social welfare services will probably need to increase from $8 million in 1954 to $19 million in 1959, reflecting mainly development of community services, growth of population and increase in the assistance programs.

D LABOR [44]

Singapore's labor force already has a surplus of unskilled and a shortage of skilled labor. We therefore recommend that the Labour Department, in cooperation with the Department of Education, emphasize the training of workers by development of youth guidance, apprentice training and employment services until such time as other local resources assure that there is an adequate and continuing supply of skilled labor. Legislation would be needed to encourage and regulate voluntary apprentice training in suitable centers and in approved firms. Plans for the further training of apprentices or older semi-skilled workers to higher levels of skill should be coordinated with the programs for technical education and the Singapore Polytechnic.[45] The Labour Department should also provide for vocational rehabilitation, training or retraining of disabled and handicapped workers. The present central employment services should be expanded by establishing branch exchanges.

Our studies suggest that the health of young entrants into the labor force should be protected by stricter controls than are practiced at present, as by conditioning the issuance of work permits on initial and periodic health examinations by the Medical Department and on matching the physical fitness of the young person and the requirements of the prospective job.[46]

Sound management-labor relations should be fostered—by continued encouragement of trade union development, orderly negotiation and conciliation of disputes, and educational activities on trade unionism and labor relations conducted by both the Department of Labour and voluntary agencies.

[44] For a comprehensive review of the activities of the Labour Department, see the Annual Report of the Department for 1953.

[45] See Technical Report 9.

[46] See Technical Report 10, and recommendation 4, p. 174.

Much has already been accomplished to improve the sanitary and safety conditions of work, but extremely bad conditions are still common. The mission recommends that inspection services be expanded and strengthened, and that continued and stronger efforts be made toward improvement, especially in industries with relatively high frequency of accidents and disease. Consideration should also be given to the closer coordination, if not integration, of administrative responsibilities for inspection and control activities now dispersed among the Labour and Medical Departments, the Singapore Harbour Board and other agencies. We also recommend a comprehensive review of the Labour Ordinance, particularly toward strengthening the enforcement provisions concerning hours and days of work, conditions of work, wage fixing and settlement of disputes.

Provisions for the compensation of injured workmen are said to be operating satisfactorily. Nevertheless, we recommend a study to survey the adequacy of work accident reporting and of compensation payments, and to examine the need for a change from individual employer liability to a system of compulsory insurance.

The staff of the Labour Department should be enlarged, to equip it for the expanded and strengthened program envisaged here and for more adequate compiling and reporting of labor statistics, especially with respect to occupations (classification, standards, trade testing and reporting), employment and unemployment, and costs of living—the last in conjunction with the Social Welfare Department.

Financial provisions for the Labour Department should, we believe, increase from about $0.9 million in 1954 to about $2.0 million in 1959. In these estimates we have allowed for the augmented services recommended above, for three branch employment exchanges to be developed in 1956-58 and for a training center to be built in 1956-57 and staffed progressively in and after 1957.

E   TOWN PLANNING AND HOUSING [47]

Overcrowding in the central part of Singapore, bad before the war, has become appalling. Of the population of 1.15 million, nearly half a million are living in slums, squatter areas or badly overcrowded facilities. Inade-

[47] See The Work of the Singapore Improvement Trust: 1927-1947, by J. M. Fraser, 1948; the Annual Report of the Singapore Improvement Trust, 1953; and the Annual Report, Colony of Singapore, 1953.

quate housing has become one of the main contributory causes of the dangerously high prevalence of tuberculosis.

Construction of permanent dwelling units has increased greatly in recent years, as evidenced by the following figures:

	1949	1953
Public agencies		
Singapore Improvement Trust	828	2,031
City Council	471	347
Public Works Department	342	180
Singapore Harbour Board	60	324
Sub-total.	1,701	2,882
Private agencies	685	2,376
Total	2,386	5,258

Growth of housing activity has continued since then.

The Singapore Improvement Trust (SIT) functions as the official agency for planning, improvement, public housing, etc. It develops public housing and related projects through government loans. These have aggregated nearly $100 million (through 1954).

Though the housing agencies, public and private, have been making very large and commendable efforts, new construction is scarcely keeping pace with the rapid growth of population; it certainly is not making any substantial inroads into the accumulated backlog of deficiency. The need for relief and constructive improvement is urgent.

Present impediments to commerce and industry, health progress and the amenities of living are so grave that the mission urges as vigorous a program of rehabilitation and development as resources will permit. This demands complementary large-scale activities by the public authorities (with respect to community improvement projects and sub-economic and subsidized minimum-cost housing for low income groups) and by private enterprise (with respect to economic flats, houses, shops and other commercial or industrial establishments).

A general pattern of town planning and housing will presumably be provided by the Master Plan, to be submitted before 1955 but not available to us at this writing (October 1954). Our recommendations must therefore be regarded as provisional.

The general needs seem to us to be clear: (a) general planning for the Island; (b) redistribution of residence, mainly from the center to the suburban and rural areas, with allowance for increase in population; (c) improvement in the center, with slum clearance and rebuilding at an accelerated rate, so that it will become mainly the commercial and business area; and (d) rapid development of satellite towns and suburban and rural residence.

The information available to us indicates that Singapore needs about 8,000-10,000 housing units a year to keep pace with most urgent existing needs and about 6,000 housing units a year to provide for an annual increment of 40,000 persons—apart from commercial and industrial buildings, schools, medical and other community facilities.

The mission recommends the maximum practical program of improvement in the city, and an accelerated schedule of public low-cost rental housing that will produce at least 4,000 units in 1955 and an increasing annual number thereafter, so that about 28,000 new units would be provided in the period 1955-59. Special emphasis should be given by the Singapore Improvement Trust to carrying out the Queenstown satellite town plan and embarking on similar projects. The Trust should continue its commendable research activities toward further reducing the costs of satisfactory permanent low-cost housing. Our studies indicate need for about $180 million for capital expenditures by the Trust in 1955-59 for public housing and other improvement activities.[48]

We also recommend that government encourage private industry to engage in this field of enterprise and community service by government's reiteration of its intent to confine its own activities to community development and improvement and to the production of low-cost and sub-economic housing. Private business should be stimulated to produce as many dwelling units as effective demand, labor, material and financial resources permit. We would especially emphasize the importance of producing flats and houses for ownership by people in the middle and lower-middle income groups.

[48] We expect that new low-cost rental flats can be provided by SIT for an average of $5,000–6,000 or less per unit, and new low-cost single or double story houses for an average of $2,500 or less per unit; and that the average for all new low-cost public housing may decline to (or below) $5,000 per unit. Assuming an average cost per unit of $5,000, the capital required for 28,000 units would be $140 million. Allowance of an additional $40 million has been made for other construction and improvement activities of the Singapore Improvement Trust.

F CENTRAL PROVIDENT FUND

In 1953 Singapore enacted an Ordinance (No. 34) establishing a compulsory Provident Fund, similar to that in the Federation (see p. 160), estimated to cover about 200,000-250,000 employees. A team of experts from Great Britain is now helping to develop administrative procedures so that the program can be brought into operation in the second quarter of 1955. We believe the establishment of this Fund should be regarded as a sound first step toward a more comprehensive system of social security to be developed when employees and employers have become familiar with, and have accepted participation in, a contributory program, and when experience and skill have been acquired in administration.

III THE UNIVERSITY OF MALAYA

The University of Malaya in Singapore was established as an autonomous institution in 1949 by legislative enactments of the Federation of Malaya and the Colony of Singapore, and is sponsored and financed jointly by the two governments. It was formed, in the first instance, by absorbing Raffles College and the King Edward VII College of Medicine,[49] with combined enrollments of 450. It has achieved academic and professional recognition at home and abroad.

In many respects, the University is the apex of educational and cultural institutions for both the Federation and Singapore. There are strong pressures within Malaya for it to expand further so that it can accommodate increasing numbers of men and women seeking higher education for cultural values and as preparation for careers in public administration, teaching, medicine, other professions, and in business. Its enrollment is already approximately 1,000 and may be expected to reach 1,500 in the next five years.

University authorities and officers of the two governments have carefully considered the future of the University and its finances. They have drawn up tentative plans,[50] but many uncertainties which cannot be resolved at this time make a definitive blueprint impossible.

[49] The general plan for the University was laid down in the Report of the Commission on Higher Education in Malaya (Sir Alexander Carr-Saunders, Chairman), 1948. For current status, see the Fourth Annual Report, University of Malaya, 1952-53.

[50] See White Paper No. 23 of 1954, Federation of Malaya; No. 36 of 1954, Colony of Singapore.

We have no doubt that funds ought to be made available to enable the strengthening of the faculties of arts and science and considerable expansion of their student enrollments. The department of education should be equipped for substantial increase in the number of students preparing for careers as teachers. The medical school should be enlarged to produce at least 100 graduates a year as soon as practicable,[51] and preferably should become capable of producing 125 or even 150 a year in order to make a maximum contribution to the needs of the public health and medical programs of the Federation and the Colony.[52] A second medical school, presumably to be located in Kuala Lumpur, may become necessary but we believe this decision should be postponed for a few years. Establishment of a faculty of agriculture, which has been under consideration, we suggest be put off until the need is clearer than at present, relying for the next few years on development of the facilities at Serdang in the Federation and on institutions overseas for the training of specialized personnel in this field. Plans for the proposed faculty of engineering have gone so far that we assume they will be implemented, though we have some reservations about the urgency of this move in view of the costs involved and the opportunities for engineering education in the United Kingdom and elsewhere. Various teaching buildings and hostels are needed in Singapore, and faculty salaries have to be adjusted to the new (Ritson) schedules. In addition, we assume the development of one or more University faculties or colleges at Kuala Lumpur.

We have taken the indicated needs into account in deriving our estimates for the years 1955-59, allowing latitude for alternatives in the development plan, and recognizing that at this time we cannot gauge reliably what effects, if any, the prospective establishment of the Nanyang (Chinese) University in Singapore will have on the program of the University of Malaya.

In view of resources otherwise available to the University,[53] we recom-

[51] As recommended in the Report of the Committee of Enquiry on Medical Education in Malaya (Sir David Lindsay Keir, Chairman), Singapore, 1954.

[52] The expanding dimensions of those programs are presented in Technical Report 10. The estimates for the government medical departments include provisions for the clinical teaching facilities needed by the expanded medical school.

[53] General endowment funds, private donations and accumulated funds, a grant of £ 1 million hitherto available from the Colonial Development and Welfare Fund, and amounts to be realized from sale of existing properties—aggregating about $11 million toward the estimated needs of the next five years.

TABLE 3 Summary of Public Expenditures for Specified Social Services, Singapore

(Million $)

Social services	Expenditures (or income)							(Est.)		Recommendations			
	1947	1948	1949	1950	1951	1952	1953	1954	1955	1956	1957	1958	1959
Education[1]													
Annually recurrent	3.8	5.2	7.3	8.9	14.0	17.0	19.5	27.9	35.3	41.9	48.7	57.2	64.9
Capital	0.2	0.4	0.5	2.3	2.3	2.3	1.4	10.0	16.2	11.0	11.0	11.0	11.0
Gross total	4.0	5.6	7.8	11.2	16.3	19.3	20.9	37.9	51.5	52.9	59.7	68.2	75.9
Less income (fees, etc.)	0.2	0.3	0.3	0.3	0.5	0.5	0.6	0.7	0.8	1.1	1.4	1.4	1.6
Net total	3.8	5.3	7.5	10.9	15.8	18.8	20.3	37.2	50.7	51.8	58.3	66.8	74.3
Public health and medical care[2]													
Annually recurrent	9.5	10.2	11.6	12.5	13.9	19.4	22.0	26.1	34.4	36.4	39.4	42.5	44.6
Capital	0.8	1.0	0.8	0.8	0.5	2.3	3.5	10.6	7.8	8.0	7.2	7.4	6.4
Gross total	10.3	11.2	12.4	13.3	14.4	21.7	25.5	36.7	42.2	44.4	46.6	49.9	51.0
Less income (fees, charges, etc.)	n.a.	2.0	2.0+	2.0+	2.3	2.8	2.9+	1.8	3.8	6.0	8.0	10.0	12.0
Net total	n.a.	9.2	10.4	11.3	12.1	18.9	22.5	34.9	38.4	38.4	38.6	39.9	39.0
Social welfare[3]													
Annually recurrent	n.a.	1.3	1.1	1.7	2.3	3.7	5.8	7.7	9.2	12.3	14.1	16.2	17.9
Capital	n.a.	0.0+	0.1	0.0+	0.1	0.3	0.1	0.6	0.9	1.0	1.4	1.4	1.2
Total	n.a.	1.3	1.2	1.7	2.4	4.0	5.9	8.3	10.1	13.3	15.5	17.6	19.1
Labor[4]													
Annually recurrent	0.1	0.1	0.1	0.2	0.5	0.6	0.7	0.9	0.9	1.2	1.6	1.9	2.0
Capital	0.0	0.0	0.0	0.0	0.0	0.0	0.0	0.0	0.0	0.5	0.7	0.0+	0.0
Total	0.1	0.1	0.1	0.2	0.5	0.6	0.7	0.9	0.9	1.7	2.3	1.9	2.0
Total[5]													
Annually recurrent	13.4[6]	16.8	20.1	23.3	30.7	40.7	48.0	62.6	79.8	91.8	103.8	117.8	129.4
Capital	1.0[6]	1.4	1.4	3.1	2.9	4.9	5.0	21.2	24.9	20.5	20.3	19.8	18.6
Gross total	14.4[6]	18.2	21.5	26.4	33.6	45.6	53.0	83.8	104.7	112.3	124.1	137.6	148.0
Less income (fees, charges, etc.)	n.a.	2.3	2.3	2.3	2.8	3.3	3.5	2.5	4.6	7.1	9.4	11.4	13.6
Net total	n.a.	15.9	19.2	24.1	30.8	42.3	49.5	81.3	100.1	105.2	114.7	126.2	134.4

[1] Includes Department of Education and Singapore Polytechnic. Excludes education activities of other government agencies, and grants to the University of Malaya.

[2] Includes Colony Medical Department, City Council Health Department and Rural Board. After 1953, excludes markets, abattoirs and cemeteries. All figures exclude water supplies and sewerage in the city.

[3] Includes Department of Social Welfare, contributions to voluntary agencies and expenditures from trust funds.

[4] Department of Labour only.

[5] Excludes: grants to the University of Malaya; government loans to and other operations of the Singapore Improvement Trust; other housing activities; water supplies and sewerage; broadcasting and other public informational services; and current expenditures and accruing liabilities for pensions.

[6] Excludes social welfare expenditures this year.

SOURCE: Technical Reports.

mend that grants of approximately $5 million be provided for development of plant and equipment in 1955-59, plus, for annually recurrent expenditures, $5.5 million in 1955, increasing by $0.4 million per annum thereafter, to about $7 million in 1957. The apportionments between the Federation and Colony Governments should be determined by them in light of the specific plans that will be developed.

These estimates are minimal with respect to capital development funds. They may be approximately adequate if supplemented by a new grant (of, say, £ 1 million) from the Colonial Development and Welfare Fund. If such a grant is not forthcoming, the capital amounts to be provided by the two governments should be reconsidered.

PART **IV**

FINANCING AND ORGANIZATION OF DEVELOPMENT

CHAPTER 8

FINANCIAL RESOURCES FOR DEVELOPMENT

We may now consider the expenditures, both recurrent and capital, called for by our recommendations, plus those to which the two territories are committed, in relation to the financial resources which may reasonably be expected to be available for a public development program during 1955-59. This requires an assessment of the probable course of public revenues and other public financial resources and of both categories of expenditure. It would be presumptuous, as well as misleading, to present such an assessment, covering so long a period, with any degree of assurance or claim to precision. So far from doing so, we call attention to the fact that our assessments are based on a variety of assumptions and involve a very large element of conjecture because of the many uncertain variables which affect both revenue and expenditure. They are therefore to be considered only as indicative of the financial prospects which presently seem reasonable. Even with this limitation, some such forecasts are of value, indeed are essential, as a guide to financial policy and the planning of expenditure. We claim no more for our particular forecasts than that they fairly reveal the difficult financial context in which, we believe, development planning in both territories must proceed during the next few years. These forecasts, as we have earlier cautioned, should be reviewed periodically in the light of changing circumstances, and financial policies and development planning should thereupon be adjusted accordingly.

Two further comments are necessary:

1. We are concerned with the total financial resources and the total financial requirements of the governmental sector. To consider separately the finances of the Federal Government, the State and Settlement Governments and other public agencies in the Federation, on the one hand, and of the Colony Government, the City Council and other public agencies in Singapore on the other, would lead to a diffused and disjointed picture of the over-all public finance position and prospects in each of the two territories. The picture would be further complicated by inter-agency

189

transactions and by the fact that, in the fiscal situation of the public sector as a whole, deficits in one agency may be affected by surpluses in another.

In assessing the present and prospective public financial position we have, therefore, for convenience of presentation and for the sake of clarity, eliminated inter-agency transactions on both the paying and receiving sides and consolidated the receipts and expenditures of all the governmental bodies and public agencies in each of the territories, as explained in the Statistical Appendix in Part V. The figures presented for 1949-1953, therefore, differ from the published accounts of the governments in the two territories.

2. We have addressed ourselves, essentially, to a program of development technically and financially capable of achievement in the course of a five-year period. The advance scheduling of such a program in terms of annual goals is not practicable; such decisions must be made year-by-year in the light of changing circumstances and considerations. Our primary interest, then, is in five-year aggregates of public investment expenditure and of resources available to meet that expenditure. Nevertheless, to confine discussion to five-year aggregates would, we believe, obscure the increasing difficulty of the financing problem for both territories which appears probable during the next few years. The prospect is one of steadily rising recurrent expenditures, especially for social services, fairly static revenues and limited borrowing possibilities. To reveal the extent of this problem more clearly, we have presented annual breakdowns of recommended capital and recurrent expenditures and of our estimates of available financial resources. While we believe that these figures represent a reasonable timing of development expenditure in relation to prospective financial resources, we recognize that such year-to-year estimates are in large measure arbitrary and that the apparent precision in the phasing of our recommendations is artificial.

I FEDERATION

Since the end of the boom period which followed the outbreak of the Korean War, the Federation's financial position has deteriorated in the face of declining revenues, the heavy financial burden of the emergency and mounting expenditures in other fields, especially for social services. Table 1 shows a consolidation of the finances of Federal, State and local governments and of quasi-government enterprises and entities since 1949.

TABLE 1   Consolidated Public Finances of the Federation of Malaya

(*Million $*)

	1949	1950	1951	1952	1953	1954 (budget estimates)
Revenue	327	469	796	784	665	593
Recurrent expenditure						
Economic services	37	41	45	65	78	75
Social services[1]	54	57	93	118	131	159
Defense, police, emergency . .	82	101	217	287	296	250
Other	155	152	181	209	237	219
Total	328	351	536	679	742	703
Revenue less recurrent expenditure	−1	+118	+260	+105	−77	−110
Capital expenditure	71	59	111	167	156	249
	−72	+59	+149	−62	−233	−359
Contributions and grants from United Kingdom . . .	44	28	2	7	6	68
Over-all surplus (+) or deficit (−), excluding borrowing[2]	−28	+87	+151	−55	−227	−291

[1] For explanation of slight differences between these figures and those shown in Chapter 7 on the Social Services see notes to Table 2(A) in the Statistical Appendix, Part V.

[2] Since the Table includes the revenues and expenditures of municipalities and public agencies as well as capital expenditures from loan funds, the surpluses or deficits differ from those shown in the Federation printed accounts.

The deficits of recent years have been met in part by grants from the United Kingdom but mainly by domestic and foreign borrowing and, in 1953, through a reduction in government cash and foreign investments. The further reduction in liquid government assets expected in 1954 is likely to prove to be considerably less than the above figures would suggest, since the fiscal accounts for 1954 can be expected to show revenues somewhat higher and expenditures substantially lower than estimated.

Present revenues and other domestic sources of finance are only just about sufficient to cover current expenditure at the present level, including that arising from the emergency. Outlays directly attributable to the emergency, over and above what might be considered the cost of a normal police and defense establishment, were estimated in 1954 at about $170 million, that is, rather more than one-quarter of all current expenditure. Only external assistance through grants and loans has enabled the Federation to carry the very heavy burden of the emergency and yet maintain a large program of capital expenditure. Expenditure directly attributable to the emergency has been estimated at $138 million for 1955; what it will be in the succeeding years will largely be governed by political factors, external as well as internal, and consequently is not susceptible of even rough estimation.

In the circumstances, we have concluded that our best course is to draw up a program which, but for the emergency, could be financed from domestic sources. We realize that emergency expenditure will probably continue for some time to be a heavy charge on the budget, limiting the contribution to development which revenues would otherwise make. But, on the other hand, we have made no allowance for possible assistance from the United Kingdom to the Federation in the form of grants or loans in aid of the emergency or for developmental purposes; neither have we taken account of the possibility for external borrowing. We recognize that circumstances may well compel a re-examination of the recommended development program, leading to its curtailment or its extension over a longer period. In any event, even on the most optimistic assumption about the emergency, the funds likely to be available for development purposes will be extremely limited. We accordingly consider it essential that additional revenue be raised and that expenditures be carefully allocated and strictly controlled.

A REVENUE PROSPECTS

About 70% of public revenue in the Federation comes from import and export duties and income taxes. In 1953 these sources provided 30%, 18% and 24% of current revenues respectively. Their trend will, therefore, largely determine the Federation's revenue position over the next few years. All three are closely related to the fortunes of the rubber and tin industries.

A decline in the income of both industries seems probable during the next five-year period, and the consequences for public revenues are unlikely to be offset by a compensating growth in income and profits in other sectors of the economy. For purposes of calculation we have assumed a rubber price for RSS No. 1 of 75 cents per lb. in 1955 and of 65 cents in the following four years. We believe that a conservative estimate of prospective rubber revenues is justified in view of the uncertainties of the rubber market and the competition from and possible improvements in synthetic rubber. We have assumed a decline in the volume of rubber exports during 1955-59, in accordance with the estimates of the Rubber Growers' Association, which are based on the assumptions that targets of the smallholders' replanting program will be achieved, that estates will replant about 60,000 acres a year and that yields of old rubber trees will fall somewhat.

As regards tin, we have assumed that during the next two or three years world production will decline to about world consumption levels and that, under the International Tin Agreement, Malaya's share of this production would be between 45,000 and 50,000 tons, or, say, 47,500 tons. We have also assumed a fall in tin prices to about $350 a picul (133⅓ lbs.) ex smelter in Singapore; this lies in the lower third of the range of prices proposed in the Agreement.

Export Duties

We have assumed that the rates of duty on rubber will remain unchanged at prices below about 75 cents per lb. For tin and other exports we have assumed a continuation of the present schedule of export duties. On these assumptions we estimate that, because of higher average rubber prices, the revenue from export duties will be somewhat higher in 1955 than the 1954 level of around $100 million and will decline thereafter to about 85% of the 1954 figure. We would expect that most of this decline would occur over the next two years as a result of a narrowing of margins between natural and synthetic rubber prices, and a downward adjustment of tin production under the International Agreement. Thereafter, for the latter part of the 1955-59 period, we have assumed that export duty revenues would be reasonably stable, pending the rise in rubber production expected to start in the early 1960's as a result of replanting.

Import Duties

The 1955 level of import duties is likely to be higher than the 1954 figure of about $200 million because of recent increases in and additions to the import duty schedule. Thereafter, a steady downward trend until

1959 or 1960 seems probable since, in our view, some decline in imports for domestic consumption can be expected in the course of the next five years. In 1953 and undoubtedly also in 1954 the expenditure on consumption and investment for Malaya as a whole was larger than the gross national product, the difference being financed in part by drawing on public and private savings accumulated during the boom. As a result, the volume of imports for domestic consumption is probably at a level higher than can be sustained after these accumulated savings are run down. However, these balances are still high and because of this, and allowing for growth in the national income, it is reasonable to assume that there will be no sudden decline in imports. The effect on revenue from import duties may come even more gradually since most of the revenue is derived from commodities for which the demand is fairly steady. We therefore assume that between 1955 and 1959 the yield will fall by only $10 million, from an estimated $215 million to about $205 million.

Income Tax

The problem of forecasting income tax revenue is particularly difficult because of the inadequacy of information on income and income distribution, uncertainties regarding trends of gross income and costs in particular industries, and prospective changes in the pattern of production in the rubber and tin industries. But it is clear that the yield during 1955-59 at present tax rates will be lower than the revised estimate of $140 million for 1954.[1] This figure includes $16 million collected in Singapore in 1953 but not brought to account by the Federation until 1954.

The government has estimated revenue from income tax in 1955 at $125 million. The rise in export income in the latter part of 1954 and the prospect of higher average rubber prices in 1955 than in the preceding two years may be reflected in somewhat larger income tax collections in 1956 than in 1955. Our rough calculations, based on our assumptions regarding the course of rubber and tin prices and production and on a variety of other relevant data, suggest a downward trend thereafter to a level of the order of $110 million in 1959 at present rates of tax. In making

---

[1] The initial budget estimate, as included in Table 1, was $110 million. This, however, did not allow for collections made in Singapore in 1953 on behalf of the Federation but transferred in 1954. Actual collections in the Federation in 1954 have also been above the initial budget estimates.

these calculations we have taken into account the increasing effectiveness in assessment and collection of the tax.

Other Sources of Revenue

In addition to revenues from export and import duties and income tax, there is a long list of lesser revenue sources of Federal, State and local governments and quasi-governmental agencies which together yield a substantial amount. It is obviously impossible to make individual forecasts for all such items over a five-year period, so we have merely assumed a small but steady annual increase in total receipts on the basis of present rates of tax, fee or charge.

B RECOMMENDATIONS FOR INCREASED REVENUE

We have taken as a basis for calculation the following trend and orders of magnitude of total public revenue, at present tax rates, for the period 1955-59 (in millions of dollars):

1955	1956	1957	1958	1959
635	625	610	605	610

Comparable actual revenues in 1953 were $659 million and for 1954, probably about $615 million.[2]

In our opinion, the Federation cannot carry out a significant program of economic and social development at these levels of revenue, even on the assumption that the amount of external assistance in grants or loans would equal total emergency expenditure. Consequently we believe it essential that steps be taken to increase public revenues.

Individual Income Taxes

We think that the government can no longer afford its present relatively low effective rates of tax on individual incomes. The scheduled rates range from 3% on the first $500 slice of chargeable income to only

[2] These figures differ slightly from those in Table 1. Differences are due to the exclusion here of the income from the rubber research cess (expenditures from which are also excluded in the subsequent expenditure estimates) and to revision in the 1954 estimates for (a) income tax revenues previously mentioned; (b) revenue from tin and rubber export duties, which increased; and (c) revenues from import duties, to allow for some adjustment in the 1954 estimates and for the effects of subsequent increases in the rates of duty.

30% on the slice exceeding $50,000, while personal allowances and deductions[3] are higher in relation to per capita national income than in many countries. A married man with two children and an income of $10,000, for instance, pays tax at an effective rate of less than 5%, while one with an income of $100,000 pays only 22% of it in tax. We accordingly recommend that the tax on individuals be raised so as to bring substantially more revenue than is yielded by the present rates. In our view, the maximum rate should be higher than 30% and the scale should be made steeper in the higher income brackets. Personal allowances and deductions should be reduced, but since any reduction would add to the number of taxpayers, the potential additional revenue should be weighed against the additional load which would be thrown on the Inland Revenue Department.

State and Local Revenues

Revenues collected by the States and Settlements and local governments should also be increased. These revenues, which come mainly from land rents, forest revenue, license fees, rates (other than those levied by the three municipalities) and fees and charges for goods and services, appear to us to be low. It may be that the financial relationship between the Federal Government and the State and Settlement Governments has not been conducive to full use by the latter of the sources of revenue at their disposal. Local pressures for expanded and improved education, health and other social services have largely been met by increased Federal grants. We cannot emphasize too strongly that Federal finances can carry the burden of acceding to these pressures only to a limited extent if essential and urgent expenditure in other directions is not to be jeopardized; we believe this limit has nearly been reached. On the other hand, we fully recognize the need and importance of expanding and improving the social services. While the Federal Government should contribute substantially toward their cost, the demand at State and local levels should be accompanied by a willingness to assume a larger share of the cost than at present.

In the preceding chapter the mission has proposed a practical program for expanding the social services. We have also recommended that the rate of expansion in education, medical and health services be geared to the rate at which State and local revenues can be increased for these purposes,

---

[3] $3,000 for a resident taxpayer, $2,000 for his wife and varying amounts for children depending on their number.

so as gradually to reduce the share of the expenditure met from Federal sources. It is estimated that with the proposed program, the revenue from social service fees could be increased from about $5 million in 1954 to about $15 million by 1959. In addition, it would be necessary for State and local governments to add to their revenues for these services by an amount rising from about $3 million in 1956 to about $25 million in 1959. We believe that this is feasible. Local rating has been little developed and offers considerable revenue possibilities through reassessment of rateable values and the levying of higher percentage rates, and by expanding the system of local rating consequent upon the steadily enlarging network of local government.[4] The greatest possible use should be made of specific rates levied for, and identified with, services for which there is a popular demand. Those license fees and other fees and charges which have not been increased during the last few years in line with the fall in the value of money are further sources of additional revenue.

Effect of Recommendations

Assuming that higher individual income tax rates are imposed and that additional State and local revenues are found, we may take the following figures of total public revenue during 1955-59 as a basis for planning (in millions of dollars):

1955	1956	1957	1958	1959
635	630	640	650	665

Given this revenue trend and making favorable assumptions about the level of external assistance and the course of emergency expenditure, it should be possible for the Federation to maintain a significant rate of public investment and still manage its fiscal situation. However, if revenues fall short of our forecasts, if the costs of the emergency should greatly exceed the actual amount of external assistance or if other expenditure requirements should be greater than now seems reasonably likely, it may become necessary to look for additional tax revenues in order to maintain the proposed programs of economic and social development. Such additional revenue can in our opinion be found by increasing import duties and taxes on company profits. But import duties were only recently increased and higher company taxation has disadvantages from the stand-

[4] The reassessment might be done by a local committee in the first instance.

point of its effect on company saving and private investment. We feel it inadvisable therefore to suggest heavier taxation on these sources just now, except as a last resort. Should financial circumstances prove so much less favorable than we have assumed as seriously to jeopardize the programs of public development, we believe that Malaya's long-term interest in maintaining the programs would justify such additional taxation.

Company Taxation and Import Duties

We have estimated roughly that a 10% profits tax on companies (which would not be deductible from dividends for purposes of individual income taxes paid by shareholders), apart from the present income tax of 30%, would yield between $20 million and $25 million a year in additional revenue. Such a tax would not add to the burden of nonresident British companies, since it would presumably be allowed for relief from taxation in the United Kingdom. It would, however, be an additional burden on companies registered in Malaya. Should such a tax become necessary, we think it would be advisable to minimize its effects on small-scale establishments which, as we have noted elsewhere, are fairly characteristic of local enterprise and which seem likely to continue to predominate in the further development of Malayan industry. We would therefore recommend that any additional tax be applicable only to a company's taxable income above a certain minimum level, say $50,000, and that the tax on profits between $50,000 and $100,000 be at a lower rate than on profits above $100,000. This would, of course, reduce the yield below the $20 million to $25 million a year which we estimate could be realized from a flat tax of 10% on all companies. The difference might be made up through some further increases in the schedule of import duties.

Coordination of Income Taxation in the Federation and Singapore

The recommended increase in individual income taxation and the possibility of an increase in company taxation in the Federation raise the question of the financial and administrative difficulties that would result if rates of income taxation differed in the Federation and in Singapore, in view of the fact that the two territories are virtually a single economic unit and now have a unified income tax administration. Although Singapore's financial position is presently much stronger than the Federation's, we believe that it too will need more revenue to finance its development program. We have elsewhere recommended a like increase in individual income tax rates in Singapore and the question of further taxation on company income may also become an issue there. With joint consideration and adoption of changes in rates no difficulty would arise. But so long as the two territories remain under separate governments, with elected majorities in both Legislatures, the difficulties arising out of different rates may well have to be faced at some point; it seems unlikely that the fiscal policies of the two governments will always coincide and that, when they differ, the one will be willing to be circumscribed in its policy by the financial position and fiscal policy of the other.

C RECURRENT EXPENDITURE ESTIMATES

In projecting expenditures during 1955-59, outlays directly attributable to the emergency have been omitted for the reasons already given; economic and social services have been estimated on the basis of the 1954 provisions plus the estimated cost of implementing the mission's recommendations in these fields; and allowance has been made for small but continuing increase for administrative, "normal" police and defense, and miscellaneous expenditure. Since the 1954 estimates which were taken as a base have proved to be somewhat higher in total than actual expenditure —partly no doubt because of a decline in costs since they were prepared— we have reduced the total of our expenditure projections, excluding pensions and debt service, by 5%.

TABLE 2 Recent and Proposed Recurrent Expenditure
on Economic Services, Federation

(*Million $*)

	1953	1954	1955	1956	1957	1958	1959
Transport and communications[1]							
Roads	24.7	25.5	25.6	25.7	25.9	26.0	26.1
Road transport	1.4	1.5	1.5	1.5	1.5	1.5	1.5
Civil aviation	3.2	2.2	2.3	2.3	2.4	2.4	2.4
Marine	2.0	1.9	2.0	2.0	2.1	2.1	2.2
Meteorology	.6	.3	.4	.5	.5	.6	.6
Other	—	.1	.1	.1	.1	.1	.1
	31.9	31.5	31.9	32.1	32.5	32.7	32.9

TABLE 2 (continued)

(Million $)

	1953	1954	1955	1956	1957	1958	1959
Other economic services							
Agriculture[2]	6.1	5.3	6.1	6.7	7.0	7.3	7.6
Veterinary	2.1	2.2	2.4	2.5	2.5	2.5	2.5
Forestry	4.6	4.9	5.5	5.6	5.6	5.6	5.6
Cooperative development	1.6	1.3	1.5	1.6	1.7	1.8	1.9
Drainage and irrigation	10.4	7.7	8.8	9.3	9.6	10.1	10.7
Fisheries	.7	.7	1.0	1.1	1.1	1.1	1.1
Game	.3	.4	.4	.4	.4	.4	.4
Mines and Geological Survey	2.0	3.2	3.8	4.0	4.0	4.0	4.1
Industrial Research Inst.	—	—	—	—	0.3	0.5	0.5
Surveys	5.9	7.3	7.4	7.5	7.5	7.6	7.6
RIDA	4.6	4.0	3.5	3.0	3.0	3.0	3.0
Machinery	.3	.4	.4	.4	.4	.4	.4
Total	70.5	68.9	72.7	74.2	75.6	77.0	78.3

[1] Exclusive of posts and telecommunications, the net revenues from which are included in the revenue estimates with other public commercial services.

[2] Includes estimates of recurrent expenditures involved in proposals for an agricultural marketing division, subsidies for coconut replanting, a land-use survey, and pilot smallholder cocoa and oil palm projects.

Tables 2 and 3 summarize recommended recurrent expenditure in the various economic and social fields, the bases and details of which are discussed elsewhere.

TABLE 3 Recent and Proposed Recurrent Expenditure for Social Services, Federation

(Million $)

	1954	1955	1956	1957	1958	1959
Education	92.3	97.0	105.0	115.0	125.0	134.0
Medical	56.8	57.1	59.5	62.6	65.9	68.9
Social welfare	4.8	5.8	6.2	6.3	6.6	7.0
Labor and others	5.5	6.3	6.8	7.4	8.0	8.5
Total	159.4	166.2	177.5	191.3	205.5	218.4

On the basis of these estimates, the projected total current expenditures are summarized in Table 4, together with estimated trends of revenue, reflecting the increases proposed by the mission.

TABLE 4 Estimates of Prospective Revenue and Recurrent Expenditure, excluding Emergency Expenditure and External Aid, Federation

(Million $)

	1954	1955	1956	1957	1958	1959
Recurrent expenditure						
Economic services	69	73	74	76	77	78
Social services	159	166	178	191	206	218
Administration, police and						
defense and miscellaneous .	269	273	277	281	285	289
	497	512	529	548	568	585
Reduced by 5%	472	486	503	521	540	556
Pensions and debt service[1]						
(net)	37	40	50	55	60	66
Total recurrent expenditure.	509	526	553	576	600	622
Rounded total	510	525	555	575	600	620
Revenue (reflecting mission's						
recommendations)	615	635	630	640	650	665
Revenue surplus[2]	105	110	75	65	50	45

[1] Debt service includes sinking fund only in 1954; net interest credit in this year included in revenue.
[2] Excluding capital expenditure, emergency expenditure and external assistance.

D PROSPECTIVE CAPITAL ACCOUNTS

According to the preceding forecasts, it is estimated that with the proposed increases in taxation and with the recommended levels of recurrent expenditure (excluding expenditures directly attributable to the emergency), government savings from current revenue from domestic sources would run from just over $100 million in 1955 to about $45 million in 1959.

The mission estimates that an additional $60 million a year could be raised through borrowing from internal sources. This would be in addition to loans already raised by the Central Electricity Board, of which an unspent balance, estimated at about $25 million, is available in 1955. It is expected that the bulk of domestic funds available for loans to the government would be from the Employees Provident Fund, net contributions to which have been about $60 million a year. With the possibility of some decline in wage rates and some drop in employment in the tin industry the figure may be somewhat lower over the next few years; we have therefore assumed that about $50 million annually would be available from the Fund.

Another source of public borrowing is the deposits of the Post Office Savings Bank. The net increase in deposit liabilities was $12 million in 1952 and $8 million in 1953. These deposits may continue to be a source of public borrowing, especially if the policy of investing the greater part of them abroad is modified. We have assumed that between the Post Office Savings Bank and various private sources the government could raise at least an additional $10 million a year in loans.

With available loan capital of about $85 million in 1955 (including the unspent credits of the Central Electricity Board) and of about $60 million a year thereafter, the revenues available for public capital expenditure (exclusive of withdrawals from reserves) may be estimated as follows (in millions of dollars):

	1955	1956	1957	1958	1959
Current revenue balance	110	75	65	50	45
Government borrowing	85	60	60	60	60
Total	195	135	125	110	105

The borrowing estimates can be considered conservative. We believe, however, that such estimates are justified for planning purposes in view of the potentially large margin of error in projecting revenues and recurrent expenditure, and because we have omitted both emergency expeditures and external assistance. To the extent that borrowing possibilities are more favorable, the very tight financial position of the Federation will thereby be relieved. But even excluding the costs of the emergency and allowing for a determined effort to increase public revenues, it is difficult on the basis of our assumptions to see how income and borrowing together can produce more than an average of some $130 million to $135 million a year for public investment during most of the 1955-59 period.

E RECOMMENDED GOVERNMENT CAPITAL EXPENDITURE

Individual items of recommended capital expenditure in the economic and social fields over the next five years have been presented in the preceding sections of the report and are also discussed in greater detail in the various Technical Reports. These recommendations have, of course, been formulated with an eye to prospective public resources available for capital expenditure and to the priorities among the many competing demands upon public finances. The mission has tried to outline a program of capital expenditure which, within the limitations of resources, will make the largest possible direct contribution to what seem the most logical and promising lines of economic development and will at the same time give realistic recognition to the needs and pressures for, and the important indirect contributions to be derived from, additional social services.

It should be noted that in many cases the bases are lacking for an accurate estimate of capital costs and that the estimates presented are often only very rough approximations, sometimes being little more than token figures.

The mission's recommended program of public capital expenditure is summarized in Table 5.

TABLE 5 Recommended Public
Capital Expenditures, 1955–59, Federation

(Million $)

	1955	1956	1957	1958	1959	Total
Transport and communications						
Ports	4.4	10.1	9.3	6.8	1.8	32.4
Railways	4.7	6.1	5.8	5.8	1.5	23.9
Roads and road transport.	19.2	18.1	19.0	19.5	18.5	94.3
Civil aviation	0.5	0.7	0.2	0.2	—	1.6
Posts	0.9	0.9	0.9	0.9	0.9	4.5
Telecommunications	3.2	2.9	3.9	3.8	3.8	17.6
Broadcasting	0.1	0.1	0.4	0.6	0.6	1.8
Meteorology	0.1	0.2	0.1	0.1	—	0.5
Surveys	0.8	0.2	—	—	—	1.0
Agriculture, forestry, fisheries						
Agriculture Department	1.1	0.7	0.4	0.4	0.3	2.9
Veterinary Department	0.6	0.3	0.3	0.1	0.2	1.5

TABLE 5　(continued)

(Million $)

	1955	1956	1957	1958	1959	Total
Forestry Department	1.1	1:0	1.3	1.2	1.0	5.6
Land-use survey	0.1	0.8	0.8	0.8	0.8	3.3
Pilot cocoa and oil palm schemes	—	0.5	1.0	1.0	0.1	2.6
Drainage and irrigation	10.0	10.0	11.0	12.0	12.0	55.0
Cooperative development	0.2	0.1	0.1	0.1	—	0.5
Fisheries Department	1.0	0.8	0.4	0.2	—	2.4
Rubber replanting grants to estates and smallholders	15.0	20.0	25.0	30.0	35.0	125.0
Mining						
Mines Department	0.4	0.1	0.1	0.1	0.1	0.8
Geological survey	0.2	0.2	0.2	0.2	0.2	1.0
Aeromagnetic survey	—	0.7	0.7	—	—	1.4
Industrial Research Institute	—	0.5	0.5	—	—	1.0
Rural and industrial development	3.0	3.0	3.0	3.0	3.0	15.0
Power						
Central Electricity Board	26.7	14.9	10.0	10.0	10.0	71.6
Penang	6.4	5.4	2.4	.5	.5	15.2
Social services						
Education	10.0	11.0	11.0	11.0	11.0	54.0
Medical and health	4.6	8.2	9.8	9.6	4.8	37.0
Social welfare	0.8	0.7	0.6	0.5	0.5	3.1
Other social services[1]	1.1	1.2	1.1	1.1	1.1	5.6
Works						
PWD workshops	1.0	2.0	1.0	0.5	0.5	5.0
Sewers and water supply (including Penang)	6.5	8.0	10.0	12.0	14.0	50.5
Govt. buildings and housing	7.0	7.0	7.0	7.0	7.0	35.0
New village resettlement	2.0	4.0	5.0	2.0	1.0	14.0
Other capital expenditure						
Loans to Housing Trust and Building Society	2.5	2.5	4.0	4.0	4.0	17.0
Loans to local governments	.5	.5	1.0	1.5	1.5	5.0
Petaling Jaya development	1.0	1.0	1.0	1.5	1.5	6.0
Census	—	—	2.0	—	—	2.0
Miscellaneous	12.0	12.0	12.0	12.0	12.0	60.0
Total	148.7	156.4	162.3	160.0	149.2	776.6
Rounded total	150	155	160	160	150	775

[1] Including the Labour Department and the Federation's share of the University of Malaya's program (net of approved Colonial Development and Welfare grant).

These rates of proposed capital expenditure are slightly above the rates of capital outlay on revenue and capital accounts of the governments and government entities (excluding public security and emergency and additions to stocks) in 1952 and 1953. The totals in those years were $116 million and $122 million respectively. Budget estimates for 1954 show a substantial increase in comparable capital expenditure to rather more than $200 million. It seems probable, however, that the actual accounts for 1954 will show capital outlays far short of this estimate.

The preceding estimates of financial resources available for public investment in 1955-59 are short of the total recommended expenditure by the following amounts (in millions of dollars):

	1955	1956	1957	1958	1959	Total
Estimated availability of financing for public capital expenditure	195	135	125	110	105	670
Recommended capital expenditures	150	155	160	160	150	775
Deficit (−) or Surplus (+)	+45	−20	−35	−50	−45	−105

The mission believes that an over-all deficit of this magnitude can be safely financed from the available balances of the government, about $220 million at the end of 1954, if, as recommended, measures are taken to ensure a continuing ordinary revenue surplus through higher taxation and prudent expenditure policies.

II SINGAPORE

In contrast to the Federation, Singapore's public finances have been consistently favorable over the past several years. For the period 1949-53 inclusive, ordinary revenues were sufficient to cover the entirety of capital and recurrent expenditures. Borrowing by the Singapore City Council during 1951-53 was more than counterbalanced by accumulation of reserves by the Colony Government and public agencies.

The budget estimates for 1954 again show a substantial current surplus, although this time it is estimated at less than total capital expenditure. Actual expenditures of the Colony Government are, however, reported to be below the estimates and the final accounts of the Colony for 1954 are expected to show an over-all surplus rather than the deficit of $26 million shown in the initial estimates.

TABLE 6   Consolidated Public Finances of Singapore

(Million $)

	1949	1950	1951	1952	1953	1954[1] (estimates)
Revenue						
Income tax	30	27	51	73	103	70
Import duties	40	44	58	62	64	62
Excise, stamp and other duties and						
taxes	13	15	22	24	23	23
Licenses	7	8	11	12	13	12
Local government rates	8	9	11	13	17	18
Revenue from property and net						
interest receipts	5	5	10	11	11	8
Fees and charges	10	11	15	16	19	23
Surplus of commercial undertakings .	17	21	26	25	28	28
Miscellaneous	7	4	7	11	7	6
	137	144	211	247	285	250
Grants from U.K.	—	—	1	—	1	10
Total revenue	137	144	212	247	286	260
Expenditure						
Economic services	4	4	4	6	6	8
Social services[2]	19	25	34	41	49	64
Defense and police	15	12	20	33	28	39
Pensions, etc.	5	5	5	5	6	7
Sinking funds	7	8	8	10	11	12
Administrative and miscellaneous . .	55	52	57	57	60	68
Total recurrent expenditures . .	105	106	128	152	160	198
Revenue less recurrent expenditure . .	+32	+38	+84	+95	+126	+62
Capital expenditure	21	32	57	84	79	133
Over-all surplus (+) or deficit (−) . .	+11	+6	+27	+11	+47	−71

[1] These figures are based on the initial budget estimates of the various governmental bodies included in the consolidation. Revised figures for all these bodies were not available when the report was completed but the actual accounts are expected to show a much more favorable position for 1954 than these figures indicate.

[2] For explanation of slight differences between these figures and those shown in Chapter 7, see note to Table 2(B) in the Statistical Appendix, Part V.

The consolidated financial results since 1949 of the Colony Government, the City Council and its commercial departments, the Rural, Education and Hospital Boards, the Singapore Improvement Trust and the Singapore Harbour Board,[5] are shown in Table 6.

Although these figures reflect a favorable financial position for the years through 1953 and the accounts for 1954 seem likely to show a similar situation, they also give warning of less comfortable fiscal prospects in the future. Of particular concern are the leveling-off of revenues and the steady rate of increase in expenditures, especially for social services. The actual results for 1953 were somewhat less favorable than the figures suggest, since income tax revenue included $16 million collected by Singapore on behalf of the Federation in 1953 but not transferred until 1954.

Upon careful consideration of revenue prospects, of the funds necessary to meet commitments already made by the government for social services to the rapidly growing population, and of reasonable financial requirements for other government services, it is evident that Singapore's financial situation will become increasingly difficult over the next five years.

The following discussion presents a summary of the bases for this conclusion.[6]

Revenue Prospects

More than half of the combined revenues of public bodies in Singapore comes from income taxes and import duties collected by the Colony Government.

Income Tax. The mission has found, as might be expected, a fairly close correspondence between the trends of total Malayan trade, including profits of the entrepot trade, and income assessed for taxation in Singapore. There is, however, a considerable time lag between the earning of taxable income and the assessment and collection of the tax on it; for example, it is roughly estimated that of the total Singapore collections in 1953, about 35% was on incomes earned partly in 1950 and mainly in 1951, and about 40% on incomes earned partly in 1951 and mainly in 1952. In other words,

---

[5] The fiscal year of the Harbour Board is July-June while that of the others is January-December. The Harbour Board accounts have, however, been taken as if they were for the calendar year with, e.g., 1948-49 taken as 1949, etc.

[6] Forecasts, unless otherwise stated, are in millions of Malayan dollars.

the 1953 tax collections of $87 million (excluding amounts transferable to the Federation) still reflected to a considerable extent the relatively high income levels of 1951 and early 1952. The drop in collections to around $70 million in 1954 indicates that the influence of boom period earnings on subsequent tax revenue had largely disappeared.

Over the next few years we would expect income tax revenue, at present rates, to remain fairly close to the present level. The prospect of some decline in total Malayan trade over the next few years is likely to be reflected in lower income tax revenues. It seems reasonable to expect, however, that the reduction in revenue will be largely offset by increasing efficiency in income tax administration and by a growth in economic activity and income not directly related to external trade. The government has estimated 1955 income tax revenue at $70 million and we have taken this figure as a basis for calculation in the period 1956-59 also.

Import Duties. We have assumed a slight downward trend in import duties during 1955-59, in line with our expectation of a decline in total Malayan imports for domestic consumption in this period. As in the Federation,[7] we expect that the decline in yield in Singapore will be proportionately smaller than the reduction in total imports. Only liquors, tobacco and petroleum are dutiable in Singapore; of these the volume of petroleum imports seems likely to increase rather than decrease, and while liquor and tobacco imports may show some decline, we would not expect this to be proportionately greater than for Malayan imports as a whole. It therefore seems reasonable to assume that the annual revenue from import duties will remain within 5-10% of the present level.

Other Revenues. For other revenues of the Colony Government, the City Council and other governmental bodies and public agencies, we have assumed a gradual increase in most items. We believe this is reasonable for most revenue sources, in view of the steady growth of the city and the expansion of governmental services. The net revenue from commercial undertakings seems likely to increase substantially as a result of recent and prospective additions to the capacity of existing public utilities, the acquisition of the telephone service and the increase in rental housing to be built by the Singapore Improvement Trust. The main exception to this upward trend is to be found in net interest receipts; these are likely to be supplanted by net interest payments as a result of additional borrowing and a decline in reserves. On the whole we would expect that a rising

[7] See p. 193, *supra.*

trend in revenue, at present tax rates, would more than offset any decline in import duty revenues, resulting in a small increase in Singapore public revenue as a whole over the 1955-59 period.

On these assumptions we estimate total revenues in Singapore as follows (in millions of dollars):

1955	1956	1957	1958	1959
250	250	260	260	270

Expenditure Estimates

The mission has prepared estimates of what it considers the probable public recurrent and capital expenditures implicit in its various recommendations and in commitments already undertaken in the administrative, economic, commercial and social services.

It may be stated at the outset that these expenditures, while reasonable in relation to the prospective needs of the rapidly growing population of Singapore, add to figures which seem likely, at present tax rates, to be beyond the prospective financial resources available from domestic sources for public expenditure. The financial requirements created by the needs of the growing population are particularly heavy in the fields of education and medical and health services, and housing, sewerage, water supply, public utilities and other municipal services.

The cost of meeting the commitment of the government to provide educational facilities for the entire population of primary school age (7-12 years), together with needed provisions for additional secondary and vocational education, would, according to our calculations, more than double the recurrent costs of education over the next five years and would require a large capital outlay for additional schools and equipment. Most of this increase, as discussed elsewhere, is simply a matter of the arithmetic of present educational commitments and the prospect of an increase in the primary school-age population over the next five years by as much as 50%.

The estimates of financial requirements for medical and health and social welfare services and housing, while large, are by no means excessive in relation to the problems in these fields. Indeed, the provision for housing construction by the Singapore Improvement Trust no more than keeps pace with population growth, without catching up on arrears.

The estimated costs of additional electricity, gas, water, harbor and other utilities and sewerage again are based on minimum requirements in relation to prospective growth in demand.

Besides these social and commercial services, the mission has included in its estimates of needed expenditure some provision for additional economic services, which are relatively small, as might be expected in a large urban center, and for the various other recurrent and capital outlays involved in maintaining the administrative establishment.

As in the case of the Federation, the budget estimates for 1954 have been taken as the starting point for calculations of estimated expenditure. The latter, therefore, largely reflect price and cost conditions in late 1953 when the 1954 budget estimates were prepared. In view of subsequent reductions in costs, an over-all deduction of 5% has been made in the total recurrent estimates. It should also be noted that many of the estimates are only rough approximations, in the absence at present of any basis for more reliable calculations. Some of the amounts included for capital expenditure are indeed little more than token figures.

The bases of the mission's estimates of reasonable public financial needs

TABLE 7　Prospective Recurrent Expenditure, Singapore

(Million $)

	1953 (actual)	1954 (estimates)	1955	1956	1957	1958	1959
Economic services[1]	6	8	9	10	10	11	11
Social services							
Education	19	29	35	41	47	55	63
Polytechnic Institute	—	—	—	1	2	2	2
Medical and health	22	26	34	36	39	43	45
Social welfare and other[2] . . .	8	9	12	16	18	21	23
Administration, police and defense and miscellaneous	88	107	115[3]	107	109	111	113
Sub-total	143	179	205	211	225	243	257
Less 5%	(143)	170	195	201	214	231	244
Pensions and debt service[4]	17	19	19	21	23	26	28
Total recurrent expenditure .	160	189	214	222	237	257	272
Rounded total			215	220	235	255	270

[1] Increases are mainly to cover recurrent expenditures involved in recommendations for additional services in agriculture, industry, fisheries, civil aviation, meteorology and road maintenance.

[2] Including the Labour Department and the University of Malaya.

[3] Includes exceptionally, for 1955 only, $10 million for special defense expenditure.

[4] Net interest payments are included only in 1957, 1958 and 1959. For 1953 and in the figures for 1954–56 estimated net interest receipts are included on the revenue side.

TABLE 8 Prospective Capital Requirements, Singapore

(Million $)

	1955	1956	1957	1958	1959	Total (1955–59)
Economic services						
Civil aviation	10.0	8.0	—	—	—	18.0
Kallang Bridge, and approaches	3.0	5.0	4.0	1.0	—	13.0
Other roads	0.5	2.0	4.0	4.0	4.5	15.0
Sewers	4.3	8.1	8.7	4.7	5.0	30.8
Fish and produce markets . .	—	1.0	2.0	1.0	1.0	5.0
Industrial Research Institute .	—	0.5	0.5	—	—	1.0
Quarantine stations	0.7	0.8	0.6	0.5	—	2.6
Abattoirs.	0.5	0.5	—	—	—	1.0
Meteorology	0.3	0.1	—	—	—	0.4
Total	19.3	26.0	19.8	11.2	10.5	86.8
Social services						
Education	11.0	11.0	11.0	11.0	11.0	55.0
Medical and health	7.8	8.0	7.2	7.4	6.4	36.8
Polytechnic Institute	5.2	—	—	—	—	5.2
Social welfare and others[1]. . .	1.4	2.0	2.6	1.9	1.7	9.6
Total	25.4	21.0	20.8	20.3	19.1	106.6
Commercial services						
Improvement Trust housing .	24.0	30.0	36.0	42.0	48.0	180.0
Electricity	21.1	17.2	14.9	14.3	8.7	76.2
Gas	0.6	0.9	4.1	4.1	0.1	9.8
Water	13.7	11.3	6.0	1.0	1.0	33.0
Harbour Board	5.0	10.0	5.0	—	—	20.0
Posts and telecommunications .	3.2	3.8	4.5	5.3	6.2	23.0
Miscellaneous	2.0	2.0	2.0	2.0	2.0	10.0
Total	69.6	75.2	72.5	68.7	66.0	352.0
Miscellaneous	11.0	12.0	13.0	14.0	15.0	65.0
Grand total	125.3	134.2	126.1	114.2	110.6	610.4
Rounded total	125	135	125	115	110	610

[1] Including the Labour Department and Singapore's share of the University of Malaya's program (net of approved Colonial Development and Welfare grant).

in Singapore over the next five years have been presented in the appropriate sections of Parts II and III and are discussed further in the various Technical Reports. They are summarized in Tables 7 and 8 for comparison with prospective public revenues and other available public financial resources. As noted previously, the result is a considerable gap between prospective needs and resources. Means for closing this gap will be considered at the conclusion of this section.

As in the case of the financial results and the revenue projections presented previously, the estimates of expenditure requirements are a consolidation of projected financial needs of the various authorities and public agencies in Singapore, namely the Colony Government, the City Council,[8] the Education and Hospital Boards, the Improvement Trust and the Harbour Board.

In summary, the preceding estimates would result in an excess of recurrent and capital expenditure over revenue in the period 1955-59 as shown in Table 9.

TABLE 9   Summary of Singapore Financial Prospects

(Million $)

	1955	1956	1957	1958	1959
Revenue	250	250	260	260	270
Recurrent expenditure	215	220	235	255	270
Balance	+35	+30	+25	+5	—
Capital expenditure	125	135	125	115	110
Excess of total expenditure over revenue	90	105	100	110	110

Public borrowing in Singapore (all by the City Council) has amounted in the past few years to around $30 million annually. Additional borrowing opportunities should be created by the establishment of the Employees Provident Fund, which is expected to begin operations in 1955. It is assumed that the Fund's balances will be invested for the most part in Malaya, since its liabilities will be almost entirely there. With the mobilization of savings through the Fund, with some additional borrowing from private individuals and institutions, and with the investment of a larger proportion of Post Office Savings Bank deposits in Singapore rather than abroad, domestic borrowing possibilities can be put at about $40 million in 1955 and about $50-60 million a year thereafter.

Part of the accumulated balances of the Colony Government will also

[8] Which is to become the City and Island Council and to encompass the functions of the present Rural Board.

be available. At the end of 1954 the "free" reserves of the Colony are likely to amount to around $185 million (after making allowance for the capital cost of acquiring the telephone undertaking). In addition, reserves of the Singapore Harbour Board available for financing part of the proposed port improvement program can be put at about $15 million. In our view, these reserves could be safely utilized to the extent of about $100 million over the next five years.

With these estimates of borrowing and utilization of reserves the preceding estimated deficits could be covered to the extent shown in Table 10.

TABLE 10   Covering of Estimated Singapore Deficits
by Borrowing and Use of Reserves

(*Million $*)

	1955	1956	1957	1958	1959	Total
Excess of total expenditure over revenue . . .	90	105	100	110	110	515
Domestic borrowing	35	55	55	55	55	255
Utilization of reserves	55	45	—	—	—	100
Uncovered deficit	—	5	45	55	55	160

Mission's Recommendations

The figures in Table 10 clearly indicate that the preceding estimates of revenue and expenditure cannot be accepted as a realistic basis for future planning. They imply excessive dependence on external financial assistance and would in a few years place the government in the position of having to devote its entire revenue to recurrent expenditure with no margin of saving for capital purposes.

It seems essential, therefore, that the gap between revenue and expenditure be reduced to manageable proportions. This could be achieved by increasing revenues, cutting expenditures or a combination of the two.

On the revenue side, as in the Federation, we recommend an increase in the present low effective rates of individual income tax by raising the maximum rate of tax considerably above 30%, by a steeper graduation of rates for the higher income brackets and by reducing the personal allowances and deductions for dependents. We have not tried to propose specific changes in rates, allowances or deductions but we do recommend that the objective should be a substantial increase in the present yield from personal income tax. To preserve the advantages of uniform rates and of a joint tax administration, the schedule and allowances and deductions should, we suggest, be revised in consultation with the Federation.

This proposed increase in income tax will not, however, suffice alone. We suggest raising, and more effectively collecting, the charges for in-patient hospital care. We also recommend an increase in the education rate and in other fees, licenses and charges. It seems reasonable to expect that approximately $10 million a year in additional revenue could be realized from these sources by 1959. This sum, plus the revenue from a higher personal income tax, would reduce by about $85 million the previously calculated uncovered deficit of $160 million for the five-year period, leaving a gap of about $75 million.

On the basis, then, of the preceding estimates and recommendations the prospective financial position may be summarized as shown in Table 11.

TABLE 11   Revised Estimates, Singapore

(Million $)

	1955	1956	1957	1958	1959	Total
Revenue						
Previous estimates	250	250	260	260	270	
Additional income tax and other revenue . .	—	20	21	22	23	
Revised estimates of revenue	250	270	281	282	293	
Recurrent expenditure	215	220	235	255	270	
Surplus of revenue over recurrent expenditure	35	50	46	27	23	181
Capital expenditure	125	135	125	115	110	610
Excess of total expenditure over revenue . . .	90	85	79	88	87	429
Less:						
Domestic borrowing and use of reserves . .						355
Uncovered deficit						74

While these revised estimates would indicate an uncovered deficit of about $75 million for the five-year period, it is to be noted that no allowance has been made for any additional financing from external sources in the form of Colonial Development and Welfare grants from the United

Kingdom and possibly of external borrowing. Moreover, our estimates of revenue and domestic borrowing may prove conservative, especially if the levels of Malayan trade are higher than we have anticipated. And some of the items of expenditure may fall short of our forecasts because physical limitations may prevent spending at rates which would otherwise be desirable.

On the other hand, should our revenue forecasts prove overly optimistic or borrowing possibilities more limited than we now think it reasonable to expect, it may become necessary to consider further economies, additional revenue measures and perhaps a somewhat greater reduction in reserves than has been suggested.

Suggested economies in our proposed public investment program might include about $10 million over the five-year period in capital expenditures for buildings and equipment in the social service fields, to be achieved by the adoption of somewhat less expensive construction standards than now proposed, and a reduction by about 10% in the proposed capital expenditure on roads and posts and telecommunications, resulting in a saving of about $5 million for the five years.

The mission does not suggest a reduction at present in the recurrent social service expenditures included in the preceding estimates for 1955-59. We believe that the figures for health and medical services, social welfare and vocational training are not excessive in relation to the needs of the Colony and that the services recommended in these fields are essential to the fostering of satisfactory economic as well as social development. The same may be said of the recommended large capital outlay for the Singapore Improvement Trust. With regard to the proposed expenditure on primary education, the largest item in the increasing recurrent requirements for social services, we do not feel able to suggest reduced expenditure in view of the very large "hump" to be expected in the rate of increase in the primary school-age population during the next few years, and the commitments which have been made to provide universal education in this age group. But if suggested reductions in our expenditure estimates should prove insufficient, it may be necessary to give further consideration to ways of reducing those commitments.

The chief source of additional revenue, should that become necessary, would be an increase in taxation of company profits. We estimate that an addition of 10% to the present rate of company taxation would yield an additional $15 million or more annually, if the additional tax is not deductible from dividends paid to shareholders. In view, however, of the adverse influence of higher taxation of company profits on savings from earnings and on new investment by companies registered in Singapore, we believe that this means of securing additional revenue should not be resorted to unless financial developments make it unavoidable. In this event we would recommend concessions for small-scale enterprise similar to those suggested in the discussion of the Federation.

CHAPTER 9

ORGANIZATIONAL AND INSTITUTIONAL PROPOSALS

In this concluding chapter we consider certain broad institutional and organizational measures which we believe will be conducive to the further development of the Malayan economy and will facilitate the continuing analysis of Malaya's economic problems and the planning and execution of public investment programs.

Our main recommendations in this respect are concerned with the administrative arrangements, chiefly in the Federation, for the formulation of development plans and economic policies; with the financial relationship between the Federal and State and Settlement Governments in the Federation; and with currency and banking institutions and a framework for a coordinated monetary and credit policy for Malaya as a whole.

1 ORGANIZATION FOR DEVELOPMENT PLANNING

We remarked in Chapter 2 that development must be closely planned and controlled if the Federation is to husband its straitened resources and be able to meet the challenge presented by a restricted national income and a fast-growing population. To achieve this, certain organizational changes appear to be necessary, in addition to the modifications in the present financial relationship between the Federal and the State and Settlement Governments recommended subsequently. It seems to us, moreover, that the impending constitutional advances may, of themselves, require these or similar organizational changes, since the existing machinery and procedures may well be found to be inappropriate or inadequate with an elected majority in the Federal Legislative Council.

Economic Committee of the Executive Council

Coordination of all proposals concerning economic development must be the ultimate responsibility of the Federal Executive Council. We consider that this coordination would be more effectively achieved if it were made the special responsibility of a small committee comprising those members of the Executive Council most closely and directly concerned with economic development. A small committee would be able to give closer and more frequent attention to the many problems in this field than could the full Council and would, incidentally, relieve the other members of detailed consideration of these problems, thus giving more time for matters for which they have particular responsibility.

We accordingly recommend that an Economic Committee of the Executive Council be set up, to consider all development proposals involving significant expenditures from government funds, and to recommend to the full Council which proposals should be implemented and in what order of priority. The Committee should also review the progress made on development projects being undertaken. But it should have a broader function than this if it is to serve its purpose. Many matters, such as land use, taxation, tariff policy, the encouragement of private enterprise and so forth, closely affect economic development without making any direct call on public funds. All such matters, and, in general, all major matters of economic significance should be the concern of the Committee and the subject of its consideration and recommendation to the full Council.

The Committee should, we propose, consist of the Financial Secretary and the Members for Economic Affairs, Natural Resources, Transport and Communications, and Works. Other members of the Executive Council would be coopted to the Committee on occasions when matters of particular concern to departments in their portfolios are to be discussed. We suggest that during the coming stage of constitutional advances the Financial Secretary should preside over the Committee, in view of his particularly close concern with, and the influence of fiscal policy on, economic development.

Association of State and Settlement
Governments with the Economic Committee

The State and Settlement Governments have a close interest in economic development and on them is conferred the executive authority in many of the most important fields of government. We accordingly recommend joint consultation from time to time between the Economic Committee and representatives of the State and Settlement Governments on economic development matters of particular concern to the States and Settlements. A formal permanent consultative body for this purpose would not seem to be necessary; we suggest, however, that meetings be held not less than twice a year for the discussions we have in mind.

Secretariat for the Economic Committee

The Committee will require a Secretariat if it is to function properly. Economic planning is at present a function of the Economic Division of the Treasury. But this is only one of several responsibilities assigned to the Division which has, we believe, been so burdened with administrative duties as not to be able to give its planning function the detached and constant attention essential for satisfactory performance. We recommend that this Division be reorganized and strengthened to serve as a Secretariat to the Committee. In particular, the Secretariat's duties should be:

1. to assess each year the finance likely to be available for all public investment projects during the next few years, including those of State and Settlement Governments, local governments and public agencies as well as of the Federal Government;

2. to review, in the light of this assessment and without concerning itself with engineering or other technical aspects, all development proposals submitted by the Federal departments or requiring Federal financing and to coordinate them into a program of recommended priorities for consideration by the Economic Committee;

3. to keep informed of the progress of all approved development projects and report thereon periodically to the Committee;

4. to initiate, with the Committee's approval, such studies and surveys in the economic field as may appear to be necessary, employing outside consultants if that seems expedient; and

5. to submit to the Committee all major matters of economic significance, with such data and analysis as may be required for proper consideration.

The Secretariat should not be required to assume responsibility for any of the day-to-day work of the Treasury and should have no administrative duties other than those narrowly arising from its secretariat functions. To serve the Committee effectively, it must keep well informed on trends in the economy. Where there are gaps in Malayan economic statistics, the Secretariat should seek to have them filled by the appropriate departments.

Although administratively part of the Treasury, the Secretariat should be responsible to the Economic Committee.[1] It should be headed by an official of status not inferior to that of head of a major Federal department and should have a small, well-qualified technical staff of economists and such other professionals as experience may show to be necessary.

Elsewhere we have recommended that the land-use survey team should be responsible to the Head of the Secretariat.

Technical Advisory Committee on Development

To assist the Secretariat in its task of reviewing and coordinating development proposals, and to associate departmental heads more formally with the planning of economic development, we further recommend the appointment of a Technical Advisory Committee consisting of the heads of the Federal departments most closely connected with economic development, under the chairmanship of the Head of the Secretariat. The departments we have in mind for representation on the Committee are Agriculture, Drainage and Irrigation, Forestry, Geological Survey, Lands, Mines, Survey, Treasury and Works. The Committee would thus have substantially the same membership as the Federal Lands Advisory Committee which was appointed in 1952 with wider terms of reference than its title suggests. The tasks with which the committee was charged include "formulation of the principles on which the utilization of land, water and other resources in the Federation of Malaya should be based," and "advising the High Commissioner and State and Settlement Governments on the basis for planning the integrated development of the Federation of Malaya in its varied land and water resources." This Committee has not yet, however, got into its stride, largely because it was not provided with an adequate secretariat, and we suggest that it should be disbanded as unnecessary if the Technical Advisory Committee we have recommended is appointed.

Rural and Industrial Development Authority

RIDA was conceived as an agency to develop rural areas and thus to raise the economic level of the Malays, who are preponderantly rural, but

[1] This duality need not lead to organizational difficulties so long as the Financial Secretary remains Chairman of the Committee. In the event that a Cabinet Office is set up in a further stage of constitutional advance, the desirability of transferring the Secretariat to that Office might be considered.

when effectively constituted in 1950 it assumed the wider responsibility of promoting rural and industrial development as a whole.[2] Its functions have been stated to be twofold—"to promote economic development proper through improved methods of production, processing and marketing" and "to assist the rural population to improve its living conditions by the provision of better essential services and amenities."[3] It was incorporated by statute as from the beginning of 1954 with somewhat enlarged powers but substantially unchanged functions. The whole of its funds—some $10 million up to the end of 1953—has been provided by the Federal Government.

RIDA's activities have fallen into four main categories. It has been a financing agency, providing medium- and long-term credit for a variety of small enterprises and, more recently, for housing projects, as well as short-term seasonal credit for cooperative societies. Secondly, it has itself provided and operated certain services, notably a boat building yard in Trengganu, a rubber factory in Johore and tractor services in all but two of the States and Settlements. Thirdly, it has made grants for the construction or improvement of small electricity and water supplies, minor roads, community centers and schools. In providing funds for these last three purposes, it has insisted on self-help in some measure from the community benefited, either in the scheme for which the grant is given or in some other appropriate scheme in the same community.

Fourthly, in cooperation with government departments, RIDA has provided a number of training courses, in various trades, commercial subjects and general rural economy. It is now establishing a Training Division to coordinate all its activities in this field.

Through these activities RIDA has undoubtedly made a substantial contribution to the development of the Federation. Some of this contribution has, however, been made by operating in the same fields as government departments and other public agencies, while leaning heavily on them for technical advice and assistance. If our recommendations for the coordination of development proposals are accepted, it will fall to the Economic Committee of the Executive Council to recommend what additional funds should be allocated to RIDA for these activities. In our view, RIDA could contribute most effectively to development by directing its activities more to fields not occupied by other agencies of government; and

[2] RIDA Progress Report up to 31st December 1951, page 3.
[3] RIDA Progress Report up to 30th June, 1952, page 5.

foremost among such activities we would put that of providing finance and guidance to small enterprises.

Organization for Development in Singapore

We see no need for an Economic Committee and Secretariat in Singapore. We recommend, however, that the small branch in the Secretariat which deals with development matters be strengthened and that each year it assess the finance likely to be available for public investment projects during the succeeding few years, and review all proposals submitted by Colony departments in the light of this assessment, without concerning itself with their engineering or other purely technical aspects. The projects of the City Council and public agencies must, of course, be taken into account. A report on the financial assessment and the review should be submitted to the Executive Council (or Council of Ministers). The branch should also keep itself informed on the progress of all approved Colony development projects and prepare progress reports for the information of the Executive Council (or Council of Ministers).

II FINANCIAL RELATIONSHIP IN THE FEDERATION BETWEEN FEDERAL AND STATE AND SETTLEMENT GOVERNMENTS

The financial powers and responsibilities of the Federal and State and Settlement Governments are regulated by the Federation Agreement. The Third Schedule to the Agreement allocates certain sources of revenue to the States and Settlements. In the main these include certain excise duties; revenue from lands, mines and forests; licenses, fees and charges for goods and services supplied or rendered by State and Settlement departments; revenues of local authorities other than municipalities; and profits distributed by the Currency Commission. All revenues not specifically allocated to the States and Settlements are Federal, and these include the main sources of revenue: import and export duties and income tax. Only the Federal Government is empowered to borrow.

Another Schedule to the Agreement sets out the heads of expenditure to be met from Federal and State and Settlement revenues respectively. The lists contain a number of common heads; in general, the Federal list comprises, insofar as these common heads are concerned, expenditure on Federal headquarters, research, and Federal institutions and works, while the residue of the expenditure on the common heads is left to the States and Settlements. A Federal institution or work is not defined. Both lists leave room for expenditure on unspecified subjects by including, as a last item, "Any other Department, staff, institution, research or work."

The excess of State and Settlement expenditure over revenue from the sources allocated to them is met by lump sum Federal grants determined annually. The Agreement neither prescribes the method by which these grants are to be determined nor gives any guidance on it. How much shall be granted to each State and Settlement for the ensuing year is a matter for annual discussion; the amount of the preceding grant is necessarily taken into account, but the Federal Government's financial prospects and commitments weigh heavily in determining the total amount which can be allocated. In 1954 slightly more than two-thirds of all State and Settlement expenditure was defrayed from these lump sum Federal grants.

The Agreement gives the Federal Government extensive powers of control over States' and Settlements' budgets and finance. The States and Settlements are required to submit estimates of their revenue and expenditure to the Federal Government and must obtain prior Federal approval before including new heads of expenditure or certain new items of expenditure in the estimates. Moreover, they may not add to the number of pensionable posts (other than minor posts) or alter the salaries and emoluments of such posts without Federal approval. The High Commissioner is empowered to make orders, binding upon the State and Settlement Governments, to give effect to these provisions of the Agreement.

The States' and Settlements' estimates of expenditure are also indirectly subjected to the approval of the Federal Legislature by the requirement that they shall be revised if the sum allocated by the Federal Legislature is less than the sum applied for.

The Agreement further provides that any excess of States' and Settlements' revenue over expenditure at the end of the financial year shall lapse to the Federal Government.

Experience during the six years since the Federation was established has shown this system of financial relationships to have many disadvantages and to be unsatisfactory to both the Federal and the State and Settlement Governments. The executive authority vested in the States and

Settlements in many of the most important fields of government, the policy-making powers which they have in practice enjoyed, and the system of lump sum grants have combined to give the States and Settlements considerable power to determine levels of expenditure in these fields, particularly in the social services, without being fully responsible for finding means to defray the expenditure. The division of authority in the Federal Agreement is such that, notwithstanding the powers of control given to it, the Federal Government can be put in the position of having to pay the piper for tunes called by the States and Settlements. Secondly, the distribution of expenditures over a wide field is largely determined by the States and Settlements, though the national interest may require, for example, that more be spent on economic services and less on social services. Thirdly, the system gives little or no financial independence to the State and Settlement Governments, limited incentive for the development of the sources of revenue under their control, and small encouragement to a proper attitude towards economy, for once the amount of the Federal grant has been determined, the benefits of any saving would accrue to the Federal Government. Fourthly, the determination of the amount of the federal grant is a perennial source of contention. And lastly, planning is made more difficult by uncertainty about the size of the Federal grant from year to year.

In other federal systems, experience has shown that there is no final solution to the perplexing problem of how best to allocate revenues between the federal and regional governments so that each shall have the revenues needed for the discharge of its responsibilities; modifications become necessary because of changed conditions, and are made from time to time. This necessity has now risen in the Federation; substantial modification of the financial arrangements prescribed in the Federation Agreement is, in our view, essential to the best management of the Federation's financial resources and to the more effective use of these resources for the development of the country.

There are two approaches to the problem. One is to make the State and Settlement Governments fully responsible for both policy and execution in certain fields, and to allocate to them a constitutionally prescribed share of Federal revenue, supplemented perhaps by grants, so that, with their own sources of revenue, they would be enabled to meet their obligations. The alternative is to devise within the present constitutional framework a system of Federal grants which, while giving the State and Settlement Governments more financial independence, would not have the undesirable features of the present comprehensive lump sum grants.

The first approach would require fundamental constitutional changes. In addition, it is open to the objections that a satisfactory, practicable scheme for the allocation of a share in the major sources of Federal revenue to the eleven States and Settlements could not be devised and that it would make for less coordination in development instead of the closer coordination which we believe to be essential. We therefore recommend the alternative.

Specifically, we make the following recommendations:

1. The Federal lump sum grants should be discontinued;

2. The Federal Government should make specific grants to the States and Settlements for education and for medical and health services, as recommended in Chapter 7, to be used—in accordance with a predetermined pattern of sharing costs—in carrying out long-range Federal programs; the States and Settlements should be required to submit annual estimates for prior Federal approval, and controls should be instituted to assure that Federal funds are used only for federally approved plans;

3. The Federal Government should make specific grants for the full amount of States' and Settlements' expenditure on drainage and irrigation, agriculture, forestry and veterinary services. Prior Federal approval of State and Settlement estimates of expenditure on these services should be required, and the Federal grant would be the amount of the approved estimate or the expenditure actually incurred, whichever were the less;

4. The Federal Government should similarly make specific grants for capital expenditure for "new villages." We have elsewhere remarked on the importance of ensuring the permanent success of the resettlement scheme.

5. With the exception of profits distribution by the Currency Commission, the State and Settlement Governments should continue to retain revenues from the sources now allocated to them, including revenues derived from services financed by specific Federal grants. (The Federation's share of the distributed profits of the Currency Board or of a Central Bank in the event of its establishment is more appropriately a Federal revenue; the historical reasons for distributing such profits among the States and Settlements appear to be no longer valid.)

6. To enable the States and Settlements to meet the difference between their remaining recurrent expenditure and revenue from the sources allo-

cated to them, and to provide them with a margin for capital expenditure (other than on services financed by specific Federal grants), the Federal Government should make an annual per capita grant to each State and Settlement. The grant might be per head of the whole population of the State or Settlement or per adult only. In either case, the enumeration in the 1947 or subsequent census should be used until such time as the annual estimates of population have become sufficiently reliable to be used in the intercensal years. The per capita grant should be the same for all States and Settlements and should be announced annually by the Federal Government before the States and Settlements prepare their estimates for the year in respect of which the grant is to be made. For the purpose of framing the long-term programs for education and medical and health services, the State and Settlement Governments would, however, require to know the probable amount of the grant during each of the five or six years.

7. Supplementary grants should be made for a period of years to the less advanced States of Kelantan, Pahang, Perlis and Trengganu to enable them to raise the standard of services other than those financed by specific Federal grants.

8. For a period of not more than three years, special grants should be made to any State or Settlement which would be seriously embarrassed by the introduction of the new system of grants. The purpose of these special grants would be to give a breathing space for adjustments to the new system, and the grants should be reduced progressively each year.

9. Consideration should be given to the allocation of additional sources of revenue to the States and Settlements. We particularly have in mind motor vehicle license fees.

10. When the Federal Government's financial position permits, each State and Settlement should be granted a sum sufficient to provide it with working balances of reasonable amounts. Ownership of these balances will contribute to the greater financial independence of the States and Settlements which we consider to be desirable.

11. The States and Settlements should retain any surplus of revenue from the sources allocated to them and from nonspecific grants over their expenditures on services not financed by specific grants and should be free to apply them to aided or nonaided services.

Under this system, the Federal Government could more effectively plan and coordinate the expansion and improvement of economic and social services, and could more effectively control the expenditures of Federal funds on them, while the States and Settlements would be fully responsible for the services not financed by specific Federal grants. It would not be consistent with this responsibility to require them to obtain Federal approval for increases in their estimates of expenditure on these services.

To adopt these recommendations would require amendment of the Federation Agreement. Although they imply substantial changes in the present financial arrangements, we believe them to be in harmony with the intention of the Agreement.

III MONETARY AND FINANCIAL INSTITUTIONS

The Malayan dollar is legal tender in both the Federation and Singapore and also in the Colonies of North Borneo and Sarawak and the State of Brunei. The currency is issued and redeemed by a currency board freely and exclusively in exchange for sterling and is consequently backed at least to 100% by sterling assets. The rate of exchange is two shillings, four pence per Malayan dollar (equivalent to three Malayan dollars per one U. S. dollar). The currency issue is less important in the total Malayan money supply than bank deposits because of the relatively well-developed banking system and banking habits.

The currency and banking systems in Malaya are further described in Technical Report 12, where we note the especially close and direct correspondence between movements in international trade and payments and in general internal financial liquidity under the present currency and credit arrangements.

With this close linking of internal liquidity to external economic and financial relationships there is no possibility for exchange crises or loss of confidence in the currency. The system worked well in the course of Malaya's past economic development when the money sector of the economy was largely dominated by external capital and revolved around foreign trade and production for export, when banking facilities were provided chiefly by overseas banks, when labor moved into and out of Malaya with the rise and fall in the activity of the export industries, and when distinctly domestic activity was largely for subsistence or organized in small family units.

The dominant position of the export industries of course continues. But the Federation and Singapore—considered together as an economic unit—have now reached a stage of development where this largely external orientation of the economy has been and is being modified by such factors as a wide and growing volume of monetary transactions and of local capital and enterprise; a settled labor force; indigenous banking facilities at least as important as those afforded by overseas banks; and a need, as the inflow of new private external capital has declined, to depend increasingly on internal savings for further investment in the development of Malaya's resources.

A Central Bank of Malaya

In the mission's view these changes in the economy call for a modification of the present currency system to permit a measure of deliberate management of the money and credit situation, with the object of fostering a more favorable climate for the further development of domestic enterprise. As the instrument for this management we recommend the establishment of a Central Bank of Malaya.

The Central Bank would replace the Currency Board as the currency authority. It should operate under conditions which would prevent any threat to the link between the Malayan dollar and sterling, either in terms of exchange stability or of full convertibility. It would serve both the Federation and Singapore and, possibly, the three British Borneo territories now in the Malayan currency area, unless they elected to have their own currency. These and other features of the Central Bank's constitution and the scope and character of its operations are set forth in Technical Report 12. Our presentation is, however, in general terms and as a preliminary to the establishment of a Central Bank we suggest that the two governments enlist the assistance of United Kingdom monetary authorities or the International Monetary Fund for a detailed enquiry into the problems of central banking in Malaya and for advice on the provisions of the legislation to establish the bank.

Ideally, perhaps the most important element of a more favorable financial climate would be a substantial degree of insulation from the wide and periodic fluctuations in the export trade which are directly translated domestically into alternating periods of speculative boom and depression. These fluctuations are probably an important cause of the Malayan investor's marked preference for a highly liquid assets position and a very flexible form of business organization. This in turn distorts the structure of interest rates and makes it difficult and expensive to raise long-term capital, favors the quick turnover of commodity dealing rather than substantial fixed investment, and is undoubtedly among the factors fostering a preference for small family enterprise over a large, continuing and impersonal form of business organization.

We recognize, of course, that since the export industries are the main pillars of the economy it would be idle and dangerous to attempt to maintain any substantial degree of internal stability irrespective of the fluctuating fortunes of rubber, tin and the entrepot trade. In an economy heavily dependent on foreign trade, like Malaya's, the margin for monetary management without upsetting the balance of payments is very narrow. Within limits, however, it could be widened somewhat by a central bank policy of keeping the level of foreign exchange reserves, on the average, sufficiently above the "safety" level so that a sort of stabilization fund in sterling would be available. This would permit appropriate monetary and credit policies which could ease domestic adjustments to external fluctuations without endangering the balance of payments and foreign exchange position. In addition, the very existence of a central bank as a lender of last resort might influence significantly the prevailing attitude toward liquidity, beginning with the local banks and spreading through the various channels of credit and capital, thereby encouraging relatively greater interest in longer-term as compared with short-term investment.

Monetary management through a central bank might also permit economies in the average amount of sterling which in the long run the currency authority, banks and governments would otherwise hold, and so make possible some additional local investment. We do not believe this to be a large potential source of financial resources for domestic investment. However, the possibility that some small part of the sterling assets held as cover for the currencies of the dependent territories might be invested in locally issued securities has recently been recognized in principle, subject to the circumstances of individual territories, by authorities in the United Kingdom.

The central bank might also promote a wider market for government securities than now exists due, among other reasons, to the present illiquidity of that type of asset; manage the overseas and domestic assets of the governmental bodies, probably preferably as their agent rather than within the balance sheet of the central bank itself; and also act as agent for governmental authorities in floating new bond issues and in improving their coordination and timing. It might determine an appropriate range of security maturities and yields conducive to a more active security market, enlisting the assistance of the governments in meeting the need for such a range, supplemented possibly with central bank issues should authority for such issue be found desirable; and serve as agent of the governments in administering foreign exchange regulations and perhaps also in supervising the observance of satisfactory standards of commercial banking, which should be established by statute.

In pointing to the potential contributions of a central bank, we must at the same time emphasize the danger that it may be used to over-expand credit. The consequences of an irresponsible pressure on a central bank and of abuse of monetary independence have been learned by many countries to their sorrow. There are no monetary "tricks" by which a country can maintain a scale of private and public investment in excess of the flow of capital from domestic saving and from abroad. Any attempt to do so can lead only to dissipation of foreign assets, progressive inflation, misdirection of investment, exchange crises and a loss of investors' confidence.

Safeguards against this danger should be incorporated in the central bank's constitution; we believe that there can be greater assurance of their effectiveness in Malaya than in many other countries, for the joint participation of at least two governments in the central bank should limit the scope for the exercise of political influence by any single government.

The mission is convinced that there is a real and present economic case for the establishment of a central bank in Malaya. But if this were not so, if the Malayan economy were not yet ready for it, there might nevertheless be sound reason to establish a central bank now. A central bank has become the symbol of monetary independence, without which political independence is thought to be incomplete. At the same time it must be recognized that a central bank can only gradually move toward the complete and effective exercise of its functions. If first-hand experience of the responsibilities and limitations of monetary management can be gained during the present period of political transition, some of the financial mistakes and excesses which elsewhere have at times marred the early years of newly independent governments may be avoided.

A further—and powerful—argument for a central bank is one which scarcely emerges from any discussion of particular problems of economic stabilization or monetary management. There are two Malayan governments, sharing a single economy, closely and inevitably unified by the interlocking of trade and finance. In a common central bank may be found the most effective focus of thinking for the Malayan economy as a whole, a center in which the Federation and Singapore can be brought together in relation to many issues of economic policy which, although they involve monetary questions, go far beyond them. The bank should be strongly and ably staffed as rapidly as possible with this objective in view; assistance in this respect might be obtained from the Bank of England and the International Monetary Fund. In this role as a center for economic study and thinking about the course of development and the problems of the Malayan economy as a whole and as a source of advice and guidance to the two governments, a central bank could, we believe, make perhaps one of its greatest contributions.

An Industrial Credit Institution

We have elsewhere expressed the view that there will be an increasing need for a specialized industrial credit institution to provide medium- and long-term capital for private industrial enterprise and that this need will be the greater and more imminent if the present availability of industrial capital, sustained by the liquidity carried over from the boom period, proves to be a passing phase. While the need for such an institution does not appear urgent at the moment, we suggest that the proposed Central Bank give continuing attention to the availability of capital for sound industrial expansion. It should also give early consideration to the appropriate form of organization and the role of an institution for industrial financing.

We suggest the following guides in connection with this matter:

1. The industrial credit institution should be pan-Malayan in scope, serving both the Federation and Singapore, but in its financial resources and management it should be independent of the government of either territory.

2. To ensure such independence, it would be preferable that the voting equity in the institution be privately owned. Accordingly, we suggest that the possibility of securing the participation of the commercial banks as well as of other private investors be explored at an early stage.

3. The capital requirements of the institution could be determined only after a careful assessment of the needs of industry as they become more apparent. We would not, however, expect that the initial paid-up capital

would need to be large. In addition to the amounts raised by the issue of voting stock to private interests, we suggest that funds might be obtained by borrowing from the Central Bank.

4. We do not believe that the institution should be subsidized; rather, its interest charges should be sufficient to provide a reasonable return on the capital, including that invested by the Central Bank, as the volume of lending operations builds up.

5. We would expect the bulk of the institution's business to be in loans for industrial enterprises. We believe, however, that financing procedures should be flexible and we would not rule out the possibility of equity participation in sound new industrial ventures, provided that reasonable efforts to secure the entire equity capital from private sources have been unsuccessful. In such cases, we believe that the institution should limit itself to minority participation and that it should dispose of its equity holdings to private investors as soon as practicable. We would also not exclude lending operations outside the industrial field for such purposes, for example, as the establishment or expansion of large agricultural enterprises or for new mining ventures. We do not believe, however, that the institution should engage in lending to small-scale agriculture; for this type of financing, as previously indicated, we support the proposal for a separate specialized credit institution at the apex of cooperative credit societies and intermediate cooperative banks.

6. It is hardly necessary to emphasize that the institution's lending should be based on careful evaluation of the technical, organizational and financial merits of the projects to be financed. Assistance in the evaluation of projects and of creditworthiness might be obtained from the proposed Industrial Research Institute, which we have elsewhere recommended, and from the commercial banks. The institution will nevertheless require its own small but capable and experienced staff of technicians and financial analysts. While the assumption of risk will obviously be necessary if the institution is properly to perform its role of fostering private industrial expansion, it is essential that from the outset the institution establish a reputation for objectivity, care and soundness in its financing operations.

PART V
TECHNICAL REPORTS; STATISTICAL APPENDIX

MAP 4

MEAN MONTHLY RAINFALL

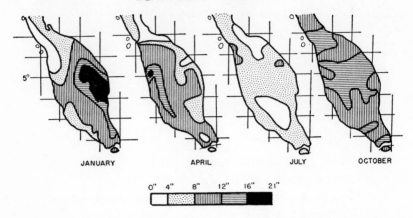

JANUARY   APRIL   JULY   OCTOBER

0" 4" 8" 12" 16" 21"

MEAN ANNUAL RAINFALL

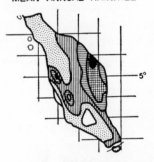

MEAN MONTHLY & MEAN ANNUAL DISTRIBUTION OF RAINFALL IN MALAYA

(by courtesy of the Director of the Malayan Met. Service, Mr. I. E. M. Watts (author) and the University of London Press; figure adapted from "Equatorial Weather Analysis" by I. E. M. Watts, in press)

0" 80" 100" 120" 140" 160" 200"

JUNE, 1954

TECHNICAL REPORT 1
AGRICULTURE AND FORESTRY

I ENVIRONMENT

A CLIMATE

The climate of Malaya is characterized by abundant rainfall, high humidity and a generally uniform high temperature.

The Malayan seasons are marked by the northeast monsoon, from October or November to February, and the southeast monsoon, from May or June to August or September. These correspond roughly to winter and summer in northern latitudes. Most of the west coast and the inland regions receive their maximum rainfall during the periods between the monsoons, while the east coast's maximum rainfall comes during the northeast monsoon. January and February are likely to be dry over the northern portion of the country, and July is a dry month over much of the west, center and southeast.

The greatest annual fall is recorded for the east coast at over 120 inches; the average fall inland ranges from 80 to 120 inches and is somewhat less in the northwestern and southwestern regions than elsewhere. There is considerable variation both in annual fall and seasonal distribution.

Evaporation data, of value in agricultural, irrigation and drainage practice, are very sparse for tropical regions generally. Their lack in Malaya is thus all the more to be deplored. Fortunately free-water-surface evaporimetric data have been collected recently from the three reservoirs, McRitchie, Pierce and Seletar, in Singapore. The average annual evaporation for the three stations for the years 1948-53, in inches, totalled 60.72, 61.76, 62.03, 68.10, 66.13 and 64.45, respectively. In view of the high humidity and heavy rainfall of Singapore, this evaporation loss may be considered high.

The 24-hour mean relative humidity for the year ranges from about 84% (Alor Star, Kuala Lumpur, Malacca and Singapore) to about 89-91% (Cameron Highlands and Frazer's Hill, respectively). Under these comparatively humid conditions, annual crops recover much more rapidly from

235

diurnal wilting in dry spells during the growing season than they do in the dry tropics. But the occasional periods of low humidity do have an inhibiting influence on growth and vigor. The 24-hour means hide the fact that for some hours on dry days the saturation deficit may be quite high, and this, in conjunction with temporarily low available soil moisture and the high temperature of air and soil, may adversely affect the functions of transpiration and growth.

Temperature conditions are generally uniform seasonally, the range being 2°-4°F. only. On the other hand, the diurnal range is more marked, being about 12°F. on the coast and 18°F. inland at the higher elevations. Over the period 1931-40, the mean monthly maximum temperature at Alor Star, a northwestern coastal station, was 88.6°F. and the minimum 73.1°F. Corresponding data for Kuala Lipis, a central station, were 83.3°F. and 71.3°F., and for Cameron Highlands, a hill station, 73.2°F. and 56.5°F.

B   GEOLOGY, PHYSIOGRAPHY AND SOILS

Geology and Physiography

About half of the Federation's 51,000 square miles is made up of granite and other igneous rocks. The high mountains are predominantly granitic. Basic rocks of volcanic nature, mostly basaltic, are widely distributed in

---

Key to Map 5: Geology

AGRICULTURAL STATIONS

1. Gajah Mati
2. Ayer Itam
3. Bukit Mertajam
4. Simpang Lima
5. Selama

PADI EXPERIMENT STATIONS

22. Telok Chengai
23. Bukit Merah
24. Titi Serong
25. Talang
26. Sungei Manik

6. Kuala Kangsar
7. Ayer Tawar
8. Degong
9. Tanah Rata
10. Raub
11. Telok Datok
12. Cheras
13. Rembau

27. Jelebu Padi Test Station
28. Ampang Tinggi Padi Station
29. Pulau Gadong
30. Melor
31. Kota Bharu
32. Tanjong Malim Fruit Nursery

14. Kuala Gemeroh
15. Sungei Udang
16. Tangkak
17. Ayer Hitam
18. Temerloh
19. Pekan
20. Kuantan
21. Kuala Lipis

33. Federal Experiment Station, Port Swettenham
34. Central Federal Experiment Station, Serdang
35. Federal Experiment Station, Pontian
36. Johore Bahru Canning Research Station

MAP 5

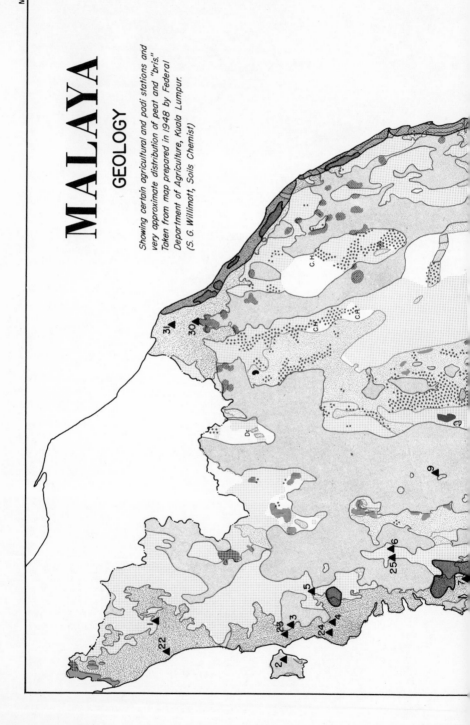

MALAYA

GEOLOGY

*Showing certain agricultural and padi stations and
very approximate distribution of peat and "bris."
Taken from map prepared in 1948 by Federal
Department of Agriculture, Kuala Lumpur.
(S. G. Willimott, Soils Chemist)*

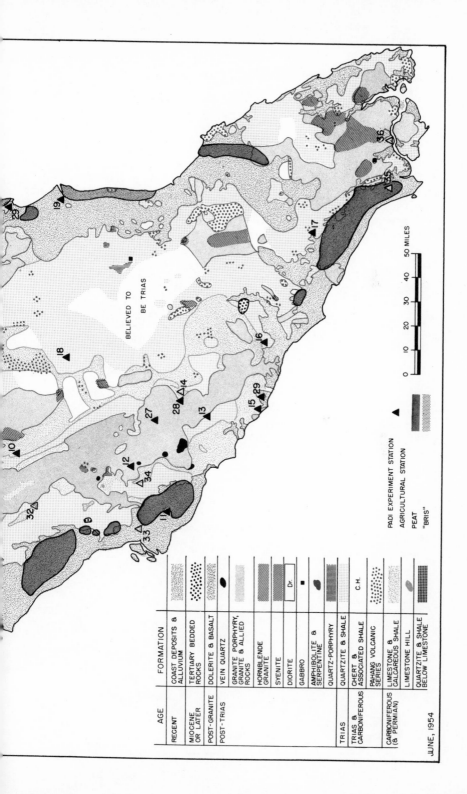

AGE	FORMATION
RECENT	COAST DEPOSITS & ALLUVIUM
MIOCENE OR LATER	TERTIARY BEDDED ROCKS
POST-GRANITE	DOLERITE & BASALT
POST-TRIAS	VEIN QUARTZ
	GRANITE PORPHYRY, GRANITE & ALLIED ROCKS
	HORNBLENDE GRANITE
	SYENITE
	DIORITE
	GABBRO
	AMPHIBOLITE & SERPENTINE
	QUARTZ-PORPHYRY
TRIAS	QUARTZITE & SHALE
TRIAS & CARBONIFEROUS	CHERT & ASSOCIATED SHALE
	PAHANG VOLCANIC SERIES
CARBONIFEROUS (& PERMIAN)	LIMESTONE & CALCAREOUS SHALE
	LIMESTONE HILL
	QUARTZITE & SHALE BELOW LIMESTONE

BELIEVED TO BE TRIAS

PADI EXPERIMENT STATION

AGRICULTURAL STATION

PEAT

"BRIS"

Dr.

C.H.

0 10 20 30 40 50 MILES

JUNE, 1954

the center and east, although their total area is small. Sedimentary rocks older than the granite—the triassic and the carboniferous and possibly permian formations—constitute rather less than a third of the area. Of the remainder of the country, the greater portion is alluvium, with a relatively small representation of tertiary sedimentaries. Most of the soil so far developed for agriculture, including rubber, coconut and padi, is provided by the alluvium and by the sedimentary rocks older than the granite.

On both sides of the Malayan peninsula there are wide alluvial plains extending inland toward the foothills and a semi-central series of ranges and massifs. The plains on the western side are wider—running inland up to about 50 miles—than on the east side where the maximum width is only about half as great.

Soils

No systematic detailed study has been made of the development, distribution and classification of the soils of Malaya, although the subject has been dealt with in several papers published in Malayan journals.[1]

In general, there is a wide range of soils suitable for agricultural purposes. But because of the heavy rainfall, much of the soil is of low fertility and the application of fertilizers is either desirable or essential for both annual and perennial crops. It is significant that such perennial crops as oil palm and rubber are fertilized as a matter of routine on the more progressive estates. The undulating character of a large proportion of the land from the littorals to the foothills, in combination with the heavy rainfall, also makes the soils in these areas especially susceptible to erosion when cultivated unless careful conservation practices are observed.

C VEGETATION

The vegetation is tropical evergreen rain forest in a number of forms, both tall and short, depending upon such factors as elevation, soil moisture and drainage. In its primeval condition the whole of the peninsula was covered in forest; despite appearances, particularly of the ribbon development along the major roads and the railway, man's activities have seriously

---

[1] See, for a tentative classification of the major soils, G. Owen, "A Provisional Classification of Malayan Soils," 1951, *Journal Soil Sci.* II: 1:20-41 reprinted as Vol. 13, Communication 274, Rubber Res. Inst. Malaya.

affected only about 20-25% of the great expanse of woody vegetation.

Botanically and ecologically the vegetation is related to that of Borneo, Sumatra, Java and other areas of western Malaysia. Upwards of 8,000 species of flowering plants have been recorded, at least 2,500 being trees occurring in places at the rate of about 100 genera to an acre—an amazing richness even for the tropics.

The vegetation may be divided into three general groups of forest communities. The first includes those conditioned and perhaps controlled by edaphic features. These comprise mangrove-swamp, beach, peat-swamp, semi-swamp and riverine fringing forests, as well as forest and scrub vegetation of limestone and quartzite outcrops. Approximately 560 square miles of mangrove-swamp forests occur on mud flats on the west coast and in sheltered river mouths on the east coast; they are commercially important as sources of poles, fuel and charcoal. The extensive eastern beach forests are useful chiefly as protection against wind-blown sand. The peat-swamp, semi-swamp and riverine fringing forests carry useful timber.

The second group consists of communities of the lowland, hill and montane regions, including the Lowland, Hill and Upper Dipterocarp forests, the montane Oak forests and montane Ericaceous communities. The first category comprises the extensive forests of the plains and foothills up to about 1,000 feet, estimated to cover about 17,280 square miles on forest reserves and state land and to have been removed from, or impaired on, an additional 7,880 square miles, mostly state land. These forests yield the bulk of commercial timber, but also cover land of value in future agricultural development. The Hill and Upper Dipterocarp forests lie between 1,000 and 4,000 feet (somewhat lower nearer the sea) and together occupy about 11,400 square miles, of which 4,060 are in reserves. The montane Oak forests lying between 4,000 and 5,000 feet are of little commercial value, while the montane Ericaceous communities, over 5,000 feet, have only a protective and aesthetic value.

There are, finally, the secondary largely man-induced communities which, besides rubber, oil palm, coconut, kampong fruit trees, padi and other crops, include lalang (*Imperata arundinacea Cyr.*), bamboo, and gelam swamp-forests. These have developed on land that has carried one or another of the primary communities already noted. Lalang is a rank, troublesome, vigorous grass which is costly and difficult to eradicate; if protected against fire it is invaded by pioneer shrubs such as Melastoma and Lantana, and is in time reduced by the shade of the woody growth.

Bamboo forms communities created by shifting cultivation, firing and grazing; more widely spread are secondary bamboo communities on land formerly cultivated but which has reverted to natural vegetation. Gelam swamp-forests occur on alluvial or peat flats allegedly where development of peat-swamp forest has been hampered by fire.

II UTILIZATION OF NATURAL RESOURCES

Past Practices

Malaya's natural resources have been exploited much less than those of many another country with generally similar climate, soil characteristics and vegetation and with a kindred history of agricultural and mining development. This is in part attributable to the fact that the heavy and relatively well-distributed rainfall, high humidity and high temperature, subject to only slight daily or seasonal variation, makes the soils less susceptible to serious sheet erosion and down-cutting. In part it is due to the remarkably rapid recuperation of the vegetation after disturbance. And it is true that the intensity and extent of disturbance is mild compared with that experienced in many other tropical regions in recent times.

However, mistakes have been made and are still being made in the use of Malaya's forestry, agricultural, mineral and water resources. Fortunately, it is still possible to take steps leading to a solution of the problems of utilization and conservation.

Significant examples of past errors include the following:

1. Peat areas have been planted to rubber even though stands are liable to heel over with the wind, exposing the root system, as oxidation and a gradual sinking of the level of the peat takes place. So far investigations of satisfactory techniques for padi cultivation on peat soils have not been particularly fruitful, but these peat areas might have supported pineapple, coffee, various kampong fruit and other food crops, vegetable gardens (notably *Colocasia* and sweet potato) and, where they are less than one foot deep after drainage, oil palm and coconut.

2. While coconut does very well on the organic clays and related types, if rather less well on the shallower peats, some littoral sands and sandy loams of the "bris" on the east coast have also been planted to coconut; the yield has been poor and, in some instances, the trees have deteriorated and

died. It is likely that more careful reconnaissance would have revealed localities, both coastal and inland, better suited to coconut.

3. Shortly after limitations were placed on rubber acreage in 1931, sloping terrains were cleared of jungle and planted to pineapple. Erosion and deterioration ensued, and by now much of these erstwhile pineapple areas, taken over by lalang and similar growths, has been lost to cultivation. Equally disturbing, however, is the fact that steep slopes in various States still are cleared of their natural vegetation for what must be short-term crops of pineapple; some particularly striking examples are to be seen in the Cameron Highlands. Since it has been known for some time that some of the peats, mucks and organic clays are suitable for pineapple, this is all the more to be deplored.

4. Bananas are cultivated on steep slopes in many regions, notably in Negri Sembilan and in parts of Johore and Pahang. Since the crop is a heavy feeder, the particular methods of cultivation practiced take a severe toll of the soil. Where irrigation is poorly controlled, erosion soon follows.

5. Upland tea—notably in the Cameron Highlands but also elsewhere in country of broken topography generally—has been developed upon a terrain so steep and rugged that only the most efficient and costly soil and water conservation measures, both biological and mechanical, could prevent deterioration and soil erosion. As the yields are low and the costs of production high in comparison with lowland tea, and as many of the estates are poorly managed and little instruction is given to smallholders, good management and conservation practices are almost wholly lacking. Thus upland country of value as a catchment area for water is gradually being destroyed.

6. Kampong and other types of smallholder farming have been allowed to develop along the banks of a number of rivers, notably the Perak, the Pahang and the Kelantan, during the last half-century. Although the rapid regeneration of vegetation along the banks has kept erosion within bounds, there are many areas of local deterioration which are likely to spread. The sand and silt load in some of the rivers has increased as a result of cultivation along their banks; stretches navigable by river craft early in the century are now navigable by sampan or similar craft only.

7. There are many cases of the unfortunate effect of tin mining upon agricultural resources both in upland and lowland localities. Localized land damage is of course to be expected in view of the economic advantages of exploiting the valuable tin deposits. But in the past there has also been

MAP 6

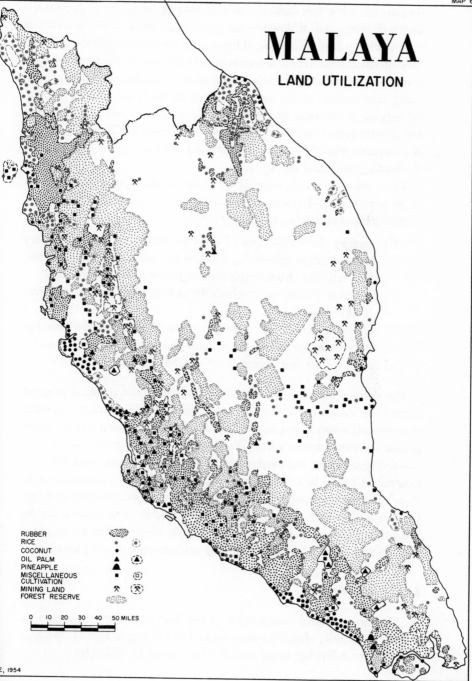

MALAYA
LAND UTILIZATION

RUBBER
RICE
COCONUT
OIL PALM
PINEAPPLE
MISCELLANEOUS
CULTIVATION
MINING LAND
FOREST RESERVE

0   10   20   30   40   50 MILES

ME, 1954

considerable secondary damage due to inadequate measures to prevent the silting of rivers and of downstream agricultural lands. This, however, is now much less true, as a result of the control measures required under the Mining Enactment. There nevertheless remain the problems of rehabilitating land degraded by mining operations, and of devising suitable policies which take account of the national interest in the exploitation of mineral deposits but at the same time minimize the adverse effects on agricultural and forestry resources. These problems are discussed in Chapter 4, Part II, in connection with the mining industry and also later in this section under the heading "degraded lands".

In an effort to repair some of the errors of the past and to plan for better use of natural resources in the future, a Federal Land Advisory Committee was established in 1952 to:

(i) consider the preparation of a comprehensive resource-inventory of information concerning land, water and other resources and their inherent characteristics, potentialities and economic uses;

(ii) formulate principles on which the utilization of natural resources should be based;

(iii) advise the Federal and State Governments regarding the planning of the development of the country in its varied resources; and

(iv) advise on the best potential use of land and water resources.

For various reasons the Committee has made little practical progress toward the objectives for which it was established. Its terms of reference encompassed a very broad field of guidance in the planning and coordination of economic development. We have elsewhere suggested an alternative arrangement for this purpose, under which the Federal Land Advisory Committee would be replaced by a Technical Advisory Committee to include the various departments concerned with economic development (see Chapter 9, Part IV). Also within this administrative arrangement for development planning and coordination we have recommended a specialized team to undertake land-use surveys and guidance in land-use planning.

Land-Use Survey

The recommended composition of the land-use survey team and its immediate priority objectives are indicated in Chapter 3, Part II. We suggest that the following broad qualifications would be desirable:

1. An agriculturist with a good knowledge of tropical agriculture and experience in the development of tropical land;

2. An ecologist[2] with tropical experience and an appreciation of the interplay of agriculture, forestry and irrigation requirements;

3. A pedologist whose principal training and experience is as a "soil surveyor," rather than as a laboratory pedologist;

4. A cartographic draftsman/surveyor experienced in map compilation from aerial photographs, including the mapping of vegetation, soil and other required features; and

5. An agricultural economist experienced in the economics of production in tropical and monsoon agriculture, and in the interrelationships of production and market factors as they affect land-use planning.

We have suggested that additional specialists, as needed, be made available by the various departments. It may also be found necessary, finances and recruiting possibilities permitting, to consider later the addition of another agriculturist, ecologist and pedologist to the team. We would expect that the Department of Agriculture would provide laboratory assistance and facilities for the physical and chemical analyses of soil samples. Two assistant draftsmen, probably employable locally, would also be needed for the cartographic work. And the team would of course require a supporting staff for clerical, secretarial and other duties and an adequate number of vehicles and other equipment.

It is probable that aerial photography will play an important role in facilitating the work of the survey in both broad and detailed reconnaissance. We recommend contracting for the services of a company which specializes in aerial photography and its interpretation for land-use survey purposes. The whole of the Federation has already been photographed from the air on a scale of 2½ inches to the mile for topographical mapping; these photographs will undoubtedly be useful for broad reconnaissance purposes, although this should be verified by specialists. They would not, however, be suitable for detailed reconnaissance where photography at a contact scale of 1/10,000-1/15,000 would be required for selected areas.

Initially, we suggest that the survey team spend about six months studying, in consultation with appropriate departments, available information relevant to the survey problem and in undertaking some prelimi-

---

[2] While we have suggested in Chapter 3 that the general agriculturist be the leader of the team, considerations of experience and personal qualifications may make it preferable to place the ecologist in charge.

nary reconnaissance to determine the general physiography of the country and the broad outline of land-use patterns and potentialities. On the basis of this initial study, a first demarcation might be made of different regions according to their varying land-use promise, and a selection made of areas for further examination in accordance with the priorities of the survey.

Following this, the logical procedure of the survey would appear to be along the following lines:

1. Broad reconnaissance of the regions given high priority in the survey, with the object of mapping the broad patterns of soil and vegetation, drainage and other general features affecting land use, and of selecting areas for study in greater detail. Interpretation of the existing air photographs, with additional photography on a comparable scale as necessary, should be included in this broad reconnaissance phase for the mapping work of the cartographer/surveyor and his assistants.

2. Detailed reconnaissance, including new aerial photographs on a larger scale and their interpretation, together with detailed on-the-ground examinations. The object of such detailed reconnaissance would be the mapping and evaluation of soils, water resources, drainage, vegetation and other information necessary to land-use planning.

By the end of the third or fourth year we would expect the broad reconnaissance work to have been completed. Progress in the more detailed reconnaissance would of course be much slower, but within this same period it should also be possible to complete much of what is needed along these lines to achieve the indicated immediate priority objectives. Completion of the detailed reconnaissance of all the more promising land-use potentialities emerging from the broader survey would necessarily require a considerably longer period.

It should be emphasized that such a survey is only one important aspect of detailed land-use planning and the preparation of specific development projects. The results of the survey must also be related to the work of research and experimentation in particular crops and techniques of cultivation, of engineering and other technical aspects of irrigation, drainage and communication requirements, of economic studies of marketing possibilities and relative costs and benefits of alternative land uses, etc. These aspects of land-use planning would not be the primary responsibility of the land-use team but rather of the Agriculture, Forestry, Drainage and Irrigation and other departments. In the detailed reconnaissance phase of the survey, close collaboration would therefore be necessary between the survey team and the departments responsible for related investigations and the further planning necessary for the formulation of specific programs and projects.

To what extent additional air photography may be needed can be decided only after expert evaluation of what is already available and a preliminary study by the survey specialists. The mission was not in a position to estimate requirements and costs and the allowance in our expenditure recommendations of $3 million for this purpose up to 1959 is little more than a token figure. In general, modern techniques in photography and interpretation greatly facilitate land-use surveys. They may, however, be of more limited value in the Malayan environment than in many other areas, because of the prevailing high proportion of periods of unsatisfactory visibility, the unproven suitability of the infra-red technique and the uneven results with panchromatic film in tropical rain forest conditions, and the generally more difficult problems of interpretation due to the heavy cover, broken topography and wetness. It is possible, therefore, that detailed on-the-ground investigations will play a greater part in a land-use survey in Malaya than in areas more favorable for photographic analysis.

III AGRICULTURAL DEVELOPMENT

We have set forth in Chapter 3, Part II, the broad outlines of our recommendations for agricultural development, giving particular attention to the problems of the rubber industry and have commented on the more important conclusions and recommendations of the recent Mission of Enquiry into the Rubber Industry of Malaya. We add here a few comments which supplement the discussion of rubber in Chapter 3, and devote the remainder of this section to the situation, problems and development possibilities for crops other than rubber.

Rubber (Hevea brasiliensis L.)

Financial Assistance. In the Chapter 3 discussion of the Rubber Enquiry's proposals for tax concessions and financial arrangements intended to encourage replanting by smallholders and estates, we stated our conclusion that the advantages to be gained under those proposals would not justify the cost to the government. We reached that conclusion for the following reasons.

FIGURE I

RUBBER PRODUCTION AND CONSUMPTION
(MILLIONS OF LONG TONS)

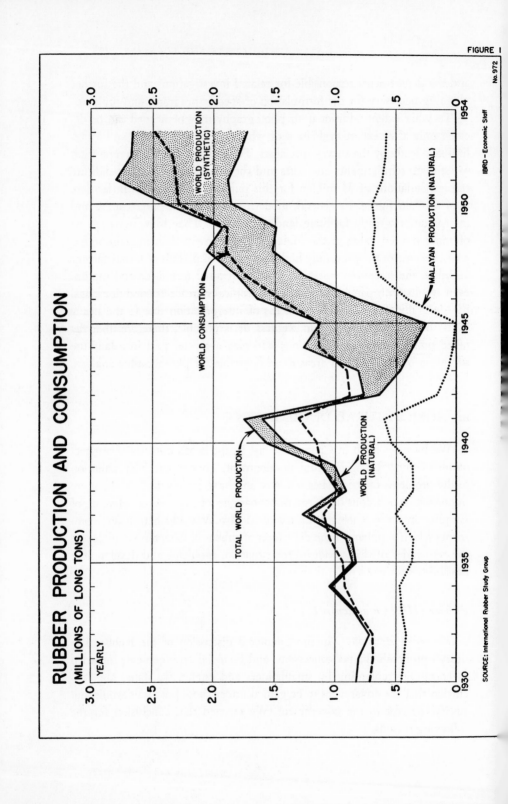

YEARLY

WORLD PRODUCTION (SYNTHETIC)

WORLD CONSUMPTION

TOTAL WORLD PRODUCTION

WORLD PRODUCTION (NATURAL)

MALAYAN PRODUCTION (NATURAL)

SOURCE: International Rubber Study Group

IBRD – Economic Staff

No. 972

First, with regard to smallholders, there is undoubtedly a strong case for financial assistance from the government to encourage replanting. But there is little reason to expect that a reduction or abolition of the export duty would by itself induce a significant increase in replanting by small-holders, principally because the whole of the benefit of lower export duty is unlikely to be passed on to them. Any benefit received would of course be important, but it would be small in relation to a smallholder's total income, low as it is, and it is improbable that smallholders' decisions concerning replanting rest on such close accounting concepts that they would be materially affected. And as for new planting, there seems to be no lack of demand for new land for the purpose, although actual new planting falls far behind this demand, mainly because of restrictions on alienation of new land for rubber. One way to ensure that the additional return resulting from a reduction or abolition of the duty on smallholder rubber is actually used for replanting would be to increase the smallholder replanting cess correspondingly, using the additional proceeds for additional replanting grants. The need for and desirability of such additional grants are discussed later. The Rubber Enquiry did not, however, recommend this procedure, and it would mean raising the smallholder cess above that proposed for estates, thereby giving rise to difficult administrative problems. As a means of stimulating replanting, the very limited effect of a reduction or abolition of the export duty, as such, in the smallholder sector of the industry does not appear to justify the loss of revenue to the government. Since this sector produces about two-fifths of domestic rubber exports, the loss at a price of 65 cents would be $12-14 million annually.

In the estate sector of the industry, some of the estates classified as "superior" by the Rubber Enquiry undoubtedly find difficulty in financing a satisfactory replanting program. By and large, however, they are probably able to continue financing an annual 3% rate of replanting at present tax rates at rubber prices of 65 or even 60 cents per pound, and their position will be further strengthened as areas already planted in high-yielding trees mature. For these estates, the need for tax concessions or other forms of assistance does not appear critical to the maintenance of satisfactory replanting programs unless rubber prices should fall very low indeed. Although some reduction in taxation or a contribution toward replanting costs would improve the financial position of these estates, assistance to the extent proposed by the Rubber Enquiry and the establishment of a replanting cess and fund do not appear necessary to secure satisfactory replanting by the majority of estates in the "superior" group.

The situation is otherwise in the remainder of the estate sector. At the other extreme from the "superior" estates are those with only 10% or less of their area in high-yielding rubber. These estates have done little or no replanting, even during the boom period of very high rubber prices, which suggests a deliberate policy of drawing off the maximum possible immediate returns at the expense of steadily declining yields and deterioration of the estate. For such estates, tax concessions alone would merely permit increased withdrawals of current earnings without long-run benefit to the estates themselves or to the national economy. This could be prevented by coupling the tax concessions with a compulsory replanting cess. But a cess of 4½ cents a pound, as recommended by the Enquiry, credited to these estates in accordance with their production, would not provide individual estates within the group with anything like the funds needed to make up reasonably quickly for long neglected replanting and to assure, say a decade hence, a satisfactory proportion of mature high-yielding trees. Investment well in excess of the yield from the cess would seem to be required and experience gives little confidence that it would be forthcoming, either with the estates' own or borrowed funds.

Much of this poorest estate acreage, then, seems destined to continuing deterioration while it is operated under present policies. This group seems to need some form of selective assistance, concentrated on those estates prepared to undertake replanting at the high rate necessary for their rehabilitation. In a great many of these cases rehabilitation could probably be accomplished only through liquidation and absorption by interests prepared and able to invest in a major replanting program within a short period and to wait during the maturing period to enjoy the financial results.

The "intermediate" group of estates seems to be composed mainly of estates which carry on replanting as financial conditions permit but, because their mature high-yielding acreage is still relatively small, find it difficult at competitive rubber prices and present taxation to replant at satisfactory rates and still give some return on the capital invested in them. Their problem is to keep to a planting schedule at competitive price levels which will bring them into the "superior" group. For these estates, as we have noted in Chapter 3, there appears to be a strong economic case for tax concessions or other assistance which would supplement their own replanting expenditure by an amount sufficient to permit them to finance at least a 3%, and possibly for a time a higher, rate of replanting. But we have also pointed out that this group represents only about 15% of the entire rubber area, including smallholders.

In Chapter 3, we stated that we had also not adopted a proposal for financial assistance advanced by the Rubber Producers' Council. Under this proposal, the present schedule of export duty would be maintained but the government would retain only so much of the receipts as corresponded to a 2½% ad valorem rate, regardless of the price of rubber. The balance collected on exports of estate rubber would go to an estate replanting fund, for credit to the account of individual estates in accordance with their production. The Schedule II cess would continue to be collected and paid into the replanting fund. Funds would be released from the accounts of the estates in accordance with replanting expenditure undertaken subsequent to 1946.[2a]

The advantage of this proposal over that of the Rubber Enquiry is that it would mean a much smaller reduction in government revenue, at prices below 68 cents. But it has several disadvantages. There would be no steeper progression of export duty rates at higher rubber prices, as suggested by the Rubber Enquiry and endorsed by the mission. The government's revenue would be based on a 2½% ad valorem rate no matter how high the price of rubber, while the increase in collections resulting from the present progression of duty as rubber prices increase would accrue entirely to the credit of estates. At the lower ranges of rubber prices, with which we are principally concerned, the main disadvantage of the Council's proposal is that the estates in greatest need of assistance when prices are low would receive far less than they need to maintain a satisfactory rate of replanting. For example, at rubber prices ranging from 60 to 65 cents the collections for the replanting fund per pound of rubber would be between 1.5 and 2.375 cents only, whereas the Rubber Enquiry has shown that even its proposal of a 4.5 cent cess would not be enough for satisfactory rates of replanting by the "intermediate" and "poorer" estates. A further disadvantage of the Council's proposal, as with the Rubber Enquiry recommendations, is that the collections for the replanting fund would be credited to particular estates irrespective of their willingness to utilize these funds

[2a] These proposals were revised after this section of the report was drafted. The revised scheme would have raised the government's share of the proceeds of export duty to a maximum of 5% ad valorem at prices for rubber of 70 cents a pound and above. The criticism of the scheme contained in the next paragraph, however, still applies generally in spite of this revision.

to replant and to forego the income from existing trees while waiting for the newly planted high-yielding varieties to mature.

Smallholdings.[3] Only about 10% of the smallholding area in rubber is of fairly recent planting. About two-thirds of the rest is in trees of over 25 years of age and more than half over 33 years old. Mainly because of advanced age, the yield from existing trees on smallholdings is expected to decline steadily, according to the Rubber Enquiry probably from 20-50% in the next decade.

The major difficulties for the smallholder in checking this deterioration through replanting are the labor and capital required to remove the old trees and to substitute and care for the new plants, and the loss of income during the maturing period of the new stand.

The smallholders' export cess and replanting fund were instituted in late 1952 to assist in rehabilitation of smallholdings. Unlike the proposal of the Rubber Enquiry for estates, the smallholders' cess (4½ cents per pound) is not credited to a particular holding but goes into a common fund from which allowances are paid for approved replanting. Payment is made in installments as the steps needed to bring the new trees to maturity are satisfactorily completed. Smallholders are eligible for allowance on up to one-third of their area or up to 5 acres where they hold less than 15.[4]

The program aims at the replanting of 500,000 acres by 1959; this would bring the area planted in new rubber trees to about one-third of the present smallholder acreage.

In its first two years the program has been behind the targets (first installments were paid or approved on 27,000 acres as compared with a target of 40,000 acres in 1953 and on 33,000 acres compared with a target of 50,000 acres in 1954).[5]

The objective of 500,000 acres by 1959 may not be fully achieved and is probably as high as is administratively feasible in view of the growing size and complexity of the task of periodically checking on the compliance with replanting standards and care of the new trees necessary for eligibility for each installment of the replanting allowance.

[3] Smallholdings are officially defined as holdings under 100 acres. However, only a small proportion of these are over 25 acres. The great majority are less than 10 acres and a large proportion are less than three acres. Smallholdings are estimated to account for 45% of rubber acreage and about 40% of 1953 production.

[4] The allowance may also be paid for replanting with an alternative crop, subject to approval by the Rubber Replanting Board.

[5] The annual targets increase from 40,000 acres in 1953 to 90,000 acres in 1959.

In addition to the task of administration, other obstacles may hinder the program.

One of the most disturbing is the difficulty of controlling infestation of replanted areas by lalang, a noxious grass which spreads rapidly and deprives the young rubber plants of moisture, nutrients and space. A very large proportion of the area replanted under the smallholders' program is reported to be seriously infested already. Really effective control appears to require complete eradication of the grass before new trees are planted and vigilance in preventing its reappearance. As yet, sodium arsenite spraying is the only means of control both effective and economical. But this chemical is subject to very strict regulation because of the serious risks of poisoning to human beings and livestock, mainly through water pollution; it is therefore unsuitable for general use. Other known means of effective control are prohibitively expensive or otherwise impracticable.

The Replanting Board, the Rubber Research Institute and the Department of Agriculture are acutely aware of the lalang problem. We can only urge the support of their continuing efforts to find a remedy and hope that they will be successful in time to prevent serious interference with the pace of the program. If and when such a remedy is found, however, its use will raise the direct cost of smallholder replanting.

It is not yet clear precisely what level of allowance will induce replanting on a scale commensurate with the targets, especially in view of the scheduled annual increases in the latter. According to the Chief Officer of the program, a large part of the applications has come from "those most intensely keen to replant and who have few disabilities to hamper them."[6] He has noted that the former allowance of $400 per acre was far from commensurate with the sacrifices involved, especially on the part of the small operator, in the actual replanting and bringing to maturity of the new trees and in the loss of income while the trees mature. The burden of labor, often including hired labor, necessary to deal with lalang has probably been greater than expected and in many of the replanted smallholdings the necessity for fencing to prevent damage by livestock has added to cash requirements. Because it was far from certain that the replanting targets could be achieved in these circumstances, the grant per acre was recently increased to $500.

The Rubber Enquiry estimated that, at a rubber price of 70 cents, the

[6] The Rubber Industry (Replanting) Board, *Report on Operations by the Chief Replanting Officer for the period 1st November, 1952 to 31st December, 1953, p. 44.*

smallholder's net loss of income per replanted acre over the seven-year maturing period is about $650, after deducting the saving in labor resulting from the fact that the replanted acre is no longer tapped. Where the tapping would have been done in any case by unpaid family labor, the loss in cash income would be considerably larger. In addition, the direct cash outlays for replanting one acre are estimated at about $160, assuming no need for fencing, no particular problems of lalang control or other difficulties requiring outside labor. Actually, both outside hired labor and fencing may often be necessary.

Padi (Oryza sativa L.)

Official figures of padi acreage, production and average yields per acre in the Federation are as follows:

TABLE 1. Padi Acreage, Production and Average Yield,[1] Federation

	Acreage (Thousand Acres)	Production (Thousand Tons)	Average Yield per Acre (Pounds)
Av. 1926–30	662	309	1,046
Av. 1931–35	740	509	1,541
Av. 1936–40	745	543	1,633
Av. 1948–50	865	575	1,409
1950–51	864	703	1,823
1951–52	799	541	1,518
1952–53	825	700	1,901
1953–54	835	647	1,737

[1] Acreage and average yield figures prior to 1940 are not strictly comparable to those after 1948, since the former are based on planted area while the latter are for harvested area. The difference is, however, not significant.

In spite of their statistical limitations, these figures clearly show the marked upward trend of padi acreage, production and yields per acre over the last 25 years. The fact that there has been a slight decline in acreage since the 1948-50 period may be attributed to special circumstances, especially to the fact that the immediate postwar increase in acreage was very large and rapid, stimulated by high rice prices, and that, thereafter, cultivation was adversely affected by the attraction of alternative employment during the 1951 and 1952 rubber and tin boom, by recruiting for the security forces during the emergency, and by particularly adverse weather conditions in the 1951-52 season.

In Chapter 3, Part II, we noted the emphasis placed on increased rice production in governmental agricultural policy, the results of which are reflected in the rice production figures; indicated our view that in the further planning of agricultural development greater consideration should be given to the relative advantages of other crops in comparison with rice; recommended that new land development for rice and other crops be given increasing emphasis; and emphasized that we have in mind a broadened and expanded program of agricultural development rather than a curtailment of attention to increased rice production. As we have pointed out, further expansion of rice production in both existing and new areas is bound to be of high priority in any soundly conceived program of agricultural development.

With Malaya's potentialities for further expansion in padi acreage and for increased yields per acre, there seems every reason to expect that the long-term upward trend in rice production can be maintained into the foreseeable future. But to do this, governmental measures to foster additional rice production will continue to be at least as necessary as in the past.

An indication of the contribution of government irrigation programs to the expansion of rice production is the fact that of the total planted padi acreage of 864,000 acres in 1950-51, about 225,000 acres, or over 25%, were within areas where irrigation works have been established or improved by the Department of Drainage and Irrigation, largely during the last 20 years. And the 85,000 planted acres within these irrigated areas in 1950-51 exceeded by about 60% the acreage planted to padi in these same areas prior to the construction of the irrigation works.[7] Since 1950-51 there has been a further large increase in the area under controlled irrigation.

Other governmental measures to improve and extend padi production have included breeding, selection and distribution of improved seed; experimentation and development of improved techniques for sowing, cultivation, and disease and pest control; testing and subsidized distribution of fertilizers; investigation of mechanical cultivation possibilities for padi; and provision of mechanical cultivation services to padi growers on a small scale through RIDA.

Recommendations. We can only commend the excellent work that is

[7] Annual Report of the Drainage and Irrigation Department for the year 1950-51. Appendix E, pp. 60-69.

being done along these lines and limit our comments, additional to those in Chapter 3, to a few matters in connection with the various rice programs of the government.

1. Excellent results have been attained in Kelantan through use of chemical fertilizers; increases in yield up to 30% have been reported. On the basis of this experience, programs of subsidized distribution of fertilizer have been conducted in Kelantan and for similar soils in Trengganu. Subsidies amounted to $8.00 per 100 lbs. in 1952-53, $6.00 in 1953-54 and $4.00 in 1954-55. The indications are that cultivators in these areas are becoming "fertilizer-minded" and we believe that the benefits to be realized justify continued use of subsidies to foster and strengthen this trend. Testing and experience are probably now sufficient to warrant extension of the program into Kedah and possibly other padi areas. The funds required are relatively small and we believe that the long-term advantages of establishing the use of fertilizer as a customary practice among an increasing number of padi cultivators justifies a further increase in the appropriations for this purpose. Whether the present subsidy rate of $4.00 per 100 lbs. is adequate should be decided on the basis of the 1954-55 experience. Wider testing of fertilizers for the various regions, soils and major strains of padi should also be encouraged.

2. While we are aware that efforts are being made to multiply the more promising padi varieties to provide growers with pure strains of higher-yielding and resistant seed, we suggest that this work might be facilitated by some addition to staff. It may be noted in this connection, however, that the development of improved strains was interrupted by the war and that in many cases further time is required to produce adequate supplies of improved seed developed from postwar selections and trials. The Department of Agriculture has attempted in some cases to accelerate the process of developing such supplies for distribution; we believe it has been well advised to refrain from doing so where acceleration is not fully justified by adequate selection and trial work. Unsatisfactory experience by growers with prematurely distributed seed would result in an unfortunate setback to the whole program for improving rice varieties. According to data submitted to the Rice Production Committee, it is expected that seed resulting from selection and breeding work started during 1947-52 will become available for distribution over the period 1955-62.

3. Very little of the present padi acreage produces more than one crop per year. The mission supports the view that there is considerable scope

for an extension of "double-cropping," especially in Province Wellesley, Kelantan, Trengganu and Malacca. Given early maturing varieties of padi for this purpose, there are still many other requirements for substantial development in this direction, including careful scheduling of the main and seasonal crops, adequate and properly utilized water supplies, the application of fertilizer and (perhaps the most difficult requirement) a willingness on the part of the cultivators to modify their annual work pattern to a double cycle of cultivation. Special inducements have been suggested for this purpose but these are difficult to administer and may lead to neglect of the main crop in order to take advantage of the particular benefit attached to the second crop. For these reasons extension of double-cropping will probably be slow but it should nevertheless receive continued emphasis in the research and extension programs of the Department of Agriculture.

4. Continuing attention should also be given to the practical and economic possibilities of introducing rotational and green manure crops into padi production. This again would mean a modification of work patterns on lands where only padi is now cultivated. It is encouraging, on the other hand, that off-season production of crops other than padi is practiced in many areas, particularly in Malacca, Selangor and Province Wellesley; the main off-season crops are chilies, ginger, soya, vegetables and maize.

5. While considerable attention has been given to the possibilities for mechanizing padi cultivation, it is recognized that, with an adequate and increasing labor force and limited alternative employment possibilities, the justification for mechanization must rest on grounds other than the saving of labor. It is possible that mechanized cultivation would result in consistently higher yields through deeper plowing and more effective weed control, that opportunities for double-cropping would be enhanced through faster and more closely scheduled mechanized soil preparation and that mechanized harvesting and threshing would improve the quality of rice and increase the possibilities of using padi straw for livestock feed and other purposes, instead of burning it. But until the advantages are more definitely established we believe the use of mechanical equipment should remain on its present largely experimental basis. Mechanical cultivation is likely to prove practicable only if it can be adopted for areas of considerable size and in localities where the arrangement of plots, soil and sub-surface conditions, water supply, irrigation works and weather conditions are

suitable. It would seem that, given the circumstances of Malayan padi cultivation in small plots and with sufficient labor, the economic possibilities and advantages for mechanized cultivation on an extensive scale are likely to be limited. The provision of mechanized soil preparation services, however, appears to be a promising means of facilitating double-cropping, although it is recognized that this is only one in a complex of conditions necessary to encourage double-cropping on a larger scale. Experiments with mechanization should be continued and it might be helpful to draw on experience with mechanization in other areas, e.g., under the somewhat similar climatic conditions of parts of British and French West Africa or in larger rice producing areas, such as Japan, where there has been a considerable and rapid increase in the use of small-scale mechanical equipment in padi cultivation.

6. It has been suggested that a special rice branch be established in the Department of Agriculture. We do not, however, believe that there is any real need for this as long as close coordination is maintained within the Department among the activities associated with padi research and extension.

7. In general, the research and experimental work on padi cultivation is praiseworthy and it is discouraging that the funds and facilities for this work are being reduced. The greatest need is for an expansion in the extension services in order to transmit the results of research and experimentation to the cultivators. This need, and the problems and possibilities involved, are discussed subsequently under Extension Services.

Coconut (Cocos nucifera L.)

From an estimated 606,000 acres planted to coconut in 1935,[8] the total acreage has shrunk to about 500,000 acres, of which an estimated 375,000 acres belong to smallholders.

Annual production of copra is about 152,000 tons; net imports are about 10,000 tons. From this total, about 97,000 tons of coconut oil are produced, of which approximately 56,000 tons are exported. Of the remainder, about 7,000 is used in soap making and the balance is consumed as edible oil.

The coconut has developed principally on the heavy clays and some of the shallower peats of the west coast, both near the sea and inland, although elsewhere it normally thrives on well-drained sandy loams or even lighter

[8] D. H. Grist, *An Outline of Malayan Agriculture*, Kuala Lumpur, 1936.

soils. Yields per acre vary greatly according to site: under conditions of good drainage, adequate nutrients and good management, as on the better estates, average yields may range from 1,600 to 2,000 lbs. of copra per acre, but on smallholdings, where natural conditions and husbandry are poor, the per acre yield may be as low as 500 lbs.

Remarkably high yields, up to 20-25 piculs (2,600-3,300 lbs.) per acre, have been reported for special types of "talls" grown under favorable conditions of climate and soil and receiving effective attention from the time of their establishment. Returns are reportedly almost as high for selected and well-treated "dwarfs" in the same sites; these have become increasingly popular for underplanting of "talls" needing replacement. Some estates have introduced the "dwarf" varieties or have begun to convert from "talls" to "dwarfs," with apparently satisfactory results so far. The "dwarfs" are generally planted at 108 palms per acre compared with 50 for "talls," and reach bearing maturity in about 7-8 years. They show a high proportion of self-pollination and are thus comparatively pure genetically, whereas the "talls," being cross-pollinated, exhibit much diversity in their growth and fruiting character.

While the yields on the more progressive estates indicate considerable promise for the future of coconut, the low yields of the smallholders' acreage show the inevitable result of lack of attention to planting materials and to establishment, cultivation and harvesting. For both estates and smallholdings there is a need for more information regarding varieties, responses to fertilizers and cultural treatment, and pests and diseases. The smallholdings also need a program for the rejuvenation of a large proportion of the stands. Little replanting has been done in smallholder areas, and palms have often been established on soils most unsuitable for economic production.

Recommendations. Coconut research in recent years has received little if any official attention, although nongovernmental groups have made some efforts in this direction. The mission recommends that the government and these groups together plan an intensive series of investigations into the varietal, response and management aspects of production. A coconut research center of not less than 1,000-1,500 acres should be established in a suitable locality, and cooperative trials should be organized on estates in the several producing regions. A specialist officer should be appointed to direct this work.

For the smallholdings, a replanting scheme with approved planting material on selected acreage is recommended. A site survey is a prerequisite to such a project. It is suggested that the coconut replanting project in Ceylon might serve as a guide and that an officer of the Department of Agriculture might visit that project. It supplies smallholders with approved seedlings of suitable varieties raised in a number of centrally situated nurseries. A government subsidy helps to finance the raising of seedlings, inspection of plantings and provision of technical advice to smallholders.

Assuming that it would cost $1.00 to produce a seedling, that "talls" at 30 x 30 ft. (50 per acre) were to be supplied, that the project were to begin in 1956 by covering 1,000 acres at a subsidy of $30 per acre, that 2,000 acres were added the second year, 3,000 the third and so on, by 1961 a total of 21,000 acres would be covered at a subsidized cost of $630,000 over the six years; in 10 years 55,000 acres might be covered for a total subsidy of $1.65 million. Although this seems small compared with the 300,000-370,000 acres probably demanding attention, it would be a step in the right direction and its demonstration value should justify the expenditure.

Oil Palm (Elaeis guineensis Jacq.)

The oil palm demands high and well-distributed rainfall and well-drained soil, and in general responds excellently to the Malayan climate. The fruit is produced in large numbers on bunches weighing 50 to 70 lbs., the oil occurring in the fleshy outer portion or pericarp and the kernel being contained in a nut surrounded by pericarp. The oil content of a bunch is about 16% to 18% of its total weight, the kernel content being only 5%.

There are three principal types; *dura,* whose fruit has a medium-thick shell and 35-55% pericarp by weight, the well-known "Deli" variety being widely grown in Malaya; *tenera,* whose fruit has a thin shell and 80% pericarp; and *pisifera,* whose fruit is without shell and has either a very small kernel or none, a very well-developed pericarp with a high oil content, but which is usually sterile.

The industry in Malaya is organized on an estate basis, and gives direct employment to about 15,000 workers. About 100,000 acres are planted to oil palm, divided among just over 60 estates ranging in size from 10 acres to over 16,000. Some of the more progressive estates average 1½ tons of oil per acre. Production for 1953 was 49,098 tons of palm oil and 12,669 of kernels, while net exports were 49,502 tons of palm oil and 12,613 of palm kernels. Acreage and tonnage have both increased gradually over the past few years. Almost all oil produced is exported, virtually none being used locally, except for about 6,000 tons per annum consumed by Lever Brothers (Malaya) Ltd. in their modern soap and oil factory in Kuala Lumpur.

In Malaya the palms usually come into bearing when about four to five years old, the better yields being obtained from about the 11th year until about the 25th to 30th. The trees reach 35 ft. to 45 ft. in height thereafter, making harvesting of the bunches difficult and expensive. It costs three cents to harvest a bunch at 10 ft., whereas at 25-30 ft. the cost is 12 cents. This fact, together with the heavy cost of replanting—an estimated $400 to $500 per acre—should make the short-stemmed "dumpy" palm developed by Jagoe and his colleagues particularly valuable to the industry when once certain deficiencies, such as the production of an insufficient number of good fruits per bunch, are remedied.

Production of a high quality oil of low free fatty acid content (2-3%) requires planned, properly timed harvesting, and processing within 24 hours. This calls for heavy, complicated machinery and equipment, a competent and sufficiently large staff and a network of roads and estate railways to bring in the fruit rapidly and without undue bruising. In addition, capital requirements are considerable. Consequently, the notion is prevalent in Malaya that the oil palm is essentially an estate crop, unsuitable for production by smallholders. Another reason advanced for this view is that the palms should be in large and compact blocks, not scattered widely over kampongs as are coconut and tree fruits generally.

Having regard to the high quality of estate and factory management, the congenial climatic conditions and the range of soils available, it can be concluded that the oil palm has a promising future in Malaya.

Problems of selection of tall and "dumpy" varieties of high yield, resistance to disease, and control of diseases and various insect pests exist and will continue to be present.

Recommendations. An unsuccessful approach has been made by the Director of Agriculture to the industry groups which have undertaken oil palm research, suggesting the establishment of a central oil palm research station, primarily to develop improved planting material and later to study the agronomy of the crop and its nutritional needs. In the circumstances, the mission recommends appointment of a specialist officer to continue, full-time, the basic studies hitherto conducted by the Department. A suitable officer might be recruited from West Africa. As one of the more promising means of diversification of agriculture, the crop is so important that continued official support should be given to the investigations financed by the industry.

It has been remarked that arguments against the production of oil palm by smallholders have been advanced locally. Admittedly there are problems of maintaining standards of fruit production and processing and both experience and capital are required. Yet it should be remembered that in West Africa the production of palm oil from "wild" palms is the prevailing practice. While the circumstances and setting of Malaya are quite different, the mission nevertheless recommends that a carefully planned pilot scheme, covering both the production and the processing aspects of the industry, be undertaken in a suitable locality. Acreage in oil palm should not exceed 1,000-2,000, and smallholders should be assured of sufficient land to permit the raising of food and cash crops during the period in which the palm is maturing. A special study should cover such aspects of the project as location, dimensions, number of smallholders, area to be allocated per family for palms, food and cash crops, organization for clearing the jungle and establishing the stands, financial assistance, facilities for transportation and processing of the fruit, etc. If necessary the views of experienced producers outside of Malaya could be sought. An officer capable of organizing the development of the project should be assigned to it from the outset.

In connection with milling facilities for smallholders, the mission has considered the possibility of the "Pioneer" type of mill developed in West Africa, but has concluded that it would not be appropriate without modification. As the yields in Malaya may be expected to be much higher than is possible in West Africa, the mill for a 1,000-2,000 acre pilot project would have to be fairly large and might cost about $1.3 million. As an alternative to erection of a new mill, consideration might be given to the feasibility of locating the project near an existing estate with available facilities for processing the crop.

Pineapple (Ananas sativus Schult)

The pineapple industry's difficulty is that it expanded rapidly by emphasizing low cost production rather than quality. In a seven-year period about the 1930's, exports increased by 70%,—but by the mid-1930's progressive price reductions had brought the industry to the verge of bankruptcy. Poor conservation practices, wasteful and unscientific methods carried over from the early days of pineapple production when it was a "catch" crop rather than a "sole" crop, caused erosion and deterioration of the soil, making it useless for permanent cultivation for many decades. In the prewar years, the government and a representative packers' association cooperated to bring about sounder production practices and improved factory techniques in the canning of the fruit, but they had not made much headway when the war broke out. During the war and the occupation, the industry received a setback through loss of planted areas to lalang growth and destruction or damage to all but one of the 17 prewar canneries.

The postwar reconstruction of the industry has been directed, with some success, at production of good quality fruit based on planned development, sound agricultural methods, the working out of a proper balance between smallholder and estate cultivation and regulation of prices for various grades of fruit; modernization of processing and canning and development of by-products; and reorganization of the industry and regulation of marketing.

Exports of canned pineapple rose from 4,099 tons, valued at $3.65 million, in 1948 to 17,391 tons, valued at $19 million, in 1953.

Since 1951 there has been a cess on exports, the proceeds going toward improvement of the industry and the financing of two pineapple experimental stations, concerned with both production and processing aspects, in Selangor and South Johore.

The present area of about 25,000 acres is rather less than half what it was prewar. Of the 16,000 acres in Johore, about 6,000 are farmed by smallholders; of the balance of the acreage, all in Selangor, all but 400 acres are smallholdings. Pineapple-growing is largely a Chinese enterprise, so that the removal of large numbers of Chinese to the "new villages" and the dangers facing those working on outlying areas in Johore have to some extent retarded expansion of production. Another limiting factor is that peat land must be drained before being planted to pineapple.

All in all, the future of the industry is promising, but there are still some unsolved problems, particularly in connection with producing a better quality and more uniform fruit.

A variety more suitable for canning than the present standard "Singapore Canning" (Singapore Red Spanish) must be found. "Sarawak" grows too large, a condition which might be remedied by closer planting (2 x 1 x 4 ft: 2 rows, for hand cultivation by smallholders; 2 x 1 x 6 ft: 3 rows, for mechanical cultivation on estates, giving 14,520 and 13,068 plants per acre, respectively), and by special hormone spraying. Appearance and flavor of the chief grades of the pack should be improved and possible by-product uses for presently discarded materials should be studied.

Treatment of peat and muck soils should be improved. For peat, this means extensive and deep drainage, timed so that there will be neither excessive removal of moisture during periods of comparative drought, nor waterlogging during and after periods of excessive rain. Such diseases as green wilt, red wilt and heart rot require better control under field conditions. Nutrient needs of the various pineapple soils must be determined, so that the most suitable chemical fertilizers can be applied at the right times.

A solution must be found for the production and harvesting difficulties of smallholders, who cannot supply enough fruit of uniform quality and ripeness at a time. In this connection, continued study should be made of the practice advocated by the Department of Agriculture of spraying the crop with a growth-promoting substance 9 to 15 months after planting; this reportedly stimulates appearance of flowers about six weeks later and results in fruit ready for harvesting 150 days after spraying. Finally, an improved transport system should be worked out, to minimize damage to fruit by bruising and to facilitate its collection from smallholders within a given radius of a factory.

Recommendations. The government and the industry should in every way possible support the field and factory studies at the experimental stations. It would be wise to assign an officer exclusively to this work. The mission cautions, however, against a very quick expansion of present acreage, in view of the technical and organizational problems. Improvement of amount and quality of estate and smallholder yields would contribute more effectively to the rehabilitation of the Malayan industry than a much expanded but less efficient production.

Cocoa (Cacao: Theobroma Cacao L.)

Cocoa has received serious attention in Malaya only since 1948, following a report on its potentialities.[9] Fortunately for Malaya, the Director of Agriculture, responsible for following the broad principles of the report, has had wide experience in cocoa in West Africa.

The Department's policy has been to assure availability of a reasonable

---

[9] E. E. Cheeseman, "Report on Potentialities for the Cultivation of Cocoa in Malaya, Sarawak and North Borneo," H. M. Stat. Off., London, 1948.

supply of suitable planting material and to ascertain the localities most congenial to cocoa before attempting any but experimental production. As a result, much has been learned of the responses of varieties from several regions of the world and the promising behavior, to date, of West African *Amelonado*. Trials with a range of established shade crops and under thinned primary and secondary jungle indicate that probably the more satisfactory responses are made under the indigenous communities, and especially on the deeper, better drained soils derived from granite. Soils from the Pahang volcanics may prove to be even better.

Apart from small-scale trials with a variety of soils and canopies in the east, center and west, practical testing of cocoa under the guidance of the Director of Agriculture has been carried on since 1951 chiefly by Malayan Cocoa Ltd., on its estate at Jarangau, about 30 miles from Kuala Trengganu on the east coast, in the vicinity of the Federal experimental station at which both cocoa and oil palm are being studied. Cocoa has been planted on 126 acres, 51 acres to *Trinitario* and 75 to *Amelonado*; of the latter, about 54 acres are commercial plantings. A further 55 acres of *Amelonado* were planned for 1954. Much has been learned regarding suitable light and soil moisture conditions, raising of seedlings in nurseries under forest conditions and transporting them to the planting site, sowing at stake, espacement, fertilizer requirements, and diseases and pests. Considerable experience has been gained in budding techniques and in the use of cuttings; if the latter prove generally successful, propagation by that method would contribute to a rapid expansion of the crop should that come to be desirable. From estimates given to the mission, it appears that the costs over a period of four years—the tree requires four to eight years to reach bearing age— would be in keeping with those for other tree and palm crops. If the baskets used in lifting seedlings produced in nursery beds could be dispensed with, there would be a saving not only of their high cost (about 14 cents each), but also in the cost of transport. So far, *in situ* sowings have suffered much damage from rodents and ants but initial experience with open-footed seedlings indicates that they may provide a solution.

It has been estimated that Malaya is capable of producing 100,000 tons of cocoa bean per annum.[10] This would call for about 300,000 acres, which could be developed in perhaps three decades. The east coast is probably the best location but there may also be many suitable localities in the west and in the center. In view of favorable world market prospects and the

[10] Cheeseman, *op cit.*

promising possibilities for cocoa in Malaya, its expansion should be given every encouragement.

Among the more critical problems to be solved are thinning of forest to achieve optimum conditions at lowest cost; reduction in cost of transplants; spacing to assure a high yield with minimum expenditure on planting material, general maintenance and harvesting; fertilizing at lowest cost for maximum response; effective ways to combat insects and other pests.

Recommendations. While experiments under established shade plants, including rubber, should continue, it is probably safe to assume that the best results will be achieved in thinned primary or secondary forest in suitable locations. Experimental testing of the removal of some or all of the dominants from the forest, the better to control both light intensity and soil moisture, and nutrients, should be given serious attention.

The Department should be strengthened by the appointment of an officer with a background of research in cocoa production, to replace an officer recently lost to the Department.

A soil survey of regions likely to be hospitable to cocoa should be made as soon as possible.

A steady, systematically planned expansion of cocoa production by estate interests is to be expected and it should receive the cooperation and guidance of the Department. Cocoa also lends itself particularly well to production by the smallholder and the mission recommends that as soon as possible selected smallholders be introduced to cocoa production via a pilot program in proximity to an estate or experimental station. What we have in mind initially is something less than a full-fledged smallholder scheme; our thought is that since cocoa is for all practical purposes a new crop, it is advisable to introduce it on a limited scale, thus minimizing the difficulty of stimulating interest in a further trial should the first fail to come up to expectation. If it should be successful, it would be all the easier to start on a broader smallholder's program. The program should be planned and guided by an officer experienced in cocoa production, preferably from West Africa or Trinidad, who should be recruited as soon as possible.

Tea (*Thea sinensis L.*)

Tea has never been a major product of Malaya. However, acreage of both lowland and upland tea rose from just under 3,000 acres in 1934 to somewhat over 9,000 acres in 1949, thereafter dropping slightly. About 3.78 million lbs. of tea were produced in 1952, about 1.6 million lbs. of which were exported and about 2 million sold locally. Acreage of upland tea has increased comparatively fast, especially in the Cameron Highlands. Lowland tea is rated as "common black Ceylon" grade but upland as "medium Ceylon." However, a progressive lowland estate yields an average of 1,200 lbs. per acre at a cost of about 90 cents per lb., while the yield of a comparable upland estate averages 675 lbs. per acre at a cost which may be as much as $1.19–$1.34 per lb. Lowland tea clearly has the better economic future, the difference in price between "common" and "medium" grades not being sufficient to offset the great disparity in yield and cost of production.

For uplands tea it is necessary to solve problems of blister blight and to reduce production costs. The uplands also present a special problem of soil conservation. Broken physiography, steep slopes and shallow and erodible soils make orthodox terracing and contour furrowing difficult if not impossible. It remains to be seen whether contour planting, selective weeding and strategically placed mechanical erosion controls can solve this problem.

Recommendations. Although world consumption of tea is said to be rising and present prices are very favorable, price recessions most readily occur in the "common" tea grades such as those grown in Malaya. The mission recommends limited and gradual expansion of lowland tea; but the heavy cost of merely maintaining the soil in the uplands—quite apart from maintaining its fertility—and the low yield obtained under any but progressive management, argue against expansion of upland tea production. The Federal and Pahang State authorities should consider whether some of the more eroded properties should not be withdrawn from production.

For want of funds the Department of Agriculture has had to limit tea research. Its work on suitable "jats," pruning and fertility responses has been most useful to the industry. We urge that investigations be continued, preferably in collaboration with the leading estates.

Coffee (Coffea liberica Hiern)

Malaya's small (about 9,000 acres) commercial coffee area is planted entirely with "liberica," a long-lived variety with a relatively high yield but a low quality bean. It is grown without shade and, except for one estate in Selangor, is entirely a smallholders' crop. The peak production year was 1905, when an export crop of about 14 million lbs. was grown. As coffee prices fell and interest shifted to rubber, coffee acreage decreased and coffee became largely an interplanted "catch" or mixed crop. By 1952 coffee was planted on only 9,561 acres, just over half of the 1934 acreage, although prices in recent years have been high.

On mucks and clays and on certain "improved" peats there is promise of expanded production, especially if coffee production on "improved" peat is up to expectations. Estate production must still be regarded as experimental. The race of the variety must be improved to increase yield while maintaining resistance to environmental factors and disease; maintenance of soil fertility and techniques of tending and pruning require study.

Recommendations. Research by the Department of Agriculture has been limited because of a shortage of funds; it should be increased as soon as possible. Rapid expansion should not be attempted either by smallholders or estates. Improvement in processing would probably result in a more widely acceptable, better quality product but for some time the yield is likely to be absorbed locally.

Tobacco (Nicotiana tabacum L.)

Tobacco has long been cultivated for local use. About 30 years ago the Department of Agriculture encouraged small-scale production but advised against large acreage, because of the difficulty of obtaining a cured leaf satisfactory in texture, aroma and burning quality. By 1940, however, a total of about 5,850 acres in numerous small plots was planted to tobacco, the expansion probably being accounted for in part by an increase in duty on imported manufactured tobacco. Acreage fell sharply to about 1,300 acres by 1948; recently it has been increasing again, to an estimated 3,000-4,000 acres. Much of the tobacco is grown not as a "sole" crop but as an interplanted "catch" crop. Chinese in the new villages are now taking greater interest in tobacco because of its good cash return.

The most common variety is the local large-leafed Deli (Sumatra) type, yielding rather dry papery leaves with little aroma; yields range from 650 lbs. to nearly 1,000 lbs. per acre. It is doubtful that a first-quality leaf could be produced under local conditions of high rainfall and poor soils. The local crop suffers from the usual tobacco diseases such as mosaic, bacterial wilt and frog-eye (Cercospora).

While unquestionably more home-grown tobacco could be used in local cigarette, cigar and pipe tobacco manufacture, numerous problems of selection, fertility, disease and curing must be solved before a thriving, if small, export industry can be developed.

Recommendations. The mission recommends that the Department of Agriculture resume its studies of tobacco; the crop's future is promising, provided its quality is improved through more efficient husbandry and treatment of the leaf. It would be advisable to engage a specialist with experience in the development of better grades of tobacco under similar climatic conditions. In the meantime expansion should be planned, gradual and limited.

It might be possible to interest an organization such as the British-American Tobacco Company in undertaking production on a partnership basis with local interests, and perhaps in aiding studies related to both the growing and the processing aspects of production.

Pepper (Piper nigrum L.)

Pepper, a smallholder crop, has been cultivated in Malaya since 1790, although production has never been large. Abandonment of land under pepper in Singapore and Johore has been one cause of the relict lalang patches so common in some parts. Yields of 2-3 lbs. (dry pepper) per vine in the fifth to seventh year have been recorded, the yield for the first five years being much less. The vines may bear for at least 12-18 years.

Prices have been very high since the end of the last war but little advantage was taken of them in Malaya.

For the future, better management practices must be worked out, because the Chinese cultivators' habit of "clean weeding" does steady damage, especially in undulating sites. Maintenance of fertility is also a problem. The better type of well-drained forest soil fed with organic matter, burnt earth and wood ash produced the best returns before the use of fertilizers.

Recommendations. In view of the steady increase in demand, production should be put on a better-planned basis, giving consideration to cover crops and other means of soil and water conservation. Efforts should be made to obtain the cooperation of Chinese and other growers in stopping the practice of "clean cultivation," and the Department of Agriculture should conduct experiments aimed at determining the crop's response to various fertilizers and methods of soil husbandry.

Manila Hemp (Musa textilis Nee; Abaca)

Although the Department of Agriculture has experimented with a range of fibers, including ramie, Urena and jute, only manila hemp so far promises to be of commercial interest, and even this requires further investigation before its expansion can be considered advisable. Soils whose fertility is maintained by manures and fertilizers are capable of producing several varieties of fibers, the tensile strength and other characteristics of which can meet minimum requirements acceptable for export purposes. Several estates are producing hemp on a small scale.

Fertility of the better soils must be maintained and improved if commercially worthwhile yields are to be obtained. While there is promise for limited, planned expansion, this presupposes solution of problems of selection, soil types, fertility, and details of management and processing. If the threat of "bunchy-top," a virus disease in the Philippines and North Borneo, materializes, it might entail destruction of stands and some years of fallowing or planting to annual crops. The stem rot caused by *Marasmius sp.*, which results in serious defoliation, has been observed in Selangor and Pahang in conditions of high humidity; it requires watching lest it spread.

Recommendations. Investigations should continue, particularly with respect to varietal selection, responses to fertilizers and interplanting with young rubber. No great expansion is advocated at present.

Food Crops, Vegetables and Fruit

Food crops grown for subsistence and sale (for example, sweet potato, groundnut, yam, Colocasia, maize, soya bean and sundry pulses, sago and tapioca (largely for feeding pigs)) are estimated to cover roughly some 60,000 acres (of which about one-third is tapioca). Market garden vegetables are reported grown on about 13,000 acres, exclusive of vegetables produced for kampong consumption. Various fruits, apart from pineapples and bananas, are said to account for some 100,000 acres in the kampongs and elsewhere. It appears likely that these are all underestimates.

There is great promise for the production of additional food crops, fruits and vegetables for home consumption; there is plenty of available land and a great demand. Production for market, however, requires special consideration because of the hazards of over-production and slumps in the market. Various disease and pest problems face the grower and much needs to be learned regarding varieties, fertility and husbandry.

Recommendations. The Department of Agriculture should be supported in its efforts to improve varieties and production of some of the more important food crops such as groundnuts, soya bean (of great potential significance), sweet potato and maize.

Market garden vegetable production has been aided by the Department's work on such crops as onion, cabbage, potato (upland areas), tomato and beans, and these investigations should be continued and extended. Guidance should be provided to market gardeners in the Cameron Highlands, to avoid extensive soil deterioration.

The Department has also worked on kampong fruit (durian, rambutan, mangosteen and citrus) and has sold many plants of improved varieties to kampong holders. The mission recommends that this activity be intensified so that plant distribution can be increased many-fold in the course of the next five years.

Bananas, planted to an estimated 40,000 acres, are a very valuable food crop and find a ready market. Unfortunately, they are often grown on steep slopes after removal of primary or secondary jungle and, being a heavy feeder grown without regard to approved conservation practices, they speedily reduce soil fertility and may even induce erosion. The Federal Government should consider with the State authorities the desirability of prohibiting banana cultivation on hillsides or, if this would create political difficulty, at least of requiring that approved conservation practices be followed. Since the prescription of conservation requirements and their policing would add to the already heavy responsibilities of the State agricultural staff, prohibiting hillside cultivation seems the better alternative.

IV ANIMAL HEALTH AND PRODUCTION

General

The climatic and vegetation characteristics of Malaya are not congenial to livestock production. There are no natural pastures, and agricultural activities are directed more to tree crops and padi than to dry land annual crops. Since annual crops are limited, there has been little appreciation of the need for farmyard manure and compost. Moreover, except for buffaloes and other cattle used in some States in preparing padi fields, little use has been made of animal power. In general the people have little interest in livestock, apart from the Chinese, who raise pigs in conjunction with poultry and fish, and the Indians, who raise milch cattle.

Nevertheless, the nucleus of a livestock industry has been established. During the occupation the small but thriving industry received a serious setback, but is now on the upgrade, as shown by Table 2.

TABLE 2   Livestock Population, Selected Years, 1934-53

(Thousands)

Year	Buffalo	Other Cattle	Goats	Sheep	Pigs	Equines
1934	196.85	293.2	252.1	1	370.0	—
1939	217.0	287.7	300.0	31.0	599.0	.6
1946	170.6	242.3	129.1	23.1	252.5	.7
1953	242.8	279.2	288.7	26.3	306.1	.65

¹ Included with goats, 1934.

It is estimated that with existing pasturage, fodder, food residues, management and advisory services Malaya could support a total of 280,000 buffalo, 350,000 other cattle, 500,000 goats, 50,000 sheep and 600,000 pigs.

Classes of Livestock

Buffalo. There are two types of buffalo in Malaya, the wide-horned Kerbau or Malayan swamp buffalo of Siamese origin and the curly-horned Indian Surti or Murrah. The former is many times more numerous and is used in plowing and fertilizing of padis and, by the Chinese, in hauling timber. The Murrah type is raised for its milk by Sikhs on the west coast.

Other Cattle. Besides a small proportion of cattle of Indian origin owned by Indians, the cattle are of the so-called Siam-Kedah breed, moderate-sized, general purpose, draft-and-beef production animals originally found largely in Kedah, North Perak, Kelantan and Trengganu. There are small numbers of Bali cattle, introduced chiefly for slaughter. European breeds such as the Jersey and Holstein (Friesian) have been brought in for milk production, but have been found to be unsuited to the humidity, temperature, rainfall and nutritional conditions.

Efforts to improve breeds include importation of cattle from Pakistan, a plan for paying premiums to owners of selected indigenous bulls which are allowed freely at stud (Kelantan), and compulsory castration of scrub bulls (Kelantan and Kedah). Attempts to improve the so-called grazing reserves and to develop new ones have been fortuitous and the results negligible. Only pilot schemes and demonstrations of the value of establishing fodder grasses on kampongs are likely to make any lasting impression on the typical cattle owner.

Goats and Sheep. Indigenous sheep in Pahang and Kelantan are remarkably resistant to the environment and the low nutritional level. Breeding stock has been imported from Indonesia and India, with emphasis on meat breeds. Indians on the estates keep goats for milking. Production of both goats and sheep has a promising future, for there is a growing demand for goat meat and mutton from local sources.

Pigs. Almost wholly in the hands of the Chinese, pig production is based on the local Chinese pig upgraded by the Middle White. Breeding stock is provided from the Agricultural Department's studs, most farmers being still unwilling to breed pure-bred Middle Whites. The sequence of tapioca and vegetable production, pig-rearing and fish culture practiced by the Chinese is of great economic importance. Disrupted by the transfer of thousands of Chinese farmers to the new villages during 1950-52, this sound system of intensive farming is again getting under way. When the emergency is over, pig production should fast overtake the prewar figure, assuming the availability of enough largely home-produced bulk foods and concentrates; if most of the concentrates must be imported, production is likely to be much less attractive economically.

Poultry. Poultry is primarily a kampong industry, but several large farms have been established in recent years. Among introduced breeds the Rhode Island Red continues to be the favorite, but various others are becoming more popular. Usually little interest is shown in breeding beyond the first cross with the local birds. Ducks of improved quality (Pekin and Khaki Campbell) are beginning to show promise for such crossing. Ranikhet (Newcastle disease: avian pneumoencephalitis) took a very heavy toll of indigenous and crossed birds just after the war, but an intensive vaccination program has been most successful; during 1953 the Veterinary Department treated 3.25 million birds. It appears that this free service has been the major stimulus to interest in the rearing of poultry. Another useful contribution has been the introduction of the "chemical implant" method of caponization of cockerels.

While the decline in rubber and tin prices is reported to have diverted some interest to poultry farming, much remains to be done to build a thriving industry.

Livestock Products

Livestock products, besides meat, include hides and skins either dried, salted and tanned locally or exported raw, milk and ghee. The total annual production of fresh cow and buffalo milk is an estimated 2.5 million gallons, a negligible quantity.

Prices of livestock are very high compared with those before the war, although some slight drop in pig, beef, mutton, poultry and egg prices has recently come about. For 1953 the total value of domestic livestock based on average current market prices and taking into account the distribution, age and condition of the animals, was estimated by the Veterinary Department at $194.5 million.

While several States are almost self-sufficient with respect to fresh meat, the country generally must import animals for slaughter. But in 1953, as compared with 1952, imports of all classes of animals except pigs decreased, more animals of all classes except sheep and pigs were slaughtered, and livestock production rose. Allowing for differences in the average carcass weight of imported and local stock, the Veterinary Department estimates that the country supplies about nine-tenths of its fresh beef, about half the fresh mutton and nine-tenths of the fresh pork. Large amounts of chilled and frozen beef, mutton and pork are still imported annually from Australia.

Pests and Diseases

Malaya has eliminated most of the major bacterial and virus diseases responsible for epizootics and has facilities for the control of sporadic diseases. But animal health is still impaired by parasites and deficiency diseases. A survey of parasitological and nutritional problems and a program for their solution are needed.

Malaya is completely free from the major cattle diseases (rinderpest, foot-and-mouth, blackquarter, anthrax and tuberculosis). The authorities are aware that this fortunate state of affairs will continue only if protective measures against their introduction are continued. Recently the country has had minor and local troubles only: haemorrhagic septicaemia as the principal cattle disease; Helminth parasites, responsible for much loss in general vigor in all classes of animals; sodium arsenite residue from weed-killing operations, toxic to livestock; rabies; and melioidosis and contagious ecthyma to a limited extent in goats.

A new Veterinary Research Institute has been established at Ipoh (Perak), to which a grant of £ 94,000 was made from Colonial Development and Welfare funds. The Institute will address itself principally to preparation of vaccines and examination of field specimens but will eventually undertake basic research into livestock health and welfare. Other important recent services include preparation of 2.3 million doses of vaccine against ranikhet, for distribution not only locally but to all British colonial territories in Southeast Asia.

Problems and Recommendations

Several problems confront the development of the livestock industry. Sufficient pasturage and fodder must be available to maintain all forms of livestock in good condition during the rainy and the drier periods of the year. This would include bulk and concentrates for pigs, and grain and other foods for poultry, as well as pastures, fodder grasses and crop residues for buffalo, other cattle, goats and sheep. Natural pasturage can be established, as the Veterinary Department is demonstrating at Kluang and Paroi, but the difficulties and economic implications require investigation before it can be advocated as an extension measure. Kampong fodder grass establishment and use, while admittedly presenting extension problems, appears more feasible.

The Department of Agriculture and the Veterinary Department have long been aware of a deficiency of some kind in certain non-alluvial east coast areas, notably in the northern part of Kelantan where lameness and loss of condition in cows have been noted. Preliminary studies suggest that perhaps a mineral deficiency, possibly of phosphorus, is involved. The problem calls for study from the standpoint of animal metabolism, soil characteristics, natural vegetation and supplementary foods, and it must be determined whether the deficiency can practicably and economically be corrected.

Periodically it is proposed that there should be an effort to "ranch" cattle on a scale sufficiently large to attract estates and perhaps some quasi-official organization such as the Colonial Development Corporation. In view of the time and money involved in preparing even rough pasturage, producing fodder grasses and establishing an economically worthwhile herd, neither private enterprise nor a quasi-official organization is likely to be attracted, despite the present high price of livestock products. The problem is one that demands attention, however, and probably it could be attacked nowhere better than on the Central Animal Husbandry Station at Kluang.

There is, finally, a problem arising from the attitudes of the various population groups toward livestock: the Malay is interested mainly in buffalo, among cattle, and his interest in goats and sheep is limited; the Chinese is not interested in animal husbandry apart from the vegetable-pig-poultry-fish sequence; and the Indian's interest in cattle is confined to milk production. An educational campaign should be conducted to convince kampong owners of the advantages of livestock production, and should include demonstration at readily accessible official centers in the various States. Further, a group of carefully selected cultivators should serve as models, being assisted in keeping livestock on their own properties with a minimum of official help. Although some useful study has already been undertaken on the buffalo, it would be worthwhile to intensify and extend it; the study should cover breeding, nutrition and management aspects.

Pasture management, including production of special fodder grasses such as Guinea (*Panicum*) and Napier (*Pennisetum*) has received no more than localized attention. The Department of Agriculture's intensive work at Serdang should be tied in with the more extensive work of the Veterinary Department at Paroi and the Central Animal Husbandry Station at Kluang. The mission recommends the appointment of at least one experienced or well-trained pasture management officer. He should be understudied by several officers from both departments who might eventually take over his responsibility. Pasture management elsewhere in the Commonwealth generally is the responsibility of departments of agriculture, but there is no reason why in Malaya the Veterinary Department should not take over chief responsibility from the already over-burdened

Department of Agriculture, provided that the departments collaborate closely. The pasture management officer should be attached to the department given such responsibility. Further, the government should ask FAO for the services of a pasture management consultant experienced in subtropical or tropical pasture investigation, who could serve in Malaya for perhaps a year, during which he might lay the foundation of a progressive research and extension policy.

The Veterinary Department is responsible for encouraging production, improving breeds and preventing or eliminating disease in all classes of livestock except pigs and poultry; for these latter groups, the Department of Agriculture undertakes responsibility for production and improvement. The mission endorses the policies and accomplishments of the Veterinary Department in enabling Malaya to meet an increasing proportion of its meat, milk and poultry products needs and in providing healthy animals for agricultural work. It particularly commends the policy of not trying to breed beyond the limits of Malaya's environment and capacity for management, attempting rather to improve quality by selection from local stock and judicious introduction of equivalent types of other Asian, and perhaps African blood, avoiding introduction of animals from regions able to support larger and more productive animals.

The Department of Agriculture is conducting useful investigation and demonstration work in poultry and pig production and has brought about wide acceptance of the Middle White pig, alone or crossed with the Chinese pig. The mission recommends, however, that there be closer association with the Veterinary Department in pig and poultry research, demonstration and extension work. It also recommends that the Veterinary Department associate itself more directly with the Department of Agriculture's efforts to encourage the carrying of other livestock by smallholders and others. Since such closer collaboration will increase demands on the staff of both departments, additional personnel may be required.

v   FOREST RESOURCES

Policy

One of the principal objectives of forest policy has been that the country as a whole and each State and District shall be permanently self-supporting in timber and other forest produce. A related objective is the conservation of water and soil resources by establishing protective reserves in selected localities, even if the intrinsic value of their timber is low. The national interest requires continued adherence to these wise principles of conservation and management.

Forest Estate

Forests cover 37,452 square miles of Malaya, of which 12,496 have been constituted forest reserves for one purpose or another. About 30% of total reserves is unproductive, reserved for protective purposes only.

Management programs have been drawn up for over 6,000 square miles of reserves, much of the useful prewar work having been lost during the occupation and the emergency. These plans are in operation notably in Pahang, Malacca, Johore and Kedah, and in the principal mangrove forests in all States. There are also State programs for controlling the exploitation of nonreserved forest on State lands.

Little reafforestation is undertaken by planting, the total area being only 4,554 acres made up largely of indigenous planting in forest and, to a lesser degree, by trial establishment of exotics (pines and Eucalyptus principally) at the higher elevations.

Value of Forest Products

The yields for major products in 1953, expressed in terms of the true volume in solid cubic feet, were (in thousands):

Heavy hardwoods (durable in contact with the ground) . 4,311
Other timbers 41,277
Poles 4,103
Firewood 11,191
Charcoal 4,144
_____
Total 65,026

About 51% of the total came from forest reserves, the rest from State land; of the heavy hardwoods, 54% derived from the reserves, and of the other timbers, 45%.

Timber exports in 1953 exceeded those for all prior years except 1950.

Exports in 1953 of graded sawn timber (principally to the United Kingdom and Australia) from the Federation and Singapore equalled 82,855 tons (of 50 cubic feet), while ungraded sawn timber exports totalled 24,886 tons. The f.o.b. value of these categories of sawn timber was about $13 million in 1952 and about $19 million in 1953. Of total exports, 45% was sawn in the Federation.

The forests have for many years shown a surplus of revenue over expenditure, rising since 1946 from $230,064 to a record $5,467,771 in 1953. Gross revenue for the latter year was just over $10.6 million, derived almost entirely from timber and fuel. Less than $220,000 was expended for silviculture and only about $145,000 for research, extremely modest expenditure for the valuable work accomplished. The Department's conservation, management, silviculture, exploitation and research practices are of comparatively high standard, especially in view of the moderate size of its staff.

Sawmilling Industry

Sawmilling, established in the 1930's, is one of Malaya's most important industries. It provides direct employment for about 20,000 men, plus an equal number engaged in working on the timber, so that in all about 150,000 persons depend upon the industry. At the time of the mission's visit, there were over 350 sawmills in Malaya, of which only about 80 were sizeable. The industry's annual production is valued at about $70 million, although it reached $100 million during the boom years.

Because of the initially low level of prevailing wages, Malayan timber used to be among the cheapest available anywhere. But more recent events have led to uneconomic development: during the boom period too many mills were built and many drew materials from as much as a hundred miles away. Security considerations and the risks involved in working some forest areas led variously to the basing of mills in towns rather than forests, to a concentration of logging in some areas, making for longer hauls to the mills, to marked increases in loggers' wages, and to inadequate supervision. Because emergency regulations prohibit workers from taking their food into the forests in many areas, the working day is only about four hours despite the high wages. Logging and milling have been inefficient, not having kept pace with requirements and with the rising wages, and finally, rail and sea freights have increased, as have timber royalties, while timber prices in the overseas markets have declined.

As a consequence the industry is in a parlous state and requires reorganization. To this end we endorse the proposal, made by some in the industry, that a timber trade advisory council should be set up. The council would advise on such matters as licensing; royalties and rail transport rates; distribution of log supplies; inspection; and maintenance of grades, quality and trade names. All branches of the industry should be represented, and official representation might include the Treasury, Public Works and Transport. The proposed council would give better representation to the interests of the industry and would provide opportunities for an expression of its views. Necessary funds might be raised by means of a cess on sawmill production. The council might also consider and recommend ways of fostering the use of tractors in logging operations and of replacing the large amount of obsolete milling facilities with modern equipment. These appear to be the most effective long-run possibilities for reducing production costs. Tractors are especially needed to prepare approach roads and drag logs from stumps, leaving the winch lorry commonly used for this purpose to transport logs from collection points. Difficulties created by the emergency and reportedly encountered by contractors seeking acceptable hire-purchase terms now limit the use of tractors.

The advisory council might also consider ways of improving export marketing, perhaps through cooperative sales, transport, storage and loading at the ports and handling methods, and ways of reducing costs.

Regeneration Operations

The acreage covered by essential silvicultural treatment, aimed at establishing more valuable crops of timber, is at present far too small.

The annual coupe (the total acreage in the reserves which could be cleared annually without risk of felling more than could be grown in the same period by the forest as a whole) ranges from 45,000 to 50,000 acres. This assumes a 70-year rotation, during which young regeneration would be brought to maturity under the "shelterwood" system. To achieve this objective and to provide an enhanced economic return at the end of the rotation, regeneration fellings and related operations are required after removal of the timber. Timely "improvement" operations could result in a yield, by the end of the 70-year rotation, of two to three times that from the same type of forest not subjected to silvicultural treatment. Ideally the work should be performed at a rate which keeps abreast of current exploitation and cuts into the backlog built up during the past decade; this would call for an expenditure of about $1.5 million per annum, based on an estimate of $30 for each acre of the annual coupe. Expenditure on regeneration work was only about $210,000 in 1953, and although this was more than twice the 1952 expenditure, it is far short of adequacy if Malaya is to become and remain self-supporting in timber. But other demands on public funds for the time being make it impracticable to carry out regeneration at a rate commensurate with the rate of felling. In Chapter 3 of Part II, we have recommended an increase in these annual expenditures to about $600,000.

Reserve Areas

By far the greatest proportion of the valuable forests are at the lower levels, below 1,000 feet elevation, and extensive forest reserves have accordingly been established at this elevation in all the States and Settlements. It is probable that the size and number of reserves in the lower elevations will have to be reduced appreciably over the next few decades, to make way for agricultural development. The objective should be to assure the maximum return from the reserves consistent with agricultural development needs, and this demands a planned completion of exploitation of the reserves and conversion of the residual forest to agricultural uses. It is therefore most important that the Federal and State and Settlement Governments determine the basis of selection for reduction or elimination of reserves and the necessary schedule for exploitation.

To make up for the losses in timber potential, the Hill and Upper Dipterocarp reserves, between 1,000 and 4,000 feet elevation, will have to be utilized on a planned basis and subsequently regenerated. The best methods of exploitation and the most economic means of extraction should be studied in the near future.

The montane forest reserves at the higher elevations, 3,500 to 5,000 feet, are of little economic value because of the small size and tortuous form of the trees. We recommend that the Department experiment on a more intensive basis than heretofore with trial replacement by some of the more promising exotic species, such as *Pinus insularis, Eucalyptus robusta* and *E. decaisneana* which might yield small, straight material for a range of agricultural needs, including fuel. Kenya, Southern Rhodesia and South Africa might supply information regarding other exotic species of some value.

VI RESEARCH, EXTENSION AND EDUCATION

A RESEARCH AND INFORMATION

Throughout the preceding parts of this report recommendations have been made for particular research projects. For convenience, some of the more important of these recommendations are gathered together here.

The standard of research in agriculture, veterinary services and animal husbandry and forestry is satisfactory, and in some instances high, but growing demands for agricultural diversification make it essential that this activity be expanded.

The Federal Government has a responsibility to ensure that sufficient well-qualified research workers are available to speed solution of some of the more pressing problems, as well as to provide opportunities for locally domiciled persons, trained in research, to acquire experience under skilled direction. Limited numbers have, in fact, been sent overseas with official support for all their training in research or for specialized instruction and experience. It is suggested that the numbers be increased as soon as more men with the necessary basic training and aptitude for research become available.

It is extremely difficult to attract experienced research staff to under-developed countries in a status of political transition. Thus it is desirable that the more senior officers be given every support and encouragement to induce them to remain as long as regulations and policy permit; the opportunity to collaborate in research activities with men of reputation will further serve to attract staff.

Agriculture

Further research is required on padi;[11] the coconut and oil palm industries; cocoa; the possibilities of stimulating and improving production of pineapple, coffee, tea, pepper and tobacco; pasture management; and rehabilitation of mining areas for agricultural purposes. This would entail additional funds for staff, equipment and other facilities.

[11] Among the research problems of padi, it would be most helpful for future planning purposes if the issue of the suitability of peat lands for padi cultivation could be more clearly resolved. The experience in Japan in this connection might be helpful and we would also suggest consultation with rice experts of FAO.

The government should investigate the possibility of interesting commercial firms, such as Imperial Chemical Industries, Unilever, and the British-American Tobacco Company in making available trained personnel on secondment for research in fields in which they are directly concerned. The various companies which maintain their own research personnel in Malaya should be invited to collaborate with the government in commodity research, particularly on the oil palm and cocoa.

The recently established Agronomic Branch of the Department is closely related to the Research Branch in its objectives and activities; it also has associations with extension work. It is particularly important, therefore, that the research and experimentation being conducted by the new branch be given every possible support.

Veterinary Medicine and Animal Production

The Veterinary Department has done praiseworthy work on livestock pests and diseases. It is equally commendable that its research has not been confined to veterinary medicine but has extended to husbandry and livestock production. To the extent permitted by staff and facilities, it has also worked on the establishment and management of pasturage.

The mission endorses the Department's plans for studies in parasitology as well as "deficiency," a limitation on livestock development caused by some environmental factor or combination of factors, acting sometimes through the vegetation. The necessary staff might be made available through the United Nations technical assistance program or under the Colombo Plan; otherwise, the studies should be financed by the government.

Forestry

The Forestry Department has done considerable research into conservation and production problems, and we believe that this work should be supported on an increased scale. Progress in finding additional commercial uses for Malayan forestry products and possibilities for more extensive propagation of commercially useful timber varieties would be of great significance for the economy in view of the very rapid rate of tree growth in the Malayan environment. This warrants continuing research emphasis on silviculture, botany of forest trees, entomology and pathology as well as studies of timber mechanics, durability, preservation, technology and chemistry. We may also mention specifically the importance of further investigation into uses of timber for pulping and fiber board manufacture, improved means of timber extraction and more effective methods of milling.

Agricultural Meteorology

Although the climatic conditions in Malaya are said to be relatively uniform, it is desirable that the meteorological authorities, in collaboration with the Agricultural, Veterinary, Forestry and Drainage and Irrigation Departments, direct more attention to the collection of data bearing on the major climatic factors of significance to the work of these departments. Rainfall data are too infrequent for parts of eastern Malaya, among others; intensity of rainfall is rarely measured; evaporation records exist for Singapore reservoirs and one or two other centers only; and sunshine duration and wind force information is sparse.

It is recommended that the meteorological authorities and the other departments concerned formulate proposals designed to fill the gaps in the present data on prime meteorological factors of significance in agriculture and related subjects. These proposals will undoubtedly call for additional funds for equipment and perhaps for additional observers and other staff; reasonable additional expenditure would be justified in view of the contribution which a better knowledge of climatic factors could make to agricultural research and practice.

Irrigation and Drainage

For a number of years, interrupted by the war, the Department of Drainage and Irrigation has taken river gaugings and made other hydrological studies. The present status of these measures and studies, and proposals for their expansion are discussed in Technical Report 2 on irrigation and drainage.

"Degraded" Land

We have noted the continuing conflict of interest between land use for alluvial mining and for agriculture and forestry, and have indicated our view that there is a strong presumption that the extraction of valuable mineral deposits, even though it damages land for agricultural and forestry purposes, is in the national interest, provided the damage is localized and does not create secondary dangers of erosion and silting over an extensive area of actually or potentially valuable agricultural land. We do not, however, minimize the importance of rehabilitating localized degradation from mining. Present land-reconditioning requirements imposed on mining lessees are not usually a really satisfactory answer. Much more research and experimentation is necessary to determine what measures will actually restore the lands to a satisfactory cultivable state. This is a matter on which several governmental departments should collaborate, especially Agriculture, Forestry, Mining, Geological Survey and Drainage and Irrigation, perhaps through a small interdepartmental team.

Such research is a prerequisite to the approach to the land degradation problem elsewhere suggested, in terms of particular mining areas considered as a whole rather than of individual mines. And it should be recognized that an extended period will be required for the investigations necessary to develop effective rehabilitation methods.

The general lines of investigation should be somewhat as follows:

1. A reconnaissance survey to determine the major types of degradation and the nature of the locales in which they are to be found;

2. Sampling of such major types to determine shortcomings of the soils through profile, physicochemical and biological analyses;

3. Field testing of selected types of degraded soils with, *inter alia,* the following objectives:

a. To throw light on the rate and extent of improvement in edaphic conditions through biotic reaction on the several types of soils by both natural plant succession and selected preparatory vegetation;

b. To determine the influence of such practices as drainage, soil preparation to improve aeration and other physical factors, and manuring with chemical fertilizers, organic materials, etc. Experimentation in these practices should be related to selected kinds of crops and trees;

4. Experimental rehabilitation of a small region of degraded soils not only to study the practical application of the results of preceding research and investigations but also to guide the planning of such programs on a larger scale and to determine what practices should be observed in the course of mining operations to facilitate subsequent rehabilitation.

Research Advisory Committee

The mission suggests that the government consider the appointment of a small research advisory committee, centered in London, on which distinguished scientists would be invited to serve. Their function would be to take a special interest in, and advise on, the agricultural and related research problems of the Federation. This committee would supplement the general assistance given to research in Malaya by the Colonial Advisory Research Committee for Agriculture and Forestry, by directing its advice and efforts to Malaya alone.

B EXTENSION SERVICES

Agricultural Extension (Field Branch)

There is a Field Branch of the Department of Agriculture with a small advisory Federal section centered in Kuala Lumpur and a corps of Agricultural Officers, Assistant Agricultural Officers, Agricultural Assistants, and Junior Agricultural Assistants distributed among the States and Settlements. A major obstacle to the application of agricultural policy is that this branch is woefully inadequate, not because of a lack of interest or efficiency, but because its personnel is much too thinly spread. There are too few fully trained or experienced Agricultural Officers, and the lower staff levels are also seriously short, down to the lowest grade.

It is unfortunately true that even if funds as requested by the Department had been appropriated, there would be difficulty in filling posts as rapidly as desirable. It would certainly be necessary to draw senior officers from overseas to begin with and junior staff would have to be trained, at Serdang and elsewhere, on a scale not previously attempted. But there is no question that additional staff is needed.

The present establishment of 18 agricultural officers in the Field Branch is too few to bring about any significant agricultural development. Government should bring in a number of officers from overseas and should at the same time send abroad for training a number of selected Malayan-born students. Although the government's stated target for 1959 is 22 agricultural officers, 27 would be a better target, having regard to the problems to be solved.

The mission also recommends an increase in the number of Agricultural Assistants. These officers are one of the principal needs in extension work; they and the Junior Agricultural Assistants should be in close and constant contact with the cultivators in padi fields and kampongs, guiding, encouraging, demonstrating and gradually bringing about greater interest in quality and quantity of production. The number of Agricultural Assistants proposed for 1959 in the Department's "1951 Reorganization Proposals" should be raised, although the mission realizes that the training of so many men is likely to create difficulties at Serdang, assuming enough suitable candidates were attracted to the course.

Junior Agricultural Assistants are lamentably short; these, the most junior of the trained staff, could play a more important role in extension duties than they do. It is recommended that not only should the present establishment of 154 be increased toward a goal of 250 (the Department's goal for 1959 is only 170) but that a more satisfactory course of training should be provided, as proposed later in this report.

Of course, the employment of additional staff will not, by itself, accomplish the objective of bringing home to the cultivator a practical conception of the improvements he might make in his farming. Opportunities for instruction and intellectual stimulation must be provided for all grades of officers: for the senior staff, conferences, technical literature and refresher courses overseas; for the junior ranks, short courses of instruction, suitable literature, competitions, and so on.

Although all aspects of extension work are important, some activities now demand more than the ordinary degree of attention. These include padi production and kampong agriculture—food crops, vegetables, fruit and livestock husbandry.

Special mention may be made of the subject of extension services to kampong agriculture since this offers a challenging and promising field for improvements by way of increased production. In addition to such crops as rubber, padi, coconut and fruits and livestock and poultry, there are those peculiar to the kampong: areca, sago, nipah, pandanus, kapok, gambier, tuba (Derris), cloves, pepper and pulses. Increased production depends on the government's skill in directing the energies and interest of the cultivators, and this in turn requires better knowledge of other than purely agricultural aspects of the kampong economy. The Departments of Agriculture and Drainage and Irrigation and the Veterinary Department have long been aware of the need for such studies but have not had the funds and staff, simultaneously, to undertake them.

The field is so vast that the mission cannot attempt detailed recommendations. We do, however, urge thorough studies of the kampong communities and their special agricultural and related problems. The officers selected to undertake the studies, who should be extension officers of the Department of Agriculture, should be particularly fitted by outlook and experience to win the goodwill and cooperation of the kampong dwellers. They should also work closely with personnel of such government agencies as Social Welfare and Public Health. We suggest further that the Federal and State authorities set up joint working parties to propose practicable methods of inducing kampong cultivators to take advantage of educational, demonstration and other facilities available to them in the crop and livestock fields; for improving demonstration techniques and making them more widely available; and for supplying cultivators with seed, plants, livestock and equipment at reasonable cost. Unless the government gives sympathetic consideration to requests for additional staff needed to put into effect the recommendations of the working parties, it is unlikely that any appreciable progress can be made. In any event, increased production from the kampongs will at best come very gradually.

Closely connected with increases in agricultural production are improvements in feeder roads and in marketing and credit facilities. These are discussed elsewhere in the mission's report.

Veterinary and Animal Production Extension Service

Veterinary services and animal production demonstrations and publicity have considerably restored the once decimated livestock of Malaya. These services have been accomplished by a comparatively small Department. If the livestock population is to be raised to its prewar level and beyond, the Department must be strengthened.

Assistant Veterinary Officers form the most significant part of the staff responsible for field services. We recommend that the establishment of 38 be raised to 44. Veterinary Assistants and Veterinary Attendants play an important role in aiding the Assistant Veterinary and other senior officers in extension and other field duties. In many localities the duties of these officers also extend to animal production services. The existing establishment of 47 Veterinary Assistants and 62 Attendants should, we recommend, be raised to 67 and 72, respectively. The Department should make the necessary arrangements for their training.

Forestry Field Services

Although the Department of Forestry has no responsibility for "extension" comparable to that of the Department of Agriculture and the Veterinary Department, it has important field duties: the conservation, management and improvement of forest reserves and the administration of forest exploitation on State land. For these duties it has a staff with university or equivalent training in forestry, supported by subordinate field staff trained in Malaya. As the work in forestry intensifies, the need for trained staff increases. The forest estate is so important that the Department must have adequate staff.

Five additional posts should be added to the present establishment of 39 senior officers. The increase is necessitated by the intensification of forestry work following on the development of several forest districts. A corresponding increase should be made in the subordinate staff.

Plant Protection Service

The mission concurs in the recommendation of the Department of Agriculture that a Plant Protection Service be established. It further recommends that the service be established promptly, to guard against the potential danger from virus, bacterial and fungus diseases brought to Malaya by aircraft or vessels.

C EDUCATION

Agriculture

Government assistance is given to locally domiciled persons for higher education in British and Australian universities and courses are offered to subordinate staff at the College of Agriculture at Serdang. Recently, consideration has been given to establishing a Faculty of Agriculture of the University of Malaya and to the question of whether, in that event, the three-year and one-year courses at Serdang for Agricultural Assistants and Junior Agricultural Assistants, respectively, should be continued.

Having considered the matter from the standpoint of educational advantage and the best use of public funds, the mission has concluded that a Faculty of Agriculture is not urgently needed and might well be considered an eventual rather than an immediate objective. It would be better educationally, as well as less costly, to continue awarding scholarships to overseas universities[12] than to create a Faculty for the training of a limited number of candidates a year. Even were other British Southeast Asian territories to send their candidates to the Faculty, probably no more than 12 or 16 could be absorbed per year in the several services in the first five years and probably fewer thereafter. Even a small Faculty, largely supported by the Department of Agriculture and situated at Serdang where many facilities are available, would entail an estimated capital cost of from $500,000 to $1 million over the first five years, and recurrent expenditure of $250,000–$300,000 per annum.

We do, however, recommend that the senior course at Serdang be reviewed, to see whether it can accomplish its objective more effectively, and whether additional teaching staff, equipment and other facilities should be provided. We understand that the Department is undertaking to do just this, improving the content and providing more satisfactory instruction, having in mind the possibility that the course may be taken over by the University.

As an alternative to the immediate establishment of an agricultural faculty, we suggest that the University might take over the Serdang three-year course for a time. This would give the University time to determine how an agricultural faculty might best be staffed and supported, and an opportunity to gain some experience in practical administration. The standards of the present course might be raised by the provision of somewhat better laboratory and other facilities and by a strengthening of the staff. If desirable, the successful candidates might be granted a diploma by the University.

The one-year course for Junior Agricultural Assistants suffers from being given along with the senior course at Serdang. Not only is an undue burden placed on the teaching staff but facilities are also inadequate. Moreover, it is psychologically unsound to have in a single center students of senior and junior status and of different ultimate prospects in the Department. As the one-year course is essentially a practical one, it could readily be given at another center, where padi, rubber and other crops could be studied in the field, something not possible at Serdang. The Department has in mind the re-siting and general improvement of the content of this

[12] £ 400 per annum for unmarried men, £ 600 for married men, for periods of from two to four years, depending upon the individual and the university selected.

course: its intentions, as communicated to the mission, appear to be sound in principle and detail.

Consideration should be given to the question whether biological or rural science courses should be offered in the schools. While the mission recommends that the advice of experts in this matter be sought, we caution against indiscriminate introduction of so-called "courses in agriculture," since these often develop in the student a dislike of anything associated with the farm. This usually is due in part to the handling of the subject by teachers not well trained themselves, and also to unimaginative "practical" assignments.

Interest in agriculture should be stimulated by broadcasts on extension subjects and by the encouragement of organizations similar to the young Farmers' Clubs in other countries. The Departments of Agriculture and Education might collaborate on appropriate programs of this kind.

Veterinary Medicine and Animal Husbandry

Veterinary, Research and super-scale Officers must possess the M.R.C.V.S. qualification or its registrable equivalent. Deputy Veterinary Officers and Assistant Veterinary Officers must hold a degree or diploma awarded by a recognized university in India or Pakistan. Veterinary Assistants and Laboratory Assistants are locally-trained men, who have obtained a Cambridge School Certificate; no other grades receive local training.

The mission considers the present arrangements for the overseas training of all senior grade officers to be satisfactory and recommends their continuation. Even if a Faculty of Agriculture were established at the University, we would not recommend a course in veterinary medicine there; experience and materials for satisfactory training are lacking. We suggest that the scope and duration of the training of Veterinary Assistants might be reviewed: with the new Research Institute at Ipoh and steadily improving facilities elsewhere there appears to be no reason why the standard of this course should not be raised.

Forestry

Locally domiciled persons, suitably qualified educationally and otherwise, are sent for advanced training in United Kingdom or Australian universities. Subordinate staff is given a short course at the Forest Research Institute at Kepong.

The program of overseas training for the higher branches of the Department should continue to receive government support. As the training in Australia appears to offer some advantages, it is recommended that efforts be made to arrange for the conferring of a degree in forestry after successful completion of two years of forestry study for candidates who have taken two years in basic sciences at the University of Malaya. Such an arrangement has been made with Oxford.

We have no specific recommendations with respect to the Kepong course for subordinate staff, which is apparently well organized and adequate.

VII FINANCIAL REQUIREMENTS

The implications of the preceding recommendations in the agricultural fields in terms of additional staff and financial requirements may now be summarized. It should be noted that the estimates of staff and cost are only rough approximations and are presented as illustrative of what appear to be reasonable requirements. The estimates of recurrent expenditures are expressed as additions to the recurrent expenditure for the establishment as it existed in 1954.

Department of Agriculture

Senior Officers

1. Agricultural Officers, including one officer each for the proposed oil palm, cocoa and coconut replanting projects . .   10
2. Agronomists   2
3. Research Officers
   Coconut and Oil Palm   1
   Cocoa   1
   Soils   1
   Padi   1
   Others   2
4. Agricultural Economists (Marketing)   2
5. Lecturers for training programs   2
                                                              —
                  Total   22

Other Staff	Agricultural Assistants	Junior Agricultural Assistants
Field (Extension)Branch . .	32	74
Research Branch	18	9
Agronomy Branch	16	25
Education Branch	4	2
Total	70	110

Recurrent expenditure required for personal emoluments and other purposes (including an agricultural marketing division, pilot smallholder projects for cocoa and oil palm, subsidies for padi fertilizer and for coconut replanting, and recommended additions to research, training and extension services) may be estimated to increase by about $2 million during the five years.

Capital expenditure requirements for the five-year period as a whole, mainly for buildings and equipment (including a new training center for Junior Agricultural Assistants) and for the recommended pilot oil palm and cocoa projects, may be put at about $5 million.

Veterinary Department

Senior Officers

Research

Parasitologist 1

Biochemist 1

Pasture Research 1

Assistant Veterinary Officers 6

Total 9

Other Staff

Veterinary Assistants 20

Veterinary Attendants 10

Total 30

The additional annually recurrent expenditure may be estimated to increase by about $300,000 per year. Capital expenditures for the five-year period for buildings, equipment and quarters; establishment of an animal husbandry station on the east coast and purchase of livestock seem likely to be about $1.5 million.

Forestry Department

Senior Staff 7

Other Staff 50

Recurrent expenditure, including the salaries of additional staff and an increase in silviculture expenditure by about $400,000 a year, may be estimated to increase by about $700,000. Capital expenditures, mainly for forest roads, reclamation of degraded lands and buildings and equipment, may be estimated at about $5.5 million.

Land-Use Survey

Annually recurrent expenditure requirements may be estimated to rise to about $250,000 while total capital expenditures, including the cost of aerial photography, may be put roughly at about $3.3 million over five years.

TECHNICAL REPORT 2

IRRIGATION, DRAINAGE AND RIVER CONSERVANCY

Background and History

Irrigation and drainage programs of the Drainage and Irrigation Department are among the most important activities being carried on for the development of Malayan agriculture. The Department is also responsible for river conservancy. Irrigation programs account for more than half of all public expenditure for water control purposes. Drainage schemes, concentrated in the western coastal areas, are for the improvement and protection of land under rubber, coconut and other crops. Heavy silting of rivers has necessitated flood mitigation, silt retention and other river conservation works; the establishment and maintenance of such works is of continuing importance, but the task of the authorities in this field has been lightened by measures of control prescribed under the Mining Enactment and by soil conservation measures applied in agriculture and forestry.

Modern efforts at drainage date from the latter part of the nineteenth and early twentieth centuries; the Wan Mat Saman Canal is an example of these. The first of the modern irrigation schemes, that at Krian, dates from about 1892, although a canal was constructed in that area before 1880 in an unsuccessful attempt to bring water to the padi lands.

In 1913 an Irrigation Branch of the Public Works Department (PWD) was formed; its functions were confined to investigation. In 1921 it became the Hydraulics Branch of the PWD and its functions were enlarged to include the investigation and collection of data concerning the conservation of rivers. Meanwhile, in northern Kedah, drainage schemes were being undertaken by an Irrigation Branch of the State PWD. Catastrophic floods in 1926 led to much greater river conservancy activities. In the 1930's, as a result of the findings of a Committee of Inquiry on rice production, the Hydraulics Branch was detached from PWD and given departmental status as the Drainage and Irrigation Department (DID).[1]

---

[1] The abbreviation DID is commonly used in referring to both Federal and State Departments of Drainage and Irrigation and to their combined activities.

Federal-State Responsibility

Responsibility for drainage and irrigation is divided between the Federal DID and corresponding departments in the States and Settlements.

The Federal Department in effect works on a joint basis with the State and Settlement Departments. The Director has full executive and administrative control of Federal works and activities, while in the States and Settlements he functions in an advisory capacity but with direct access to DID heads on technical matters. He is responsible for the control and accounting of all DID expenditures from the Federal ordinary and loan budgets; performance of the work is supervised by State and Settlement officers in their territories.

Construction activity on drainage and similar works is handled by the staff of the departments concerned and with equipment owned by the departments, except for the building of concrete structures, performed on a contract basis. The equipment at the disposal of DID includes more than 90 dragline excavators, 10 river dredges and a variety of mechanical equipment such as tractors, graders and other earth-moving machinery.

The DID staff at headquarters and in State and Settlement posts as of December 31, 1954 consisted of 740 persons, including 59 senior administrative officers and 498 subordinate technical staff; 20 of the senior officers and 54 of the technicians are attached to headquarters, a number of whom are posted from time to time to the States and Settlements to assist in carrying out special projects as may be necessary. The volume of work that can be undertaken in any State depends upon the number of engineers on the particular State's establishment. The posting of staff is a Federal responsibility but acceptance rests with States and Settlements.

Relationships between members of staff functioning under this dual arrangement are extremely good. This is probably due in large measure to personal factors, to earlier associations and to community of interests. In the course of time some of these cementing influences may disappear and unless others take their place problems arising from division of responsibility will multiply. But even the utmost in good will and desire to make things work is not likely to overcome all of the handicaps imposed by the present system.

The Department faces special recruitment problems arising out of the nature of its activities. The work of the technical staff is often arduous in the extreme. It may involve months in isolated areas cut off from normal amenities, and long periods of work in unhealthy jungle swamp. These hardships, which are not common to other engineering departments, act as a deterrent to young men who might otherwise consider employment with DID. It may be necessary to offer higher salaries or special field allowances to prospective employees.

Development of activities in irrigation, drainage, river conservancy and the like is reflected in expenditures given in Table 1. The gradual increase in activity up to 1939 was interrupted by the war and Japanese occupation, when projects under construction were halted and works in general were allowed to deteriorate; much of DID's effort in the early postwar years had to be devoted to restoration.

TABLE 1   Total Expenditures of Federal and State/Settlement Departments of Drainage and Irrigation

(*Thousand $*)

Year	Expenditure	Year	Expenditure
1932	862	1950	7,912
1939	2,050	1951	9,729
1946	2,345	1952	12,446
1947	4,979	1953	15,739
1948	6,648	1954	20,000[1]
1949	4,800		

[1] Based on budget estimates. Actual accounts for 1954 will undoubtedly show a lower figure.

SOURCE: Figures 1932, 1939 and 1946–53 from Department of Drainage and Irrigation.

Since 1950 there has been a significant increase in programs. This reflects the Six-Year Draft Development Program (1950-55) under which both Federal and State Drainage and Irrigation Departments undertook to construct 59 irrigation schemes for the improvement of 300,000 acres of existing padi land and the development of some 100,000 acres of new land.

In 1953, under an additional program, DID submitted plans for 34 irrigation schemes, 10 drainage schemes and six projects for river conservancy. Capital expenditures under this program during 1955-59 are estimated at just over $50 million, including about $32 million for irrigation, $7 million for drainage, $8 million for river conservancy, $3 million for additional plant and equipment and $1 million for surveys and research purposes.

Irrigation

About 60% of DID's total expenditures is concentrated on irrigation, primarily for the purpose of expanding padi production. Effort and expenditure have largely been directed to providing or improving irrigation for already cultivated padi areas, where production can be raised more quickly and simply than by opening new land; the problems and delays incident to land clearance, colonization and the establishment of transport, communications and other community facilities are avoided.

But while given much less, and perhaps inadequate, emphasis in the DID programs, the development of new land has not been neglected. The Tanjong Karang project in Selangor, involving 100,000 acres, about half of which are irrigated, is nearly completed and largely under cultivation. About 20,000 acres of new padi land have been opened in the Sungei Manik project in Perak since 1933 and a number of other projects have made provision for considerable additional new land development. A start has now been made on the first stage of the Trans-Perak irrigation project in Perak where, subject to further investigation by consulting engineers, an area of 180,000 acres of additional land is expected eventually to be brought under cultivation, mainly in padi.

In 1949 the government agencies concerned estimated that about 600,000 acres of padi land could be improved by irrigation and that about 763,000 acres of unused land, mainly swamp jungle, could be developed for wet padi cultivation. More recent estimates indicate that over half of the latter area is overlaid with peat, much of it to a considerable depth, on which the practicable possibilities of successful padi cultivation are as yet uncertain.

Between 1949 and 1953 some 200,000 acres of padi land were improved by irrigation and about 40,000 acres of new land were brought into cultivation. Irrigation works serving a further 50,000 acres of existing padi lands and 20,000 acres of new land were expected to be completed in 1954. The total area for which irrigation facilities were established or improved during the six years 1949-54 is therefore estimated at 250,000 acres of already cultivated land and 60,000 acres of additional land.

For the period 1955-59 the DID program includes 34 irrigation projects, both improvement of existing works and construction of new ones, to affect an estimated 200,000 acres or more of presently cultivated padi area and 70,000 acres of new undeveloped land. Some of this would be attributable to projects started prior to 1955 but scheduled for completion during 1955-59.

The DID estimates the capital cost of its proposed 1955-59 program at about $32 million. This estimate is undoubtedly much too low, since it excludes costs outside DID's jurisdiction, especially in new land development: construction of access roads, payments to settlers for land clearance work, additional initial grants to settlers for subsistence if necessary, and water supplies, schools, dispensaries and other community requirements. Some part of annually recurrent appropriations for the DID should also properly be charged to capital outlay.

While during the same period the area to be improved or opened up is estimated to be about 270,000 acres, it is not entirely accurate to relate this improvement to the capital outlay to be made in that period. Part of this addition to the irrigated area will result from the continuation or extension of projects undertaken prior to 1955, and therefore to some extent should be attributed to expenditures made prior to 1955. Similarly, some of the expenditure proposed for 1955-59 will be for projects whose construction would extend beyond that period.

A cost-benefit analysis is further complicated by the fact that there appears to be a wide variation in per acre costs among projects. Moreover, many projects are designed both to improve existing land and to develop new land, and the per acre costs and benefits for the one differ substantially from those for the other. There is also wide variation in the per acre maintenance costs of different projects, while information on the economics of cultivation is so limited as to preclude any evaluation of the net benefit realized by cultivators in relation to the capital expenditures involved.

Accordingly, an accurate cost-benefit analysis of the irrigation program is not possible and a financial and economic assessment can be made only in terms of gross returns in relation to capital expenditure; even this can be done only in fairly rough and approximate figures.

DID's information on its capital outlays on irrigation projects suggests that a fairly representative per acre cost figure for DID activities on projects included in the proposed 1955-59 program would be somewhere between $100 and $125 per acre of land within the irrigation areas. The higher figure in this range may be taken, to allow for the imputation to capital works of some part of the Department's recurring expenditure. On the basis of experience it may be assumed that about 75% of the padi land within the irrigation areas would be irrigated and planted and therefore the cost per planted acre may be taken at about $170. For a number of individual projects, per acre cost appears to be much higher but the land affected by them is only a small part of the total acreage. The figure would make no allowance for the non-DID expenditure involved in opening new land, such as cost of land clearance, subsistence allowances for settlers where necessary, access roads, outlays for tools and seed, milling and marketing installations, provision of housing and community facilities, etc. No inclusive estimate is available for such new land development but the figure might run to two or three times that incurred by DID alone.

Definite information is also lacking as to anticipated additional output as a result of irrigation. On the basis of experience, however, it seems reasonable to estimate such additional annual output from existing padi lands at about 60-70 gantangs[2] (about 335-390 lbs.) of padi per acre on the average, while a comparable production figure for newly opened padi land would be about 330 gantangs (about 1,850 lbs.) per acre. Assuming that a price for domestic padi, related to imported rice prices, would be about 50 cents per gantang, this would mean an increase of about $35 per acre in value of output from already cultivated land and of about $165 per acre from the newly opened land under cultivation.[3]

These calculations are obviously only approximate and provide no more than a rough basis for economic and financial appraisal. They suggest, however, satisfactory rates of direct annual gross return in relation to capital, which would appear to justify the capital outlay involved. While the gross return per unit of capital expenditure in irrigating already cultivated land is considerably smaller, relative to cost, than in developing new land, it may be noted that nearly all of the increased productivity in the former represents a net gain: little additional operating labor or expense on the part of the cultivator is necessary and the only regular expense is the annual cost of maintaining the irrigation works, on the average about $5.00 per acre.

While there appears to be no question of the economic and financial justification of most of the proposed capital outlays on irrigation, the neces-

[2] One gantang of padi averages about 5.6 lbs.

[3] This figure as an average gross return per planted acre does not allow for additional output and income to be expected from such commodities as fish, poultry and goats and other subsidiary activities which are of considerable significance in the usual agricultural pattern. The figure would also be affected to the extent that part of the land were to be used for other crops or other production purposes with a higher or lower gross average annual output as compared with padi.

sity of carefully allocating the limited resources of the Federation suggests that the necessary data should be more systematically collected and that for individual projects there should be a more careful analysis of estimated economic and financial benefits in relation to total costs (including costs other than those under DID jurisdiction). It would seem advisable that an officer of the DID be sent abroad to study techniques of cost-benefit analysis under environmental conditions somewhat similar to Malaya; e.g., in Japan or in East Pakistan, where considerable work on irrigation project analysis has been done with the assistance of FAO.

We have pointed out that while our estimated DID capital outlay figure of $170 per planted acre for the 1955-59 program may be taken as fairly representative for most of the land area involved, for some of the projects (involving irrigation of some 10,000-15,000 acres, mainly of existing padi land) the per acre capital requirement is much higher. It is impossible to arrive at a precise and uniform figure of maximum cost per acre beyond which the economic justification for an irrigation project would be doubtful. The benefits in additional produce vary from project to project, as does the annually recurring cost of producing the additional output and of maintaining the irrigation works. But as a rough rule of thumb we would suggest careful reconsideration of projects for which the public capital requirements per acre of land to be irrigated (including costs other than those incurred by DID) would be much above $200 per acre for already cultivated land and much above $600 for the total public and private cash costs per planted acre of new padi land development. The capital cost of schools and other social services should not be taken into account in assessing the justification of new land development projects, in any case in which the provision of such services can properly be considered part of a national program for the expansion of the social services.

As previously noted, the estimated DID capital expenditure on irrigation projects for the 1955-59 period amounts to about $32 million. The addition of costs of land clearance payments, initial subsistence grants to settlers, community facilities and all the other public and private non-DID cash costs involved in new land development would undoubtedly bring the figure to $45 million or more. On the other hand, part of the colonization and settlement expenditures will undoubtedly be incurred in the years following 1959, and another part of these would presumably be met by the settlers themselves. The figure might be reduced by economies realized through greater concentration of DID effort, discussed below, and through reconsideration of the justification of some of the projects for which cost-benefit analysis may indicate very high investment requirements relative to returns. Such capital expenditures incident to new land development as feeder roads, schools, water supplies and medical facilities are included elsewhere in our financial recommendations. Accordingly, as an approximate estimate, our recommended program for 1955-59 includes $35 million for capital expenditures on irrigation works.

In Chapter 3 of Part II we recommend a progressive shift toward more emphasis, proportionately, on the opening of new land. A start in this direction should be possible during 1955-59 within the limit of our recommended outlays on irrigation. A substantial change in emphasis is likely to be practicable, however, only after 1959, as a basis is established for extensive development of the Trans-Perak project and as land-use surveys and other planning aspects of projects to extend the area of cultivation progress.

In connection with the irrigation programs, special mention should be made of the important contributions of the Department of Agriculture, which collaborates in the surveys and is responsible for testing the soils in areas to be irrigated. This work has been carried out under the handicap of quite inadequate staffing, which has often prevented proper coverage by soil testing on some of the larger projects. Soil testing and analysis is of special importance in planning of land utilization and crop patterns in individual projects. This is especially so where the land is divided into small individual holdings, since variations in the quality of soils may result in an inequitable distribution of land and unsatisfactory crop patterns. For this, as for many other of the responsibilities of the Department of Agriculture, we recommend that provision for adequate staffing and facilities be made, including the establishment of experimental stations on the larger new land development projects.

Drainage and River Conservancy

The proposed 1955-59 DID program includes estimated capital expenditures of $6.8 million on 10 drainage projects, mainly in Selangor and Johore, and $8.4 million on six programs of river conservancy, including the purchase of dredging equipment. Substantial outlays for these purposes are essential for the protection and development of Malaya's agricultural and other natural resources, in view of the nature of the climate, topography and soils. While the mission was not able to examine the drainage and river conservancy projects individually and in detail, the programs as a whole appear to us well justified and we have included these estimates of capital expenditure in our proposed program.

Land drainage is a major problem for all the west coast States and Settlements. Drainage of padi land is usually associated with irrigation schemes and is maintained under these schemes. Drainage works also cover extensive areas of coconut, rubber and kampong lands. The lands involved are constituted Drainage Areas under the Drainage Works Enactment and maintained under the supervision of the DID. In 1953, there were 26 Drainage Areas, covering a total of 288,000 acres along the coasts of Perak, Selangor and Johore.

Before the first Drainage Rate Enactments in the former Federated States in 1909, drainage was left to the initiative of private land owners and was consequently haphazard and uncoordinated. The purpose of existing schemes is to provide comprehensive drainage for defined areas and to develop and improve agricultural land within their boundaries.

In the past, most of the schemes have been undertaken in Perak and Selangor; attention has recently turned to the west coast of Johore, where cultivated areas need protection and large areas can be reclaimed and developed.

The nature of the drainage problem and the steps necessary to deal with it are illustrated by the Senggarang and Sri Menanti projects combining 68,000 acres in Johore. The areas involved consist largely of smallholdings under coconut, developed in a haphazard manner over many years. Drains were constructed without a general plan and with no thought to the future. Much of the inland portion was covered with peat; subsequent shrinkage lowered this area to the point where drains became of little value. The clearing of land at some distance from the sea resulted in a more rapid run-off and flooding of rivers, while at the sea coast the absence of effective bunds and control gates permitted tidal water to invade the drains, preventing the escape of flood waters from the interior.

The job to be done consisted of the construction of coastal bunds and tidal control gates, the improvement of interior drainage and the bunding of rivers, notably the Sungei Sembrong, to prevent flooding. The first stage of the Senggarang project was completed in 1952. It was declared a Drainage Area and a Drainage Board was formed. Work continues on other parts of this project and on Sri Menanti.

Government policy with regard to the financing of drainage schemes differs from that relating to irrigation: customarily the annual rate charged covers not only maintenance but interest and amortization of capital. Maintenance, interest and amortization totalled $766,000 in 1953; drainage rate collections slightly exceeded this sum.

The Drainage Works Ordinance provides for the appointment of a Drainage Board for each Drainage Area. The Boards make recommendations to the State and Settlement Governments on matters of concern to their respective areas; in practice they exercise considerable administrative authority.

The rapid development of agriculture and mining over the past 50 years has caused serious deterioration in the condition of Malaya's rivers. Land clearance has resulted in increased run-off, while silt from mining and from soil erosion on denuded land has raised the level of river beds, with consequent flooding of low-lying areas. Silt retention works had to be erected in some areas to protect settlements, and at Ipoh and Kuala Lumpur deviation and canalization of rivers became necessary as silting from upstream mining caused serious flooding. Although soil conservation measures and the control of silt from mines have reduced the amount of silt entering river beds, flood mitigation and silt retention schemes, river deviation and maintenance and improvement of natural waterways remain an essential part of DID's activities.

Flood mitigation works are being maintained on the Kinta River at Ipoh and Batu Gajah, on the Sungei Bernam at Tanjong Malim and on the Klang River at Kuala Lumpur. Silt retention and prevention works in recent years have included river training and erosion control projects and construction of bunds, spillways and checkdams.

A number of river deviation projects are being carried out by mining companies under the supervision of DID. The largest of these involves a 25-mile deviation of the Kinta River below Ipoh to permit the mining companies to exploit the rich tin deposits in the present river bed.

Research and Statistics

Comprehensive and long-term information on rainfall and run-off in river basins is essential to efficient planning and use of water for irrigation, hydroelectric development, and for domestic and industrial use. It is also required for the design of land drainage schemes and flood control works.

Rainfall records are obtained from more than 900 stations, of which nearly two-thirds are located in Selangor, Perak and Johore. Coverage is thin on the east coast. Effective coverage in most catchment areas is poor, owing to the small number of stations on higher jungle-covered ground.

The systematic gauging of rivers was started in 1910 and by 1941, 33 gauging stations had been established, all but two located on two rivers in Perak and Selangor. Additional stations were established after the war, largely in Johore, but parts of Johore and all of Kedah, Kelantan, Trengganu and Pahang are still inadequately served.

We recommend that 10 more stations be established so that more adequate data on these areas, and especially on the Kelantan, Trengganu, Pahang and Perak rivers, may be obtained. The cost, including the stations and required vans, launches, instruments and other equipment, may be estimated at close to $1 million.

There is a related need for detailed and systematic collection of other statistics and technical data of economic and engineering significance, particularly to enable the more thorough evaluation of projects we have recommended. In 1953, a DID branch was set up to deal with hydrological and other records but shortages of staff, funds and office equipment have precluded much progress. The present staff consists of an engineer and one permanent and three temporary junior officers; the engineer has had other duties and consequently little time to devote to this branch. We support the Department's view that additional staff (two senior officials and several senior and junior technicians) is essential to the efficient functioning of the unit. At least one of the senior officials and some of the technicians should be trained in economics and statistics. The total increase for salaries should be about $115,000 annually.

Coordination and Planning

The engineering and technical efficiency of the DID staff is of a high order, and cooperation within the Department is good despite the dual responsibility and control referred to earlier. There is, however, some evidence of lack of over-all planning of projects where a number of departments are concerned.

In several of the States a committee to advise on irrigation and drainage matters has been established. It usually includes the State Secretary, the State officers concerned with irrigation and drainage, agriculture, forestry and mines, district officers and representatives of estates and smallholders.

The addition of a representative of the Public Works Department would be desirable; officials concerned with education, public health and social welfare should be co-opted as necessary. Each State and Settlement should establish a similar committee to plan and coordinate irrigation and drainage work and other measures of land improvement and reclamation, including settlement of newly opened areas.

There is no comparable coordinating body on the Federal level. Consultation between DID and heads of other departments is often on an ad hoc basis, as contrasted with the careful over-all consideration of projects that a committee can give. We have accordingly recommended in Chapter 9 certain organizational measures designed to ensure closer cooperation in the planning and execution of development programs generally.

Efficiency and Timing of Operations

The completion of irrigation and other projects has in many instances taken longer than would seem desirable or necessary. This appears to be due to inability under the existing administrative arrangements to concentrate men and equipment for the most efficient operation.

The amount of equipment that DID can make available to any State or project must be related to the size of the staff on the establishment of the State concerned. The desire of each State to have as much work as possible under way may result in equipment being distributed too widely for most efficient utilization. At the time of the mission's visit, for instance, 47 construction jobs were in progress. It is almost impossible to concentrate staff and equipment in order to expedite completion of any given project.

A greater centralization of authority over personnel and equipment would be in the interest of both the States and the Federal Government. It would permit concentration of effort and would lead to a better balance of personnel and equipment, to greater efficiency and increased output.

This might be achieved either by vesting complete control and direction of both staff and equipment in the Director of the Federal Department, or by employing additional staff, attached to and under headquarters direction, to supplement construction forces operating under State or Settlement authority. Under the first alternative, no additional staff would be required. According to the Director of DID, the program projected through 1959 can be carried out with the force now available, provided it is effectively deployed. Centralization of control would give mobility to construction personnel without interfering with maintenance and operation of completed works; for these the necessary staff could be specifically retained or assigned.

It should be emphasized that what is proposed would not mean a drastic revision of State programs. It would mean some rearrangement of priorities and deferment of some projects in the interest of earlier completion of others. The net result should be greater efficiency, larger output and, in the long run, more work completed in all the States and Settlements.

Summary of Financial Requirements

In our program, we have allowed for DID capital expenditures of $55 million. This includes $35 million for irrigation, $8 million for river conservancy, $7 million for drainage, and $5 million for miscellaneous purposes, including plant and equipment to meet specific needs, additional gauging stations, research facilities, and surveys and investigations. The figure for irrigation allows for some expenditure outside DID jurisdiction involved in new land development, but does not allow for access roads, schools, dispensaries and other social and community facilities; these are included under separate heads in our estimates of financial requirements.

For salaries and other annually recurrent DID expenditures we have projected an increase from the figure of $7.7 million in the budget estimates for 1954 to $10.7 million by 1959.

TECHNICAL REPORT 3 *LAND TENURE*

I FEDERATION

The constitutional structure, the difference in religion, tradition and economic level between the Malays and Chinese, and the Muslim law of inheritance combine to make land problems in the Federation peculiarly complex.

Land Legislation and Land Administration

General Problems. In land matters, among others, the Federation Agreement of 1948 gives the Federal Government legislative power but confers the whole of the executive authority on the State and Settlement Governments. The Federal legislative power to ensure a common policy in land matters has, however, not yet been exercised to any important extent; there is consequently no uniform land code for the country as a whole, and State and Settlement laws enacted before 1948 remain in force. This lack of uniformity extends to the system of land administration.

The four former Federated Malay States (Negri Sembilan, Pahang, Perak and Selangor) have a common land code. Each of the other five States has its own law, although these are similar in essentials since the separate enactments were largely based on the code of the former Federated States. The two Settlements have not yet adopted the Torrens system[1] of registration in force in the States and, instead, follow the less efficacious system of registering deeds. Neither have they yet codified their land legislation.

Unification of land legislation throughout the Federation is clearly desirable. Accordingly, we have recommended, in Chapter 3, Part II, that a Federal land code be enacted as soon as circumstances permit. This should be done after State and Settlement legislation and land alienation policy directives have been studied and collated.

[1] A system under which the certificate of title establishes an indisputable right of ownership to the land registered.

306

The property in and the control of all land in the States as yet unalienated is vested in the Ruler. Most alienated land is held in perpetuity, subject to the payment of a fixed annual rent and, in the case of agricultural land, to certain express or implied cultivation conditions. The Land Code of the former Federated States and the separate State enactments also permit alienation on a leasehold basis, and the trend in recent years has been to alienate land on this basis rather than by way of a grant in perpetuity. Little precise information was available to the mission on the lease policy of the various States, but it appears that leases for agricultural land are usually given now for periods of 60 to 99 years.

Land administration is the responsibility of the State and Settlement Governments with consequent differences in standards of performance. These standards are said to have fallen since the war and particularly since the emergency. The Japanese occupation left a legacy of a large number of unregistered land transactions and, in some districts, of lost registers. These difficulties had to be dealt with. Thereafter, preoccupation with the emergency and the extensive resettlement scheme prevented close attention to land administration; inspection and survey work were made difficult or impossible by terrorist activities. Nonetheless, it is probably fair, in general, to say that some of the deterioration must be ascribed to insufficient training and the reduced supervision and direction of land office work compared to prewar practice.

The matters mainly requiring attention are delays in dealing with applications for land, the arrears in registration and the too ready resort to issuance of temporary occupation licenses.

Delays in dealing with applications for land are frequently attributable to the lack of clear directives on land-use policy; this is discussed elsewhere. The other matters mentioned are dealt with below.

Good land administration is of fundamental importance to the general administration of the country and is a precondition of a sound land-use policy. Where land administration is not of high calibre, resolute attempts should be made to improve it. Granted that the emergency will hamper the work of land offices, we believe much can nevertheless be done by better training and closer supervision and inspection. Except in Perlis, Kelantan and Trengganu the staffs of land offices are reported to be numerically adequate in most cases; an improvement in the quality of their work is required.

In Chapter 3, we recommended that the Commissioner of Lands' office be strengthened. The Commissioner should have sufficient staff to keep in close touch with the senior Land Officers in the State and Settlement secretariats, and to make frequent visits to land offices, as well as to act on or assist in carrying out those of our recommendations concerning land legislation and land administration which the governments decide to adopt.

We also recommended the appointment of a senior Land Officer in the secretariats of the States (Negri Sembilan, Perak and Selangor) which lacked such officers at the time of our visit. It would be their responsibility to deal with land matters in the secretariat, under the State Secretary, to inspect land offices and to give training in land office subjects by personal advice and through organized courses. In States where the post already exists but the incumbent is required to perform other functions, e.g., in Kelantan, where the Advisor on Lands and Mines is also State Financial Officer, arrangements should be made to shift such other duties to other officials, to permit the land officer to concentrate on land work.

Thirdly, we have recommended the creation of a specialist cadre of land officers, under the control of the Commissioner of Lands, from which there would be no transfer to other branches of the administration. Limitation of the duties of these officers to land work and their membership in a specialized Federal career service in which the Commissioner of Lands would be senior would, we believe, foster the necessary coordination and cooperation on matters of land policy and administration common to the States and Settlements.

Recording of Rights and Other Land Office Work. Separate registers for smallholders are kept in most districts of the States, while ownership and other interests in town lands and estates of more than 10 or 15 acres are recorded in State central registers which are maintained by more highly qualified staff. In some States, however, registration of title exists only nominally, or has greatly deteriorated in practice.

In the States of Kelantan, Perlis and Trengganu, title registrations are considerably in arrears, principally due to understaffing of land offices, and, perhaps, añ insufficient sense of urgency. Certificates of title were not issued by the land offices as fast as surveys were made, with the result that information became outdated and resurveying necessary. In Kelantan, only one-quarter of the holdings has been properly surveyed and registered. Some 400,000 lots lack either proper titles or current registration. Title registration teams under Federal supervision are to be sent to the various districts of the State to bring registration up to date, a task which will take several years. Similar measures are under consideration in Perlis, where 26,000 lots are without proper title. It may also be necessary to take steps to accelerate the work of survey and registration of some 50,000 lots now in progress in Trengganu. The technical difficulties in these former unfederated States can be easily explained. The description of the original titles, such as the Grants Lama in Perlis, was often vague so that documents had to be recalled and replaced by surveyed titles. When registration was finally started, the owners did not appear, being afraid of the rent fixing which was associated with the registration procedure. As time passed, the difficulties increased. On the death of each unauthorized occupant, his heirs seized a portion of the holding, thereby causing excessive fragmentation. In Perlis, usurpation of the holding by the strongest heir is still frequent.

It is not necessary to recommend that the registers in these States be brought up to date, since steps to this end are already being taken or are in contemplation. The mission wishes, however, to emphasize the importance of doing so in the shortest possible time, not only in these States but also in districts of other States where arrears exist. We also wish to stress the importance of distributing estates as quickly as possible and ensuring that changes of ownership resulting from death are promptly recorded. In many districts the number of undistributed estates is very large, while in others the number of applications filed is reported to be less than might be expected in view of the size of the population. Closer contact between land offices and registrars of death would make for an improvement in this respect.

As mentioned earlier, the two Settlements have not yet adopted registration of title. Instead, they follow the more complicated and less efficacious method of registration of deeds. Title is evidenced by a complex of instruments, so that a purchaser wishing verification of title must have a time-consuming and expensive examination of the records made. He must also ascertain that a possessory title has not been established by occupation. A further result of the present system is that many transactions between smallholders have not been registered, while acquisition proceedings have shown that many heirs have neither taken out letters of administration nor had the land in question transferred to them by register.

As an essential step toward the introduction of title registration, the boundaries or holdings in both Settlements are being surveyed; the work was nearly finished at the time of the mission's visit. A committee for reorganizing registration has been set up in Penang and was studying the procedures for the immediate introduction of title registration.

The mission strongly endorses the intention to change over to the Torrens system in the two Settlements and recommends that this be done with as little delay as possible. The change will not only introduce a better system of registration but will also make for uniformity throughout the Federation. Although additional staff will be required, we consider that this should not be allowed to stand in the way of the change. Survey work already completed will lose more and more of its value the longer registration is delayed.

Since the Government of Singapore is also considering the introduction of title registration, consultation and cooperation between the respective Commissioners of Lands would be of value to both the Federation and Singapore.

The various land laws of the States all embody in greater or lesser degree old Malay customary law that ownership depends upon cultivation. The Land Code of the former Federated States provides, for instance, for the forfeiture of country land if half of the area covered by the title is not continuously cultivated in a proper manner for three consecutive years,[2] and the Land Rules prescribe fines for cultivators who fail to plant at the proper time. Steps are already being taken, on the recommendation of the Rice Production Committee,[3] to enforce cultivation conditions for padi land more closely and to revest title to neglected padi land in the State. Enforcement in other cases might well be difficult until the general level of cultivation practices has been raised by agricultural extension work; we see no reason, however, why title to all abandoned country land should not be revested.

A defect in present land administration is the ease with which temporary occupation licenses can be obtained. These licenses ought to be issued only if there are solid reasons for not granting title, as in cases where the area in question has been earmarked for mining purposes or for a town site or has not yet been surveyed. In some of the States with backlogs in title registration, the temporary occupation license has, however, become a permanent feature of the system of land holding and in many instances such a license is issued without investigation of the application.

[2] In the case of padi land, the fraction is three-quarters and the period two years.

[3] A committee appointed by the Federal Government in November 1952 to consider ways of increasing rice production.

It is to be expected that as land administration is improved and registers are brought up to date, a much stricter policy in respect of the issue of these licenses will be followed.

Lastly, in regard to land administration, it would be most useful if an alphabetical card index of the names of all registered land owners were maintained by the central land office in each State. Such an index would show the concentration of land ownership and, with proper cooperation between district and central offices, would be of value in dealing with applications for land. It is recognized that additional staff and cost would be required to compile and maintain such an index, but we believe that consideration should be given to whether its usefulness would outweigh this disadvantage.

Urbanization of Agricultural Land. The growth of towns and the consequent adjustment of boundaries brings land alienated for agricultural purposes within the town boundaries. The Land Code of the former Federated States provides that in these circumstances the land shall be freed from cultivation conditions, but does not reserve for the State any part of the increment on the value of agricultural land which is developed for other purposes.

The mission considers that part, at least, of this increment should accrue to the State. How the increment should be assessed and whether the State should receive the whole or only part of it is a matter requiring more attention than we were able to give. We recommend that the matter be studied further. In the interest of uniformity, any pertinent legislation should be Federal.

Malay Reservations and Areas under Customary Tenure

Malays in the Federation are afforded special protection in the possession of their land by State and Settlement legislation designating large areas as Malay reservations or areas under customary tenure. The legislation provides that no non-Malay may acquire land in these areas from a Malay[4] and that none but Malays may be granted land in the reserved areas.

The first Malay Reservation Enactment was promulgated in the Fed-

[4] A Malay is defined in the Malay Reservation Enactment as "a person belonging to any Malayan race who habitually speaks the Malay language, or any Malayan language, and who professes the Muslim religion." Immigrants from Indonesia come within this definition. The Kedah Enactment also covers Thais.

erated Malay States in 1913. Similar legislation was enacted in Kelantan in 1930; in Kedah in 1931; in Perlis in 1935; in Johore in 1936 and in Trengganu in 1941.[5] There is no Malay reservation legislation in Malacca and Penang, but the Malacca Customary Rights Ordinance, which dates back to 1886, has a similar effect. The Customary Tenure Enactment of Negri Sembilan of 1909 also gives protection to cultivators belonging to any of the tribes. There are no reservations in Penang (including Province Wellesley). The Malay reservations are shown on Map 7.

The purpose of this legislation is to protect existing Malay ownership, not to exclude non-Malays from the reservations. Non-Malay shopkeepers continue to live and work in the reservations and even non-Malay cultivators can be found in them. Moreover, non-Malays are permitted to retain land held before the various enactments came into force and, usually, to transfer land to other non-Malays.

The original legislation made it impossible for a Malay to transfer or lease his land to a non-Malay but did not prevent his pledging the land as security. This loophole allowed effective control to pass to non-Malay moneylenders and shopkeepers, the Malay remaining owner in name only; in 1933 the Malay Reservation Enactment of the former Federated States was accordingly amended to forbid charge or lease to a non-Malay and to prevent a creditor's seizing the land in discharge of a debt. Similar measures were taken in other States. These provisions have no doubt had the effect of restraining thriftlessness, but at the same time they have deprived Malay smallholders of credit facilities for productive purposes; public or cooperative credit sources do not yet provide an adequate substitute. A recent amendment to the legislation, made by the Federal Government, goes some way toward remedying this by enabling land within the reservations to be mortgaged to certain public and quasi-public credit institutions.[6] We recommend that consideration be given to a similar amendment to the Negri Sembilan Customary Tenure Enactment.

Malays regard the reservations as necessary to safeguard the hold of Malay cultivators on their land because of their otherwise relatively disadvantageous economic position in comparison with financially stronger non-Malay interests. The position of the Malays is especially vulnerable in

[5] In Trengganu no Malay reservations have been designated but Malays have special privileges under this Enactment.

[6] The Chief Secretary, the Rural and Industrial Development Authority, the Housing Trust, the Rubber Industry (Replanting) Board and the Federal and Colonial Building Society.

MAP 7

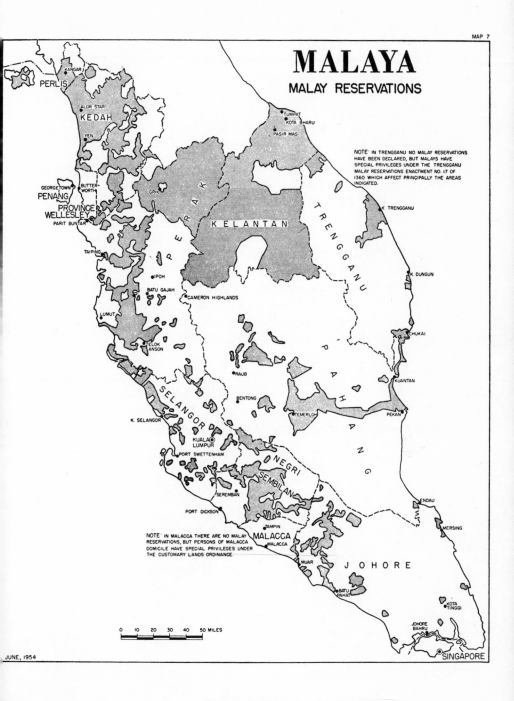

MALAYA
MALAY RESERVATIONS

NOTE: IN TRENGGANU NO MALAY RESERVATIONS HAVE BEEN DECLARED, BUT MALAYS HAVE SPECIAL PRIVILEGES UNDER THE TRENGGANU MALAY RESERVATIONS ENACTMENT NO. 17 OF 1360 WHICH AFFECT PRINCIPALLY THE AREAS INDICATED.

NOTE: IN MALACCA THERE ARE NO MALAY RESERVATIONS, BUT PERSONS OF MALACCA DOMICILE HAVE SPECIAL PRIVILEGES UNDER THE CUSTOMARY LANDS ORDINANCE.

PERLIS
KANGAR
KEDAH
ALOR STAR
YEN
GEORGETOWN
PENANG
PROVINCE
WELLESLEY
BUTTER-WORTH
PARIT BUNTAR
TAIPING
IPOH
BATU GAJAH
LUMUT
TELOK ANSON
PERAK
GRIK
KELANTAN
TUMPAT
KOTA BHARU
PASIR MAS
TRENGGANU
K TRENGGANU
K. DUNGUN
CHUKAI
KUANTAN
PEKAN
CAMERON HIGHLANDS
RAUB
PAHANG
BENTONG
TEMERLOH
SELANGOR
K. SELANGOR
KUALA LUMPUR
PORT SWETTENHAM
NEGRI
SEMBILAN
SEREMBAN
PORT DICKSON
JAMPIN
MALACCA
MALACCA
MUAR
BATU PAHAT
JOHORE
ENDAU
MERSING
KOTA TINGGI
JOHORE BAHRU
SINGAPORE

0 10 20 30 40 50 MILES

JUNE, 1954

areas where congestion of population on the land and accompanying sub-division and fragmentation of holdings weakens the bases of the culti-vators' economic independence. In such circumstances the loss of holdings by cultivators to dealers, moneylenders and investors in land is a common phenomenon in Asia. In congested areas within the Malay reservations such a process would undoubtedly be facilitated if the transfer, lease or charge of land by Malays to non-Malays were permitted. The reservations, therefore, represent a justifiable means of protecting the economic status of Malay cultivators in areas where pressure of population on the land has already developed or is definitely in prospect.

The situation may be different in reserved areas which are only sparsely settled and more distant from centers of rural congestion but which have definite potentialities for development. Development activity in such areas, either through governmental projects or by private initiative, may be im-peded by the reluctance of Malays to move any considerable distance from their established communities, by the limited availability of private Malay capital, and by the check on the flow of non-Malay capital resulting from the restrictions on non-Malay land ownership and land use. This may be of relevance not only to the problem of land development for agricultural purposes but also, for example, to the exploitation of mineral resources by non-Malay mining companies.

This is a complex problem, in view of the need to protect the position of the Malay cultivators and provide reasonable opportunities for the ex-pansion of their areas of cultivation without interfering with a desirable development of natural resources which could otherwise take place. Specific recommendations are particularly difficult because of the limited informa-tion on development opportunities in those parts of the Malay reservations which are as yet underdeveloped and which are unlikely in the near future to be needed as a safety valve for existing or accumulating pressure of Malay cultivators on the land. For those parts of the Malay reservations where there is little imminent prospect of extensive development by Malays, we recommend a re-examination of the present policy concerning land use by non-Malays. Surveys of new agricultural land potentialities and promising mineral possibilities, recommended elsewhere, should provide guidance in this re-examination. In the long run, however, only con-tinuous progress in the fields of education and improvement in the institu-tional arrangements will strengthen the economic position of the Malays, and the mission has recommended continued efforts along these lines.

Subdivision, Fragmentation and Land Consolidation

Minute subdivision and fragmentation of agricultural land is common in countries where distribution of property is governed by the Muslim law of inheritance. This law makes no distinction between real and personal property and prescribes elaborate and precise rules for distributing the property of a deceased person. The application of these rules often creates a multiplicity of co-owners of holdings, some with extremely small shares, and leads often to minute subdivision of land itself. Physical subdivision of the deceased's land among the heirs is not required by Muslim law, but transfer of one heir's share to another must be voluntary, and the law protects shares of minors.

Land registers in many parts of the Federation give abundant evidence of extensive fragmentation. How far this has been carried and the extent to which it has led to actual subdivision of the land have not yet been a subject of detailed study. Physical subdivision must, however, be less than the division recorded in the registers since in many cases it would be quite impracticable to subdivide into the minute shares shown by the registers.

Fragmentation leads to uneconomic holdings, concealed unemployment, increased indebtedness, reduced productivity of the land, the abandonment of very small plots which become breeding grounds for pests and, in general, has a disintegrating effect on an agricultural community. In rubber areas the joint ownership of small holdings makes agreements on replanting schemes more difficult or actually impossible and also leads to overtapping.

In Chapter 3, Part II, we commented on the undesirable consequences of fragmentation, and indicated that both religious and secular authorities were aware of the problem. We were encouraged to hope that the problem can and will be solved in a manner acceptable to all.

Experience has shown that attempts to persuade the heirs to agree to voluntary transfer of shares to reduce fragmentation and subdivision have limited success. The heirs usually cling to their shares, not for economic considerations, but because of the prestige which attaches to land ownership. Legislation appears to be the only practicable solution.

The State of Kelantan has already adopted this approach. Section 37A of the Kelantan Land Enactment of 1938 restricts the subdivision of lots in the following terms:

"37A. (i) From and after the coming into force of this Enactment, except in the case of land situated within the limits of a town or village constituted under this Enactment or any previous land law—

(a) no land which exceeds 250 square depa[7] in area shall by survey be subdivided in such a manner that any of the resulting subdivisional lots shall be less than 250 square depa in area, and

(b) no land which is 250 square depa or less in area shall be subdivided, and

(c) no transaction shall be registered in respect of any land which would have the effect of creating undivided shares of such size that, if the land were to be subdivided by survey according to the size of such shares, the area of any resulting subdivisional lot would be less than 250 square depa.

(ii) His Highness the Sultan may in any particular case by order in writing grant exemption from any of the above provisions and thereupon the land referred to in such order may be divided or such shares in the land created as may be set out in such order and not otherwise."

This restriction was acceptable to the religious authorities in the State. The minimum size prescribed by it—the equivalent of one-quarter acre—is admittedly far too small. Nevertheless, the Enactment has considerable importance in that it has established a precedent for restricting the subdivision of land.

We have recommended Federal legislation patterned on the Kelantan Enactment but leaving the minimum area to be determined by State and Settlement Governments, since this should vary with crop and locality. The legislation should also void any private unregistered agreements which are not consistent with its provisions. This legislation need not, and should not, await the survey which we recommend later. Minimum areas prescribed by State and Settlement Governments after the proposed legislation has been promulgated can later be altered if the survey should show this to be necessary. We have also recommended Federal legislation designed to preclude subdivision of land alienated in the future.

A corollary to the prescription of minimum sizes for smallholdings is the provision of adequate credit facilities to enable the single heir to buy out the shares of the others; absent such facilities, there will be resort to unregistered illegal private arrangements, as is now frequently the case in the Tanjong Karang scheme.

[7] In Kelantan, 1,000 square depa = 1 acre.

While effective measures can be taken to restrict further subdivision of land already cultivated and to prevent subdivision in newly opened areas, the consolidation of lands already excessively subdivided presents an extremely difficult and complex problem. There are instances of voluntary consolidation by the exchange of plots between owner-cultivators. Such voluntary exchanges should be encouraged with the assistance and guidance of local officials and notables. They are, however, unlikely to make a significant contribution to the solution of the problem. Basically, the excessive subdivision of land results from the interaction of the Muslim law of inheritance, population pressure and underemployment in a given area. The condition can be effectively ameliorated only if alternative livelihood is provided through the opening of new areas of cultivation and an expansion of nonagricultural economic activity. In view of the rapid growth in population and the limitations of resources, it would seem a counsel of perfection to suggest that the rate of new employment opportunities can so outdistance population growth that there can be a significant reduction in the number of cultivators on already cultivated lands. Nevertheless, consolidation measures designed to eliminate uneconomic holdings should be considered wherever possible, particularly where it is proposed to provide irrigation in densely populated areas; without consolidation the benefit to be derived from irrigation would be reduced and there would be no substantial improvement in the economic position of cultivators in the area. There will be cases in which a project for land development can provide some relief for population pressure in other areas; in such instances a scheme for land consolidation should be linked to the project. It must, however, be admitted that such possibilities are likely to be small in relation to the size of the problem of existing fragmentation.

Tenure Conditions and New Settlement Schemes

Satisfactory tenure conditions are clearly an element of first importance in any scheme to open up new land for cultivation.

Recent practice has been to alienate land in economically sized smallholdings on leases up to 99 years, as in the Tanjong Karang scheme. Provided that the land may not be subdivided, this is undoubtedly a satisfactory basis. Other forms of tenure might, however, be more appropriate for large schemes, such as the proposed Trans-Perak irrigation scheme, particularly where possibilities of large-scale mechanized farming exist; these will no doubt be considered when the schemes are being planned.

An alternative we have in mind is an adaptation of the organization of the large and successful Gezira cotton scheme in the Sudan. The essence of this scheme is that the state provides the land and the water, the tenants are responsible for the cultivation operations, and a state-owned but autonomous board provides agricultural supervision and management as well as seasonal finance for the tenants, and is responsible for harvesting and marketing the cotton crop. The net profits[8] on this crop are divided in fixed proportions among the three parties. The individual tenant's portion of the tenants' total share of the net profits is determined by the amount and grade of the crop produced on his tenancy. No rent is paid by the tenant and the food and fodder crops grown on the tenancy are entirely his own. Tenancies are annual but renewable each year if good cultivation practices have been followed. The land is partly owned by, and partly under compulsory lease to, the government. Plowing is done by the board but the cost is recovered from the tenant.

A scheme organized in this way secures the advantages of efficient agricultural management and large-scale marketing, while avoiding the disadvantages of the plantation system. Clearly much modification of the organization found suitable for cotton-growing in the Sudan would be required to adapt it to a rice-growing or other scheme in Malaya. The mission nevertheless believes this form of organization to be worthy of consideration.

Tenancy Security

Tenancy is not only a feature in the areas of old settlement such as Kedah and Province Wellesley but has also spread to areas of more recent settlement, such as Krian, where smallholders were settled on an irrigation scheme in the early years of the present century. The principal cause of this spread of tenancy has undoubtedly been excessive subdivision of land, although improvidence has also played its part. Moreover, where land is held by a multiplicity of owners, another feature of minute subdivision, it is not infrequently rented to tenants for cultivation.

Tenancies are generally granted for one year and are not registered.

---

[8] Gross proceeds of sales less the cost of processing, selling and shipping the crop.

Before the war, renewal of the tenancy was a matter of course, provided the tenant fulfilled his obligations. Since the war, however, diminished respect for tradition and the pressure of demand for land by a fast growing population have combined in some regions to lead land owners into conditioning renewal of the tenancy upon an increase in the tenant's obligations. In some areas this change has introduced a new factor in Malayan agriculture—the extreme insecurity of the tenant cultivator—which will have serious social and economic repercussions if it is not checked.

Traditionally, rent is paid in kind after the harvest, either in a fixed amount of produce or as a proportion of the crop. However, a growing number of land owners are demanding rent in cash and in advance; as an illustration, it may be mentioned that petition writers in Alor Star (Kedah) stock printed forms which contain a provision that rent is payable in cash in advance. Sometimes rent for the next season is demanded at the end of the current season's harvest. Tenants unable to meet these terms will have no land to cultivate in the coming season.

This practice of requiring cash rental in advance makes necessary increased borrowing by tenants and puts an added strain on the financial resources of cooperative societies. Officials of two such societies in Kedah interviewed by the mission reported an increased volume of applications for loans for this purpose. Should this practice spread, normal cooperative activities may be jeopardized and part of the benefit of credit facilities made available to cooperative societies by government or under government guarantee would go to the landlords.

Where tenants faced with demands for advance cash payment are not members of cooperative societies, they are forced to borrow from shopkeepers and thus become still more dependent upon the *padi kuncha*[9] system; even those who are members of cooperative societies would probably have to borrow under this system, since loans from the former are unlikely to cover the full amount of the rent. This close interrelationship of tenure arrangements, indebtedness and the *padi kuncha* system indicates the need for an integrated approach to tenure and marketing.

The position of the tenant is further impaired by the fact that the change to cash rent is frequently associated with rent increase. Investigation in some districts of northern Kedah and in one district of Province Wellesley revealed such rent increases ranging from 30% up to as much as 100%, not counting the concealed rent increase in the form of interest on money

[9] See footnote 9, p. 79.

borrowed to make advance payment. The fact that tenants will have to sell their padi immediately after the harvest, when the price is lowest, will mean an additional loss to them.

In addition, the change from rent in kind to cash rent of an amount fixed in advance shifts to the tenant what had previously been the landlord's share of agricultural and/or price risks. This by itself is a significant change in the landlord-tenant relationship.

While there is insufficient information for anything like a complete picture of present owner-tenant relationships, there is nonetheless substantial evidence that they have deteriorated. Immediate action should be taken to establish a minimum of security for the tenant until increased knowledge of the essential facts provides the basis for an integrated approach to the whole problem of the Malayan agrarian structure. Since the traditional rent level in Malaya is not high by comparison with other Southeast Asian countries, for the present, effort should be directed toward the maintenance or re-establishment of traditional rents.

The mission accordingly has recommended (Chapter 3, Part II) Federal legislation to give an efficient tenant cultivator security in his holding. He and his family should have a right to continuous occupation of the land provided he continues to pay rent and to observe the terms of the last tenancy agreement, except that if the agreement requires advance payment of rent in cash, the tenant should have the right, instead, to make the customary payment in kind of a share or a fixed quantity of the crop. However, the tenant and his family would not have the right to continue in possession if the landlord can show:

a. that the tenant has not paid rent in accordance with the terms of the agreement (or has not made the customary payment in kind where he has elected to do so) or has acted contrary to the rules of good husbandry; or

b. that the landlord himself, his wife or his children intend to cultivate the land personally (in which case a year's notice should be given to the tenant); or

c. where the tenant has died, that the landlord cannot reasonably be expected to continue to let the land to a member of the deceased's family.

To arbitrate disputes arising out of this legislation, we further recommend that the legislation provide for the setting up of tenancy security committees at the *mukim*[10] level. The committee might consist of the *Penghulu*,[11] the Cooperative Officer or another suitable person as chairman and two members drawn from a panel of persons well acquainted with local conditions and representing land-owners and tenants respectively. Its work should be supervised by the District Officer. The right of appeal from the committee's decisions should be allowed either to a committee at the district level, a District Court, or a special Land Court with a judicial officer sitting with two assessors.

Initially, the tenancy security committees should not be required to deal with more than the clear-cut facts of occupancy and the re-establishment of traditional conditions; more intricate matters, such as compensation claims for improvements on termination of a tenancy, would best be left until the committees have gained experience and are functioning well.

New Villages

Some of the Chinese population resettled in "new villages" were agriculturalists who had settled before the war, but in the main they were townspeople, tin mining workers or rubber tappers who had gone into the countryside voluntarily or otherwise during the Japanese occupation. Many were driven there by food shortages. Few had obtained title to the land on which they settled. Living in isolated communities, often beyond close administrative control, these people were exposed to terrorist intimidation and extortion and became an important source of supplies, information and recruitment to the terrorists. As a security measure, they were moved into some 550 compact communities, which now have a population of about 570,000 persons, mainly Chinese but some Malays and Indians as well.

This operation, involving the resettlement of about 10% of the total population of the Federation and provision of basic services, was a remarkable achievement. Hardship was lessened by the coincidence of the resettlement with the rubber and tin boom, which enabled many of the resettled persons to find employment at high wages. It was also reduced by the policy of resettling them, wherever possible, near to the areas where they lived so that they could continue in any employment they had. The mission visited a number of these villages and was greatly impressed by the success

[10] A subdivision of an administrative district.
[11] The official in charge of a *mukim*.

achieved. As was inevitable in so sizeable an operation carried out with speed in difficult conditions, some of the villages were badly sited and have no economic future; these are, however, reported to be only a minority. Resiting for such cases seems essential and in our financial estimates we have made token provision for this.

The terms of leases offered to resettled persons in some States are considerably less favorable than the customary terms. In Johore, for instance, leases for only a 21-year period have been offered. In Kedah, where title to most agricultural land is generally granted in perpetuity, and shop lots are leased for 60, 90 or 99 years, the resettled persons have been offered only 30-year leases for all classes of land; moreover, an annual rent of $5 a *relong* (0.7 acres) is charged as against the usual maximum of $1 a *relong* for first-class padi land. This is true of Selangor also: instead of the usual 99-year lease for agricultural land and 30-year lease for house sites, resettled persons (other than those in the Tanjong Karang scheme) are given only 30-year leases and are made to pay a substantially higher rent than usual. In the Settlement of Penang, the leases offered, whether for agricultural or other land, are for 33 years only, but in this case the usual rent is charged. Disposition of the land during the first 10 years of the lease is, however, prohibited. The Settlement of Malacca offers more favorable terms; there, resettled persons can obtain land on a 30-year lease renewable for a further 30 years. The rent charged is the customary rent and the premium required is only nominal.

Little information is available to show the extent to which resettled persons have applied for title to agricultural lots and house sites and what proportion of the applications has been approved. The mission understands, however, that the applications have been disappointingly few. This may be ascribed to a variety of reasons: the land offered may be unsuitable for the type of agriculture chosen, i.e., it may not be profitable for market gardening; some of the resettled persons may be accustomed to living on their holdings and may dislike living in a village some distance away; living in a village is more expensive than living in an isolated area, since payment has to be made for services such as sanitation and water; having been compulsorily settled, the people have the assurance that they will not be moved and, in these circumstances, are satisfied with a temporary occupation license, which is less costly than a surveyed title; leasehold may not appeal to persons who in China were accustomed to ancestral land; and lastly, some may have a feeling of political insecurity.

Some of these reasons have nothing to do with the terms on which titles are offered. But insofar as reluctance to seek title can be overcome by the offer of more favorable terms, this should be done.

Field Work on Certain Aspects of Land Tenure

The lack of data relative to tenure conditions, subdivision and fragmentation has been mentioned earlier in this report. We believe an examination of present land policy and its economic and social effects to be of considerable importance and therefore have recommended that a survey be made of the system of land-holding in the Federation.

The survey should have well-defined terms of reference.

We suggest that they include the following:

(a) the extent of tenancy, particularly in the padi areas, and the content of tenancy agreements (amount of rent, the form in which rent is paid, period of the agreement, etc.);

(b) the contributions of the landlord and tenant to production in comparison with their respective returns;

(c) the origins and effects of subdivision and fragmentation of land and the interrelationship between subdivision, tenure arrangements and the *padi kuncha* system; areas of advanced fragmentation should be compared with the more recently settled areas;

(d) rural indebtedness, including the mortgaging of land; and

(e) the respective merits of different farming systems as applied to the cultivation of the principal agricultural crops.

The Food and Agriculture Organization of the United Nations might be able to assist the Federation in carrying out the survey, and in giving advice on policy matters in the light of its results. Should our recommendation for the survey be accepted, the Federation Government will no doubt consider whether it wishes to seek this assistance.

II SINGAPORE

Land Administration

The Commissioner of Lands' office deals with matters of land alienation and acquisition, the collection of land rents, registration of deeds and other routine land administration work. The Singapore Improvement Trust, established by ordinance in 1927 "to provide for the improvement of the Town and Island of Singapore," acts as agent for the government in all matters connected with planning, housing and land use. Any change in the use of private land or buildings is subject to approval by the Trust, which also acts as adviser to the Commissioner of Lands in matters affecting the use of Crown land.

The Constitutional Commission recommended a single Ministry responsible for "Housing, Lands, Administration of the adjacent Islands, Town Planning and Local Government." The adoption of this recommendation would undoubtedly make for closer coordination of the separate agencies concerned with land matters.

Over 90% of the privately-owned land in the Colony is held in perpetuity or under 999-year lease. Policy has, however, recently been changed and urban land is now customarily leased for 99 years, agricultural land for 60 years. In order to extend the area under leasehold and facilitate planning, the government has recently bought tracts of freehold land for conversion into leasehold parcels.

Title Registration

The introduction of title registration is one of the most important tasks confronting the Government of Singapore in the field of land tenure.

An expert in the field of title registration was recently invited by the government to study the relevant legal and administrative conditions in the Colony and to advise on the registration of titles to land. The mission has seen his report and, as indicated in Chapter 3, shares his view that a system of title registration should be adopted, and that there would be advantages in modifying the strict application of the Torrens system to the extent of recognizing title claims founded on undisturbed physical occupation for a prescribed period in certain well-defined circumstances. As a means of encouraging registration of transactions with respect to land, it was recommended that a claim to title based on adverse possession for 12 years from the date of last registration, and thereafter affirmatively asserted by the trespasser, should prevail over any other claim to title based on an unregistered transaction. An adverse possessor for the statutory period might also succeed to the title of any registered owner who, although he had not alienated any interest in his land during that period, had not in that time filed an assertion of ownership equivalent to registration.

The ground has been well prepared for the introduction of title registration by a very complete survey, and the staff in the offices of the Chief Surveyor and the Commissioner of Lands should be able, with some limited reinforcement, to cope with the transitional difficulties. The high standard of surveying and the fact that Singapore is primarily urban may even justify the introduction of an advanced system of title registration, including registration of easements and, ultimately, government guarantee of the title. We suggest that this should be considered.

Express Conditions in Agricultural Leases

Sixty-year agricultural leases are being substituted for some 10,000 temporary occupation licenses granted to smallholders. With a view to increasing food production, the Food Production Committee has proposed that these leases contain certain restrictive conditions designed to further the Committee's policy and that they be subject to cancellation for failure to observe these conditions and to follow the advice of the supervisory staff. Very low rents are proposed, since the restrictive conditions would clearly reduce the value of the land to the lessee. The proposal has two other disadvantages: considerable administrative expenditure might be incurred in enforcing the conditions, while any change in the Committee's policy might require amendment of provisions in a large number of leases. For these reasons the mission considers that it would be better to give effect to the food production policy by some other means.

The significance of fisheries in Malaya is perhaps best illustrated by their contribution to food supplies. Domestic fish supplies probably account for about 15% of the value of domestic food, and something near 10% of the value of all food consumed. The gross value of fish production is not far below that of domestic rice. Fish is the one primary source of animal protein acceptable to people of all races and creeds. Consumption has been rising rapidly in postwar years; present average per capita consumption in the Federation is 2⅓ ounces a day (53 lbs. per annum). A substantial further increase is considered desirable by nutrition authorities in Malaya.

Measures to increase production and improve distribution of fish accordingly deserve high priority in the development program.

Production

In 1954, 110,000 tons of marine fish and 25,000 tons of fresh water fish were produced for human consumption in the Federation. Another 15,000 tons of fish were processed for use as fertilizer.[1] The catch in Singapore-licensed boats going through the wholesale markets amounted to 4,500 tons.

Production has increased substantially in postwar years. Commercial landings in the whole of Malaya rose from 862,000 piculs[2] in 1947 to 1.9 million in 1954 (see Table 1). The rapid expansion of the earlier years was checked in 1951 and 1952 by poor fishing seasons along some parts of the coast and by measures necessitated by the emergency, which reduced the number of fishermen and restricted activities. Increasing mechanization, however, prevented the more drastic decline that would otherwise have occurred. The 1953 fishing season saw a substantial improvement as conditions became more normal. Postwar expansion was largely confined to the Federation, where commercial landings in 1953 were nearly double those in 1947; the output of the fisheries of Singapore made much less progress during this period.

[1] Annual Report of the Department of Fisheries, 1954.
[2] One picul = 133-1/3 lbs.

325

TABLE 1   Official Commercial Landings of Fish

(*Thousand piculs*)

State/Settlement	1947	1948	1949	1950	1951	1952	1953	1954
Perlis	19.5	43.8	43.9	33.7	28.7	41.1	26.0	43.1
Kedah	63.5	128.0	133.7	176.6	175.1	115.6	93.1	121.7
Penang	81.1	85.4	81.6	76.0	63.8	57.0	46.8	65.9
Perak.	231.6	269.4	310.0	325.2	303.1	331.6	440.8	547.4
Selangor . . .	58.5	118.6	111.8	136.0	105.4	109.6	121.9	286.7
Malacca. . . .	37.4	39.8	41.5	28.2	19.3	36.6	34.9	67.7
Negri Sembilan.	3.1	2.7	2.3	2.4	3.5	3.5	3.4	5.4
Johore	83.6	58.5	101.3	117.9	111.0	108.0	101.8	137.4
Trengganu . .	53.7	83.9	160.7	173.2	139.2	167.0	265.4	240.6
Kelantan . . .	34.6	35.1	102.5	133.8	163.6	56.1	55.7	65.9
Pahang	36.1	28.6	119.2	100.9	113.4	224.4	170.4	187.9
Singapore[1]. . .	159.2	161.5	170.7	171.0	166.0	162.3	169.7	168.7
Total . .	861.9	1,055.3	1,379.2	1,474.9	1,392.1	1,412.8	1,529.9	1,938.4

[1] "Auction market landings" only.

SOURCE: Department of Fisheries.

There are considerable seasonal variations in landings. Peaks of production generally occur in May-June and again in September-October. Landings are usually low in the months of December to February, especially on the east coast, where the northeast monsoon makes it difficult to launch and land craft. In Perlis and Kedah, landings also decline during the southwest monsoon in July and August. Greater use of mechanized craft and the construction of better landing facilities would assist materially in overcoming these seasonal shortages.

The number of persons engaged in fishing has fluctuated considerably; it increased from 48,000 in 1947 to a peak of nearly 77,700 in 1950 (see Table 2). In 1954 some 49,500 fishermen operated off the coasts of Malaya; more than two-thirds were Malays, somewhat less than one-third Chinese, and less than 2% were of other nationalities, primarily Indian and Thai.

In addition to persons directly engaged in fishing, a considerable number are employed in industries and services related to fishing, or depend on income from the fishing industry.

Malaya's sources of marine fish are located in the South China Sea, the Straits of Singapore, the Straits of Malacca and the eastern extremity of the Indian Ocean. The industry is mainly based on intensive fishing of

TABLE 2   Number and Nationality of Fishermen, Federation

Nationality	1947	1948	1949	1950	1951	1952	1953	1954
Malay	34,359	50,312	55,329	56,184	51,927	27,630	37,406	33,679
Chinese	13,278	17,582	19,903	20,791	21,560	22,044	17,893	15,173
Indian	495	474	512	387	353	532	378	388
Thai.	34	28	330	189	213	131	292	228
Portuguese	5	41	68	101	53	49	62	64
Other	18	2	6	3	67	12	4	—
Total	48,189	68,439	76,148	77,657	74,173	50,398	56,035	49,532

SOURCE: Department of Fisheries.

inshore waters. The craft used, mostly small nonmechanized units, are unsuitable for long voyages and Malay fishermen are not accustomed to operations requiring prolonged absence from their homes.

Nonmechanized inshore fishing requires a minimum of harbors, port facilities, market and processing outlets. But there is evidence that 30-40 years of intensive commercial operations along the coasts of Malaya may be leading to overfishing. It will be necessary to fish further afield, which will call for larger craft and for better facilities on shore.

Chinese vegetable gardeners commonly combine pig and poultry farming and fish breeding with vegetable production. Several species of Chinese carp are popular. Experimental work is being carried on and demonstration ponds are used to encourage the production of several species of nonindigenous fish.

Three important varieties of fish are produced in padi fields, irrigation canals and drains in all parts of Malaya. One of these, *sepat siam* (*Trichogaster pectoralis*) is exported in salted form. The other two, *keli* (*Claricas batrechus*) and *aruan* (*Ophiocephalus striatus*), are chiefly consumed locally as fresh fish. Annual production has been valued by the Department of Fisheries at approximately $10 million.[3]

In the mangrove swamp area of southwestern Singapore, brackish water ponds are formed by means of bunds; each pond is drained by a sluice gate. Cone-shaped bag nets attached to these gates catch shrimp, prawn and crabs as the water flows out at low tide. There are about 900 acres of such ponds and a potentially available area of several thousand acres.

[3] Memorandum prepared for the mission by the Department of Fisheries.

The fresh water and brackish water facilities and operations, particularly the ponds, are capable of very considerable expansion but more research and education are required.

Methods of Fishing

Gear. Marine fishing is carried out with various types of moving and stationary nets, hand lines, troll lines, or traps. Fresh water fish in ponds and rivers are captured mainly with portable traps of rattan and bamboo. Seine nets, cast nets and, in large rivers, small fishing stakes are also used.

Boats. Most fishing boats used in coastal waters are propelled by sails, oars or paddles. In 1954 there were 17,787 such boats in operation, compared with only 4,052 powered boats (see Table 3). The nonpowered boats operate from, and in many instances in, shallow water.

The northeast coast of Malaya has long sandy beaches and the fishing areas are some 10 miles off shore. Boats must be able to weather rough seas and stand the strain of being launched and beached on exposed shores. The largest are up to 45 feet in length and have a seven-foot beam. These larger boats are, however, limited in number and in use; most fishing craft, even in this area, are smaller.

From the east coast of Johore around Singapore and up the west coast to Perlis, much of the fishing is done close to shore with hand lines, cast nets or small nets. The *sampan* is the most popular boat in this area, whereas larger boats are used in the Straits of Singapore and Johore and along the northwestern coast from Perlis to Perak.

The traditional craft and equipment of native fishermen are well built and serve their purpose but are primitive and inefficient by modern standards. Their area of operation is limited and output per man is low compared with that of mechanized craft: the average output of fish per fisherman in all Malaya in 1949 was about 2,200 lbs., whereas in Perak, where mechanization of the fishing fleet is most advanced, it was as high as 5,700 lbs.

A Fisheries Department comparative study of the operating efficiency of the motorized Pangkor fleet in the west and that of nonmechanized east coast units indicates a relatively high and constant rate of production for the former while the nonmotorized eastern fleets attain the average efficiency of the Pangkor fleet only at peak periods.[4] However, some allow-

[4] Department of Fisheries.

TABLE 3   Number of Licensed Fishing Boats

	Federation		Singapore		Total	
	Powered	Nonpowered	Powered	Nonpowered	Powered	Nonpowered
1947. . . .	114	16,101	229	1,301	343	17,402
1948. . . .	191	19,501	267	1,386	458	20,887
1949. . . .	327	21,466	231	1,490	558	22,956
1950. . . .	811	21,993	168	1,831	979	23,824
1951. . . .	709[1]	20,196	254	1,933	963	22,129
1952. . . .	1,775	20,810	582	2,047	2,357	22,857
1953. . . .	1,570	21,037	613	2,432	2,183	23,469
1954. . . .	4,052	17,787	592	2,572	4,644	20,359

[1] Not including Kelantan.

SOURCE: Malayan Statistics, May 1954.

ance must be made for differences in fishing conditions in the two areas.

In the past few years considerable progress has been made in motorizing the industry. In 1954, 3,594 more powered craft were licensed than in 1948 but the total of 4,052 was nevertheless only about 20% of all fishing craft in use. Mechanization of fishing craft and the provision of adequate harbor facilities will contribute more than any other factor to increased production of Malayan fisheries; training of crews to handle the craft will have to keep pace.

Harbor Facilities

The future of Malayan marine fisheries depends upon their ability to operate in waters considerably beyond those now being fished. Experiments based at Singapore and Penang have established several potential fishing grounds. One runs across the mouth of the Gulf of Siam; another extends in a north-south direction about 80 miles off shore from Trengganu, while a third runs east and west 20 miles off the coast of Pahang. Trawlers 80-100 feet long are needed to work these grounds.

A fourth extends north and west from Penang in an arc between the northern tip of Sumatra and the Langkawi Islands. This, too, is accessible only with craft larger than those commonly in use in Malaya. Such craft require adequate harbor facilities.

In establishing these facilities, relevant considerations are proximity to fishing grounds and availability of fishermen who can be trained for this type of fishing. These factors and the practical necessity of combining fishing needs with other requirements lead us to suggest the possibility of developing facilities at the ports of Kuala Trengganu and Kuantan in the east and Kuala Kedah in the west.

Ideally, ports for the fishing operations we envisage should have approaches which will accommodate craft with a draught of 9½-10 feet even at low tide. In view of the extent of silting in the ports mentioned (as indeed in most east coast ports) and of the Federation's limited financial resources, it is unlikely that this standard can be met in the near future. It should, however, be possible to improve approaches sufficiently to permit access at high tide to ships of that draught.

Port facilities should include piers or wharfs alongside which fishing craft may lie at any tide level and which will permit unloading of fish simultaneously with loading of ice and stores. Space should also be provided in the immediate vicinity for offices, a wholesale fish market, an ice factory and refrigeration facilities, and for parking of trucks. An area should be set aside for the repair and maintenance of nets and gear. The ports must also be able to provide adequate water and fuel services. Good harbors concentrate fishing activities and this in turn is likely to encourage the establishment of secondary industries, by-product plants and servicing agencies of many kinds.

The Fisheries Department has strongly advocated the development of a third east coast port, Kuala Besuṭ. But according to D. F. Allen's report on the Minor Ports of Malaya, maximum depth at this port is only 3½ feet at high tide because of a bar at the estuary; the other ports mentioned offer a much greater depth. To bring the approaches up to the desirable standard would be very costly; this consideration should be carefully weighed against benefits anticipated from developing Kuala Besut.

Prices and Markets

Price charts published by the Department of Fisheries indicate that prices generally declined from 1947 to mid-1949, rose to a peak early in 1953 and again declined. For most varieties, supplies have not met demand and prices have reflected the conditions of a sellers' market. In 1953 the average price of first quality fish was about 75% above the 1948 level; second and third quality fish showed less increase. It is significant that fluctuations since 1948 have closely paralleled changes in rubber prices and in economic activity in general.

Fish are landed at more than 300 points along the extensive coast line, making it possible to supply large numbers of consumers fairly quickly. Considering that many landing points lack marketing, preservation and processing facilities, marketing is reasonably efficient. Coastal cities have an obvious advantage over inland cities in this respect. Prices vary considerably among localities and have as a rule increased more in the interior than along the coast. The Fisheries Department estimates that the cost to the housewife is on the average of about $2\frac{1}{4}$ times the price received by the fisherman; in Ulu Kelantan the margin is as much as 600%.

The increase and variations in prices seem to suggest not only inadequacy of supplies, but also uneven and in places costly distribution. One answer to the problem would appear to be more fish; this in turn argues for motorized boats to tap new fishing resources and harbor facilities to extend operations. But there are also marketing problems which call for more services: for improved transport, refrigeration and, in places, processing facilities. There is a need for auction markets at many centers where volume justifies such selling methods.

A new development in the field of marketing is the Kelantan Fish Marketing Scheme initiated by the Department of Fisheries. Its purpose is to increase output, improve distribution and assure a fair price to both consumers and fishermen; it is also designed to provide participating fishermen with producer goods at reasonable prices. The scheme is financed by Colonial Development and Welfare funds and is operated on a cooperative basis.

The first fish handling depot at Bachok went into operation in September 1954. Its facilities include shop and office premises, a sorting shed, stores for ice and for dried and wet fish and a fish processing factory. Two motor boats collect the catch from fishing boats at sea, which enables fishermen to extend their operations and speeds up the handling of the catch. Fish purchased by the depot are packed in ice and dispatched to cooperative or other stores or agents inland; any surplus is processed or put into storage.

The depot buys fish at a price agreed upon by a committee of head fishermen participating in the scheme. Its selling price allows for a margin sufficient to cover its operating costs and overheads, repayment of loans and a profit to be distributed among participants in the scheme.

It is proposed to establish a number of such depots at various points along the coast and ultimately to bring the entire Kelantan fishing industry into the scheme.

Future Development

Research. The exploitation of marine fisheries calls for a program of development involving many aspects of production, transportation and distribution. Such a program must be based on adequate research. Research should begin with the study of marine fishing resources, including an analysis of what has happened in tributary waters and what should be done to arrest exploitation and restore productivity. It must include exploration, to assess the magnitude and distribution of resources further afield. There must also be research and experimentation in methods, types of equipment and other aspects of marine fishing. Facilities for research on marine fisheries are being developed in Singapore, where the Southeast Asia Regional Research Station is under construction.

As regards fresh water fishing, the industry is closely tied in with agriculture and the peasant economy of the padi field and vegetable gardens. Here it is a matter of experimenting with varieties of fish, culture operations, conservation of fertility and restocking. Fish breeding stations and restocking are essential parts of this program. Fresh water fisheries research is to be undertaken in the proposed Commonwealth Fish Culture Research and Training Institute, which may be established in Malacca with Colonial Development and Welfare funds. The Federal Government also intends to establish a fry and fish culture demonstration and training center at Penang.

Research on production is fundamental to a development program; it must be accompanied by research on methods of preservation and processing to assure the best utilization of supplies. It is also important to study transportation, merchandizing, distribution, consumer demand, costs and the like.

It may be necessary to follow research with pilot plant demonstrations before new processes and new products are accepted and produced commercially.

Improved statistical reporting is basic to administration, policy decisions and the whole program of development. The Department has already done a good deal in this field but more and better statistics are still needed.

This does not necessarily mean greater expenditure; substitution of sampling for complete enumeration was instituted in 1952 but is not yet fully developed.

Education and Extension. If production is to be increased and anything like the industry's potential contribution to national welfare realized, an intensive program of education and demonstration must be carried on. This is particularly important because of the change from small-scale to commercial operations now in progress in Malaya. There should be at least one, possibly two, schools to teach modern commercial fishing methods, including the use of gear and boats, care of fish, and sanitation in relation to boats, markets and processing plants; refrigeration and preservation adapted to local needs; design and construction of fish ponds; fish breeding, rearing and fattening techniques; restocking of rivers and river conservation. Supplementing the schools, extension and demonstration work should be undertaken among the fishermen.

Port Facilities, Equipment and Secondary Industries. A comprehensive long-range development program should include improvement of unloading places and shore facilities at many points throughout Malaya. At smaller centers these improvements need not be elaborate or expensive; at the larger ports facilities such as those outlined above should be considered. The government will have to provide basic shore facilities; capital for the purchase of fishing equipment and the establishment of processing and auxiliary industries and services must come largely from private sources with the continued financial assistance of the Rural and Industrial Development Authority.[5]

Cooperation. Fishing itself, as well as ownership of boats, provision of credit, operation of motor transport, marketing and simple types of processing could be organized on a cooperative basis. Local societies should not, however, be established without adequate discussion and study of their possibilities and limitations, and of the responsibilities of members, or without making provision for adequate training of the societies' officers.

Execution of the Program. The Fisheries Department, under a Director of Fisheries, is pan-Malayan. Its headquarters are at Penang and it has four regional stations in the Federation, Kuala Trengganu, Kuantan, Penang and Malacca. In Singapore there is a Fisheries Division of the Department of Commerce and Industries, administered by a Deputy Director under the guidance of the Director of Fisheries at Penang.

[5] For a discussion of the activities of RIDA, see Chapter 9.

The Department's permanent establishment is 14 senior and 41 subordinate officers. In addition, a staff of 14 is to be employed in the two new research stations. Four senior posts were vacant in the Department at the time of the mission's visit owing to lack of funds. The unfilled posts were those of senior specialists in research and extension work on marine and fresh water fisheries, the technology of fish handling and processing, and in the economics of marketing and distribution; the approved post of Principal of the projected Fisheries School had also not yet been filled. Furthermore, it was considered doubtful that available funds would permit recruitment up to the full establishment of the two research stations.

The Department is now reasonably well equipped with craft for work at sea, but office and other facilities on shore are inadequate. A small building program has recently been begun.

The Department considers that it can carry out an effective program for the next few years, if it is allowed to recruit up to its approved establishment of technical senior officers and some additional junior staff, and if it is provided with the requisite facilities and equipment. The mission recommends that every effort be made to meet these requirements.

Singapore

The Colony has some problems that are peculiarly its own. It has become increasingly obvious in recent years that the waters adjacent to Singapore have been fully exploited. Maximum in-shore fishery production appears to be about 4,000 tons and actual output in 1952 was 3,428. Since this is but a fraction of the quantity consumed in Singapore, it has been necessary to import fish from the Federation and from Indonesia, as well as to exploit the off-shore fisheries.

The most notable development has been the exploitation of distant waters by mechanized craft. There has been a substantial increase in the number of motorized units, the total reaching 613 in 1953, compared with a third as many a few years earlier. Trawling by several units operating in pairs appears likely further to increase the off-shore fishery returns; these amounted to 2,085 tons in 1952.

Production by Singapore fishermen has been helped by a Fisheries Loan Fund of $400,000, administered by a Fisheries Loans Board. This fund, together with the facilities of a Fishing Materials Suspense Account, is used in part to make bulk purchases of supplies such as fishing gear and pressure lamps for resale to fishermen. It has been devoted principally to assistance in the purchase of motors and of larger and more powerful fishing craft. Encouraged by this support, private industry has also invested in modern craft and gear.

There are five auction markets in Singapore and numerous retail outlets, ranging from large retail markets to individual street hawkers carrying their wares in baskets. A study conducted by the Department of Fisheries in 1953 indicated that improvement of distribution is required at both the wholesale and retail levels. There are not enough wholesale points and retail equipment is frequently deficient. In particular, wider use should be made of ice and refrigeration. Plans for the establishment of fish-landing facilities and a large wholesale market were under consideration at the time of the mission's visit. A site for this project has been reserved in the Kallang area. The mission supports these plans and has included a token amount for their execution in its proposed program.

TECHNICAL REPORT 5 *MINING*

I TIN MINING

Any appraisal of the mining industry must be largely confined to tin mining. Other metals and minerals are produced (see Map 8) but their aggregate value is small in comparison with tin (see Table 1) and their contribution to Malaya's economy and external trade almost insignificant. While expanded production is possible, it is difficult to foresee an increase of a magnitude sufficient to offset the consequences of any appreciable decline in tin production.

Tin mining employed 88% of the mining industry's labor force of 41,661 in 1953; it consumed 72% of all electricity used in the Federation and directly contributed about 12-15% of government revenues. The gross value of tin production in 1953 was equivalent to 20% of Malaya's total exports in that year.

Malaya accounts for about one-third of world production of tin and

TABLE 1   Approximate Value[1] of Mineral Production, 1949-53

(Million $)

	1949	1950	1951	1952	1953	1954
Tin	261.57	352.89	487.34	458.45	343.37	360.52
Coal	7.93	8.52	7.84	7.87	8.59	6.74
Gold	0.90	1.87	1.73	2.01	1.86	2.13
Iron ore	0.13	8.92	18.71	24.35	21.38	24.92
Bauxite	—	—	—	0.30	2.13	3.42
Ilmenite	0.02	0.05	0.58	0.48	0.70	1.24
Wolframite	0.02	0.04	0.40	0.57	0.90	0.22
Scheelite	0.13	0.04	0.20	0.30	0.29	0.24
Tantalite-columbite	—	0.05	0.16	0.40	0.69	2.00
China clay	0.08	0.06	0.07	0.05	0.04	0.84
Quarried stone	3.67	3.33	3.20	4.22	5.76	5.76
Total	274.45	375.77	520.23	499.00	358.71	408.03

[1] Actual value for tin and coal; assumed value in Gazette notification for bauxite and ilmenite; assumed value for quarried stone; declared value of exports of other minerals.

SOURCE: Information supplied by Chief Inspector of Mines, Mines Department, Federation of Malaya.

336

MAP 8

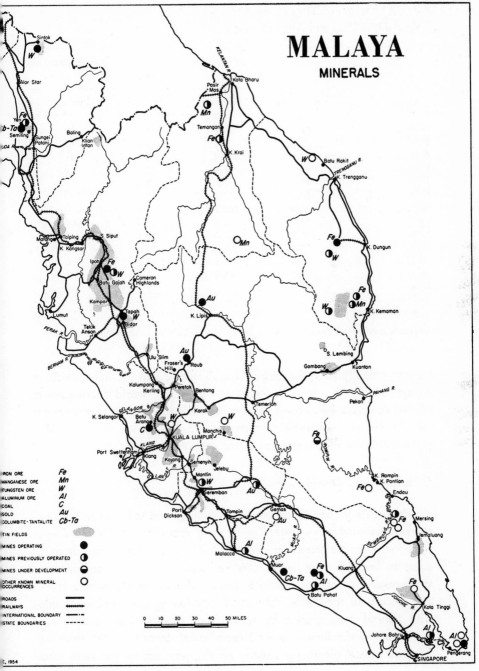

MALAYA
MINERALS

IRON ORE *Fe*
MANGANESE ORE *Mn*
TUNGSTEN ORE *W*
ALUMINUM ORE *Al*
COAL *C*
GOLD *Au*
COLUMBITE-TANTALITE *Cb-Ta*

TIN FIELDS

MINES OPERATING

MINES PREVIOUSLY OPERATED

MINES UNDER DEVELOPMENT

OTHER KNOWN MINERAL
OCCURRENCES

ROADS

RAILWAYS

INTERNATIONAL BOUNDARY

STATE BOUNDARIES

0   10   20   30   40   50 MILES

1954

TABLE 2   Exports of Tin-in-Concentrates,
Export Duty Paid and Average Prices

	Exports		Duty paid	Average Singapore price of tin
	Thousand tons	Million $	Million $	$ per picul
1930.	62.1	76.0	9.1	73
1933[1]	23.9	37.7	4.9	100
1939.	52.2	100.2	13.1	114
1940.	81.3	177.4	23.3	130
1946.	10.3	29.5	3.6	—
1947.	26.4	94.3	13.8	—
1948.	44.8	203.7	29.7	—
1949.	55.4	264.1	38.5	295
1950.	57.7	354.0	52.1	367
1951.	57.4	505.5	76.2	527
1952.	57.7	465.1	69.6	480
1953.	56.7	345.9	50.6	364
1954.	60.8	347.6	52.7	354

[1] Prewar lowest.

SOURCE: Bulletin of Statistics Relating to the Mining Industry of Malaya; Mines Department, Federation of Malaya.

exports virtually its entire output (see Tables 2 and 3). Malayan tin is always assured of a market, owing to the uneven world distribution of known resources and, because of the favorable mode of occurrence of the ore, the industry is capable of competing in any market in the world if given reasonable encouragement by the government.

Occurrence and Distribution

Tin occurs principally as cassiterite (SnO_2) and is found in both primary and secondary deposits. The primary deposits occur as lode formations in rocks; the secondary deposits, known as "alluvial" or "detrital," occur in beds of gravel, sand, clay and silt. The alluvial deposits have their origin in intrusions which carried the tin minerals into cracks and fissures in the rocks. Subsequent weathering and erosion, coupled with natural concentration by water from the abundant rainfall, have given rise to the formation of large alluvial deposits in the river valleys and coastal plains, particularly on the west side of the main range

FIGURE 2

TIN PRODUCTION AND CONSUMPTION
(THOUSANDS OF LONG TONS)

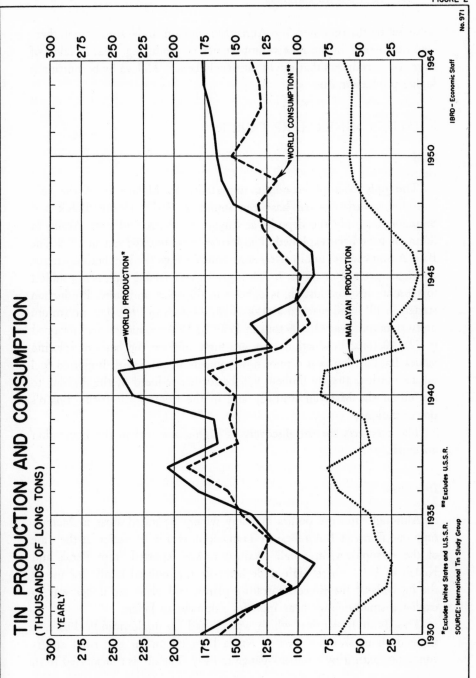

YEARLY

WORLD PRODUCTION*

WORLD CONSUMPTION**

MALAYAN PRODUCTION

*Excludes United States and U.S.S.R.   **Excludes U.S.S.R.

SOURCE: International Tin Study Group

IBRD – Economic Staff

No. 971

levels set by the proposed Tin Agreement remains to be seen. If not, there could be a shift in the relative importance of producing areas in favor of lower cost producers that might ultimately benefit Malaya by permitting it higher production quotas.

II OTHER MINERAL RESOURCES

Coal

The only coal of economic importance in Malaya is of the sub-bituminous variety. Coal has been found in Perlis, Johore, Perak and Selangor, but only the deposits at Enggor in Perak and Batu Arang in Selangor have been exploited. The former were worked out in 1928. The Batu Arang coal occurs in two seams which are worked by both open-cast and underground methods. It is low-grade, very friable and, being subject to spontaneous combustion, is difficult to transport and store. Production started in 1913 and reached a peak of 781,000 tons in 1940. The maximum postwar output was 416,000 tons in 1950; by 1954 production had dropped to 225,000 tons. Production costs are high, and on the basis of calorific values Batu Arang coal cannot now compete in price with imported fuel oil. Its market, already limited, will be further reduced by the decision to use oil in the Malayan Railway and in the Central Electricity Board's power stations.

The prospects for the discovery of high-grade coal in the Federation are small.

Iron Ores

Although iron ore occurs in many widely separated areas in Malaya, only one mine, at Bukit Besi in Trengganu, was in operation at the time of the mission's visit. Small production was reported from Perak and Kedah in 1953, where high-grade hematite is produced locally for use in the jig beds of the tin-concentrating plants, and plans are under way to exploit a small deposit near Ipoh for shipment to Japan.

The Bukit Besi mine, which was opened up in the middle 1920's, is situated about 17 miles west of Kuala Dungun on the east coast and is connected with it by a narrow-gauge railway. The ore is transported from the mine in small 12-15-ton cars and is transferred to ships by lighter. It is hematite-magnetite and is of relatively high grade, ranging from 55% to 63% Fe. In 1954 production was 1,212,780 tons and 1,039,430 tons were exported to Japan.

Mining is by open-cast method. The mine is well mechanized and has recently installed a washing plant. Reserves are estimated to be of the order of 7-9 million tons; an extensive program of prospecting and development now being carried out may disclose additional reserves. Other known deposits in Trengganu are at Bukit Tasek and Bukit Anat Sal; these reserves are probably not large. The ore has a grade of 50% Fe.

An area around Ulu Rompin, 37 miles south-west of Pekan in Pahang, is being actively explored by a mining company. Indications are that it contains reserves of some 20-30 million tons of high-grade iron ore, possibly averaging 60% Fe. Annual production of two million tons is projected.

Total proved reserves in Malaya are approximately 25 million tons with a further 20 million tons in the "probable" and "possible" categories. Most of these reserves lie within the mines of Bukit Besi and Ulu Rompin.

Little, if any, iron ore is used in Malaya apart from a few hundred tons used as "jig ragging" in the tin industry. The consumption of pig iron is relatively small; most of the foundries have access to local scrap, and imports of pig iron in 1954 were only 750 tons. Imports of semi-finished iron and steel products were also comparatively small. The absence of substantial demand, coupled with lack of domestic coking coal, precludes the establishment of a steel industry. Malayan iron ore mining is thus dependent on export markets. Japan, which is experiencing difficulties in meeting its requirements, especially of high-grade iron ore, would appear to be the logical market.

Additional geological work and prospecting are required to determine whether the known widely scattered deposits are interrelated and whether there may be other deposits.

Bauxite

There are a number of known occurrences of bauxite, particularly in the southern half of the peninsula. Some production has been recorded in

Johore and Malacca, but is now confined to a deposit at Telok Ramunia in Johore, where output is at the rate of about 20,000 tons per month; the bulk of this is exported to Japan. The mine is fully mechanized, a washing plant has been installed, and the final product averages about 58% Al_2O_3 and less than 4% silica. Known reserves are small.

Aluminium Ltd. holds a controlling interest in a lease of approximately 3,000 acres near Pengerang, a short distance from the Telok Ramunia mine. The bauxite is of good quality, averaging around 54% Al_2O_3 and 5% silica. The company is planning a treatment plant and will ship the product to Japan. Other deposits in Johore which have been mined in the past, largely by Japanese interests, are at Bukit Pasir, Perigi Acheh (Kim Kim), and Sri Medan, the latter associated with iron ore. All of these are small and are for the most part worked out.

No deposits of a size sufficient to maintain an aluminum industry are known. Although a number of small deposits with reserves of a few million tons may possibly be found, the future of bauxite mining must depend upon its ability to export at competitive prices.

Manganese

All known deposits occur in the States of Trengganu and Kelantan, but at the time of the mission's visit manganese was not being produced. The ores are chiefly pyrolusite and psilomelane and are probably due to secondary concentration following the weathering of the surrounding rocks. In some places iron ore is found in association with manganese. The origin of the deposits precludes the possibility that they extend to any depth.

The grade of ore as mined was appreciably lower than that normally acceptable to the iron and steel industry. The deposits at Gual Priok in Kelantan average around 37% Mn, those at Machang Stahun in Trengganu approximately 25% Mn and 25-30% Fe. Perhaps the most promising deposit is at the headwaters of the Sungei Aring in Kelantan. Little is known about it, and its inaccessibility and the emergency have prevented prospecting and development. Since large high-grade deposits are available in India, Africa and elsewhere, the prospects for production of manganese in Malaya are not promising unless the grade of deposits proves much higher than that mined in the past.

Tungsten

The tungsten ores of Malaya, wolframite and scheelite, are usually found in association with tin and gold ores. In a few places, however, mines have been opened for their wolframite and scheelite content alone, notably at Bukit Kachi, Sintock in Kedah and the Chendrong Concession mines in Trengganu for wolframite, and at Pulai in Perak for scheelite. Small quantities of very high grade scheelite are obtained as a by-product from the mining of gold at Raub in Pahang.

Columbite-Tantalite

Columbite occurs in alluvial deposits associated with tin; the greater part of the output comes from the Semeling district in Kedah. In 1953, 52 tons of concentrate were produced, averaging 74.2% combined oxide in the ratio of four parts of columbium to one of tantalum. During the war some production was also developed in Bakri in Johore. Small amounts of columbite have been observed in tin concentrates from widely scattered areas. Tin slags from both smelting companies contain appreciable quantities of the combined oxides of tantalum and columbium. The recent rise in demand with consequent high prices has stimulated interest in these slags, and in 1953 19,269 tons were exported with a reported value of $3.5 million. The slags contain approximately 6% to 7% of the combined oxides in almost equal ratio.

The slags are extremely complex and the results achieved in their treatment are not yet definitely known. Should the extraction of columbium-tantalum prove profitable, a substantial additional source of these metals would become available.

Gold

Apart from small quantities of gold obtained from tin dredging and gravel pump mines, almost the entire output comes from one lode mine at Raub in Pahang. The deposits are a series of small lenticular ore shoots in steeply dipping veins of quartz and brecciated shale, which form part of an extensive reef system in a highly folded area extending along the eastern side of the main range. Prospects for a moderate expansion of operations in this area appear to be good, but the price of gold relative to present production costs is not conducive to optimism. Moreover, the emergency renders prospecting hazardous.

Ilmenite

Ilmenite (Fe O Ti O_2) is obtained solely as a by-product of tin mining. The cleaning and upgrading of crude tin concentrates to a marketable grade yields a residue locally known as "amang," which is largely ilmenite. The amang is cleaned by washing or passing through magnetic separators to recover the ilmenite. Only exports are recorded. Production depends largely on the output of tin and the market demand for ilmenite. Since production costs are relatively low, Malaya should be able to sustain its position in a competitive market. Associated with the amang are zircon, monazite and other rare earths; the possibilities of making marketable concentrates of these should be fully investigated.

Nonferrous metals

Malaya has no recorded production of lead, zinc or copper; minor amounts of mixed sulphides containing a high proportion of copper are, however, being recovered at the lode mine at Sungei Lembing as a result of introducing flotation and tabling in the clean-up circuit of the mill.

Building Stone, Road Metal, Clays and Shales

The extraction of stone, sand and gravel does not come under inspection by the Mines Department nor are they covered by mining leases; only permits for their removal are required. Much of the material is produced under the direction of the Public Works Department. On the whole, Malaya has an abundance of stone, gravel and sands for ordinary construction needs. Requirements of ornamental stone are small and are met by imports.

Clays and shales suitable for the manufacture of bricks, tiles and coarse earthenware are widespread. Bricks and tiles of good quality are produced at Batu Arang, but transportation costs limit their market.

Cement

A modern plant at Rawang began operation in July 1953, using shale from Batu Arang and local limestone and imported gypsum. The possibilities of future expansion are good.

China Clay

China clay is mined on a small scale near Tapah in Perak and at Cheras in Selangor. The material is suitable as a filler for the local manufacture of rubber goods and the production of lower grades of chinaware. Large supplies are doubtless available in other parts of the Federation, particularly in the Tronoh and Bidor districts of Perak.

Outlook for Mineral Diversification

The prospects for developing a major mineral industry in Malaya in addition to tin mining are not encouraging. This does not imply that the country is incapable of increasing its output of other minerals. Tin has been given priority and relatively little attention has been directed to the prospecting and development of other minerals. Large areas of the country have not been thoroughly prospected, due to inaccessibility and difficult terrain. But much of Malaya, insofar as it is known geologically, is underlain by granites, which are not usually favorable for the occurrence of metaliferrous mineral deposits.

Prospecting in most parts of Malaya by ordinary visual means is exceedingly difficult. Rock outcrops are rare and jungle covers large areas, making accurate geological mapping by ground traverse methods difficult and slow. There has not been sufficient geological work to indicate rock relationships, which might be a clue to potential prospecting areas. Upon completion of work in progress at the time of the mission's visit, some 21% of Malaya will have been mapped geologically. Emergency conditions have prevented anything but the most cursory examination of areas other than those in proximity to closely patrolled or well-guarded localities.

Most of the minerals produced in Malaya are obtained as by-products of the tin-mining industry, or are being produced under the stimulus of world emergency demand. For the most part deposits are small, and, with the possible exception of iron and bauxite, do not permit large and low-cost production over an extended period of years. The country itself has only a small metal-using industry and in world markets Malayan minerals face competition from sources closer to the major industrial centers. For these reasons Malaya's mineral strength must continue to rest on a strong, healthy tin-mining industry.

III GOVERNMENT AGENCIES AND THE MINING INDUSTRY

Responsibility for development of the mineral resources of any country rests jointly on government and industry. The government's role is to encourage the orderly development of these resources and to create conditions that will attract private capital for their development; industry must provide the capital and technical skills necessary for efficient mining operations. Knowledge of the extent of resources is essential to orderly development and planning, yet for reasons already stated geological mapping, exploration and prospecting in Malaya have not kept pace with the exhaustion of commercially exploitable deposits.

Two agencies of the Federal Government, the Mines Department and the Geological Survey, both under the Member for Natural Resources, are directly concerned with the mineral industry as it affects the welfare and economy of the country. The Mines Department is specifically charged with the administration of mining legislation and with advising the Federal and State Governments on all technical aspects and policies relating to the industry. The Geological Survey is primarily concerned with the detailed geological study of the country and the preparation of maps and reports, so that data relating not only to the geological areas, but to soils, ground water resources and other matters pertinent to engineering works may be available. The work of the Geological Survey has been hampered in the past by lack of trained staff and inadequacy of suitable quarters and laboratory facilities; the construction of new headquarters with Colonial Development and Welfare funds, as well as the provision of additional staff should, however, do much to strengthen the Survey.

The mission endorses the development plans put forward by the

Director of the Geological Survey but suggests that more emphasis be given to the economic geology of known mining areas and adjacent areas. Plans for detailed mapping of the whole country should not be abandoned, but in view of the many difficulties in the way of surveying and mapping and the shortage of trained and experienced staff, we think first priority should be given to extending the knowledge of areas known to contain mineral resources. It is suggested that a Division of Economic Geology be set up under an assistant director, whose first task should be to assemble and train a small staff.

The possibility of using modern techniques of aerial magnetometer and geophysical and photogeological surveying should be considered, directed particularly to determining the contact between the granites and the sediments. The United Nations Technical Assistance Administration has furnished technical advice on this matter, and its consultant has recommended the aeromagnetic survey of several areas. That agency has also provided funds for a team of geophysicists to survey potential mining areas. It is recommended that the results of geophysical surveys already carried out be carefully studied by the government, if necessary in consultation with outside specialists, to determine whether the proposed expenditure on aeromagnetic surveys is warranted.

The mission does not feel competent to advise in these matters but would point out that certain difficulties inherent in Malaya's geological history, physiography and rugged terrain may preclude successful results.

Much of the geological program for the next few years is to be financed by means of Colonial Development and Welfare grants. The mission attaches great importance to the continuance of a strong Geological Survey and, to ensure this, suggests that the Federal Government should assume the responsibility for staff expenditures before or when the grants come to an end.

The mission also endorses in general the Mines Department program, which includes the erection of new mineral dressing and research laboratories, estimation of ore reserves, and research into mining methods, particularly as they affect the exploitation of lands on the higher slopes. The Mines Department has already done promising work in devising methods and equipment for increased recovery of tin and of by-products. The mission recommends that this work be expanded and that the industry be guided into adopting improved methods. We are aware of the reluctance of the industry, particularly of the Chinese sector, in this respect but believe that existing mining legislation could be invoked to ensure reasonable conformity to proved suggestions.

The paucity of accurate information regarding proved and potential tin reserves has already been noted. In the mission's view, the Mines Department, in cooperation with the Geological Survey, should give priority to a detailed economic survey of these reserves. The survey should include a compilation of statistics on land worked out and abandoned and land "worked over," but still under lease, which might be reworked under improved marketing and operating conditions. These data would also be required for the study of the rehabilitation of mining lands recommended earlier.

TECHNICAL REPORT 6 *POWER*

1 FEDERATION

Organization of Electric Power Supply

No installation for the generation of electric power may be operated in the Federation without a license from the Central Electricity Board (CEB). These are granted for as long as 21 years, subject to cancellation for noncompliance with their conditions. The Board is empowered, in certain circumstances, to close down a public installation[1] if it is able, without loss, to supply the licensee with power at a rate below his current generation costs.

At the time of the mission's visit, about 25 licenses had been granted to public suppliers by CEB. The Perak River Hydroelectric Power Co., Ltd., (PRHE) is the largest licensed power undertaking in the Federation, with an installed capacity of about 77.7 MW.[2] Other large licensees are the Kinta Electrical Distribution Company (a distribution subsidiary of PRHE), and Huttenbachs Ltd. There are about 22 small licensees operating diesel units with an aggregate capacity of about 1 MW.

Special provisions of the Electricity Ordinance relate to the Electricity Supply Department of the Municipality of George Town (in Penang), which enjoys greater freedom than other licensees.

CEB's present policy is to encourage private participation in the power field where this will assist in the development of the country. It does not encourage new public plants in localities where it can provide power at lower cost; in such cases even existing diesel plants may be shut down.

It is the mission's view that CEB should continue to use its authority with restraint. Otherwise, private participation may be rapidly eliminated

---

[1] Defined as an installation operated by a licensee for the supply of electrical energy to any person other than the licensee.

[2] Megawatt = 1,000 KW. Figures and data in the text and tables, apart from projections of the mission, are drawn from the CEB Annual Report, 1952-53; Penang Annual Report, 1951-52; PRHE Annual Report, 1952-53; and records of the Federal Departments of Mines and of Machinery.

and CEB may defeat its own basic objective of promoting economic development.

Installed Capacity

A breakdown of capacity by type of prime mover and ownership is shown in Table 1.

TABLE 1   Power Installations by Type of
Prime Mover and Ownership, 1954

(*MW*)

	Public Utilities	Mines	Others	Total
Steam	134	17	2	153
Oil engines	24	125	103	232
Hydro-power	29	8	—	37
	187	150	105	442

Steam and diesel installations account for over 90% of the Federation's power capacity; hydroelectric power is largely concentrated in Perak for tin mining consumption. The public utilities own less than half of the total installed capacity. The extent of self-sufficiency in power is explained partly by the remoteness of some enterprises from public utility systems, partly by the inability of the latter to meet the increasing demand of postwar years as it developed, and partly by the Chinese miners' traditional independence. Of the 150 MW owned by the mining industry, tin mining accounts for possibly 135-140 MW; it utilizes, in addition, some 70 MW of the capacity of public utilities. Rubber estates and sawmills account for a large part of the 105 MW of capacity owned by nonmining enterprises.

The distribution of power installations in the Federation is shown in Table 2.

The main public utility undertaking in the first area is the Electricity Supply Department of George Town (Penang) which supplies the Island of Penang and provides power for distribution by Huttenbachs through its high tension network in Province Wellesley.[3] In Kedah, a considerable

[3] Messrs. Huttenbachs were taken over by the CEB on January 1, 1955.

TABLE 2 Regional Distribution of Power Installations, 1954

(MW)

Area	Public Utilities	Mines	Others	Total
Penang, Province Wellesley,				
Kedah and Perlis	20.9	4.0	22.0	46.9
Perak	81.4	73.0	21.0	175.4
Selangor, Negri Sembilan,				
Malacca and Johore	78.9	61.0	60.0	199.9
Kelantan, Trengganu and Pahang	5.8	12.0	2.0	19.8
	187.0	150.0	105.0	442.0

number of privately owned stationary engines are in use, mainly by rubber estates and sawmills.

The second and third areas are the main areas of consumption. Perak is supplied largely by PRHE, the third area mainly by CEB. In Perak, the towns of Ipoh and Batu Gajah are supplied by CEB with power purchased in bulk from PRHE, and a number of small towns and villages are supplied by Huttenbachs and other, minor, undertakings. Many small tin mines operate their own power plants.

The main installations of public utilities in the northeastern area are in the State of Kelantan. The CEB diesel power station in Kota Bharu feeds the town and the surrounding agricultural area. The Eastern Mining and Metals Company's mines in Dungun (Trengganu), and the Pahang Consolidated Company's mines in Sungei Lembing (Pahang), have their own power installations with total installed capacity of 6 MW.

The installed capacity of public utilities is unusually high in relation to peak loads, as shown below:

	Peak Load (MW)	Installed Capacity (MW)	Ratio of Installed Capacity to Peak Load
CEB			
Central network	40	68.9	1.67
Diesel stations	10[1]	18.1	1.81
PRHE	67	77.0	1.15
Penang	10	17.0	1.70
Minor undertakings	5	6.0	1.20
		187.0	

[1] Bulk supply to Johore Bahru from Singapore, 2.4 MW peak, not included.

The high ratios are attributable to the fact that: (a) some of the steam power sets are obsolete and are used only as standby equipment; (b) hydroelectric installations cannot be fully utilized in periods of low water supply; and (c) some diesel stations are provided with standby units. It is CEB's policy to provide standby units; once installed, these are often required for normal service to meet an increase in demand.

The number of units generated by the public utility companies in 1953-54 was 726 million KWH.[4] Statistics of other power generation are not available, except for electricity generated by private mining installations. On the basis of oil consumption, however, it may be estimated that industrial power installations produced electric and mechanical power equivalent to approximately 670 million KWH; of this, 550 million KWH may have been in the form of mechanical power.

Estimates of Future Power Requirements

The tin mining industry took two-thirds of the units sold by public utilities in 1952-53. Special consideration must therefore be given to the industry's probable demand when estimating future power requirements, as well as to the usual factors of population growth, industrial expansion and improvements in the standard of living.

Prospects for a significant increase in Malayan tin production are not encouraging. In view of the fairly close relationship between the industry's demand for power and the level of tin production, it would be unwise to assume any large increase in demand from this source. In view of this and other relevant factors, it would not be practicable to estimate power requirements beyond the next five years. Neither is it feasible to take into account a possible expansion in privately owned power installations. This analysis is therefore confined to the public utilities, which are expected to supply most of the increased requirements of the Federation.

Power for mining operations other than tin has for the most part been supplied not by public utilities but by private generating plants; this will probably continue to be true, since the mine sites cannot be economically reached by the public utility systems.

Rubber estates are large users of mechanical power but many are located too far from transmission lines to be economically reached by the public utilities. Some of the rubber mills now generating their own power

[4] CEB Annual Report, 1953-54, page 55.

FIGURE 3

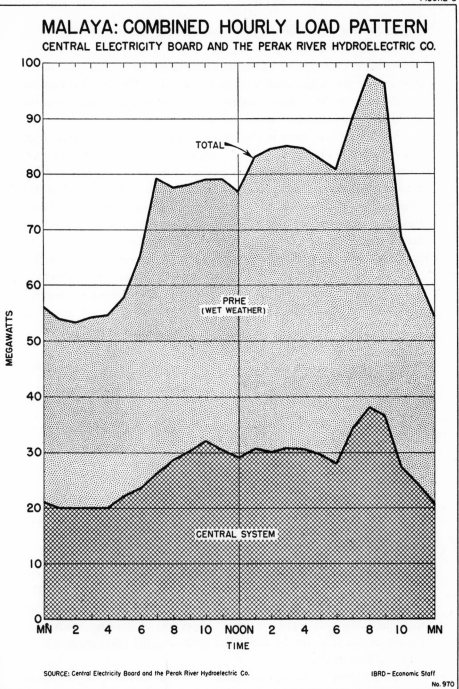

MALAYA: COMBINED HOURLY LOAD PATTERN
CENTRAL ELECTRICITY BOARD AND THE PERAK RIVER HYDROELECTRIC CO.

TOTAL

PRHE
(WET WEATHER)

CENTRAL SYSTEM

MEGAWATTS

TIME

MN 2 4 6 8 10 NOON 2 4 6 8 10 MN

SOURCE: Central Electricity Board and the Perak River Hydroelectric Co.

IBRD – Economic Staff
No. 970

might, however, be encouraged to take electric power from the public utilities if rates were attractive.

Domestic consumption of electricity accounts for a large part of the demand on the public utilities systems, other than PRHE. This demand can be expected to expand steadily; the facilities for renting domestic appliances offered by the utilities will increase it.

CEB has forecast a rise in the demand for power from its systems from 208 million KWH in 1952-53 to 432 million KWH in 1957-58. Its figures do not appear unreasonable except possibly with respect to the dredging sector of the tin mining industry. The CEB estimates are based on the consumption of dredges to be built or converted to electrical drive during the next five years, for which firm commitments for power had either been made or were being negotiated. The estimate assumes that all dredging companies will proceed with their conversion and construction plans and that no dredges receiving power will become idle. In view of the uncertain prospects for tin this may prove an overoptimistic assumption. Table 3 shows a breakdown of the CEB estimates.

TABLE 3   Estimated Power Requirements of the CEB System

(Million KWH)

	Consumption		Generation
	1953	1958	1958
Domestic light and power, commercial lighting, etc.	69	143	171
Industrial power	49	124	149
Tin mines			
Dredges	41	115	138
Other	49	50	60
	208	432	518

Domestic and lighting requirements are estimated to increase over the five years by about 100% and industrial requirements by some 150%. The estimate for future industrial consumption is based on the assumption that electricity will replace a large proportion of existing mechanical power; as this may also be somewhat optimistic, the estimates should be reviewed frequently.

The situation in the area served by PRHE is, however, very different.

While sales of PRHE increased by 63% from 1948 to 1953, the increase from 1952 to 1953 was only 1%.[5] This was due to the closing of a number of mines and a reduction in the activity of others. Consumption in this area over the next five years has been estimated on the basis of no substantial increase in consumption by mines but a 100% increase in the towns served by the Kinta Electrical Distribution Company.

Service is now restricted on the Island of Penang during peak hours when the Prai steam plant owned by the Municipality of George Town is running at full load. The construction on the Island of a new 30 MW steam station is planned and 2.5 MW of diesel capacity is meanwhile being installed there as an interim measure. On the basis of unrestricted supply the load is expected to increase at a rate of about 9% a year to a peak load of 13 MW and generation of 52 million KWH in 1958. Loads will continue to be largely domestic and traction.

The loads of the minor utilities are expected to double over the next five years.

Table 4 summarizes the mission's projections.

Assuming losses and station consumption of 20% of output, about 1,030 million KWH would have to be generated to meet the estimated demand of 822 million KWH in 1957-58.

TABLE 4 Projected Increase of Peak Loads and Sales of Energy in the Public Utility Systems, 1952-53 to 1957-58

	1952–53		1957–58	
	Sales (Million KWH)	Peak Load (MW)	Sales (Million KWH)	Peak Load (MW)
CEB Central System	157	38	326	76
Diesels	26	6	41	12
Johore Bahru	8	2	37	4
Bulk Supplies	17	4	28	8
	208		432	
PRHE	287	52	300	55
Kinta	13	8	26	16
Penang	30	8	40	13
Minor Utilities	12	4	24	8
	550		822	

[5] The increase from 1953 to 1954 was 12%, mainly due to increased mining activity.

The following capacity is now available, under construction or projected:

CEB		Megawatts
Central network		
Steam		
Available.	66.5	
Under construction	40.0	
Projected	20.0	
	126.5	
Hydroelectric (maximum)	2.3	128.8
Diesel stations, available		15.7
Diesel stations, projected		8.1
		23.8
PRHE (with subsidiary)		
Steam, available.	50.0	
Hydroelectric, available	27.0	
(maximum 27 MW, in dry season 11 MW only)		
Diesel, available	0.7	77.7
Penang		
Steam, available.	17.0	
Steam, projected (replacing present plant)	30.0	30.0
Minor utilities		
Diesel, available		4.4
Diesel, projected		2.0

Both the CEB and PRHE systems will thus have capacity to meet the anticipated demand.

Indigenous Power Resources

The Batu Arang collieries have a potential of about 40,000 tons of coal a month. Production is, however, much lower, since the price is no longer competitive with fuel oil or imported coal. The coal has a low heat content (9,000 BTU per lb.), and contains 12% of ash and 20% of moisture. The Connaught Bridge thermal station has been designed to make use of either domestic coal or fuel oil, largely as a protection against an inordinate rise in the price of fuel oil. When the second half is completed in 1956, the station could absorb the entire maximum output of the Batu Arang collieries, if the use of domestic coal should come to be considered desirable. Consequently, new power stations need not be designed to use domestic coal.

Approximately 100,000 acres of peat swamps lie between Selangor and the Bernam River near Tanjong Karang. The peat has a heating value after drying of 8,500 BTU per lb. Consideration has been given to using peat for power generation in a large station to be erected specifically for this purpose. Any such plan should be approached with caution. Experience with the use of peat for power generation has varied; the cost of extracting, transporting and drying the material must be determined with accuracy before a large-scale project is undertaken. This particular case presents a number of difficult problems, such as drainage of the site, which is only a few feet above sea level, and the high cost of clearing the jungle and digging peat bogs 10 to 20 feet deep.

Wood is abundant and is commonly used as a domestic fuel, largely in the form of charcoal. Its increased use in Malaya for industrial purposes might be considered.

The potential hydroelectric resources of the Federation have not been adequately investigated. The Drainage and Irrigation Department keeps regular hydrographical records of some of the main rivers, but available information is inadequate and shortages of staff have prevented expansion of the work. Topographical and geological surveys for power development have been made in a few locations, mainly in the Cameron Highlands and on the Triang River, but further investigations are necessary before suitable sites can be established.

Estimates made by CEB put the unharnessed hydroelectric potential of the country at approximately 250-260 MW, including the Cameron Highlands; in view of the paucity of basic information, these estimates must be considered as very tentative.

Existing and Proposed Power Installations

Hydroelectric Plants. The only large hydroelectric generating plant at present in operation is the Chenderoh Power Station, owned by PRHE. Its installed capacity is 27 MW; in the dry season its generating capacity drops to 11 MW. The annual output is 200 million KWH. CEB owns a small station with a capacity of 2.3 MW at Ulu Langat which produces 10 million KWH per annum. Other small plants of similar design are operated chiefly by mining companies.

The most important hydroelectric development now under consideration by CEB is the Cameron Highlands Scheme, to be situated in Perak. The proposed plant would supply power for distribution through both the PRHE and CEB systems. It is estimated that maximum capacity cannot be economically used until the combined maximum peak load of the CEB and PRHE systems reaches 262 MW (present estimates anticipate a combined peak load of around 140 MW in 1958). In view of the fact that during the dry season the capacity of the Cameron Highlands plants would fall to 80 MW and that of other hydroelectric plants in the two systems to 12 MW, thermal capacity of 170 MW would be required to meet peak loads at all times. This requirement would be considerably reduced if provision were made in the Cameron Highlands Scheme and in other new hydroelectric schemes for adequate storage, to assure a higher proportion of firm power.

The Cameron Highlands project should be planned for development in stages consistent with the quantities of power which can be economically used by the networks. This requires coordinated planning between CEB and PRHE, and full consideration of the combined characteristics of the two systems.

Another, much smaller project on the Triang River in Negri Sembilan is in the early stages of study. The site is in thick jungle and must be cleared before detailed surveys can be undertaken. We recommend that this be pressed forward.

The Federal Drainage and Irrigation Department is considering a few irrigation schemes which may provide some power. These are still in the study stage and it is not possible at this time to estimate their effects on power supply.

In Chapter 4, Part II, we have urged more attention to the possibility of establishing small hydroelectric plants which could be connected into existing networks. The geography of the western side of the peninsula seems particularly suitable for such installations.

Steam Power Plants. Malaya is relatively close to oil-producing centers. Thermal and diesel plants now largely supply the Federation's power needs; thermal plants are likely to continue, for some time to come, to be an important part of any power expansion program, particularly for carrying base loads; present prospects of developing large storage hydroelectric projects are not encouraging.

Several relatively large steam plants are under construction or planned:

the second half of the new Connaught Bridge station, the proposed Malacca Power Station to be built near Tanjong Kling, and a new power station near George Town.

Diesel Plants. CEB has a program for steady expansion of diesel capacity in outlying areas. At the end of the 1953-54 fiscal year the total installed capacity of diesel generating plants was 18.7 MW; generating equipment with a total capacity of 5.1 MW was on order and during the year capacity of 3.0 MW had been added.

The cost of diesel power is relatively low, ranging from about 3.6 cents to 4.6 cents per KWH in typical installations, exclusive of depreciation and interest. The cost of power produced by privately owned diesel installations is at present almost competitive with power purchased from public utilities; this may make the displacement of privately generated power by public utility supplies difficult and may limit the possibilities of expansion of their networks.

Networks

The existing 66 KV transmission system and proposed extensions, and the proposed 132 KV system are shown on Map 9. The 132 KV system is planned in connection with the development of the Cameron Highlands hydroelectric scheme. It will consist of 130 miles of double circuit transmission lines, including two step-down transformer stations. The estimated cost of this installation, $20.2 million, could probably be justified when the project is operating at full capacity; it is doubtful, however, whether a 132 KV line is economically justifiable at low capacities.

There are two separate 66 KV systems, one operated by CEB, the other by PRHE. The CEB system consists of approximately 120 miles of line with projected extensions of about 45 miles. The PRHE system consists of 54½ miles of double circuit line; no substantial expansion is contemplated. The two systems are at present about 73 miles apart. Interconnection may be made in the future, but development depends largely upon the availability of new economical sources of hydroelectric power.

The 33 KV CEB system totals about 220 miles of line. This is the main system used for supplying tin mining and large industrial consumers. The extensions planned are largely for the purpose of providing power to a number of tin dredges. This part of the program, together with proposed extensions to the 66 KV system north of Kuala Lumpur, should be

MAP 9

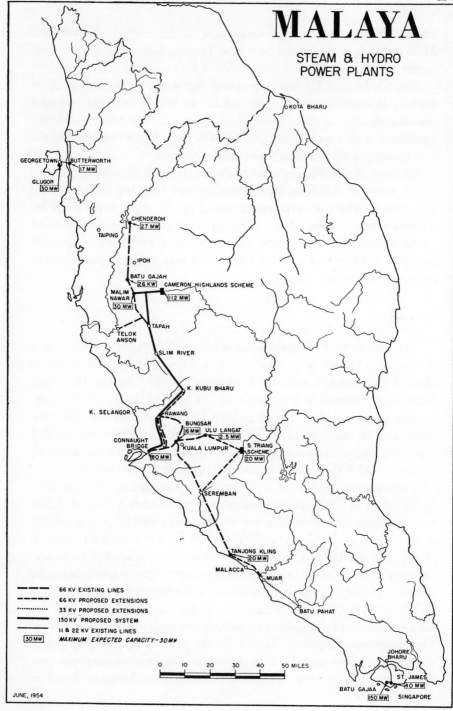

MALAYA

STEAM & HYDRO
POWER PLANTS

GEORGETOWN BUTTERWORTH
17 MW

GLUGOR
30 MW

KOTA BHARU

CHENDEROH
27 MW

TAIPING

IPOH

BATU GAJAH
26 KW   CAMERON HIGHLANDS SCHEME

MALIM
NAWAR   112 MW
30 MW

TAPAH

TELOK
ANSON

SLIM RIVER

K. KUBU BHARU

K. SELANGOR   RAWANG

BUNGSAR
16 MW   ULU LANGAT
2.5 MW

CONNAUGHT
BRIDGE
80 MW   KUALA LUMPUR

S. TRIANG
SCHEME
20 MW

SEREMBAN

TANJONG KLING
20 MW

MALACCA   MUAR

BATU PAHAT

– – –	66 KV EXISTING LINES	
- - - -	66 KV PROPOSED EXTENSIONS	
··········	33 KV PROPOSED EXTENSIONS	
———	130 KV PROPOSED SYSTEM	
——	11 & 22 KV EXISTING LINES	
30 MW	MAXIMUM EXPECTED CAPACITY – 30 MW	

JOHORE
BHARU

ST. JAMES
40 MW

BATU GAJAA
150 MW   SINGAPORE

0   10   20   30   40   50 MILES

JUNE, 1954

reviewed and limited to those lines which are likely to be self-liquidating investments.

PRHE has a 22 KV system consisting of 134 miles of single and double circuit lines. This system is adequate for the time being and no major extensions are contemplated. CEB uses this system for bringing bulk supply from Singapore to Johore Bahru.

CEB has an extensive 11 KV system and contemplates substantial extensions in anticipation of the development of industrial and commercial loads. On Penang all power is transmitted on an 11 KV system, part of which consists of underground cables. An overhead line of this voltage supplies power in Province Wellesley for distribution in small towns and villages along the coast.

Both CEB and PRHE have substantial installations of 6.6 KV lines which are to be extended as requirements develop.

Power Rates

Average rates charged by the major utilities in 1952-53 for various categories of supply are shown in Table 5.

TABLE 5 Average Income per KWH Sold by Major Power Companies, 1952-53

(Cents per KWH)

	CEB			PRHE[1]	PENANG
	Central system	Diesel	Bulk supply		
Domestic light . .	27.97	29.96	24.55	26.5	24.65[2]
Domestic power .	7.50	8.09	6.32	8.1	7.60[2]
Domestic light and power	9.91	9.30	8.43	—	—
Commercial light .	27.82	30.03	23.45	21.5	—
Commercial power	7.37	8.06	5.97	7.5	8.15[2]
Public lights . . .	17.61	18.52	16.83	—	21.4
Mines	5.30[3]	—	—	5.95–6.55	—
Dredges	5.32[3]	—	—	4.0–5.80	—
Traction	—	—	—	—	6.0

[1] Including 1.5 cents fuel surcharge.
[2] Including 1.25 cents fuel surcharge.
[3] Including a fuel surcharge discontinued late in 1953. The current effective rate is 4.75 cents per unit.

A sliding scale tariff, based on consumption, is generally applied. The differential between rates for various categories of supply is not as great as is normally encountered in other countries. It is recommended that tariff schedules be revised to give a better balance between the various rates.

Development Programs

CEB's program for the five years 1953-54 through 1957-58 may be summarized as follows:

		(Thousand $)
Additional generating capacity		
20 MW steam station at Malacca	16,456	
Diesel plant	2,124	
Hydroelectric scheme at Robinson Falls with maximum capacity of 2 MW	1,000	19,580
Extensions and improvements to transmission lines and networks		24,951
Appliances for hire to consumers		1,000
Staff quarters		4,760
Offices		2,100
Miscellaneous and unforeseen items including purchase of existing installations		6,168
		58,559

In addition, CEB has residual funds totalling $39 million from the previous program.

The estimates for several of the items in the program, and in particular for the new Malacca station, are provisional.

We have already recommended the review of some of the proposed extensions to transmission lines and networks. The only other comment we have to offer on the program is that the amount included for staff housing appears to be high. We understand, however, that CEB's housing policy is largely determined by that of the Federal Government.

PRHE plans renewals and extensions at an estimated cost of some $8 million.

Penang's 1954-60 program is estimated to cost $25 million, of which $5 million was to have been spent by the end of 1954. The principal items are a 30 MW station and extensions and improvements to transmission lines and networks.

Financial Position of the Major Utilities

The financial results of CEB's operations for the years 1949-50 to 1953-54 and its balance sheets as at the end of the years 1949-50 to 1952-53 are summarized in Table 6.

PRHE sells 90% of its output at low rates to tin mines. The company has, nevertheless, consistently operated at a profit in recent years and in 1952-53 paid a dividend of 6% (less tax) on its ordinary stock, after providing for depreciation and making modest additions to reserves. Its

TABLE 6   Central Electricity Board

Summarized Revenue Accounts

(*Million $*)

	1949–50[1]	1950–51	1951–52	1952–53	1953–54
Income from sales of electricity	13.09	15.64	20.20	22.14	24.28
Other income	.55	.60	.76	1.19	1.31
	13.64	16.24	20.96	23.33	25.59
Generation, distribution, administration and					
other expenses	10.09	12.98	16.52	16.97	16.51
Provision for depreciation	1.75	1.86	2.00	2.18	4.34
	11.84	14.84	18.52	19.15	20.85
Net revenue	1.80	1.40	2.44	4.18	4.74
Interest on debentures and advances . . .	.04	.31	.76	1.20	1.88
Dividend to Federal Government	1.20	1.20	1.20	1.52	1.53
Transfers to reserves:					
General reserve	.50	—	.28	—	—
Insurance reserve	.06	.06	.20	.20	.20
Reserve for increased cost of replace-					
ment of fixed assets	—	—	—	1.10	1.20
	1.80	1.57	2.44	4.02	4.81
Balance of net revenue	—	.17[2]	—	.16	.07

[1] The CEB's fiscal year runs from September 1 to August 31.
[2] Debit.

TABLE 6   Central Electricity Board—*Continued*

Summarized Balance Sheets

(*Million $*)

	1949–50[1]	1950–51	1951–52	1952–53	1953–54
Fixed assets					
Balance at beginning of year	29.95	36.21	50.93	69.62	89.06
Expenditure during year (net) . . .	6.26[3]	14.72[3]	18.69	19.44	20.73
	36.21	50.93	69.62	89.06	109.79
Depreciation provisions	10.27[4]	12.05	14.45	16.33	19.39
	25.94	38.88	55.17	72.73	90.40
Current assets less current liabilities,					
deposits and provisions	7.53	5.62	.10	5.04	2.42
	33.47	44.50	55.27	77.77	92.82
Representing—					
Capital	30.00	30.00	30.00	38.06	38.32
Debentures stocks and advances	2.91	14.05	24.34	37.32	50.79
Insurance reserve	0.06	.12	.32	.52	.72
General reserve	.50	.33	.61	.61	.61
Reserve for increased cost of replacement					
of fixed assets	—	—	—	1.10	2.30
Unappropriated revenue	—	—	—	.16	.08
	33.47	44.50	55.27	77.77	92.82

[3] Includes $.878 million and $.786 million in respect of capital expenditure charged to renewals provision in 1949–50 and 1950–51, respectively, and transferred to fixed assets in 1952–53.

[4] Includes $8.59 million transferred from the Federal Government's accounts and allowed for in the take-over values. The (written-down) value of the assets taken over was $29.95 million less $8.59 million.

operating results should continue to be favorable, provided tin production in its concession area does not seriously decline.

The Electricity Supply Department of the Municipality of George Town (Penang) sells the greater part of its output at relatively high rates for domestic consumption. The net revenue, after providing for generating, distribution and administrative expenses, is sufficient to cover interest on loan capital and sinking fund installments. The Department follows the English municipal practice of providing for the redemption of loan capital in lieu of depreciation of fixed assets. Modest contributions are, however, additionally made to a reserve fund for renewals.

Organization of CEB

The present organization of CEB appears to give insufficient importance to financial management, and inadequate attention to the compilation of statistical data on the production and consumption of energy in the Federation. It is accordingly suggested that consideration be given to strengthening management on the financial side and setting up a small statistical branch.[6]

II SINGAPORE

Electricity

The Colony has had electric power since 1929. Table 7 shows the generation and consumption of electricity for selected years.

TABLE 7 Electric Power Generation and Consumption in Singapore[1]

Year	Units Generated (Million KWH)	Units Sold (Million KWH)	Number of Consumers	Peak Load (MW)
1939	60	51	28,255	16.3
1950	187	158	43,419	34.5
1951	209	174	47,404	33.3
1952	216	184	51,954	35.5
1953	278	237	58,371	55.4

[1] Excluding power generated by privately owned sets.

The Electricity Department of the City Council, which operates the two Singapore stations of St. James and Pasir Panjang, sells power in bulk to CEB for distribution in Johore Bahru. Sales in 1954 amounted to about 11.5 million KWH, absorbing capacity of 2.4 MW. This demand is expected to increase to 40 million KWH by 1958. It is unlikely that CEB's maximum demand within the next ten years will require more than 15 MW of capacity; since this can be supplied by the Electricity Department without difficulty, the present arrangement should be continued.

[6] The CEB created a new post of comptroller toward the end of 1954 to strengthen its Financial Division.

Gas

War and the Japanese occupation caused considerable damage to Singapore's municipal gas works in Kallang. Rehabilitation began in 1946; in 1951 a water gas plant was added to the gas retorts on which the plant was originally based. A further extension, now under construction, will enable the gas works to produce about 800 million cubic feet of blended gas by 1956.

Demand for gas has risen parallel with demand for electricity, as indicated by Table 8.

TABLE 8   Gas Manufactured in Singapore, 1940-53

(Million cu. ft.)

1940	331
1947	227
1950	357
1951	423
1952	475
1953	536

TECHNICAL REPORT 7
TRANSPORT AND COMMUNICATIONS

---

1 GENERAL REVIEW

The geographic and physical features which determine the pattern of the transport and communications system in Malaya are the narrow peninsula, stretching south from the frontier with Thailand, with long coast lines on the east and the west, and a mountain range through the center dividing the country into distinct eastern and western parts.

The main transport routes by coastal waters, railway, road and air, and the communication channels by post, telegraph and telephone stretch south and north through the length of the peninsula, but connections between eastern and western parts of the country are few. Rivers flow east and west from the watershed but, left unharnessed through the ages, are now mostly unnavigable, so that inland water transport is negligible.

The transport and communications systems are complete in their main arteries, which serve all parts of the country. In the eastern half, however, these arteries still carry comparatively little traffic, and, except for the main east-west trunk road, are of a lower standard of construction than in the west. There are not enough branch routes, especially in the eastern half, and too few feeder roads in all areas. The Federation has one short land frontier with Thailand; it is crossed by two roads and two railway lines, the latter carrying international traffic and traffic between Prai and Kelantan in cooperation with the State Railway of Thailand.

The link between Malaya's inland transport system and overseas transport is supplied by three main ports, Singapore in the Colony of Singapore, and Port Swettenham and Penang in the Federation. Connections with all parts of the world are exceptionally good, particularly through Singapore, one of the most important world junctions of ocean and air traffic.

Coastal shipping connects the three main ports with a large number of minor ports on both coasts, among them Malacca, a trading center of some significance. The three main ports and the lesser ports of Port Weld, Telok Anson, and Port Dickson on the west coast and Tumpat at the

377

northern end of the east coast, have railway connections. All the west coast ports have direct links with the main road system, but few of the east coast ports have inland road branches, although they are interlinked by a second-class coastal road.

The railway system consists of a main line running the length of the western half of the country from Singapore to Prai, opposite Penang, and to the Thailand border, and another main line from Gemas Junction to Tumpat, the port of Kota Bharu, capital of Kelantan, serving the interior of the eastern half of the country. The western line connects all the western state capitals and principal towns, except Malacca, as well as the main ports and minor coastal ports already mentioned.

The main road system in the west follows the railway closely and a network of secondary roads connects the smaller towns. The east has a main coastal road but many sections of it are of substandard construction and its traffic has to cross several rivers by ferry. One lateral trunk road connects east and west across the center and the two road systems join at the southernmost end of the peninsula.

A network of internal air lines, based on Singapore, connects the principal towns and provides links between east and west across the mountain barrier. It also serves Malacca, whose rail connection was despoiled during the occupation. A well-developed feeder system operated with light aircraft serves a number of interior centers.

This pattern of parallel coastal shipping, rail, road and air routes has generated intense competition and this in turn has given rise to resentment among transport operators and criticism of each others' methods of operation. Preferential treatment by government of some of the competing forms of transport has been alleged. Most of the criticism is uninformed and much of it is unfounded; in particular, the allegation of preferential treatment rests on a misconception of the duties and functions of government. A better spirit of understanding among operators would be of benefit to them as well as to the public.

The keen competition among the different forms of transport should in itself be sufficient answer to the charges frequently made that monopolies exist and should be controlled, coupled with suggestions for the introduction of yet more competition. The size of the country and of its population, and the volume of traffic offered at present or expected to develop in the foreseeable future, are not such as to leave room for more competition. The duplication of air services and of urban, suburban or local road transport services as development objectives must therefore be rejected.

The inland transport system as a whole, with its three overseas outlets, enjoys a well-balanced distribution of traffic loads on its main routes. Through traffic between inland and sea routes naturally seeks the junction where the inland route is shortest, since sea transport is cheaper than land transport. All three ports should be able to handle their traffic without failure, congestion or interruption. We cannot, therefore, support the view sometimes expressed, that development would best be concentrated on Singapore.

II PORTS[1]

A FEDERATION

Port Swettenham

Port Swettenham, situated near the center of the most developed area of western Malaya, was built as a railway port during the years immediately preceding World War I. A business and residential township has since grown up around the port. The site of the port installations is not ideal for shipping, since berthing and turning operations require special caution. Inland connections by rail and road are good. The port's traffic has outgrown its capacity; its two ocean berths, one coastal wharf, one lighter wharf and a number of small pontoon jetties in addition to six river anchorages are insufficient to handle the steadily growing traffic. The shore installations are cramped, transit, storage and railway sheds as well as shunting and storage sidings having been concentrated within a small area.

Despite setbacks in the two world wars and a major depression, traffic has expanded substantially since the opening of the port in 1911 (see Table 1). The upward trend has continued in recent years and, although fluctuations may be expected, it is safe to predict that traffic through the

[1] Unless otherwise stated, the conclusions and recommendations are based on, and supplement and elaborate, those contained in the following reports:

Report on the Major Ports of Malaya, D. F. Allen, May 1950;
Report on the Minor Ports of Malaya, D. F. Allen, October 1952;
Report of the Federal Ports Committee, April 1952;
Supplementary Report of the Federal Ports Committee, Nov. 1952.

TABLE 1 Port Swettenham

Year	Tonnage of Cargo Handled		
	Inward	Outward	Total
1929[1]	440,779	161,059	601,838
1932[2]	192,540	115,673	308,213
1939	384,590	152,568	537,158
1947	259,536	248,105	507,641
1949	342,105	271,030	613,135
1951	551,934	268,105	820,039
1953	594,726	310,979	905,705

[1] Prewar highest.
[2] Prewar lowest.

SOURCES: D. T. Allen; Report on the Major Ports of Malaya; Annual Reports of the Malayan Railway Administration.

port will continue to increase with the further development of the country.

The Federal Ports Committee recommended the construction of three new berths at the North Klang Straits site where, according to the Committee, "the operation of a new wharf is a practical and economic proposition, and where almost indefinite expansion is possible." The Committee considered unsound the proposal to construct additional berths in the present port, since they would congest the port still further, besides causing extensive dislocation during the construction period. Hence the present project is the building of three berths in deep water in the North Klang Straits, five miles seaward from the present port. The total estimated cost of the berths and their associated installations is $26 million.

The outstanding advantage of the North Klang Straits project is its site alongside deep water. Its shortcomings, insurmountable by any revision of the present design, are the unavoidable duplication of parts of the port's administrative and operational structure, of the labor force and handling equipment; shipping and merchants will have to establish branch offices in the new port area. The construction of new land approaches, consisting of considerable lengths of railway and road embankments, of sewerage, water, light and power lines, all in difficult terrain, and, most of all, the necessary bridging of the Klang River will be very costly; moreover, the bridge will impede river traffic. Housing and transport problems for staff and labor will have to be solved and a new town area developed on swampy ground. Further, the project itself shows undesirable features, recognized by the designers, which can only be rectified at a substantial increase in cost.

The existing site would admit three additional ocean berths, bringing the total to five. Its only, but important, disadvantage is the need for dredging to maintain sufficient depth of water. The space behind the quays in which the congestion occurs varies in depth from 650 ft. at the coastal wharf to an average of over 1,400 ft. at the existing ocean wharf. This compares not unfavorably with Singapore, where the total depth of 1,800 ft. also accomodates additional berths around a dock basin. The removal of the shunting and storage sidings to a location outside the port area proper, the construction of a deck over the foreshore behind the quays and its utilization for the erection of transit sheds would leave the rest of the port free for further building and would solve all problems of space and handling. (See Map 10). The scheme could be carried out without interruption to the use of existing installations. It should not include the removal of the passenger station from its present site, which is convenient for operation and for public service alike.

The mission believes that, when worked out in detail, this alternative scheme would show a saving on construction costs, as well as on recurrent administrative and operating costs, compared with the North Klang Straits project.

The mission endorses the need for increased capacity at Port Swettenham. But having regard to the deterioration in the Federal Government's financial position since the Federal Ports Committee recommended the North Klang Straits project in April 1952, and to the inadequacy of financial resources for all essential development needs, we recommend that the possibility of providing this increased capacity at lower capital and recurrent costs as we have suggested be fully investigated before the North Klang Straits project proceeds further.

At various times, government-appointed commissions, committees and consultants have endorsed the continued operation of the port as part of the Malayan Railway, an arrangement which results in appreciable economies. No new factors have emerged to require reconsideration of this advice. Neither in importance nor in size does the port warrant a separate, autonomous port authority. We support the recommendations made by the Federal Ports Committee in its supplementary report (a) that a Port Board be created; (b) that a statutory obligation be imposed to make the port available to goods carried by rail, road or water without discrimination; and (c) that a sinking fund be established to amortize capital expenditure on the extensions. We further suggest that, with a view to ensuring appropriate integration, the fusion of the proposed Port Board with the existing Railway Board into a single Railway and Harbors Board, under the chairmanship of the General Manager, be considered.

Penang

Penang is a lighter port serving both the Island of Penang and the mainland, and having an important entrepot trade. The port has excellent anchorages in sheltered deep water, but water depths alongside quays are difficult to maintain. The connection between the island and the mainland for passengers, mails, parcels and vehicles is maintained by ferries owned and operated by both the Penang Harbour Board and the Malayan Railway. Vehicle traffic has grown spectacularly in recent years.

The port facilities on the island consist of a two-berth wharf at Swettenham Pier, two lighter basins and lighter landing stages along Weld Quay and in Penang creek. Wharf and lighter basins are controlled by the Harbour Board; the lighter stages are free but, owing to silting, only usable at high tides. At Butterworth on the mainland, north of the mouth of the Prai River, the Harbour Board has a jetty and a ferry pier, and a number of private piers, including those of oil companies, are lined along the shore. South of the river mouth, at Prai, is the Railway port, complete with quays, lighter basin, cranes, transit and storage sheds, and rail and road approaches, but badly silted up. Private lighter jetties stretch along both banks of the Prai River upstream. The port's installations are thus spread over three distinct areas.

A number of projects for improvements and extensions have been under consideration since the end of the war, including the Weld Quay Scheme, for improving lighterage facilities; the Ferry Scheme, for the provision of new ferry terminals and the replacement of the obsolete ferryboats now in use; and several schemes involving the construction of deep water wharfs. In addition, plans for increased storage accommodation are now being implemented or considered.

The Federal Ports Committee took the view that capital expenditure on deep water berths was not warranted now or in the near future, but it recommended that the necessity for deep water berths—which may be provided by remedial works at Prai—be re-examined in 1957. The Committee also advised that improved lighterage facilities at Weld Quay were required immediately and that provision of further storage space should continue. We endorse these conclusions. The Ferry Scheme, which was outside the Committee's investigations, is an important additional requirement.

The consulting engineers have recommended that the Weld Quay Scheme, including the construction of a ferry terminus, be carried out in five stages. The estimated cost of the full scheme is $3 million, excluding the ferry terminus. The first stage, the rebuilding of the Japanese wharf at an estimated cost of $550,000, is already in progress. The other stages, and the order in which they should be undertaken, were under discussion at the time this report was written. Whatever is decided, it appears advisable to schedule the works on quays, extensions and ferry terminals in such a way that neither the construction nor the operation of the one is impeded by the other.

The Ferry Scheme is becoming urgent because of growing traffic and over-age vessels. The ferryboats are wartime landing-craft, varying in type and size, adapted as far as possible for service between the existing terminals, but now of insufficient capacity and expensive to operate and maintain. A separate ferry service for passengers, parcels, mail and horses, but not for vehicles, is maintained between Penang and the Railway terminus at Prai.

The project for the new ferry service provides for seven new double-end ferryboats at a cost of $6.44 million, a two-berth terminal at Penang costing $1.83 million and single-berth terminals at Butterworth and at Prai at a cost of $840,000 each. The complete project would thus require $9.95 million. The consulting engineers recommend completion of the scheme in three stages, as follows:

		(Thousand $)	
Stage 1.	Complete service Penang-Prai		
	Half Penang terminal, say	1,000	
	Prai terminal	840	
	3 new ferryboats	2,760	4,600
Stage 2.	Part service Penang-Butterworth		
	Remainder of Penang terminal	830	
	Butterworth terminal	840	
	2 new ferryboats	1,840	3,510
Stage 3.	Complete service Penang-Butterworth		
	2 new ferryboats		1,840

The project provides for vessels of increased capacity and speedier turn-round. It would also divide the traffic to and from the north and to and from the south of the Penang terminal, thereby speeding this traffic and at the same time eliminating the bottleneck at the river crossing on the mainland.

The execution of the complete project in stages will give it flexibility; portions could be postponed should traffic not increase to the extent expected. The mission's recommended program for 1955-1959 leaves the third stage to be undertaken at a later date.

Close consideration should be given to the layout of vehicle traffic lanes and pedestrian pavements at the Penang terminal: a system of one-way traffic routes around a center island on Weld Quay might be adopted and it may prove desirable to move the site of the terminal to a point midway between side streets. It will be necessary to provide a railway booking office and accommodation for luggage handling at the terminal for through passengers on the main line; suitable accommodation for a cab rank is also essential. These points should be decided, after consultation with the departments concerned, before the final design is approved.

The future Port Authority (see below) will have before it the choice among different solutions for the provision of new deep water berths, sometime after the next few years. A re-examination of the improvement of Prai in 1957 has already been recommended by the Federal Ports Committee. Certain pertinent points must be stressed here. There is already a port complete in all its sections, quays, cranes, transit sheds, storage warehouses, rail, road and inland water connections, fully equipped but lacking the required depth of water alongside the quays. The consulting engineers' investigations, including tests in a model tank, show that a depth of 26 ft. can be provided and economically maintained through the construction of walls to an 800-ft. entrance and the dredging of a five-fathom channel. Although the depth of 26 ft. would allow about 75% of the ships calling at Penang to moor at Prai quays, it must be admitted that this would not be good enough to justify the expense of approximately $7 million for the necessary work. However, no attention appears to have been given to the possibility of training the river upstream of the port so as to strengthen the current sufficiently to obtain the extra depth required. It is recommended that this aspect be studied (including a tank test) by the consulting engineers. The navigation problem has already been studied by an expert and it may here be mentioned that conditions similar to those at the entrance to Prai exist in many other world ports.

The establishment of a Penang Port Authority to embrace the present separate organizations has been decided upon by the Federal Government on the recommendation of the Federal Ports Committee, and preliminary steps have been taken to bring this about. Experience elsewhere prompts the suggestion that the new authority should use the existing resources in administration, premises, staff, shore and floating equipment to the greatest extent consistent with economical and efficient operation of the whole port, simplifying where overlapping occurs, scrapping where duplication exists. The aim must be to achieve a practical level of unification in operational and financial structures, without creating rigidity. To superimpose an entirely new administration on what exists would not solve the problem. The extent of the port area, the volume of traffic, the amount of revenues and operation expenditures could not support that type of reorganization. The separate authorities now operate with commendable energy and efficiency, each in its own sphere, and they have two or three generations of experience behind them; their simple fusion should result in reduced recurrent expenditures, increased efficiency and elimination of friction.

The close link which has existed for many years between the Singapore and Penang Harbour Boards has allowed the common use of some items of equipment and of specialist staffs. Similarly, operation of Prai Port by the Malayan Railway Administration has permitted the common use of workshops and equipment, and engineering and operational staff by port and railway. Appropriate agreements between the new port authority and the Singapore Harbour Board and the Malayan Railway should be based on maintaining what is good and economical in the present organization.

Malacca

Malacca is Malaya's fourth largest town, with a population of 60,000 and a well-developed hinterland. This provides some justification for the urging of certain groups that more use should be made of Malacca as an ocean port. Malacca cannot, however, claim to be more than a port for coastal shipping and, to a small extent, a lighter port for ocean ships. It is true that there are coast lines elsewhere in the world where ocean ports are as close together as Malacca is to Port Swettenham and Singapore. However, the hinterland of Malaya's west coast ports is so limited that there is in fact no case for another fully developed ocean port. In these circumstances, there is great force in the Conference Lines' contention that the addition of Malaca as a regular port of call is not justifiable.

Wars, economic depression and terrorist activities have hit Malacca inordinately. As a coastal port it has suffered greatly from silting; maintenance, neglected before the war and abandoned during wartime occupation, has not been sufficiently restored to avoid further loss of depth over the bars and in the channels. The railway link, removed during the war, has not been replaced. It must be realized, however, that there never was a physical connection between rail and port, and direct transshipment between railway wagon and ship or lighter has never been possible. Some neglect in providing road connections is at present being made good, and Malacca has also received some compensation in an airport and regular internal air services.

The activities of the port have steadily declined in the past 30 years. Up to and about 1935, more than 500 ships of over 75 tons called annually; by 1939 the number had dropped to 400; since the war, calls have fluctuated around 250 a year. Calls of purely coastal vessels of 75 tons and under have remained fairly constant throughout the years at between 2,500 and 3,000 per annum. The sizes of both classes of vessels have been very much smaller in postwar years, no doubt as a result of deterioration in the port's conditions. Total traffic handled through the port is at present around 100,000 tons a year. It has been asserted that, given improved facilities, it might easily reach 500,000 tons, but very likely this is overoptimistic. Besides, part of any increase would be traffic diverted from other ports and inland transport routes.

After consideration of all factors, elaborated in numerous reports and memoranda by committees, chambers of commerce, local authorities, shipping, trade and engineering experts, we recommend that the port of Malacca be brought up to a standard admitting coastal vessels with a draught of up to 9 ft. 6 ins. and a length of 150 ft.

We endorse the recommendation in the reports of the Federal Ports Committee and D. F. Allen that a moderate scale of port charges be introduced but we hesitate to concur in the further recommendation that a small port department and a port advisory committee be established, since the need for these is not apparent. Should the recommendation be implemented, however, the scale of port charges should be such as to cover any additional expenditure resulting from the establishment of the port department as well as to make a substantial contribution toward dredging and other maintenance costs.

The Federal Ports Committee and D. F. Allen both recommended that the Shipping Freight Conference should allow member lines to substitute, at intervals, a call at Malacca for one at Port Swettenham or Penang, that the so-called "arbitrary" (a supplementary charge) be reduced and that through bills of lading to and from Malacca be issued. These measures would have contributed to an increase in Malacca's activities and it is to be regretted that the Conference felt unable to agree to them.

Minor Ports

D. F. Allen's report on the Minor Ports of Malaya deals with all aspects of the small coastal ports. With the exception of one or two ore lighter ports, these serve Malaya's coastal trade exclusively. The cargoes moved in and out do not exceed 4,000 tons per month in any of the small ports, except in Telok Anson, which has considerable fuel traffic in bulk. Most of them, especially those on the east coast, are in a worse condition than they were before the war. The aim should be to restore their utility to prewar standards. This will require some surveys, much dredging, improved lighting and buoyage in a few cases, and regular maintenance of restored channels. In Chapter 5, Part II, we recommended such improvement in specific coastal ports.

The main requirement will be dredging. Since the end of the war only one dredger has been operating, for about eight months of the year at Malacca, for the remaining months at various other points of the coasts. By the end of 1954, the dredging fleet available was to consist of two self-propelled hopper grab dredgers, each with a maximum capacity of 600 cubic yards per day. These units are highly efficient but their capacity is too low to cope economically with the heavy dredging requirements. They do, however, permit rapid and cheap transfer from one site to another. The total dredging program involved in the restoration and maintenance of the recommended 9 ft. 6 ins. depths would require one additional hopper grab dredger of the existing type and two larger suction dredgers. These requirements, together with appropriate measures to ensure regular surveys and training of nautical personnel, must have high priority. The cost is estimated by the Marine Department at $2.5 million for the suction dredgers and $500,000 for the grab dredger. A small additional sum will be required for appropriate training establishments.

Additional facilities for the fishing industry are desirable in many of the minor ports: greater depth, taken care of in the dredging program; jetties for landing the fish and loading provisions, ice and gear, with adjacent space for the repair and maintenance of nets and gear; processing and storage buildings (to be provided by private enterprise); and transport inland (discussed in the section on road transport).

The construction of a fishing harbor at Chenering Head or Pulau Kapas off the Trengganu coast has been considered in the past and the former is recommended by Allen. Recently the development of the excellent natural anchorage at Pulau Redang further north has been under consideration. The need for such a fishing harbor is, however, related to further development of the use of large fishing vessels, for which considerable time will be required; these projects are therefore believed to be of future importance and not of sufficient urgency at present to be included in the five-year investment program.

The administration of the minor ports is divided between the Federal Government, the States and the Railway Administration. In principle there is nothing wrong with this division. It is, however, important that the present responsibility and powers of the Director of the Federal Marine Department should remain unimpaired if the efficiency of dredging and survey work is not to suffer. The creation of boards and advisory committees for these small ports should not, in general, be encouraged. Consideration should, it is suggested, be given to the levy of a charge for the use of channels on which there is considerable public expenditure for maintenance.

B SINGAPORE

The port facilities are distributed over three areas, Keppel Harbour, the Western Roads and the Eastern Roads, the latter being subdivided by a detached mole into Inner and Outer Roads. The wharves, *godowns* (warehouses), tugs and shore facilities for loading and unloading in Keppel Harbour are under the jurisdiction of the Singapore Harbour Board, a government-owned, self-supporting, autonomous corporation, subject to government control in matters of concern to the community as a whole. The facilities at the oil installations on islands adjoining the Western Roads were constructed and are maintained and operated by the oil companies. The general control of shipping throughout the port and all shipping operations in the Roads are in the hands of the Marine Department of the Singapore Government, which is also responsible for all navigational aids and signal stations. The Public Works Department is responsible for all dredging operations in the Roads, for the maintenance of the detached mole, and for the structural maintenance of lighthouses and beacons.

This division has existed ever since the port constructions in the first and third areas came into being by the side of the existing Roads facilities. The system has developed well and has satisfied authorities, operators and users. It may be added that the handling of traffic to and from anchorages in the Roads follows a traditional pattern still in extensive use along all Far Eastern coasts. There appears to be no good reason to change it at present. We do, however, recommend that consideration be given to the reallocation of responsibility for the maintenance of depth of water in the Roads and for approaches, inland waters and seashore moorings. The private operation of the oil depots appears sound and requires no further comment or recommendation.

Keppel Harbour

Since the Report on Major Ports was written, repair of war damage to wharves, sheds and port equipment has been virtually completed, wrecks and debris have been removed and channels and anchorages cleared, at a total cost of approximately $15 million. The labor position has been stabilized, a protective police force satisfactorily established, and mechanical handling has made rapid progress. The dues and charges structure has been brought up to date and compares favorably with those of other world ports.

Although there is now no congestion in the port, either in shipping or in shore operations, and the turn-round of vessels is satisfactory, the wharves are used almost continuously and there is no margin in berthing capacity. Berths for ships and transit sheds for their cargo must generally be allocated well in advance of scheduled arrivals to make sure that the ship's berth at the quay and the shed where the cargo is to be handled are close together. Some ships arrive early or late, and where there is little or no margin, vessel and transit shed may in such cases often be far apart. This results in additional handling and transport of cargo. An up-to-date port must have a margin to meet irregularities in ship arrivals and departures.

A number of shipping companies feel handicapped by the lack of wharf cranes. Others, which operate their vessels with a sufficient number of ships' derricks, fear that the installation of wharf cranes might result in an increase in port charges. These conflicting interests could perhaps be reconciled by installing wharf cranes on certain quays and making a charge to vessels using them. We recommend that the advantages and feasibility of this possibility be considered. Mechanization of handling on the quays and in the sheds has proved of benefit to the Harbour Board and to shipping, and will, no doubt, continue to be developed.

The harbor has one disadvantage: the limited depth of space behind the wharves. As a consequence, the Singapore trade has to use storage sheds away from the port area, although there is only one road to carry the traffic to and from the harbor. The virtual certainty that road traffic congestion will increase in the densely built-up Singapore area must always be kept in mind. It must be accepted that a large proportion of the incoming and outgoing traffic will have to be moved by rail. It has been suggested at various times that direct transshipment between ship and railway wagon could be reduced or even abandoned. This suggestion cannot be supported: direct transshipment will have to remain a feature of the port's loading and discharging operations in the interest of a properly balanced inland transport system.

Traffic through the port has steadily developed since its reopening after the war. Table 2 shows that it has reached a level well above the best prewar years.

While total tonnage of cargo handled during the last two years is slightly less than in 1951-52, the number of vessels berthed and their net registered tonnage have continued to increase. The present level of traffic leaves little margin of capacity and the Harbour Board is accordingly planning an extension of deep-water quayage.

The plan, known as the East Lagoon Scheme, provides for the ultimate addition of nine berths of a total length of 5,600 ft. of quays for ocean-going vessels. It provides for the reclamation of a considerable area by using the spoil available from dredging. Experiments carried out by consulting engineers have shown that tidal currents will allow unhampered entrance and exit to and from the berths and that little dredging will be needed to maintain the required depth of water. The intention is to carry out the construction in three phases and to provide three new berths in each phase. The initial phase, which would include the break-water, would involve the heaviest amount of construction work and expenditure. In its final shape the project should leave open the space required for a possible future railway extension, as proposed later in this report.

TABLE 2   Singapore Harbour Board Traffic, Years ending June 30

	Vessels Berthed		Tonnage of Cargo Handled		
	No.	Net Reg. Tons	Inward	Outward	Total
1932–33[1] .	2,868	9,127,142	1,049,432	1,113,977	2,163,409
1937–38[2] .	3,231	9,756,410	1,807,444	1,576,559	3,384,003
1946–47. .	1,519	4,551,388	1,839,892	1,117,033	2,956,925
1947–48. .	2,100	5,558,517	1,848,828	1,366,022	3,214,850
1948–49. .	2,528	6,979,978	1,863,407	1,744,878	3,608,285
1949–50. .	2,885	8,204,558	2,148,421	1,913,540	4,061,961
1950–51. .	2,873	8,144,343	2,608,915	2,338,357	4,947,272
1951–52. .	3,231	8,970,803	3,150,430	2,504,693	5,655,123
1952–53. .	3,698	10,398,970	2,901,583	2,455,466	5,357,049
1953–54[3] .	3,714	10,907,940	3,000,331	2,618,589	5,618,920

[1] Prewar lowest.
[2] Prewar highest.
[3] Tonnage statistics after February 1954 compiled on revised basis; 1953–54 figures therefore not strictly comparable with those of previous years.

SOURCE: Singapore Harbour Board Annual Report.

A provisional estimate of costs made in 1953 shows a total of $40 million, of which the first phase would require $20 million, the second, $11.2 million and the third, $8.8 million. The greater part, if not the whole, of this expenditure can be met by the Harbour Board from its own resources. It is recommended that, unless a recession in the port's traffic should occur, the first phase be scheduled for construction within two to three years.

The Roads

The Roads are divided into three areas, the Outer Roads, an open natural anchorage in deep water, accessible to the largest ocean ships, and the Inner Roads, separated from the former by a detached mole in whose shelter lighters and coastal vessels with a draught of not more than 15 ft. are able to operate in all seasons, and the Western Roads which are used quite extensively by ocean shipping (apart from the oil depots). The anchorages in the Roads are available to all ships without payment of dues. Cargoes are handled by a large fleet of lighters and other craft of local construction, operating to and from the banks of the various rivers that flow into the Roads, or the tidal basin and quays of Telok Ayer, which latter are managed by the Harbour Board on behalf of the government. Landing charges are made for the use of the quays in the basin but not for use of the rivers.

Between 30,000 to 40,000 ships and craft use the Roads each year, of which about 5,000 are ocean-going vessels. The registered tonnage of the latter is more than double that of the ships using the harbor. The total tonnage of all ships, ocean and coastal, is well over 20 million net registered tons a year. As most of the traffic is free, no exact figures of cargo handled are available, but about half a million tons pass over the Telok Ayer quays in a year, and it is estimated that not less than this tonnage passes into the Singapore River and creeks.

The detached mole was constructed in 1901 at a cost of $15 million. The Outer Roads never require dredging, the Inner Roads only at intervals of many years, but dredging of basin, berths and river approaches is regularly necessary. The total cost of dredging, including administrative and other maintenance and depreciation expenses, is around $750,000 per annum. Against this expenditure the revenue from Telok Ayer Basin amounts to some $350,000 only, while registration of boats, junks and *tongkangs* provides only $12,500 per annum.

A case could be made for a simple scale of dues and charges to be paid by shipping and for modest additional charges on licensed lighter operators. Any consequent increase in the cost of moving goods would be infinitesimal, but because of the importance of the entrepot trade to Singapore, the psychological effect of new or additional charges cannot be ignored. For this reason and also because of the relatively small amount of additional revenue that would be produced, we are not in favor of requiring any additional contributions towards the cost of providing and maintaining works and services in the Roads.

III RAILWAYS

The Malayan Railway

Railway development in Malaya began with short lines built to connect the tin mining areas with the west coast. The State Railways of Perak and Selangor grew from these beginnings and in 1901 were amalgamated to form the Federated Malay States Railways. By 1903 the longitudinal line between the central mountain range and the west coast had been completed from Prai to Seremban; it was then extended southward, first to Gemas and then, in 1909, to Johore Bahru at the southern tip of the peninsula. The Singapore Government Railway, which had been opened in 1903, was acquired by the Federated Malay States Railways in 1913. The next extension was a branch line northward from a point near Prai, and by 1918 the railway ran from Singapore to Padang Besar on the border with Thailand. A small gap across the Straits of Johore was closed when a causeway between Singapore Island and the mainland was built in 1923. The framework for the railway system was finally completed in 1931 by a line from Gemas through the eastern states of Pahang and Kelantan to Sungei Golok. The railway joins the Thailand Railway both here and at Padang Besar in the west. At the outbreak of World War II, the Federated Malay States Railways were an outstanding example of an efficient railway undertaking.

The railway was despoiled, damaged and neglected during the Japanese occupation. Reconstruction was a very formidable and costly task but it has been tackled resolutely and resourcefully and was expected to be virtually completed by the end of 1954. From 1948 onward, the Railway Administration (see below) had to contend with the added difficulties caused by terrorist attacks on trains, stations and telecommunications. These attacks have so diminished that they no longer have a seriously adverse effect on railway operation. The emergency is, however, likely to hamper operations and affect working results in some degree as long as it lasts.

At the end of 1953, 984 route miles were open to traffic, and equipment included 194 locomotives, 298 coaches and 5,664 wagons.

The Malayan Railway Administration, the successor of the former Federated Malay States Railways, is a corporation established by statute, but by virtue of the Federation Agreement its property is vested in the Chief Secretary. The Railway is thus a department of the Federal Government. The General Manager is responsible to the Member for Transport. He is advised by a Railway Board, of which he is chairman. The railway budget requires the approval of the Legislative Council. This form of organization has worked remarkably well in the past; it has the advantages of simple control, speedy action, a compact, inexpensive top administration and it safeguards the public's interest. Being a government department the Railway Administration lacks the flexibility of a fully autonomous corporation, but this has never proved a serious drawback, nor could it easily and quickly be remedied. The recommendation offered is, therefore, to leave the railway organization as it is. As recommended earlier, consideration should be given to the creation of a single Railway and Harbours Board.

The Railway has reached a high standard in administration, both operating and engineering, in rolling stock and equipment, in service and maintenance. It compares very favorably with the world's systems, and no reorganization measures need be suggested in any field. Training of local staff to occupy posts of higher responsibility is now proceeding; it may consequently become desirable within the five-year period ahead to redistribute functions near the top of the hierarchy. It has been necessary so far to employ one additional senior official for every four or five on the establishment to assure continuity during prolonged periods of overseas leave. Since this practice adds to administrative costs it is suggested that consideration be given to delegating authority, where possible, to a well-trained assistant to act during the leave of his senior officer. The opportunities of securing some reduction in staff in this way would, it is recognized, be greater if short periods of overseas leave were granted annually (with air transportation) instead of the present long periods every three years.

Table 3 shows that mineral traffic, generally carried in train loads at low cost to the railway and therefore at low rates to the industries, is relatively small. General merchandise of numerous different classes in widely varying consignments, carried at high cost to the railway, accounts for almost three-fourths of all traffic. There are no seasonal or daily peaks. The percentage of revenue from general merchandise compared with the

TABLE 3   Railway Goods Traffic, August 1954

Class	% of Tonnage	% of Ton Miles	% of Revenue
General merchandise .	65.7	75.0	73.9
Rubber	14.9	11.0	13.5
Coal and coke	8.1	4.5	4.0
Tin and tin ore . . .	3.5	3.2	3.7
Other minerals . . .	7.5	5.8	3.8
Livestock	0.3	0.5	1.1
	100.0	100.0	100.0

percentage of its ton mileage appears to be low and in many instances certain classes are carried at little, if anything, more than bare haulage costs. This is a natural consequence of the keen competition. Bulk products such as rubber, tin and tin ore appear to be carried at remunerative rates, but their volume is low in relation to the total. The fares and rates structure is well adapted to the traffic demands and possibilities, but the Table suggests that constant and continuous research on the traffic position is necessary.

The Railway's revenue accounts for the years 1948 through 1953 and its balance sheets as at December 31st of each of these years are summarized in Tables 4 and 5.

The Federal Government decided in 1953 that the capital provided by it and its predecessors prior to a date in 1951 should be treated as an investment in the equity of the railway and should receive a dividend only to the extent that the railway earned a profit on the equity. Loans subsequent to that date bear interest at rates determined by the High Commissioner. According to figures provided by the Railway Administration, the "investment in the equity" up to the end of 1953 amounted to $178.7 million, while advances bearing interest totalled $4.5 million. The remainder of capital expenditure, amounting to $66 million, was financed from railway revenue.

A survey of capital assets was being made at the time of the mission's visit. When it has been completed, assets lost as a result of the war will be written off, and that part of reconstruction and rehabilitation expenditure which is represented by capital assets will be written into the Capital Account.

TABLE 4 Malayan Railway: Summarized Revenue Accounts, 1948-53

(Million $)

	1948	1949	1950	1951	1952	1953
Revenue						
Railway	33.40	33.49	36.65	44.01	45.75	50.20
Ports	3.12	3.38	4.31	7.12	7.99	8.32
	36.52	36.87	40.96	51.13	53.74	58.52
Interest	.69	.69	.69	.69	.63	.40
Revenue arrears	.15	.19	.40	.27	.01	—
Appreciation and profits on sales of investments	.42	—	.29	.01	—	.43
Released and retrieved stores and materials	.27	.25	.25	.39	.28	.34
Miscellaneous	—	—	—	—	.73	.89
	38.05	38.00	42.59	52.49	55.39	60.58
Expenditure						
Railway	29.64	29.55	31.10	37.62	43.98	43.29
Ports	2.22	2.89	3.87	6.23	6.99	7.02
	31.86	32.44	34.97	43.85	50.97	50.31
Special expenditure						
Capitalized	.14	.64	.71	.25	.24	—
Not capitalized	.25	.66	1.12	1.65	1.47	.38
Transfers to reserves						
Renewals	4.62	2.99	4.02	.98	1.07	8.60
Uncompleted works & services	—	—	—	1.27	1.03	.26
Miscellaneous	—	.21	.27	.60	—	.55
Depreciation and loss on investments	—	1.06	—	1.66	.17	—
Arrears on salaries	1.18	—	1.50	2.23	.35	.35
Interest on capital	—	—	—	—	.04	.13
Miscellaneous	—	—	—	—	.05	—
	38.05	38.00	42.59	52.49	55.39	60.58

SOURCE: Public Accounts of the Federation of Malaya.

The policy in regard to provision for renewals is to make annual contributions from revenue to a renewals reserve at the rate of 3% of the total estimated replacement cost of all major wasting assets. In 1946 and 1947, the contributions were based on the 1941 estimated replacement value of $112 million. In 1948 this was arbitrarily increased by 50% to $168 million. The net revenue during the years 1948 through 1953 was insufficient,

TABLE 5 Malayan Railway: Summarized Balance Sheets, 1948-53[1]

(Million $)

	1948	1949	1950	1951	1952	1953
Assets						
Cash	1.54	.47	.76	1.62	2.55	2.37
Investments						
Sterling	21.80	20.69	21.09	19.43	9.83	10.29
Rupee	.51	.51	.51	.51	.51	.48
Local loans	.29	.39	.42	.62	.84	1.06
Nonmarketable	—	.08	.08	.08	.28	.28
Stores	9.53	8.29	7.49	9.64	13.50	13.49
Advances, debtors and debit						
balances	3.65	4.30	3.75	6.55	5.36	4.81
	37.32	34.73	34.10	38.45	32.87	32.78
Reconstruction and rehabilitation						
expenditures	—	51.50	57.77	63.26	70.35	80.86
Capital account expenditure . .	242.15	243.31	244.05	244.84	246.64	249.21
	279.47	329.54	335.92	346.55	349.86	362.85
Liabilities						
Creditors, deposits and credit						
balances	9.90	4.94	4.47	5.97	6.82	6.13
Federal government	.66	2.90	4.92	10.07	11.07	7.31
Reserves						
Reconstruction & rehabilitation	—	4.70	3.39	1.85	1.12	.89
Renewals	27.98	21.91	20.77	16.90	11.04	15.80
Arrears of salaries	—	—	—	1.25	—	—
Uncompleted works and						
services	—	—	—	1.27	1.71	.98
Miscellaneous	.09	.28	.55	1.15	1.12	1.67
	37.32	34.73	34.10	38.45	32.87	32.78
Advances from Federal Government						
for reconstruction and						
rehabilitation	—	51.50	57.77	63.26	70.35	80.86
Capital receipts	242.15	243.31	244.05	244.84	246.64	249.21
	279.47	329.54	335.92	346.55	349.86	362.85

[1] As at December 31.

SOURCE: Public Accounts of the Federation of Malaya.

however, for full provision to be made on this basis, except in the year 1953, and over the six years the net shortfall amounted to $6.54 million. On the completion of the survey of assets it will be possible to make an estimate of the replacement cost of assets actually in use and thus to provide for renewals on a sounder basis than at present.

The revenue accounts from the postwar years do not provide a sound basis on which to assess future results. Even in 1953, when reconstruction was well advanced and operating conditions were more favorable than at any time since the reoccupation, emergency measures, such as reduced speed of trains, nightly withdrawals of maintenance staff, pilotage and protection, were still in operation and affected working results. Under normal working conditions railway revenue should be expected not only to meet operating costs but also to provide adequately for replacements and a moderate return on the capital invested in the undertaking. This should not be beyond reach. If necessary, consideration should be given to a slight increase in passenger fares and rates for goods traffic; the risks of some loss of traffic to competing forms of transport must, of course, be carefully weighed.

The program prepared by the Railway Administration consists of the following projects:

1. Normal goods and marshalling yards extensions to accommodate growing traffic in industrial centers and new development areas, estimated at $1.5 million a year. The mission has, however, allowed only $1 million a year for this purpose in its proposed program.

2. The replacement of a number of steam locomotives by diesel locomotives. Unit for unit, diesel locomotives cost very much more than steam locomotives but one of the former is capable of doing the work of two or three of the latter, and the savings on operating costs can be substantial. The estimated cost of this project is $8 million over an initial change-over period, of which $2 million would be charged to renewals.

3. Rolling stock rehabilitation. Carriage and wagon stocks have not yet been fully restored; to bring them to a level consistent with regular and economical operation will require an expenditure of $4 million for carriages and $3.2 million for wagons in 1955-56.

4. Development of Port Swettenham, discussed earlier.

5. Replacement of temporary shop buildings at the central workshops at Sentul at an estimated cost of $4.5 million.

6. Staff housing. The additional amount required is estimated at $500,000.

7. Provision of permanent facilities for staff training at an estimated cost of $600,000. The present facilities are temporary and inadequate for intensified training of local staff.

We recommend an immediate study of the desirability of substituting diesel for steam traction to a much greater extent than is provided for in the railway program. A number of facts *prima facie* favor diesel traction: the division of the system into two main lines; the subdivision of the west coast line into equal distances, all of a length permitting the operation of the principal passenger and goods trains to timetables based on 12- and 24-hour turn-rounds; uniformity in the volume of traffic and in the weight of trains; and the present age distribution of the existing stocks of steam locomotives, requiring replacement in sufficiently large lots. Special attention should be given to the feasibility of adopting a single standard type of diesel locomotive, using one for light local trains, and two, coupled together, for heavy long-distance passenger and through goods trains. A timetable revision to make the most of the smallest number of units should be studied at the same time. The acceleration in service might have its influence on the turn-round of wagons and as a result make possible a reduction in the number required.

We further recommend that the operation of existing branch lines by small passenger units, one unit per line, without signalling or staffing of intermediate halts, be investigated.

A scheme for an east-west railway is unlikely to become a live issue unless prospective development in the eastern part of the country makes it worthy of further study. Nevertheless, the project should not be shelved altogether; the cost of constructing a single track railway would in all probability be below that of a two-lane main road.

Development Problems in Singapore

There is a steady increase of traffic in Singapore's streets. Plans for a redistribution of part of the city's population to suburbs and satellite towns in the Island are being studied. Workers living in the new suburbs and satellites will have to be moved to and from town daily during short peak periods.

In areas where there is no railway line, bus services radiating from many directions would probably be best suited to deal with this special type of suburban traffic; short suburban railway branches would be far too expensive to construct and operate. A circular line serving the outlying satellites would also be expensive and would not serve every township equally well.

Where there is a railway line and the suburbs and new towns have a population of 10,000 or more, the mass traffic at peak hours and the reduced traffic in off-peak periods should undoubtedly be carried by rail. This would involve the movement of large numbers of passengers through the Singapore railway terminus within a short space of time. The present terminus could handle this traffic, but the single main street between the station and the business center could not be expected to carry the additional load of vehicular traffic expeditiously. This aspect should be carefully weighed when planning future sites for suburbs and satellites.

If a population of, say, 200,000 or more were to be settled in the railway belt, it would become necessary to provide a railway extension between the present railway station in Singapore and a point as close as possible to the center of the city near Clifford Pier. The project would not be difficult to carry into effect nor need it be expensive. Most of the requisite land is now vacant. The few sections of buildings that would have to be razed are old and of low value. It is not proposed that such a project be included in the development program at this stage, but it is suggested that a belt of land along the future alignment be reserved and that no structures be erected or replaced within this belt.

IV ROADS

A FEDERATION

There are 6,200 miles of metalled roads in the Federation, not counting the city streets of Kuala Lumpur, Penang and Malacca. The trunk roads and several other main roads, 2,200 miles in all, are maintained at the expense of the Federal Government and 4,000 miles of link roads at the expense of the States and Settlements. State engineers and their staffs have a dual responsibility as State and Federal divisional officers. The Federal Public Works Department has a separate road section staffed by road engineers at its headquarters in Kuala Lumpur, but there are no similar separate sections in the State departments. No clear pattern of responsibility exists for feeder roads to villages.

The main road system is excellent. Design, construction and maintenance are generally of the highest standard. The roads section of the Federal Public Works Department has up-to-date workshops, laboratories, stone quarries, modern plant and equipment and an able and experienced engineering, research and administrative staff.

The two main Federal trunk roads, north-south from the Thailand border to the Johore causeway and east-west from Kuantan to Port Swettenham are given primary attention. Federal roads leading off these arteries and State roads receive attention which varies from State to State. The present policy is to maintain the two main trunk roads to a standard permitting four-wheel vehicles up to eight tons laden-weight, six-wheel vehicles up to 12 tons, and to set for a number of other main and branch roads a standard that has caused loads to be restricted.

The outstanding advantage of road transport is that passengers and goods are carried from door to door. This advantage is seriously reduced if the same load cannot be transported on all links. Traffic density on the less important roads is lower than on the main trunk roads, and where additional restriction is required by reason of somewhat lower construction and maintenance standards, it ought to be in speed rather than in load.

In general, traffic on the Federation's roads, outside of Kuala Lumpur, Penang and a few other centers, is still light. There are 93,000 vehicles registered in the Federation, or 15 for each of the 6,200 miles of metalled roads. Only two or three of these are lorries; seven or eight are private cars and two or three are motorcycles, the remainder being taxis, buses, trailers, caravans, road rollers, etc. A high proportion of these vehicles normally runs within city limits. Counts of traffic on the main north-south trunk road on a normal day showed an evenly distributed traffic density of 32-79 vehicles per hour in one direction, 60-115 vehicles per hour in both directions, the higher figures representing traffic at the approaches to the larger towns. Two-thirds of the vehicles were private cars, less than one-third lorries and buses. This is well below the average capacity of a well-aligned two-lane road, which can be put at 300 vehicles per hour, rising to 700 vehicles in a peak hour.

A seven-year development program begun in 1953 concentrates the main efforts on realignment, widening, raising in flood areas, strengthening of bridges, elimination of level crossings, and minor improvements, on many sections of the two main trunk roads; major deviations for by-passing towns are not included. The cost is estimated at $145 million, of which $75 million is for road improvement and $20 million for bridges on the north-south road, $29 million for road improvement east of Kuala Lumpur, $16 million for a dual carriageway between Kuala Lumpur and Port Swettenham and $5 million for a new bridge at Klang on the east-west road. About $10 million of this program has been scheduled for expenditure after 1959. The program will also require additional recurrent expenditure on staff for a number of years, rising from $56,000 a year to a maximum of $346,000 a year after three years and declining to $221,000 a year toward the end of the program.

A program for the construction and improvement of inland roads has also been prepared, the priorities being as shown below:

	(Million $)
1. Sekinchang—Utan Melintang, new, 32 miles	4.5
2. Kuantan—Kota Bharu, improvement, 242 miles	9.0
3. Malacca—Kendong, improvement, 25 miles	5.0
4. Batu Pahat—Muar—Malacca, improvement, 37 miles	5.6
5. Grik—Kroh, new, 30 miles	5.0
6. Mersing—Endau, improvement, 24 miles	1.2
7. Gemas—Rompin, new, 12 miles	3.6
8. Bahau—Menkuang on Triang, new, 34 miles	10.2
9. Endau—Rompin, new, 11 miles	2.2
10. Rompin—Pekan, improvement, 55 miles	5.5
11. Various new sections to open up agricultural development areas	10.5
	62.3
Less: expenditures to the end of 1954 on items 1 and 2	3.0
	59.3

A weak feature of the program is the absence of a coordinated plan for the development of feeder roads. The construction of this type of road should be given as high a priority as the most necessary sections of the main and secondary road program. Feeder roads can be built most economically and quickly by the local population. They could provide the labor to clear the route, level the ground, dig the drains and build simple culverts and bridges from tree trunks felled on the site. Surfacing will be required, for which a layer of gravel, laterite or quarry waste would be adequate. We recommend that an intensive drive be made to add substantial feeder road mileage in this way, the Federal Government to provide such technical advice and grants in materials or money as may be necessary. The cost to the budget should not, on average, exceed $5,000 a mile. Where a local government authority exists, it should be made responsible for drawing up a program of feeder road construction in the area and ensuring its execution.

The merit of the items included in the road program is unquestionable and sooner or later they will have to be carried out. But provision for the whole of the program cannot be made within the limit of the financial resources likely to be available to the Federation in 1955-59 without displacing other items in the over-all development program of higher priority than some of the items in the road program. The road program must accordingly be pruned, and in the mission's view this can be done with the least detriment to economic development by deferring costly realignments of sections on the main trunk roads. In the present circumstances the benefits would be incommensurate with cost.

The mission accordingly recommends:

1. That priority be given to the development of feeder roads.
2. That the main trunk road program be limited to essential improvements, to sections liable to serious flood damage, to dangerous stretches and to weak bridges. These improvements should be so scheduled that no additional staff, temporary or permanent, would be required.
3. That the program for inland and coastal roads as detailed above be recast to include only items 1 to 6 inclusive, 9 and 10 and, in place of item 11, a provision for access roads leading from existing main roads to the perimeter of agricultural development schemes. Roads within such schemes should be built as an integral part of the schemes.

The over-all road program would then be as follows:

	(Million $)
Feeder roads, rising from $500,000 to $1 million a year . .	4
Main trunk roads program	50
Inland roads	35
Access roads to agricultural development schemes (token) .	5
	94

B SINGAPORE

City Roads

City roads radiate from a very small central business area to the city boundaries; they are well spaced and generally of ample width. In Chapter 5, Part II, we recommended the construction of sidewalks and the covering of all open monsoon drains, at an estimated cost of about $3 million.

Another major development project, already scheduled, is the construction of a road across the present site of Kallang Airport, which will be closed in 1955. This will provide an additional outlet eastward from the city center in an area where the traffic is densest. The cost is estimated at $13 million, including a bridge over the Kallang River and construction and realignment of approaches. It would appear advisable to build the bridge with four traffic lanes, two bicycle tracks and two footpaths, and to construct the foundations of abutments and piers for two additional traffic lanes at a future date. This could be done at comparatively little additional cost now, leaving the future widening to be carried out by accommodating bicycle and pedestrian tracks on brackets.

In addition to the two major projects, we have made allowance in our recommended program for $8 million over five years for various street construction and widening projects.

Island Roads

Extensions to the city's main radial roads and new approach roads to the Paya Lebar Airport are being widened, strengthened, realigned or newly built to keep in step with traffic developments. The projects scheduled for 1955-58 and their estimated cost are as follows:

(Million $)

1. Nine miles of dual carriageways on the Island's main trunk road 1.11
2. Improvement of road connecting West Coast Road and Jurong Road 55
3. Realignment of sections of the Changi, Tampines, Thomson and Clementi roads 1.54

For these and other miscellaneous island road construction expenditures during 1955-59 we have made provision in our estimates of $4 million.

v ROAD TRANSPORT

Road transport in the Federation and in Singapore is well organized and shows healthy progress. Fifty thousand vehicles are licensed in Singapore, and 93,000 vehicles in the Federation. In Singapore the control of road traffic is naturally centralized, but a large measure of decentralization exists in the Federation. The rules and regulations governing road transport are based on United Kingdom experience and practice and are similar in both territories.

A FEDERATION

First organized in 1937, road transport control was re-established shortly after the liberation of Malaya in 1945 and has since operated under the abnormal conditions created by the need for reconstruction and by terrorist activities. Despite these handicaps it has attained a commendable degree of order and efficiency. For all practical purposes the road transport industry began its development after the war. The complexity of the situation made it necessary to confer upon the Commissioner of Road Transport far-reaching, in some cases absolute, powers; they have, however, been used equitably and with restraint.

The inexperience and ignorance of hosts of would-be participants in the early stages of the growing road transport industry have, in Malaya as elsewhere, led to harmful practices and methods, such as nonobservance of company laws, neglect of accounts, incorrect bookkeeping, failure to provide for depreciation, payment of dividends out of capital, indiscriminate borrowing, unlawful subletting of permits, operation of unauthorized routes, unlicensed traffic, overloading and overcrowding, nonobservance of timetables or fare schedules, insufficient checks on payment of fares or freight charges and neglect in the maintenance of vehicles. Several years of control, guidance and education have, however, succeeded in creating a well-ordered system, and on the whole it can be said that established road transport operators provide a good service. Nevertheless, malpractices persist. To halt deliberate evasion of the regulations, we have recommended in Chapter 5, Part II, a strengthening of reenforcement staff of the Road Transport Department, and additional patrol equipment for traffic police.

A new road transport bill was to come before the Federal Legislative Council shortly after the mission's visit. It would authorize appeal from the decisions of Registrars and the Commissioner, hitherto unavailable. It is recommended that consideration be given to the inclusion of a clause covering the "obligation to carry" traffic offered, without discrimination among persons, groups of persons, or consignors of merchandise.

The bill would introduce a zoning system. There would be 24 zones in the Federation; all road haulers issued with new "A" (public carrier) or "B" (limited carrier) licenses would be restricted to operation within one zone, or within 25 miles from base, while those issued with new "C" (private carrier) licenses would be restricted to two adjacent zones or 50 miles from base.

It is extremely doubtful whether this would be an improvement on the existing system. The present system of one route, one bus line, and the authorization of goods services according to business or traffic requirements, has great advantages over the zone system.

The Federal Legislative Council has appointed a select committee to inquire into means of furthering greater participation by Malays in the road transport industry. The matter undoubtedly deserves attention but the means to achieve the end require the most thorough and careful consideration. Incentives hastily designed to bring about such greater participation would inevitably delay progress toward the elimination of the malpractices referred to earlier and might undo much of what has already been achieved in this respect.

B SINGAPORE

Buses and taxis provide public transport, supplemented by *tri-shaws*[2] in the city area. Country buses are restricted to routes terminating at selected points inside the city not far from the perimeter. The system is satisfactory, and there is no immediate need for a unified public transport system throughout the Island. Illegal taxis, operated by private car

[2] A bicycle with a side-car for one or more passengers.

owners, should be vigorously suppressed, in the interest of an orderly transport system.

Within the city limits the bus services are operated by a private company, the Singapore Traction Company; rural bus services in the Island are run by nine small companies while three private companies are licensed to operate bus routes from Singapore into the Federation. The standard of operation is reasonable. Premises, maintenance shops and garages of the smallest companies are often primitive; they could be improved by pooling resources but, short of compulsory amalgamation, little can be done to bring this about.

The services of the Singapore Traction Company are good: operation is efficient, the fare structure reasonable, timetables effective and properly observed, equipment, offices, workshops and garages and other premises in good condition. It is quite certain that none of these could be materially improved if the company were taken over by public authorities. The authorized share capital of the company is £ 790,697, and net current assets at the end of 1953 were £ 420,572. It is clear, therefore, that the purchase of the company would require a large sum. In view of the many needs for development in other fields it would appear wise to extend the company's charter for another term of seven years from 1955, as provided for in the Singapore Traction Ordinance. Within that period the unification of road transport in the Island may materialize and the rural bus routes may by then be advantageously amalgamated with the city lines. The agreement between the government and the company gives effective means of controlling the company's services to the public.

Traffic Problems

Traffic congestion in the streets of Singapore appears to be acute and there is a growing parking problem. We have recommended that uninterrupted pedestrian pavements should be provided and that the open drains should be covered. We further suggest that traffiic rules affecting bicycles and *tri-shaws* be more strictly enforced, and, if necessary, amended. But while this would assist materially in reducing congestion in the roadway, it would not solve the waiting and parking problems. The use of back alleys behind business premises for loading and unloading is being investigated. The ultimate solution of the parking problem may be construction of multi-story car parks, but for the more immediate future a careful survey of the central area may disclose suitable open spaces for parking. The availability of parking space should be taken into account by the town planning authority in approving sites and designs for large new office buildings.

The problem of traffic congestion would be even more acute were it not for the fact that a large proportion of the passenger cars and commercial vehicles used in Singapore are of the smaller types. The desirability from the traffic point of view of continuing to encourage the use of smaller vehicles should be borne in mind whenever any changes in the taxation of motor vehicles are being considered. The Singapore Traction Company should be encouraged to continue testing double-decker buses as a contribution toward reducing traffic congestion; the test made with a single double-decked vehicle cannot be considered conclusive.

An extensive experimental scheme of one-way traffic routes is now in operation. It works smoothly, but has probably been carried to excess; many detours are very long, and there are a number of wide avenues where two-way traffic might be restored without creating additional junction and crossing problems.

vi CIVIL AVIATION

Regional headquarters are situated in Singapore under a Director-General and include a department responsible for civil aviation work in the Colony of Singapore. The Federation's department is in Kuala Lumpur. Control and supervision of air traffic, of safety and maintenance and all related activities, are well coordinated.

The cost of the regional headquarters is shared by the two governments and each government bears the cost of its own department. Regional headquarters cost approximately $1.1 million in 1953, the Singapore department $600,000, and the Federation department $1.5 million. Revenues jointly earned were about $900,000, mostly from aircraft landing fees. These fees are modest at present; a 25% increase would bring them to the level of Hong Kong and other Far East regions. It is recommended that an increase of this order be considered.

International air services are centered on Singapore, a junction for world air lines to all continents. Penang Airport is used by lines to Thailand and Sumatra. Internal air transport is provided by regular passenger, mail and cargo services between the main centers and by feeder services, which carry passengers and parcels only, and link the smaller towns and rubber, tin and other production areas with the main routes. In 1954, 162,140 passengers passed through the Federation's airports and landing grounds, some 3,384 tons of cargo and 436 tons of mail.

Internal air services are provided by Malayan Airways, a private company with head offices in Singapore, and the Malayan Railway operates feeder services with light aircraft.

In Chapter 5, Part II, we noted the need for replacement of Malayan Airways' present fleet. The company's charter expires on April 30, 1957. In the circumstances, a decision must be made at once on extension of the charter. Acquisition of the undertaking by the two governments would necessarily displace high priority items from the development programs; moreover, it is unlikely that a nationalized air line could improve on the present high standards of operation and maintenance and it might well have higher administrative and operating costs. For these reasons we have recommended that the company's charter be extended with such modifications as may be appropriate. We have also recommended that the company be required, as a condition of the extension, to give preference to applications by residents of Malaya in allotting any new capital that may be issued. It is understood that this is in fact the company's intention.

The feeder services, now provided by a fleet of five "Beaver" light one-engined aircraft, are an essential link in inland transport. They are supplementary to the main route services and by their nature they require different methods of operation. These services must be continued, even at the cost of a subsidy, as they are in several cases the only link between outlying areas and the rest of the country. Within a few years the fleet will become due for replacement, preferably by a light type of two-engined aircraft. A recommendation is made elsewhere that these services be more widely used for the carriage of mails.

vii   AIRPORTS

A   FEDERATION

There are at present eight fully-equipped airports in the Federation, six in the west, at Kuala Lumpur, Penang, Ipoh, Taiping, Alor Star and

Malacca, and two in the east, at Kota Bharu and Kuantan. In addition, 37 landing grounds are available to regular feeder services.

Kuala Lumpur Airport, the largest in the Federation, is sited conveniently near the town. Its runway of 6,000 feet is of sufficient length for foreseeable needs, but the approaches to it are obstructed, at one end by industrial buildings, at the other by a railway embankment. It has been designated by various air lines as an emergency alternate to Singapore and it has been suggested that Kuala Lumpur might be used for a once-weekly service to London. As the present approaches make it unsuitable for the larger types of aircraft used on long-distance air routes, the proposal has been made that the airport should eventually be moved to a new site, some distance from the town. Apart from the question of cost, this solution would sacrifice the present advantage of proximity. A better solution would appear to be to relocate the railway line to the southwest (See Map 11). The cost would probably not exceed one-fifth of the cost of a new airport.

It is recommended that this alternative be studied as a possibility for the future and that, if it be favored, provision be made to restrict building or other permanent development on the site of the eventual new alignment of the railway line.

The Civil Aviation Department has submitted a development program which provides for a moderate expansion of facilities. The major items in the program are as follows:

	(*Thousand $*)
Navigation aids	160
Aerodrome fire services	194
Runways, taxiways and lighting	845
Telecommunications	100
Aerodrome staff quarters	500
New landing strips	250
	2,049

B SINGAPORE

The present international airport of Kallang is to be closed when the new airport at Paya Lebar comes into operation, probably during 1955. Attention is rightly concentrated on the early completion of the new airport. Its layout will meet the requirements of frequent and heavy air traffic, and sufficient space will remain available to double capacity when

MAP II

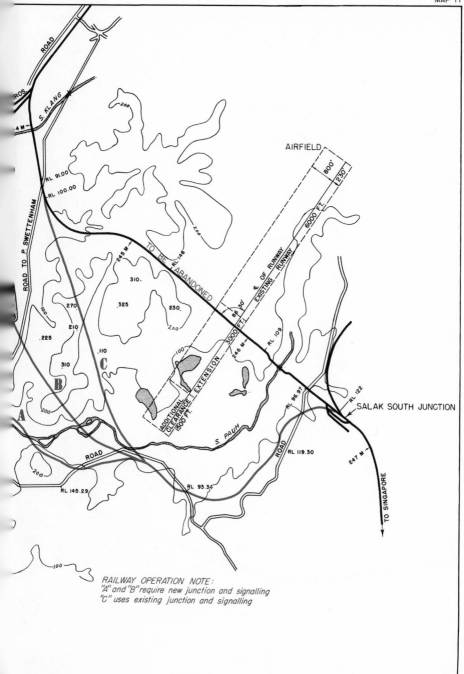

AIRFIELD

800'

230

6000 FT.

& OF RUNWAY

EXISTING RUNWAY

ROAD

S. KLANG

24 M

ROAD TO P. SWETTENHAM

RL 91.00

RL 100.00

200

245 M

TO BE ABANDONED

RL 145

310.

325

230.

270.

225

210

110

310

B

C

A

100

200

100

200

200

84° 30'

3000 FT.

246 M

RL 109

ADDITIONAL CLEARANCE EXTENSION

800 FT.

S. PAUH

RL 96.97

RL 122

SALAK SOUTH JUNCTION

ROAD

RL 119.30

247 M

TO SINGAPORE

RL 145.29

RL 93.34

100

RAILWAY OPERATION NOTE:
"A" and "B" require new junction and signalling
"C" uses existing junction and signalling

KUALA LUMPUR
AIRPORT EXTENSION

SHOWING POSSIBLE DEVIATIONS BETWEEN SALAK
SOUTH JUNCTION & PORT SWETTENHAM JUNCTION

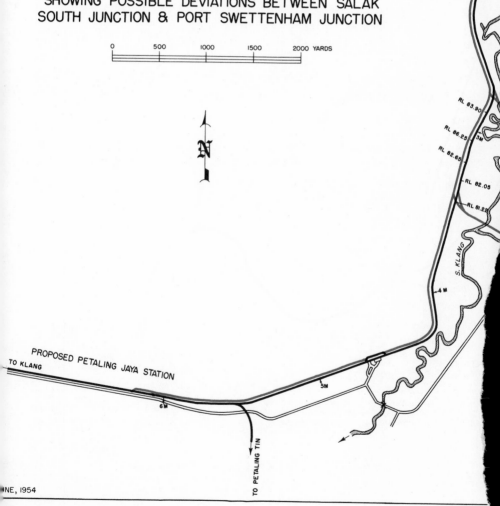

| 0 | 500 | 1000 | 1500 | 2000 YARDS |

NE, 1954

this becomes necessary. The total cost to completion will be approximately $38 million. Up to the end of 1953, $15 million had been spent or committed and a further $4 to $5 million was to be spent in 1954.

The permanent terminal building, through which a growing number of passengers from outside Malaya will pass, has yet to be designed. It is a most important part of the project and deserves expert attention. Too many of the large airport terminals of the world show defects in operation. To avoid such defects in Singapore's new terminal it is suggested that the advice of an architect-engineer versed in air terminal requirements be obtained.

VIII POSTAL SERVICES

The postal services of the Federation and Singapore are combined in a pan-Malayan postal organization under a Postmaster-General, with headquarters in Kuala Lumpur. The services in Singapore are under the jurisdiction of the local Director of Posts whose authority extends to the post offices on Christmas Island and the Cocos-Keeling[3] Islands.

The organization is efficient; it handles all the usual ancillary services, operates a savings bank and, in addition, issues licenses and makes registrations and payments for the government. Figures prepared by the Federal Department show that after allowance is made for services rendered to other government authorities without charge, it pays its way. Comparable figures for Singapore were not seen.

Transport of mails by air, rail and road is regular and speedy. It is recommended that regular use be made of scheduled feeder air services to rural areas. Ocean mails are forwarded from Singapore by the fastest services available; there is, however, great irregularity in the arrival of sea mails from the United Kingdom and in the times taken in transit. It is accordingly suggested that the British postal authorities be asked to forward outward mails to Malaya by regular fast shipping lines, and by intermediate ships only if their time schedule assures earlier arrival.

The Federal program for the expansion of postal facilities over the next five years, made necessary by the steady increase in number of communications handled, consists of the following projects:

[3] Christmas Island and the Cocos-Keeling Islands are in the Indian Ocean, respectively some 190 and 600 miles south and southwest of the western tip of Java.

(*Thousand $*)

Replacement of major post offices at Kuala Lumpur,
Penang, Ipoh, Johore Bahru and Kuala Trengganu;
new post office at Petaling Jaya; and extension of
Kuala Lumpur stores   4,957
Replacement of minor post offices   1,163
New minor post offices   1,117
Equipment for the above   224
                                                    ───────
                                                      7,461

While these projects are reasonable and necessary, the mission, having regard to other demands on the financial resources likely to be available, recommends that they be spread over a longer period by carrying forward $3 million to the next program.

The growth of the population and business activities in the city and rural districts of Singapore will require in the coming years annual capital expenditure of about $300,000 for additional branch offices, extensions and equipment. This is normal, essential development.

IX   TELECOMMUNICATIONS

The Department of Telecommunications, with headquarters in Kuala Lumpur, is pan-Malayan; it is in charge of public telegraph and telephone services in the Federation and Singapore, with the exception of the local telephone service in Singapore. This service, which includes the Johore Bahru exchange on the mainland, was formerly owned and operated by the Oriental Telephone & Electric Company but was to be taken over by the Singapore Government on January 1, 1955. Thereafter, the Singapore system was to be placed under a Singapore Telephone Board, the Johore Bahru exchange to be taken over by the Telecommunications Department.

The telecommunications systems are exceptionally well developed, defense and security needs having demanded extensive and reliable services. A modern V.H.F. (Very High Frequency) radio circuit covers Malaya and a teleprinter service links Singapore with centers in the Federation. The telegraph and radio telephone services with other countries are adequate to meet all demands with a sufficient margin in capacity. The Telecommunications Department also maintains, against payment of costs, special circuits and equipment on behalf of the Broadcasting, Civil Aviation and Meteorological Departments and the Malayan Railway.

The system has perforce been overdeveloped to some extent and it might therefore appear that expansion could be slowed down. This is indeed the case for special systems required by military and police authorities which serve the public too. These forced developments have, however, also served to educate the public in telephone-mindedness and future expansion will need to keep pace with growing public demand.

Telegraph

The public telegraph service in Malaya, as elsewhere, operates at a loss and is subsidized by the telephone services. This aid from the one to the other is small and must be accepted. The improvements scheduled for 1955-59 are estimated to cost $800,000; of this amount $440,000 is for voice frequency installations, $360,000 for teleprinter apparatus.

The 1953 accounts show telegraph operating costs of $1.8 million, revenues at $1.2 million; for the teleprinter, $416,000 and $377,000 respectively. It is reasonably certain that the operating economies which will come with telegraph development, and the increased revenues expected from teleprinter expansion will together cause a slight reduction in the deficit of the public telegraph service. The teleprinter account may be expected to become self-supporting in some three to four years.

Telephone Services, Federation

The program scheduled for 1955-59 provides for:

	(Thousand $)
1. New exchanges, automatic, manual, rural	8,376
2. Subscribers' connections and plant	12,400
3. Trunk lines and junctions	10,092
4. Exchange buildings	2,071
5. Stores, workshops and garage buildings	280
6. Vehicles for service and maintenance	814
7. Housing of staff	3,800
8. Training school	900
9. Offices, welfare and training	49
10. Training equipment	227
11. Police radio equipment	2,500
12. Police vehicles maintenance and service	228
	41,737

Revenue from telephone services amounted in 1953 to $12.8 million; the net operating surplus after provision for depreciation and a subsidy to the telegraph services was $2.5 million.

The number of telephone subscribers now exceeds the level at which experience indicates that it becomes economical to replace a simple rental by a tariff of fixed rental plus a charge per call. The introduction of this system is now under consideration. There is no doubt that revenues will continue to rise as the population grows and economic development proceeds. Modern equipment, operating and administrative methods will also help to reduce expenditure. It will be advisable to adapt the pace of development to needs, the more so as the financial revenues available for development are very limited. It is accordingly recommended that the program be spread over a period longer than five years. Should circumstances warrant, the program might be accelerated at a later stage. Non-revenue-earning projects, and particularly police communications, should be strictly scrutinized and limited to essentials.

Telephone Services, Singapore

At present the trunk exchange is attached to the local exchange and operated by the telephone company on behalf of the Telecommunications Department. The demands for telephone service in Singapore City and Island outstrip present capacity; both local and trunk exchanges require extensions and renewals.

Local Exchanges. The conclusions and recommendations concerning local exchanges only, presented in a first report by Mr. H. V. Knight of the British Post Office to the newly established Singapore Telephone Board, were available in March 1954. The future requirements as set out in this report are well reasoned and lucidly explained and the mission endorses them in full. It is therefore recommended that this first report be taken as the basis for the development program. Capital requirements are estimated at $22 million for the period 1955-59, rising from $3 million in 1955 to $6 million in 1959. Capital expenditure per new line connected amounts to $800. Net revenue per line, after provision for depreciation, is $70-$80 a year. The capital expenditure may therefore be expected to yield sufficient new revenue to pay its way.

Trunk Exchange. The present trunk exchange is inadequate. This has been realized by all concerned and plans for a new exchange have been prepared and certain equipment has been ordered. The 1954 estimates of the Colony provided $480,000 for equipment and $240,000 for building. Construction has, however, been held up pending a decision on the future management of the exchange. Whatever the decision may be as to future control there is a clear and pressing need for a new exchange, and it should not, and need not, be delayed until the decision is taken.

The question as to management is whether to follow the existing pattern which would result in operation of the exchange by the Singapore Telephone Board on behalf of the Telecommunications Department, or whether the Department should have sole responsibility. After due consideration of all aspects we recommend that the local and trunk services be separated and that the trunk exchange be made the responsibility of the Telecommunications Department.

The ideal location for a local exchange is a central position in relation to its cable network; this is usually the center of a business area, where land is expensive and space limited. The location of a trunk exchange is governed by totally different requirements and the proposed new site, in the Newton Circus area, is well chosen. The retention of both exchanges under one roof in Singapore would be uneconomical and should not be considered. Public demands on trunk services between Singapore and the Federation are heavy—as large as, if not larger than—total internal demand for trunk connections within the Federation. These demands are easier served if the terminals at both ends are operated under a single authority. Methods of service and operation are different for trunk and local services and it is better to divide them functionally rather than geographically. The need for interchangeable staff, standardized equipment and plant, is among factors favoring the vesting of responsibility for trunk services in one department. If the Singapore trunk exchange were to be operated by the Telephone Board, duplication of many sections in the administration, accounts, control, operation, engineering and stores departments would be necessary. For these reasons we consider that the trunk exchange and services should be the responsibility of the Telecommunications Department alone.

x BROADCASTING, METEOROLOGICAL SERVICE, AND SURVEYS AND MAPPING

The programs submitted by these departments are as follows:

	Broadcasting	(Thousand $)
Federation		
Kajong, additional transmitter		200
Penang, additional transmitter and permanent studios		350
Ipoh, new station		600
Malacca, modern studios and replacement of equipment		500
		1,650
Singapore		
Completion of modernization of administrative and studio premises		1,250
	Meteorological Service	
Pan-Malayan		
Station detecting equipment		102
Federation		
New station at Kluang and transfer of Kuala Trengganu station		129
Housing for staff at airfields distant from towns . . .		276
		405
Singapore		
Requirements for new Paya Lebar airport		291
	Surveys	
Federation		
Continuation of national grid plan		5,000
New headquarters building		1,000
		6,000

The mission has no comments to offer on these projects. A suggestion is made in Technical Report 1 that more attention should be paid by the Meteorological Service to the collection of data bearing on some of the major climatic factors of significance in the agricultural, veterinary, forestry and irrigation and drainage fields.

The Present Scope of Secondary Industries

The secondary industry of Malaya covers a very wide range of activities, most of which are so fragmented and so intimately bound up with primary production and entrepot trade that it is not easy to sum up either the present state or the future prospects of industrial development. The only comprehensive view available is that given by the 1947 census figures of persons engaged in secondary industries, which are set out (in a re-arranged form) in Table 1. In 1947 secondary industry as defined in the Table accounted for over 9% of the Malayan working population—a high figure for Asia, probably exceeded only by Japan, India, and Hong Kong. Expansion since 1947 has apparently been, on balance, at a rate no more than commensurate with the rate of growth of the total working population, and although some significant new enterprises have been established the general structure and character of secondary industry seem to have changed very little.

Malaya lacks cheap sources of power; the availability of new land for settlement and the profitability of tin, rubber and trading have tended both to keep wages relatively high and to attract capital into nonindustrial avenues. In these circumstances, any secondary industry has had to meet a very severe test before it could be considered worth while as against the alternatives which Malaya's good fortune offered. With few exceptions, the industries able to meet this test have been those with a decisive margin of "natural" protection in terms of location: secondary industry has typically taken the form of activities, associated directly or indirectly with Malaya's role as primary producer and trader, which need to be performed on the spot or which are specially sheltered by high transport costs. This is generally true of each of the five groups of industries shown in the Table:

(1) *Handicrafts.* These activities occupy idle hands and hours in rural households, make special use of local skills, and/or rely on the need for close worker-customer relations. Their labor force consists mainly

of own-account workers and unpaid family helpers. This group accounts for nearly one-third of the "industrial" working population in the Federation, but is comparatively less important in Singapore.

(2) *Processing.* The processing industries depend chiefly on the advantage of converting local raw materials into less heavy and more transportable forms. In each case a great volume of material is handled at

TABLE 1   Workers Engaged in Secondary Industries, 1947

(*Thousands*)

	Federation	Singapore	Malaya
1. *Handicrafts*			
Attap-making and ratan ware	21.0	1.2	22.2
Tailoring, dressmaking, etc.	11.2	5.9	17.1
Goldsmithing, etc.	8.8	2.7	11.5
Handloom weaving and other	5.2	0.8	6.0
Total	46.2 (32.3%)	10.6 (15.8%)	56.8 (27.0%)
2. *Processing*			
Rubber milling, packing, etc.	16.0	5.5	21.5
Tin smelting	0.4	0.3	0.7
Sawmilling, etc.	7.9	1.6	9.5
Rice, coconut, palm oil milling, etc.	9.5	1.6	11.1
Fish curing and other . .	2.6	0.1	2.7
Total	36.4 (25.4%)	9.1 (13.6%)	45.5 (21.7%)
3. *Food, Drink and Tobacco*			
Bread, biscuits, etc. . . .	6.7	2.6	9.3
Other food preparations .	7.6	1.7	9.3
Beer, soft drinks, etc. . .	1.1	1.1	2.2
Tobacco and cigarettes . .	2.8	0.2	3.0
Total	18.2 (12.7%)	5.6 (8.4%)	23.8 (11.3%)
4. *Engineering*			
Railway workshops . . .	3.0	—	3.0
Dockyards, etc.	1.5	11.8	13.3
Motor vehicle workshops, etc.	8.4	6.6	15.0
Electrical installation and repair work	1.2	1.8	3.0
Foundries, forges, etc. . .	8.9	5.8	14.7
Total	23.0 (16.1%)	26.0 (38.9%)	49.0 (23.3%)

TABLE 1   Workers Engaged in Secondary Industries, 1947—*Continued*

(*Thousands*)

	Federation	Singapore	Malaya
5. *Other Manufacturing*			
Bricks, tiles, etc.	2.4	1.4	3.8
Soap	0.6	0.7	1.3
Metal containers, etc. . .	0.7	1.1	1.8
Rubber and other footwear	3.4	2.7	6.1
Other rubber goods . . .	2.3	2.0	4.3
Furniture, etc.	3.8	2.5	6.3
Newspapers, printing and photography	3.9	3.6	7.5
Miscellaneous	2.3	1.6	3.9
Total	19.4 (13.6%)	15.6 (23.3%)	35.0 (16.7%)
GRAND TOTAL	143.2 (100.0%)	66.9 (100.0%)	210.1 (100.0%)
PERCENTAGE OF TOTAL GAINFULLY OCCUPIED POPULATION	7.5%	18.7%	9.3%

SOURCE: Census, September 1947—"Population by Industry" (persons, male and female). Building industry and gas, water and electricity supply workers have been excluded. "Factory" workers on rubber estates (11.9 thousand) and on coconut and oil palm estates (4.6 thousand) have been included, the figures being taken from the Census "Population by Occupation" tables. Workers in the Singapore Naval and Harbour Board dockyards (10.7 thousand) were counted under other headings in the Census, and have here been added from Labour Department statistics. The figures have been rearranged from the Census headings. In a number of instances both the Census classification and the description here given are not very reliable.

a very low cost per unit in relation to the price of the commodity. But Malaya (especially Singapore) has also been able to attract these commodities for processing from neighboring countries, partly by virtue of superior technical facilities and partly as an outgrowth of the historical development of the entrepot trade. Indeed, the trading aspect of the goods imported for processing and re-export is at least as important as the value of their processing, as such, but the two activities are inseparable.

(3) *Food, Drink and Tobacco*. In the third group, the advantages of location are in the case of foodstuffs chiefly a matter of spoilage with time (e.g., bread baking, canning locally-grown pineapples). Nevertheless, Singapore's biscuit manufacturers, to whom these advantages hardly apply, have managed to capture most of the domestic market and also

to acquire a small (and diminishing) export trade, mainly in Indonesia. Beverage manufacture, which has greatly increased in recent years, relies on avoiding the costs of foreign shipment of a bulky article, while local tobacco manufacture is almost entirely dependent on the freedom of locally-grown leaf from excise duty.

(4) *Engineering.* The fourth group ranges from primitive blacksmith shops to foundries and dockyards capable of major engineering tasks. Although the majority of enterprises in this group are small workshops primarily engaged in repair and part-replacement work, the demand for which is strongly localized, there are some larger establishments, especially in Singapore, which produce a wide range of engineering and metal products. The largest engineering firm in Southeast Asia has its headquarters in Singapore, where machinery, iron and steel castings, ships and boats, constructional steel work and a wide range of other engineering products are made. This firm also has two factories in the Federation which serve the mining industry. The Singapore Harbour Board has substantial engineering establishments, as has also the Malayan Railway in the Federation. The latter is planning to manufacture an increasing proportion of its requirements of rolling stock. In addition to these larger establishments, there are a number of small engineering firms and workshops producing machinery such as gravel pumps, tin ore dryers, rubber milling and sheeting machinery, boilers, etc. The ship and boat building industry is capable of supplying nearly all the requirements of Malaya in small motor-driven and other craft and it also supplies Borneo and other adjacent territories. Singapore has a considerable and well-equipped motor industry engaged in assembly and maintenance work, including a large assembly plant owned by a firm of Canadian motor-car manufacturers. Several firms in the Federation build bodies for buses and commercial vehicles. Steel tanks and drums and various kinds of steel pipe are produced by a factory in Singapore and firms both in Singapore and the Federation manufacture wire netting, barbed wire and similar products.

(5) *Other Manufacturing Industries.* In the fifth group, apart from the localized need for printing and newspaper services, the natural shelter of transport costs predominates. The local manufacture of bricks and concrete building materials supplies nearly all the market (though

Indian roofing-tiles still manage generally to compete successfully against the local product). Cement manufacture, established in 1952, supplies about a third of the Malayan demand from a factory at Rawang, but it may be necessary to establish another factory at a more southerly site in order successfully to meet foreign competition in Singapore. The manufacture of metal containers and a number of other metal products and also of glass bottles, is expanding (these products are bulky in relation to their materials). Soap, made from local materials, meets most of the domestic demand (its manufacture is largely associated with oil milling, but a large modern factory was recently established by an overseas firm at Kuala Lumpur). The manufacture of rubber footwear, hose, belting, cycle tires and tubes, etc., has the advantage (within the Federation) of using a local material which is obtained duty free; although some lines of production are expanding, the consumption of rubber by Malayan manufacturers has on the whole been declining in recent years, partly as a result of import competition and partly because the considerable export sales of rubber footwear have been falling off. Two other significant exceptions to the rule of transport cost shelter are the manufacture in Singapore of flashlight batteries for export (by an American factory) and of cotton and rayon yarn (by a Chinese factory, established in 1953, which is the only important textile enterprise in Malaya).

All this adds up to a very substantial body of industrial activity—dependent in large measure, it is true, on Malaya's primary production and trading, but itself making an important contribution to the success of those undertakings. The range of products and skills and the qualities of enterprise and hard work already evident in Malayan secondary industries offer a very good basis for further progress. The existing stage of development has been reached almost entirely without the aid of tariff protection[1] or other "artificial" assistance. In spite of Malaya's high costs, the country has achieved a degree of industrial progress beyond that of most of its neighbors, partly because its major producing and trading activities have

[1] Singapore is an entirely "free port", except for revenue duties on liquor, tobacco and petroleum for local consumption. The Federation's import duties cover a wider range of goods (recently extended), but their purpose is still almost entirely the collection of revenue and hitherto their protection effects have been small. The island of Penang, in the Federation, is also a "free port."

themselves called in special measure for ancillary industrial services, and partly because their profitability has furnished both savings for industrial capital formation and living standards for a varied industrial market.

Some Special Features of Malayan Industrial Enterprise

For an understanding of the problems of future development, some special features of the existing industries must be noted:

1. Very small-scale enterprise is the rule. No private manufacturing firm in Malaya employs more than a few hundred workers; the average firm has perhaps 20, the majority less than 10. In the Federation nearly 40%, and in Singapore more than 10%, of the "industrial" labor force consists, not of wage-earners, but of own-account workers and unpaid family helpers.

2. With only a score or so of important exceptions, the capital, management and skill in Malayan industrial enterprises are Asian. European capital has tended to concentrate on the plantations, mines and commerce of Malaya, while the Chinese have taken a leading part in its industry. Not only in Singapore, where it might have been expected, but also in the Federation, 80-90% of industrial employers are Chinese (the remainder mainly Indian), and more than three-quarters of the wage-earners are also Chinese. The basis for the assembly of capital for an enterprise, and also for the acquisition of industrial skills, is predominantly the coherence and traditions of the Chinese family or clan.

3. Levels of technical equipment and of working efficiency are enormously varied, even where standard processing operations are concerned. Ingenuity and improvisation are often called upon to work miracles. This makes for success chiefly in small-scale enterprises. On the other hand, there are many examples of well-equipped and efficiently conducted enterprises under Asian management, and it would be a mistake to judge industrial efficiency in Malaya in terms of "spit and polish," or to imagine that Western standards of horsepower per worker are always a good rule in a very different economic environment.

4. Although systematic evidence is hard to find, it does seem that "turnover" among industrial enterprises is very considerable, the percentage of failures normally quite high. This may be partly a

matter of the relative ease of starting new ventures in a situation which often calls for relatively low capitalization. It is also probably the result of the general instability of the Malayan economy, and of a tendency to look for "speculative" profits rather than steady returns. Further, small enterprises often become indebted to moneylenders, at very high interest rates which both reflect and increase the risks of failure.

The Problem of the Future

In the coming years and decades the growth of population is likely to outstrip by far the absorptive capacity of the "staple" activities—rubber and tin production, and entrepot trade—on which Malaya now depends. Unless equally productive alternatives continue to be developed, the Malayan standard of living may gradually drift from its present relatively high "rubber" level back toward the "rice" levels prevailing in much of the rest of Asia. At the same time as land suitable for the extension of agricultural settlement is gradually occupied, an increasing proportion of the population will have to find employment elsewhere if it is not to remain idle or underemployed.

This prospect—so very different from Malaya's past, or even its present, but already unfolding itself—very strongly suggests the need for a greater emphasis on industrial development. It means, in the first place, that the tests which secondary industries have had to meet, before they could be considered worth while from the viewpoint of the Malayan economy as a whole, may in future be less severe, if the alternatives offered are less favorable. But if it is to sustain or to raise Malaya's living standards, industrial development must not merely provide some sort of work for idle hands: it must provide work productive and profitable enough to justify the wage levels that go with Malaya's present living standards. Can enough industrial opportunities be found—at prevailing Malayan labor costs, or not too much below them—to absorb a larger proportion of the rapidly growing labor force?

The Range of Industrial Opportunities

As we have seen, existing secondary industries are concentrated in fields in which Malaya enjoys a special natural advantage, largely associated with the "staple" economic activities. It is reasonable to consider first what greater industrial use might be made of locally-produced materials.

Unfortunately, on the basis of present technology, Malaya's typical natural resources do not seem to lend themselves to really major projects of industrial development. Malaya is not a natural center for a large rubber-manufacturing industry, exporting to the markets of the world. Rubber is light and compact in relation to its value and therefore inexpensive to ship. The rubber itself is usually a small part of the cost of such major rubber products as automobile tires, and other requisite materials for tire manufacture would have to be imported. Since rubber normally gains in weight and bulk in the course of manufacture, rubber-using industries are more advantageously located near centers of consumption. Tin is a very minor component in most of its industrial uses, and transportation costs are also comparatively low. There have been suggestions that tin-plate might be manufactured in conjunction with an iron and steel industry based on Malaya's high-grade iron ore deposits, but the absence both of coking coal and of cheap power rules this out as an economic proposition. Besides, a steel industry would require very large amounts of capital in relation to the labor it would employ. This is true also of the manufacture of pulpwood and paper, but in any case Malayan hardwoods and grasses appear to be generally unsuitable for present commercial pulping processes. In this case research is proceeding in various parts of the world (including some chemical research recently begun by the Federation Forestry Department) which may eventually change the picture. Known mineral deposits other than tin and iron ore are not large enough to support substantial processing industries.

Apart from the possibility of important technological or geological discoveries, it would seem that Malayan industrial development, in the future as in the past, must take the form of fairly small advances along a very wide front, chiefly for the home market and neighboring export markets, rather than the establishment of a few big new industries. In this context, the outlook is reasonably promising. The existing processing and manufacturing industries based on local materials are in many cases in urgent need of technical improvement; given that, there are still considerable possibilities of extending their operations. The coconut product industry suggests several opportunities—e.g., milling in Malaya of a higher proportion of the available copra (including development of solvent extraction), refining of coconut oil (now mostly exported in its crude state), manufacture of dessicated coconut, development of coir fiber production and related manufacturing activities, increased manufacture of better grades of soap and of other toilet preparations. The manufacture of rubber goods for the domestic market should be capable of expansion, perhaps especially in the field of foam rubber products, and there is almost certainly room for one modern tire factory producing the most common types and sizes of tires for cars and trucks. Processing of crude rubber, as such, offers few further opportunities of development along present lines, but research may reveal methods of chemical or physical modification of natural rubber to make it more suitable for particular purposes (especially those in which synthetic rubber now has the upper hand). The work already done on "cyclized" rubber suggests one such opportunity.[2]

In the wood-working industries, greater production of better-class furniture, pre-fabricated joinery, veneers and plywoods should be possible. The manufacture of cement and clay building materials should continue to expand. Pineapple canning is also capable of expansion if fruits of improved quality and uniformity can be developed, especially since the industry is still producing only a fraction of its prewar output. The processing of fish, including its canning and the manufacture of pastes and by-products, is a field almost entirely unexploited in Malaya, although much research will be needed before it can be known what the possibilities are. Research and imaginative enterprise could also undoubtedly reveal many minor possibilities of industrial development based on agricultural, mineral and marine resources at present unknown or neglected.

Among industries dependent on imported materials, the light engineering and other metal-working industries probably offer most scope for expansion. Judging from the beginnings that have been made, one would expect a development of simple (but increasingly elaborate) assembly work and motor body building, the fabrication of more parts and machines for use in local industry, and the manufacture of a much wider range of household articles and fittings and other metal products. There is perhaps not a great deal more scope for new developments in the food, drink, and tobacco industries, though local milling to replace the large

---

[2] "Cyclized" rubber is a chemically-modified form of natural rubber, said to be superior as a material for the soles of shoes and other purposes. A pilot plant for the production of sufficient quantities for commercial testing is being set up in England by Rubber Technical Developments Ltd.

quantities of wheat flour now imported is a possibility. The Malayan market would probably support the establishment of modern weaving, knitting and garment-making factories, now conspicuously absent, which would incidentally also provide a local market for the yarn already being manufactured in Singapore. Facilities for dyeing, printing and finishing the fabrics produced would also be needed. In view of the great variety of Malayan tastes, the types and quantities of goods to be produced would have to be very carefully planned. The successful operation of a few light manufacturing enterprises, even in export markets (e.g., batteries, boot polish), suggests that similar miscellaneous opportunities remain to be exploited.

The foregoing remarks are intended merely to illustrate the range of industrial opportunities in Malaya, and should not be construed in any sense as recommendations. Indeed, conclusions regarding particular industrial ventures could not possibly emerge from the kind of investigation which the mission was able to undertake. Moreover, final judgment about particular ventures must rest chiefly with the private entrepreneurs who, in the Malayan economy, are likely to remain the principal initiators and agents of industrial development. Our concern is rather with depicting the general pattern of prospective development and with the broad government policies which need to be pursued in order that the economic climate and background facilities for industrial enterprise should be as favorable as possible in this new phase of industrial development for which Malaya's changing situation calls.

Necessity for Modern Organization and Techniques

The major conclusion that emerges even from a very general survey is that, in order to make sufficient progress, Malayan secondary industries, which have concentrated for the most part in fields where they had a localized natural advantage, must move into lines which meet more direct and open competition with the industries of other countries, on the basis of cost and quality. Of course, close attention will have to be paid to the local advantages which the Malayan economic and physical environment offers, and these will continue to determine the directions of successful development, but even where Malayan materials can be used the margin of natural advantage is likely to grow smaller as development extends. The manufacture of plywood, for example, is in this sense a much more competitive business than sawmilling; cakes of toilet soap are further removed from the original coconut than are bars of washing soap; foam rubber can be processed from latex in the United States, although the latex itself must be processed or treated in Malaya. Every advance of the engineering industries into new and more elaborate operations invites more direct comparison with the costs of similar operations in the production lines of North American, European, Japanese and Indian factories; a Malayan textile industry must, for instance, face on the one hand the experience and equipment of Manchester and on the other hand the low wages of Bombay.

Malaya is not wealthy enough to afford in most instances the outlay of capital which is reflected in the American or even the British ratios of installed horsepower to industrial workers. On the other hand, if present living standards are to be anything like maintained, Malayan labor is expensive by Asian standards, although still cheap in terms of Western wage-rates. As pointed out in Chapter 6, Part II, the natural goal of Malayan industrial development, in these circumstances, is some sort of intermediate position between East and West.

The question then to be answered is whether Malayan industrial entrepreneurs and workers are in a position to seize upon and operate successfully the kinds of industry and technique that need to be developed. American industries can pay high wages not only because they are highly capitalized, but also because their operations fit together, one helping the other; because they are efficiently and scientifically managed; and because their workers are well trained and industrious. Industries in many underdeveloped countries can afford only low wages, partly because they have comparatively less capital equipment, but also because they lack the advantages of reciprocal industrial help and because both their management and their labor force are not sufficiently trained or effective in the jobs they have to do. In these respects, Malaya can already claim to be in advance of much of the rest of Asia. But it is here that most remains to be done, and the degree of success of industrial development in Malaya will turn largely upon how well it is done. In Chapter 6 we have set forth our analysis of the requirements for industrial progress. They may be summarized here by saying that the hope of industrial development in Malaya, to help maintain or raise living standards in the face of rapid population growth, rests upon the application of modern methods of organization and techniques in widening industrial fields that must become increasingly competitive with foreign industries, both in the Malayan home market and to some extent in export markets. This application is partly a matter of private initiative—of which there seems to be no lack—and partly a matter of government policies to foster the conditions in which private initiative can be successful. The prospective role of government has been outlined in Chapter 6.

It must be emphasized, however, that the income from primary production and trading will continue for a very long time to be the basis of Malayan living standards and the indispensable background of industrial development. Income from these sources not only helps to provide industrial capital and a prosperous home market for manufactures, it is also the source of foreign exchange with which Malaya can buy food and other requirements (including materials for local manufacture) from abroad, enabling the secondary industries to concentrate on the home market rather than go out to face the keener competition of world export markets. Anything that tends to jeopardize Malaya's "staple" activities will also tend to depress living standards and secondary industries; equally, measures to promote the success of those activities are among the most important ways of promoting successful industrial development.

Protective Measures

In Chapter 6 we have indicated the circumstances in which some degree of tariff protection may be suitable and desirable. The Federation's revenue duties (which in September 1954 were in many cases increased in rate and widened in coverage) automatically offer a margin of protection for some local industries, since they are not accompanied by excise duties on the corresponding local products. But it is clear from what has been said in Chapter 6 that the protective effects and possibilities of the tariff should be deliberately recognized and systematically reviewed. Administrative arrangements to accomplish this review, to provide for proper investigation of applications for protection, and to ensure safeguards against its abuse, are recommended later in this report.

We do not recommend the use of quantitative import restrictions for protective purposes (beyond their present function as an adjunct of sterling area exchange control), because we believe that their general use would eliminate desirable elements of international competition. Moreover, quantitative restrictions almost inevitably result in trading rigidities and undue advantages for the firms to which import quotas are allotted. We were told by some Malayan manufacturers that quota restrictions are needed to prevent overseas suppliers from defeating the object of protective duties by "dumping" their goods at uneconomic prices in an effort to destroy local competitors. Other countries have found that any such attempt can be forestalled by provisions in the customs law for quick imposition of temporary "anti-dumping" duties, should this prove necessary. We recommend that the Federation adopt similar provisions as a precautionary measure, and as a reassurance against fears which in Malaya seem to be more widespread than the facts generally warrant.

In some countries, including a number of British colonies, new enterprises have been granted protection even against internal competition by licensing requirements which limit the number of new entries to an industry. The problem with which these requirements are intended to deal is a very real one—for example, the local market may be too small to support more than one or two efficient factories, yet a dozen enterprises may spring up, most of them doomed to failure. This problem is perhaps especially acute when tariff protection is granted with a certain scale of factory operations in view. However, any industrial licensing system in Malaya, with its large body of versatile entrepreneurs and its inter-racial problems, would encounter almost insuperable difficulties, even apart from the dangers of too great a restriction of healthy competition. We recommend that official limitations on new entries to secondary industries should not be imposed, unless in very exceptional circumstances. It should be possible to achieve much of the purpose of such limitations by making available realistic advice on market opportunities, as we recommend below.

One question that will become more important with the increasing significance of the Federation tariff is the position of manufacturers in Singapore and on the island of Penang in relation to the mainland markets. In any case, if only for the avoidance of physical overcrowding, the population and industries of Singapore should in the long run spill over across the causeway into Johore, and we believe that it is wise to recognize this prospect in Singapore's town-planning. Migration to the mainland from Singapore would also help to widen the market inside the Federation customs area. Although in the long run this is a movement to be encouraged, economic policy should not ignore the fact that Malaya is essentially an economic unit. We have therefore recommended that manufacturers in the free ports be relieved of Federation customs duties on their mainland sales, and have suggested possible methods of policing this concession and of mitigating any consequent adverse effect on Federation revenues. More serious is the fact that duty-free admission of Singapore manufactures would presumably be at least a technical infringement of the most-favored-nation clauses of the General Agreement on Tariffs and Trade.[3] However, there may be ways of avoiding this difficulty in the special circumstances of Malaya, and they should certainly be explored.

We also recommend that steps be taken to ensure that mainland manufacturers are not burdened with import duties on major items of their raw materials or capital equipment. With the present structure of the Federation tariff, this question does not appear to arise in any important cases, but it may demand more attention in the future.

Education and Training

The general progress of education in Malaya, and especially the progress of the English schools, will undoubtedly be a major factor making for more rapid industrial development. But Malaya can afford to maintain its educational plans only if the economy is prosperous, and much of the economic value of the education will be lost if a proper place is not given to the types of education and training, in and out of school, that contribute directly to industrial efficiency. This is not only because modern industry is so dependent on special skills—from those of the machine operator in a production line to those of the machine-tool maker, and beyond to the professional skills of the chemist and engineer—but also because an education system which does not give a conspicuous place to manual and technical achievements is likely to encourage social attitudes, such as the prestige of the "white collar" job, which are out of harmony with industrial development.

In the past, very little attention has been paid in Malaya to the training of an industrial labor force because skilled workers have normally come

---

[3] Under the General Agreement on Tariffs and Trade, the United Kingdom Government has accepted certain obligations on behalf of dependent territories. These do not impose any restrictions on the revision of tariff rates, except that under the most-favored-nation provisions the margins between preferential and general rates of duty cannot be widened beyond those in force on 10th April 1947 (Articles I and II). However, the products of all contracting parties are entitled to national treatment in internal taxes, charges, and other regulations affecting sale or distribution (Article III). There are also provisions regulating the use of quantitative restrictions on imports for the protection of local industries (Article XVIII).

as immigrants from China. Such training as there is consists mainly of the passing on of skills from one worker to another, typically a part of the Chinese "family" system, and of internal training schemes introduced by a few large firms which have been somewhat discouraged by the difficulty of retaining workers once they have been trained. There is no standard system of apprenticeship leading to regulated or easily recognizable trade qualifications. Both the Federation and Singapore have made a beginning toward developing technical schools, and this will be carried further in Singapore with the opening of the Polytechnic Institute. The subject of vocational education is discussed further in Technical Report 9 on Education.

We must emphasize that one of the greatest obstacles to the general development of an efficient scale of factory operation is the absence or inadequacy of publicly available training facilities and publicly recognized trade qualifications for skilled industrial workers. Higher forms of technical and professional education are equally important, though for the time being these gaps can often be more readily filled by sending Malayans overseas for training or by importing qualified personnel from overseas. To some extent the gaps in training facilities for skilled workers can also be made good in this way—for instance, admission under the immigration regulations was granted for a limited period to some skilled workers needed in connection with the recently established Singapore spinning factory. No doubt similar arrangements will be made in other suitable cases, but this can only be a temporary expedient and is not a practical substitute for new education and training facilities to produce the skilled workers and technicians that are needed.

Technological and Market Research

Up to the present there has been practically no Malayan research effort devoted to problems directly bearing on Malaya's industrial future. Experience in other countries shows that systematic research, in industrial as in other spheres, often pays for itself many times over.

We recommend the establishment, on a Malayan basis, of an Institute of Industrial Research, to investigate both the technological and economic aspects of secondary industries in Malaya. It should be pan-Malayan, because the industrial problems of Singapore and the Federation are so inter-connected that separate (and still more, rival) organizations in the two territories would involve an obvious waste of very scarce scientific resources. It should probably devote the greater part of its efforts and budget to technological inquiries, but it should also be concerned with the market and other economic problems of the industries it studies, if only to make sure that its technological work is concentrated at points most likely to give fruitful results. Its permanent staff should be highly qualified, but quite small, and should regard itself as a nucleus around which can be collected outside experts and experienced industrialists from overseas to work on particular problems for varying periods. In some cases it should be possible to obtain these experts through the facilities of the Colombo Plan and the United Nations technical assistance programs. The Institute should have its own laboratory facilities, and should be prepared to set up pilot plants to determine the practicability of industrial processes, but a considerable part of its work would consist of assembling knowledge gained elsewhere and bringing it to bear on Malayan problems.

The problems the Institute might study would include the identification, processing and industrial uses of materials actually or potentially available from local sources; the testing and standardization of industrial products; the improvement of industrial techniques and the utilization of by-products; the solution of specific technical difficulties encountered by Malayan industrial enterprises; and the estimation of costs and market opportunities in Malaya for particular industries whose establishment may be contemplated.

The results of this work would be made available in various ways, ranging from the publication of technical brochures to the confidential communication of the outcome of research commissioned by private firms at their own expense. Some of the work would be done at government request, as a contribution to particular problems of policy—e.g., in connection with applications for tariff protection, or other forms of government assistance. The Institute would need to cooperate closely with government departments and other organizations already engaged in allied survey and research work. However, the Institute itself should not be administered as a government department, since the nature of its work would require flexibility and scientific independence.

The costs of such an Institute can only be guessed at, especially since it is impossible to say in advance what portion of its expenses might be borne by international agencies or private commissions, but they should not be very great. The mission considers that it would be reasonable to contemplate a capital outlay of perhaps $2 million on buildings and laboratory equipment, and recurrent expenditure of perhaps $1 million annually when the Institute is in full operation.

We suggest that, if our recommendation is accepted in principle, problems of the establishment and staffing of the Institute should be discussed in the first instance with the International Bank for Reconstruction and Development, which has had experience with similar projects in other places.

Industrial Finance

The mission found great difficulty in obtaining any general picture of the availability and character of finance for industrial enterprise. It is predominantly a matter of private transactions which take place within circles of varying degrees of intimacy among the Chinese community. Most Chinese enterprises appear to have begun on a small "family" basis, and to have been built up (where they have been built up on any scale) chiefly by reinvestment of profits. Many of the larger ones are constituted as private companies, and some of these include an element of capital contributed from wider circles. The relatively few European industrial enterprises have mostly been established with overseas capital (even when they are incorporated in Malaya); in only a handful of cases were their shares issued on the Singapore stock market.

The banks have shown themselves willing to provide short-term credit for industrial working capital to reputable firms against the security of commodities or other good collateral, but it is unlikely that the volume of this business is large. Interest rates charged by the banks range from $4\frac{1}{2}\%$ per annum to more than 6%. We were unable to gather any systematic evidence as to how large a part Chinese and Indian money-lending may play in industrial finance, but it is probably considerable among the smaller enterprises, at interest rates which are often very high and which vary greatly according to the standing or circumstances of the borrower. Except for limited financing by the Colonial Development Corporation and RIDA, there appears to be no institutional source or regular channel for medium- and long-term capital for industry.

The apparent availability of capital may be a passing phase, associated with the accumulation of savings out of the profits of the 1950-51 tin and rubber boom. It may also be partly because not enough Malayan entrepreneurs are yet aware of the advantages of operation on an efficient factory scale. We believe that new institutional arrangements for industrial finance will become necessary and have suggested elsewhere that the proposed Central Bank give early consideration to this need. We have indicated broadly the institutional arrangements for this purpose which we believe should be considered. Meanwhile, we have also suggested that in appropriate and carefully investigated cases the government should, if necessary, be prepared to guarantee bank advances to sound industrial projects of substantial importance. Such guarantee should be approached cautiously, since the contingent liability involved might easily lead to a false sense of security, and since government officials are probably not in as good a position to assess industrial risks as would be the staff of an independent financial institution. Where such guarantees are given for substantial sums the government may be obliged to take steps to safeguard its interests (e.g., by appointing an experienced member of the business community with a watching brief as an official nominee on the board of directors) but it would be well advised not to intervene in the management of the enterprise. We would stress that such guarantees should be given very sparingly and only where the inadequacy of alternative financial sources is clearly established.

Experience as to the availability of finance for projects considered worth while by the proposed Institute of Industrial Research should in the future be an important guide to the adequacy of sources of industrial capital.

Economic Stability

In more indirect ways than the facilitation of industrial finance, the governments and the Central Bank should be able to help industrial development maintain a steadier course in the face of fluctuations in Malaya's main export markets.[4] But any violent fluctuations in the price of rubber, and to a lesser extent in the price of tin, are inevitably unsettling for Malayan secondary industries competing with foreign industries; it is hard to prevent industrial wage rates moving to some extent in sympathy with the prevailing rates in the rubber and tin industries, and the competitive position of secondary industries against foreign suppliers tends to

---

[4] See Technical Report 12 on Currency and Banking.

shift up and down accordingly. For industries serving a home market with little prospect of foreign competition, this does not matter—when rubber is booming, for example, and wages are high, they can afford to raise their prices to offset higher costs. But as industrial development brings a wider range of Malayan industries into direct competition with foreign suppliers, any serious instability of Malayan costs must present more difficult problems.

Fortunately, the rubber and tin markets promise in future to be more stable than in the past. Industrial wage rates may also be less influenced by the fluctuations of the major primary industries if the Malayan labor force is looking more and more to industrial employment to absorb its annual growth. Further, the circumstances that make for high rubber and tin prices should also often make for higher costs in foreign industries as well as in Malaya. By adopting a more steeply progressive scale of export duties at higher ranges of rubber prices (which we recommend elsewhere), the Federation Government should be able to cut off a good deal of the internal effects of rubber price movements. There is also some case for erring slightly on the generous side in the granting of tariff protection, so as to provide a margin for cost fluctuations.

Although we recognize the risks of instability to which internationally-competitive secondary industries are exposed in an economy dominated by one or two primary export commodities, we think that, given sympathetic attention to the economic situation of secondary industry in the framing of fiscal, monetary and other policies, the difficulties should not be insuperable. And the progress of industrial development will itself reduce the risks, by reducing the extent to which the Malayan economy is dominated by its staple exports.

Overseas Enterprise

Malaya has imposed no restraints on overseas enterprise and capital movements (beyond those which are general to the sterling area). Clearly this policy should be continued, not only because any inflow of capital is a useful contribution to the financing of Malayan development, but also because the technical "know-how" of overseas firms is often almost indispensable for successful industrial development in particular directions.

In some instances, overseas technology and facilities for technological advancement are needed to make an important contribution to Malayan industrial development, but overseas firms are reluctant for political or other reasons to invest large sums in Malayan ventures. We recommend that in such cases the governments invite the participation of these firms through management contracts assuring adequate managerial authority to the contracting firms and establishing a suitable basis of remuneration (e.g., profit-sharing, either alone or combined with a fixed fee) over a mutually satisfactory period. It is desirable, though not essential, that the managing firm should have some stake in the capital of the undertaking. Capital requirements which the managing firm is not prepared to meet should, if necessary, be contributed or guaranteed in the first instance by the government, but from the beginning local investors should be encouraged to participate as fully as possible and the object should be eventually to dispose of any government interest to private shareholders. Rubber manufacturing and textile projects are two examples which come readily to mind as possibilities for the use of this approach, which has been successfully employed in a number of instances by underdeveloped countries.

Provisions of the Income Tax Law

Several underdeveloped countries, including some British colonies, have adopted what is often called "pioneer industry" legislation, under which new industries may be granted exemption from income tax on their profits for a period of years, special concessions in depreciation allowances, and other tax privileges.

In Malaya all enterprises are allowed to offset losses over the previous six years against current profits in the assessment of taxable income. Initial depreciation allowances are 10% of the capital expenditure in respect of buildings, and 20% in respect of other capital expenditure; thereafter, annual depreciation is allowed for buildings at the rate of 2%, and for various kinds of industrial capital equipment at rates ranging from 5% to 20% (calculated on the original cost of the asset as reduced by the initial and annual depreciation allowances of previous years).

We believe that general concessions along the lines now followed are likely to be more effective in Malaya in encouraging industrial development than any attempt to distinguish "new" industries as such under "pioneer industry" legislation. New Malayan industries should mostly grow out of the wide range of existing enterprises, and special tax concessions to "new" industries would, in our opinion, involve invidious comparisons of a very difficult and unnecessary kind. Generous depreciation allowances automatically favor the industries and enterprises that are developing most rapidly in terms of the acquisition of capital assets.

Administrative Arrangements

In Singapore, the Department of Commerce and Industry is responsible for measures to encourage industrial development. It is ready to assist in the acquisition of factory sites and generally to give a helping hand to new enterprises. Although its staff on the industrial side may need to be gradually expanded, it does not appear that any major changes in organization or responsibilities are called for.

A special feature of Singapore's industrial planning is the Master Plan now being prepared for the broad lines of development of the island and for the zoning of land-use, including provision for the setting aside of special areas for factory development. Two such areas have already been established. One is an "industrial estate" owned and managed by the Colonial Development Corporation, the center of activity for the factories to which the Corporation has contributed finance. The other is an area developed by the Singapore Improvement Trust, on which several factories are now operating; sites are made available on 99-year lease, the lessees being responsible for the erection of factories. Most of the important new industries established in Singapore since the war are located in those two areas. The concentration of factory development in areas of this kind has considerable advantages, not only from a town-planning viewpoint, but from the point of view of technical cooperation and economy in the provision of ancillary services. In the Federation, a special industrial area is being developed at Petaling Jaya, near Kuala Lumpur. We thoroughly endorse this policy and recommend that consideration be given to extending the concept of the "industrial estate" along lines which have proved successful in the United Kingdom and elsewhere, by official construction of factory space for rental or hire-purchase by private firms. This is a particularly effective way of overcoming difficulties of industrial long-term finance, and probably less risky than the making of loans to particular firms.

Singapore's administrative problems in relation to industry are comparatively simple compared with those of the Federation, since the latter has many scattered industrial centers to consider, as well as problems of tariff policy which do not arise in Singapore. The handling of industrial development matters is at present shared between the Economic and Trade Divisions of the Federation Treasury, both under the supervision of the Member for Economic Affairs. Elsewhere we recommend the establishment of an Economic Secretariat, absorbing some of the functions of the Economic Division, and including among its functions consideration of the broader issues of industrial and other forms of development. In addition, an organization is needed to handle the more specific administrative aspect of industrial development.

We recommend that alongside the Trade Division there be established a Division of Industrial Development. Under the supervision of the Member for Economic Affairs, the duties of this Division should include all the detailed work involved in reviewing the protective aspects of the Federation tariff, investigating applications for protective duties, and keeping an eye on the efficiency and selling prices of protected industries to make sure that protection is not being abused. It should handle requests by local industries for relief from duties affecting their procurement of materials or equipment; assist in the investigational and other work associated with negotiations with overseas enterprises; advise upon cases in which questions of government guarantee of industrial finance may arise; act as a center of liaison between the proposed Institute of Industrial Research and the government, and as a channel through which arrangements can be made for the dissemination, in appropriate cases, of the Institute's research results, at the State and district level throughout the Federation. It should cooperate with the Departments of Education and Labour in planning the development of vocational education and training. It should also be responsible for working out plans for "industrial estates" along the lines already discussed and should otherwise facilitate the acquisition of factory sites. Generally, the Division of Industrial Development should be the point of contact between secondary industries and the government, and should especially seek to help new enterprises with the official and other initial problems of their establishment.

TECHNICAL REPORT 9 *EDUCATION*

FEDERATION[1]

I INTRODUCTION

Public education has become a primary function of government in Malaya and already occupies a position of considerable magnitude and high priority in the budget. Nevertheless, further increases in education costs must be anticipated: present educational needs are only partially met and the school age population is growing at a rate which may not be exceeded by that of any country in the world. Complicating factors are the rapidity with which the demand for education emerged after World War II, the racial and linguistic complexity of the population, and the urgent social and political—as well as economic—needs precipitated by the imminence of self-government. Rising costs of education are not peculiar to Malaya; they present problems in many countries, especially in those with economies not yet extensively developed.

A sound program of education will not be possible without solution of the technical problems, many of which are outside the scope of this report; neither will a sound program be possible unless it is within the resources of the nation, having regard for other demands on the economy. To achieve a balanced perspective it is helpful first to look backward, to recall the evolution of public education in Malaya, to review the diligent efforts already made to resolve the perplexing problems, and to re-examine the potentials and probable costs of alternative proposals for the future.

Secular education began in Malaya under the stimulus of British missionaries and administrators a century and a half ago. The first school

[1] A preliminary draft of this part of the Technical Report was made available to the Federation Government on request of the High Commissioner in July-August 1954. The Government subsequently submitted a White Paper on Education Policy (No. 67 of 1954) to the Legislative Council, and it was adopted on October 7, 1954. Though there are some differences on important details, the broad educational policies and objectives, the main priorities and the principal elements of the financial program in the White Paper are in substantial agreement with the recommendations developed in this Report. The White Paper did not become available to the mission in time for incorporation of specific comparisons here, but some major items are noted in Chapter 7.

was established in Penang in 1816 by the efforts of the Church of England with financial assistance from the East India Company. It was attended by children of all races, with English the language of instruction; there were vernacular sections and branch schools in outlying districts, instructing in the languages the children spoke at home. Here was the beginning of the present-day pattern.

For a long time there was general indifference toward both English and vernacular education but interest slowly awakened and many schools of both types were established. Malay, Chinese and Indian vernacular schools multiplied, and the Christian churches continued to receive financial assistance from the government and to provide English education. The government also established and operated schools.

Before World War II there were few schools that could not take more pupils than were enrolled. The Chinese had largely developed their own schools to meet their needs and desires, and many sent their children to China for advanced education. The Indians, who lived mainly on rubber estates, were provided with at least rudimentary schooling in accordance with the requirements of a labor ordinance. In the case of the Malays, attendance for four years was made compulsory for boys early in the century when it became evident that their school enrollment was developing very slowly.

An amazing change of attitude toward education occurred during the Japanese occupation. Families of all races became eager to have their children educated. The burden on the disrupted and partially damaged schools was greatly increased by a shortage of teachers and by the needs of older children whose education had been interrupted by the war. The difficult task of reopening the schools first fell to the British Military Administration. In April 1946 the schools were transferred to the Education Department of the newly formed Malayan Union which included the nine Malay States and the Settlements of Penang and Malacca.[2] The Department was faced with problems of organization and with a rapidly expanding school population. Before the war about 263,000 children had been in school throughout the Malay Peninsula; in January 1946 there were approximately 266,000; by March, at the close of the British Military Administration, 309,000, and the number was climbing rapidly.

According to the 1947 census, 62% of the population 15 years of age and over was illiterate (43% of the males and 83% of the females).

[2] Singapore became a separate Colony.

In February 1948 the constitutional change from Union to Federation established a new division of responsibility for education. The Federation Agreement assigned to the Federal Government responsibility for a common policy and a common system of administration for primary, secondary and trade school education, and direct obligation for technical and higher education and the training of teachers; to the State and Settlement Governments, executive authority for the primary, secondary and trade schools. This division still obtains.

An educational crisis began to be evident as the postwar rise in enrollments and costs gained momentum. There were extensive considerations of policies and principles to be followed—by a Central Advisory Committee on Education established in 1949; a committee on Malay education (Mr. L. J. Barnes, Chairman); a study team on Chinese education (Mr. W. P. Fenn and Dr. Wu Teh-Yao); and by a Special Committee appointed to recommend legislation. National education policy was crystallized late in 1952 with the passage of a comprehensive Federal ordinance. It set as an eventual goal free compulsory six-year primary education for children 6+ to 12+ and the establishment of national primary schools. The national schools would be open to children of all races with the medium of instruction either of the official languages at the option of the people in the area. In Malay-medium schools, English would be taught to every pupil from the beginning of the first year; in English-medium schools, Malay would be taught from the beginning of the third year. All national schools would be required to provide facilities for the teaching of Tamil or Chinese (Mandarin) when parents of 15 or more children of the same linguistic standard ask for it. Provision would also be made for religious or, with pupils whose parents have no religion, moral instruction.

With the enactment of the Education Ordinance, 1952, the Federal Government committed itself to enlightened but admittedly ambitious goals which were frankly recognized as possible of attainment only in the course of decades. The technical difficulties in implementing the Ordinance became increasingly clear within a year. Enacted at a time of national prosperity, the cost implications had been considered only in vague and general terms though it was plainly evident that the program carried a potential financial commitment several times as large as then current education costs. With the decline in world rubber and tin prices new economic situations and needs developed which have compelled a careful review of the outlook for education.

The government has made great efforts to meet the wide and intense postwar demand for the education of the unusually large proportion of the population which is of primary school age (20% of the total in 1954, and rising). Despite an increase in school enrollments from 400,000 to over 700,000 between 1947 and 1953 and in public expenditures from $16 million to $95 million, further expansions in both still must be expected. In the government and aided schools there are places for only 56% of the children of primary school age and 6% of those of secondary school age, and the true percentages of school age enrollment are even less because many in the schools are overage. Education is now widely regarded as equipment for a livelihood, and ever-larger numbers of families demand places for their children in primary school, make sacrifices to keep their girls as well as their boys in school, and want secondary and technical, post-secondary or university education for their young people.

There are also other reasons to expect rising costs. Modernization of vernacular education, which has lagged qualitatively behind English education, calls for higher expenditures. Though government financial support to the Chinese schools is now more generous than formerly, it still does not cover as large a portion of their operating expenses as does the aid given to English schools. The Chinese also ask for equality of treatment with Malays and Indians in the availability of free primary education. Everywhere in the Federation and among all racial groups there is mounting demand for English education, which costs the government at least twice as much per pupil as vernacular education. Finally, the primary school age population is expected to increase by more than 40% between 1954 and 1960—from 1.2 million to 1.7 million. The prospects for offsetting economies are limited.

This outlook has precipitated an issue of national political as well as economic policy. Government and community leaders, preparing for an elective legislature and self-government and confronted by the urgent need to weld the more or less disparate racial groups into one nation, regard education as an essential means for the Malayanization of the population.

The technical, economic and political problems are interrelated and lead to more or less common questions. What should be the immediate pattern of the education program? How much and what kinds of education do people want? How much do they need for literacy, for vocational purposes, for civic ends? How much is feasible? How much is compatible with the resources of the economy? How are the costs to be financed?

This report does not undertake to answer all such questions. It attempts to help those who must face them and be responsible for the decisions.

II THE PRESENT SYSTEM OF EDUCATION

A GENERAL SUMMARY

Primary education, designed as a six-year course for children between the ages of 6+ and 12+, is provided by the States and Settlements in primary schools and in the primary departments of comprehensive schools having both primary and secondary classes. Enrollments include some younger and many older children, attendance of the latter being extensively permitted because education was badly interrupted during the occupation and enrollment has been grossly incomplete in the "correct" school ages.

Most primary schools are of the vernacular type, identified by the language used as the medium of instruction—Malay, Chinese (using Kuo Yu (Mandarin)) and Indian (using various languages, mainly Tamil). The remainder are English. With minor exceptions, the Malay, Chinese and Indian schools are attended only by Malay, Chinese and Indian children, respectively, but children of all races attend English schools and study together.

General secondary education is provided only in English and Chinese schools, both of which charge fees. The English schools have a five-year course (Forms I-V) which leads to the Cambridge School Certificate. Malay, Kuo Yu and Tamil are offered as subjects. A small number of pupils continue in post-certificate university preparatory classes (Form VI). The Chinese secondary schools provide a six-year course (three years of junior middle and three of senior middle school), with instruction in the medium of Kuo Yu. English is taught as a subject and is increasingly used for part of the instruction.

Primary and secondary schools are commonly identified according to the type of financing and management. *Government schools* are those financed and managed by the Federation or the States and Settlements. *Aided schools* are managed by voluntary agencies; they meet government standards and receive financial grants from the government. Many private schools, mainly English and Chinese, receive no aid from the government.

Registration of all schools and teachers is required. Admission of schools to the register depends on observance of standards with respect to management, facilities, health and safety, submission of curricula, financial accounting and nonengagement in political activites.

Many schools operate only one session a day despite acute need for expansion of enrollments. Even if teachers were available, double sessions would not be generally feasible because most of the population is rural and many children live where transportation is limited or where schools are wholly lacking.

Education for girls has lagged and the educators have been making special efforts to expand it. Schools were originally organized as boys' or girls' schools, but girls are admitted to boys' schools where there are none for girls. Coeducational schools have recently been established.

School health services are provided by the medical departments of the States and Settlements.

Specialized training on the secondary level is provided in various kinds of institutions and through diverse arrangements. Much of it is teacher training. There are some junior technical (trade) schools, and one-year courses are given at the College of Agriculture and at the School of Forestry.

Post-secondary education is provided at the Technical College, Kuala Lumpur, and the College of Agriculture. There is a new Military Academy. A large number of men and women teachers in the English schools attend part-time normal classes. There are also a few commercial schools. In August 1954 a two-year residential college to train teachers for the English schools was opened at Kota Bharu, Kelantan. In addition a teacher-training college is operated at Federation expense in Kirkby, England, and arrangements have been made for a second such college to begin operation in 1955. Both the Federation and Singapore are served by the University of Malaya which offers professional training in education, medicine, dentistry and pharmacy.

B MAJOR ELEMENTS OF THE EDUCATION SYSTEM

English Schools

English is the language of instruction in English schools. They are closely patterned in curriculum and extracurricular activities on schools in the United Kingdom and have an importance in Malaya disproportionate to their number or enrollments. English education is in great demand for the economic and political advantages it affords. It is a means of becoming prepared for admission to institutions of higher learning at home and abroad. English schools maintained or aided by government funds have been quickly responsive to Western standards and to improvements in teaching methods and in the scope and content of courses. In turn they have served to raise the levels of both the vernacular schools and the English private schools.

In 1953 in a total enrollment of 102,666 in government and aided English schools, Malays numbered 26,091, Chinese 52,484, Indians 21,090 and other races 3,001. Most English schools are located in urban areas and have large Chinese enrollments because the Chinese population is heavily concentrated in cities. The teachers are also of many races. Of 3,605 on the staffs of government and aided schools in 1953, "European" (mainly British but including French, Italians, Germans and Americans) numbered 195, Malays 273, Eurasians 327, Indians 1,135, Chinese 1,587, and others 88.

Government aided English schools are for the most part managed by missionary bodies assisted by liberal government grants.[3] The women of Malaya owe a great debt to the Missions in advancing their educational opportunities and providing schools acceptable to parents when the education of girls was counter to tradition. In 1953 about 75% of the girls attending English schools were in Mission schools.

Most government and aided English schools offer both primary and secondary education. The combined courses cover eleven years, at the end of which pupils should be prepared for the Cambridge School Certificate Examination.[4] A few schools have added special classes (Form VI) of 20 months to prepare for entrance to the University of Malaya and of 24 months to prepare for entrance to universities and other institutions of higher learning overseas. Some of the private English schools carry the

---

[3] The Christian Brothers (French), the Dames de St. Maur of the Convents of the Holy Infant Jesus (French), the American Methodist Mission, the Church of England, the Canossian Roman Catholic (Italian) Order, the Plymouth Brethren, the Mission Etrangeres (French) and the Roman Catholic Mission. For terms of grants from the government see pp. 454-455.

[4] The Overseas School Certificate Examination of the University of Cambridge Local Examination Syndicate is adapted to Malaya but with the standard remaining on Cambridge School Certificate level. A test in oral English is added. The school certificate is requisite to many types of employment and is essential for those intending to teach in English schools.

pupils to School Certificate level, but there are others that are mainly nursery schools and kindergartens with a year or two of primary work for children whose families plan to send them abroad for further education. The private schools serve a useful function in providing English education for those who cannot meet the strict age or study requirements of the government and aided schools.

Multi-lingualism presents special difficulties. In a single entering class the pupils may come with great diversity of language; some may speak and understand only one and some only another among half a dozen or more Asian languages or dialects. Through the "direct" method of instruction, they soon acquire an essential understanding of classroom activities and a simple common English vocabulary. All through the primary school years much stress is laid on spoken English. The period of greatest difficulty comes perhaps in the later years when the content of the course shifts from mainly factual and objective to more conceptual and abstruse subjects.

Until 1952 the first seven years were called the primary course, with the following four years secondary; now only the first six years are classified as primary with a five-year secondary course. There has been some experimentation with acceleration of the brighter children to complete the primary course in five years by special instruction rather than by double promotion.

The government and aided English schools make special provision for Malay children selected on merit from the Malay vernacular schools. Two years of special work with emphasis on English prepares them to join the regular classes of English schools at the sixth year level. Some of the schools have hostel provisions for these students. In 1953, 3,766 entered the Special Malay Classes and 4,407 were accepted for admission in 1954. There is no similar special provision for the children attending Chinese or Indian schools. About one child in seven in primary schools is in an English school.

The secondary English school course is academic in nature, with the languages offered as elective subjects mainly Asian: Malay, Kuo Yu and some of the Indian languages. General science, domestic science, physics and chemistry have been added as rapidly as teachers and laboratory facilities have become available. Enrollments in the secondary English classes diminish substantially from the first to the fifth year, as shown below by the September 1953 enrollments. The recent increases in primary enrollments are still reflected only in the first years of the secondary schools.

School Year[a]	Govt. & Aided	Private	School Year[b]	Govt. & Aided	Private
1	12,422	6,919	7	10,060	3,168
2	10,262	4,548	8	9,081	2,106
3	9,231	4,672	9	6,774	1,418
4	13,083[c]	4,879	10	5,470	767
5	12,476[c]	4,816	11	3,044	165
6	10,481	4,075	12–13[d]	282	62
Total	67,955	29,909	Total	34,711	7,686

[a] Since 1952 the primary years have been known as Standards I–VI. When the course was seven years the classes were Primary I and II followed by Standards I–V.

[b] Secondary school years are known as Forms I–VI. Until 1952 the secondary classes were Standards VI–VIII, School Certificate and post-Certificate classes.

[c] Includes the enrollments in Special Malay Classes.

[d] Since these are September enrollments, the number in the post-certificate course (Form VI) has already been reduced by those who have left to enter the University of Malaya.

In view of the large demand for places in the government and aided English schools, admissions to the first year are largely restricted to the six to eight year age group, with preference currently given to those who are in their eighth year and would be too old to be eligible the following year. This factor and a system of dropping children who fail of promotion in two subsequent years make those attending nearer true primary age than in any other type of school. At the end of the last primary year the pupils take an examination set by the school for admission to the first secondary year. At the close of the 1953 school year nearly four-fifths of the pupils who were candidates passed the examination. There is currently discussion of setting a common examination for all schools.

There were 4,584 teachers on the staffs of all English schools in 1953, of whom 389 held a university degree; 3,922 had completed the general secondary (School Certificate) course but of these 1,779 were untrained or only partially trained (1,162 were in part-time normal classes); and 273 had not completed a secondary school course.

The government and aided English schools expanded rapidly between 1946 and 1954. For example, 19 new schools were opened in 1952, bringing the total to 106, and 167 new classrooms (including 17 science rooms) were added to old schools.[5]

All English schools charge fees, generally higher in private than in government and aided schools. In the latter they are $2.50 a month for primary classes and $5.00 for secondary. Special provision is made for free places and scholarships. In 1953 these aggregated 19,245 or 19% of enrollments; by race, the proportions were: Europeans and Eurasians, 2.2%; Malays (including the selected children who transferred from vernacular schools), 72.6%; Chinese, 16.8%; Indians, 7.9%; other Malaysians, 0.3%; and others, 0.2%.

The costs of maintaining a primary school pupil at government and aided English schools are about $200 a year for the primary years, $300-400 for the secondary years, and $1,000 for the Form VI post-certificate classes. Form VI classes are small and have well qualified and highly paid teachers.

Malay and Indian Schools

It has long been the policy of the government to encourage and provide education for the Malays. More children attend Malay than other types of schools, 342,163 out of total enrollment of 776,739 in all the schools of the Federation in September 1953. There were 2,055 Malay schools, of which 1,622 were government schools, 423 were aided by the government,[6] and 10 were private unaided schools.

[5] In connection with costs to be considered later, the following are standard specifications for English school facilities: A classroom to accommodate 40 children is 675 square feet in area which gives each child 15 square feet, with 75 square feet for the teacher, blackboard and cupboards. Provision has also to be made for corridors, verandahs and assembly hall, lavatories, office space, storage space, craft rooms and, in the case of secondary schools, special rooms for science, domestic science, art and geography, with the result that at least 45 square feet per child must be allowed when planning a school building. Quarters for teachers must also be provided in many cases. In many areas it is not possible to obtain bids which work out at less than $10,000 for one classroom of the simplest type of construction. (Annual Report, 1952, Department of Education.) In some localities bids on these specifications were as high as $15,000 per classroom in 1954.

[6] Rural interest in Malay education has been shown by the development of Ra'ayat or "people's" schools. These are built at the initiative of the people of small villages. A village or group of villages submits a request for a government grant to help build a school and to pay the salaries of teachers. If the plan meets approval, the Department of Education advises on the site and assists in recruitment of teachers. When such schools prove of permanent value they may be taken over by the government.

The government Malay school system provides free primary education. There are no Malay general secondary schools and only a few offering vocational or trade courses. Malay education has a strong rural bias, attempting to combine lasting literacy and such subjects as gardening, handicrafts, nutrition and domestic science adapted to the needs of the home environment. All Malay children receive religious instruction either in school or after school hours in mosques.[7]

Indian schools are similar in many respects to the Malay schools. They provide education for the 11% Indian minority in Malaya and are the fewest in number of any type of school. Their September 1953 enrollment was only 43,434. All Indian schools are primary schools, and Tamil is the medium of instruction in most of them. Some schools teach in Hindi, Punjabi, Malayalam, Telegu, Gujerati or Gurkhali but these are not usually aided schools. Indian education is free (except in a few private schools). This is a result of the Labour Ordinance requiring the owners of estates and mines to maintain schools for their employees' children if there are 10 or more between the ages of 7 and 14. Federal and State/Settlement Governments as employers of Indian labor also opened free schools for Indians, mainly in urban centers where their labor forces were concentrated. In 1953 when there were 869 Indian schools, 694 were estate schools with about 60% of the Indian school enrollment.

Both Malay and Indian schools are mainly rural schools offering six-year primary courses, although only a fraction actually provide the full six;[8] and, in 1953, 101 Malay schools and 29 Indian schools had a seventh year for those intending to become teachers. Malays may be employed at the age of 14 and Indians at the age of 16 as "pupil teachers" after completion of their own primary school course.

There are two Malay teacher-training institutions operated by the Federal Government, one for men (Sultan Idris Training College, Tanjong Malim) and one for women (The Malay Women's Training College, Malacca). They are classified as secondary education, and offer three-year courses for pupils from Malay primary schools. These training colleges have been used as a focus for improving teaching in Malay schools. There are no Indian teacher-training institutions.

[7] Muslim religious schools are under the State/Settlement departments concerned with Malay religious affairs and are not financed through the Department of Education or the education funds.

[8] There were sixth year classes in 478 of the 2,055 Malay schools and in 518 of the 869 Indian schools.

The rural schools face common difficulties in finding teachers who are willing to serve in remote one- and two-teacher schools. Still more difficult is the provision of instruction in English for both types of schools, and in Malay for the Indian schools, where only part-time services of specially trained teachers are required.

It is evident from the following tabulation for government and aided schools in 1953 that the number of pupils enrolled decreases rapidly in successive school years. In that year only 88 Malays and 627 Indians were attending private vernacular schools. Seventh-year classes for those intending to become teachers were attended by 1,085 Malays and 116 Indians.

School Year	Malay		Indian	
	Number	Percent	Number	Percent
1	106,597	31.4	18,313	42.9
2	73,971	22.0	8,360	19.6
3	63,539	18.8	5,925	13.9
4	46,872[a]	13.8	5,005	11.8
5	32,191[a]	9.4	3,113	7.3
6	14,847	4.6	1,914	4.5
Total	338,017	100.0	42,630	100.0

[a] The fourth and fifth year classes were diminished by 6,176 pupils attending Special Malay Classes in English schools.

There were no teachers with university degrees in Malay and Indian government and aided primary schools in 1953. In the Malay schools, 3,275 had been teacher-college trained and another 161 had completed secondary courses; 8,571 had not completed secondary courses but 2,136 had been trained. In the Indian schools only 9 out of 1,504 teachers had completed secondary courses and 695 had been trained.

In addition, 249 teachers of English taught in 314 Malay schools and 47 in Indian schools, and 34 teachers of Malay in Indian schools.

Rural Malay and Indian school buildings are usually simple in structure. The teachers themselves make much of their own education apparatus.

The annual cost to government of Malay and Indian school education is approximately $80-100 per student.

Chinese Schools

Chinese schools in Malaya have a different origin and history from Malay, Indian or English schools. Because there was no provision for their schooling, the Chinese living either temporarily or permanently in Malaya established their own schools (as well as giving generous financial support to English schools). Some schools were organized by individuals and some by groups, generally using teachers trained in China and textbooks from China which were readily available and familiar to the teachers.[9] Trends in both education and politics in China were felt in Malaya. The shift from the use of various home dialects to instruction in Kuo Yu in China was followed by a similar change in Malayan Chinese schools. The nationalist movement in China led to Kuomintang political propaganda among the overseas Chinese of Southeast Asia.

After World War I the Government of Malaya, which previously had been quite indifferent to the Chinese schools, became actively interested. For the first time, some of the schools were given a limited amount of aid —a small sum for each student enrolled. The Chinese schools came under the Protector of Chinese; an officer of the Protectorate was attached to the Education Department and was given the title of Assistant Director of Education (Chinese). After World War II Chinese schools were brought under the Department of Education.

The establishment of the People's Republic in China and the beginning of the emergency in Malaya caused renewed attention to be given to the Chinese schools. The rise of nationalism in Malaya as the country moves toward self-government and independence, and continued discussion of improvement and expansion of the educational system and of its role in unifying and welding the races into a single Malayan nation, have made education, and particularly the education of the Chinese, a leading political issue.

It will be seen later (p. 473) that the distribution of government expenditures on education for the several racial groups closely approximates racial proportions in the population. Nevertheless, there being only three government Chinese schools, the Chinese are said to believe that their education is still largely provided on their own initiative and at their own expense, and that they are treated less generously than other racial groups.

[9] Textbooks prepared for use in Malaya are now being introduced, following intensive study and revision of the curricula.

With only a few exceptions fees are required in Chinese schools, generally larger than those charged by government and aided English schools. The government spent $95,000 in 1953 for reimbursement of fees for "necessitous" children in Chinese schools. A recent change (1952) provides much more generous aid to qualifying Chinese schools but still does not bring it to the level of aid to the English schools.[10]

The Chinese schools offer both primary and secondary education. Kindergarten often precedes the primary course of six years (not all schools offer the full primary course). The secondary school course is also six years; the first three comprise "junior middle school" and the final three years "senior middle school." Some senior middle schools, including one Federal Government school (Green Lane, opened in Penang in May 1952), offer two-year teacher-training courses known as "senior normal" classes.

There were 1,214 Chinese schools in 1953: 3 government, 846 government aided, 53 operated by public corporations, and 312 unaided private schools. Of the total, 47 provided secondary school courses but only nine of these included senior middle as well as junior middle school and 43 also had primary departments.

In the data on Chinese school enrollments by school years in 1953, given below, it will be noted that there is a large decrease from year to year in both the primary and secondary schools; and that the total enrollment in the final three years of secondary school was very small.

School Year	Primary[a]		Secondary[b]	
	Number	Percent	Number	Percent
1	64,949	29.6	6,765	45.6
2	51,732	23.6	4,562	30.6
3	41,126	18.8	2,321	15.6
4	28,622	13.1	653	4.4
5	20,620	9.4	373	2.5
6	12,244	5.5	166	1.3
Total	219,293	100.0	14,840	100.0

[a] Excludes 15,853 enrolled in night primary classes and 895 children in kindergarten.
[b] Excludes 533 in senior normal classes.

[10] For a comparison of government aid given to Chinese and English schools see pp. 454-455.

There were 5,972 teachers in Chinese schools in 1953. Of these, 362 held university degrees, mainly from Chinese universities; 2,233 had completed either junior or senior middle school courses (924 were trained teachers); 3,377 had not completed secondary school courses although more than one-third were trained. In addition there were 1,308 teachers of English and 698 teachers of Malay.

Chinese school buildings vary from the most modern type to the small private school in a converted private house with little or no provision for sports or outdoor activities.

The cost to the government of educating a child in a government Chinese school averages more than $200 a year, and in an aided primary or secondary school $60. The cost will increase in the aided schools since the government has assumed responsibility for all further salary increments and allowances arising from incremental increases.

New Village Schools

The emergency Resettlement Scheme created the need to provide schooling for the children in a population of nearly 600,000. In the three years 1951-53 classrooms and teachers' quarters were built in 367 "new villages." The schools are mainly Chinese; 282 schools taught English and Malay as subjects in 1952. Large sums of money were raised by the Malayan Chinese Association for new village schools in the first years and the Legislative Council appropriated special funds for aid to these schools. Arrangements were made by the Federal and State/Settlement departments of education for the training of teachers who, as a whole, lacked the minimum qualifications required of teachers in other Chinese schools. By the end of 1953 many of the new village schools were well enough staffed and equipped to be eligible for grants-in-aid given to Chinese schools instead of having to make application under the special aid plan for new village schools.

The enrollment in new village schools in 1953 was 66,263—Chinese 51,854, Malays 4,001, Indians 348 and others 60.

Grants-in-Aid

The types of schools which are aided by government and the terms on which the voluntary agencies qualify for a grant are set out as follows:

Types of Schools	Qualifications	Assessment of Grant
English Schools	Buildings, equipment and staff must be of the same standard as those in government schools and buildings must stand on land reserved and sanctioned for educational purposes.	The difference between the approved expenditure and the approved income from school fees is made up by the government. Approved expenditure includes staff emoluments, employers contributions to staff Provident Funds and a capitation grant to cover maintenance.
Malay People's (Ra'ayat)	Permission is given by government to build Ra'ayat schools in rural, out-of-the-way areas and whenever possible government helps with the cost of buildings and in the provision of properly qualified teachers.	Government pays the salaries of teachers at rates applicable to their qualifications. In many areas a "hard-lying" allowance is paid. Schools may charge fees and supplement salaries.
Malay Schools on Estates	These schools are for the children of labor forces on estates. Estates provide the managers and the buildings and employ the teachers, all to be approved by government.	Government reimburses the management for the salaries of the teachers. These are the same as for teachers of equivalent qualifications and experience in government vernacular schools. There are no school fees.
Indian Schools	These schools must have approved managers, buildings and teachers. The buildings are provided by the management.	(As for preceding)
New Village Schools	These schools are for the children of resettled or regrouped populations and must have approved managers, buildings and teachers. The buildings are provided in part by government.	Government pays the salaries of the teachers at certain agreed rates.
Chinese Primary Schools (Fully Aided)	These schools must have approved managers, buildings and teachers, follow an approved curriculum, use approved textbooks and conform to government regulations in the treatment of teachers. The buildings are provided by the management.	The salaries are the same as for teachers of equivalent qualifications and experience in government vernacular schools, government pays a salary-grant-in-aid consisting of half the sum of the initial salaries and the cost of living allowances plus the whole of the annual salary increments and the employers' contributions to the Provident Fund. School fees may not exceed the amount necessary to meet the remaining portion of the salaries and small incidental expenses.

Types of Schools	Qualifications	Assessment of Grant
Chinese Schools (Capitation grant-aided)	These schools must have approved managers, teachers and buildings and conform to government regulations. The buildings are provided by the management.	Capitation grants are paid at three rates for primary schools and two rates for middle schools, depending on the standards of accommodation and teaching.
Chinese Schools on Estates and Mines	(As for preceding)	A grant of $50 a month is paid toward the salary of each teacher. One teacher to 30 pupils is permitted.

Government pays the full salary of teachers of English and Malay in Chinese aided schools; if part-time teachers are employed, payment is at an hourly rate. A flat grant of $400 per month is given for each senior normal (teacher-training) class in an aided Chinese secondary school, and no school fee is charged the students.

In all cases there must be a definite need for the school.

Teachers and Teacher Training

A great shortage of qualified teachers has been common to all types of schools in the 1946-54 period of rapid expansion. To remedy this a large number have been given training while teaching. Centers have been established in all the States and Settlements where the teachers attend sessions on a nonschool day (Saturday or Sunday) over a period of three years. In some cases, if the teachers are too remote from such a center, concentrated courses are given during vacation periods or the teacher takes a correspondence course provided by the Department of Education. Like the school system itself, this is a four-part arrangement with separate classes for those teaching in Malay, Indian, Chinese and English schools. There are also two-year courses for the teachers of English in vernacular schools, designed for improvement of the teachers' own English and for instruction in the principles and methods of teaching English.

Part-time teacher training is recognized as a necessary but undesirable expedient until such time as there can be established enough teacher-training institutions to sustain a corps of trained teachers adequate to the needs of the country.

There were only two government teacher-training institutions in Malaya, one for Malay men and the other for Malay women, until 1952 when the Green Lane School for teachers in Chinese schools was opened (see p. 452). In 1954 a residential teacher-training college for English school teachers was opened at Kota Bharu. In December 1951 a two-year training college had been organized in Kirkby, England; with the co-operation of the Government of the United Kingdom, a former teacher-training college was made available for the training of Malayan students. (A second college in England is planned for 1955.) It is estimated that the cost per student, including travel allowances and bursaries (scholarships), is only slightly more than the prospective costs of the new college in Malaya, which in its first years of operation will depend heavily upon a staff recruited from overseas.

Further provision to train teachers for the higher primary and secondary classes of the English schools is made through the award of teaching bursaries, up to $1,800 a year each, at the University of Malaya. These carry the student through four or five years, depending upon whether study for a Diploma in Education follows the three-year pass degree or the four-year honors course. Those with an honors degree and the Diploma are qualified to become Education Officers. A five-year plan was started in 1952 with the intention of producing 225 graduate teachers at the rate of 45 a year but because of financial stringency the plan has been severely curtailed.

The government and aided English schools employ many nonnationals who obtained their training outside of Malaya, drawing heavily upon the United Kingdom and other parts of the Commonwealth. In 1953-54, 31 teachers were recruited from India and Pakistan on contract for three years, mainly to teach science and mathematics in the secondary schools.

The two training institutions for Malay teachers (see p. 449) offer three-year residential courses. In addition to providing professional training, the courses extend the general education level of the students. Since 1948, the teaching of English has been included. These colleges try to equip their students to become leaders in introducing new educational methods and to participate in community activities.

Prior to the Japanese occupation most of the teachers in Chinese schools came from China or were trained there. More recently some of the Chinese middle (secondary) schools have offered two years of full-time teacher training (senior normal courses). The Green Lane (government) School draws upon its own junior middle school where the students receive more than half of their instruction in English. In 1953, of 533 attending senior normal classes, 158 were at Green Lane. There is no substantial current supply of university-trained teachers for the Chinese schools.

The educational requirements for admission vary greatly for the teacher-training institutions: for the Malay, it is Malay primary education; for the Chinese, three years of Chinese junior middle (secondary) school; and for the English, School Certificate at the completion of the basic secondary English school course.

The number of teachers attending full-time courses of training instruction in 1953 were as follows:

English (two-year course, Kirkby, England) 300
Malay (three-year courses, Malay training colleges) 614
Chinese (two-year senior normal classes, in senior middle schools) 533
Indian (no institutional training provided) . . . . —

Total 1,447

Part-time or intensive training classes had the following enrollments:

English 1,162
Malay
   Normal classes 2,277
   Preliminary[a] 3,585
Chinese 495
Indian 434
Teachers of English in vernacular schools 660

Total 8,613

[a] Given during a three-year probationary period to those who have completed primary courses, and preliminary to the normal courses.

The training status of teachers in the various types of schools in 1953, excluding the 1,447 students in full-time training institutions and those preparing to be teachers of English in vernacular schools, may be summarized as follows:

	Teachers by Type of School				
	English	Malay	Chinese	Indian	All
Trained	2,582	5,333	2,477	731	11,123
Untrained	840	832	2,984	399	5,055
In training	1,162	5,862	495	434	7,953
Total	4,584	12,027	5,956	1,564	24,131

In the government and aided schools untrained or partially trained teachers are placed whenever possible in schools where they may benefit from association with well-trained teachers and under competent principals. The Federation has been fortunate in the recruitment of many young men and women with a sense of dedication and vocation who are eager to improve their competence.

The salaries paid teachers in government and aided English schools are higher than those paid in Malay, Indian and aided Chinese schools. The teachers of English in vernacular schools, with only one year short of School Certificate in English schools as qualification, are paid on an intermediate scale.

Until the 1952 revision of aid given to Chinese primary schools, the teachers were poorly paid and uncertain that their employment would be for more than one year. The new type of aid, which is related to teachers' basic salaries and increments, makes their emoluments similar to those of teachers in the Malay and Indian schools and is contingent upon the schools providing greater security of employment.

Adult Education

Government and Government Aided. The Federal and State/Settlement departments of education operate a modest program of adult education—mainly instruction in English but also some in technical, domestic science and commercial subjects. Enrollment was 3,452 in 1952, and 500 higher in 1953.

In July 1951 a Federal Adult Education Association was formed; branch associations had been established in all States and Settlements by the close of 1952. There are now (1954) about 70. The government has assisted these voluntary bodies since 1952 by grants-in-aid to the latter for teaching costs and to the Federal Association for administrative costs, training of teachers and preparation of materials. The amounts provided in 1952 and 1953 and allocated in 1954 were:

	1952	1953	1954
Federal Association	$ 60,000	$ 78,700	$ 44,000
State and Settlement Associations	195,359	321,300	256,000

The initial objectives have been elimination of illiteracy, increased use of English and promotion of civic consciousness. The Malay literacy program was greatly assisted by Dr. Frank C. Laubach[11] who visited Malaya in May 1952, trained about 290 literacy teachers and prepared a follow-up reader for new literates.

The Malay literacy campaign was started in the summer of 1952; 850 classes had been formed before the close of the year, with 300 additional classes in English and 42 in other subjects and a total enrollment of approximately 34,000. In December 1953 there were far fewer classes: Malay literacy, 515; English, 250; and others (including Chinese and Tamil literacy and Malay as a second language), 35. The reduction reflected the more limited funds for classes for a full year compared with only the last months of 1952. With $100,000 less allocated by the government for 1954, the program is being reinspected for methods of improving administration, the possibility of laying more stress on Tamil and Chinese literacy and the establishment of a general community development program in which adult education will be an integral part.

Another development in adult education, assisted by a government grant, has been the founding of Women's Institutes. Lady Templer, wife of the High Commissioner, 1952-54, fostered the movement in Malaya and its initital development was stimulated by her continued personal interest. Although not conducted in formal classrooms, these institutes, patterned on those of the United Kingdom, are designed to broaden the interests of the Malayan women—many of whom have led a traditionally secluded life—and to increase civic consciousness and group activity. The programs include needlecraft, handicrafts, cookery and nutrition according to the interest of the group.

Nongovernment. It will be recalled that in 1953 there were 15,853 attending primary classes in private Chinese night schools. A few schools offer English or commercial subjects.

In 1953 the Malayan Chinese Association established classes in Chinese literacy, English and other subjects. There were 693 classes with 22,526 enrolled, but at the end of the year the Association announced that lack of funds made it necessary to suspend the program temporarily.

[11] Dr. Laubach, an American, is widely known in the field of language teaching for his development of methods quickly enabling illiterates to read and write.

Technical Schools

Only very limited school facilities for technical and vocational training have been provided in the Federation. Business firms have not displayed any eagerness to recruit from the schools; they have preferred on-the-job training. Chinese firms have traditionally employed those known to management—friends, relatives and associates.

There are four Junior Technical Schools offering three-year technical and trade training. A fifth (the Technifactory at Kuala Lumpur) concentrates on cabinet making. None provides apprentice training but all provide pre-apprentice training. English and technical subjects are taught. Enrollments have increased from 414 in 1950 to 723 in 1953. By type of course the 1953 enrollments were: radio mechanics, 11; electric installation, 82; machine shop practice, 433; carpentry and building, 118; tailoring, 29; and cabinet making, 50. Of the 723 enrolled in 1953, 378 had free places or scholarships (Malays 306, Chinese 65, and Indians 7). Malays numbered 561 of the total attending. There are hostel accommodations for nearly 500 students.

The costs of machines and tools, materials used, and instructors recruited from outside the country make the cost of this type of education approximately $600 for a student-year, offset slightly by income from the paid work of the schools and from school fees.

The schools have also provided special courses giving basic training for men of the Malay Regiment, trade training for special constables taking their discharge from the force, and classes that are part of the program operated by the Rural and Industrial Development Authority (RIDA). RIDA has established courses of instruction with a more rural bias or designed for those engaged in fishing. Evening classes have been given for apprentices and for others employed in the trades.

Post-Secondary Education

Post-secondary education is provided by the University of Malaya, located in Singapore but jointly supported by the Federation and Singapore Governments, the Technical College, the College of Agriculture, Kota Bharu Teacher Training College, and a new Military College which is part of the military establishment.

A number of Malayans go abroad for further education and training, some on scholarships, some privately and others as part of government employee training. In addition there is the Federation teacher-training college in Kirkby, England.

The Technical College. This college, located in Kuala Lumpur, is a Federal institution under the Department of Education. It provides a four-year course in surveying, architecture, and in civil, mechanical, electrical and telecommunications engineering. Established primarily to meet government requirements for technical personnel, the enrollment is made up largely of technical apprentices for the Departments of Public Works, Drainage and Irrigation, Telecommunications, and Survey, and some for the Malayan Railways, the Central Electricity Board and the Municipalities. During 1953 there were 231 government technical apprentices, two State scholars, and only six private students. The courses do not undertake to qualify tne students for full professional recognition (i.e., they are not prepared to take the accrediting examinations given by the engineering and other professional institutions of the United Kingdom).

Scholarships and Overseas Study. Some scholarships are awarded to students as individuals, not conditioned on joining or continuing in the public service. But more scholarships and arrangements for study overseas are for those already in or planning to join the public services, to fill the government's needs for personnel with improved qualifications and training in specialized fields.

In 1953, 69 students attending the University of Malaya held teaching bursaries aggregating $125,472; 22 held medical bursaries of $36,338; and 62 held arts and science bursaries of $94,836.

Apart from the 300 students at the Malayan Teachers College at Kirkby, England, in 1952 there were 158 overseas scholarship holders of whom 49 were in universities and colleges in the United Kingdom, 82 in Australia, 17 in New Zealand and 10 in India (data for 1953 not available). Federal, State or Settlement Government, British Council, Colonial Development and Welfare Fund, Colombo Plan and other scholarships had been awarded to these students.

For the three-year period 1950-52, the major scholarship awards by the Federal Government and by the States and Settlements were as follows:

	Number of Awards			Expenditures on Higher Scholarships ($)		
	1950	1951	1952ᵃ	1950	1951	1952
Federal Government . .	72	76	181	484,445	569,104	565,402
States	32	60	43	206,859	302,845	303,175
Settlements	8	20	15	4,000	18,628	48,142
Total	112	156	239	594,114	890,577	916,719

ᵃ Excludes students attending the Malayan Teachers College, Kirkby, England.

C SOME GENERAL STATISTICS

Expansion: 1947-53

The rapid expansion of the education system in the postwar years is summarized in Table 1 which shows enrollments, schools and teachers in the primary schools of Malaya—government, aided and private. It is not possible to compile similar data for secondary education because of year-to-year variations in statistical practices of including or excluding teacher training and other vocational enrollment. It may be noted, however, that in 1953, when secondary school enrollment was about 57,600, it was only 7.5 percent of the combined primary and secondary enrollments.

Between 1947 and 1953 the average enrollments for all schools (primary and secondary) rose from 120 to 175 pupils per school (in English schools from 310 to 430, Malay from 140 to 167, Chinese from 124 to 206, and Indian from 42 to 50). In addition to the large proportionate increase in average enrollments in the Chinese schools, some of the older urban English aided schools more than doubled or trebled in size and several now have more than 1,000 pupils (primary and secondary) each. The ratio of pupils to teachers remained remarkably constant for all types of schools combined—about 32:1; but there was a decline in the ratio for Malay schools and an increase for the others.

Variations among the States and Settlements

School enrollments in terms of percentages of the school age population, primary and secondary, vary considerably among the States and

TABLE 1   Primary Enrollments, Schools and Teachers, 1947-53, Federation

Pupils, Schools and Teachers by Type of School[1]	1947	1948	1949	1950	1951	1952	1953
Pupils Enrolled							
English	61,059	67,827	72,906	82,946	92,072	91,604	97,864
Malay	170,693	206,223	271,909	265,335	287,413	309,526	338,105
Chinese	180,999	179,851	198,126	210,336	199,414	213,683	236,041
Indian	35,479	35,456	38,743	38,833	37,100	38,859	43,257
Total . . .	448,230	489,357	581,684	597,450	615,999	653,672	715,267
Schools							
English	197	210	224	244	253	272	325
Malay	1,231	1,321	1,432	1,609	1,772	1,955	2,055
Chinese	1,379	1,362	1,338	1,319	1,168	1,199	1,215
Indian	843	890	889	881	861	854	869
Total . . .	3,650	3,783	3,883	4,053	4,054	4,280	4,464
Teachers							
English[2]	2,327	2,646	3,003	3,279	3,646	3,959	4,584
Malay	5,127	6,242	7,956	8,250	9,377	10,398	12,027
Chinese	5,179	5,328	5,187	5,425	5,540	5,068	5,956
Indian	1,152	1,267	1,341	1,388	1,410	1,464	1,564
Total . . .	13,785	15,483	17,487	18,342	19,973	20,889	24,131

[1] All schools—government, aided and private, excluding Malay religious schools.

[2] Includes both primary and secondary school teachers, not separable because most English schools have both departments.

SOURCE: Department of Education.

Settlements and there are also differences in the proportions attending the various types of schools. Many factors have influenced the development of education, and many are involved in any comprehensive explanation of the present situation. When comparing enrollments it is interesting to note some correlations which seem to suggest that the patterns of development have been influenced by factors of urbanization, racial composition and the length of time the States have been in the general education system (the former Unfederated States have been within it only since the end of World War II). (See Appendix Table 1). Unfortunately the analysis cannot be carried far for lack of economic indices for the States and Settlements.

TABLE 2 Primary School Enrollments, September 1953, Federation

Area or Pupil Group	Estimated Primary Population[1]	All Schools		Enrollments					
				Government and Aided Schools				Private Schools	
		Number	%[2]	English	Malay	Chinese	Indian	English	Vernac.
Johore	175,000	104,172	59.5	5,915	49,195	39,082	4,344	4,637	999
Kedah	129,000	65,682	50.9	3,188	44,231	13,894	3,259	792	318
Kelantan	99,000	48,751	49.2	1,711	43,867	2,275	185	145	568
Malacca	57,000	36,253	63.6	5,205	19,229	7,704	1,208	971	1,936
Negri Sembilan .	64,000	42,262	66.1	5,167	16,747	14,949	3,310	1,535	554
Pahang	56,000	36,414	65.0	2,794	20,248	10,976	1,090	888	418
Penang	103,000	68,113	66.1	11,969	22,260	26,276	3,414	2,883	1,311
Perak	223,000	145,179	65.3	16,090	57,820	48,936	12,378	7,593	2,362
Perlis	16,000	8,873	55.5	552	6,748	1,205	15	165	188
Selangor	169,000	112,818	66.6	14,792	29,829	42,162	13,427	9,934	2,674
Trengganu	50,000	30,747	61.4	422	27,843	1,763	—	366	353
Federal Institutions	—	150	—	150	—	—	—	—	—
Total	1,141,000	699,414	61.0	67,955	338,017	209,222	42,630	29,909	11,681
Boys	570,000	448,039	78.4	41,955	209,219	141,423	25,574	22,230	7,678
Girls	570,000	251,374	44.0	26,040	128,799	67,799	17,056	7,679	4,003
Children of Correct No. .	1,141,000	576,317	50.5	62,428	485,404			28,485	
Primary School Age % .	100.0			5.5	42.5			2.5	

[1]See Appendix Table 3.

[2]Percent of estimated primary school age population.

SOURCE: Department of Education.

TABLE 3 Secondary School Enrollments, September 1953, Federation

State/Settlement or Federal	Secondary "Educative" Population[1]	Enrollments					% of Secondary "Educative" Population				
		Total	All	English Govt. & Aided	Private	Chinese	Total	English All	English Govt. & Aided	Private	Chinese
Johore	26,000	5,968	4,044	3,357	687	1,924	23.0	15.6	12.9	2.6	7.4
Kedah	19,500	1,769	1,501	1,200	301	268	9.1	7.7	6.2	1.5	1.4
Kelantan	15,000	884	675	675	—	209	5.9	4.5	4.5	—	1.4
Malacca	8,500	3,304	2,502	2,305	197	802	38.8	29.4	27.1	2.3	9.4
Negri Sembilan	9,500	3,760	2,909	2,571	338	851	39.5	30.5	27.0	3.5	9.0
Pahang	8,500	2,023	1,562	1,535	27	461	23.8	18.4	18.1	0.3	5.4
Penang	15,500	11,144	6,880	5,734	1,146	4,264	71.7	44.2	36.8	7.4	27.5
Perak	33,500	13,980	10,728	8,283	2,445	3,252	41.6	31.9	24.6	7.3	9.7
Perlis	2,500	136	136	136	—	—	5.4	5.4	5.4	—	—
Selangor	25,500	13,569	10,781	8,316	2,465	2,788	54.1	43.0	33.2	9.8	11.1
Trengganu	7,500	399	351	271	80	48	5.3	4.7	3.6	1.1	0.6
Federal Institutions	—	656	656	656	—	—	—	—	—	—	—
Total	171,500	57,592	42,725	35,039	7,686	14,867	33.5	25.0	20.5	4.5	8.5

[1]20% of population between 13 + and 18 + years of age.

SOURCE: Department of Education.

Primary Enrollments. In September 1953 total primary enrollments in all the schools of the Federation were 699,414,[12] equal to 61.3% of the primary school age population, 57.7% in government and aided schools and 3.6% in private schools or, alternatively, 8.6% in English schools and 52.7% in vernacular schools.[13] Enrollments in the primary schools of the States and Settlements and percentages of school age population enrolled by type of school are given in Table 2 and Appendix Table 1. Selangor, with the highest proportion enrolled, 67%, also had the largest proportion in private schools, 7%–8%; Kelantan had the smallest percentage enrolled, 49%, and the smallest private school enrollment, less than 1%. English school enrollments were highest in Selangor, 14.6%, and lowest in Trengganu, 1.5% of the primary school-age population. Data on schools and teachers in the States and Settlements are shown in Appendix Table 2.

Secondary Education. Secondary enrollments varied even more than primary school enrollments (Table 3). For the Federation as a whole, there were 57,592 enrolled in secondary schools and classes in September 1953, 33.5% of the so-called "secondary educative" population (171,500, 20% of the secondary school age population)—25% in English and 8.5% in Chinese schools.[14] Penang had the highest percentage, 71.7% (44.2% English, 27.5% Chinese), and Trengganu the lowest, only 5.3% (nearly all in English schools). Some States with a large proportion of Malays and relatively few Chinese have little or no Chinese secondary education, and pupils wishing to enroll in senior middle schools must go elsewhere.

Primary Enrollments by Sex and Age

Table 2 shows that in a total of 699,414 enrolled in primary schools, 448,039 were boys and 251,375 girls, giving a boy:girl ratio of 1:0.56. The ratio varies somewhat by type of school: in English government and aided schools, 1:0.62; in English private schools, 1:0.35; in government and aided Malay and Indian schools, 1:0.62; and in Chinese schools, 1:0.48.

Table 2 also shows that of the total primary enrollment 576,317 were of correct school age (6+ to 12+); conversely, nearly 18% of the chil-

[12] Differs slightly from the corresponding figure in Table 1 because of difference in months when the counts were made.

[13] Percentages based on the school age population estimated by the Department of Education. See Appendix Table 3.

[14] *Ibid,* as for the primary school age population.

dren were either too young or too old for their classes. More detailed tabulations (in Annual Reports of the Department of Education) show the wide range of ages within each school year. The 1952 enrollments by age in the first year of primary school show the wide range in all schools taken together and the much narrower range in the government and aided English schools where greater selectivity can be practiced:

Types of School	Age in Years						
	−6	6–8	8–10	10–13	13–16	16–20	20+
All types	8,763	91,080	53,113	24,364	2,081	2,168	1
Government and aided English schools .	24	8,034	1,491	15	—	—	—

The vernacular schools continue to have the difficult problem of teaching a large proportion of overage children throughout the primary course.

Enrollments and Race

The number enrolled in each type of vernacular school, and in the case of the English and new village schools enrollments by race, have already been given. The total enrollments by race for all government and aided primary and secondary schools closely parallel the racial composition of the population, as may be seen in the following comparison for September 1953:

	Percentages by Race				
	Malay	Chinese	Indian	Others	Total
Population .	49.2	37.7	11.7	1.4	100
Enrollments .	51.7	38.9	9.0	0.4	100

Distribution by School Years and "Wastage"

The attainment of lasting literacy is generally believed to require at least four years of schooling, if not five or six. The extent of "wastage" or premature withdrawal from school cannot be assessed with complete accuracy by comparing simultaneous enrollments in the various school years because total attendance has been increasing rapidly, greatly swelling the numbers in the first school years.[15] A better indication of how long the pupil stays in school may be illustrated by the following figures which show, for all primary schools, enrollments in advancing school years in the successive calendar years 1948-53:

Year	School Year	Total	English	Malay	Chinese	Indian
1948. . . .	First . .	160,244	10,532	80,963	49,067	19,682
1949. . . .	Second .	129,464	10,561	62,387	46,085	10,731
1950. . . .	Third . .	113,020	11,291	54,483	40,356	6,890
1951. . . .	Fourth .	85,906	11,461	41,525	27,888	5,040
1952. . . .	Fifth . .	67,271	14,896	28,781	20,750	2,845
1953. . . .	Sixth . .	43,565	14,556	14,847	12,244	1,918

The rapid decline in the total enrollment is striking. The number in the fourth school year in 1951 was only 54% of the number enrolled in the first school year in 1948; and in the fifth year it was only 42%. The percentage decline is slightly larger in the Malay and much larger in the Indian schools.[16] In the English schools the numbers increased in successive years, particularly in the fifth year when nearly 4,000 children transferred from Malay schools to join the Special Malay Classes in the government and aided English schools.

International Comparisons

As a result of the large expansion of education in Malaya since the war, the current provisions and enrollments compare favorably with those in many countries of Asia and other continents. This is evident when international comparisons through objective indices are made with adequate regard for circumstances that affect need for education, capacity to

[15] Enrollments by school years were shown for the different types of schools in preceding pages. For all types of schools combined, the percentages in each class in 1952 decreased as follows: 1st year, 27.6%; 2nd, 19.6%; 3rd, 16.4%; 4th, 12.9%; 5th, 9.5%; 6th, 5.7%; 7th, 3.2%; 8th, 2.1%; 9th, 1.4%; 10th, 0.9%; 11th, 0.5%; and 12th, 0.1%.

[16] A small proportion of the decline between the first and second years is not really "wastage" because it represents transfer of children (especially underage children) from vernacular to English schools.

provide it or obstacles to be overcome.[17] Malaya's progress in education is neither the most nor the least notable among the non-self-governing territories or the underdeveloped countries of the world. It is highly commendable, however, in light of the difficulties that result from extremely rapid growth of child population and the complexities inherent in utilizing four types of primary and two types of secondary schools.

III EXPENDITURES FOR EDUCATION

Total Expenditures: 1947-54

The postwar expansion of education in the Federation is reflected in the public expenditures. From $16 million in 1947, they have risen to $95 million expended in 1953 through the Federal and State/Settlement de-

TABLE 4 Expenditures by the Departments of Education, 1947-54, Federation

(*Million $*)

Expenditure or Income	1947[1]	1948	1949	1950	1951	1952	1953	1954[1]
Annually recurrent .	15.8	28.9[2]	30.1	32.1	50.4	57.5	83.5	92.3
Capital charges . .	0.2	0.3	2.1	1.7	4.5	6.5	11.7	9.3
Gross total[3] . .	16.0	29.2[2]	32.2	33.8	54.9	64.0	95.2	101.6
Income from fees[4] .	0.5	0.6	1.2	0.7	0.8	1.0	1.2	2.6
Net total . . .	15.5	28.6[2]	31.0	33.1	54.1	63.0	94.0	99.0

[1] Comparable expenditures not available for the specified year; the figures given are based on budget estimates—the 1954 figures on revised estimates, April 1954.

[2] Includes arrears of salaries and cost of living allowances for August–December 1947.

[3] Excludes current expenditures and accruing liability for pensions.

[4] Estimated, except 1948 and 1949 actual receipts.

SOURCE: Estimates supplied by Department of Education; expenditures from Annual Reports of the Department.

[17] For details of international comparisons, see for example, Preliminary Report on the World Social Situation, United Nations, 1952; and Special Study on Educational Conditions (Non-Self-Governing Territories), United Nations, 1954. Useful indices include percent of total or school-age population enrolled in primary schools, secondary schools, or both; ratio of teachers to total or school-age population; rate of improvement of literacy. Among the major factors that must be taken into account are national economic resources; urban-rural distribution of populations; racial and linguistic complexities; proportion of the total population in the school ages; rate of growth of total and school-age population.

partments of education. The corresponding estimates are nearly $102 million for 1954.[18] Thus, in the period 1947-54, when total enrollment in government and aided schools (primary and secondary) increased by about 100%, expenditures by the education departments increased by more than 500%. Revenue from fees has been relatively small; it is now less than 3% of the gross expenditures, as shown by Table 4.

Expenditures for education by other departments of government (Agriculture, Medical, RIDA, etc.) are about $1.5 million; grants to the University of Malaya about $2.9 million; and subventions to the adult education associations $300,000. Thus, governmental expenditures for education are about $106 million. Private expenditures by aided agencies and institutions are probably about $7 million, increasing the total to about $113 million. There are no reliable estimates of the amounts spent by unaided private agencies, mainly the private English and the unaided Chinese schools. It seems probable that the gross total for public and private education is about $120-140 million for 1954.

TABLE 5   Classification of Education Expenditures, 1949-53, Federation

(*Million $*)

	Expenditures[1]				
Class of Expenditure	1949	1950	1951	1952	1953
Primary schools	20.7	23.3	34.7	39.6	55.6
Secondary schools	3.3	4.1	5.0	7.0	10.6
Post-secondary education[2]	0.1	0.2	0.7	1.0	0.1
Teacher training	0.5	0.5	1.0	0.7	2.9
Other vocational	0.3	0.3	0.4	0.4	0.7
Board & lodging	0.5	0.5	0.8	1.0	1.1
Maintenance (buildings) & equipment	1.1	0.8	0.9	1.6	1.6
Scholarships (overseas & regional) .	0.3	0.2	0.5	0.5	1.6
Administration	1.6	1.7	2.6	2.4	4.3
Miscellaneous	1.6	0.4	1.0	1.2	5.0
Capital (buildings & equipment) . .	2.1	1.7	4.5	6.5	11.7
Total	32.1	33.7	52.1	60.9	95.2

[1] Includes expenditures from funds voted through Department of Education and other agencies. Excludes some Federal items not available by class of expenditure, and current expenditures and accruing liability for pensions.

[2] Excludes grants to the University of Malaya.

SOURCE: Annual Reports, Department of Education.

[18] These costs do not include expenditures or accruing liability for pensions.

Classification of Expenditures: 1949-53

The expenditures made by the Federal and the State/Settlement departments of education in the years 1949-53 are summarized in Table 5 according to class of expenditure. Over the five-year period 1949-53, the pattern of expenditures has changed somewhat, mainly with a proportionate increase for capital items. Exclusive of the latter, the proportionate expenditures were substantially the same in 1953 as in 1949; there was a slight decrease in the percentage for primary schools (from 69% to 67%), a corresponding increase for secondary schools (from 11% to 13%) and a major proportionate change for post-secondary, teacher training, etc. (from 4% to 6%).[19]

Expenditures by Type of School: 1948-53

The trends in government expenditures by type of school are shown for 1948-53 in Table 6. All of the figures show increases, the largest being incurred for Malay and English schools and the smallest for the Indian schools. The three major changes in this period of expansion were (a) the

TABLE 6 Government Expenditures by Type of School, 1948-53, for Government and Aided Schools[1], Federation

(Million $)

Type of School	1948		1949		1950		1951		1952		1953	
	Amt.	%	Amt.	%	Amt.	%	Amt.	%	Amt.	%	Amt.	%
English . .	11.7	44	12.6	40	13.8	41	21.9	41	22.6	38	34.9	38
Malay . .	12.2	45	15.3	49	16.0	48	23.0	43	25.3	42	34.1	37
Chinese . .	1.1	4	1.4	4	1.7	5	3.6	7	6.7	11	13.7	15
Indian . .	1.9	7	2.1	7	2.1	6	2.9	5	3.2	5	3.7	4
New Village	—	—	—	—	—	—	2.2	4	2.3	4	6.1	6
Total .	26.9	100	31.4	100	33.6	100	53.6	100	60.1	100	92.5	100

[1] Excludes miscellaneous expenditures incapable of allocation ($2.3, $0.7, $0.1, $0.5, $0.9, and $2.7 million, for 1948–53, respectively).

SOURCE: Annual Reports and special tabulations, Department of Education.

[19] The last would appear much larger if account were taken here of the Federation grants to the University of Malaya.

slightly more rapid expansion of expenditures on English than on Malay schools, so that by 1953 these were equal; (b) the development of new village schools (since 1951); and (c) the more than ten-fold increase in government aid to Chinese schools.

Expenditures by Race: 1953

Government has assumed different degrees of financial obligation for the several types of schools, providing all the funds for some and only giving aid to others. Current practices are subject to much criticism; it is said that there are inequities in expenditures among the several racial groups.

Much of the discussion is confused because government expenditures by type of school are often taken to be equivalent to education expenditures by race. This is not valid, as becomes evident when expenditures for all government and aided schools in 1953 are examined by race as well as by type of school (see Table 7) taking into account the fact that more than one-half of all the pupils in the English schools and more than nine-tenths in the new village schools were Chinese. The results may be com-

TABLE 7   Public Expenditures for Education, by Race, 1953, Federation

(Million $)

Type of School[1]	Race				
	Malay[2]	Chinese	Indian	Others	All
English[3]	8.85	17.90	7.20	0.95	34.90
Malay	34.10	—	—	—	34.10
Chinese	—	13.70	—	—	13.70
Indian	—	—	3.70	—	3.70
New Village[4]	0.30	5.75	0.05	—	6.10
All Schools	43.25	37.35	10.95	0.95	92.50[5]

[1] Includes government and aided schools; data not available to separate primary and secondary schools.

[2] Includes Malaysian.

[3] Includes *pro rata* distribution, by enrollment, of gross costs and of fees remitted for free places. Total free places were 19,245–10,982 in primary and 8,263 in secondary English schools. Of the total free places, 14,022 were for Malays, 3,240 for Chinese, 1,513 for Indians and 470 for others.

[4] *Pro rata* distribution of costs according to enrollment.

[5] Excludes $2.7 million which cannot be allocated.

SOURCE: Department of Education, special tabulation. Amended to agree with White Paper No. 67 of 1954.

pared with the racial composition of enrollments and population as follows:

	Percentages by Race				
	Malay	Chinese	Indian	Others	All
Enrollments in all government and aided schools	51.7	38.9	9.0	0.4	100.0
Government expenditures for education	46.8	40.4	11.8	1.0	100.0
Total population	49.2	37.7	11.7	1.4	100.0

The striking result is that the departures from equality are relatively small. It may be assumed that the same would be true of proportions in the school-age population if the figures were available.

Allocations among States and Settlements: 1954

The uneven levels of education among the States and Settlements (see p. 462) invite attention to the allocations in the 1954 budget. Of a total of $102 million,[20] nearly $75 million were allocated specifically to the State/Settlement departments—$69.1 million for annually recurrent charges and $5.7 million for special and capital expenditures.[21] Comparisons of budget allocations and population in the States and Settlements are summarized in Table 8, which shows what proportion of the school-age population was enrolled in September 1953 and what proportion of funds budgeted for education in all States and Settlements was allocated to each. Perak, with 19.5% of the population, has a slightly higher proportion of the total education funds, 20.8%. Three States (Selangor, Negri Sembilan and Pahang) and the two Settlements (Penang and Malacca) each have a

[20] Including amounts assigned to the Federal Department of Education and provided from the Education Development Fund. This fund, established under an Ordinance of February 19, 1953, receives an amount equal to the proceeds of the fees imposed under Part III of the Registration and Licensing of Businesses Ordinance, 1953. The Board in charge of the EDF may spend the money for the training of teachers, provision of buildings and new equipment for educational purposes and generally for the advancement of education in the Federation. In 1953, the receipts amounted to $5.547 million.

[21] Large proportions of the difference between $102 million (total) and $75 million allocated to the States and Settlements will be spent during the year in connection with the programs planned and operated by them. It is not possible at this point to estimate the proportions. It is assumed, however, that the budget allocations give a reasonably accurate picture of totals available for the several State and Settlement programs.

substantially higher proportion of the funds than of population. Of the remaining five States, Johore and Perlis have slightly lower than proportionate percentages of the funds, and Kedah, Kelantan and Trengganu receive percentages that approximate (more or less) one-half their proportions in the total population. The proportionate allocations for annually recurrent charges are similar to those for total funds; the allocations for special and capital expenditures show considerable departures from this pattern—especially the very high proportions for Perak (35%) whose education system is expanding rapidly, and the low proportions for Penang (4.5%) and Malacca (0.9%) which already have extensively developed facilities.

The data in Table 8 suggest that budget practices and provisions tend to work as much toward preserving as toward reducing inequalities in educational achievements among the States and Settlements.

TABLE 8 Comparison of Population and Allocation of Education Funds to States and Settlements, 1954, Federation

(All figures in %)

| State/Settlement | Population[2] | Percentage Primary Enrollment[3] | Education Funds[1] | | |
			Annually Recurrent[4]	Special and Capital[5]	Total
Perak	19.5	65.3	19.6	35.0	20.8
Johore	15.3	59.5	13.4	14.4	13.4
Selangor	14.9	66.6	17.5	20.2	17.7
Kedah	11.3	50.9	6.0	9.9	6.3
Penang	9.0	66.1	13.3	4.5	12.6
Kelantan	8.7	49.2	4.6	3.1	4.5
Negri Sembilan	5.6	66.1	8.3	7.5	8.2
Malacca	5.0	63.6	6.7	0.9	6.3
Pahang	4.9	65.0	6.6	2.6	6.3
Trengganu	4.4	61.4	2.7	1.0	2.6
Perlis	1.4	55.5	1.3	0.9	1.3
Total	100.0	61.0	100.0	100.0	100.0

[1] Allocations in the budget for 1954.
[2] Estimated mid-year population, 1953. Total, 5,705,952.
[3] In all primary schools (government, aided and private), September 1953.
[4] Personal emoluments and other charges annually recurrent.
[5] Other charges, special expenditures, and Public Works Department, non-recurrent.

SOURCE: Department of Education.

iv ALTERNATIVE PATTERNS AND COSTS: 1955-60

In view of the outlook for rapid expansion of education and much higher costs in the future, the mission explored various alternative patterns. The implications of four, among many which have been considered, deserve inspection. With various combinations and compromises to which they lend themselves, these four appear to provide the minimum and maximum boundaries for potential educational achievements and costs. They also take account of the major alternative proposals considered or advocated by responsible official and nonofficial leaders in Malaya, and of the patterns which have emerged from our own studies of the problem.[22]

A THE PROSPECTS AT CURRENT LEVELS OF EXPENDITURE

The rise of education expenditures to the $100 million level in 1954 precipitated the view in certain official quarters that the Federal Government could not afford to provide substantially larger amounts in 1955 and subsequent years, and that the education budget would have to be kept at approximately this figure unless other sources of funds could be found. Even without expansion, costs would automatically rise to about $115 million per annum by 1959 because of normal increments in the salaries of trained teachers and larger increases for those who complete training. We have therefore examined some of the consequences of holding education costs at these levels, considering various possibilities for English and vernacular schools and for primary and secondary education.

If the present school system were not expanded but enrollment had to keep pace with the school-age population, the government and aided primary schools of 1954 would have to accommodate about 40% more pupils by 1959 or 1960.[23]

If we assume that the schools can absorb an increase of only 5-10%, enrollment would decline from 56% of primary school-age population in 1954 to about 41-43% in 1960.[24] This would be a serious retrogression in

---

[22] The mission is indebted to the Department of Education for estimates of prospective enrollments and costs on specified assumptions.

[23] Enrollments would have to increase from 667,000 in 1954 to 935,000 in 1959 and 948,000 in 1960. These are equal to 56% of 1.20 million in 1954, of 1.64 million in 1959 and of 1.695 million in 1960.

[24] Estimates of school-age population used throughout our report are based on data furnished by the Department of Education. The estimates developed by the Registrar of

primary education. Secondary education enrollment would not be adversely affected because (as a result of birth and death rates of the war years) the population of secondary school ages is expected to show in these years a temporary increase followed by a decrease in numbers (see Appendix Table 3).

Calculations were also made to see how much expansion of English primary education would be possible with fixed total expenditures. For this estimate the enrollment and costs of vernacular schools were held at the 1954 level (except for automatic salary increases), and English academic secondary education was reduced so that by the end of 1960 it would account for only 20% of the total enrollment in primary and secondary English classes. It developed that English primary enrollment could be increased from about 73,000 in 1954 to about 96,000 in 1960. But English academic secondary enrollment would have to decline by about 10,000 pupils, thus drastically reducing the number who would become available for Form VI, teacher-training colleges, technical and pre-university education, university education in Malaya and overseas, the professions, public service, etc. Primary school-age enrollment would decline at the rate of about 2% a year: from 56% in 1954 to 40% in 1960.

If English education were expanded by 10% a year (still holding enrollment in vernacular schools at the 1954 level and English academic secondary education at 20% of total English enrollment in 1960), the costs would increase from the $100 million level to about $126 million in 1960. The increase of over 100% in English primary enrollment (from 73,000 to 152,000) would be accompanied by a decline in total primary school-age enrollment to 44% in 1960.

The mission concluded that such retrogressions in enrollment of primary school-age population would be undesirable and unacceptable, and that education expenditures would have to rise substantially above the $100 million level.

Statistics are somewhat lower (e.g., 927,000 instead of 1.141 million children of primary school ages in 1953). Both series are shown in Appendix Table 3.

Total enrollment in government and aided primary schools in 1953 equalled 58% of the primary school-age population, and 56% in 1954. About 17% of the places in the primary schools (and about 9% in the secondary schools) were occupied in 1953 by overage children. Thus, enrollment of children of primary school ages was about 48% in 1953 and is about 46% in 1954. If the lower (Registrar's) estimates of school-age population were used, school places would equal 71% (instead of 58%), and enrollment of pupils of true primary ages would be 59% (instead of 48%) for 1953.

B   MAXIMUM EXPANSION OF THE PRESENT EDUCATION SYSTEM

Though the availability of funds fixes a limit on the expansion of resources for education, the supply of teachers is an even more rigid limiting factor. Unless teacher-pupil ratios are to increase without regard for qualitative standards, enrollment is limited by the number of young men and women that can receive the prerequisite education, the number that can be recruited and trained as teachers, and the years involved in such preparation. With present standards and practices, the maximum feasible expansions and the costs involved are estimated as follows:

	1954	1959	1960
	Enrollments (Thousands)[a]		
English[b]	107	214	240
Vernacular[c]	594	983	1,033
Total	701	1,197	1,273
	Expenditures (Million $)[d]		
Annually recurrent			
English[b]	32.1	64.2	72.0
Vernacular[c]	56.7	89.7	94.3
Sub-total	88.8	153.9	166.3
Capital	7.3	16.5	15.3
Total	96.1	170.4	181.6

[a] In government and aided schools.
[b] Primary and secondary.
[c] Primary only.
[d] Exclusive of technical and vocational institutions and teacher training.

Thus, if the maximum effort were made to enlarge the capacity of the present education system and the program were undertaken at once, total enrollment in government and aided schools (primary and secondary) could be expanded from about 700,000 to 1.2 million in 1959 and nearly 1.3 million in 1960. This includes a doubling of enrollments in primary and secondary English schools and an increase in vernacular school enrollment from about 600,000 to over 1 million in the same period. The number of teachers would have to increase from about 24,000 in 1953 to about 36,000.

Assuming that pupils in academic secondary schools might be 20% of total enrollments, the maximum achievement by 1960, 1.273 million, would include 1.018 million in primary and 255,000 in academic secondary schools. These would be 60% of the primary and 34% of the secondary school ages, respectively. If the number of academic secondary school pupils were held to the so-called "educative" standard (20% of the population of secondary school ages), the 1960 enrollments would be 1.118 million in primary and 155,000 in academic secondary schools, and 66% of all children in the primary school ages would be in school.[25]

If, in the alternative, the academic secondary school enrollment were arbitrarily limited to, say, 50,000—by reference to the numbers needed for post-secondary education, industry and commerce, public service, etc.— the primary school enrollment would be 1.223 million or 72% of the primary school-age population.[26]

Such a program of maximum educational development would involve nearly a doubling of expenditures for primary and secondary schools in the next six years. With allowance for costs not included in the tabulation (teacher training, vocational education, administration and miscellaneous items), the total public cost would be increased from $100 million in 1954 to about $200 million in 1960.

We do not regard this as a practical program. The estimates are useful, however, in fixing upper limits on enrollments and costs.

C THE NATIONAL SCHOOL PROGRAM

Potential Costs

The general magnitude of costs implicit in the national school program may not have been fully appreciated when the Education Ordinance, 1952, was enacted. At a minimum annual cost of $200 per pupil, primary education for a population of a million children of primary school ages (1952) would cost $200 million a year. Academic secondary education (at $350 per pupil a year) for 20% of the number in primary classes would add $70 million a year. Other education costs[27] would bring the total to at

---

[25] The percentages in these paragraphs ignore enrollment of overage children—they are based on places in school—and thus overstate percentage enrollments of children of correct school ages.

[26] The alternatives presented in these paragraphs are not all equally practical of achievement, and they would result in somewhat different costs from those shown in the tabulation.

[27] Teacher training, technical and vocational education, university education, building costs, administration, etc.—apart from medical inspection and care, meals, boarding, clothing and transport included in the Ordinance.

least $300 million a year—five times the public expenditures for education in 1952, and equal to 50% of expenditures on all public services exclusive of the emergency. If we take account of the expected growth of primary school-age population (from about 1 million in 1952 to 1.7 million in 1960) the estimate is increased to about $500 million a year six years hence. Since the number of children would still be increasing rapidly, higher education costs would be in prospect for subsequent years.

Of course, these potential expansions and expenditures are not achievable—for lack of teachers, even if the costs could be met.

Maximum Practical Development

It is pertinent to consider what may be achievable as a maximum practical program for national schools. The calculations assume: the maximum practical program of teacher training; conversion of all existing English schools into English-medium national schools; assignment, from 1955 onward, of English-trained teachers one-half to English and one-half to Malay-medium national schools; secondary enrollment restricted to become 20% of primary enrollment in national schools; and Form VI limited to 1,000 students. The estimates are as follows:

	1954[a]	1959	1960
	Enrollments (Thousands)[b]		
English-medium	73	127	139
Malay-medium	—	78	96
Total	73	205	235
	Expenditures (Million $)[c]		
Annually recurrent			
English-medium	15	25	28
Malay-medium	—	13	15
Sub-total	15	38	43
Special and capital	6	14	14
Total	21	52	57

[a] Present English-medium primary schools, convertible into national type schools.
[b] Excludes other primary schools and all post-primary education.
[c] Exclusive of the costs of teacher training, all post-primary education, and all nonnational primary schools.

On this basis it appears possible to have places in national type primary schools for about 235,000 children in 1960—about 14% of the primary school-age population of that year. The Department of Education estimates that the percentage could be doubled in each of the next two five-to-seven-year periods (28% in 1965-67 and 56% in 1970-74).

With such a maximum development program, annual costs would increase by about $35 million a year by 1960. With allowance for teacher-training facilities, the increase becomes about $40 million a year. At that time, and for the next decade or longer, the primary schools of Malaya would still be mainly of the vernacular rather than of the prospective national types.

This exploration confirms our impression that the full national school program must remain in the category of a long-term objective.

D   EXPANSION WITH PRIORITY FOR ENGLISH SCHOOLS

Finally, we turn to consideration of a development program focussed on expansion of English-medium education and improvement of vernacular education. In this exploration we assume that both the "English" and the "vernacular" schools would increasingly take on many characteristics of national type schools, and we would emphasize that these terms as used here and later should be interpreted accordingly. Since the results of this inquiry form the basis of major recommendations, some of the details are included.

The estimates were prepared according to the following general specifications: [28]

1. English education to be developed as rapidly as possible;
2. Maximum practical program of teacher training (English school standards) to be undertaken;
3. Academic secondary school enrollments to be restricted so as to become 20% of primary enrollment in English schools; and Form VI enrollment to be fixed at 1,000 students, thus limiting the use of trained teachers at post-primary levels;
4. Other primary school enrollments (vernacular) to be expanded so that total enrollment in all primary schools (English and vernacular) remains at 56% of primary school-age population (as in 1954); and
5. Qualitative improvements in vernacular education to be effected by improved teacher training and through increased emoluments and grants-in-aid.

The principal results are summarized in Table 9.

[28] Supplementary technical specifications are stated in the footnotes to Table 9.

TABLE 9—Estimated Enrollments and Expenditures for a Maximum English-Priority Development Program, 1954-60, Federation

Type of Education or Expenditure	1954	1955	1956	1957	1958	1959	1960
	Estimated Enrollments (Thousands)[1]						
Primary schools							
English	73	94	115	133	154	179	200
Vernacular	594	622	650	682	710	738	766
Total primary . . .	667	716	765	815	864	917	966
Post-primary schools or classes							
English secondary, academic[2]	34	34	34	34	34	35	40
English nonacademic[3] . .	1	1	(1)	(1)	(1)	(1)	(1)
Chinese secondary[4] . . .	16	(16)	(16)	(16)	(16)	(16)	(16)
Form VI[5]	1	1	1	1	1	1	1
Total post-primary .	52	(52)	(52)	(52)	(52)	(53)	(58)
Total	719	768	817	867	916	970	1,024
Annually recurrent[7]	Estimated Expenditures (Million $)[6]						
Primary schools							
English	16.5	20.9	25.9	30.2	35.0	40.7	45.7
Vernacular	56.7	60.7	64.8	69.2	73.3	77.3	81.2
Total primary .	73.2	81.6	90.7	99.4	108.3	118.0	126.9
Secondary and Form VI	16.0	16.0	16.0	16.0	16.0	17.1	19.3
Teacher training[8] . . .	2.4	3.1	6.2	7.7	7.7	7.7	7.7
Other vocational, etc.[9]	0.7	1.0	1.3	1.6	1.9	2.2	2.3
Improvement factors[10] .	—	1.0	2.0	4.0	6.0	8.0	8.0
Total annually recurrent . . .	92.3	102.7	116.2	128.7	139.9	153.0	164.2
Capital[11]							
English[12]	5.0	4.3	4.8	5.3	6.0	7.5	6.8
Vernacular	2.3	2.4	2.4	2.4	2.4	2.4	2.3
Teacher training[13] . . .	2.0	4.5	4.0	—	—	—	—
Other[14]	—	2.0	3.0	4.0	5.0	4.0	4.0
Total capital . . .	9.3	13.2	14.2	11.7	13.4	13.9	13.1
Total[15]	101.6	115.9	130.4	140.4	153.3	166.9	177.3
Less income from fees .	2.6	3.0	4.0	5.0	6.0	7.0	8.0
Net total . . .	99.0	112.9	126.4	135.4	147.3	159.9	169.3

Footnotes to table on next page.

[1] In government and aided schools. Excludes nonaided private schools. Includes overage pupils, since the figures are places available for pupils. Excludes enrollments in teacher-training and in vocational schools.

[2] Estimates held constant, 1954–58, in lieu of a decline resulting from the specifications.

[3] Includes the technical schools and the Technical College. The parentheses indicate that increase of unspecified size is to be expected after 1955.

[4] No estimate available of enrollment in government and aided Chinese junior and senior middle classes after 1954. The parentheses indicate that the number is arbitrarily held here at the 1954 level.

[5] Arbitrarily held at 1,000. The number can be increased by 100 or 200 a year after 1955, to become 1,500 or 2,000 in 1960, to meet the national need for qualified candidates for teacher training, other professions, public services, commerce and industry, etc.

[6] *Assumes*: Present salary and supplementary provisions plus increase in personal emoluments in vernacular schools; annually recurrent costs of instruction per pupil of $200, $400 and $1,000 in English primary, secondary and Form VI classes, respectively; and $100, $90 and $80 in Malay, Indian and Chinese vernacular schools, respectively, except as modified by improvement factors.

[7] Includes annually recurrent and special charges (except equipment for new buildings).

[8] *Assumes*: (a) Continuation of Kirkby; (b) operation of Kota Bharu College in 1954, and Penang and Johore Bahru Colleges in 1956; (c) a second Kirkby in 1955 if another college is not developed in Kuala Lumpur or elsewhere in Malaya; (d) annual recurrent costs of $1.6 million for Kirkby and $1.5 million for each of the others, with a two-year course and training 150 teachers a year; and (e) $400 per student a year for part-time normal training classes.

[9] Trade and technical schools, cadets, education for special constables, allowances for teachers receiving university scholarships, etc.

[10] Additional improvements in vernacular education ($1.1 million a year after 1955) and in adult education, trade schools, etc.

[11] English school buildings at $10,000 per classroom of 40 additional pupils; others at $2,000–$4,000.

[12] Primary, secondary and Form VI.

[13] $4.0 million per teacher-training college, and $500,000 for a second Kirkby.

[14] Other vocational installations, nonacademic secondary schools, and improvement of existing buildings.

[15] Administrative and related costs are allocated with functional categories.

SOURCE: Department of Education, special calculation.

English school primary education can be expanded to accommodate about 200,000 pupils in 1960. With sufficient increase in vernacular enrollment to keep the total primary places (English and vernacular) at the present relationship to school-age population (56%), the number in vernacular schools would increase from about 600,000 in 1954 to about 766,000 in 1960.[29] It was seen earlier that this sector could, as a practical maximum, be expanded to an even higher level—about 1.0 million. With the increases shown in the table, the number of English teachers would have to increase from 4,600 in 1953 to 8,000 in 1960 (6,000 trained and 2,000 probationer); and the vernacular teachers from 19,500 to 21,000-24,000.

Enrollment in English academic secondary schools would be held constant for several years and then would increase to 40,000 in 1960. It may be assumed that enrollment will have to increase in English non-

[29] As actually worked out in Table 9, the total primary enrollment would rise slightly in this developmental period—from 56% of school-age population in 1954 to a maximum of 59% in 1959; it would be 57% in 1960.

academic secondary schools in 1955-60, but no estimates are included here. Enrollment in Chinese secondary schools and classes may increase or decrease after 1954, depending on trends not specified in this calculation.

Total public expenditures for this program would rise from about $102 million in 1954 to $177 million in 1960. With allowance for income from school fees, the net annual total would increase from $99 million to $169 million. Since the school-age population would still be increasing after 1960, on the stated assumptions there would be further increases after that year—presumably rapid increases because both the secondary school-age population (which is expected to decline between 1956 and 1960) and the primary population would be increasing.

The extent to which economies could be effected and estimated costs reduced would depend mainly on policies and opportunities with respect to future levels of emoluments (salaries and other) in the public services generally and in education in particular, and with respect to the costs of school and other education buildings.

Finally, it should be observed that the teacher-training program required to make possible the indicated increase in enrollments of English primary and academic secondary schools and to provide qualified English teachers for vernacular schools would call for extremely vigorous measures in the development of the training colleges, in Malaya and overseas.

The program embodied in these estimates is probably not altogether achievable. If the maximum schedule could not be maintained and overseas recruitment could not fill temporary gaps in the needed supply of teachers, the estimates of enrollments and expenditures shown here would have to be reduced.

v A DEVELOPMENT PROGRAM

A OBJECTIVES AND GOALS

". . . The objects of education in the Federation should be:

    a. to further the growth of individuals towards the best in knowledge, skill and character which they have it in them to attain;

    b. to encourage and enable each community to occupy its rightful place in relation to other communal groups in the mixed society of Malaya;

c. to assist the formation of a unified citizen body, that is, a Malayan nation, composed of all such groups.

". . . It is implicit in these objects that, while all sections of the community should combine to form the united Malayan nation, none need lose its individuality and that the cultures of the Malay, Chinese, Indian and other inhabitants should be preserved and developed to evolve a common Malayan culture. These objects constitute the basis for the definition of the 'aim and purpose' of a national educational policy. . . .

"In order to attain these objects we consider it necessary to set as a goal the achievement of universal and compulsory education, at least at the primary stage, and we believe this should be the declared goal of the Federation toward which all should work. . . . In the Federation, as in the countries of the West, the time necessary to complete achievement of the declared goal of universal primary education may have to be reckoned in decades rather than in years."[30]

This statement of the "objects of education" in Malaya underlies the statutory policy of the Federation. It may serve as a useful guide when considering, here, measures which may be undertaken and costs that may be incurred for the years immediately ahead—measures that may contribute toward attainment of eventual goals while making maximum immediate contributions to education, and costs that may be within the means and resources of the economy.

We have already summarized the impressive achievements of public and private education in Malaya since World War II, and have indicated the major problems that confront the country in its striving toward the goals of its education policy. If the Federation's prospective financial resources permitted the ignoring of the future costs of education, these problems could be studied on professional and administrative bases alone. Unfortunately, the government must have serious concern for the $100 million level to which education costs have already risen and for the much higher levels toward which they may go within a generation. Education patterns and practices must be directed toward practical goals likely to be within the resources of the country.

While the emphasis here must necessarily be on financial considera-

[30] Report of the Special Committee . . . to recommend legislation to cover all aspects of educational policy for the Federation of Malaya. Report No. 70 of 1952.

tions, priority must be given to the education needs which are of greatest national importance—

1. Extension of education toward the goal of literacy and basic education for all—through larger enrollments, reduction of "wastage" from premature school leaving, and part-time education of adult and adolescent illiterates;
2. Continued improvement in the techniques of education, especially the vernacular, and continued adjustment of the content of education to conditions of living and to general and special vocational needs; and
3. Maximum possible contribution of education toward the national goal of Malayanization—toward welding racial and linguistic groups into a unified Malayan people and equipping them for common civic responsibilities while preserving cultural heritages.

B IMPROVEMENTS IN EDUCATION

There can be no doubt that the present multiple system of English and vernacular schools and the complexities within and among them increase the difficulties of administration and reduce the effectiveness of educational effort. Education contributes to the needs of individuals, families and the whole society, but today it also contributes to fragmentation of the population, seriously impeding the efforts of official and private groups to develop a "unified citizen body, . . . a Malayan nation." Unfortunately, the general pattern cannot be changed and improved rapidly. The best that can be done is to encourage and accelerate those practical steps that will contribute most effectively toward improvement.

The mission recommends that priority should therefore be given to the following group of undertakings: (1) the development of English schools and the teaching of English in vernacular schools, (2) maximum practical expansion and improvement of vernacular schools, (3) increase of "bridges" from the vernacular to the English schools, (4) institution of a strong program of adult literacy and further education, (5) development of technical and vocational education in relation to Malaya's program of industrial and commercial expansion, and (6) as an essential prerequisite to most of the others, maximum practical expansion of teacher training.

The specific steps that should be taken to carry out a developmental program along the indicated lines will challenge the education resources of the country and the resourcefulness of the administrators and the teaching profession. Fortunately, Malaya's educators have a tradition and a record of facing complex problems with ingenuity and vigor, and they have already explored or practiced many of the undertakings recommended.

Increase in Enrollments

In the Schools. The potentials for expansion and improvement, and the outlook for costs, are those generally indicated in one of the alternative explorations presented earlier (pp. 480-483 and Table 9). With a maximum program of teacher training, it would apparently be possible to expand enrollment in government and aided English primary schools from about 73,000 in 1954 to about 200,000 in 1960, while at the same time (a) increasing enrollment in English academic secondary schools from 34,000 (1954) to about 40,000 (1960), (b) accommodating 1,000 students in Form VI in 1955 and in each year thereafter (or increasing this number to 1,500 or even 2,000 if necessary or desirable), and (c) developing English non-academic secondary education ("modern," commercial and technical). However, the mission strongly recommends that such development should not be at the price of retrogression in primary school-age enrollment if this can be avoided. If possible, the primary vernacular schools should be expanded simultaneously so that their enrollment can increase from about 594,000 in 1954 to at least 766,000 in 1960. This would keep the total number of primary school places in government and aided schools at an approximately constant percentage (56%) of the growing school-age population. And they should be expanded as much more—up to the practical limit of about 1.0 million or more in 1960 (about 60%-70% of primary school-age population)—as may prove to be possible. If this maximum program is not achievable for technical or financial reasons, or both, we would fix an enrollment equal to 50% of primary school-age population in 1959-60 as the minimum.

The preceding estimates have not taken account of the enrollment (about 16,000 in 1954) in Chinese secondary schools. We do not have an adequate basis to judge whether this enrollment may be expected to increase or decrease in the next five years. For reasons given later, we recommend developments which should lead to these schools becoming increasingly bilingual—Chinese and English—in instruction, reducing the differences between them and the English secondary schools and encouraging transfer of pupils from the one type to the other.

In view of the relatively small prospective enrollments in secondary schools for the next six years, the mission recommends (a) preparation for considerable expansion in these schools (academic and nonacademic) after 1960, and (b) experimentation with two-year intermediate schools—with strong vocational bias—for children between ages 12+ and 14+.

Adult Education. It is clear that between now and 1960 the schools cannot be expanded sufficiently to achieve complete enrollment of the rapidly growing population of school ages or overcome the backlog of educational need. While there continues to be a large number of illiterate or partially literate adults, and while many young adults continue to attend the first years of vernacular primary schools instead of classes adapted to their age and needs, adult education must be given an important place in the program. An estimate prepared by the Department of Education indicates that an expenditure of only about $1 million a year ($250,000 to be spent directly by government agencies and about $750,000 as government grants to voluntary adult education associations) could result in virtual elimination of adult illiteracy within a generation. The mission therefore recommends a campaign for adult literacy and further education in the years immediately ahead, to be pursued vigorously even if the cost considerably exceeds these preliminary estimates.

Improvement and Unification of the School System

The mission has given first consideration to the quantitative need for primary education. This does not mean that we have subordinated the maintenance of standards and the improvement of the primary schools or the development of post-primary education. Nor have we failed to realize that the need for rapid expansion of enrollments increases the difficulties of progressive qualitative achievements and development of national-type patterns in both English and vernacular primary schools. We recommend, however, that continued effort be made to raise the level of vernacular primary education and to facilitate the transfer of pupils from vernacular schools to English schools by (1) providing more and improved English teaching and (2) extending the scope of the special transitional classes in the English primary schools to include more Malays, and to Chinese and Indian children as well. We recognize that this would lead to larger "bulges" in the English school enrollments in the fourth and fifth year levels but this development would be compatible with the increasing total enrollments in English schools contemplated by our recommendations.

With respect to the Chinese secondary schools, it should be recalled that of 14,800 pupils in 1953 over 90% were in the junior middle years and only about 2,000 completed the third year; that there were about 1,200 in the senior middle years of whom less than 200 completed the academic course; and that there were altogether only nine schools providing senior middle classes (See pp. 452-453). In view of the widespread demand for English as the medium of higher education and of national and international industry, commerce and trade, we recommend that government assist in the provision of more and improved teaching of and in English in the Chinese junior middle schools. This would be of value to the pupils who do not go beyond these first three years, and it would prepare others for completion of their secondary education in English schools. We also recommend, as an interim measure, provision of special language classes or courses in the English secondary schools for the transferring pupils. We recognize that the development of the Nanyang University in Singapore may affect the outlook for Chinese secondary schools. The Chancellor has announced that the University intends to require entering students to be equipped in both English and Chinese and will lean heavily on both English and Chinese as media of instruction. We hope the new University will adhere to these policies and will encourage the unification of the education system in the Federation.[30a]

The mission also recommends that teacher qualifications, and standards and schedules for financial treatment, move toward uniformity for all government-aided schools according to their levels of conformity to national standards.

Teacher Training

Success in the development and improvement of the education system will depend in large measure on an expanded and strengthened program

[30a] See footnote 46a, p. 514.

of teacher training. This should be dynamic, experimental and flexible in the years immediately ahead, as in the past.

Provisions for teacher training should, in the mission's estimation, be given highest priority and should include the following measures:

a. Temporary extension of part-time normal training to provide for rapid expansion of primary school enrollments;

b. Vigorous development of training colleges to meet the need for English school teachers—including the college in Kota Bharu and the colleges planned for Penang and Johore Bahru, in addition to continuance of the college operating in Kirkby, England; if one or two more colleges cannot be developed in Kuala Lumpur and elsewhere in Malaya soon, serious consideration of a second college in England;[31]

c. Review of the two present Malay training colleges, in view of the importance of Malay education and its qualitative improvement, and the need for teachers of Malay in all types of schools;

d. Consideration of the development of common training colleges to prepare teachers for English and vernacular schools, drawing students with comparable qualifications from all racial groups, training them together, and providing—in addition to a basic training—specialized training with respect to the special language and subject interests of the students; and

e. Maximum practical use of resources at the University of Malaya to prepare graduate teachers for secondary schools and training colleges, and graduates for other posts in research and administration.

Equalization among States and Settlements

We have pointed out that there are now wide differences in the educational opportunities for children in the several States and Settlements. The mission recommends that new plans for the education program be designed so as to operate toward reducing these inequalities. Federal grants to the States and Settlements should be adjusted to give special financial aid to bring enrollments up to a minimum national level (see p. 496).

[31] Plans for a second college at Brinsford in England, scheduled for opening in 1955, have been announced since this was written.

Reduction of Urban-Rural Differences

Distribution of the population in small widely scattered rural communities, lack of transportation, and the difficulties of recruiting teachers for outlying areas make more difficult the reduction of urban-rural differences in opportunities for primary schooling. The mission recommends (1) that the Department of Education continue and even strengthen the policy of offering financial inducements for specially competent trained teachers to accept posts in rural schools; (2) that the present program to provide language teaching in rural vernacular schools be extended as rapidly as possible—if not by special teachers on part-time arrangement because of travel difficulties, then by trying to recruit for the rural vernacular teaching force general teachers who have attended English schools; (3) further development of rural English schools to serve regional rather than local areas, some such schools to have all primary years, some only the first four years, to teach up to the level of durable literacy and basic education, and others with only the three last years, including special classes for children transferring from vernacular schools;[32] and (4) until (3) can be effected, transfer of more rural children to urban English schools, extending to Chinese and Indian children the present practice for Malays.

Reduction of "Wastage"

Premature school leaving is the most serious cause of loss and extravagance in education. The present rates of such "wastage" defeat the purpose for which a large part of all expenditure for primary education is now incurred. Until compulsory education becomes feasible, it may not be possible to increase the retention rates greatly. If there were improvement in the economic status and security of low-income families, especially in the rural population, there might be marked reduction in the withdrawal of young children from school but this must come as the result of broad economic changes and is outside the scope of education *per se*. The mission believes, however, that measures can be taken that will help reduce "wastage," and recommends vigorous steps (1) to educate parents on the long-run value of keeping their children at school for at least four years

---

[32] The mission recognizes that (3) involves working out appropriate plans for transportation, hostels and selection of pupils.

and preferably for five or six, and (2) to improve education, make transfer from one type of school to another possible, and make education more readily available in rural areas, particularly in the States with least educational opportunities. The mission also recommends the elimination of fees at the primary school level as soon as practical, particularly where local rates for education become payable. If other promising means can be devised for reducing premature school leaving they should be utilized even if they involve substantial expenditures.

Adaptations to Needs of the Economy

The education system has a long history of adjusting the content and focus of the primary and secondary school to changing needs. This policy will no doubt be followed in the future. The primary school will continue to have first concern with literacy and basic education. Since for the next five years most of the pupils will not go beyond the primary level, the principal role of the primary school will be to prepare them for their rural or urban living. The secondary school will have the main responsibility for equipping a relatively small number who proceed up the education ladder and eventually become prepared for posts in education, other professions, commerce, industry and public services.

The mission recommends that as the secondary schools and their enrollments increase, their form and content should have regard for the emerging needs of the economy. They should include more scientific, technical and commercial courses. As the commerce and industry of Malaya develop, the trade schools should increasingly provide for apprenticeship training and make effective use of the workshops of industry. The places provided in academic secondary schools and in university preparatory classes will have to expand to the number necessary to meet the national need for the professions and public services, as well as the rising cultural level.

Higher Education

The development of education in the next 5-10 years will no doubt continue to rely on the University of Malaya as the main resource for higher education in Malaya. In Chapter 7, Part II, the mission recommends continuing grants from the Federation (and from Singapore) to support the University and encourage its expansion. We also recommend generous provision of bursaries, the greatest practical use of the University facilities for the preparation of graduate teachers and qualified incumbents of other posts, and participation by the Department of Education in planning the development of University colleges and faculties at Kuala Lumpur. In addition, we recommend that Malaya continue to make extensive use of overseas universities for study in many special fields in which it is neither necessary nor feasible to develop university facilities in Malaya. We also hope that the prospective Nanyang University, whose plans apparently have not yet taken altogether definitive form, will prove to be a valuable additional resource for higher education within Malaya.

Capital Costs of Buildings

We have been struck by the unduly wide diversity and variation in school facilities. The costs range from a few hundred dollars for a simple open structure with an atap roof, a few benches, tables and blackboard, to $18,000 or more per classroom for permanent steel and concrete buildings with extensive modern facilities and equipment. The one extreme probably hampers and discourages teaching; the other becomes a serious drain on financial resources, competitive with capacity to expand the whole education system. We recommend that the Federal and State/Settlement departments of education and the construction agencies seek ways to narrow the extremes—by providing better facilities and equipment for rural schools, and by adopting for urban areas standards that can be met by capital costs substantially below $10,000 per classroom.

Administration

Expansion and development of the education system along the lines we recommend demand a comprehensive review of the administrative structure and practices, especially in light of proposed changes in financing.

At the Federal level, there appears to be urgent need for various improvements:

(a) To simplify administrative relations between the Federal Department of Education and other Federal and State/Settlement authorities and agencies, presumably by more delegation of responsibility to the Department to act within a framework of adopted policies;

(b) To equip the Department to provide the States and Settlements more comprehensive and up-to-date information about Federal standards and regulations;

(c) To increase the present minimal and insufficient number of central administrative personnel and to add an adequate staff of school inspectors;

(d) To increase the central resources for the compilation and analysis of operating data and the preparation of resulting information for the Federal and the State/Settlement departments;

(e) To conduct a more extensive program of research and developmental studies over the whole field of education (particularly with respect to the problems of multi-lingualism and the teaching of languages, perhaps through an Institute for Education Development—within the Federal Department—with its own staff) to study practices, curricula, schoolbooks and other teaching aids, to perform evaluative and developmental studies and field experiments, and to prepare research and educational reports; and

(f) To authorize the Federal Department to establish consultative or advisory committees of nonofficial individuals engaged in education activities and informed on education problems and needs, and to utilize such committees in the review of operations and development of new plans.

At the State/Settlement level, similar needs may obtain and we recommend they be studied with an eye to developments in the Federal Department.

C FINANCING THE FUTURE PROGRAM

Cost Sharing Policy

The program outlined as desirable for 1954-60 would involve public costs increasing by about 10% each year over the preceding year. With the specifications stated earlier (see pp. 480-483), the gross cost would increase from about $102 million in 1954 to about $167 million in 1959 and $177 million in 1960; the net cost (allowing for income from fees) would rise from about $99 million to about $160-169 million. If vernacular education were expanded sufficiently so that the total primary enrollment increased as a percent of school-age population despite rapid growth of that population, the annual costs would be still higher. The maximum attainable by the system of government and aided schools by 1960 (pp. 477-478) is apparently total enrollment equal to 72% of the children in the primary school ages; this would bring the gross cost to about $190 million in that year. Since the primary school-age population would continue its rapid increase after 1960, costs would still be moving upward if the enrollment percentage were not permitted to fall back. Economies in salary scales and other emoluments and reductions in unit costs for new buildings might lower these estimates but would not change the general order of magnitude. If this program should prove to be not wholly attainable the costs may climb to, say, $140-160 million a year by 1959-60.

If the costs of education had to remain wholly charges on the Federal revenues (or nearly so), the suggested program would demand larger expenditures than the foreseeable financial resources of the Federal Government could be expected to carry, and such a program could be undertaken only by endangering or sacrificing other important Federal activities. However, world experience in the financing of education suggests it is neither necessary nor altogether sound that an education program operated mainly by the States and Settlements should be wholly or even primarily financed by the Federal Government. Sound administrative policy and financial necessity both argue for a reallocation of education costs between the Federal and the State/Settlement Governments. The mission believes that, as education expands, the rising costs should increasingly be met by funds raised in the States and Settlements and in their localities. On this basis public demand for education may have a larger opportunity to be truly reflected in the public provision of the service; willingness and readiness to pay the costs would increasingly express demand and its satisfaction, and would invite increased local participation by the public in the design and operation of the program.

A pattern which involves the sharing of costs by two or three levels of government, especially for a rapidly growing and changing system of education, requires, first, a clear allocation of functional assignments and, second, a schedule of future financial responsibilities.

We believe that a logical division of education functions in Malaya should start with agreement that primary and secondary education and supplementary part-time adult (literacy and vocational) education should be provided by the States and Settlements and by their local authorities and voluntary agencies, and that higher levels of education, teacher training, technical education, and other functions which need not or cannot be operated separately in each State or Settlement should be functions of the Federal agency.

We also believe that the assumption of financial responsibility by the States and Settlements, and by local authorities, would have to be gradual. When financial sharing is first undertaken the Federal Government would have to continue to provide substantially all of the funds; it could become responsible for a decreasing share only on a progressive basis. Since the total education costs would be increasing rapidly Federal funds might not decrease—indeed, might increase—in amount even though decreasing as a share of the total.

We are strongly of the opinion that Federal grants for the education functions of the States and Settlements should be on a predetermined pattern, so that for the next 5-10 years the Federal Government can know approximately how much money it will have to provide year by year, and the State and Settlement Governments can know how much of the increasing cost they will have to finance.

Pattern for Federal Grants

Assuming a policy of sharing costs, the mission recommends that the Federal Government provide (a) the appropriations required annually for the operations of the Federal Department of Education, and (b) an annual appropriation (for annually recurrent, special and capital expenditures) to be allotted as education grants to the several States and Settlements, to be used by them in conjunction with State/Settlement/local voluntary funds for purposes approved by the Federal Department of Education.

More specifically, the mission recommends that the annual Federal appropriation for grants should increase between 1954 and 1960 as may be necessary and feasible in support of the developmental program but that after 1955 it should become a decreasing percentage of total expenditures under Federally approved State/Settlement plans so as to be not more than, say, two-thirds or three-fourths of the total by 1960—the proportion depending primarily on an estimate of the capacity of the States and Settlements to meet education costs. If two-thirds, the Federal appropriation for grants might remain at an approximately fixed amount in and after 1960, except that it should not fall below 50% of total expenditures under Federally approved State/Settlement plans. If the Federal share in 1960 is fixed at three-fourths, it should decline toward two-thirds or one-half in subsequent years as total costs increase.

The mission further recommends that the State and Settlement Governments, with or without sharing by their local authorities or by approved voluntary bodies, be expected to provide such funds, in addition to grants from the Federal Government, as may be necessary to meet the costs of the education program under their Federally approved plans, as well as all funds for purposes outside the content of the approved plans.

As a basis for further development of the education program, the State and Settlement Governments should be required to submit general long-term plans for their several education programs, including general estimates of establishments, personnel, enrollments and costs. After review by the Federal Department of Education, the Executive Council and the Legislative Council, the Federal Government should indicate its intent with respect to finances for a period of years. Thereafter, the States and Settlements should submit specific and detailed annual plans, to be utilized by the Federal Government in developing annual estimates of appropriations and of grants to the several States and Settlements.

There are many possible patterns for the formulae to be used in allotting grants to the States and Settlements. The particular one employed would have to be developed after careful study. One such pattern may be used to illustrate how some of the problems may be solved. The Federal appropriation for grants would be divided into two portions. Part one might equal the aggregate amount expended for education by the States and Settlements in 1954, or some major fraction (67%, 75%, 80%, or 90%) of such aggregate amount, and be allotted *pro rata* in accordance with expenditures in 1954. Part two, the remainder of the Federal grant appropriation, would be allotted on the basis of need for Federal aid in carrying out the Federally approved education plan for the year in each State and Settlement. These adjustment allotments should be made with regard for (a) the short-term and long-term goals of the total program, (b) the objective of attaining minimum national education standards throughout the Federation, and (c) the intent to achieve equality in Federal grants per school-age child in all States and Settlements by 1960 (or somewhat later if not feasible by that year).

Our recommendations intend that all Federal grants be matched by non-Federal funds in predetermined proportion. For example, if the target is a minimum of 25% sharing by the States and Settlements in 1960, the Federal program might require that non-Federal funds shall constitute not less than the following percentages of total State/Settlement expenditures under Federally approved plans: 1957, 5%; 1958, 10%; 1959, 20%; and 1960 and thereafter, 25% (or more).

The grant program might specify that the non-Federal matching requirement for each year shall be not a single percentage but a range of percentages, lowest for the poorest State or Settlement and highest for the wealthiest—for example: 1957, 2½%; 1958, 5-15%; 1959, 10-30% and 1960, 15-35%. Such a variable matching requirement would adjust the Federal aid to the fiscal capacity of each State and Settlement—that is, to the relative need for financial aid from the Federal Government. If such a provision were adopted, it should to the maximum extent practicable utilize objective indexes of fiscal capacity and financial need.

A grant program of the kind outlined could give the States and Settlements assurance of having the financial resources to proceed in 1955 on the basis of their 1954 education program, and could give each State and Settlement a longer-term basis on which to plan its program for 1955 to 1960 and beyond. Each would be on notice as to the share of its total education costs it may expect to receive from the Federal Government and the share it would have to raise.

A grant program such as is envisaged here would require orderly and predetermined procedures. In addition to policy formulation and declarations by the Federal Government, the Federal Department of Education (after consultation with the State/Settlement departments) should develop and periodically revise regulations for the procedures and practices to be observed; it should receive and review annual plans from the States and Settlements and develop estimates of allotments; and, after approval by the Federal Government, should make the allotments. When necessary, upon finding that allotments for a fiscal year are insufficient to carry out Federally approved plans, it should prepare and submit estimates for supplementary Federal appropriations. It should require annual (and, if necessary, more frequent periodic) statistical, financial and other reports from the States and Settlements with respect to operations and expenditures under these plans. And it should require a State or Settlement to return, or it should deduct from future allotments, any expenditure of

Federal funds found by the Department not to be in accordance with the Federally approved plan of the State or Settlement or with any relevant ordinance, enactment or regulation, or found to exceed the Federal percentage share of the approved State or Settlement expenditures.

Some General Implications

The proposals outlined above would have certain broad consequences for the education program and for Federal-State/Settlement relations. In addition to clarifying the allocation of responsibilities, they would lay a basis for development of education in accordance with declared national policies and presumably with the resources of both the Federal Government and the States and Settlements. They would also invite increased participation by the public in determining education policy, practice and finance, especially with respect to primary, secondary and adult education.

At the Federal level, the proposals would require a separation of Federal education funds from the annual lump sum grants made by the Federal Government to the several States and Settlements. The Federal financing of education would then become more readily controllable by the Federal Government. The separation would permit placing on the States and Settlements (and on their local authorities) clearer and more substantial responsibilities for specified education functions and finance.

At the State/Settlement level, responsibility for certain major education functions would become more clearly assigned, and with it increased financial responsibility—little at first and more with each passing year, especially if the expenditures for primary, secondary and adult education continue to grow.

Such a program might require new agreements to give States and Settlements, and their local authorities, larger and more diverse revenue sources than are now available to them. It would also require a vigorous and extensive program in the States and Settlements for the development of local and regional authorities competent to assume responsibility for education and to levy and collect local rates for general functions of local government (including education) or for education alone. Such a development would require considerable time and might proceed at an uneven pace in the several States and Settlements. The suggested financial arrangements therefore include a six-year period, 1955-60, or a five-year period, 1956-60, within which the States and Settlements might equip themselves to take over one-third or one-fourth the cost of the expanding education program and, if education continues to expand, to meet up to one-half of higher costs in succeeding years. To whatever extent the assigned responsibilities for education or its financing were not delegated to local or regional authorities, they would remain with the State/Settlement Governments. The development of local rates for education should, of course, proceed with due regard for the fiscal resources of localities, lest by placing excessive responsibilities on poor areas inequalities in the development of education be continued or even made greater.

TABLE 10   Illustrative Financing of the Education Program, 1954-60, Federation

(Million $)

Expenditures and Sources of Funds	Estimated Expenditures						
	1954[1]	1955	1956	1957	1958	1959	1960
Maximum Practicable Program							
Gross expenditures	102	108	118	128	140	153	167
By Federal Dept.[2] . . .	10	11	12	13	14	15	17
By St/Stl/loc	92	97	106	115	126	138	150
From Federal funds	92	97	98	98	99	99	100[3]
From other sources[4]	—	—	8	17	27	39	50[5]
Source of funds:							
Federal	99	104	110	111	113	114	117
St/Stl/loc	—	—	4	12	22	33	44
Fees	3	4	4	5	5	6	6
Minimum Recommended Program							
Gross expenditures	102	107	116	126	136	145	152
By Federal Dept.[2] . . .	10	11	12	13	14	15	15
By St/Stl/loc	92	96	104	113	122	130	137
From Federal funds	92	96	98	99	100	102	103[6]
From other sources[4]	—	—	6	14	22	28	34[7]
Source of funds:							
Federal	99	103	110	112	114	117	118
St/Stl/loc	—	—	2	9	17	22	28
Fees	3	4	4	5	5	6	6

[1] Revised estimates. Excludes present expenditures from other than Federal funds.
[2] Estimated as (uniformly) 10% of gross expenditures, on the basis of Table 9.
[3] Maximum (two-thirds of expenditures by States and Settlements and localities).
[4] States and Settlements, localities and fees.
[5] Minimum (one-third).
[6] Maximum (three-fourths of expenditures by States and Settlements and localities).
[7] Minimum (one-fourth).

Illustrative Allocation of Education Costs

The patterns of expenditures and sources of funds that may result from our recommendations are illustrated more specifically in Table 10, where two alternatives are shown.

The maximum practical program in the upper part of Table 10 takes account of the estimates in Table 9 and the recommendations in the preceding pages and reduces the dollar figure on the assumption that the maximum developmental program is not wholly achievable. The allocation of funds assumes that by 1960 the Federal grants would not exceed two-thirds of the education expenditures by States and Settlements. The gross expenditures shown here would enable government and aided schools to provide enrollments equal to 53-55% of the primary school-age population of 1959-60.[33]

The *minimum recommended program* in the lower part of the Table correspondingly indicates the gross expenditures if expansion cannot quite keep pace with growth of primary school-age population and— instead of maintaining enrollment equal to 56% (the 1954 level)—succeeds in providing in government and aided schools primary school places equal to only 50% (820,000 in 1959 and 847,500 in 1960), divided 10% in English and 40% in vernacular schools.[34] Also, the allocation of funds here assumes that Federal grants would not exceed 75% by 1960.[35]

With the maximum practicable program, gross expenditures would rise from about $102 million in 1954 to about $167 million in 1960. Total Federal expenditures would rise from $102 million (gross) in 1954 to $117 million (net) in 1960; and they would rise thereafter only with respect to (a) further increases in appropriations to the Federal Department, and (b) increases in grants when total State/Settlement expenditures exceed $200 million (i.e., when Federal grants of $100 million become less than 50% of total Federally approved expenditures by all States and Settlements). Expenditures by the States and Settlements would rise from $92

[33] The percentage enrollment would depend on whether reductions from the dollar levels of Table 9 apply to the English or the vernacular education or are divided between the two.

[34] Secondary English enrollments may have to be assumed to rise to 40,000 in 1960 for academic and nonacademic schools and classes.

[35] The total dollar amounts shown in this part of the Table are estimated to be approximately sufficient to meet the objectives indicated here and earlier only if suggested economies are observed with respect to capital costs and other major items of expense and if expenditures are carefully controlled.

million to $150 million and, in addition to income from fees, the States and Settlements would have to find $33 million in 1959 and $44 million in 1960. Thereafter, their funds would have to increase according to further expansion of education expenditures. These estimates may or may not be beyond the resources of the Federal Government but there is a high probability they would be beyond the means of the States and Settlements and their localities.

With the somewhat more modest minimum recommended program, gross expenditures would rise to $145 million in 1959 and $152 million in 1960. The cost to the Federal Government would be about the same as for the somewhat larger program, but the States and Settlements would have to raise only two-thirds as much—about $22 million in 1959 and $28 million in 1960.

These results suggest that if the Federation can, as a minimum, expand primary education so that enrollment in government and aided schools does not fall below 50% of the growing school-age population in 1959 and 1960, the Federal costs may be within the foreseeable resources of the Government, and the States and Settlements may be able to raise, as their share, one-fourth of their expenditures by 1960. Further expansion would depend basically on the development of additional financial resources for education by the States and Settlements and their localities.

SINGAPORE

I INTRODUCTION

Shortly after the end of World War II, the Government of Singapore announced its aim to provide free primary education for all children between the ages of 6 and 12 and secondary education for a limited number. As a result of great effort, applied with imagination and supported by relatively large appropriations, substantial progress has been made toward these ends. Singapore must now chart a course for the future, having special regard for primary education of the rapidly growing child population and for expansion of post-primary education to meet vocational and cultural needs.

Though two-thirds of Singapore's adult population was illiterate before the war, there was little public demand or provision of education for children or adults. After the Japanese occupation, however, there emerged intense desire for education and a place in school for every child; the people of Singapore wanted at once or within a decade what western countries had slowly achieved in the course of a century.

Singapore's prewar schools were part of the larger heterogeneous system of the Straits Settlements and the Federated Malay States—English and vernacular schools; government, aided and private. Government schools were relatively few and some nongovernment schools received a varying degree of financial aid. There were 71,800 children enrolled in primary and secondary schools in 1941, but the government bore the main financial burden for only the 23,300 who attended government English and Malay schools or generously subsidized English schools operated by missions. It made only a small annual financial contribution ($6-7 per pupil) for another 11,200 children who attended aided Chinese or Indian schools. More than half of all the pupils were in private or nonaided schools, mainly Chinese schools supported by fees and private philanthropy. Both English and Chinese schools offered academic secondary education but enrollments were small and relatively few completed the full course. Higher education was provided by Raffles College which awarded a three-year certificate and a Diploma in Education, and by the King Edward VII College of Medicine which gave education and training in medicine, dentistry and pharmacy. The Technical College in Kuala Lumpur accepted students from Singapore, but those wishing to achieve higher qualifications in technical fields had to go overseas.

During the occupation some of the schools continued to operate, with Japanese as the language of instruction. Enrollments dwindled, staffs became greatly reduced in numbers, and secondary education was discontinued except for some night classes. In 1944 all school fees were waived, but attendance remained small or negligible.

When the British returned to Singapore in September 1945, they found that many of the schools had been used for other purposes or had been damaged, destroyed or looted. Textbooks and equipment were in short supply. Large numbers of children had never been to school or had had their education interrupted. Under the direction of the Military Administration, schools were immediately reestablished and by the end of the year there were as many children in school as before the war. On April 1, 1946, when civil government was restored, an important change was made in the administration of education. Separate Directors of Education, educators instead of civil servants, were appointed for Singapore and the Malayan Union. They replaced the prewar Director of Education of the Straits Settlements who had also been Adviser on Education to the Federated Malay States though his headquarters had been in Singapore.

In August 1947, the government accepted in principle obligation to provide—by as rapid stages as possible—a six-year course of free primary education, junior technical schools, post-school certificate classes in secondary schools to prepare students for institutions of higher learning, and a college to train teachers for all types of schools.

An extensive survey of current and future educational needs of the Colony led to a *Ten-Year Programme* presented in 1949. It was expected that between the census year 1947 and 1959 the primary school-age population, reflecting the impact of the high postwar birth rate, would rise from 163,000 to 222,000 and that the secondary school-age population would increase from 62,500 to 78,000. Enrollments in 1949 were only 109,700 in primary and 8,300 in secondary schools. Allowing for a continued preference for vernacular education by as many as 70,000 in 1959, the Programme foresaw as a 10-year goal the following numbers of new schools: 150 primary schools (100 government and 50 aided),[36] nine secondary schools, two-three vocational schools, and four-five special schools (for handicapped and retarded children) to be operated in conjunction with the Medical and Social Welfare Departments.

Before the Programme was undertaken, however, it was reassessed the following year and was expanded by a five-year *Supplementary Education Plan* calling for 90 schools (18 a year) more than had been first estimated. Provision of secondary education was also reappraised, and proposals were developed for programs of adult education to meet literacy, vocational and cultural needs.

Execution of the plan has been at a rapid but uneven pace. First priorities have been given to what has been regarded as the essential foundation—primary education, teacher training, and secondary education of an academic type to supply the teaching and other professions.

In many respects the expansion and development of education presents less difficulty in Singapore than in the Federation. The Colony is small and compact; about two-thirds of the population is urban; and funds have been more or less readily and regularly available.

[36] The 1949 Programme intended that parents should have a choice between English and other language media in regional schools for children of all races.

The mission's survey in 1954 comes after five years' implementation of the Ten-Year Programme and at a time when Singapore is reviewing its achievements and reformulating its needs. This year for the first time Singapore has more places in the primary schools than children in the 7+ to 12+ primary age group. There are secondary school places for about one-fifth of its children of secondary school ages. It is raising teaching standards and is adjusting to the changing needs of the economy by extending vocational and technical training.

Singapore is a busy, prosperous cosmopolitan center. Its population has grown from 800,000 at the end of the war to nearly 1¼ million in 1954, and its high birth rate and low death rate ensure further rapid growth, even if there is no net in-migration. Its commerce and industry, competitive on the markets of the world, demand technical competence of its business managers and increasing productivity of its workers, but there is a surplus of unskilled and a shortage of skilled labor. The education system will therefore be under great pressure to expand in the years ahead. Pressures for expansion will also result from the growth of self-government, and from the increasing faith in education, within Singapore and in the neighboring countries of Asia, as a means to cultural growth and maturity.

Thus, the future of education in Singapore has to be assessed and planned not only by economic but also by social and political criteria. Its costs must be viewed in relation to perspectives for the needs and capacity of the economy and weighed against other demands on common resources.

II   THE PRESENT EDUCATION SYSTEM[37]

Like the Federation, Singapore has four types of primary schools, classified by language of instruction as English, Chinese, Malay and Indian. Some are government schools (only English and Malay); some are private schools, assisted by government grants (English, Chinese and Indian); others are nonaided private schools. The government English and Malay and the aided English schools provide free primary education for Malayan-born pupils who are of proper age for their school years; these schools now have places for nearly one-half the total primary enroll-

[37] In the following discussion, as in the preceding pages describing the schools of the Federation of Malaya, levels of primary school work are referred to by school year. Secondary schools and courses are those between primary and university levels.

ment. All other registered schools (except those admitting only Europeans) receive a special contribution with respect to pupils qualified for free education, reducing the fees for these pupils by the amount remitted in government English schools.

More than 90% of the primary school enrollment is in the English and Chinese schools. Formerly there were many more children in Chinese than in English schools, but the numbers are rapidly becoming equal. Malay and Indian schools combined have less than 8% of the total enrollment.

Secondary education in Singapore, as in the Federation, is mainly of the academic type and is provided only in English and Chinese schools—government English, aided English and Chinese, and private. Fees are charged by all types. About three-fifths of the secondary enrollment is now in the English schools.

Two methods are used for making grants to schools that qualify for government aid: (a) payment of a per capita amount based on the average number of attendances; and (b) payment of an amount equal to the difference between salaries (teacher and staff) and income from fees, plus a small capitation allowance for maintenance costs, and payment of up to 50% of approved capital improvements. Chinese schools are now (December 1954) the only ones receiving grants solely on a capitation basis, although Indian schools received this type of aid until 1950.

Many school buildings are used for double sessions. Each session has a separate administrative and teaching staff, and each is usually counted as a separate school. In alternate years the sessions are shifted from morning to afternoon so that the disadvantages of the afternoon session are shared.

Radio broadcasts are extensively used as teaching aids. The Singapore Broadcasting Department offers school programs in English, Chinese, Malay and Tamil, and almost half of the schools are equipped with receiving sets.

Physical education and sports are encouraged in all schools. School health services are provided by the Colony Medical Department and the City Health Department.

English Schools

English school education is in high demand in Singapore, as in the Federation, because of the opportunities for employment that are opened by a command of English and for the preparation it affords for higher education at home and abroad. Government and aided English schools offer substantially the same education. The private schools serve the useful function of extending the availability of English education by accepting pupils who are too old for admission to the government and aided schools or who cannot keep up with their classes. The aided schools, mainly Roman Catholic or Protestant mission schools, continue to encourage the education of girls—especially beyond the primary levels.

The school children are of many races,[38] and they first come to school with little or no knowledge of English. Both spoken and written English are therefore given much time and emphasis in the curriculum which is closely patterned on the schools of the United Kingdom, with adaptation to the local social, civic and geographic scene. The study of Asian languages is included in the primary school course to meet the cultural needs of the Chinese, Malay and Indian children; current plans call for further similar provision in the secondary school classes.

Government and aided English primary schools have for many years made possible the transfer of a few selected students from Malay schools by providing special two-year transitional classes concentrating on the study of English. Since 1948 special classes have admitted pupils from Chinese and Indian schools.[39]

The fees in English government and aided schools are $2.50 per month for children in primary schools not eligible for free education, and $4.00 and $3.00 per month for boys and girls, respectively, in secondary courses.

[38] Following are the racial compositions of the Singapore population and the English school enrollment in 1952 (latest available):

Race	Singapore (%)	English Schools (%)
Chinese	77.1	79.4
Malaysian	12.2	6.8
Indian	7.4	9.2
Other	3.3	4.6
All	100.0	100.0

[39] It is not possible to cite the numbers in 1953 because figures for "Special Classes" include a second type of special classes, those for overage pupils; 763 were in both types of special class, 423 Chinese, 326 Malays and 14 Indians. In 1951, 135 Malays transferred from Malay schools to the transitional classes, and 68 transferred in 1950.

Of approximately 71,000 enrolled in English schools in 1953, 60,500 were in primary classes and 10,500 in academic type secondary classes. The primary school course was reduced from seven to six years in 1953. It is estimated that 55% of the pupils who complete the primary course in government English schools and over 90% of those in aided English schools continue into secondary classes. In the government schools selection is made by examination; in the aided schools pupils may continue in the same institution by promotion.

Government secondary schools are planned as separate institutions, but in the period of rapid expansion of schools, both primary and secondary classes have been given in some schools as an interim arrangement. In aided and private schools secondary courses are usually given in "comprehensive" schools having both primary and secondary departments. Of 11 government schools offering secondary courses in 1953, seven (including one junior technical school) were for boys, two for girls, and two were coeducational; of 37 aided schools with secondary classes, 22 were for girls and 15 for boys. Seventeen private schools also had secondary classes. The 10,401 pupils in English academic secondary classes in 1953 included 7,051 boys and 3,350 girls, with the following distributions by type of school: government schools, 2,095 boys and 552 girls; aided schools, 3,324 boys and 2,641 girls; and nonaided schools, 822 boys and 157 girls.

Secondary schools prepare pupils for the Cambridge School Certificate Examination[40] at the end of the fourth year.[41] The number who pass this examination each year is of great moment because it is the necessary qualification for English school teachers and for other professional requirements. In 1953, 925 or 72% of the 1,284 candidates passed the examination. Since 1951 post-certificate classes (the equivalent of Form VI in United Kingdom schools), which prepare for the Cambridge Higher School Certificate Examination, have been offered in some schools for those wishing to meet the requirements of the University of Malaya and British universities. In 1953 they were offered in two government and four aided schools. As yet few pupils have entered for the full Higher School Certificate Examination although a larger number have entered for parts of the examination.

[40] See p. 445.

[41] Note the divergence of practice in Singapore and in the Federation. In the Federation the reduction of the primary course to six years was accompanied by an extension of the secondary school course from four to five years for school certificate preparation.

Secondary school enrollments in 1953 are shown below by secondary school year and type of school. The large numbers in the first years reflect the recent greatly increased provision of English primary education, particularly in government schools. Not all schools carry the pupils as far as the school certificate (only 19 of the 32 aided schools).

Type of Secondary School	School Years					
	1	2	3	4[a]	5–6[b]	All
Government Schools . .	1,321	1,092	572	407	65	3,457
Aided Schools	2,469	1,682	1,086	620	108	5,965[c]
Nonaided Schools . . .	494	281	188	36	—	979
Total	4,264	3,055	1,846	1,063	173	10,401

[a] School certificate classes.
[b] Post-certificate classes.
[c] An additional 56 were enrolled in commercial courses.

There has been limited experimentation with "modern" type secondary schools offering both academic and technical and vocational courses.

English Secondary Technical Education. Plans and programs for secondary technical education have emerged within the last five years, in response to increasing industrialization in a period when restrictions on immigration have limited the supply of skilled labor formerly available from China. Demand for technical and vocational education has been less pressing than for academic education because much of the employment in Singapore has been on the "family" system, with relatives or members of a clan being engaged and trained by skilled artisans. Recent surveys indicate that there is considerable need for well-trained technical school students.

There is only one government Junior Technical School, a former trade school reorganized in 1951 on the pattern of secondary technical schools in the United Kingdom. The first two years of the three-year courses include English, mathematics, geography, history and physical training. The third year is largely devoted to workshop practice, with a continuation of English and mathematics. The school aims to provide sound technical training for boys who will become apprentices. A department of engineering offers motor or general mechanical, electrical and radio courses, and a building department offers domestic engineering (plumbing) and carpentry. The enrollment has increased from 108 in 1948 to 190 in 1953. Tuition is $3.00 a month but about 25 pupils are usually given free places. Two more schools of this type are planned for the near future.

Government also aids a trade school (St. Joseph's) under the management of the Order of St. Gabriel and operated primarily for boys who present social problems. The 1953 enrollment was 104. Instruction is given in general mechanics, carpentry, printing and tailoring.

A Nautical School was opened in August 1952 to train seagoing personnel for Ministry of Transport Certificates. Enrollments were restricted to deck officers with sea experience, higher grade engineer officers and junior grade engineers with workshop experience. The initial enrollment was 18; in 1953 it was 35.

In July 1954 the Department of Education added to its staff an Assistant Director of Education (Technical), a former principal of a technical institute in Nigeria. This new appointment reflects increasing concern with technical subjects in secondary schools and craft instruction in primary schools. Primary school crafts are now viewed not only as a means of self-expression but also as part of a program to develop manual skills and dexterity.

The establishment of the Singapore Polytechnic (see p. 520) will greatly increase the provisions for secondary technical education, and later may be expected to help fill the pressing need for qualified teachers of technical subjects.

Chinese Schools

The Chinese schools of Singapore shared a common development and history with those of the Federation until 1946, and still have many similarities in management, length of courses, and curriculum (see pp. 451-453). School fees ranging between $3.00 and $10.00 a month are commonly charged; there are usually additional charges that may be from $3-$80 a year. Under the free education scheme the fees of eligible primary pupils are reduced by $2.50 a month and the school is reimbursed by the government. Despite government grants-in-aid given to many of the Chinese schools, they are still the only schools supported to any considerable degree by their own racial groups in Singapore. "They have been able to carry on with comparatively little government help, but only with increasing difficulty and by strict economy on buildings and equipment, and—what is more serious—on teachers' salaries."[42]

The amount of government grant to Chinese schools, paid on a capitation basis, was determined for some years by the establishment of three grades for primary and two for secondary (middle) schools. The schools were assessed according to their efficiency and compliance with the Education Code. In December 1953, the government proposed[42] substantially increased rates of aid and establishment of a fourth grade of aid for which primary schools previously not aided might become eligible, contingent upon the schools providing a good working knowledge of English as well as Chinese[43] and turning out good citizens of the Colony. The government announced it would continue to pay the salaries of teachers of English in the aided Chinese schools. The new schedule of grants came into force from January 1, 1954, changing the capitation grants as follows: (a) primary departments: Grade I, from $20 to $40; Grade II, from $14 to $30; Grade III, from $10 to $20; proposed Grade IV, $10; (b) secondary departments: Grade I, from $36 to $75, Grade II, from $24 to $50; and for normal classes in secondary schools from $50 to $75.

Grants were made to 111 of the 273 registered Chinese schools in operation in 1953, covering about 68% of the Chinese school enrollment. By September 1954, 203 of the 277 registered schools were receiving the increased grant-in-aid with respect to 8,254 pupils in secondary departments and 55,830 in primary departments.[44]

In 1953, 2,977 were enrolled in kindergarten and 68,825 in primary classes. Approximately 40% of those who complete the six-year primary course continue with secondary school work.

The curriculum of the Chinese secondary schools is subject to approval by the Department of Education and standards are maintained by government examinations. English is the only second language offered and in some schools it is the language of instruction in science and mathematics. In 1953 all but two schools were equipped with science laboratories. Western type courses in general science or the correlation of the sciences have

[42] Chinese Schools—Bilingual Education and Increased Aid. White Paper No. 81 of 1953.

[43] It was suggested that the time devoted to the teaching of English and other subjects taught in English should be at least one-third of the total teaching time in the primary school, one-half in the junior middle and two-thirds in the senior middle school. (*Op. cit.*)

[44] The government has proposed a further change, offering the Chinese schools the same grants as are provided the English schools. This is now (December 1954) under negotiation with the school authorities.

not been generally introduced. In recent years a few pupils from the Chinese secondary schools have presented themselves for the English Cambridge School Certificate Examination. Since 1952, a considerable proportion of the graduates have sought admission to English schools after completing the senior middle school course (about 80 in 1954).

Secondary education was given in 10 schools in 1953, nine of them government aided. Five schools accepted both boys and girls, two were for boys only and three for girls only. The total enrollment was 7,470 (including 58 in senior normal classes). It will be noted from the secondary enrollments by school year given below that relatively few complete the three secondary years of the junior middle schools, and that the number completing the full six-year general academic course is extremely small.

	Junior Middle			Senior Middle		
School Year	7	8	9	10	11	12
Enrollment	3,132	2,032	1,196	612	249	249
Total		6,360			1,110	

The number of boys attending secondary schools is substantially larger than the number of girls; in the junior middle schools there were 4,205 boys and 2,155 girls, and in the senior middle schools 701 boys and 409 girls. Many of the pupils are old for their place in school; 3,548 pupils in junior middle classes were 15 years of age or over, and 469 in the senior middle classes were 18 or older, including 160 who were 20 or over.

Before 1947 the government gave financial aid to the Chinese secondary schools offering normal courses, but there were no government teacher-training courses. Most of the teachers had been recruited or trained in China.[45] The low salaries paid to teachers of Chinese and the insecurity of their tenure have been detrimental to the stability of the Chinese schools. First steps to raise a special fund for old age and social welfare benefits for the teachers were not taken until 1951.

Department of Education administration of the Chinese schools is in the hands of a Chief Inspector of Chinese schools who has a staff of seven

[45] As recently as 1949 over 70% of the teachers of Chinese and 18% of the teachers of English in Chinese schools had been born outside of Malaya, the great majority in China. (Department of Education Annual Report 1949, p. 91.)

inspectors. There is also a Liaison Officer who has no administrative responsibility but is a link between the Department and the management committees, supervisors and staffs of the Chinese schools.

Political activities in some of the Chinese secondary schools have continued to be an unfortunate aspect of Chinese education. In 1950 communist documents and seditious materials were found in two schools, and in the spring of 1954 students of seven schools were involved in demonstrations against National Service.

Malay Schools

Prior to the introduction of the free education scheme in 1949, Malay schools were the only government schools offering free education. Most of them offered four years of primary work with a practical bias and only six out of 39 offered a fifth year; three of those provided a sixth year, mainly for pupils intending to become teachers. The scope and content of the course has been greatly revised in the last five years. English, which had been taught in only one school and some Saturday morning classes before the war, is now taught in several schools. Formerly the pupils learned to read and write in both Jawi (Arabic) and Rumi (Romanized Malay), but now only Rumi is taught.

In 1951 the Department of Education announced that Malay schools would operate with Malay as the language of instruction for only the first three years, then a gradual change-over to English would take place, with a seven-year course preparing for English secondary schools. A few selected Malay children still continue to transfer from Malay schools to special classes in government and aided English schools.[46]

Between 1947 and 1953 enrollments in Malay schools increased from 6,463 to 9,236. The proportion of girls has risen from 21% to 38% (only 16% were girls in 1941). Many pupils are overage; in 1953 over 10% were between 13 and 19 years of age, an improvement over 1952 when more than 18% were in these ages. About one-third of the enrollment was in the rural area of Singapore. There were 37 school buildings, 22 of which were used for both morning and afternoon schools. All except one were government schools; an aided school was managed by the Shell Company of Singapore, Ltd.

A Malay craft school for girls, opened in 1952, offers instruction in

[46] See p. 506.

cooking, sewing, housewifery and home nursing. In 1953 a craft school for boys opened with an enrollment of 45 who were taught simple woodworking.

A teacher in a Malay school is required to have only a primary school education but in 1953 more than half of the teachers had been trained at the Malay teacher-training colleges in the Federation.

Indian Schools

Indian schools, like the Malay schools, offer only primary education. Instruction was in Tamil in all except two of the 23 schools operating in 1954. There is little estate labor on the Island of Singapore and Indian schools have not been extensively developed; until 1954 enrollments never reached 1,500 in registered schools. More Indian children attend English than Indian schools. In 1953, when the total Indian school enrollment was 1,271 in 21 schools, only 184 children were in classes beyond the third year.

All Indian schools were government aided in 1952, but in 1953 there were two nonaided schools. Grants-in-aid, originally given to mission schools on a capitation basis, now cover the cost of teachers' salaries, a capitation grant for maintenance of buildings, and the cost of up to three textbooks a year for each child. This change was precipitated by financial and managerial difficulties in nonmission schools in 1949.

Six mission schools are managed by the Ramakrishna, Roman Catholic and Methodist missions. Other schools are managed by committees. For many years the nonmission schools have had difficulties in maintaining reasonable standards of work, in recruiting suitable teachers and in enlisting efficient management.

Not all Indian schools provide the full six-year primary course. The curriculum has been expanded to include arts, crafts, nature study and music. English was introduced in 1950 and was taught in nine schools in 1953. Only primary education is necessary to qualify for teaching in an Indian school.

Post-Secondary Education

The University of Malaya, located in Singapore and founded in 1949 as a pan-Malayan institution, incorporated the former Raffles College and the King Edward VII College of Medicine. It is organized in three faculties, arts, science and medicine, and awards a postgraduate diploma in education. The University and the Teachers' Training College (see p. 517) are at present the only post-secondary institutions.

Plans for a polytechnic institute are well advanced. Initially it is intended to provide part-time instruction for men and women who are employed but wish to gain additional skill or more advanced knowledge. Study will be on a post-secondary but not a university level.

Nanyang University, a new private Chinese institution being organized in 1954, is scheduled to admit students in 1955. The first three faculties are to be arts, science and commerce. Dr. Lin Yu-Tang, Chancellor, has announced that knowledge of both Chinese and English will be required for admission, and that both languages will be used by the University, depending upon the courses offered.[46a]

Of a total enrollment of 965 at the University of Malaya in 1953, 381 were Singapore students, 286 men and 95 women. The enrollments by faculties or departments were medicine, 145; dentistry, 24; pharmacy, 12; science, 62; arts, 129; and nine postgraduates working toward a diploma in education.

There being no post-secondary technical training institutions in Singapore, those desiring more advanced technical training study in the Federation of Malaya or overseas. The Technical College in Kuala Lumpur had an enrollment of 21 Singapore students in 1953; 12 were studying civil engineering, six telecommunications engineering, and three surveying. One student was attending the College of Agriculture in the Federation. An additional 38 were pursuing technical studies outside of the country.

In 1953, 159 students assisted by fellowships, scholarships and studentships, were studying overseas in a great variety of fields.[47] Many of them were government employees selected to increase their competence in specialized fields of service. An additional 625 were known to be studying abroad. Of these 784, 303 were in the United Kingdom, 381 in Australia and 100 in the United States.

[46a] Since this was written, political, educational and financial differences with the Executive Council of Nanyang University have led to the resignation of Dr. Lin Yu-Tang (April 1, 1955) and of eleven members of the faculty. Plans for the University are presumably in the course of reformulation. (*Straits Budget,* various issues; and *New York Times,* April 7 and 18, 1955).

[47] The sources of the awards were: Singapore Government, 111; Colonial Development and Welfare Fund, 7; Colombo Plan, 28; Australian Imperial Forces Nursing Scholarships, 2; U. N. (Technical Assistance), 1; and the U. S. Government, 10. In 1952 there were only 83 students abroad on scholarships.

Teachers and Teacher Training

The need for teachers, acute in many countries, has been a pressing problem in Singapore because of the rapid expansion of schools. Various means have been employed for teacher recruitment and training in recent years, with many unavoidable compromises in standards. The eventual goal is primary schools staffed by graduates of a teacher-training college and secondary schools staffed by university graduates. The recruitment and training of teachers occupies an urgent priority in plans for the future.

The teachers in Singapore's schools vary greatly in their preparation, from those who have completed only a six-year primary course to those who hold the highest university degrees. Many received their training in part-time normal classes attended outside of teaching hours; some at the secondary school level; others attended teacher-training colleges or hold university diplomas in education.

In 1953, of the 5,360 teachers in primary and academic secondary schools, 2,724 were teaching in English schools, 2,276 in Chinese schools, 311 in Malay schools and 49 in Indian schools. Forty-five percent (2,432) were trained; the rest were untrained or partially trained.[48]

The qualifications of the teachers in the English and Chinese schools are set forth in Table 11. It will be noted that while there were 605 university graduates, 1,016 had not completed secondary courses. The secondary school course for those in the English schools is at least of Cambridge School Certificate level, and in the Chinese schools "completed secondary course" includes teachers who attended normal courses given in the secondary schools and not the general secondary course of six years.

Of 307 teachers in Malay government schools (excluding four teachers in the aided school), 162 had been trained in the Malay teacher-training colleges in the Federation, 41 were part-time normal class trained, nine were untrained and 91 were probationary teachers recently out of primary schools who were receiving instruction while teaching. After three years the successful probationary teachers become eligible to attend the training colleges or to teach and receive further part-time training.

There were 49 Indian school teachers, 23 trained and 26 untrained. The former were mainly primary school graduates who had received their

---

[48] Compared with a teaching force of 2,527 in 1947, with 1,185 (47%) trained and 1,342 (53%) untrained; and 5,008 in 1952, with 1,976 (39%) trained and 3,032 (61%) untrained.

TABLE 11 Teacher Qualification in English and Chinese Schools, 1953, Singapore

Qualification	English Schools				Chinese Schools			English and Chinese Schools
	Govt.	Aided	Non-aided	All	Teachers of Chinese	Teachers of English	All	All
Teachers in Primary Schools								
University graduate								
Trained	10	13	5	28	41	1	42	70
Untrained . . .	2	10	15	27	51	9	60	87
Completed secondary course								
Trained	570	293	8	871	390	30	420	1,291
Untrained[1] . .	667	288	100	1,035	517	187	704	1,739
Secondary course not completed								
Trained	23	8	—	31	415	—	415	446
Untrained[1] . .	104	25	88	217	280	59	339	556
Total. . .	1,356	637	216	2,209	1,694	286	1,980	4,189
Teachers in Secondary Schools								
University graduate								
Trained	101	93	5	199	32	1	33	232
Untrained . . .	7	23	23	53	138	25	163	216
Completed secondary course								
Trained	34	104	—	138	15	13	28	166
Untrained[1] . .	35	55	31	121	32	30	62	183
Secondary course not completed								
Trained	—	1	—	1	2	—	2	3
Untrained[1] . .	—	3	—	3	1	7	8	11
Total . . .	177	279	59	515	220	76	296	811

[1] Including partially trained teachers attending part-time normal classes (954 in 1952).

SOURCE: Annual Report, 1953, and special tabulation, Department of Education.

training in part-time normal classes. Six of the untrained teachers were attending normal classes in nearby Johore Bahru in the Federation. Classes provided by the government in 1948-50 were discontinued in 1951.

Expenditures for teacher training have until recently been a relatively small part of the education budget. Total expenditures between 1949 and 1953 increased from $35,000 to $553,000, with the latter including $485,000 for English schools (both government and aided), $50,000 for Malay schools, and $18,000 for Chinese schools (no expenditures for Indian schools).

Teachers' Training College

Before the last war there was no English teacher-training college in Singapore; one was planned early in the century but was never established because of failure to attract prospective candidates. The English schools were staffed either by trained teachers from other countries, teachers who held a diploma in education from Raffles College (in Singapore) or those who were trained in normal classes designed for primary or post-primary teachers. The Malay training colleges to train Malay teachers were established to serve all of Malaya including Singapore, and they continue to allocate places to Singapore students; in 1953 their enrollments included 25 men and 7 women.

A Teachers' Training College was finally established, admitting students for a full-time certificate course for English school teachers in 1950. The Department of Education planned to lengthen the original two-year course to three years for those admitted in 1953, but a shortage of teaching staff made it necessary to continue on the two-year basis. The College also serves as a center for part-time normal training courses for both English and vernacular school teachers. Its facilities are grossly inadequate and greatly overtaxed. The planned replacement has already begun.

The number in training at the College rose from 191 in 1948-49 (it was used for part-time normal training before the organization of the full-time training course) to 1,922 in 1953-54. The enrollments by type of course were 151 in the full-time certificate course; 1,125 in part-time normal courses for teachers in English schools; 52 in a part-time post-normal course; 380 in part-time courses for vernacular and continuation school teachers;[49] and 214 in a full-time course for Chinese school teachers.[50]

The Department of Education is greatly concerned lest the rapid expansion of the English schools result in too great a dilution of the teaching staffs by untrained teachers. It has been experimental in the recruitment

---

[49] Continuation schools were originally English schools started after the war for overage children. Now they are mainly aided schools offering "less formal academic" courses and are staffed by slightly underqualified teachers.

[50] White Paper No. 20, of 1954.

of teachers and in its training program. In 1952 an intensive three-month course was substituted for the first year of the three-year part-time normal training, but this was not considered a successful means of shortening the training period and was not repeated. In 1953-54 recruitment of teachers was greatly accelerated by admission of married women and special categories of slightly underqualified teachers. A new post-normal training course has been offered to raise the qualifications of the normal trained English school teachers and to meet the requirements of the new Singapore Education Service Scheme. On the other hand, since the students in part-time normal training are already teaching in the schools, the pressure of current need for teachers in the primary schools has been so great that the authorities have been reluctant to encourage large numbers to take full-time training which would postpone their availability in the schools.

The secondary school program will not be under severe pressure for expansion until 1960 (see p. 533). Steps are now being taken to provide a corps of university trained teachers. The number of bursaries for study at the University of Malaya has been increased from 13 in 1953 to 100 in 1954, and their value has also been increased in an effort to attract more candidates. Current estimates of requirements are 29 graduates of various types in 1955, and an annual increase in this number thereafter up to 50 (including need for normal replacements), with approximately one-third of the staff for the new secondary schools being qualified in science.

A solution has not yet been found for the training of highly qualified supervisors and inspectors of schools. There is also a shortage of school administrators to meet the needs of the new schools.

In 1953 for the first time the government offered full-time training for teachers for the Chinese schools. It started two senior normal classes (with an enrollment of 74) similar to the senior normal courses it had aided in Chinese schools, and it prepared a plan (to be undertaken in 1954) for an experimental two-year full-time training course for those holding senior middle certificates to prepare teachers for the junior middle schools.

Adult Education

Adult education in Singapore is sought mainly by those hoping to gain economic advantages. The study of languages, especially English, is regarded as a means of occupational and professional advancement.

Vocational Education. Government evening classes for the public are offered by the Department of Education in two centers with a combined enrollment of about 1,500. The classes and attendances in 1953 were as follows:

a. At Raffles Institution: 10 classes with an average attendance of 179 in shorthand, bookkeeping, accounting and English; three classes, attendance 23, for masters, gunners and helmsmen of local coastal vessels;

b. At the Junior Technical School: 13 courses with enrollment of 1,000-1,300 in electrical, marine, mechanical, radio and structural engineering, mathematics, builders' quantities, building construction, plumbing, gas fitting, carpentry, woodwork and drawing. The students are trained for the Examinations of the City and Guilds of London Institute.

Fees of $3.00 a term ($9.00 a year) were charged for all classes except the nautical classes, which were free.

In response to the needs of the construction industry a school of building was opened in 1953 at the Junior Technical School. It has been giving a full-time three-months' day course in bricklaying and plastering and in theory and drawing. The trainees receive a subsistance allowance. Training in woodwork and metalwork was also provided for a few crippled youths at the same school.

Various government departments and services have their own training and apprenticeship schemes. The Public Works Department and Telecommunications make use of the Technical Training College at Kuala Lumpur for the training of their apprentices. Practical instruction in major and minor trades is given at H.M. Dockyard. The Electrical Department gives instruction and training in ship and factory installations, workshop repair work, the maintenance of high and low tension overhead and underground distribution systems and substation work.

In addition to government provision of technical and vocational training there were 51 proprietary institutions in 1953 with an enrollment of 8,865 students: 5,383 attending commercial classes, 1,956 English and the remainder studying art, music and various other subjects.

Many employees of private firms receive their training on the job. Much of it is insufficient for the development of highly specialized skill or competence. A few firms offer recognized apprenticeship schemes; one large organization has had a five-year training plan for apprenticeship in various trades, with a consultant technical officer advising on the studies the apprentices should take.

The field of technical and vocational training has been open to study and review in the light of changes in business and industrial organization and an emerging demand for a more highly skilled labor force, greater productivity and better trained supervisors, foremen and managerial staff. Plans for the establishment of the Singapore Polytechnic[51] are based on an expression of employer willingness to utilize its training and interlock apprenticeships with the courses offered. In its first years the new Polytechnic expects to offer part-time or concentrated courses for those who are employed. It is intended that the level of the courses will lead to the certificates of established professional institutes. An analysis of the labor force and employers' needs has suggested first priority for commerce, management studies, engineering and architecture, with applied arts and women's departments second. At the outset general education courses would play an important part in bringing to the requisite post-secondary level the prospective applicants now employed, many of whom have not completed secondary courses.

Illiteracy

The designers of the *Ten-Year Programme* and the *Supplementary Education Plan* (1949-50) took account of the 1947 census finding that 53% of all adults 15 years of age and over were totally illiterate. They therefore proposed a modest but supposedly practical program of adult literacy classes. Government subsidy was to be given to the voluntary agency already working in the field of adult education (the Peoples Education Association, which later became the Adult Education Council).

Before launching a literacy campaign in 1952, experimental work in language teaching was carried on by the Department of Education. Singapore was visited by Dr. Frank C. Laubach, consultant to the Committee on World Literacy, who worked out a set of four charts and preliminary reading material in Romanized Malay to be used in connection with Malay literacy courses.

The grant to the Adult Education Council stipulated that classes were

---

[51] Report of the (Dobby) Committee on a Polytechnic Institute for Singapore, 1953; Report on Singapore Polytechnic, by A. W. Gibson, 1954.

to be carried on in any vernacular language or in English. Of the 251 classes organized in 1952, 167 were in English, 81 in Mandarin, two in Tamil and one in Malay. They were called not literacy but language classes and were not confined to illiterates. The attendance consisted of truly illiterate persons only in the rural areas, where most of the vernacular classes were held.[52] In 1953 there was a slight expansion of English and vernacular language classes but little was done in establishing further education classes and the Department of Education reports that there was little public demand for them or appreciation of their value.[53]

It would appear that, unless adult illiteracy is much lower now than is suggested by the 1947 census, the progress of education in the intervening years and other information, only a meager program has been carried on to deal with it and that much remains to be done, particularly in publicizing the possibility of becoming literate and in improvising ways of reaching illiterate women as well as men.[54]

iii POSTWAR EXPANSION

The large expansion of education since World War II appears in the data for 1947-54 summarized in Table 12. Total primary and secondary enrollments rose from about 87,000 in 1947 to over 180,000 in 1954. The largest increase, absolute and relative, occurred in the English schools where the total enrollment now nearly equals that in the Chinese schools.

The number of registered schools has doubled in the period 1947-54, and all types show the increase. The sharp rise in the number of English schools in 1950 reflected the first effective implementation of the amended *Ten-Year Programme* for expansion of English-medium education.

The total number of teachers has grown from 2,523 in 1947 to 6,182 in 1954. The increase has been greatest in the English schools. The ratio of pupils to teachers, which rose in the period of rapid school expansion after 1949, declined slightly between 1953 and 1954 except in the Indian schools:

[52] Annual Report, 1952, page 70.

[53] *Ibid*, 1953, page 77.

[54] The illiteracy rate among females 15 and over was reported by the 1947 census as 77% and it has been noted that female school attendance has lagged far behind the male.

Type of School	Pupils per Teacher		
	1949	1953	1954
English	27	32	25
Chinese	37	39	34
Malay	31	32	31
Indian	26	28	31

The data in Table 12 are confined to the registered schools. Some nonregistered schools have been allowed to operate pending conformance to registration requirements because the need for places in school has been

TABLE 12   Enrollments, Schools and Teachers, 1947-54, Singapore

Type of School	1947	1948	1949	1950	1951	1952	1953	1954
	Enrollments[1]							
English	27,953	33,185	35,056	48,782	53,776	61,649	71,003	82,715
Chinese	51,920	55,463	66,256	70,187	74,308	71,430	76,237	85,686
Malay	6,463	7,157	7,862	8,436	8,505	8,579	9,236	10,440
Indian	919	1,012	1,315	1,486	1,272	1,205	1,271	1,541
Total	86,895	96,817	110,489	128,891	137,861	142,863	157,747	180,382
	Schools[2]							
English	68	83	94	132	128	148	175	190
Chinese	154	184	271	287	288	279	273	277
Malay	35	37	39	43	43	48	59	60
Indian	11	15	19	23	20	20	21	22
Total	268	319	423	485	479	495	528	549
	Teachers							
English	887	1,085	1,322	1,868	2,188	2,659	2,724	3,304
Chinese	1,419	1,530	1,843	1,946	2,011	1,991	2,276	2,491
Malay	190	221	248	270	306	316	311	337
Indian	27	36	47	56	47	42	49	50
Total	2,523	2,872	3,460	4,140	4,552	5,008	5,360	6,182

[1] Enrollments in registered schools only. Primary and general secondary school courses included; kindergarten, trade school and normal class enrollments in Chinese secondary schools excluded.

[2] The number of schools is not strictly comparable from year to year, being affected by changes in the classification of schools and the method of counting from time to time. For example, some schools with two sessions have been counted as one school in one year and as two schools in a later year.

SOURCE: Annual Reports, Department of Education, 1947–53; Department data, 1954.

acute. In 1948 there were 164 nonregistered schools with enrollments of 15,519; 38 were Chinese schools with 14,209 pupils and 26 were Indian schools with 950 pupils. Four nonregistered Chinese schools were permitted to operate in 1953, with an enrollment of 662; in 1954, there were three such schools with 465 pupils. In addition, 1,441 children who had not gained admission to schools were receiving informal education and some instruction in handicrafts at 15 centers operated by the Department of Social Welfare.

Primary Education

Singapore has used all of its resources and bent its energies toward providing places in school for all children of primary age. By 1954 it attained the goal of having (in public and private schools) more school places (158,500) than children between the ages of 7+ and 12+ (145,000) —though not all of this age group are in school and 32,000 in primary classes are older or younger.

The growth of primary school enrollments, exclusive of kindergarten,

TABLE 13   Enrollments in Registered Primary Schools, by Type of School, 1947-54[1], Singapore

Type of School	1947	1948	1949	1950	1951	1952	1953	1954[2]
English: Total . . .	24,162	29,128	30,943	44,256	47,151	53,407	60,546	69,315
Government	16,313	16,443	16,965	18,896	23,769	29,486	34,278	41,286
Aided				10,859	18,302[3]	18,552	19,515	20,023
Nonaided . . .	7,849	12,685	13,978	14,501	5,080[3]	5,369	6,753	8,006
Chinese: Total . . .	49,452	52,880	63,552	67,854	69,912	65,807	68,825	77,206
Aided	29,318	32,627	34,586	38,223	40,053	42,241	49,037	68,867
Nonaided . . .	20,134	20,253	28,966	29,631	29,859	23,566	19,788	8,339
Malay: Total . . .	6,463	7,157	7,862	8,436	8,505	8,579	9,236	10,440
Government .	6,463	7,014	7,708	8,436	8,505	8,579	9,236	10,440
Aided	(n. a.)	143	154					
Indian: Total . . .	619	1,012	1,315	1,486	1,272	1,205	1,271	1,541
Aided	576	810	847	1,486	1,272	1,205	1,271	1,541
Nonaided . . .	343	202	468	—	—	—	—	—
All Schools	80,996	90,177	103,672	122,032	126,840	128,998	146,350	158,502

[1] Excludes kindergarten classes.
[2] August 1954.
[3] Reflects a change in classification.

SOURCE: Annual Reports, Department of Education, 1947–53; unpublished Department data, 1954.

from about 81,000 in 1947 to 158,500 in 1954 is shown in Table 13, where the data have been compiled by type of school. Among the English schools the expansion has been almost wholly in the category of government schools; among the Chinese schools the increases are identified with aided schools, enrollment in nonaided schools having declined from over 20,000 in 1947 to 8,300 in 1954.

Secondary Education

As noted earlier, all secondary education is English or Chinese; there are no Malay or Indian secondary schools. The secondary education is almost exclusively of the academic type, a pattern which has evolved in response to need and demand. There is increasing public interest, however, in technical and commercial secondary schools or in "modern" type schools which fuse academic and vocational training.

In August 1954 there were about 21,900 pupils in registered secondary schools. This number is equivalent to about 22% of the population of 98,000 in ages 13 to 16, inclusive. This percentage is somewhat misleading, however, because many of the secondary pupils are overage—particularly in the Chinese schools (see p. 511).

Table 14 shows the growth of secondary school enrollments from 5,900 to nearly 22,000 between 1947 and 1954 by type of school. It will be noted that enrollments increased substantially in government (English) and in

TABLE 14   Enrollments in Registered Secondary Schools, by Type of School, 1947-54[1], Singapore

Type of School	1947	1948	1949	1950	1951	1952	1953	1954[2]
English: Total . . .	3,431	4,057	4,113	4,526	6,625	8,242	10,457	13,400
Government .	{3,189	{3,604	1,500	1,743	2,137	2,664	3,457	4,354
Aided			2,613	2,783	4,105	5,027	6,021	7,278
Nonaided . . .	242	453	(n. a.)	(n. a.)	383	551	979	1,768
Chinese: Total . . .	2,468	2,583	2,704	2,333	4,396	5,623	7,412	8,480
Aided	2,415	2,529	{2,704	2,252	{4,396	{5,623	{7,412	{8,480
Nonaided . . .	53	54		81				
All Schools	5,899	6,640	6,817	6,859	11,021	13,865	17,869	21,880

[1] Excludes enrollments in trade schools and normal classes in Chinese schools.
[2] August 1954.

SOURCE: Annual Reports, Department of Education, 1947–53; unpublished Department data, 1954.

both types of aided schools (English and Chinese). The number in all English schools increased by 290% and in Chinese schools by 240%. The English schools had 58% of the total enrollment in 1947 and 61% in 1954.

IV EXPENDITURES FOR EDUCATION: 1947-54

Total Expenditures

The postwar expansion of the education system, evidenced by rapid growth in schools and enrollments, has been made possible by large increase in the government's financial support. Appropriations were $4 million in 1947; they rose to $21 million in 1953. Supplementary expenditures by aided schools from their private funds, $1.5 million in 1947, were nearly $8 million a year in 1952-53. As Table 15 shows, government expenditures on education will probably nearly double between 1953 and

TABLE 15 Expenditures on Education, 1947-54[1], Singapore

(Million $)

Expenditure or Income	1947	1948	1949	1950	1951	1952	1953	1954[2]
Public								
Annually recurrent[3]	3.8	5.2	7.3	8.9	14.0	17.0	19.5	27.9
Capital charges .	0.2	0.4	0.5	2.3	2.3	2.3	1.4	10.0
Gross total .	4.0	5.6	7.8	11.2	16.3	19.3	20.9	37.9
Income from fees .	0.2	0.3	0.3	0.3	0.5	0.5	0.6	0.7
Net total . .	3.8	5.3	7.5	10.9	15.8	18.8	20.3	37.2
Private[4]	1.5	1.6	3.4	5.9	5.8	7.9	7.5	7.5[5]
Public and private								
Total	5.3	6.9	10.9	16.8	21.6	26.7	27.8	44.7

[1] Includes expenditures by the Department of Education (and the Education Board) and the Department of Public Works. Does not include expenditures by other departments, grants to the University of Malaya, or current expenditures and accruing liabilities for pensions.

[2] Revised estimates (July 1954). Later revisions indicate that actual expenditures may be only $24.5 million annually recurrent and $6.6 million capital.

[3] Includes: personal emoluments (PE); other charges annually recurrent (OCAR); and other charges, special expenditures (OCSE). OCAR includes grants-in-aid and OCSE capital grants to aided schools.

[4] Private expenditures by agencies operating government-aided schools.

[5] Preliminary estimate.

SOURCE: Department of Education.

1954, reflecting large increases in capital expenditures (new buildings) as well as in recurrent charges, special expenditures and grants.[54a]

Net expenditures by the government have grown much more rapidly than population:

Year	$ per capita	Year	$ per capita
1947	4.05	1951	15.16
1948	5.51	1952	17.46
1949	7.65	1953	18.08
1950	10.74	1954	31.66

Classification of Expenditures

All major categories of expenditure show large proportionate increases (Table 16). The largest amounts have, of course, gone into the development of the primary schools. The expenditures for secondary schools have

TABLE 16 Classification of Government Education Expenditures, 1949-53 [1], Singapore

(*Million $*)

Class of Expenditure	1949	1950	1951	1952	1953
Primary schools	5.1	6.0	10.0	11.3	12.2
Secondary schools	1.2	1.2	1.9	2.3	3.4
Post-secondary education	0.2	0.0+	0.0+	0.1	0.1
Teacher training	0.0+	0.1	0.2	0.4	0.6
Other vocational	0.1	0.2	0.2	0.3	0.4
Maintenance (buildings) and equipment	0.0+	0.0+	0.0+	0.1	0.1
Scholarships (overseas and regional)	0.0+	0.1	0.2	0.3	0.4
Administration	0.5	0.5	0.5	0.7	0.8
Miscellaneous	0.0+	0.0+	0.2	0.4	0.4
Capital (buildings and equipment)[2]	0.7	3.1	3.1	3.6	2.5
Total	7.8	11.2	16.3	19.3[3]	20.9

[1] Includes expenditures by the Department of Education (and the Education Board) and the Department of Public Works. Does not include expenditures by other departments, grants to the University of Malaya, or current expenditures and accruing liabilities for pensions.
[2] Includes capital expenditures and capital grants to aided schools.
[3] Does not check total of column because of rounding.

SOURCE: Annual Reports, Department of Education.

[54a] See footnote 2, Table 15.

nearly tripled since 1949; those for teacher training have increased even more rapidly but are still a relatively small proportion of the total. Post-secondary budgets have decreased but this has been more than offset by increases for regional and overseas scholarships. Expenditures for admin-istration have been surprisingly static, considering the large expansion of the system as a whole. In general, the functional distribution of noncapital expenditures has remained substantially unchanged in this period of rapid growth. Capital expenditures (directly by the government and through grants to aided schools) have been considerable but the increase in level between 1949 and 1950 was only little more than maintained in 1951-52 and was followed by a decline in 1953. A large increase will occur in 1954.

Expenditures by Type of School

The following tabulation summarizes government expenditures for the various types of schools during 1949-53:

(Million $)

Type of School	1949	1950	1951	1952	1953
English[1] . .	6.54	9.57	13.50	16.18	17.26
Chinese . . .	0.55	0.74	1.68	2.00	2.47
Malay . . .	0.69	0.80	1.05	1.02	1.09
Indian	0.05	0.11	0.11	0.11	0.11
Total . .	7.83	11.22	16.34	19.31	20.93

[1] Includes expenditures for post-secondary and vocational education, and scholarships (overseas and regional).

SOURCE: Annual Reports, Department of Education.

While the total increased from $8 million to $21 million, uniformly about five-sixths was spent for English schools. The amount spent on Chinese schools rose at an even faster rate than total expenditures, increasing nearly five-fold and rising from 7% to 12% of the total. Expenditures for Malay schools increased in absolute amount but decreased proportionately, from 9% of the total to 5%; and expenditures for Indian schools changed little in amount or as a percent of the total.

Grants to Aided Schools

It has been noted that Singapore's reliance on aided private schools has undergone changes in the postwar years, and government aid, per school and per pupil, has been frequently modified. The net effects in terms of public expenditures are summarized in Table 17.

The upper portion of the tabulation summarizes government grants to aided schools by type of school during 1947-53. The total grants to primary and secondary schools have increased nearly six-fold—more than four-fold for the English, fourteen-fold for the Chinese and ten-fold for the Indian schools.

The middle portion of the Table shows the increases in the grants expressed in dollars per pupil in the aided schools, reflecting the policy to improve those schools and to reduce the burden of fees.

The lower portion of the Table relates grants to total governmental expenditures for education. For all aided schools, grants since 1949 have accounted for about 30% of total government education expenditures. Since growth of total expenditures has been accompanied by development

TABLE 17   Government Grants to Aided Schools, 1947-53, Singapore

Type of Aided School	1947	1948	1949	1950	1951	1952	1953
	Total Grants (Million $)						
English	0.91	1.31	1.98	2.32	3.10	3.47	3.88
Chinese—total	0.16	0.26	0.47	0.65	1.55[1]	1.83	2.29
Direct grants-in-aid . .	0.16	0.26	0.27	0.29	0.64	0.70	0.82
Teachers of English . .	—	—	—	—	0.45	0.61	0.79
Grants in lieu of fees . .	—	—	0.20	0.36	0.46	0.52	0.68
Indian	0.01*	0.01*	0.01*	0.08	0.10	0.09	0.09
Total	1.08	1.57	2.46	3.05	4.75	5.39	6.26
	Grant per Pupil in Aided Schools ($)						
English	76	109	154	169	216	225	227
Chinese	6	7	9	21	45[1]	37	47
Indian	7	5	5	57	67	73	67
	Grants as % of Total Expenditures for Each Type of School						
English			30	24	23	22	22
Chinese			85	88	92	91	93
Indian			11	77	87	82	82
All types	[2]	[2]	29	27	29	28	30

* Less than 0.01.
[1] Rate of aid doubled this year.
[2] Total expenditures by type of school not available for 1947 and 1948.

SOURCE: Annual Reports, Department of Education.

of government English schools, grants to aided English schools have fallen from 30% to 22% of the total spent for all English schools. And since the government does not directly operate any Chinese schools, the grants reflect total expenditures, with the exception of administrative costs, for schools of this type. Similarly, over 80% of all expenditures for Indian schools are in the form of grants.

Net Cost per Pupil in English and Technical Schools

Since English education has been playing an increasingly expanding role, it is important to be aware of the rising costs of providing education in English primary, secondary and technical schools. Table 18 shows net costs per pupil.

TABLE 18 Net Cost per Pupil, by Type of School, 1947-53, Singapore

($)

Type of School	1947	1948	1949[1][2]	1950	1951	1952	1953
Government English schools	106	182	211	154	214	247	166[3]
Aided English schools—total	78	112	172	191	248	256	268
From government funds	76	99	157	172	219	228	235
From mission or private funds .	2	12	15	20	29	28	33
Government Junior Technical School	805	707	603	685	694	913	881
Aided Junior Trade School	n. a.	n. a.	n. a.	n. a.	542	509	591

[1] Includes expenditures for arrears of salaries.
[2] First year of "free" education program.
[3] See text comment on this figure.

SOURCE: Annual Reports, Department of Education.

For the government English schools, primary and secondary, costs rose from $106 per pupil in 1947 to $247 in 1952 and then fell to $166 in 1953. The Department of Education ascribes this fall to a temporary concatenation of factors (increase in enrollments, reduction in teacher-pupil ratio, etc.), expecting the annual net cost per pupil to tend to become about $240 in the primary and about $500 in the secondary schools.

For the aided English schools, costs were lower in 1947 but are now about the same as in the government schools. It will be noted that, though not government-owned or managed, the aided schools receive nearly 90% of their total net costs from the government.

In the case of the government Junior Technical School, net cost per pupil fell from $805 in 1947 to a low of $603 in 1949 and has been much higher since then. In St. Joseph's (aided) Trade School, net cost has been $500-$600 per pupil.

v THE DEVELOPMENT PROGRAM AND ESTIMATED COSTS

A THE GOVERNMENT'S PROGRAM

The education needs of Singapore are determined in large measure by four factors: growth of population, increasing desire among all racial groups for literacy and higher levels of education, demand for English education, and need for technical and vocational training. The Colony is committed to giving first priority to six years of primary school education for all children 7 to 12 years of age. This carries in its train priority commitments for expansion of academic secondary education and teacher training to make possible expansion of the primary schools. Development of nonacademic education and adult literacy, and possibly extensive improvement of qualitative standards, must therefore take secondary roles though Singapore's economic needs dictate that they cannot be neglected.

All planning for education is colored by the postwar rapid growth of population. Whether or not this rate of growth continues into the longer future, the next 5-10 years will see a large increase in the population of primary and secondary school ages, reflecting the high number of births and the low number of infant and child deaths since the war. If Singapore undertakes to meet its declared obligations, the education system must expand and expenditures must rise rapidly.

Primary School-Age Population

The school-age population is now growing at an even faster rate than the population as a whole. In the years 1954-70, total population is expected to increase by about 50% (from 1.2 million to 1.8 million).[55] In the same period primary school-age population will probably more than double;

[55] Based on projections prepared by the Department of Statistics, Singapore, assuming no net migration and continuance of the mortality rates of 1947 and the fertility rates of 1947-51.

children in the ages 7 to 12, inclusive, numbering 145,000 now (1954) will number about 293,000 in 1970.[56]

The six-year primary school-age population (ages 7 to 12) decreased from 140,000 in 1950 to 131,000 in 1952, and then began to rise, to 134,000 in 1953; the decline and the subsequent small increase in these years reflect the effects of low birth rates and high death rates during the Japanese occupation. The further growth of this population group is expected to be extremely rapid between 1954 and 1960, averaging nearly 18,000 (about 9%) a year; these years include progressively more and more of the children born after the war when birth rates rose to unprecedented levels and death rates declined sharply. This is expected to be followed by a moderately rapid but steady rate of growth in the years 1960-70—an increase of about 3,000-4,000 a year in the school-age population in 1960-65, and about twice as large an annual increase in the next succeeding five-to-six years—reflecting the uniform birth and death rates assumed for the statistical projections.

The primary school enrollment in 1954 is 158,500. This exceeds by 13,500 the estimated number of children in the six-year group of ages 7 to 12 (145,000)—the group for which the government has made a commitment to provide primary education.[57] The excess places are occupied by children 6+ (i.e., age 6-7) and 13+. The primary schools therefore no longer have a backlog of insufficient places with respect to the children of true primary school ages. However, the present number of available places is less than the number of children in the six-year group 6 to 11 (164,000), in the seven-year group 6 to 12 (183,000) or in the eight-year group 6 to 13 (209,000). Consequently, the task of providing places for the increasing primary population will be even greater if the age of entry is 6+ instead of 7+, and if education is to be made available for seven or eight instead of six years.

New Primary Schools and Teachers

Considering only the most conservative of the primary school-age populations, the six-year group in ages 7+ to 12+, the new schools and teachers needed to keep pace with population growth are as follows:

[56] White Papers, Nos. 20 and 25 of 1954.

[57] The estimates for the six years in ages 7 to 12 inclusive are not strictly coterminous with estimates for a six-year school-age population 7+ to 12+ (which means, in general, from age 7¼ to age 13¼). However, the difference is not taken into account here.

Year	School-age Population (Thousand)	Needed New Schools[a]	New Teacher Recruits[b]
1953	134	—	—
1954	145	11	380
1955	163	18	600
1956	183	20	670
1957	201	18	620
1958	224	23	780
1959	240	16	580
1960	243	3	200
1965	259	3	220

[a] One school building per 1,000 increase in primary school population.

[b] Three teachers per 100 pupils, increased by annual recruitment to replace losses by resignation and retirement. (White Paper No. 25 of 1954.)

In the years of very rapid growth, 1953-59 inclusive, the school-age population is expected to increase by 106,000. To keep pace, Singapore will have to build, equip and staff in 1954-59 a total of 106 primary schools of standard design (500 pupils in each of two daily sessions per school building),[58] about 18 schools a year over this six-year period, and the education system will have to recruit about 3,630 new teachers, more than 600 per year.

In the six years 1960-65, when expansion will be much less rapid, Singapore will need 19 new primary schools, a little more than three per year, and an average of 230 new teachers per year. After 1965, the rate of development will presumably increase gradually.

To carry out this program, Singapore will have to exert great effort. Intensive planning by the Department of Education in 1953 and early 1954, in conjunction with the Lands and Public Works Department and the Singapore Improvement Trust, indicates that the sites can be found, the plans can be drawn and the building industry can have the necessary capacity—but not without great difficulty.

Recruitment and training of teachers will be even more difficult than production of the physical facilities. However, it appears that if the conditions for employment of English teachers continue to be relatively favor-

[58] This leaves a margin—for secondary and technical classes—by ignoring the 13,500 places now occupied by children not in the assumed primary group and the children of eligible ages who will not be sent to school as long as attendance is not compulsory.

able, the program can be carried through.[59] It will require, in addition to large expansion of normal classes, the replacement and increased staffing of the present Training College (this is now in progress). Indeed, if the standards of teacher qualification are not to decline seriously, the program should provide for the construction and staffing of a second training college within the seven-year period (presumably in 1957-58). The development of sufficient teachers for the primary schools will, however, have to be augmented by recruitment and training of teachers for the expanding program of secondary education, supplementing the numbers that will become available from the University of Malaya and overseas colleges and universities.

Secondary Schools

Except insofar as it is the link between the primary school and the preparation of a teacher, the secondary school has not been given high priority in Singapore's education program. The undertaking to provide a place in primary school for every child of primary school age nearly exhausts the capacity to recruit and train teachers. Secondary school education therefore has been and continues to be a privileged opportunity for a limited number of children.

Hitherto, nearly all secondary schools have been of the academic (grammar) type.[60] The secondary enrollments have increased from 5,900 in 1947 to 21,900 in August 1954, only slightly exceeding the widely used 20% standard for academic education. Most of the children among the 98,000 of secondary ages (1954) still receive no education beyond the primary level.

The secondary school-age population has been increasing in recent years at a moderate rate. It will start to feel the full impact of the postwar high birth rates in 1959 and succeeding years, when the children born in the postwar years begin to complete the primary years. The number is expected to increase to 105,000 in 1960[61] and then will rise more rapidly. If the secondary schools are to expand and keep pace with secondary population growth, development of additional schools will have to begin between now and 1960.

[59] Details are given in White Papers Nos. 20 and 25 of 1954.

[60] The nonacademic secondary schools include the government's Junior Technical School, the aided junior technical school (St. Joseph's Trade School) and the Chinese normal classes.

[61] Estimated by the Department of Statistics.

The Department of Education hopes to develop during the seven years 1954-60, inclusive, the following secondary schools:

	Number	Capacity
New academic schools	13	8,320
New Raffles Girls' School (academic) . . .	1	500[a]
Junior technical schools	2	400
Secondary-cum-technical schools	6	3,840
Total	22	13,060

[a] Additional capacity over present secondary enrollment.

Added to the present capacity of about 21,900, this would give total secondary enrollment in 1960 of about 35,000 or about 33% of the expected secondary population of that year.[62] The total academic capacity would be about 30,700 or 29%. But the nonacademic enrollments would be increased from about 300 to about 4,540, at which level they woud be equivalent to about 4% of the 1960 secondary population. Though the latter would be supplemented by the post-secondary enrollment of the new Polytechnic (to be constructed in 1954-55 and to achieve a capacity of 500 full-time and possibly 2,000 part-time students in 1960),[63] this does not promise an adequate development of nonacademic education and vocational training for post-primary children.

Cost Estimates for the Government's Program: 1954-60

The cost estimates for the education program outlined in the preceding pages for the years 1954-60 have been estimated by the Department of Education and are summarized in Table 19. Since the precise rate at which schools can be built, equipped and staffed will have to remain uncertain, the new capital expenditures have been treated for convenience as though they would be uniformly distributed over the seven years. The resulting estimates are therefore only indicative for each year; their general level and trend are more reliable.

The annually recurrent expenditures for 1954 are revised estimates

[62] The percentage would be somewhat lower if the indicated capacity should not be achieved until 1961.

[63] Report of the (Dobby) Committee on a Polytechnic Institute for Singapore, 1953.

TABLE 19 Cost Estimates for the
Government's Education Program, 1954-60, Singapore

(Million $)

Type of Expenditure[1]	1954[2]	1955	1956	1957	1958	1959	1960
Annually recurrent[3] . .	27.9	32.8	37.7	43.5	51.3	58.3	65.8
Capital charges[4]	10.0	10.0	10.0	10.0	10.0	10.0	10.0
Gross total	37.9	42.8	47.7	53.5	61.3	68.3	75.8
Income from fees[5] . . .	0.7	0.7	0.8	0.8	0.9	0.9	1.0
Net total	37.2	42.1	46.9	52.7	60.4	67.4	74.8

Breakdown of Gross Totals

	1954[2]	1955	1956	1957	1958	1959	1960
Primary education—							
total	25.00	28.50	32.10	36.70	42.65	48.20	54.00
Annually recurrent.	19.40	22.90	26.50	31.10	37.05	42.60	48.40
Capital charges[4] . .	5.60	5.60	5.60	5.60	5.60	5.60	5.60
Secondary education—							
total	9.45	10.00	10.80	11.65	12.65	13.65	14.95
Annually recurrent .	6.45	7.00	7.80	8.65	9.65	10.65	11.95
Capital charges[4] . .	3.00	3.00	3.00	3.00	3.00	3.00	3.00
Academic—total . . .	8.05	8.35	9.25	10.10	11.05	12.00	13.30
Annually recurrent .	5.95	6.25	7.15	8.00	8.95	9.90	11.20
Capital charges[4] . .	2.10	2.10	2.10	2.10	2.10	2.10	2.10
Technical—total . . .	1.40	1.65	1.55	1.55	1.60	1.65	1.65
Annually recurrent .	0.50	0.75	0.65	0.65	0.70	0.75	0.75
Capital charges[4] . .	0.90	0.90	0.90	0.90	0.90	0.90	0.90
Adult education	0.50	0.65	0.70	0.80	0.90	1.05	1.10
Teacher training—total .	2.10	2.65	2.90	2.95	3.55	3.70	3.90
Annually recurrent .	0.70	1.25	1.50	1.55	2.15	2.30	2.50
Capital charges[4] . .	1.40	1.40	1.40	1.40	1.40	1.40	1.40
Administration and							
inspection	0.85	1.00	1.20	1.40	1.55	1.70	1.85

[1] Includes only expenditures by the Department of Education and the Public Works Department. Does not include expenditures by other departments, grants to the University of Malaya or costs of the Singapore Polytechnic.
[2] Revised estimates (July 1954). See Table 15, footnote 2.
[3] Includes: personal emoluments (PE); other charges annually recurrent (OCAR); and other charges, special expenditures (OCSE). OCAR includes grants-in-aid, and OCSE includes capital grants.
[4] Annual average for the period 1954–60.
[5] Estimated.

SOURCE: Department of Education.

which allow for increase in grants to Chinese schools in accordance with the new policy recently laid down by the government.[64] The estimates for 1956-60 assume that grants will be on the pattern that now applies to government aided English schools.

With capital charges averaging $10 million a year, the recurrent charges may be expected to increase from $28 million in 1954 to $66 million in 1960, and the gross expenditures to rise from $38 million to $76 million.[65] Thus, if Singapore undertakes to carry out the indicated education commitments and obligations, it must prepare to double its public expenditures for education in six years, in addition to providing the amounts that will be needed to support the Polytechnic and the University of Malaya.

The lower portion of Table 19 shows the breakdown of the estimates. Most of the increase is, of course, associated with primary education. Together with teacher training, which is for the most part an integral part of the primary program, this accounts for $31 million of the $38 million increase in the annual gross totals between 1954 and 1960. Relatively smaller increases are associated with secondary and adult education. The increases for administration and inspection, from $850,000 to $1.85 million (from 2.2% to 2.4% of the totals) are modest but essential for the general direction and management of the whole program; indeed, they are probably too low, since it is difficult to believe that these functions can be adequately performed with less than 3-5% of annually recurrent costs.

B   COMMENTS AND RECOMMENDATIONS

In view of social, political and economic needs, the mission believes that Singapore should proceed with expansion of education having as eventual goals (a) evolution of a system of public education, with English as the common language and providing for the multiple lingual and cultural interests of the population; (b) compulsory free education for all children of primary school ages; (c) adequate provision of academic secondary and higher education; and (d) vocational training and education adequate to meet the needs of the Colony's commerce and industry.

Expansion of the present system should, we believe, proceed in general

[64] White Paper No. 81 of (December 8) 1953.
[65] See Table 15, footnote 2, for more recent estimates of actual expenditures in 1954.

along the lines already laid down by the government. First priorities should continue to be given to the primary schools, so that there will be a place in school for every child of the rapidly expanding primary school-age population. This must of necessity be accompanied by rapid expansion of academic secondary education and of recruitment and training of sufficient teachers for the primary and secondary schools. Plans for new government schools should continue to include provisions encouraging the teaching of English in accordance with the wishes of parents and the bilingual policy which has been adopted by the government.

Though these first priorities may tax the resources of the education system and the building industry, our study leads us to recommend that provisions even larger than presently contemplated should be made, when and as feasible, for (a) the education of all children from age 6+ to the employment age 14, (b) maximum practical expansion of nonacademic secondary education (technical, commercial and "modern"), (c) special classes or schools for handicapped, retarded or backward children and (d) adult literacy education. We appreciate that the key to these possible developments is capacity to recruit and train teachers and we offer some suggestions on this score later.

Primary Education

As indicated above, we recommend that the eventual goal for the primary school level should be compulsory free education for all of Singapore's children beginning with the age of 6+, and the school span should be extended eventually from six years to seven or eight years. In the interim, we suggest—as a social as well as an educational measure—that the Department of Education should experiment with two-year intermediate schools or classes for pupils who may profit from further education, especially if it is given a vocational bias. Many children between 12 and 14 who otherwise would leave school would thus be provided an opportunity for some further education and some vocational preparation, instead of being at loose ends or becoming prematurely employed.

In accordance with the bilingual policy, all practical efforts should continue to be made to extend and improve the teaching of English in all government and aided schools in order to give the pupils at least a basic competence in English and to prepare some of them for English secondary schools. In addition, sufficient special classes should be provided in English primary schools to meet the needs of qualified pupils whose parents want them to transfer from vernacular to English schools.

Under the general policy of developing bilingual education, Singapore has already proposed increased government aid for the Chinese schools. Beginning with 1954, grants were being increased as proposed in White Paper No. 81 of (December) 1953. Our study led us to believe they should be further increased by application of the same standards and schedules of financial aid as apply to aided English schools, and our cost estimates for future years were calculated on this basis. The government recently proposed such augmented aid to the Chinese schools. We believe this is a sound course, and we hope that mutually satisfactory working arrangements will be developed between the government and the schools. Provisions for the training of teachers for Chinese schools should be expanded as rapidly as practical. These views concerning the Chinese primary schools we also apply *in toto* to the Chinese secondary schools.

With respect to the Malay schools, we recommend special studies to reassess the relative values—to the Malays and to the Colony—of their bilingual pattern (initial instruction in the home language and subsequent introduction of English) as against the pattern of the English schools.

With respect to the Indian schools, our study suggests that their place in the education system should be reviewed in view of the small enrollment in these schools,[66] the difficulty of staffing them with qualified teachers, the complexity they add to administration and the general preference Indian families have shown for enrollment of their children in English schools.

Finally, we recommend that consideration be given to devising ways of absorbing into the primary schools the children who now receive their elementary education only by attending social welfare centers.

Secondary Education

As indicated earlier, the mission recommends that secondary education be expanded as rapidly as possible in the years 1955-60. The first goal should be provision of about 35,000 places in academic courses by 1960, as now scheduled by the Department of Education. The second should be provision of as many more places as practical in nonacademic courses

[66] It is 1,541 in 1954; it was 1,271 in 1953, with only 184 beyond the third year.

(commercial and "modern") and in technical schools, to prepare Singapore's children of secondary school ages for proficiency and productivity in their future employments and to provide opportunities for increasing numbers to prepare for higher education in specialized fields.

The English secondary schools should increasingly provide opportunity for the study of Asian languages and cultures, and the Chinese schools should have improved teaching of and in English. This development should be accompanied by increased aid for the Chinese schools, as recommended earlier.

Higher Education

The principal problems of higher education in Singapore are in general similar to those in the Federation and the recommendations we have made in the case of the Federation are generally applicable here (see p. 491).

Adult Education

Our study gives encouragement with respect to the outlook for full-time and part-time adult education which will become available through the Singapore Polytechnic and the training resources to be affiliated with it. The mission supports this prospective program.

We also recommend a broadening of the part-time vocational and semi-vocational adult education programs conducted by the Department of Education and the Council for Adult Education.

We are disappointed in the present program of part-time literacy and further education classes for male and female adolescents and adults because of its small size and scope. We strongly recommend rapid expansion, striving toward elimination of adult illiteracy within the next generation. We regard this as so important that we suggest consideration be given to authorizing the establishment of a special operating division within the Department of Education, so that responsibility for this field will not be left wholly or mainly to aided private agencies.

Special Provisions for Handicapped Children

Our study shows that, while a beginning has been made, not enough is being done for handicapped, retarded and backward children. We recommend expansion of special provisions so that eventually such children can receive education suited to their needs and capacities without burdening the resources for other pupils or slowing their pace. In this connection, we suggest that special studies be undertaken to develop methods of differentiating lack of educational capacity from problems of multi-lingualism.

Teacher Training

The mission recommends that the highest priority be given to expansion and strengthening of teacher recruitment and training. This is fundamental to all plans for development of education, since expansion of the education system should not outstrip the development of essential teaching resources. We endorse Singapore's declared eventual objective to have graduates of teacher-training colleges for all primary (and intermediate) teaching posts, and university graduates with diplomas in education for higher teaching levels. In the interim, the expanding education system will have to compromise with these qualitative standards in the interest of achieving essential quantitative growth, and continue to have a large proportion of teachers with only part-time normal training.

However, the system should be prepared to make a temporary sacrifice for the sake of future gain toward the declared qualitative objectives. It should press recruitment for college training, up to the capacity of teacher-training colleges, despite resulting temporary reduction in the number who may be available as probationer or part-time normal-trained teachers.

More specifically, we suggest that the development program should include the following current and additional measures for the critical years immediately ahead:

1. Temporary extension of part-time normal training, particularly in keeping with the rapid expansion of primary enrollments in the next five or six years, with conversion from part-time normal to full-time certificate courses as rapidly as practicable;
2. Expeditious construction of the urgently needed new facilities for the present Teachers' Training College and fullest possible staffing;
3. Development of a second teachers' training college in Singapore as soon as possible (if feasible, in 1957-58);
4. More extensive use of resources for the training of teachers overseas;
5. Special provision in the teachers' training colleges and/or in the

prospective Singapore Polytechnic for the training of teachers of nonacademic subjects, supplementing domestic resources for these purposes by overseas recruitment of qualified personnel on short-term or permanent contracts, with such adjustment of emoluments as may be necessary;

6. Largest practical use of the resources of the University of Malaya (degree course and Diploma in Education), with generous bursaries for students who agree to teach in government or aided English schools;

7. Utilization of qualified teachers who may be prepared by the prospective Nanyang University;

8. Maximum practical use of part-time day and evening teachers, including supplementary teaching as at present by those holding teaching posts, and employment of former teachers and—especially for science and nonacademic subjects—of qualified persons employed in commerce and industry in and near Singapore; and

9. Continuous effort toward achieving uniform standards of education, training and emoluments for all teachers in vernacular and English schools.

Administration, Research and Inspection

It is almost gratuitous to emphasize that the expansion program cannot be carried out well unless the Department of Education is adequately staffed for the study, planning and administrative tasks involved in this complex undertaking. We recommend financial provisions, and authorizations with respect to recruitment and employment of staff, that will permit the maximum that is practical toward increasing the number of personnel to adequate size. The headquarters administrative staff should be supplemented by a group of specialists for research and program planning, and by a greatly strengthened staff of inspectors—to inspect schools, to advise teachers on their work and to help in selecting promising teachers for positions of greater responsibility.

Coordination of Planning and Operations

In view of the growing complexity and importance of vocational preparation and education, the mission recommends that provision be made through an appropriately constituted advisory body to ensure not only careful planning but also effective coordination among the departments and agencies of the Colony Government, the City and Island Council and the private business community.

C ADJUSTED COST ESTIMATES FOR THE DEVELOPMENT PROGRAM

We have brought together in Table 20 estimates of the over-all costs Singapore should expect to incur if it undertakes to carry out the education program we have recommended for the years 1954-60. These have been developed by adding to the estimates in Table 19 as follows:

1. For expansion of the school program along the lines indicated in the text: $1 million per annum for capital charges, and (1955-60, progressively) $2-5 million per annum for annually recurrent costs;
2. For adult literacy classes to be operated by the Department of Education: $500,000 a year.

TABLE 20 Adjusted Estimates for the Education Program, 1954-60[1], Singapore

(*Million $*)

Type of Expenditure	1954[2]	1955	1956	1957	1958	1959	1960
	Department of Education						
Annually recurrent .	27.9	35.3	40.7	47.0	55.3	62.8	71.3
Capital charges . . .	10.0	11.0	11.0	11.0	11.0	11.0	11.0
Gross total . . .	37.9	46.3	51.7	58.0	66.3	73.8	82.3
Income from fees, etc.	0.7	0.8	0.8	0.9	0.9	1.0	1.0
Net total . . .	37.2	45.5	50.9	57.1	65.4	72.8	81.3
	Singapore Polytechnic[3]						
Annually recurrent .	—	—	1.2	1.7	1.9	2.1	2.4
Capital charges	—	5.2	—	—	—	—	—
Gross total . . .	—	5.2	1.2	1.7	1.9	2.1	2.4
Income—total[4] . . .	—	—	0.3	0.5	0.5	0.6	0.6
Net total . . .	—	5.2	0.9	1.2	1.4	1.5	1.8

[1] Exclusive of grants to the University of Malaya.
[2] Revised estimates (July 1954). See Table 15.
[3] Based on estimates in the Report on Singapore Polytechnic, by A. W. Gibson, 1954.
[4] Assumes that income from student fees will equal 7% and from business firms 20% of annually recurrent expenditures.

APPENDIX TABLE 1 Correlation of Enrollments, Racial Proportions in the
Population and Urbanization among States and Settlements, Federation

(%)

State or Settlement[1]	Enrollments,[2] September 1953							Population	
	Total Primary	English Primary	Vernacular Primary	Total Secondary	English Secondary	Chinese Secondary	Urban[3]	Malay[4]	Chinese[4]
Selangor	66.6	14.6	52.1	54.1	43.0	11.1	38.3	26.7	49.8
Penang	66.1	14.5	51.8	71.7	44.2	27.5	56.2	30.3	55.3
Negri Sembilan .	66.1	10.5	55.7	39.5	30.5	9.0	22.3	41.2	41.8
Perak	65.3	10.6	54.9	41.6	31.9	9.7	29.5	38.1	45.8
Pahang	65.0	6.6	58.3	23.8	18.4	5.4	14.4	53.8	39.2
Malacca	63.6	10.8	52.7	38.8	29.4	9.4	26.3	50.9	39.2
*Trengganu	61.4	1.5	59.9	5.3	4.7	0.6	23.5	92.2	6.9
*Johore	59.5	6.0	53.6	23.0	15.6	7.4	22.6	44.9	46.6
*Perlis	55.5	4.4	51.0	5.4	5.4	—	9.0	78.3	16.4
*Kedah	50.9	3.1	47.8	9.1	7.7	1.4	13.8	67.7	20.9
*Kelantan	49.2	1.8	47.3	5.9	4.5	1.4	7.8	91.7	5.9

[1] Arrayed according to % of primary school-age population enrolled.
[2] % of primary or secondary-educative school-age population, respectively.
[3] Census, 1947.
[4] Mid-year 1952.
* Former Unfederated States.

APPENDIX TABLE 2 Schools and Teachers, March 1953, Federation

Federal, State or Settlement	Schools					Teachers				
	English	Malay	Chinese	Indian	Total	English	Malay	Chinese	Indian	Total
Johore	36	352	233	112	733	400	1,380	1,288	159	3,227
Kedah	17	194	87	78	376	209	1,387	328	118	2,042
Kelantan	8	176	22	10	216	84	1,475	99	11	1,669
Malacca	15	102	72	33	222	265	586	326	44	1,221
Negri Sembilan . .	20	123	117	79	339	330	687	494	133	1,644
Pahang	15	182	84	31	312	155	756	377	46	1,334
Penang	43	105	111	41	300	722	912	1,041	119	2,794
Perak	75	386	281	234	976	1,170	2,164	1,866	423	5,623
Perlis	2	36	9	1	48	23	267	42	1	333
Selangor	81	149	169	233	632	1,115	1,076	1,324	453	3,968
Trengganu	2	163	19	—	184	28	714	72	—	814
Federal	2	—	—	—	2	26	—	—	—	26
Total	316	1,968	1,204	852	4,340	4,527	11,404	7,257	1,507	24,695

SOURCE: Legislative Council Paper No. 43 of 1953.

To round out these estimates for future education costs, Table 20 also shows the estimates for construction and operation of the Singapore Polytechnic, although it is intended that this institution shall be administered by an independent body outside the Department of Education.

Thus, to carry out the recommended education program, Singapore should expect and prepare for gross financial expenditures for education[67] that will increase from about $38 million in 1954 to $74 million in 1959 and $82 million in 1960. Development of the Singapore Polytechnic should be expected to add to these costs about $5 million in 1955 when constructed and about $2 million a year by 1959-60. In addition, Singapore should prepare for still higher education costs after 1960 as the population continues to grow, especially if primary education is provided increasingly in free government schools and if Singapore's maturing society and expanding economy demand provision of free secondary education, academic and nonacademic, for increasing proportions of the post-primary population.

APPENDIX TABLE 3 Estimates of School-Age Populations, 1953-60, Federation

(All figures in thousands)

Year	(A)		(B)	
	6–12	13–18	Primary (6+ to 12+)	Secondary (13+ to 18+)
1953	927	787	1,141	857
1954	962	789	1,200	860
1955	1,013	818	1,260	890
1956	1,062	837	1,325	908
1957	1,129	826	1,405	897
1958	1,216	809	1,500	880
1959	1,344	751	1,640	814
1960	1,390	718	1,695	777

SOURCE: (A) Estimates furnished by the Registrar of Statistics; (B) Department of Education estimates for September 1953 and for 1954, successively increased by percentage changes from year to year in (A). Estimates in series B used throughout this report.

[67] Exclusive of grants to the University of Malaya (see p. 184).

TECHNICAL REPORT 10

PUBLIC HEALTH AND MEDICAL CARE

FEDERATION

1 INTRODUCTION

Not long ago, Malaya was one of the unhealthiest places in the tropics. Today it is among the healthiest, comparing favorably with many countries in subtropical climates. This is one of the world's outstanding achievements of public health and medicine, a tribute to the British administrators and their medical and public health officers.

The undertaking to conquer some of the worst epidemic and endemic diseases of Malaya was stimulated by the needs of economic development. The successful expansion of tin mining, of rubber planting and agriculture generally, of industry and commerce, depended upon a reduction in the prevalence of tropical disease. Large expenditures to prevent disease and to care for the sick brought more than commensurate returns in well-being, growth of population, productivity and wealth.

As in other tropical countries, the first emphasis in the health services of the 19th century was on curative medicine. Malaya had the good fortune, however, that its development came mainly late in the century, in time to profit from the birth of bacteriology, the emergence of modern epidemiology and the development of effective methods to control tropical disease. In 1895, when four Malay States federated, medical staff had already been recruited and hospitals had already been established in the main centers of population. The discoveries of modern medicine and public health at the turn of the century were quickly applied on a large scale in Malaya. Malaria, which had been the scourge of the land, began to come under control. The wealth produced from tin and rubber, made possible in large measure by prevention of disease among the laborers, in turn provided the means for generous support of an expanding program of sanitation, construction of hospitals and recruitment of trained staff from the Western world.

546

Between 1900 and World War II, health progress in Malaya had many ups and downs; health services were affected by alternating cycles of boom and depression and by the diversion of public resources during World War I. Nevertheless, there was on the whole quite steady improvement up to the outbreak of World War II. There was a bad setback during the Japanese occupation. Local output of professional staff dried up and replacements were not available. The health of the people deteriorated—due to bad diet, general privation, abandonment of many health measures, and neglect of anti-malaria work generally and of special health services for the labor force used by the occupation authorities. When the British authorities took over early in 1946, the health picture was discouraging. The Medical Department applied itself to recover the lost ground with such vigor that by 1949 most of the wartime damage had been undone, except for the apparently new widespread prevalence of tuberculosis and the damaged health of young children—two legacies of the war that persist and create problems for the years ahead.

Health achievements are by no means complete. There are still areas of the country (e.g., in parts of Trengganu) where 50-90% of the population shows signs of malaria, where worm infestations are more or less universal, where yaws is prevalent, leprosy not uncommon or smallpox a constant threat. Tuberculosis, venereal diseases, malnutrition and a host of lesser ailments, though preventable or curable, are still widespread causes of sickness, disability and premature death more or less throughout Malaya. These are part of the unfinished business of the health program. The other part is the maintenance of what has already been done, lest indifference or neglect permit the old plagues to revive or new ones to enter the country.

Large expenditures in the past have brought a relatively high level of health, but they do not promise smaller expenditures for the future. Difficult problems have yet to be solved, and some of them involve very expensive procedures because, increasingly, they require personal services rather than environmental controls. The population is growing rapidly and there will be more people to be served, especially through costly urban services. Many hospitals and other facilities have grown old and dilapidated and need replacement. Professional staff is insufficient and, as has long been appreciated might happen, all racial groups in the population now increasingly accept and expect "western medicine," and have begun to demand clinic and hospital services exceeding the capacity of the available resources. Since health and medical services are, in the main, supported by the general revenues of government, the Federation is confronted with rapidly rising public costs.

II SOME VITAL STATISTICS FOR THE FEDERATION

Malaya was sparsely populated for a long time. Births and deaths were about equal, and population increases resulted mainly from excess of immigration over emigration. In recent years population has grown very rapidly: from 2.34 million in 1911 to 4.91 million in 1947 (the last census year) and to an estimated 5.9 million in 1954.

Fragmentary data suggest that the birth rate was in the range of 35-40 births per 1,000 persons in the 19th century and the death rate only slightly lower. Infant mortality was probably at the rate of about 300 deaths per 1,000 births or per 1,000 children under one year of age. By the early 20th century the rate of mortality was much lower, although still very high in various parts of the Malay States. For example, it is reported that on some of the first rubber plantations, there were 200 adult deaths a year per 1,000 workers about 1910. Statistics on causes of sickness and death have been highly unreliable; as recently as 1937, one-third of the deaths were reported as due to "fevers of undefined nature."

Marked decline of the death rate, with persistence and even increase of the birth rate, is in the main a postwar phenomenon. The birth, death and infant mortality rates for the years 1947-54 are shown, by race, in Table 1.

Since births are incompletely recorded, minor changes in the birth rates from year to year and in differences among the racial groups are presumably insignificant. In general, the rates are essentially the same among the various Asian groups,[1] are at least 40-45 per 1,000 of population and, with allowance for under-reporting, are probably 45-50.

The death rates have been declining sharply in all racial groups, most strikingly among the Malaysians. Rates of 10-11 per 1,000 among the Chinese and Indians are down to levels customary in western Europe and North America, though here they reflect in part the relatively low average age of the population.

These birth and death rates suggest that natural increase of population

[1] They are much lower among "others" (Europeans, Eurasians, etc.).

TABLE 1 Birth and Death Rates by Race, 1947-53, Federation

Year	All Races	Malaysians	Chinese	Indians and Pakistanis	Others
Births per 1,000 Population					
1947	43	41	44	49	22
1948	40	37	44	45	26
1949	44	43	44	49	32
1950	42	42	42	45	30
1951	44	45	42	46	31
1952	44	46	43	45	32
1953	44	45	42	44	32
1954	44	46	41	44	33
Deaths per 1,000 Population					
1947	19	24	14	16	12
1948	16	20	13	13	14
1949	14	17	12	12	14
1950	16	19	13	14	14
1951	15	17	13	13	11
1952	14	15	12	13	10
1953	12	15	10	11	10
1954	12	15	10	10	9
Infant Deaths per 1,000 Live Births					
1947	102	129	70	99	63
1948	89	111	67	88	68
1949	81	93	64	85	59
1950	102	121	74	114	67
1951	97	108	82	104	45
1952	90	101	69	108	38
1953	83	98	61	92	41
1954	83	100	59	83	47

SOURCE: Annual Report, Federation of Malaya, 1953, and Annual Reports, Medical Department, 1947–54.

is at the rate of about 30-32 per 1,000 of population (about 3%). If, as seems probable, there is more under-reporting of births than of deaths, natural increase may be at a rate closer to 3½% than to 3%.

Infant mortality is a sensitive index of health conditions in other parts of the world and it may also be in the Federation. Unfortunately, since the reliability of infant mortality rates depends on the accuracy with which both births and infant deaths are reported, the recorded rates are of uncertain value and it is difficult to determine whether they understate or overstate decline in true infant mortality. These rates show much less decline than the crude death rates for all ages.[2]

Reported maternal deaths have also declined moderately in proportion to population in Malaya, from 7.0 maternal deaths per 1,000 births in 1947 to 4.7 in 1954.[3]

With due allowance for crudities and elements of uncertainty in the mortality rates,[4] the available data nevertheless indicate general decline in mortality in the postwar years. There can be no doubt that Malaya's health progress of a half-century continues, and it is highly probable that improvements are being made at an accelerated rate.

III SUMMARY OF PERSONNEL AND FACILITIES

The resources for health and medical services in Malaya are, in the main, those provided by the Federal and State/Settlement Governments. The Federation has, in considerable measure, a comprehensive public health and national medical service whose resources are available free or with only limited charges to the population. In addition, there are private practitioners, hospitals, clinics and specialized facilities. In the urban areas these are identified with the private practice of medicine or the activities of voluntary agencies concerned especially with tuberculosis, maternal and child welfare, etc., and in the rural areas mainly with the agricultural estates and the mines.

These public and private resources provide "Western medicine" on the educational standards and the operating patterns of Great Britain. There are also many individuals who act as "native" medical practitioners, midwives, herbalists, religious healers, etc.; they practice primitive medical

---

[2] The infant mortality rates in Table 1 may be compared with corresponding rates of about 20-25 in Australia and New Zealand, 20-50 in western Europe, 25-30 in the United States and Canada, 50-75 in southeastern Europe, about 80 in Ceylon, 105 in the Philippines, 115 or more in India and 75-150 in many other countries. (U. N. Statistical Yearbook 1953.)

[3] In western Europe and the United States rates of about 1 per 1,000 live births are now common.

[4] Lacking data on age distribution of the population, it is not possible to standardize the rates for age and thus avoid effects of possible changes in age distribution that may be associated with the high birth rates of recent years. Also, since three-fourths or more of all deaths are registered without medical certification, cause of death is uncertain in one-half or more cases and analysis of mortality by cause is unrewarding.

TABLE 2   Health and Medical Personnel,[1] March 1954, Federation

Personnel		Number	Population per Practitioner[2]
Physicians[3]	Total	631	9,200
Government		274	21,200
Private		357	16,300
Dentists	Total	630	9,200
Qualified	Sub-total	68	85,500
Government		44	132,000
Private		24	242,000
Registered	Sub-total	562	10,300
Government		1	—
Private		561	9,500
Pharmacists		6	96,900
Sanitary Inspectors		134	43,400
Medical Assistants[4]		1,020	5,700
Nurses	Total	1,289	4,500
Senior[5] and certificated[6]		757	7,700
Partially trained		337	17,300
Assistant nurses		151	38,500
Dental nurses		44	132,000
Technical Staff	Total	88	66,100
Laboratory assistants		63	92,300
X-ray technicians		11	529,000
Dental mechanics		14	415,000
Midwives[7]		501	11,600

[1] Excludes personnel in mission establishments; numbers not available. Also excludes physicians and others in administrative posts.

[2] Ratios based on population estimate of 5,814,700 as of Dec. 31, 1953.

[3] Registered for clinical services; with degrees recognized locally and overseas. Exclusive of physicians in administrative and research posts.

[4] Persons with advanced medical training below the university level.

[5] With training equivalent to that in the metropolitan country.

[6] With certificate recognized locally but not overseas.

[7] With training equivalent to that provided overseas, or with certificate recognized locally.

SOURCE: Medical Department.

arts inherited largely from the pre-scientific knowledge and superstitions of earlier Asian cultures, including the ancient indigenous medicine of Southeast Asia and the medicine brought to Malaya by the Chinese.

Personnel and Facilities

Total health and medical personnel in the Federation, exclusive of those in administrative posts and of nonregistered or nontrained practitioners, are summarized in Table 2. These are, in effect, the persons available for more or less direct personal health and medical services to the

TABLE 3   Hospitals, Health Centers and Dispensaries, April 1954, Federation

Type of Institution	Institutions	Beds	
		Number	Per 1,000 Persons[1]
Hospitals Total	213	18,027	3.1
Government Sub-total	67	11,930	2.1
General[2]	30	8,537	1.5
District[3]	37	3,393	0.6
Private Sub-total	146	6,097	1.0
Estate	120	5,477	0.9
Mission	1	85	0.01
Maternity	25	535	0.09
Specialized units (government)			
Maternity and child welfare[4] . .	477	120	0.02
Tuberculosis[5]	8	637	0.1
Venereal diseases[6]	12	—	—
Leprosy[7]	4	3,470	0.6
Mental	2	4,200	0.7
Dispensaries[8] (government)	169	—	—
Mobile units[9] (government)	75	—	—

[1] Ratios based on population estimate of 5,814,700 as of Dec. 31, 1953.
[2] Institutions equipped to deal with all general, medical and surgical cases.
[3] Smaller hospitals which refer severe or complicated cases to general hospitals.
[4] 104 main and 372 sub-clinics, and the 120-bed maternity hospital at Penang.
[5] Four institutions with beds; three clinics and 1 BCG vaccination unit.
[6] Clinics and dispensaries.
[7] Three settlements and one camp.
[8] Institutions primarily for the treatment of out-patients.
[9] Total staff, 75.

SOURCE: Medical Department.

population. In March 1954, there were 631 physicians in government service and private practice to serve 5.8 million people—one per 9,200 persons. There were about as many dentists, a few registered pharmacists, 134 qualified sanitary inspectors, over 1,000 medical assistants, nearly 1,300 nurses with various levels of training, less than 100 trained technicians and about 500 trained midwives.

Similarly, the hospital and other institutional facilities of the Federation are summarized in Table 3. Exclusive of specialized institutions, there were (in April 1954) 213 hospitals with a total of over 18,000 beds, equivalent to about 3.1 beds per 1,000 persons. Less than one-third of the hospitals were governmental but they had two-thirds of the beds.[5]

The institutions that are classified as hospitals are highly diverse. At the one extreme, there are many private hospitals with only a few beds each, the most meager equipment, limited secondary staff and a part-time attending physician; at the other, there are the fully equipped and staffed large modern institutions represented by the government general hospitals at Penang (694 beds), Malacca (628 beds) and Johore Bahru (600 beds).

The hospitals, specialized institutions, dispensaries and mobile units maintained by government are supplemented by a variety of private (proprietary and nonprofit) institutions and facilities other than hospitals— mostly small and meager, and their total number not recorded—for the care of ambulatory patients, acute cases needing short-term bed care, or chronic cases needing long-term institutional or primarily domiciliary maintenance and supervision.

Distribution among the States and Settlements

The distribution of registered private physicians and of government physicians throughout the country is shown in Table 4; their numbers have been related to the populations of the several States and Settlements. There are about 16,600 persons per registered private physician in the country as a whole, but the ratio ranges from about 7,000 in Penang to about 124,500 in Trengganu (in the latter there are only two registered private physicians although the population of the State is nearly 250,000 persons). Government physicians average about one for 21,000 persons, with much less variation in the ratio from State to State than obtains for private practitioners.

---

[5] On the average the government hospitals had 178 beds, the private hospitals 42 beds, and all hospitals 84 beds.

TABLE 4   Physicians in the States and Settlements, March 1954, Federation

State/Settlement	Popula-tion[1] (Thousands)	Physicians[2] Private	Govern-ment	Persons per Physician[3] Private	Govern-ment	Both
Perak	1,117	74	49	15,100	22,800	9,100
Johore	875	40	46	21,900	19,000	10,200
Selangor	847	89	47	9,500	18,000	6,200
Kedah	646	16	26	40,400	24,800	15,400
Penang	512	71	33	7,200	15,500	4,900
Kelantan	494	6	7	82,300	70,600	38,000
Negri Sembilan	321	17	24	18,900	13,400	7,800
Malacca	283	19	16	14,900	17,700	8,100
Pahang	281	8	16	35,100	17,600	11,700
Trengganu	249	2	7	124,500	35,600	27,700
Perlis	81	1	3	81,000	27,000	20,300
All	5,706	343	274	16,600	20,800	9,200

[1] Mid-year 1953.

[2] March 1954. "Private" includes only registered physicians by place of registration; less than the total (357) for the Federation shown in Table 2. "Government" includes only physicians engaged part- or full-time in general or specialized clinical service; it excludes administrative officers and those in tuberculosis settlements, mental disease hospitals, leprosaria, port quarantine, research, etc.

[3] Ratios slightly understated because calculated against estimated populations of mid-year 1953.

SOURCE: Medical Department.

Taking all physicians, private and government, together, there is about one for 9,200 persons, and the ratio ranges in the several States and Settlements from 4,900 (Penang) to 38,000 (Kelantan). The maximum is nearly eight times the minimum, but most of the States are within the range of 8,000-20,000 persons per physician. In other words, the distribution of government physicians is such as to reduce the variations though still leaving a comparatively wide range in the ratios.

The distribution of hospitals is shown in Table 5. The private Chinese maternity institutions serve mainly Chinese but also admit women of the other races. Many of the estate hospitals serve as general community hospitals but tend to have limited clientele. The government hospitals supply 2.1 beds per 1,000 persons in the Federation as a whole, from a minimum of 0.7 (Kelantan) to a maximum of 3.9 (Negri Sembilan). The total of 222 general hospitals, private and governmental (exclusive of the tuberculosis, mental, leper and other specialized institutions), has over 18,000 beds,

TABLE 5 Hospitals in the States and Settlements[1], Federation

State or Settlement	Private Hospitals[2]				Government Hospitals[3]				All Hospitals		
	Hospitals and Maternity Homes[4]		Estate Hospitals		General		District		Number	Beds	
	Number	Beds	Number	Beds	Number	Beds	Number	Beds		Number	Per 1,000 Persons[5]
Perak	3	142	28	1,305	8	2,292	4	306	43	4,045	3.6
Johore	—	—	13	462	4	1,306	5	602	22	2,370	2.7
Selangor	3	241	29	1,280	2	642	6	995	40	3,158	3.7
Kedah	—	—	13	1,087	3	888	2	111	18	2,086	3.2
Penang	11	223	3	205	1	694	7	589	22	1,711	3.3
Kelantan	—	—	4	82	1	276	2	73	7	431	0.9
Negri Sembilan . .	1	25	17	919	2	760	5	477	25	2,181	6.8
Malacca	4	45	21	206	1	628	4	150	30	1,029	3.6
Pahang	—	—	4	172	6	731	—	—	10	903	3.2
Trengganu	—	—	1	50	1	200	2	90	4	340	1.4
Perlis	—	—	—	—	1	120	—	—	1	120	1.5
All	22	676	133	5,768	30	8,537	37	3,393	222	18,374	3.2

[1] Total hospitals and beds differ slightly from numbers in Table 3 because of differences in dates on which national and State/Settlement counts were made.
[2] December 31, 1952.
[3] April, 1954.
[4] All Chinese maternity hospitals or homes except one hospital in Selangor and two in Penang.
[5] Ratios slightly overstated because calculated against estimated populations of mid-year 1953.

SOURCE: Medical Department.

about 3.2 per 1,000 persons in the Federation. The variations are from 0.9 per 1,000 in Kelantan to 6.8 in Negri Sembilan. Disregarding the lowest and highest ratios, the range is from 1.4 beds per 1,000 in Trengganu to 3.7 in Selangor. Considered by standards applied in many countries of the world, these ratios suggest that there are generally sufficient hospital beds in Malaya as a whole, but shortages—ranging from mild to severe—in some of the States.

IV GOVERNMENT ESTABLISHMENTS AND ACTIVITIES

A THE GOVERNMENT ESTABLISHMENTS

In accordance with the terms of the Federation Agreement, 1948, medical and health functions are divided between the Federal Government and the States and Settlements. The Federal Government performs the national and multi-State/Settlement functions and operates institutions which serve the whole Federation or several States/Settlements; the State/Settlement Governments operate most of the intra-State/Settlement health and medical facilities. The Federal functions are financed directly by the Federal Government, and the State/Settlement functions by Federal funds provided through lump-sum grants. The municipalities and other local bodies raise and spend relatively small additional amounts for public health and related functions.

The government medical departments provide preventive and sanitary services for communities and special groups in the population and, in addition, diagnostic and treatment services for the sick. The public health and the medical and hospital functions are largely integrated at each level of government.

The Federal Medical Department is generally responsible, under the Member for Health, for the health and medical programs of the Federation. It is directly responsible for over-all planning, port health and quarantine services, research, the recruitment of professional staff and their posting to the State/Settlement Governments, training of personnel (this function is shared with the State/Settlement departments), maintenance of central stores which supply all the government departments, and direct operation of the four leprosy settlements, the two mental hospitals of the Federation and the two general hospitals in the Settlements.

The State/Settlement medical departments are largely independent, controlled by the respective State/Settlement Governments. Their annual estimates for health and medical services are reviewed by the Federal authorities, and the Member for Health and the Director of Medical Services advise on plans and programs. There is considerable lattitude, however, in the operations of the State/Settlement departments and local authorities, despite the fact that nearly all of the funds are provided by the Federal Government.

The budgets of the medical establishments now provide for about 3,215 personnel; of these, 1,678 are for the Federal Department and 1,537 for the State/Settlement departments.

The State/Settlement departments carry the main load of operating responsibilities—they provide the major sanitary and other preventive services and they operate the general hospitals (except the two in the Settlements), the district and lesser hospitals, the clinics, dispensaries and welfare centers. In effect, they offer—up to the capacity of their medical facilities— general public medical services for any in the population who request and need care.

In addition to their services for in-patients, all government hospitals operate out-patient departments. There are also fixed and mobile clinics and dispensaries. The services for the ambulatory sick are without fee. Charges for in-patients vary among the hospitals and are graduated according to the type of accommodation.[6] Government employees and members of their families are charged at reduced rates, usually about one-half the standard rates. Ward charges cover all professional services as well as bed, diet, nursing, medicines, etc., and are considerably less than operating costs.

B ACTIVITIES OF THE MEDICAL DEPARTMENTS

The operation of hospitals, clinics and dispensaries accounts for a large part of the work of the Federal Department and is the main activity of the State/Settlement medical departments. Some of the principal details will be

[6] Charges for the third class wards are small or nominal ($0.50-$1.50 per day) and are frequently remitted; many of these wards are entirely free. Charges in the second class wards are commonly $2-$5 per day. In the hospitals that have first class rooms, the charges are usually $8-$10 per day. In a few places there are single-bed rooms, costing $12-$15 per day. All of these are ordinarily all-inclusive charges, though some States require extra payments for X-ray, laboratory and other items from first class, or from first and second class, ward patients.

summarized later. Brief notes here may suffice to indicate the scope of other services performed by the medical departments.[7]

Port Health and Quarantine

The Federal Department reviews incoming passenger and pilgrim ships, quarantines deck passengers when such action is indicated, performs vaccinations, inspects aircraft, water boats, lighters, etc. The Department is especially concerned with preventing the importation of dangerous infectious diseases—yellow fever,[8] smallpox, plague, cholera, etc.

Sanitation and the Control of Malaria and Other Diseases

Sanitation and the control of malaria and other diseases are among the main activities of the medical departments, particularly because of the never-ending need to control malaria. In large urban areas, malaria is efficiently controlled; in the smaller towns and in rural areas it is still prevalent. Except for an unexplained rise in 1951-52, malaria admissions to hospitals and clinics, deaths and fatality rates have been declining—admissions from over 22,000 in 1947 to less than 10,000 in 1954, deaths from 736 to 111, and deaths per 100 cases from 3.3 to 0.9. The known cases and deaths are, of course, only a small fraction of the total that occur. Control measures, guided by the Malaria Advisory Board, include extensive activities in education, drainage and mosquito control, house and area spraying with DDT and other residual insecticides, prophylactic and suppressive treatment, clinic and hospital care of acute cases, surveys and research. Control is greatly complicated by new agricultural drainage and irrigation undertakings and by resettlement of population.

Hookworm and other infestations are still widespread, but there is no reliable estimate of prevalence or incidence. In the hospital and dispensary returns for 1953 there were at least 6,400 in-patients and 166,000 out-patients treated for amoebiasis, other protozoal and unspecified dysenteries, hookworm and round worm, and nonspecified helminth diseases.

Activities to improve housing, to provide latrines and drainage, and to

[7] Details are given in the Annual Reports of the Medical Department.

[8] A potential insect vector is present in Malaya and international air transport is increasing.

extend public understanding of disease control and clinical treatment continue—but unevenly and sporadically.

Leprosy

The prevalence of leprosy is not known with even approximate reliability but there is no doubt that it is high and extensive. Special facilities for the isolation and treatment of lepers are provided as follows:

	Beds	Average Daily Patients (1954)
Leper Settlement, Sungei Buloh .	2,650	2,427
Leper Settlement, Johore Bahru .	350	389
Leper Settlement, Pulau Jerejak .	440	438
Leper Camp, Kota Bharu	40	33
Total	3,480	3,287

Various drugs are being used and research is going forward. Welfare activities are conducted in each settlement. An experiment on resettlement and encouragement of self-dependency of discharged cases in Province Wellesley apparently has been successful.

Smallpox

Smallpox is substantially under control now; there were no indigenous cases in 1953 and 1954. The medical departments perform about 300,000 vaccinations a year.

Yaws

Yaws is still widely prevalent and is extensive in some areas, especially on the east coast. In 1954, 40,000 cases were treated, apparently a small fraction of the number needing treatment. Surveys were made in 1953 in Kelantan and Trengganu under the direction of an expert provided by WHO, and an intensive penicillin treatment and control program was started in April 1954 with equipment from UNICEF and technical assistance from WHO.

Venereal Diseases

Venereal diseases are known to be widespread in the population, but there are no reliable prevalence or incidence rates for the general population or for persons examined for other conditions in the hospitals and dispensaries. The incidence of new cases treated in the hospitals and special clinics has been declining; between 1947 and 1954, new syphilis cases fell from 12,500 to 4,000, gonorrhea from 6,600 to 5,300, and other venereal cases from 2,000 to 900.

Diphtheria

Diphtheria is widely prevalent and occasionally breaks out in epidemic form. In 1953, there was a mild outbreak in Malacca: 1,182 cases with 319 deaths. Comparatively small numbers of immunizations are done. A campaign to bring infants and young children to the clinics for immunization was undertaken in 1953-54 but there has been only limited public response.

Tuberculosis

Tuberculosis continues to be widely prevalent and one of the most serious diseases in Malaya. Prevalence and incidence are not reliably known; there have been no comprehensive surveys. Most of the cases seen in the hospitals and dispensaries are pulmonary. Since the facilities for the care of the tuberculous are overtaxed and waiting lists are common, the number of cases treated is not a reliable index of prevalence.

About 2,900 beds in the government hospitals are now allocated for tuberculosis (about 23% of the beds). In addition, about 30% of the beds in general wards are occupied by tuberculosis patients. Altogether, about 5,460 (45% of all beds in hospitals) are being used for this disease. Large proportions of the cases reach the dispensaries and hospitals too late for good prognoses and, for lack of other resources for their care, are kept for six months and longer in beds intended for acutely sick persons.

Hospital in-patient admissions (all forms of tuberculosis) in government institutions have declined from 9,000 in 1947 to 6,500 in 1954; dispensary out-patient admissions have increased from 4,600 to 6,300. Treatment utilizes rest, diet, surgical intervention, and biochemical and antibiotic drugs (streptomycin with PAS, isonicotinic hydrazide, etc.).

BCG vaccination was instituted in 1951 under the guidance of a Danish team. About 109,000 persons were tuberculin tested in 1954, and about 62,100 were vaccinated (50,000 adults and 12,100 newborn).

In 1953 and early 1954 there was much public discussion of measures to relieve the hospitals of chronic tuberculosis cases, especially by development of settlements for such cases under the auspices of either the government or the Malayan Association for the Prevention of Tuberculosis (MAPTB).

A beginning was made, primarily through voluntary gifts, toward erecting the Lady Templer Hospital for Tuberculosis in Kuala Lumpur—to provide 250 beds for treatable cases and research, with supplementary settlement beds elsewhere.

Mental Disease

Except for about 190 beds for psychotics in the government hospitals, the whole of the mental health services of the Federation consists of two mental disease hospitals: the Central Mental Hospital at Tanjong Rambutan (near Ipoh in Perak State) with 3,000 beds, and (since 1952) the Mental Hospital at Tampoi (near Johore Bahru in Johore State) with 1,200 beds and with capacity up to 2,000 beds. There are no provisions for mental defectives, for prevention or after-care, and there are no out-patient clinics. Services at the two hospitals in 1954 were as follows:

	Patients 1/1/53	Admissions	Discharges	Deaths
Tanjong Rambutan	3,462	1,659	1,564	181
Tampoi	836	590	422	42
Total	4,298	2,249	1,986	223

Each institution has a very small staff and extremely limited resources for treatment.

Dental Services

Considerable progress has been made in providing dental care, especially for children, by developing fixed and mobile dental clinics, recruiting staff and inaugurating the training of dental nurses. Services provided in the clinics have increased greatly—from 102,000 attendances in 1947 to 318,000 in 1954. Most of the dental services are extractions rather than preventive care.

Development of a Dental Nurses Training School at Penang makes possible increase in dental services for school children and others without, as in the past, depleting the medical department's supply of trained nurses. Newly completed health centers are being equipped with dental facilities, new school dental clinics are being opened, and mobile dental clinics are being added.

Maternity and Child Welfare

The maternity and child welfare field is one of the most rapidly growing areas of medical department activity. In recent years, in-patient (maternity) and out-patient (maternal and child) services have been as follows:

	1949	1952	1953	1954
Admissions to maternity wards[9]	37,741	47,360	40,833	46,692
Attendances at welfare centers	633,638	983,355	1,087,204	1,192,413
Home visits to mothers and children	271,553	419,939	500,866	470,510

The government hospitals now have about 1,175 beds (in a total of 12,000) allocated to obstetrics. Resources for preventive and curative services on an ambulatory basis have been increased; permanent maternal and child welfare centers have grown from 58 in 1949 to 100 in 1954, and subsidiary centers from 80 to 401. Each center is normally under the supervision of a health sister, with a staff of health nurses and trained midwives. Prenatal services are provided; advice is given on infant feeding and hygiene; mild diseases of children are treated; and midwifery services are provided for the rural areas through salaried or subsidized midwives. Red Cross and St. John's welfare teams assist in the work in the New Villages and in rural Malay communities.

Nutrition

Technical research studies on nutrition and on the nutritional status of the population are being carried out with limited resources at the Institute

[9] There were 280 maternal deaths in hospitals in 1949, 378 in 1952, 368 in 1953 and 385 in 1954.

for Medical Research. Surveys which have been undertaken have not, however, been completed.

It is commonly reported that there is now no marked nutritional deficiency in the Federation, but beri-beri is still one of the leading causes of hospital and dispensary admissions, and mild and severe cases of malnutrition of infants and young children are commonly seen in the course of hospital and dispensary rounds.[10] The adequacy of the diets of the various racial groups in Malaya, especially among the agricultural populations, has been the subject of debate.[11]

Education on nutrition is being carried forward for children in schools, in cooperation with the Department of Education, by radio and otherwise through the Department of Information and various voluntary agencies. There is supplementary school feeding in some local areas, and skimmed milk powder is distributed to some schools.

Rural Health Services

Development of a comprehensive rural health service is complicated by the emergency, especially by the removal of approximately 10% of the country's population to new villages and resettlement areas. The relocations have created new health hazards and needs, by bringing together families accustomed to living in widely scattered areas, but have also increased the opportunities for effective health service by aggregating hitherto isolated people into communities where they can be reached.

The Medical Department has formulated a tentative national rural health program and has begun to implement it. The basic plan calls for (a) trained rural midwives, one per 2,000 persons, (b) sub-district health centers, one per 10,000 persons, including a center staff and the five midwives of the area, and (c) district health centers, one per 50,000 persons, serving as a sub-district center in its locus and as headquarters for four other such centers. For a rural population of 4.5 million, 90 district health centers would be needed (and 360 additional sub-district centers). Large scale staff recruitment and training would be an essential part of the program— and this would take many years to carry out.

[10] The hospital and dispensary returns on causes of sickness and death for 1954 (Annual Report, Medical Department) show over 169,000 cases of deficiency diseases (beri-beri, malnutrition, "other deficiency states," "other specified and unspecified anaemias," etc.)

[11] The subject is discussed at length in *The Institute for Medical Research,* Jubilee Volume No. 25, Kuala Lumpur, 1951.

Eight health centers are in process of development, the 1954-55 part of the program which contemplates establishment of 25 centers between 1954 and 1960. A pilot plan in Penang (1953-54) has operated successfully. An experimental training health center is being constructed at Jitra, north of Alor Star in Kedah State, with WHO and UNICEF help; a second model health center, to be located in Malacca, is being designed for the southern part of the country.

The present and prospective rural health services are intended to be interlocked with the urban facilities, relying on the district and general hospitals for specialized medical services.[12]

Research

Medical and epidemiological research activities are largely centered in the Institute for Medical Research (IMR) in Kuala Lumpur, though some studies are also conducted in the hospitals. The IMR, part of the Federal Medical Department, is maintained by Federal funds, with financial contributions from the Governments of Singapore and North Borneo and with special support from other governments for studies of international interest. Its studies, field experiments and publications have played a fundamental role in the development of the health and medical services of Malaya, as well as making important contributions to control of tropical diseases throughout the world. The IMR prepares biological products which are especially important for Malaya or Southeast Asia and which it can manufacture at less than commercial purchase cost, and it performs routine and special laboratory examinations and tests for the hospitals and dispensaries and for private practitioners of the Federation.

Recruitment and Training of Personnel

Since Malaya continues to suffer acute shortages in nearly all categories of trained public health and medical personnel, the recruitment, education and training activities of the Federal Medical Department are of basic importance for maintenance and development of the services.

---

[12] Rural health facilities include, in addition to the maternal and child welfare centers, dispensaries and mobile units shown in Table 3, five treatment rooms, 31 Red Cross and 26 St. John's welfare teams, and 16 mission stations.

Physicians, dentists and pharmacists are increasingly becoming available from the University of Malaya but the Department still has to recruit physicians and dentists from overseas. The shortage of physicians was greatly eased by two developments in 1952-53. First, the new Registration of Medical Practitioners' Ordinance came into force, providing for provisional registration of newly qualified physicians and for their service for a year as house doctors (internes). Second, nearly 50 physicians who are not Federal citizens were recruited on contract, mainly from India. However, there are still serious deficiencies of most specialists, especially anaesthetists, pathologists and radiologists.

The shortage of nurses has been one of the most serious problems for the Medical Department. The Department has now developed three nurses' training schools—at Penang, Kuala Lumpur and Johore Bahru. A fourth may have to be established for Malay nurses on the east coast. However, in early 1954 the total number of student nurses and assistant nurses in training was still only a little over 200, considerably below even the capacity of the present schools.[13]

A beginning has been made toward filling another acute need by opening a school at Penang for the training of dental nurses on the New Zealand pattern. The recruitment standards and the training period are similar to those for student nurses. In February 1954 there were 24 in training (14 in the second year), the number being limited primarily by availability of hostel accommodations. As a supplement to the domestic program for nurses' training, the Federation has accepted an offer from Australia (under the Colombo plan) to train 50 student nurses. About one-half this number were recruited for the first year (1954).

C IN-PATIENT CARE IN GOVERNMENT HOSPITALS

In 1954, when the Federal and State/Settlement Governments were operating 71 general, district and tuberculosis hospitals with 12,700 beds,[14] they had 236,000 admissions and, with patients carried over from the preceding year, cared for nearly 245,000 cases. Having an average occupancy

[13] Present plans contemplate expansions to accommodate 250 at each of three main schools (and 100 at the Malay east coast school) so that there would be 750-850 in training each year.

[14] Exclusive of three leper settlements and a leper camp (with a total of 3,470 beds), and of two mental hospitals (with 4,200 beds).

rate of about 82%, these hospitals provided about 3.8 million in-patient days of care—equivalent to nearly 0.7 day per capita in the population. This compares favorably with the amount of hospitalization furnished in general (or in general and special) and tuberculosis hospitals in many European and American countries.[15] About one-sixth of all deaths in the Federation occurred in the hospitals.

The activities of the medical departments have increased in the postwar years and, as will appear later, their expenditures have multiplied several fold. However, though the hospitals have been greatly improved, their in-patient capacity has declined and their volume of in-patient services has not changed substantially between 1947 and 1954. This is evident from the following summary:[16]

Year	Hospitals	Beds	Average Daily Patients	Admissions
1947 . . .	65	13,403	10,431	216,091
1948 . . .	72	13,177	10,188	203,279
1949 . . .	72	13,124	10,063	204,608
1950 . . .	69	13,332	10,445	207,483
1951 . . .	70	13,143	10,360	223,287
1952 . . .	70	12,983	10,249	222,154
1953 . . .	70	12,687	10,435	233,286
1954 . . .	71	12,763	10,446	235,738

The number of admissions increased by about 9% over these years, but population grew by more than 16%. The admission rates were 44 per 1,000 persons in 1947 and 41 per 1,000 in 1954.

All racial groups in the Federation use the hospitals. The racial proportions of in-patients in 1954 were: Chinese 45%, Indians 31%, Malays 21% and others 3%—by comparison with 38%, 12%, 49% and 1%, respectively, in the population.

The allocation of beds in the general and district hospitals by type of service varies considerably from hospital to hospital. For the Federation as a whole it was as follows in 1953:

[15] The corresponding figure for 1953 was about 1.4 days per capita in the United States.
[16] Based on data compiled from Medical Department Annual Reports, 1947-53.

Service	Beds	Percent
General[17]	8,020	63
Tuberculosis	2,946	23
Obstetrics	1,228	10
Infectious	301	2
Mental	192	2
Total	12,687[18]	100

The relatively large proportion of all beds assigned to tuberculosis (nearly one-fourth) and the small proportion to (other) infectious diseases are striking. These beds for infectious cases are supplemented by 3,470 in the four institutions for lepers; the beds for mental cases in general and district hospitals are additional to 4,200 beds in the two special mental disease hospitals which are not included in these figures.

The receipt of in-patient hospital care in the various States and Settlements is summarized in Table 6. The total of 233,000 admissions is equivalent to a rate of 41 per 1,000 persons in the population, about one-half to one-third the rate common in developed Western countries. The average hospital stay is relatively long, about 16 days per admission; this is explained by the large proportion of beds occupied by tuberculosis patients who are in the hospitals for six months or longer.

The variation in admission rates among the States and Settlements is comparatively large—from 14 per 1,000 persons in Trengganu to 69 per 1,000 in Negri Sembilan; except for these two and Kelantan, the other eight States and Settlements show rates within the comparatively narrow range 36-56.

The occupancy rates, averaging 82% for the Federation, are generally within the range regarded in Western countries as desirable for general hospitals (75-85% of possible capacity). However, they are relatively low for Malaya because it has almost no seasonal variations, the incidence of disease is presumably uniform throughout the year, and these figures include the tuberculosis hospitals with long stays and more or less complete occupancy.

[17] Includes medicine, surgery, dermatology, urology, etc.

[18] Includes 120 beds in maternal and child welfare centers and 637 beds in the tuberculosis institutions.

TABLE 6 Services in Government Hospitals and Dispensaries, 1953, Federation

State or Settlement	Hospital In-Patients[1]				Out-Patient Attendances[2]					
	Admissions		Bed Occupancy (%)	Patient Days per Capita	Total			Per 1,000 Persons		
	Number	Per 1,000 Persons			Hospitals and Fixed Dispensaries	Mobile Dispensaries[3]	Total	Hospitals and Fixed Dispensaries	Mobile Dispensaries	Total
Perak	50,728	45	77	0.74	329,147	166,666	495,813	295	149	444
Johore	33,206	38	84	0.67	187,970	137,578	325,548	214	158	372
Selangor	35,033	41	87	0.66	331,423	34,774	366,197	391	41	432
Kedah	26,413	41	87	0.49	256,992	44,318	301,310	398	69	467
Penang	22,332	44	76	0.97	153,312	59,698	213,010	299	116	415
Kelantan	8,210	17	79	0.24	68,029	71,018	139,047	138	144	282
Negri Sembilan	22,018	69	88	1.20	162,541	50,815	213,356	506	158	664
Malacca	13,295	47	86	0.86	73,748	44,687	118,435	260	158	418
Pahang	15,688	56	85	0.87	161,584	61,458	223,042	575	219	794
Trengganu	3,487	14	77	0.33	103,404	78,154	181,558	414	313	727
Perlis	2,876	36	76	0.41	32,527	6,197	38,724	402	77	479
All	233,286	41	82	0.67	1,860,677	755,363	2,616,040	326	132	458

[1] Excludes admissions to leper settlements and mental disease hospitals.
[2] Excludes attendances at infant welfare centers and venereal disease clinics.
[3] Includes riverine as well as road mobile dispensaries.

SOURCE: Medical Department.

The amount of in-patient care received in the several States and Settlements (days per capita) ranges from 0.24 in Kelantan to 1.20 in Negri Sembilan.

D OUT-PATIENT SERVICES

All government hospitals have out-patient departments at which, up to their capacity, they serve all who request service. In addition, out-patient services are provided by dispensaries located in the smaller towns, by travelling motor dispensaries which operate on more or less fixed schedules on the main roads and, in five states, by riverine mobile units.

General out-patient services (exclusive of services furnished at infant welfare centers and venereal disease clinics) at first declined after 1947 and then increased again, as follows:[19]

	Out-Patient Attendances at		
Year	Fixed Dispensaries	Mobile Dispensaries	All Dispensaries
1947 . . .	1,423,402	789,767	2,213,169
1948 . . .	1,342,080	632,929	1,975,009
1949 . . .	1,348,808	642,768	1,991,576
1950 . . .	1,441,338	685,015	2,126,353
1951 . . .	1,521,334	638,350	2,159,684
1952 . . .	1,548,228	731,252	2,279,480
1953 . . .	1,860,677	755,363	2,616,040
1954 . . .	2,112,513	783,654	2,896,167

The number of services caught up with population growth in 1954 (451 attendances per 1,000 in 1947; 492 per 1,000 in 1954). The services furnished by mobile dispensaries are somewhat less than one-third of the total.

All racial groups use the dispensaries extensively; their attendances (Malaysian 42%, Chinese 38%, Indian 16%, and others 4%, in 1954) are more closely correlated with their proportions in the population than is the case for in-patient services.

Out-patient services in the various States and Settlements in 1953 are summarized in Table 6, where attendances are related to population. The rates vary widely and there is no uniform (direct or inverse) relation be-

[19] Based on data compiled from Medical Department Annual Reports, 1947-54.

tween the levels of the out-patient and in-patient rates; the volume of out-patient services is in some cases and not in others compensatory to the volume of in-patient services.

v EXPENDITURES BY THE MEDICAL DEPARTMENTS[20]

Total Expenditures: 1947-54

Public expenditures on health and medical services through the medical departments have risen rapidly in the postwar years; they increased from $18 million in 1947 to $57 million in 1953. Revised estimates indicate current (1954) expenditure of $55 million. These figures do not include the amounts expended through the Public Works Department on projects relating to anti-malarial drainage and on water supplies,[21] the health and sanitation expenditures made by the municipalities,[22] or expenditures incurred

TABLE 7 Expenditures by the Medical Departments,[1] 1947-54, Federation

(*Million $*)

Expenditure or Income	1947	1948	1949	1950	1951	1952	1953[2]	1954[2]
Recurrent & special[3]	17.9	21.7	25.8	25.8	34.2	43.8	51.2	53.0
Capital expenditures[4]	0.3	0.3	0.6	0.7	2.0	2.1	5.5	2.3
Gross total[5]	18.2	22.0	26.4	26.5	36.2	45.9	56.7	55.3
Income from fees, etc.[6]	(n. a.)	1.4	1.7	1.7	2.2	2.7	2.9	3.0
Net total	(n. a.)	20.6	24.7	24.8	34.0	43.2	53.8	52.3

[1] Includes expenditures by Federal & State/Settlement departments; does not include health expenditures made by the municipalities.
[2] Adjusted estimates for 1953; revised estimates (April) for 1954.
[3] Includes personal emoluments, other charges annually recurrent and special expenditures.
[4] Limited to public works, non-recurrent.
[5] Exclusive of current expenditures and accruing liabilities for pensions.
[6] Includes: Federal and State/Settlement income from hospital ward charges and fees; sale of medicines, etc.; quarantine fees; and reimbursements for orthopedic supplies.
SOURCE: Medical Department; and Federal and State/Settlement financial reports.

[20] Expenditures by other departments of government which provide some health, medical or related services are not available.
[21] Expenditures on public water supplies in 1953 were $18.0 million (recurrent, $7.2 million; capital, $10.8 million). The estimates for 1954 are $35.7 million (recurrent, $8.0 million; capital $27.7 million).
[22] In 1952, these were $3.3 million (Kuala Lumpur $2.1 million, Penang $1.0 million, and Malacca $0.2 million). The total was $1.23 million in 1950 and $2.10 million in 1951.

by estates and mines which, though under the supervision of the Medical Department, operate hospitals, carry out anti-malaria schemes or support medical practitioner and other services at their own expense. The expenditures are summarized in Table 7.

Taking account of population growth, these public expenditures are equivalent to $3.71 per capita in 1947, $5.51 in 1952 and $9.94 in 1953. With deduction for income from hospital charges, sale of medicines, etc., the net totals range from $21 million in 1948 to an estimate of $52 million for 1954.

Classification of Federal Department Expenditures: 1953

Of the $56.7 million ($9.94 per capita) made available by the Federal Government in 1953, $18.2 million (32%) was provided to the Federal

TABLE 8   Classification of Federal Department Expenditures[1], 1953, Federation

(Million $)

Class of Expenditure	Recurrent and Special	Capital	Total Amount	%
Headquarters	$2.7	$—	$2.7	14
Institute for Medical Research	1.5	—	1.5	8
General hospitals (2)	5.2	0.8	6.1	33
Mental hospitals (2)	3.8	0.4	4.1	22
Leper settlements (4)	2.4	0.0+	2.4	13
Tuberculosis settlement	0.8	—	0.8	4
Port health & quarantine	0.3	—	0.3	2
Medical stores	0.5	0.1	0.6	3
Limb fitting center	0.1	—	0.1	1
Gross total	17.3	1.3	18.6	100
Less adjustment[2]	0.4	—	0.4	
Total	16.9	1.3	18.2	
Less income from fees, etc.[3]	1.2	—	1.2	
Net total	$15.7	$1.3	$17.0	

[1] Revised estimates, April 1954, prior to audit of actual expenditures.

[2] Departmental estimate of amounts not expended in 1953.

[3] Income from hospital ward charges and fees, sale of medicines, quarantine fees, reimbursements for orthopedic supplies, etc. (for Federal institutions only).

SOURCE: Medical Department; and *Estimates of the Federal Revenue and Expenditure for the Year 1954.*

Medical Department. Its expenditures are classified by major function in Table 8. Headquarters expenditures, including direction of the Federal Department and of the national program, recruitment, education and training activities, etc., accounted for 14.5% of gross expenditures. Direct operation of hospitals and settlements was responsible for nearly three-fourths of the total and for more than 90% of the capital funds. Research activities, centered in the Institute for Medical Research, consumed about 8%. Direct public health activities, other than those performed by the headquarters staff, were largely limited to port health and quarantine services which used about 2% of the funds.

State/Settlement Expenditures: 1953

The expenditures made by the several States and Settlements in 1953 are summarized in Table 9. Their aggregate was 68% of the total, more than one-half of it by Johore, Perak and Selangor. The areas are arrayed by expenditures, from Johore with the largest to Perlis with the smallest, and the percentage distribution of population is shown in parallel. There is general correspondence between these percentages, but also some sharp contrasts. Johore, Negri Sembilan and Pahang had larger proportions of funds than of population. Kelantan had less than half its *pro rata* share of the funds, and Kedah and Trengganu about three-fourths.[23] The average public expenditure through the State and Settlement departments is about $6.75 per capita; the range in the States is from less than half the average ($3.28, Kelantan) to more than twice that figure ($13.62, Negri Sembilan).

Total Expenditures, Public and Private

Data are not available for a reliable compilation of public and private health and medical expenditures in Malaya. A rough estimate for private expenditures[24] is of the order of magnitude of $55 million a year. Added to

[23] The relatively small shares of the funds shown for Penang and Malacca reflect that the large general hospitals in the Settlements are operated directly by Federal Department funds. In 1953, the Federal Department spent $3.053 million in annually recurrent and special funds and $0.393 million in capital outlays for the general hospital in Penang, and $2.185 million and $0.425 million, respectively, for the hospital in Malacca. Taking these amounts into account, the expenditures in Penang become $5.607 million and in Malacca $3.360 million.

[24] Gross payments to private physicians, dentists and hospitals; private expenditures for pharmaceutical and other supplies and for other medical services; and employer expenditures other than for private physicians, dentists and hospitals.

TABLE 9   Medical Department Expenditures and
the Populations of the States and Settlements, 1953, Federation

Medical Departments	Expenditures[1]						Popula-tion (%)
	(Million $)			Per Capita		%	
	Recur-rent	Capital	Total	Amount	Index		
All	51.2	5.5	56.7	$9.94		100	
Federal	16.9	1.3	18.2	3.19		32	
State/Settlement . .	34.3	4.2	38.5	6.75	100	68	100	100
Johore	7.4	0.6	8.0	9.09	135	14	21	15
Perak	7.2	0.4	7.6	6.83	101	13	20	20
Selangor	5.5	0.5	6.0	7.11	105	11	15	15
Negri Sembilan . .	3.9	0.5	4.4	13.62	202	8	11	6
Kedah	2.9	0.6	3.4	5.33	79	6	9	11
Pahang	2.4	0.2	2.7	9.58	142	5	7	5
Penang[2]	1.7	0.5	2.2	4.22	63	4	6	9
Kelantan	1.3	0.3	1.6	3.28	49	3	4	9
Trengganu	0.8	0.3	1.2	4.73	70	2	3	4
Malacca[2]	0.8	—	0.7	2.66	39	1	2	5
Perlis	0.4	0.3	0.7	8.80	130	1	2	1

[1] Adjusted estimates, prior to audit of actual expenditures. Excludes health expenditures made by the municipalities.
[2] Expenditures exclude amounts spent on the general hospital administered by the Federal Medical Department.

SOURCE: Medical Department.

the public expenditures (Federal, State/Settlement and local), the total
for all health and medical services is probably about $115 million a year.

VI   A DEVELOPMENT PROGRAM: 1954-60

A   SOME GENERAL POLICIES

The health and medical services of the Federation have been, on the
whole, eminently effective in achieving great improvement in health and
well-being. They have made possible the survival and vigor of immigrant
workers, the natural growth of population and the economic development
of the country. Postwar expansion of the medical departments to meet
increasing need and demand for service has been large and, in the main,

on a sound course. Now, when financial problems of the Federation invite reconsideration of future plans, it is timely to assess the program and to lay out benchmarks and guidelines for the years ahead.

Expansion of Services

Despite their recent growth, the health and medical services are still seriously inadequate. The population is growing at a very rapid rate, urban concentration is increasing, and the public is requesting more "western medicine." The services will therefore become increasingly inadequate unless there is considerable expansion of personnel and facilities.

In view of the financial stringency that may be ahead, the mission believes that an expanding health program should be designed to give the maximum return at minimum cost, even if this will involve major changes in program emphases, administrative organization and operating methods.

Increased Emphasis on Prevention

Financial limitations may compel a slowdown or even a standstill in the expansion of hospital facilities for in-patients (the most expensive form of medical care) and the maximum practical shift to out-patient services (the least expensive type of diagnostic and treatment service). Even more importantly, continuing shortage of funds and personnel invite the greatest possible emphasis on preventive services, to lighten the future medical load, even sacrificing expansion of curative services if personnel or funds are insufficient for both.

Equalization of Services

Our study shows that health and medical services are very uneven among the States and Settlements and between urban and rural areas. Government operations have shown commendable tendencies to reduce inequalities in opportunities for health services, but large differences still remain. There are many historical reasons for this situation, but they need not continue to operate with as great force in the future as in the past.

We recommend that a new program make strong and directed efforts to improve and extend services where they are least adequate, aiming at attainment of at least minimum national levels in all States and Settlements. Funds and personnel should be assigned and facilities should be developed disproportionately where health needs are greatest, not where the services are most wanted or where they are easiest to provide. Administrative policy should strive for a sound balance between urban demand and rural need.

Organization and Administration

A developmental program along the suggested lines requires organization well suited to the purposes. The Federation has been fortunate in having had administrative machinery that has served it well in the past, but both the pattern and the performance need refashioning for the tasks that are ahead.

While some functions are clearly allocated to the Federal or the State/ Settlement departments, others are not. Over-all planning is uneven and systematic implementation of plans is loose; both levels of government operate general hospitals and personnel training activities; working relations between general hospitals and facilities for ambulatory patients are unevenly developed; allocation of funds is only partly related to over-all national plans; and expenditures are not tightly enough controlled to ensure that available funds are spent primarily for the priority purposes of a national program.

We believe that the allocation of functions between the Federal and the State/Settlement medical departments should be clarified. The hospital program needs more effective management on a regional basis, with the Federal Department responsible for all the central or regional general hospitals (and not merely the two in the Settlements) and with State/Settlement departments operating the other general, district or lesser hospitals as coordinated parts of regional facilities. The out-patient departments of hospitals should be enlarged, and their operation should be coordinated within the regional hospital program and with the developing program of health centers. The facilities for professional education should be unified within the Federal Department and coordinated with the Federal and State/Settlement facilities. Health education needs considerable expansion at both levels of government and a like extension in rural as well as urban areas throughout the country.

Financial Planning and Control

The mission also believes that the success of a new Federal program, laid out for a number of years ahead, will depend as much on an orderly and pre-determined pattern of finance as on program plans, organization and administrative agreements. With growing demands for services, financial stringency will bring increased competition for shares of the funds that may be available. The Federal Government should therefore reassess the health needs for the next 5-10 years, estimate the costs, and make tentative decisions on the appropriations it expects to be able to provide. It should then formulate a financial plan geared to the substantive program, introducing such financial controls as may be necessary to ensure that the Federal funds will be used solely to carry out the adopted program. It would thus provide a foundation on which both the Federal Department and the State/Settlement Governments may develop long-term plans and know what financial support they may expect for specific plans developed from year to year.

B SOME SPECIFIC NEEDS AND IMPROVEMENTS

In addition to suggesting some general policies for a new developmental program, it may be useful to refer to a few specific needs that deserve special attention and to particular modifications of program that may promise substantial improvements. We appreciate that in most instances these are concerned more with emphasis than with innovation.

Professional Staff

The key to the success of the developmental program will be expansion of professional staff—by recruitment and training. The present shortages can be only partly overcome in the next five or six years but we recommend that the Federal Department give highest priority to achieving as much as may prove to be possible.

The magnitude of the problem may be illustrated by an example. The present complement of about 700 governmental and private physicians in the Federation, including those in administrative and research posts, is equivalent to about one per 8,000 persons. Those available for clinical and related services equal one per 9,200 persons.[25] To bring the proportion down to the modest level of one per 6,000 in each State/Settlement where the ratio is now higher would call for about 345 additional physicians, more than doubling the present number of clinical physicians (274) in government service. With allowance for population growth, the number needed would be larger. Insofar as possible, recruitment should be from the reservoir of physicians now in Malaya and to be trained within the country. New inducements would have to be provided to recruit from the field of private practice. With respect to new graduates from the University of Malaya, the output is not expected to be higher than 65 a year before 1961. Even with maximum enlargement of the resources of the medical school beginning with 1955, the number of graduates may not exceed 100 a year before 1965. These graduates have to supply the needs of private practice and public service in Singapore as well as the Federation. It is therefore likely that in addition to local recruitments the Department will have to rely heavily on Malaysians trained in medicine overseas and on non-Malaysians from other countries.[26]

The shortage of dentists presents similar needs and problems.

The present and prospective deficiencies in nurses, dental nurses, hospital assistants, trained midwives, etc., are also very large. The deficiencies should be reduced as much and as rapidly as possible through the most vigorous development of the Department's training schools and facilities. The Department should, of course, continue to utilize overseas facilities as limited supplementary resources.

General Hospitals

Since the hospitals of the Federation now provide more than three beds per 1,000 persons, over-all expansion in the capacity to serve in-patients is not urgent. This is supported by the generally moderate occupancy

[25] The developed countries of the world generally have less than 2,000-3,000 persons per physician; underdeveloped countries have as many as 50,000 or more per physician. See, for example, *Preliminary Report on the World Social Situation*, United Nations, Department of Social Affairs, New York, 1952; *Statistical Yearbook, 1953*, United Nations, Department of Economic Affairs, New York, 1953.

[26] This problem is assessed in the recent Report of the Committee of Enquiry on Medical Education in Malaya, (Sir David Lindsey Keir, Chairman), Singapore, 1954.

rates.[27] Expansion will be needed, however, to meet the growth of population. It seems probable that in most places where facilities are overtaxed the situation can be greatly improved by various changes in administrative practices, e.g., earlier discharge to out-patient status for chronic and convalescent cases, earlier ambulation and shorter hospital stays for surgical and maternity cases (as is being done increasingly in western countries), and reduction in the use of general hospital beds for long-term tuberculosis cases. Some of these changes will be facilitated by increase in staff.

Our field survey showed, however, that some of the hospitals badly need to be replaced by modern institutions and that many others need modernization and better equipment. In view of the limitations on funds for capital expenditures, we recommend that new facilities be built at minimum unit costs compatible with strictly medical needs and likely to be useful for, say, 20 years rather than longer periods. If the funds that can become available in 1955-60 cannot provide all the replacements that are needed, priorities will have to be accepted; but the hospitals that will have to be used for another period of years should be temporarily improved.[28]

The expansion of the out-patient facilities is, in our opinion, equally or more urgent. Most of the hospitals of the Federation were apparently designed and built more or less exclusively for the care of in-patients. The out-patient departments are generally very small and meagerly equipped, and they are totally inadequate for their present or prospective loads. More and better physical facilities for them and larger staffing should be given high priority. Where new hospital construction cannot be undertaken, the out-patient facilities should be temporarily enlarged and improved, even— if necessary—at the expense of giving up some space used for ward beds.

As noted earlier (p. 557), the hospital services are substantially free; the ward charges, when not completely remitted, are nominal or only a fraction of the costs incurred in providing the services.[29] In view of the acute

[27] The highest rate is 88% in Negri Sembilan, but this State has the largest hospital resources in relation to population—6.8 beds per 1,000 persons, providing 1.2 patient-days of care per capita (Tables 5 and 6).

[28] Especially by re-equipment of operating theaters, surgeries, laboratories, kitchens, etc., by installation of communication facilities among scattered buildings, by improvement of quarters for professional staff, hostels for nurses and others, facilities for subordinate staff, etc.

[29] The State/Settlement average patient-day costs are generally $5-$9, and are about $7.50-$13.00 for the large general hospitals. With more adequate staffing, as proposed, the costs will be higher. The full rates for various kinds of wards are for the most part under $2-$5 per day. Government hospitals provide nearly four million patient-days of care, but they collect less than $3 million a year, an average of less than $0.75 per patient-day.

need for funds to finance the medical services, we recommend that in-patient charges be increased for government employees as well as for the general public, without interposing such high financial barriers in individual cases as to discourage needed hospital care. While still allowing for reduced or remitted charges for patients with small means, income should be expected to increase progressively from its present level (somewhat less than $3 million) to, say, $10 million a year by 1960. We do not recommend any change in the current practice of free out-patient care.

Increased efficiency in utilization of the hospitals could be achieved by regionalization. The general hospitals in Kuala Lumpur, Ipoh and Johore Bahru and one on the east coast (in Kuantan, Kuala Trengganu or Kota Bharu) should—like those in Penang and Malacca—become central Federal hospitals. Each should serve as the center of a regional Federal-State/Settlement program embracing comprehensive services and training facilities, interlocking the complete (in-patient and out-patient) general and special services of the central hospital with the more limited services of the State and district hospitals, clinics, dispensaries, health centers, etc.

Tuberculosis

Tuberculosis is absorbing a large part of all the medical and hospital resources of the government program, yet there is serious doubt whether the disease is even being kept in check, to say nothing of being conquered. With increasing urbanization, shophouse living and extreme overcrowding in many urban areas, the disease may become even more prevalent, especially in the urban population.

The first essential for a successful campaign against tuberculosis is knowledge of its incidence and prevalence, but this is lacking in the Federation. Fragmentary data suggest that there may be 300 or more cases per 10,000 in the population generally (the corresponding figure is about 13 per 10,000 in the United States), but there is no basis for a reliable estimate of prevalence, incidence of new cases, distribution in the population by race, sex, age, etc.[30] General surveys, and intensive surveys of appropriate sample populations, are urgently needed. They should be undertaken—perhaps with the advice and assistance of a team of experts from WHO—

---

[30] It is estimated by tuberculosis experts that there may be 20,000 serious cases in Kuala Lumpur alone, most of them undiscovered and untreated; and there are corresponding estimates for some other towns.

as part of a concerted attack on this disease. And such surveys should be repeated periodically, to provide a basis for assessing the successes and failures of the program.

The hospital situation in relation to tuberculosis calls for drastic action. The general hospital facilities cannot be greatly increased, nor is it sound to continue to "block" more than 40% of all general hospital beds with tuberculosis patients. The Lady Templer Hospital will bring some relief to this situation, but very little. Much more needs to be done as rapidly as possible. Nonacute and nontreatable cases should be vacated from the general hospitals; they should be discharged to out-patient departments, clinics, health centers, etc., for treatment on an ambulatory basis and transferred to sanatoria and settlements, as may in each case be appropriate. Since the facilities for such a program are now inadequate, they should be developed.

It is clearly the responsibility of the government departments to provide the facilities for out-patient care. There have been differences of opinion, however, whether government or the voluntary agencies should be primarily responsible for development of the tuberculosis settlements. On balance, we propose that this should be undertaken by the Malayan Association for the Prevention of Tuberculosis (MAPTB), with generous financial support from the Social and Welfare Services Lotteries Board,[31] and with financial as well as technical assistance from the Federal Government if the resources of the MAPTB and the Lotteries Board prove to be insufficient to finance the construction and maintenance of settlements as rapidly as they can be staffed. This program should contemplate production of facilities for the care of 500-1,000 patients in each of the next few years, until capacity is sufficient to free the hospitals for a constant flow of early and treatable cases.[32]

These proposals recognize there is no reasonable likelihood that institutional care (hospital and settlement) can be expected to become adequate in the next 5-10 years to cope on a bed-care basis with the tuberculosis problem which confronts the Federation. Consequently, we recommend

[31] The law (No. 9 of 1950) authorizing establishment of the Lotteries Board and operation of public lotteries had its origin in the need for larger funds by the MAPTB for tuberculosis control and by the Central Welfare Council for assistance to needy persons, many of them needy because of tuberculosis.

[32] The Morib project suggests that costs would be about $300,000 for construction and equipment of facilities for 100 patients and $100,000 a year for maintenance.

that the government make an extensive trial of ambulatory care on a controlled experimental basis, because of uncertainties about its value. To this end, in addition to the expansion of general out-patient facilities already mentioned, we suggest that the developmental program include provision for special tuberculosis clinics, to be located in strategic urban areas,[33] and that as many as possible of the new rural health centers be equipped to provide tuberculosis diagnostic and treatment services, with referral services to the hospitals.

The design of tuberculosis out-patient services should utilize the experience accumulated in Singapore by the Colony Medical Department and the Anti-Tuberculosis Association (SATA).

The measures outlined above would not in themselves be sufficient to cope with the tuberculosis problem, though they might succeed in keeping pace with the cases that appear or are discovered. Stronger preventive measures will also be needed. These should include vigorous programs of: (a) health education; (b) early case finding; (c) prompt ambulatory or bed care of discovered cases; and (d) an augmented program of BCG vaccination (and follow-up survey), even though its value must still rest for some years on faith and hope rather than fully demonstrated value.

We recognize that the preventive program will continue to be weak and defective unless adequate measures are taken to deal with overcrowded urban housing, one of the most serious contributory causes of the tuberculosis problem. Our recommendations for expansion of housing activities are given in Chapter 7.

Finally, the attack on tuberculosis should include provisions to assure income for families made dependent by the disease or who will be without income if the wage-earner undergoes long-continued institutional care. Experience shows that without such provision treatment is neglected, unduly postponed or prematurely interrupted. We recommend that a treatment-allowance program, like that already devised by the MAPTB, be developed by the voluntary agencies with financial support from the Lotteries Board. If this cannot proceed adequately, the Federal Government should give serious consideration to a program like that being operated successfully in Singapore.[34]

---

[33] The developmental schedule in Table 10 provides for seven such clinics. If possible, more should be added if they prove successful.

[34] See p. 602 and Technical Report 11.

Other Infectious Diseases

In addition to a more vigorous campaign for the control of tuberculosis, the mission recommends that the health authorities make new provisions to step up the attack on other widespread and debilitating infectious diseases—malaria, yaws, venereal diseases, intestinal infestations, etc.

Rural Health

The mission recommends that the new program for rural health services (p. 563) continue to be given high priority and carried forward vigorously. In addition to the centers completed and staffed in 1954, we suggest that 24 rural health centers be developed in the years 1955-60 (four per year), and a second training center be inaugurated for the development of staff needed for these and future centers.

This program should, of course, be carefully coordinated with other rural health facilities (p. 553), and with the hospitals for the care of persons whose medical needs cannot be met at home, in a clinic or health center but require hospital in-patient care.

Mental Disease

Operation of the two large mental hospitals, with less than one bed per 1,000 persons, constitutes the total program against mental disease in the Federation. (Psychiatrists have advised us that the prevalence of mental disease and deficiency is probably about the same in Malaya as in western countries. This suggests the need for about 5-5½ beds per 1,000 persons.) There are no psychiatric services in the general hospitals, and there are no clinics or consulting services for this important group of diseases. Moreover, both of the Federal hospitals are so meagerly staffed that they cannot be said to have even a minimum of essential personnel. Indeed, it is surprising that the medical staffs achieve as much as they do with the limited resources at their command. Having to operate with an excessive discharge rate in order to have places for incoming patients, and with no follow-up services, the readmission rate at the Central Mental Hospital is about 25%.

It is said in Malaya that the present mental hospitals are too large and should be broken down into smaller units. This may be a sound proposal, but it could achieve little unless recruitment and assignment of more professional staff were successful.

The Federal Department has proposed the construction of a much-needed third mental disease hospital to be located on the east coast, the two present ones being on the west coast. There seems little point, however, in undertaking a third hospital until there is at least enough staff for the present two. The new project should therefore be postponed until personnel recruitment or training has made further progress.

In addition to staffing the present facilities for more effective diagnosis, therapy (medical and occupational), rehabilitation services and follow-up, a special effort should be made to obtain staff for at least the beginnings of a mental hygiene program in the urban areas.

Nutrition

As indicated earlier (p. 563), there is no adequate body of information concerning the diet and the nutritional status of the people. It is important to remedy this deficiency, since a large proportion of the population lives on very limited diets. We recommend that the Institute for Medical Research surveys be completed, more extensive technical and clinical research be supported, and that education activities on diet and nutrition be extended.

Dental Care

The mission believes the dental health program is basically sound and would encourage its enlargement. The training school for dental nurses at Penang should be strongly supported and expanded, and provisions for dental care should be increased—with special emphasis on preventive services for children in the schools and through health centers and clinics.

Health Education

Future health progress in Malaya will probably depend more on the spread of preventive practices than on the expansion of treatment services. In addition to development of specific preventive services, we strongly recommend that the government agencies give high priority to health education. This can be the least expensive and, in the long run, the most fruitful undertaking. The program should be directed to school children, adolescents and adults, and it should be undertaken in cooperation with the Education and Social Welfare Departments and, wherever possible, with the voluntary agencies.

Research

The mission believes that the Institute for Medical Research should continue to receive generous financial support, preferably through commitments on a quinquennial basis (as in the case of grants to the University of Malaya) so that important problems can be attacked on a long-term basis. The IMR should press vigorously its research activities on prevalence and etiology of disease, and its quest for new and improved methods of prevention and treatment. It should continue to prepare biologicals that can be produced more cheaply than purchased. While continuing to be responsible for training of specialized staff and performance of highly specialized and technical services, it should be relieved of routine hospital and clinic laboratory services.

C COST ESTIMATES FOR THE PROGRAM 1954-60

Capital Development Projects

As a first step in arriving at estimates of future costs, the major capital development projects for the years 1955-60 and their resulting recurrent charges[35] have been brought together in Table 10. This compilation includes projects specifically recommended by the Federal Medical Department, with modifications suggested in the preceding pages, and an allowance of $1-1.5 million a year for miscellaneous secondary Federal projects and $1 million a year for corresponding State/Settlement projects not otherwise provided in the estimates.

The estimated capital expenditures for the six years equal $79.6 million, calling for $8.7 million in 1955 and $19.1 million in the peak year 1957. The recurrent charges resulting from these projects rise from $400,000 in 1956 to $3.8 million in 1960.

All of the projects listed in Table 10 are eminently desirable; they would

[35] Here and in Table 10, "recurrent charges" include "personal emoluments" (PE), "other charges annually recurrent" (OCAR) and "other charges, special expenditures" (OCSE).

provide badly needed replacements or new facilities. All of them should be carried out, if possible.

Priority Capital Projects

It appears probable, by present perspectives, that the discernible financial resources of the Federation for the years 1955-60 cannot afford the whole developmental program shown in Table 10. We have therefore indicated priorities for the projects which appear to be most urgent and for which funds should in any case be provided: the replacement hospital and a new nurses' hostel in Kuala Lumpur (urgently needed for training purposes), the new facilities for central medical stores, and the rural health centers and tuberculosis clinics. We have omitted from this series the new mental hospital on the east coast and replacement of the general hospitals in Seremban, Ipoh and Taiping. Though the present buildings are dilapidated and uneconomical and their equipment is grossly inadequate, they can be used for a few years more. We suggest only a postponement of their replacement. However, provision has been made (in allowances for miscellaneous secondary projects) to permit essential temporary improvements in such of their equipment as contributes directly to adequacy and quality of medical care (e.g., surgeries, operating theaters, radiology and laboratories) and expansion of out-patient facilities.

In 1955-60 priority developmental projects are estimated in Table 10 to require capital expenditures amounting to $40.4 million—$4.6 million in 1955, rising to $9.8 million in 1957, and then declining to $3.3 million in 1960. They would result in new recurrent charges rising to $3.7 million in the latter year. The division of these funds between the Federal and the State/Settlement department programs is also shown in the Table.

Estimates for the Total Developmental Program

Table 11 shows estimates for the total program for the years 1954-60. We have tried to take account of all the developments specifically recommended or implied in the preceding pages and all the projects and allowances listed in Table 10. Thus, in addition to the capital expenditures specifically listed (and the resulting recurrent charges), these estimates provide for increased recurrent and special expenditures to expand the public medical program. This increase has been calculated with respect to (a) growth

TABLE 10 Schedule of Development Projects, 1955-60, Federation

(Million $)

Project	F or S¹	1955 Cap.	1955 Rec.	1956 Cap.	1956 Rec.	1957 Cap.	1957 Rec.	1958 Cap.	1958 Rec.	1959 Cap.	1959 Rec.	1960 Cap.	1960 Rec.	1955-60 Cap.	1955-60 Rec.
General hospitals															
Kuala Lumpur															
* Hospital (replacement)²	F	—	—	4.1	—	4.1	0.5	4.2	1.0	—	1.5	—	1.5	12.4	4.5
* Nurses' hostel and training school	F	0.9	—	0.9	0.3	0.8	0.6	—	0.9	—	0.9	—	0.9	2.6	3.6
Seremban (replacement)³	S	4.1	—	4.1	—	4.2	—	—	—	—	—	—	—	12.4	—
Ipoh (replacement)³	F⁴	—	—	4.1	—	4.1	—	4.2	—	—	—	—	—	12.4	—
Taiping (replacement)³	S⁴	—	—	—	—	—	—	4.1	—	4.1	—	4.2	—	12.4	—
Mental hospital (east coast)³	F	—	—	1.0	—	1.0	0.075	—	0.150	—	0.150	—	0.150	2.0	0.525
*Central medical stores and manu-tory	F	—	—	—	—	1.7	—	1.7	0.146	1.6	0.292	—	0.438	5.0	0.876
*Rural health facilities⁵															
* Health centers (24)	S	1.2	—	1.2	0.128	1.2	0.256	1.2	0.384	1.2	0.512	1.2	0.640	7.2	1.920
* Training center	F	—	—	—	—	—	—	0.5	0.172	—	0.172	—	0.172	0.5	0.516
* Tuberculosis clinics (7)⁶	S	0.03	—	0.03	—	0.03	—	0.03	—	0.03	—	0.06	—	0.21	—
*Miscellaneous secondary projects	F	1.5	—	1.0	—	1.0	—	1.0	—	1.0	—	1.0	—	6.5	—
*Miscellaneous secondary projects	S	1.0	—	1.0	—	1.0	—	1.0	—	1.0	—	1.0	—	6.0	—
Total		8.73	—	17.43	0.428	19.13	1.431	17.93	2.752	8.93	3.526	7.46	3.800	79.61	11.937
Federal	F	2.40	—	11.10	0.300	12.70	1.175	11.60	2.368	2.60	3.014	1.00	3.160	41.40	10.017
State/Settlement	S	6.33	—	6.33	0.128	6.43	0.256	6.33	0.384	6.33	0.512	6.46	0.640	38.21	1.920

Capital and Recurrent Expenditures

*Priority projects:															
Total		4.63	—	8.23	0.428	9.83	1.356	9.63	2.602	4.83	3.376	3.26	3.650	40.41	11.412
Federal . . . . F		2.40	—	6.00	0.300	7.60	1.100	7.40	2.218	2.60	2.864	1.00	3.010	27.00	9.492
State/Settlement S		2.23	—	2.23	0.128	2.23	0.256	2.23	0.384	2.23	0.512	2.26	0.640	13.41	1.920

[1] Federal or State/Settlement, as proposed in the text (not necessarily as at present).

[2] Includes one-half of annually recurrent charges, the estimated additional costs resulting from replacing the existing hospital.

[3] Treated as replacement; no additional annually recurrent charges included here.

[4] Whether the Ipoh project should precede the Taiping project (as shown here) or vice versa would depend on rate of growth and development of these cities and their surrounding areas. One shown as a Federal (Ipoh) and the other as a State hospital (Taiping), as proposed in the text.

[5] The six-year program shown here provides for 25 centers, one of them to serve as a training as well as a service center. Estimated costs for each: health center, $300,000 capital and $32,000 annually recurrent; training center, $500,000 capital and $172,000 annually recurrent.

[6] Capital costs $30,000 per clinic. Annually recurrent charges in regular budget and not included here.

SOURCE: Medical Department; and text.

of population (at the rate of 3½% per annum), and (b) gradual improvement in health and medical resources by an annual addition of 4% to the augmented estimates.[36]

TABLE 11   Estimated Expenditures for the Total Development Program, 1954-60, Federation

(Million $)

Expenditure or Income	1954[1]	1955	1956	1957	1958	1959	1960
Recurrent and special[2] . . .	53.0	57.1	59.5	62.6	66.1	69.0	71.6
Capital expenditures[3]	2.3	8.7	17.4	19.1	17.9	8.9	7.5
Gross total	55.3	65.8	76.9	81.7	84.0	77.9	79.1
Income from fees, etc.[4] . . .	3.0	5.0	6.0	7.0	8.0	9.0	10.0
Net total	52.3	60.8	70.9	74.7	76.0	68.9	69.1

[1] Revised estimates (April, 1954). Does not include health expenditures by municipalities.
[2] For 1955–60, the estimate for 1954 increased by
  (a) 3-1/2% a year for population growth;
  (b) Adjustment of resulting figures by further increase of 4% for improvement factors (more adequate staff, training, equipment, etc.); and
  (c) Recurrent charges resulting from all new capital projects listed in Table 10.
[3] From Table 10.
[4] Estimates after 1954 based on the proposals in the text.
SOURCE: Tables 7 and 10, and text.

On the stated assumptions, annual recurrent and special expenditures would increase from $53 million in 1954 to $72 million in 1960. With the total capital expenditures shown in Table 10, the gross totals would increase from $55.3 million in 1954 to $79.1 million in 1960. Assuming income from fees, etc., increases from $3 million to $10 million (p. 579), net expenditures would rise from $52.3 million to $69.1 million. If at all possible, the Federation should find these amounts for the government's health and medical program in the next six years.

Total Costs with the Priority Program

If only the priority capital projects and allowances of Table 10 are assumed for the developmental program in 1955-60, the resulting cost esti-

[36] This allowance for improvement is intended to provide recurrent costs for needed additional staff, expansion of training programs, more and better resources for out-patient services, more adequate surgery, X-ray and laboratory services, etc.

TABLE 12 Estimated Expenditures with a Priority
Developmental Program, 1954-60, Federation

(Million $)

Expenditure or Income	1954[1]	1955	1956	1957	1958	1959	1960
	Federal and State/Settlement Departments						
Recurrent and special[2] . . .	53.0	57.1	59.5	62.6	65.9	68.9	71.5
Capital expenditures[3]	2.3	4.6	8.2	9.8	9.6	4.8	3.3
Gross total	55.3	61.7	67.7	72.4	75.5	73.7	74.8
Income from fees, etc.[4] . . .	3.0	5.0	6.0	7.0	8.0	9.0	10.0
Net total	52.3	56.7	61.7	65.4	67.5	64.7	64.8
	Federal Department						
Recurrent and special[5] . . .	17.5	19.4	22.2	25.6	30.7	32.4	33.6
Capital expenditures[3]	1.3	2.4	6.0	7.6	7.4	2.6	1.0
Gross total	18.8	21.8	28.2	33.2	38.1	35.0	34.6
Income from fees, etc. . . .	1.0	2.0	2.2	2.4	2.6	2.8	3.0
Net total	17.8	19.8	26.0	30.8	35.5	32.2	31.6
	State/Settlement Departments						
Recurrent and special[5] . . .	35.5	37.7	37.3	37.0	35.2	36.5	37.9
Capital expenditures[3]	1.0	2.2	2.2	2.2	2.2	2.2	2.3
Gross total	36.5	39.9	39.5	39.2	37.4	38.7	40.2
Income from fees, etc.[4] . . .	2.0	3.0	3.8	4.6	5.4	6.2	7.0
Net total	34.5	36.9	35.7	34.6	32.0	32.5	33.2

[1] Revised estimates (April, 1954). Does not include health expenditures by municipalities. Subdivision between Federal and State/Settlement departments estimated from adjusted estimates for 1953.
[2] For 1955–60, the estimate for 1954 increased by:
   a. 3-1/2% a year for population growth;
   b. Adjustment of resulting figures by further increase of 4% for improvement factors (more adequate staff, training, equipment, etc.); and
   c. Recurrent charges resulting from priority capital projects listed in Table 10.
[3] After 1954, priority projects listed in Table 10.
[4] Estimates after 1954 based on proposals in text.
[5] Subdivision between Federal and State/Settlement departments:
   a. For 1954, in proportion to 1953 expenditures (33 and 67%, respectively);
   b. For 1955–60, Federal portion increased progressively to 34% in 1955, 37% in 1956, 41% in 1957 and 47% in 1958–60 to allow (as suggested in the text) for shift of general hospitals from State/Settlement to Federal operation (Ipoh, Kuala Lumpur, Johore Bahru and one on the east coast). Recurrent charges resulting from capital projects added as shown in Table 10.

SOURCE: Tables 7 and 10, and text.

mates would be as shown in Table 12. The gross total expenditures would increase from $55.3 million in 1954 to $74.8 million in 1960, and the net total from $52.3 million to $64.8 million.

A breakdown of these figures leads to gross estimates for the Federal Department rising from $18.8 million in 1954 to $34.6 million in 1960,[37] and correspondingly from $36.5 million to $40.2 million for the State/ Settlement departments. These gross figures would be reduced by the expected revenues from fees and charges.

D FINANCING THE FUTURE PROGRAM

An increase of gross expenditures for health and medical services from $55 million in 1954 to $75 million in 1960, as proposed in Table 12, itself raises serious questions whether the Federation can afford even the recommended priority program. But the prospective picture is more serious than these figures indicate because the costs must be expected to go on rising after 1960 for the following reasons:

1. The estimate of $75 million for 1960 was derived by postponing badly needed capital projects involving $39 million. Otherwise, the estimate for 1960 would have been $79 million (Table 11). These projects will have to be undertaken subsequently. And by that time, additional replacements and new construction will have to be included in the estimates;

2. Some of the new and most urgent developments, especially the rural health program, would only be well started in 1955-60 (25 centers would be built in a total of 90 scheduled now, and more will be needed as the population grows);

3. Acute shortage of professional and sub-professional staff will be only partly met by the funds proposed and there will be continued shortage to be met after 1960—both for community public health and for personal medical services;

4. With the population increasing at a very rapid rate, we assume that the resources for health and medical service and the expenditures will have to be increased proportionately; and

5. If the experience of the recent past is a guide for the years ahead, we must expect that public demand for medical care will continue to rise

---

[37] Including allowance for the proposal that the Federal Department become responsible for direct operation of general hospitals in Kuala Lumpur, Johore Bahru and Ipoh.

rapidly and that there will be steady pressure for more expansion of services than is indicated by expected growth of the population.

Increasing emphasis on preventive rather than curative services can moderate the rise in public cost, but major results from such a shift in program may not be evident for a decade. In the meanwhile, it is necessary to prepare for health and medical expenditures that will rise not merely to the $75 million level, as proposed for 1960, but to the $100 million level or higher in the following 5-10 years. Nor should this be surprising, since world experience suggests that public expenditures of about $10 per capita (the present amount) are only a small fraction of the cost that may be involved in providing adequate modern public health services and Western medicine to a tropical population. In Great Britain, western Europe and Canada total costs are equivalent to about $75-120 per capita, and in the United States to about $240 per capita.

Thus, it is necessary for us to conclude that the prospective health and medical program will soon rise beyond the financial resources of the Federal Government, and that the continued development of the services along the lines recommended here will compel recourse to additional sources of revenue.

Moreover, it is not sound that a program in which two-thirds of the current expenditures and prospectively one-half, two-thirds or more of the future expenditures are made by the States and Settlements should continue to be wholly or nearly wholly financed by the Federal Government. The public demand, especially for personal medical and hospital care, should be financed in substantial measure by funds provided more or less directly by the people who seek and receive these services. This is especially indicated by the likelihood that future increases in costs will be mainly for personal services of the kinds that will be provided by the States and Settlements.

The mission therefore recommends, for health and medical services, as for education, that the present pattern of Federal financing be replaced by one that relies increasingly on a sharing of costs by the Federal Government and the State/Settlement Governments (and their local authorities). Since the States, Settlements and local bodies would have to develop new sources of revenues and new administrative institutions, the change should be effected over a transitional period that allows ample time for the adjustments. So that the development may proceed on a sound and orderly basis, the new financial program should be carried out through an agreed long-term plan which indicates areas of functional responsibility and gives ample notice of the expected financial resources to be provided by each level of government.

More specifically, we recommend that the Federal Government undertake to provide the funds required for the operations of the Federal Medical Department and an annual appropriation (for annually recurrent, special and capital expenditures) to be allotted as grant-in-aid to the States and Settlements, separate from other grants or lump-sum allocations. The latter would be used in conjunction with funds provided by the States, Settlements, local authorities and cooperating voluntary agencies for specific purposes approved by the Federal Department. For the years 1955-60, the Federal appropriations for the Federal Department and for grants should be geared to the developmental program summarized in Table 12. After 1955, however, the Federal grants should—as in the field of education—become a decreasing percentage of total expenditures under approved State/ Settlement plans; these grants should become not more than, say, two-thirds or three-fourths of the total by 1960, and should remain fixed thereafter except as they may have to increase in order to be not less than one-half of such total expenditures. The additional funds needed by the States and Settlements to carry out their Federally approved programs, or to make expenditures outside such programs, should be provided by them and their local authorities.

In parallel with the pattern proposed for education (see pp. 493-499):

1. The Federal Government should formulate general policies and plans;

2. The State/Settlement Governments should submit general long-term plans for their health and medical programs;

3. After review of these plans by the Federal Medical Department and by the Executive Council and the Legislative Council, the Federal Government should indicate its intended financial program for a period of years;

4. The State/Settlement Governments should then submit specific and detailed annual plans for review; and

5. The Federal Government should make its annual appropriations and allot grants to support the approved plans.

The grant practices and procedures and especially the matching requirements should, as far as practical and applicable, be the same for health and medical services as for education (see p. 495). Requirements as to periodic reports from the States and Settlements and the control of expenditures should similarly be the same.

As in the case of education, such a pattern for health and medical services would clarify responsibilities at each level of government; would lay a basis for development of the services according to a declared national policy and plan; would broaden the financial resources to support the program; and would invite increased public participation in the design of the program and increased responsibility in determining the scope of the public services and the amount of public money to be spent on them.

As in education, this program would require specific health and medical grants to the States and Settlements, separate from lump-sum grants; broader delegation of sources of revenue to the States and Settlements; and possibly the development of local and regional authorities to assume responsibility for health and medical services and to levy and collect rates for general functions of local government or for these services alone.

The financial schedule for the years 1954-60 which may be expected to result from our proposals is summarized in Table 13. The first three lines—showing gross expenditures for the total program, for the Federal Department and for the State/Settlement/locality Governments—are taken from

TABLE 13   Illustrative Financing of the Future Health
and Medical Program, 1954-60, Federation

(*Million $*)

Expenditures and Sources of Funds	Estimated Expenditure or Revenue						
	1954[1]	1955	1956	1957	1958	1959	1960
Gross expenditures	55.3	61.7	67.7	72.4	75.5	73.7	74.8
By Federal Department	18.8	21.8	28.2	33.2	38.1	35.0	34.6
By St/Stl/localities . .	36.5	39.9	39.5	39.2	37.4	38.7	40.2
From Federal funds	36.5	39.9	34.7	32.6	30.0	29.5	30.2[2]
From other sources .	—	—	4.8	6.6	7.4	9.2	10.0[2]
Source of funds:							
From Federal Government	52.3	56.7	60.7	63.4	65.5	61.7	61.8
From St/Stl/localities .	—	—	1.0	2.0	2.0	3.0	3.0
From fees: Federal . . .	1.0	2.0	2.2	2.4	2.6	2.8	3.0
St/Stl/loc. .	2.0	3.0	3.8	4.6	5.4	6.2	7.0

[1] Excludes present expenditures from non-Federal funds.
[2] Three-fourth and one-fourth, respectively, of total expenditures by States/Settlements under approved plans.

Table 12. The amount to be available to the latter governments from Federal funds was fixed for 1960 at the three-fourths proportion (equal to $30.2 million) suggested earlier. As a result, non-Federal sources would have to provide additional funds amounting to $10 million in that year. A trial graduation of non-Federal funds from zero in 1955 to $10 million in 1960 begins with $4.8 million in 1956 and increases to a total of $9.2 million in 1959. In view of our proposal that income from fees be increased, we have estimated that State/Settlement revenue from this source may rise from $3.8 million in 1956 to $7.0 million in 1960. In addition, the States and Settlements would have to find in the successive years 1956-60 $1 to $3 million a year. Since these amounts are relatively small, there is not the same importance here as in the field of education for the States and Settlements to develop new sources of revenue for these services. They would, of course, have to find more after 1960 if their programs continue to expand, because we have proposed that the Federal grant of $30.2 million should not increase until expenditures under State/Settlement plans approved by the Federal Government exceed twice that amount ($60.4 million).[38]

According to this schedule, the Federal appropriations would have to increase from $55.3 million in 1954 to $64.8 million in 1960, and the net Federal expenditures from $52.3 to $61.8 million. The over-all program would involve $74.8 million gross and $64.8 million net in 1960. After that year Federal appropriations should be expected to increase moderately and remain within the fiscal capacity of the Federal Government.

SINGAPORE

1 INTRODUCTION

Singapore, in 1819 a malarial swamp with 150 inhabitants, has become a vigorous and healthy metropolis with nearly 1¼ million inhabitants. It is a symbol of man's victory over tropical diseases and a living monument

[38] If the Federal share in 1960 were fixed at two-thirds instead of three-fourths, it would amount to $26.8 million, non-Federal sources would have to provide $13.4 million that year, States/Settlements/localities would have to find about $6 million in 1959 and about $6.4 million in 1960, and Federal grants would begin to increase when total State/Settlement expenditures exceeded $53.6 million.

to its sanitarians and physicians as much as to its statesmen, public administrators and private enterprisers.

Appreciating the vital need to control disease, government authorities and business leaders—first in the Straits Settlement and more recently in the Colony—have long given generous support to the Medical Department. Without this, Singapore's population could not have survived and multiplied and its commerce and industry could not have prospered.

The health progress of Singapore is especially remarkable in the light of early population growth by immigration. Hundreds of thousands of Chinese and Indians poured in, bringing with them disease, ignorance of sanitation and hygiene, and an alien culture at best indifferent and at worst hostile to Western medicine and public health. Nevertheless, the Medical Department made more or less steady progress throughout the 19th century, recruiting personnel, developing sanitation and building hospitals. However, at the end of the century, the population was about 200,000, the death rate still greatly exceeded the birth rate and population growth still depended on excess of immigration over emigration.

At the turn of the century Singapore seized the opportunity to apply the new instruments of modern bacteriology, epidemiology and medicine. Malaria was controlled, many causes of sickness and death were substantially reduced, protection against importation of epidemic disease was greatly strengthened, and the death rate began to come down. In 1922-23 the birth and death rates became equal and Singapore began to grow by natural increase of population. This growth steadily gained momentum in the next three decades, except during World War II and the Japanese occupation when health conditions deteriorated almost catastrophically. After the occupation, the health authorities quickly restored sanitary controls, again brought malaria and other endemic and epidemic diseases under control, rehabilitated the staffs, hospitals and clinics and resumed the course of health progress.

The postwar health problems were greatly lightened by the virtual end of immigration but they were augmented by the results of health achievements. Birth rates persisted at the unprecedented levels they had attained before 1941; death rates continued to decline, going down to levels hitherto unknown in the East; and the rate of natural increase of population first reached and then exceeded 3% a year. As a result, massive overcrowding substituted new problems for old.

The vital statistics of recent years are illuminating:

	1920	1931	1940	1947	1950	1951	1952	1953
(Per 1,000 persons in the population)								
Birth rate	27.5	36.4	45.0	45.9	45.7	46.2	47.5	48.7
Death rate	35.0	24.2	20.7	13.3	12.1	11.9	11.2	10.3
Natural increase	−7.5	12.2	24.3	32.6	33.6	34.3	36.3	38.4

These are crude rates which do not take account of changes in age distribution. If there is more under-registration of births than of deaths, as well may be the case, population growth is at a rate nearer 4% than 3% a year. The population, which was 418,000 at the time of the 1921 census, had increased to 938,000 at the 1947 census and is about 1.154 million now (1954).

Measured by the infant mortality rate, generally a sensitive index of public health, progress in Singapore's health has been striking:

Deaths under one year of age per 1,000 live births							
1920	1931	1940	1947	1950	1951	1952	1953
265	203	140	81	82	75	70	67

While the current rates are still very high by Western urban standards, this decline from 265 to 67 occurred in the years when the rates fell in the United Kingdom from 80 to 25-30, in the United States from 86 to 25-30, in Japan from 165 to 55, and in India from 184 to about 115. In Hong Kong, the rate was 99 in 1949 and 77 in 1952.

Health progress in Singapore may be ascribed to activities on many fronts—sanitation, health education and provision of medical care. Public expenditures for the services, provided free or at nominal charges, increased as the population grew. The increase was modest prior to World War II, because the main activities were community services. But after the occupation the population began first to accept and finally to demand Western medicine—Western physicians, dentists and nurses, hospital bed care, and clinic, dispensary and health center services—and the growth of effective demand has been almost phenomenal. Staff and facilities have been taxed to the limits of their capacities and beyond. Plans to increase capacity for service have been found insufficient almost as soon as prepared.

In 1947, Singapore developed a comprehensive program to meet the Colony's requirements in the years ahead, contemplating capital expenditures of nearly $60 million but the program was too large to be carried out. A more modest Ten-Year Medical Plan was prepared in 1948, involving $33.5 million (at 1948 price levels) for capital projects and an increase of $4 million in annually recurrent expenditures in the 10th year. But price and income levels rose rapidly, the program was curtailed and largely postponed. Although new plans and programs were devised, only partial steps were taken until 1951-52 when a real beginning was made toward doubling the resources.

A health and medical development program for Singapore is now confronted with great difficulties. It must meet three basic needs: (1) public health vigilance to hold in check indigenous tropical diseases and to prevent the importation of epidemic diseases; (2) expansion of personnel and facilities to keep pace with an expected 50% growth of population in the next 15 years and to meet the still rapidly growing demand for Western medicine; and (3) expansion of both community and personal health services and their adaptation to the overcrowding in the central city (which apparently cannot be solved in the next decade or two), the resettlement of hundreds of thousands now in the city and the development of the rural areas of the Island. These needs must be taken into account in assessing existing resources, proposed expansions and financial implications.

II RESOURCES FOR PUBLIC HEALTH AND MEDICAL SERVICES

It is the declared aim of the Government of Singapore to provide essential public health services for the community as a whole and to furnish to individuals "necessary medical care at prices within the reach of all citizens," recognizing that in "a large majority of cases this means free treatment."[39]

Responsibility for health and medical services is allocated on the pattern which applies generally to the functions of government in Singapore. Thus, Singapore has an over-all Medical Department under the Colony Government, a Health Department under the City Council and a Health Service under the Rural Board. The general magnitudes of their operations

[39] Singapore Annual Report: 1953, p. 99.

are indicated by gross expenditures in 1953 of $21 million by the Medical Department, $5 million by the Health Department and less than $1 million by the Rural Board. The total of $26 million in that year was equivalent to $23 per capita. All three authorities have some revenue from fees but their expenditures are financed mainly from rates and taxes. Since the Rural Board is not self-supporting, most of its health costs are met by the Colony Government through grants and by posting of staff from the Medical Department. There are also transfers between the Colony and City with respect to specific services and capital works.

In addition to the public authorities, health services are provided by voluntary organizations[40] and by private practitioners—physicians, dentists, nurses, midwives and pharmacists.

The professional personnel available to serve Singapore is shown in

TABLE 14 Professional Personnel, December 31, 1953, Singapore

Personnel	Government Agencies[1]				University of Malaya	Private Practice	Total
	Colony	City	Rural Board[2]	Total			
Physicians—total	132	12	5	149	18	249[3]	416
Qualified	106	12	5	123	18	249[3]	390
Housemen[4]	26	—	—	26	—	—	26
Dentists—total	16	—	1	17	7	289	313
Qualified	12	—	1	13	7	29	49
Housemen[4]	4	—	—	4	—	—	4
Unqualified	—	—	—	—	—	260	260
Nurses—total	929	74	27	1,030	—	208	1,238
Female—sub-total . . .	757	59	20	836	—	203	1,039
Qualified	324	59	20	403	—	203	606
Underqualified . . .	93	—	—	93	—	—	93
Student[5]	340	—	—	340	—	—	340
Male	172	15	7	194	—	5	199
Midwives	42	11	43	96	—	245	341
Pharmacists.	5	—	—	5	3	66	74

[1] Exclusive of personnel in the Armed Services.
[2] Employed by Colony Medical Department but assigned to Rural Board duties.
[3] Includes six in Christian mission hospitals.
[4] Internes.
[5] Prospective qualified nurses.

SOURCE: Singapore Annual Report; 1953, p. 101.

[40] E.g., Malayan Union of Seventh-Day Adventists, Royal Singapore Tuberculosis Clinic, St. Andrew's Mission Hospital, and Kwong Wai Sui Free Hospital.

Table 14. The 416 physicians, including 26 housemen (internes), who were on the register on December 31, 1953, were equivalent to one per 2,760 persons in the population.[41] Despite the extensive public medical service, 60% of the physicians were in private practice. The 313 dentists (260 of them

TABLE 15 Summary of Hospitals, Dispensaries and
Health Centers, 1953, Singapore

| | Beds | | | |
| | | | | |
Type of Facility	Number	Per 1,000 Persons	In-patient Admissions	Out-patient Attendances
Governmental				
Hospitals—Total	1,660	1.48	55,937	843,712
General hospitals	800	0.71	25,484	482,332
Special hospitals	860	0.77	30,453	361,380
Infectious diseases . . .	250	0.22	2,049	—
Maternity	240	0.22	23,807	156,984
Orthopedic	120	0.11	74	—
Venereal disease	70	0.06	2,827	146,267
Prison	160	0.14	1,159	48,981
Police training school . .	20	0.02	537	9,148
Specialized institutions	3,154	2.81	3,111	189,078
Tuberculosis	557	0.50	1,723	171,898
Leprosy settlement	793	0.71	230	17,180
Mental	1,804	1.60	1,158	—
Out-patient institutions	—	—	—	323,386
Static dispensaries (6)	—	—	—	29,934
Police dispensary	—	—	—	15,239
Rural centers (43)	—	—	—	154,887
Mobile dispensaries (5) . . .	—	—	—	42,216
School medical services . . .	—	—	—	81,110
Voluntary				
Hospitals—Total	538	0.48	3,727	84,657
Kwong Wai Sui Free Hospital[1]	400	0.36	1,662	28,500
Malayan Union Mission . . .	68	0.06	1,472	25,477
St. Andrew's Mission	30	0.03	572	30,680
Red Cross Cripples Home . .	40	0.03	21	—
Anti-tuberculosis clinic	—	—	—	152,790

[1] Provides both Chinese and Western types of medicine.

SOURCE: Singapore Annual Report; 1953, p. 103.

[41] Highly developed countries generally have less than 2,000-3,000 persons per physician, and their large urban areas commonly have less than 1,000 per physician. Hong Kong had 3,800 per physician in 1951. (See footnote 25.)

unqualified) are equivalent to one per 3,700 persons; and the nurses (all categories) to about one per 925 persons.

The number of physicians has been increasing even more rapidly than the population so that the number of persons per physician has declined from 5,420 in 1947 (173 physicians) to about 2,500 in October 1954 (460 physicians).

The hospital and related facilities available to the population in 1953 are summarized in Table 15. Altogether, there were 2,198 beds in general and special hospitals, governmental and voluntary, equivalent to two beds per 1,000 persons.[42] Nearly all of the hospitals had out-patient departments. Of the 11 hospitals, the seven government hospitals provided 75% of the beds. In addition, the Colony Medical Department operated the tuberculosis, leprosy and mental disease institutions with aggregate accommodation for 3,154 patients; and, apart from the hospitals, both governmental and voluntary agencies provided extensive clinic, dispensary, health center and other facilities for ambulatory patients.

III   ACTIVITIES AND EXPENDITURES OF GOVERNMENTAL AGENCIES

A   PUBLIC HEALTH

The health and medical authorities of Singapore operate comprehensive programs of community sanitation and public health, in collaboration with other departments of government responsible for collateral functions. These activities are summarized here.[43]

Colony Medical Department[44]

Registration of Vital Statistics. The Department compiles the Colony-wide records and reports of births, deaths, notifiable diseases, etc. (not duplicating the activities of the City Health Department within the city area).

---

[42] In developed Western countries where most of the population expects to be served by hospitals, three-four beds per 1,000 are usually needed in general and special hospitals; their large cities commonly have 5-10 beds per 1,000.

[43] More detailed accounts are given in the Annual Reports of the Medical Department (Colony) and of the Health Department (City Council).

[44] Including services provided in the rural parts of the main island and on the outlying islands.

Port Health and Quarantine. Heavy sea and air traffic from Asian and African countries renders Singapore particularly vulnerable to introduction of infectious diseases. Customary precautions are taken. In 1953, 1,614 ships and 1,321 aircraft were inspected and cleared. Of 120,087 passengers examined, 22,640 were detained for vaccination.

Control of Malaria. Singapore has succeeded in remaining free of indigenous malaria for some years. It now has about 430 miles of drains (earth, concrete and sub-soil). It continues extensive temporary ditching and oiling control of mosquitoes, and makes routine and special surveys of breeding places. Houses on the surrounding islands are periodically sprayed with DDT.

Water Supply. Piped water is now generally made available—in the houses or at public standpipes—throughout the urban area and in most of the rural areas but expansion of the service, though vigorously pursued, has not kept pace with rapid housing developments in the outlying sections. Further expansion of the supply of water and of the distribution system is urgently needed.

Sewage and Refuse Disposal. The major sewage and refuse disposal activities concern safe disposal of nightsoil and refuse, encouragement of sanitary latrine construction, and control of nuisances (breeding places of flies, use of prawn dust as fertilizer, piggeries, fowl pens, vegetable gardens, absence of sanitary latrines, inadequate drainage, etc.). Anti-insect spraying and experiments with new insecticides are being undertaken.

Smallpox. Smallpox is comparatively well controlled; there were no indigenous cases in 1953. Vaccination of infants is compulsory and efforts are made to ensure that all immigrants are vaccinated. About 39,000 vaccinations were performed in 1953 and the authorities estimate that over 60% of the population is effectively vaccinated.

Leprosy. The prevalence of leprosy is not known but probably continues to be relatively high; each new health drive and encouraging development for cure brings additional cases out of hiding. The rural area reported 48 new cases in 1953; about 1,500 cases are receiving treatment or care.

Diphtheria. Despite the usual control efforts, the number of reported cases of diphtheria continues to rise (from 288 in 1949 to 340 in 1953). Parents are urged to have their children immunized and a "drive" was conducted in 1954, with only moderate success.

Other Epidemic Diseases. Singapore has been free of the quarantinable diseases (smallpox, plague, cholera, typhus, yellow fever and relapsing fever) since 1948. Chickenpox, measles, whooping cough, poliomyelitis and typhoid fever continue to be endemic.

Venereal Diseases. Venereal diseases are apparently widespread; the trend of prevalence and incidence is uncertain. The Medical Department operates a 70-bed special hospital, out-patient clinics, a travelling dispensary for rural areas, a serological laboratory and a voluntary prophylactic service for prostitutes, and engages in educational activities for the public and for professional personnel.

Tuberculosis. Morbidity from tuberculosis is not reliably known but there is no doubt that it is very high and that tuberculosis is Singapore's most serious communicable disease. A survey scheduled for 1953 was postponed, and if possible will be conducted in 1955 or 1956 with technical aid from WHO. The trend of incidence and prevalence is disputed; reported deaths have declined from the prewar level of 229 per 100,000 (1939-41) to 72 in 1953 but it is not clear whether deaths incorrectly ascribed to tuberculosis are more or less than tuberculosis deaths ascribed to other causes.

In addition to beds for nonpulmonary cases at the General Hospital and for chronic cases at the Orthopaedic Hospital in 1953, the Medical Department provided 557 beds for tuberculosis patients at the Tan Tock Seng (Tuberculosis) Hospital, and scheduled expansion to 1,200 beds. Over 6,000 out-patients were in regular attendance at the end of 1953. Visits to the clinic increased by 40% during the year and new cases by 12½%, many of them referred by the Singapore Anti-Tuberculosis Association (SATA) clinic for free treatment at the government hospital.

The tuberculosis treatment allowance scheme, operated in conjunction with the Social Welfare Department, continues to expand. In 1953, allowances were provided to an average of 1,252 patients per month whose prognosis was good and whose return to former working capacity seemed likely.

BCG inoculations, initiated in 1951, continue to be performed but in relatively small numbers. By the end of 1953, 90,600 persons had been tuberculin tested, 35,500 had been found negative, and 35,900 (including 1,600 newborn) had been given BCG.

Mental Diseases. The problems presented by mental diseases continue to be like those in Western countries. The number of in-patients exceeds the rated bed capacity (1,804) of the mental disease (Woodbridge) hospital; other beds and facilities are not available. A psychiatric out-patient department was first established in the General Hospital in 1953 but was able to furnish only diagnostic and case-disposal services.

Maternity, Infancy and Child Welfare. Activities include prenatal, delivery and postnatal services. In addition to operation of the Kandang Kerbau Maternity Hospital (240 beds, 23,800 in-patient admissions and 157,000 out-patient attendances in 1953), the Medical Department provides extensive home visiting services in the city and rural area and operates about 50 clinic or health centers (12 main centers with resident nursing staff, eight subsidiary centers with resident midwives and 24 temporary centers on the main island, and 11 centers on the outlying islands). Five more nurse or midwife centers were scheduled to be established in 1954. The government facilities now provide for about two-thirds of all births in urban and rural areas and reach nearly all through out-patient attendance or home visiting (city: 23,800 in-patient admissions and 157,000 out-patient attendances; rural: 8,200 deliveries, 149,000 clinic attendances and 99,700 home visits). The hospital is so crowded that the stay of normal cases has been reduced from three to two days. The clinics and centers provide care for common minor ailments as well as health education services and prophylaxis against smallpox, diphtheria and tuberculosis.

School Health. School health services are of limited scope, lacking adequate staff and facilities. This situation is expected to improve when the urban health center is completed in 1955, to be operated as a joint project of the Medical Department and the medical school of the University of Malaya. School services include general examinations of children, especially entrants and leavers, physical and X-ray examinations of teachers, and X-ray and Mantoux tests of case contacts for tuberculosis. Supplementary feeding is provided for about 6,000 school children referred by the school health officers.

Dental Health. The clinic at the General Hospital, serving government employees and the general public and operated as a teaching service for the dental school, served 14,400 new cases and had 50,400 attendances in 1953. The central school dental clinic (located at the Tan Tock Seng Hospital) served 2,300 new cases (17,400 attendances) from 17 schools and other institutions, and four dental nurses stationed in schools cared for 565 new cases (5,400 attendances). In addition, dental services were being developed for expectant and nursing mothers and for preschool children at child welfare centers, and were being provided at the mental, police and other hospitals. The volume of services has been increasing annually and most of the personnel and facilities are used to capacity.

Nutrition. The government's Advisory Council on Nutrition periodically reviews nutritional needs of the population and advises on programs (dietary scales of government institutions, supplementary school feeding, enrichment of foodstuffs, etc.). Special studies are carried out by the University of Malaya. The authorities do not find evidence of widespread nutritional deficiencies, but continue to watch returns from the hospitals, clinics and schools.

Protection of Food Supply. Since most of the population depends on others for provision and preparation of their food and supports large numbers of eating houses, stalls and itinerant hawkers, protection of food supply is particularly important. The sanitary inspectors make systematic inspections of all food stores and associated premises in the rural areas and take samples for analysis. In 1953, they made about 51,000 inspections of all kinds (factories, stores, shops, stalls, hawkers, etc.). The appearance of modern food-producing factories and increased use of public markets promise improvement but production and distribution of such foods as milk, meat, bread and vermicelli present serious problems.

Occupational Health. Little is being done to safeguard occupational health. The Medical Department is pressing for authority to facilitate control of occupational hazards.

Rural Health Services. The six static and five mobile dispensaries which provide preventive, diagnostic and treatment services, had 72,000 attendances and the 43 rural centers 155,000 attendances in 1953.

Research. There are no research institutions *per se* in the Colony but some research is done in the various health and medical institutions, especially under the departments of the University of Malaya.

Recruitment and Training of Personnel. The Medical Department is very active in development of personnel. Supplementing the professional schools of the University (medicine, dentistry and pharmacy), the Department operates a school of nursing and a midwives training school, and provides training courses for assistant nurses (tuberculosis), laboratory technicians and sanitary inspectors.

City Health Department

The City Council's Department operates a program of limited scope for the city population of 800,000 (1953), complementing the services provided in the urban area by the Colony Medical Department.

Registration of Vital Statistics. The Department records and analyzes births, deaths, notifiable diseases, etc. In 1953, there were 39,322 births (49.1 per 1,000 persons), and 8,936 deaths (11.2 per 1,000)—a natural increase of 30,386 (37.9 per 1,000). The infant mortality and maternal mortality rates were 71.5 and 1.3 per 1,000 live births, respectively. Of all deaths registered, 67% were certified by physicians, 23% by inspecting registrars and 10% by the coroner.

Sanitation; Mosquito Control. Sanitary activities include: general city sanitation; maintenance and operation of drains, with special reference to mosquito control; restraint of dangers and nuisances from unsanitary kampongs and squatter areas, vegetable gardens and piggeries. Malaria control has been highly effective in the city; the death rate from this disease, which had been brought down to 22.3 per 100,000 persons by 1948, was at a new low of 4.1 in 1953. However, the disease continues to be a constant threat and danger.

Notifiable Diseases. Tuberculosis is still one of the most important of the notifiable infectious diseases. Reported cases have declined only slightly (3,219 in 1951; 2,911 in 1953), and are common at all ages of life. The registered death rate declined from 1.71 per 1,000 persons in 1951 to 1.08 in 1953.

In 1953, there were 179 cases of leprosy, 124 of typhoid and para-typhoid fevers and 341 of diphtheria (with 56 deaths) but no cases of smallpox, cholera or plague were reported. The Department vaccinated 30,373 persons against smallpox (29,218 in the first year of life), of which 28,773 were successful (nonimmunes).

A campaign for diphtheria immunization reached 29,000 in 1952 and 10,300 in 1953. A new campaign was under way in early 1954, but the Department was still having only limited success in reducing the number of nonimmune infants and preschool children.

Middleton (Infectious Diseases) Hospital. The Middleton Hospital, a free public hospital of 250 beds (see Table 2), is operated by the Health Department.

Maternity, Infancy and Child Welfare. The Department maintains five clinics, and midwife and home-visiting services. In 1953 the midwives attended 1,364 confinements, made 3,233 visits to cases discharged from government hospitals and 181 to cases not attended by a physician or midwife. Attendances at clinics by infants, preschool children and expectant mothers, and home visits to babies and expectant mothers, continue to increase— attendances rose from 137,000 in 1952 to 148,000 in 1953, home visits from 112,000 to 119,000.

Health of Staff. Three dispensaries for City Council staff provide physical examinations, certifications for sick leave and medical care for minor conditions. Total attendances in 1953 were 97,829; these were supplemented by 80 visits to homes.

Laboratories. Bacteriological and chemical laboratories perform the usual tests for diagnostic purposes, purity of food and drugs, etc.

Food Markets, Abattoirs and Cemeteries. The Health Department operates the city food markets (wholesale and retail), abattoirs and cemeteries —functions not ordinarily within the scope of a modern urban health department. These are substantial commercial operations; they account for 20% of the Department's gross expenditures, and the charges, rentals, fees, etc., provide over 80% of its revenues.

B HOSPITALS, CLINICS AND RELATED FACILITIES

Singapore maintains a comprehensive public hospital and clinic service, largely free to the public. Before World War II, there were 1,340 beds in seven general and special hospitals.[45] In 1938, these hospitals treated

TABLE 16 Services Furnished by Government Hospitals, 1938-53, Singapore

	The General Hospital			Main Hospitals[1]		
Year	Beds	In-Patient Admissions	Out-Patient Attendances	Beds	In-Patient Cases	Out-Patient Attendances
1938 . . .	750	(n. a.)	(n. a.)	1,340	25,913	87,447
1947 . . .	550	14,676	114,167	1,210	27,514	305,138
1948 . . .	600	14,683	138,801	1,348	27,367	332,427
1949 . . .	700	15,478	153,534	1,461	32,998	461,238
1950 . . .	700	17,886	162,524	1,490	40,013	433,420
1951 . . .	700	19,720	185,131	1,510	40,833	612,095
1952 . . .	700	22,753	358,769	1,540	48,550	726,310
1953 . . .	800	25,484	482,332	1,660	55,420	957,481

[1] Excludes infectious disease, tuberculosis, leprosy and mental disease institutions, and all clinics, dispensaries, health centers, etc., that are not part of hospitals.

SOURCE: Singapore Annual Reports, 1946–53; and Annual Reports of the Medical Department, 1950–53.

[45] Exclusive of the tuberculosis, leprosy and mental disease institutions, with 600, 200 and 2,000 beds, respectively.

26,000 in-patient cases, and their out-patient departments had 87,500 attendances. After the war, as the demand for Western medicine increased, overcrowding of in- and out-patient facilities became chronic. There was relatively small increase in hospital capacity between 1947 and 1953, but in-patients more than doubled and out-patients increased by 10 times the pre-war number (Table 16).

In 1953, with 1,660 beds in the government hospitals (1.5 per 1,000 persons), there were 55,400 in-patients and 957,500 out-patient attendances. These hospitals provide about 600,000 in-patient days of care a year, averaging about 11 days per patient and equivalent to about 0.5 patient-days per capita in the population. The availability of beds in voluntary hospitals does not materially change the picture. The 538 beds (end of 1953) in these hospitals increase the total capacity to 2.0 beds per 1,000 persons. The voluntary hospitals can provide, as a maximum, about 0.15 in-patient days per capita, bringing the total to about 0.65 per capita for the present population.[46] And these figures overestimate the significance of the beds in the voluntary hospitals because the largest of them (Kwong Wai Sui Free Hospital) is only partly devoted to Western medicine.

The summary of governmental and voluntary facilities and services for 1953 shown in Table 15 may be recapitulated as follows:

	Beds	In-Patient Admissions	Per 1,000 Persons[47]	
			Beds	Admissions
General and special hospitals[48]—total .	2,198	59,664	2.0	53
Governmental	1,660	55,937	1.5	50
Voluntary	538	3,727	0.5	3

	Out-Patient Attendances	
	Number	Per 1,000 Persons[47]
Clinics, dispensaries and health centers[49]—total	1,251,755	1,114
Governmental	1,167,098	1,039
Voluntary	84,657	75

[46] By comparison, the Federation, though mainly rural, has 3.2 beds per thousand, providing about 0.9 patient-days per capita.

[47] Based on an estimated 1953 mid-year population of 1,123,172.

[48] Exclusive of tuberculosis, leprosy and mental disease institutions.

[49] Out-patient services in both hospital and independent facilities.

The data on hospital services are heavily weighted by the figures for maternity care; these account for more than 40% of the in-patients and about 20% of the out-patient attendances in government hospitals.

Tuberculosis services in specialized institutions, excluded from the totals in the summary above, do not add much to the number of in-patients (because of long average stay of the tuberculous in hospitals), but increase the out-patient attendances considerably. If these attendances are added—172,000 in the Tan Tock Seng Tuberculosis Hospital and 153,000 in the Royal Singapore Anti-Tuberculosis Association Clinic (SATA)—the total

TABLE 17   Medical and Health Expenditures, 1947-54, Singapore

(Million $)

Expenditure or Income	1947	1948	1949	1950	1951	1952	1953[1]	1954[2]
	Colony Medical Department[3]							
Hospitals, Clinics, etc.								
Recurrent . . .	6.8	6.7	7.9	8.4	8.5	12.7	14.7	18.5
Capital	0.2	0.5	0.3	0.4	0.4	2.1	3.1	9.4
Gross total	7.0	7.2	8.2	8.8	8.9	14.8	17.8	27.9
Income from fees, etc. .	n.a.	0.7	0.7	0.7	0.9	1.0	1.1	1.3
Net total .	n.a.	6.5	7.5	8.1	8.0	13.8	16.7	26.6
Other Health Services								
Recurrent . . .	1.2	1.5	1.6	1.5	2.0	2.5	2.7	3.6
Capital	—	0.0+	0.1	0.1	0.0+	0.1	0.2	0.5
Gross total	1.2	1.5+	1.7	1.6	2.0+	2.6	2.9	4.1
Income from fees, etc. .	0.1	0.1	0.0+	0.0+	0.1	0.1	0.2	0.3
Net total .	1.1	1.4	1.7	1.6	1.9	2.5	2.7	3.8
All Services[4]								
Recurrent . . .	8.0	8.2	9.5	9.9	10.5	15.2	17.6[5]	22.2[5]
Capital	0.2	0.5+	0.4	0.5	0.4+	2.2	3.3	9.9[6]
Gross total	8.2	8.7+	9.9	10.4	10.9+	17.4	20.9	32.1
Income from fees, etc.	n.a.	0.8	0.7+	0.7+	1.0	1.1	1.3	1.6
Net total	n.a.	7.9	9.2	9.7	9.9+	16.3	19.6	30.5

TABLE 17—continued

(Million $)

Expenditure or Income	1947	1948	1949	1950	1951	1952	1953[1]	1954[2]
	City Health Department							
Recurrent[7]	1.5	2.0	2.1	2.6	3.4	4.2	4.4	4.9
Capital[8]	0.6	0.5	0.4	0.3	0.1	0.1	0.2	1.8
Gross total . .	2.1	2.5	2.5	2.9	3.5	4.3	4.6	6.7
Income from fees, etc.[9]	1.3	1.2	1.3	1.3	1.3	1.7	1.6+	1.6
Net total . . .	0.8	1.3	1.2	1.6	2.2	2.6	2.9	5.1
	Colony and City Departments							
Recurrent	9.5	10.2	11.6	12.5	13.9	19.4	22.0	27.1
Capital	0.8	1.0+	0.8	0.8	0.5+	2.3	3.5	11.7
Gross total . .	10.3	11.2+	12.4	13.3	14.4+	21.7	25.5	38.8
Income from fees, etc.	n.a.	2.0	2.0+	2.0+	2.3	2.8	2.9+	3.2
Net total . . .	n.a.	9.2	10.4	11.3	12.1	18.9	22.5	35.6

[1] Revised estimates.

[2] Estimates. See footnotes 50a and 50b.

[3] Includes expenditures by the Medical Department (and the Hospitals Board) and the Department of Public Works. Includes expenditures for Rural Board services.

[4] Excludes expenditures by other departments, and current expenditures and accruing liabilities for pensions.

[5] Includes contributions and charitable allowances ($200,000 in 1953 and $100,000 in 1954) not allocated above.

[6] Includes revotes.

[7] Includes annual service charges on loan accounts.

[8] Includes some items which are not new buildings, etc., classified as special expenditures.

[9] Excludes grants from Colony Government and C. D. and W. Fund.

SOURCE: For the Colony: Medical Department, Department of Public Works, and *Estimates* for the year 1954. For the City Council: Health Department, *Audited Accounts*, and *Estimates for 1954.*

(governmental and voluntary) becomes about 1.6 million, equivalent to about 1,400 per 1,000 persons, or 1.4 ambulatory services per capita in the total population in 1953.[50]

C PUBLIC EXPENDITURES: 1947-54

The growth of expenditures incurred by the Colony Medical Department in recent years is shown in Table 17, subdivided to distinguish between

[50] It may be estimated that, in addition, about 250 qualified physicians in private practice provided about 1.5 million attendances in 1953. Thus, total ambulatory services were probably about three per capita in the total population in 1953.

expenditures for hospitals, clinics, dispensaries, etc., and for health services (all other). The gross total in 1954 ($32.1 million) is nearly four times the amount spent in 1947. Most of the expenditures are for the hospitals, clinics and dispensaries; the health services account for only about one-eighth.[50a]

In the same period the City Health Department gross expenditures have increased only a little more than three-fold—from $2.1 to $6.7 million.[50b] By class of expenditure, they were as follows in 1953:

(Million $)

	Recurrent	Capital	Total
Administration and public health services	2.97	0.01	2.98
City staff medical services	0.17	0.07	0.24
Middleton (Infectious Diseases) Hospital	0.36	0.06	0.42
Markets, abattoirs and cemeteries	0.88	0.07	0.95
Total	4.38	0.21	4.59

The data for both departments (Table 17) show expansion of total medical and health expenditures from about $10 million in 1947 to nearly $39 million in 1954, and of net expenditures from $9 million in 1948 to $36 million. Related to the growing population, these figures are as follows:

	1947	1948	1953	1954[51]
Population (thousands)	938	962	1,123	1,175
Gross expenditure (million $) . .	10.3	11.2	25.5	38.8
Per capita ($)	11	12	23	33
Net expenditure (million $) . . .	n.a.	9.2	18.8	32.5
Per capita ($)	n.a.	10	17	28

Thus, gross per capita expenditures nearly doubled between 1948 and 1953 and nearly trebled by 1954, and net per capita expenditures are nearly three

[50a] Information furnished after this report was completed (and too late for incorporation in the tables here and elsewhere) indicates that actual expenditures in 1954 were as follows: annually recurrent, $19 million; capital expenditures, $5 million; gross total, $24 million. These are substantially less than the estimates for that year used in this report.

[50b] Note that these do not include expenditures for refuse collection, street cleansing, disposal of nightsoil, etc. (City Cleansing and Hawkers Department), for surface water drainage, sanitary installations, sewerage, etc. (City Engineer's Department) or for water supply (City Water Department).

[51] Estimates. See footnote 50a concerning expenditures.

times as high in 1954 as in 1948—income from fees, etc., having become a decreasing proportion of the total costs.

IV A DEVELOPMENT PROGRAM: 1954-60

The health agencies and the general governmental authorities of Singapore have given much thought to health and medical needs and, as noted earlier, have repeatedly devised and modified carefully considered developmental plans. The Ten-Year Medical Plan initiated in 1948 now has five years behind it. The residual five-year program provides benchmarks from which to estimate the adequacy of the proposals and the expenditures that may be expected for the years immediately ahead.

A CAPITAL PROJECTS

Table 18 summarizes the capital projects currently included in the program for the Medical Department. The aggregate estimate for the program is $48.7 million, of which $3.3 million had been spent by the end of 1953. With expenditures of nearly $10 million scheduled for 1954, $35.4 million remains for the years 1955-60—somewhat less than $6 million per year. Over 90% of the total is for hospitals, clinics and dispensaries; about 4% is for health service facilities and another 4% for central services and miscellaneous projects.

The more limited and shorter-range program of capital projects needed by the City Council's Health Department includes the following:

	Total	Years
	(Thousand $)	
Analytical laboratory, alterations	30	1954–55
Bacteriological laboratory, new	50	1955
Middleton Hospital, new 60-bed ward . . .	300	1956
Clinics, new (3)	420	1954–56
Urban health center, new	250	1954–55
Dispensary for staff services, new	85	1955
Sub-total	1,135	
Markets, abattoirs and cemeteries	2,864	1954–60
Total	3,999	

SOURCE: City Health Department.

TABLE 18 Capital Projects, Colony Medical Department, 1953-60

(All figures in $)

Projects	Total	Expenditures to Dec. 31, 1953	1954–60	1954	1955–60
Hospitals, clinics and dispensaries					
General Hospital . . .	13,731,135	2,066,135	11,665,000	3,585,000	8,080,000
District hospitals . . .	9,000,000	—	9,000,000	—	9,000,000
Tan Tock Seng Hospital (tuberculosis) . . .	6,990,505	15,505	6,975,000	1,105,000	5,870,000
Kandang Kerbau Hospital (maternity & women)	6,774,995	308,606	6,436,389	3,741,389	2,695,000
Woodbridge Hospital (mental)	6,005,000	—	6,005,000	100,000	5,905,000
Trafalgar Home (leprosy)	1,802,000	195,070	1,606,930	506,930	1,100,000
Dispensary and dental clinic	100,000	—	100,000	—	100,000
Orthopaedic Hospital (children's)	45,128	45,128	—	—	—
Miscellaneous	521,368	44,368	477,000	227,000	250,000
Sub-total	44,940,131	2,674,812	42,265,319	9,265,319	33,000,000
Health services					
Rural health centers .	1,327,995	182,995	1,145,000	335,000	810,000
School medical and dental clinic	480,000	—	480,000	200,000	280,000
Dental huts (2) . . .	16,000	—	16,000	16,000	—
Sub-total	1,823,995	182,995	1,641,000	551,000	1,090,000
Other					
Medical department laundry	600,000	—	600,000	—	600,000
St. John's Island rehabilitation . . .	500,000	—	500,000	—	500,000
Quarters for staff . .	406,260	406,260	—	—	—
Miscellaneous	401,395	77,395	324,000	104,000	220,000
Sub-total	1,907,655	483,655	1,424,000	104,000	1,320,000
All	48,671,781	3,341,462	45,330,319	9,920,319	35,410,000

SOURCE: Medical Department and Department of Public Works.

In the total of $4 million, nearly three-fourths is for markets, abattoirs and cemeteries and only $1.1 million is for more strictly public health and medical facilities.[52]

Thus, the total Singapore program for new health and medical capital projects in 1954-60, Colony and City Council combined, would cost about $49.3 million.[52a] Of this, $10.9 million was included in the approved estimates for 1954, and $38.4 million remains for the years 1955-60. Excluding the estimated capital expenditures for markets, abattoirs and cemeteries, the total for 1955-60 is $36.4 million.

B TOTAL COSTS OF THE GOVERNMENT PROGRAMS

The Colony Medical Department has prepared estimates of budget requirements on the assumption that it would attempt to meet the existing and prospective health needs as rapidly as possible, having regard for population growth and geographical redistribution, increasing demand for Western medicine, and the outlook for opportunities to train and recruit personnel and to expand needed preventive services. These estimates, including the annually recurrent charges that would result from the completion of the scheduled new capital projects, are shown in Table 19. Total gross expenditures would increase from $32.1 million in 1954 to a peak of $41.6 million in 1959 and to the somewhat lesser total of $40.6 million in 1960. The capital needs that can be foreseen now would then have been completed, and expenditures in subsequent years would be determined by future growth of population, health conditions and needs.

A corresponding set of estimates for the City Health Department is also shown in Table 19. These assume the scheduled completion of the capital projects shown on p. 611; and they allow for increases in annually recurrent charges resulting from the new projects and for expansion roughly in proportion to the expected increase of the city population. Alternative totals include and exclude the construction and operation of markets, abattoirs and cemeteries.

The total gross estimates for 1954-60 are brought together at the bottom of Table 19. On the stated assumptions, Singapore should expect gross expenditures for medical and health purposes to increase from about $37

---

[52] The last figure does not include various minor projects and improvements (total about $800,000) included in the 1954 budget as "special expenditures."

[52a] Exclusive of expenditures for water supplies and sewerage.

TABLE 19 Estimated Medical and Health Expenditures, 1954-60, Singapore

(Million $)

Expenditures	1954[1]	1955	1956	1957	1958	1959	1960
	Colony Medical Department						
Hospitals, Clinics, etc.							
Recurrent	18.5	23.1	24.4	26.9	28.8	30.3	31.6
Capital[2]	9.3	5.9	6.0	6.2	6.7	5.3	3.0
Total	27.8	29.0	30.4	33.1	35.5	35.6	34.6
Health Services[3]							
Recurrent[4]	3.7	4.1	4.4	4.8	5.2	5.5	6.0
Capital[2]	0.6	0.7	0.9	0.3	—	0.5	—
Total	4.3	4.8	5.3	5.1	5.2	6.0	6.0
All Services							
Recurrent	22.2	27.2	28.8	31.7	34.0	35.8	37.6
Capital	9.9	6.6	6.9	6.5	6.7	5.8	3.0
Total	32.1	33.8	35.7	38.2	40.7	41.6	40.6
	City Health Department						
With Present Functions							
Recurrent	4.9	5.3	5.4	5.8	5.9	6.1	6.2
Capital	1.8	1.8	0.6	0.2	0.2	0.2	—
Total	6.7	7.1	6.0	6.0	6.1	6.3	6.2
Exclusive of Markets, etc.[5]							
Recurrent	3.9	4.1	4.3	4.5	4.6	4.7	4.8
Capital	0.7	0.5	0.4	—	—	—	—
Total	4.6	4.6	4.7	4.5	4.6	4.7	4.8
	Colony and City Departments[5]						
Recurrent	26.1	31.3	33.1	36.2	38.6	40.5	42.4
Capital	10.6	7.1	7.3	6.5	6.7	5.8	3.0
Total[6]	36.7	38.4	40.4	42.7	45.3	46.3	45.4

[1] Estimates. See footnotes 50a and 50b.
[2] From Table 18.
[3] Includes miscellaneous items.
[4] Includes contributions to voluntary agencies as in estimates for 1954.
[5] Excludes expenditures for markets, abattoirs and cemeteries.
[6] Excludes current expenditures and accruing liabilities for pensions. Also excludes expenditures for water supplies, sewerage, etc.

million in 1954 to $45-$46 million a year in 1959-60. These expenditures may be expected to bear the following relations to population:[53]

	1954	1955	1956	1957	1958	1959	1960
Per capita ($) .	32	32	33	34	35	35	34

If the practices of past years are continued with respect to hospital charges, fees, licenses, etc., net expenditures may be about 10% less and annual per capita costs may be relatively fixed and stable at the level of about $30 in 1954-60.[54]

C REVIEW OF THE PROGRAM

Hospitals and Out-Patient Departments

The mission is impressed that the program for development of the hospitals and related facilities would enable Singapore to achieve by 1959 or 1960 a rounding-out of its governmental resources for in-patient and hospital out-patient services. At the end of the next five or six years the Colony would have substantially modern and up-to-date plant and equipment—including resources needed for the expanding faculties of medicine, dentistry, pharmacy and public health of the University of Malaya.

With the scheduled projects completed, the bed capacity in governmental hospitals[55] would be as follows in relation to the increasing population:

[53] Based on population estimates (for the Asian populations only) prepared by the Department of Statistics for the years 1952, 1957 and 1962. These estimates assume no (net) migration, and continuance of 1947 mortality and 1947-51 fertility rates.

[54] These are about two and one-half times the per capita expenditures expected for the largely rural population of the Federation (see p. 588). They are relatively small, however, compared to costs that are equivalent to about $75-$120 per capita in Great Britain, western Europe and Canada and about $240 per capita in the United States for public and private expenditures for public health and personal medical services.

[55] Includes the present facilities of the Colony Medical Department and the City Health Department and additions and new facilities in the development program. Excludes beds in independent clinics, health centers, etc., and in the tuberculosis, leprosy and mental disease institutions.

The scheduled expansions between 1954 and 1960 are as follows: General Hospital from 800 to 1,350 beds; Middleton (infectious diseases) from 250 to 310 beds; Kandang Kerbau (maternity, etc.) from 240 to 450 beds; new district or cottage hospitals, 600 beds; Tan Tock Seng (tuberculosis) from 560 to 1,200 beds; Trafalgar (leprosy) from 800 to 1,110 beds; and Woodbridge (mental) from 1,800 to 2,300 beds.

	1954	1955	1956	1957	1958	1959	1960
Population[56] (x 000) .	1,154	1,186	1,217	1,248	1,283	1,319	1,354
Beds	1,660	2,126	2,220	2,480	2,480	2,780	3,080
Per 1,000 persons	1.4	1.8	1.8	2.0	1.9	2.1	2.3

Thus, in addition to being qualitatively improved, in-patient capacity of the hospitals would be increasing vis-a-vis the growing population.

Taking into account the 0.5 beds per 1,000 persons in voluntary hospitals in 1953 (see p. 607), the expansion would reduce present overcrowding and allow for the demand for Western medicine from an increasing proportion of the growing population. However, this should not be regarded as an optimistic estimate of the future. Need and demand may grow to such an extent as to require much further expansion of in-patient capacity.

There are no fixed or universal standards by which to measure need for hospital beds, and there are none that are directly applicable to Singapore. Experience in Western countries suggests that a large urban area needs four to six beds per 1,000 persons, exclusive of beds in chronic disease, tuberculosis and mental disease hospitals. With allowance for Singapore's high frequency of maternity cases and for its inadequate housing which tends to press the sick into the hospitals, an equivalent standard might be 5-10 general hospital beds per 1,000 persons. It is therefore evident why we regard the present hospital capacity as being grossly insufficient, even while Singapore's population is in transition toward acceptance of Western medicine.

If the people of Singapore fully accepted and demanded hospital care in the Western pattern, the Colony would need at least 3,600-6,000 beds for the present population (three to five beds per 1,000), might not be able to solve its problem without twice as many (7,200-12,000 beds), and might need still more as its population increases. Expansion of hospital facilities toward these levels would involve expenditures beyond anything hitherto contemplated. And it would be an impossible undertaking for lack of professional staff, even if the physical and financial resources were available.

Singapore may have to develop a much larger hospital system than is presently proposed. But we do not advise that this be decided now. Instead, we recommend that for the next five or six years it proceed with the present program, with such augmentation as we suggest here, pressing the expansion of out-patient services and of the preventive services.

[56] See footnote 53.

The mission believes there are at least three specific respects in which projected hospital in-patient capacity may continue to be actually inadequate even though generally sufficient in the next few years:

(1) Expansion of the Kandang Kerbau Hospital from 240 to 450 beds may not be enough for maternity care if housing conditions are not substantially improved and most of the births in Singapore continue to occur in hospitals, especially if the birth rate remains at its present high level and average hospital stay for maternity cases cannot be kept at the low figure of three to four days.

(2) The construction of 10 cottage or district hospitals (scheduled for 1958-60) may be too little and too late with respect to local hospital care, especially for the outskirts of the city and for the rural areas. The mission believes that doubling of this program (costing an additional $9 million of capital funds and adding to annual recurrent costs) may become desirable or urgently necessary—for general medical, surgical and maternity in-patients and for specialized out-patient services on a decentralized basis—and may have to be undertaken in the next few years.

(3) As long as there are almost no provisions for the bed-care of non-acute patients (other than the tuberculous, leprous and mental), we have to assume that there will continue to be inefficient use of the beds in the hospitals. We therefore recommend that consideration be given to the development, on an experimental basis, of separate institutions or hospital-connected facilities for chronic and convalescent patients. These should serve to relieve the more expensive central hospitals of cases which block many beds intended for acutely sick persons. We also recommend that an effort be made to encourage voluntary agencies to build and maintain such institutions in cooperation with the Medical and Social Welfare Departments.

The capital projects for improvement of the hospitals include provision for modernization and expansion of the out-patient facilities at the Kandang Kerbau (maternity) Hospital. At the General Hospital, a new out-patient department has already been completed. These will reduce the present overcrowding but we expect that they will serve only a fraction of the increasing number of out-patients. The care of ambulatory patients will have to fall in increasing measure on the independent (nonhospital) clinics, dispensaries and health centers. This, in our opinion, would be a sound development; progressively more and more of the people to be served as out-patients should receive care at less expensive facilities conveniently located near residential areas, and only a small fraction should have to be referred to the hospitals for specialized out- or in-patient services.

Clinics, Dispensaries and Health Centers

The program for development of independent out-patient facilities is flexible, as it has to be in light of uncertain redistribution of the expanding population. The prospectus for major expansion of rural centers, especially for maternity and child welfare services, contemplates seven main centers and about 90 subsidiary nurse and midwife centers. We regard this as an eminently sound proposal, especially since one-third of the population is already located in the rural part of the Island, the proportion is growing rapidly and the rehousing program is expected to stimulate development of satellite towns. However, we are not entirely sure that sufficient provision has been made for centers in the urban areas to provide preventive and curative services for the general public and to relieve the pressures on the out-patient facilities and ancillary services of the hospitals. We also are inclined to believe that considerable expansion beyond that presently scheduled has to be contemplated for school health, medical and dental services, based on the proposed urban health center to be developed jointly by the Medical Department and the Department of Social Medicine and Public Health of the University of Malaya.

Specialized Institutions

Singapore has accommodation for nearly twice as many patients in the specialized tuberculosis, leprosy and mental disease institutions as in the in-patient facilities of the hospitals but this is not enough. The scheduled expansion—in relation to the populations estimated for 1954 and 1960, respectively—is as follows:

	Beds	
	1954	1960
Tuberculosis (Tan Tock Seng)	557	1,200
Per 1,000 persons	0.5	0.9
Leprosy (Trafalgar)	800	1,110
Per 1,000 persons	0.7	0.8
Mental disease (Woodbridge)	1,800	2,300
Per 1,000 persons	1.6	1.7

Tuberculosis. Our study leads us to believe that even more than doubling the resources of the tuberculosis institution will not suffice, in view of the undoubtedly high although uncertain prevalence and incidence of tuberculosis.[57] The evidence available to the mission suggests that, with present methods of treatment, Singapore may already have need for 10,000-15,000 beds for tuberculosis cases.[58] And it will need more for its growing population unless the disease is checked or other effective methods are introduced.

Leprosy. The local authorities estimate that the augmented provisions for resident lepers will be sufficient for the next few years. However, we note that out-patient treatment centers and staff accommodations will apparently continue to be inadequate, and we recommend that these deficiencies be met as soon as possible. In addition, there should be new and adequate provisions for education, training and rehabilitation of suitable resident and out-patient cases. We also recommend development of treatment allowances for dependents of lepers (similar to the corresponding allowances now provided with respect to tuberculosis). This program should be widely advertised in the community in order to encourage cases to come forward early in the course of disease and to remain under treatment until discharged. The possibility of developing a self-supporting settlement for discharged cases unable to reenter general community life should be explored by the medical and social welfare authorities.

Mental Disease. The figures shown above indicate that the scheduled expansion of mental disease facilities will only little more than keep pace with population growth. By contrast, the true need may be as large in Singapore as in a Western country—above five beds per 1,000 persons. We therefore expect that this part of the development program will be found insufficient, more institutional beds will have to be built and staffed, a special institution for mental defectives will be needed, and the in-patient resources will have to be supplemented by out-patient services as well as by an enlarged mental hygiene program.

[57] On December 31, 1953, 453 of the 557 beds in the Tan Tock Seng Hospital were occupied by tuberculosis patients (104 by general patients, many of them nonhospital chronic cases). In addition, tuberculosis cases were using 50 beds in the General Hospital and 100 of the 120 beds in the children's Orthopaedic Hospital.

[58] The Medical Department has knowledge of about 6,000 cases. SATA has about 9,000 cases under ambulatory treatment or home and clinic observation and believes that about 50,000 are waiting for treatment. As a minimum, at the rate of 2.5 beds per reported death, Singapore needs 2,000-2,500 beds.

Preventive Services of the Future

The mission regards the capital development program of the immediate past and of the next five to six years as, in the main, a program to wipe out Singapore's arrears and to bring it abreast of its current needs for health and medical care. We believe that it is a necessary program and that it may be nearly sufficient. However, even though it will require large sums, it may nevertheless be only prologue to continuing expansion of hospitals and related facilities in succeeding years—certainly if population and public demand for care continue to grow as anticipated. Singapore therefore has to expect to make the large capital outlays we have already indicated and provide increasing annually recurrent funds for 1954-60, and it must expect further increases in public expenditures thereafter.

The future costs of health and medical services could become heavy burdens on the revenues of the Colony, mainly because of expenditures for hospital and other services for the sick. The first recourse to avoid this eventuality is to reduce the future volume of sickness to the maximum extent practical through prevention of disease. Singapore already has a magnificent record of achievement in this respect. Insofar as it can, we recommend that it should expand preventive activities much further with the hope they will prove to be investments that will pay large future dividends. We believe that expansion of preventive services—community and personal—should be given priority even to the extent of sacrificing expansion of hospitals and other facilities for curative services if personnel or funds are insufficient for both.

In addition to continuing and strengthening well-established services (e.g., protection against importation of nonindigenous epidemic diseases, quarantine at St. John's Island, environmental sanitation, mosquito control, safeguarding of water supply, maternity and child welfare services, periodic immunization against smallpox, etc.), the mission believes there are promising opportunities with respect to:

1. More extensive immunization against diphtheria, to reduce the proportion of nonimmunes among infants, preschool and school children, and against typhoid and related diseases;
2. Broadening the protection of food supply through sanitary control of places where food is prepared for public sale, and examination and licensing of food handlers employed in public eating places or operating as hawkers;

3. Strengthening (a) the control of occupational hazards, and (b) health services for adolescents entering gainful employment;
4. Expanding the ambulatory services for venereal disease patients;
5. Enlarging the dental health services, at first especially for young children and progressively for older children and adolescents, and adding fluoride to the water supply to prevent dental disease; and
6. Making school health and medical services more comprehensive and more nearly adequate.

Tuberculosis. The mission believes that, in many respects, tuberculosis is the most serious disease afflicting the population of Singapore. Whether its prevalence is 2-3% of the population or is as high as 5% is disputed among specialists in this disease. Reliable information is not available. And we have not found it possible to determine with confidence whether or not the disease is increasing, is being held in check or is being conquered, and whether the scheduled program will be adequate. Doubts are strong and persistent, despite the extensive activities and large expenditures of the government departments and the voluntary agencies, especially the Royal Singapore Anti-Tuberculosis Association (SATA).

Hospital facilities for the tuberculous are perennially insufficient. Their increase to an adequate bed capacity would be too expensive and they could not be staffed if they could be built.

The acute overcrowding and shortage of housing in the City cannot be overcome in the discernible future. While this important contributory cause of tuberculosis prevalence persists, vigorous steps to strengthen the anti-tuberculosis program are needed. This is well appreciated by the local authorities and we would strongly encourage them to launch a new attack on this disease. We recommend consideration of the following measures: initial surveys to determine incidence and prevalence, especially among children entering and leaving school, and subsequent periodic surveys to assess progress against the disease; expansion of inexpensive clinic facilities for ambulatory care, and development of settlements for nontreatable, arrested, convalescent and healed cases that do not require acute hospital care; early case finding; hospital care for selected treatable cases up to the capacity of in-patient facilities; an expanded program of out-patient and domiciliary care and of BCG vaccination on a controlled experimental basis; health education of cases and contacts; vocational rehabilitation of discharged cases; and support of the treatment allowance program operated jointly by the Medical and Social Welfare Departments. Such a comprehensive campaign against tuberculosis should, if possible, have the technical aid of experts from international agencies, and should be carried out in collaboration with SATA and other local voluntary agencies. The resources of the official agencies might be augmented by increased grants-in-aid to SATA for care furnished without charge or at nominal rates.

Health Education. Both for the prevention of tuberculosis specifically and for over-all preventive activities in general, a program of health education of the population should be vigorously prosecuted through all available institutions and media. We believe this is likely to be one of the most useful undertakings for reduction of future sickness and medical expense.

Recruitment and Training of Personnel

It is almost gratuitous for the mission to emphasize the high priority that Singapore must continue to give to the recruitment and training of professional and sub-professional staff, striving for the most rapid practicable expansion in the categories in which there are present and prospective shortages.

We endorse expansion of the medical, dental and pharmacy schools of the University of Malaya, and our estimates have included allowances for the needed teaching facilities.

Hostels for student and graduate nurses should continue to be provided as an essential element in recruitment but the cost of new facilities should if possible be reduced. With respect to dental nurses, Singapore has utilized the resources of the Federation's school at Penang; needed expansion of the dental program suggests that the Medical Department should develop a similar training school of its own, to ensure an adequate supply of dental nurses for schools and other public institutions.

Finally, overseas recruitment of needed specialists (medical, public health and para-medical) should be pursued vigorously until the local supply becomes adequate, and overseas facilities should continue to be used for postgraduate training of selected individuals in specialties.

D ADMINISTRATION

Our review of medical and health services and their development has treated the various elements as though they were parts of an integral program, despite the fact that administratively they are under the Colony, City Council and Rural Board authorities. We have been impressed that the various activities are carried out with good cooperation but we have also been concerned over some loss of efficiency and economy, especially in utilization of staff, resulting from maintenance of separate medical and health agencies.

Viewed only as a problem in administration of public health and medical services, we would conclude that Singapore should have a single agency responsible for all governmental health and medical activities, and that this agency should be relieved of functions not primarily concerned with, or essential to, the protection and preservation of the public health or the provision of personal health and medical services. Taking account of general problems and policies of administration, however, we recognize that administrative responsibilities may have to be divided between Colony and local authorities.

The Rendel Commission[59] proposed a division of functions between the Central Government and the City and Island Council, both island-wide in jurisdiction, which would in the main keep the present allocations. We believe that it would be better to lodge responsibility for personal health and medical services (concerned with prevention, diagnosis, treatment and rehabilitation) in the Central Government, and for environmental services in the Council.[60] While some exceptions might have to be made, these general guides could provide a basis for effective integration of each group of activities and for more effective, efficient and economical administration and development of the services.

E   FUTURE COSTS AND FINANCING

From the available information it appears to the mission that the remaining five-year program for the development of health and medical

[59] Report of the Constitutional Commission, Singapore (Sir George Rendel, Chairman), February 22, 1954, Singapore.

[60] E.g., functions with respect to operation of markets, abattoirs, cemeteries and crematoria might be lodged in a department of local government concerned with commercial activities; street cleaning, refuse and nightsoil collection, sewage disposal and operation of incinerators might go to the local health department or to another Council department; the infectious disease hospital, the maternity, infancy and child welfare clinics and the performance of immunizations should be consolidated in the Central Government; and anti-malaria and other sanitary services should be unified under the Council.

services is necessary and basically sound. We believe that Singapore should in any case be prepared to meet gross costs rising from about $37 million in 1954 to at least $45 million in 1960. But, though comprehensive and ambitious, that program is in our opinion still minimal and insufficient in many respects. If the plans for recruitment and training of personnel can be enlarged, and if the Public Works Department and the private construction industry can undertake more than has been scheduled, the program should be broadened along the lines indicated by our reassessment. Estimated gross expenditures about 10% larger than those in Table 19 should in the first instance be anticipated—about $42 million in 1955, rising to about $50 million in 1960. If revenue from hospital charges, fees, etc., is increased from 5% to about 25% of expenditures, this would offset some of the increase to be expected. The adjusted estimates of expenditures and revenues for 1954 and the next six years then become as follows.[61]

(Million $)

	1954[62]	1955	1956	1957	1958	1959	1960
Annually recurrent	26.1	34.4	36.4	39.4	42.5	44.6	46.6
Capital expenditures	10.6	7.8	8.0	7.2	7.4	6.4	3.3
Total	36.7	42.2	44.4	46.6	49.9	51.0	49.9
Income from fees, etc. . . .	1.8	3.8	6.0	8.0	10.0	12.0	12.5
Net total	34.9	38.4	38.4	38.6	39.9	39.0	37.4

It is possible that the capital costs of new facilities can be reduced, even as much as 25-33%, by lowering construction standards, accepting more modest and less permanent facilities and conserving land costs by multistory design. If this is practical, it should be done in the interest of having relatively more funds for substantive services, especially preventive services.

The financing of the prospective program raises difficult questions. Singapore has an established policy of providing necessary medical services at prices within reach of all citizens. The services have been and are largely free. The mission recommends that, if the public revenues can continue to finance what is needed, that policy should continue. If they cannot, Singapore should not curtail or delimit the program. Nor should it attempt to find a major portion of the needed funds through substantial increases

[61] Exclusive of expenditures for and revenues from markets, abattoirs and cemeteries.
[62] Estimates. See footnote 50a.

of individual fees, although substantial increase in charges for in-patient services is indicated; it may be difficult to avoid making increased fees burdensome on many of the sick or interposing financial barriers against needed care, especially ambulatory care. Prompt attention for preventive purposes and for diagnosis and care early in disease are essential for prevention of future serious, disabling and expensive illness. If Singapore must find new means of financing the medical and health services, we recommend consideration of the partial financing of hospital or other personal medical services through contributory social insurance.

TECHNICAL REPORT 11
NOTES ON SOCIAL WELFARE

I FEDERATION

There are no recent annual reports for the Department of Social Welfare and no comprehensive published records of operating experiences. The following technical notes and tables therefore summarize some of the data and analyses prepared for the mission by the Department and indicate the basis of various conclusions and recommendations presented in Chapter 7, Part III.[1]

Federal Institutions

A census of institutions operated by the Federal Department as of April 1954 was compiled for our study. The data are summarized in Table 1. The total direct operating costs in 1953 were about $1.6 million, equivalent to about $0.28 per person in the Federation. These government institutions are supplemented by voluntary institutions, some of them aided by government subventions (see p. 628). The total numbers of government institutions and of persons served are relatively small; in most cases the undertakings are little more than pilot projects.

Expenditures: 1947-54

Table 2 gives a compilation of government expenditures for social welfare in the years 1947-54, separately for the Federal Department and the State/Settlement departments and for all combined. The totals have increased from $1.6 million in 1947 to $5.6 million in 1954, mainly in the Federal program.

[1] In addition to information and documents furnished by the Department and the summaries of operations contained in the Annual Reports of the Federation, we have had opportunity to study reports prepared by the social welfare officers of Johore, Kelantan, Malacca, Pahang, Penang and Perak, to make field observations in those States and Settlements and to have conferences with the social welfare officers of Selangor.

TABLE 1   Federal Social Welfare Institutions, April 1954, Federation

Type of Institution	Number of Institutions	Residents Capacity (1954)	Residents Avg. No. (1953)[1]	Operating Costs, 1953[2] Total	Operating Costs, 1953[2] Per Resident per Month
Old people's homes	9	1,996	1,791	$802,049	$37.32
Children's homes	8	735	618	408,678	55.11
"Approved" schools	4	420	321	343,480	89.17
Remand homes and hostels	3[3]	88[3]	35	21,122	50.29
Primary school for blind children .	1	75	37	n.a.	83.33[4]
Training center for blind adults . .	1	44	n.a.	n.a.	108.33[4]
Sheltered home and workshop for blind adults	1	24	16	7,139	37.19
Youth leadership training center[5] .	1	50	—	—	—

[1] For the first quarter 1954 the corresponding figures are: 1,720, 632, 360, 34, 56 and 12.
[2] Includes only administration (personal emoluments) and other charges annually recurrent.
[3] Only two institutions with a capacity of 50 operating in 1953.
[4] Estimated on the basis of experience during early development of the institution.
[5] Opened in 1954. Includes facilities to house 200 for conferences.

SOURCE: Department of Social Welfare.

The expenditures for 1953 are subdivided in Table 3 to show the breakdown between the Federal and State/Settlement Governments and among the States and Settlements. Total government expenditures in that year amounted to less than $1 per capita in the Federation—$0.70 for the Federal and $0.23 for the non-Federal operations. The expenditures among the States and Settlements ranged from one-fourth to twice the average per capita amount.

Classification of Expenditures: 1953, 1954

Data are not available to show expenditures for each type of social welfare activity. Table 4 therefore shows for 1953 and 1954 the allocations in the budgets (votes and supplementary votes), which exceed the actual expenditures for those years. The largest portions are for public assistance and for probation and related services. The Federal funds are distributed among all types of activities except home (outdoor) relief; the State/Settlement funds are principally for home relief and children's services

TABLE 2 Government Expenditures for Social Welfare, 1947-54, Federation

(Thousand $)

Expenditure	1947	1948	1949	1950	1951	1952	1953	1954[1]
	Federal Department							
Annually recurrent[2]	785	1,296	2,024	2,220	1,769	2,277	2,590	2,965
Subventions[3]	316	322	371	382	379	343	458	529
"Emergency"[4]	—	—	335	300	423	285	245	238
Sub-total	1,101	1,618	2,730	2,902	2,571	2,905	3,293	3,732
Capital[5]	539	806	369	151	383	922	718	440
Total	1,640	2,424	3,099	3,053	2,954	3,827	4,011	4,172
	State/Settlement Departments and Offices							
Annually recurrent[2]	—	—	—	—	897	1,033	1,224	1,393
Capital	—	—	—	—	28	44	74	60
Total	—	—	—	—	925	1,077	1,298	1,453
	Federal and State/Settlement Departments and Offices							
Annually recurrent[6]	1,101	1,618	2,730	2,902	3,468	3,938	4,517	5,125
Capital	539	806	369	151	411	966	792	500
Total	1,640	2,424	3,099	3,053	3,879	4,904	5,309	5,625

[1] Revised estimates.
[2] Includes personal emoluments and other charges annually recurrent.
[3] Includes related grants-in-aid through other Federal departments.
[4] Expenditures (including administrative) for collection, maintenance and despatch of dependents of detainees.
[5] Includes special expenditures, public works (nonrecurrent) and amounts earmarked from C. D. and W. Funds.
[6] Includes Federal expenditures for subventions and "emergency" functions.

SOURCE: Department of Social Welfare.

and—as also in the case of the Federal Department—for a wide variety of miscellaneous services performed by the unallocated administrative and professional staff.

Subventions

The Federal Department of Social Welfare makes grants-in-aid to various voluntary organizations and institutions. Of $202,000 available to the Department for subventions in 1954, more than one-half ($121,000) was earmarked for 27 children's homes and orphanages with capacity for 1,951 infants and children; the grants were mainly $5 a month per resident child. Smaller amounts were assigned to various youth organizations ($38,000), three old person's homes with 340 residents ($16,000), the St. Nicholas Home and School for the Blind with 45 inmates ($11,520),

TABLE 3 Government Expenditures and the Populations of the States and Settlements, 1953, Federation

| Social Welfare Departments and Offices | Expenditures | | | | | | Popula-tion[3] % |
| | (Thousand $) | | | Per Capita | | % | |
	Recur-rent[1]	Capi-tal[2]	Total	Amount	Index		
All	4,517	792	5,309	$0.93	—	100	—	—
Federal	3,293	718	4,011	0.70	—	76	—	—
State/Settlement . .	1,224	74	1,298	0.23	100	24	100	100
Perak	252	16	268	0.24	104	5	21	20
Johore	190	4	194	0.22	96	4	15	15
Selangor . . .	176	14	190	0.22	96	4	15	15
Kedah	37	—	37	0.06	26	1	3	11
Penang	80	2	82	0.16	70	2	6	9
Kelantan . . .	60	7	67	0.14	61	1	5	9
Negri Sembilan	109	13	122	0.38	165	2	9	6
Malacca . . .	132	—	132	0.47	204	2	10	5
Pahang	71	2	73	0.26	113	1	6	5
Trengganu . .	107	16	123	0.49	213	2	9	4
Perlis	10	—	10	0.12	52	0+	1	1

[1] Includes personal emoluments and other charges annually recurrent.
[2] Includes special expenditures and public works.
[3] Mid-year, 1953.

SOURCE: Department of Social Welfare. State/Settlement expenditures provided by the Treasurers through the Accountant-General.

five Chinese maternity hospitals with 563 beds ($7,200) and to a miscellany of other agencies (child welfare schools, the Red Cross Society, the Malayan Association for the Blind, the Women's Service League, the Prisoners' Aid Society, etc.). Data on private expenditures by the voluntary agencies are not available.

Related grants in 1954 through other government offices and depart-

TABLE 4   Budget Allocations of Social Welfare Expenditures, 1953 and 1954[1], Federation

(Thousand $)

Activities[2]	Federal Department				State/Settlement Depts. and Offices				All Departments			
	Amount		Percent		Amount		Percent		Amount		Percent	
	1953	1954	1953	1954	1953	1954	1953	1954	1953	1954	1953	1954
Public assistance[3]	$1,777	$1,307	33	28	$ 432	$ 386	31	28	$2,209	$1,693	32	28
Probation and "approved" school services	1,420	1,667	26	36	—	—	—	—	1,420	1,667	21	27
Children's services	1,057	507	19	11	100[4]	854	7	6	1,157	592	17	10
Youth services	299	334	6	7	—	—	—	—	299	334	4	6
"Emergency" services[5]	294	238	5	5	—	—	—	—	294	238	4	4
Services for the blind[6]	192	221	4	5	—	—	—	—	192	221	3	4
Administration and miscellaneous[7]	401	390	7	8	883	922	62	66	1,284	1,312	19	21
All	$5,440	$4,664	100	100	$1,415	$1,393	100	100	$6,855	$6,057	100	100

[1] Based on votes and supplementary votes for annually recurrent and capital expenditures.

[2] Staff training and related functions are included with other activities.

[3] Federal activities include institutional and miscellaneous services, but no regular home relief. State/Settlement activities are nearly wholly home relief in cash or kind.

[4] Includes supplementary feeding programs.

[5] Approximately one-half is estimated to be public assistance.

[6] Institutional and home relief for the blind are excluded here and are included in public assistance.

[7] Federal Department amounts include subventions to voluntary agencies. Subvention votes through the Department of Social Welfare were $199,000 in 1953 and $202,000 in 1954; through other Federal departments $265,500 in 1953 and $326,750 in 1954.

SOURCE: Department of Social Welfare.

ments (Chief Secretary, Treasury, Education and Medical) included the following:

Scouts and Guides $235,750
Women's Institutes 40,000
Cadet Corps 31,000
Red Cross Society 10,000
St. John's Ambulance Brigade 10,000

In addition, $1.35 million was voted through the Chief Secretary's Office for services with respect to the emergency, mainly for services in new villages ($400,000 to missionary bodies and $950,000 to the Red Cross Society and St. John's Ambulance Brigade).

Proposals for Capital Expenditures: 1954-60

The Federation needs a large number of new social welfare institutions, and some of the present facilities—improvised or developed after the war—are now meager, dilapidated, primitive and unsuitable. Field observations indicate that the needed improvements, replacements and new institutions would cost far more than can be considered in a practical program for the next five or six years in view of financial stringencies and shortage of professional and administrative staff.

Table 5 summarizes the needed institutions and facilities which are given priority rating by the Department of Social Welfare (May 1954).[2] The total of $3.9 million for urgent capital expenditures in 1954-60 includes only $230,000 for old persons' homes, and thus is minimal with respect to care of destitute aged persons. Nearly all of the capital projects are concerned with care of young children or with the "constructive" services.

The priority projects listed in Table 5 and their expected costs (as of early 1954) were used as a guide in developing the mission's estimate of capital expenditures (and resulting annually recurrent costs) to be budgeted for 1955-60.

Estimates of Total Expenditures: 1954-60

In accordance with considerations set forth in Chapter 7, estimates were prepared for each type of social welfare service for the years 1955-60. These are summarized in Table 6.

[2] The priority projects have specific locations, but since these are necessarily tentative they are omitted from the Table.

TABLE 5 Priority Capital Projects, Department of Social Welfare, 1954-60,[1] Federation[2]

(Thousand $)

Activity or Project	Estimated Expenditure	
	Capital	Additional Recurrent
Public assistance		
Old persons' homes, additions and replacements (2)	230	—
Probation and "approved" school services		
Remand homes and hostels (12)	878	200
"Approved" schools—Improvements (1)	80	20
New (1)	210	80
Children's services		
Homes (5)	1,033	268
Crippled children's home	170	58
Staff quarters (3)	154	—
Services for the blind		
Nursery school	150	45
Sheltered workshop	200	25
Primary school	350	85
Hostel	250	10
Colony for mentally subnormal children	200	65
All projects, 1954–60	3,905	856
Projects for 1961 and later	1,428	451
Total	5,333	1,307

[1] As of May, 1954.
[2] The Table does not give any indication of the relative priorities of the projects listed.

SOURCE: Department of Social Welfare.

Total government expenditures of about $5.6 million in 1954 ($0.95 per capita) should be expected to increase to about $7.5 million in 1959 ($1.08 per capita) and $7.9 million in 1960 ($1.09 per capita). In these totals, public assistance has been arbitrarily held after 1954 at $2.2 million, the amount estimated as needed for 1955; whether it will have to increase or may decrease after 1955 will depend upon general economic conditions as well as other factors and cannot be determined in advance. It should certainly increase substantially if the tuberculosis treatment allowance program which we have recommended is not developed adequately by the Malayan Association for the Prevention of Tuberculosis, aided by the

TABLE 6 Estimates of Government Expenditures for Social Welfare, 1954-60, Federation

(Thousand $)

Activity or Type of Expenditure	Federal and State/Settlement Departments									1954				1960			
	1954¹		1955	1956	1957	1958	1959	1960		Amount		Percent		Amount		Percent	
	Amount	%						Amount	%	Federal	St/Stl	Federal	St/Stl	Federal	St/Stl	Federal	St/Stl
Public assistance	$1,668	32	$2,216	$2,216	$2,216	$2,216	$2,216	$2,216	30	$1,282	$386	25	7	$216	$2,000	3	27
Probation and "approved" school services	809	16	954	1,049	1,074	1,189	1,269	1,304	18	809	—	16	—	1,304	—²	18	—²
Children's services	573	11	630	730	820	890	910	1,050	14	488	85	9	2	1,050	—²	14	—²
Youth services	334	7	990	1,060	1,080	1,180	1,380	1,600	22	334	—	7	—	1,000	600	14	8
"Emergency" services	238	5	200	170	140	110	100	100	1	238	—	5	—	100	—	1	—
Services for the blind	220	4	400	525	555	575	660	710	9	220	—	4	—	710	—³	9	—³
Training and research	(18)⁴	(0+)	38	50	60	80	80	100	1	(18)⁴	—	(0+)	—	100	—	1	—
Administration⁵	1,283	25	400	400	400	400	400	400	5	360	923	7	18	400	—	5	—⁶
All annually recurrent⁷	5,125	100	5,828	6,200	6,345	6,640	7,015	7,480	100	3,731	1,394	73	27	4,880	2,600	65	35
Capital facilities⁸	500		800	700	600	500	500	400									
Total	5,625		6,628	6,900	6,945	7,140	7,515	7,880									

¹ Revised estimates.
² No transfer of function or dollars from the Federal to the State/Settlement Governments shown here, though the policy intends that such transfer should have begun before 1960.
³ It is assumed that by 1960 as much as 1/3-1/2 of the funds may be subventions to the Malayan Association for the Blind or may have been transferred to the State/Settlement Governments.
⁴ Included in funds for other activities.
⁵ After 1954, specialized staff services are included with other activities.
⁶ All included with other activities.
⁷ Includes subventions to voluntary agencies.
⁸ Estimates based on staging of priority capital projects.

SOURCE: Department of Social Welfare, special calculation.

Social and Welfare Lotteries Board, or by other nonofficial agencies. Increases in the estimates for other social welfare activities have taken account of current unmet need, expected growth of population, present staff and potential capacity of the Federal training and recruitment resources, possible development of the Federal services, staging of transfers to State/Settlement Governments and development of voluntary agencies.

In Table 6 the principal transfer from Federal to State/Settlement administration is with respect to public assistance. Transfers should also be initiated by or before 1960 not only in the case of youth services, as shown in the Table, but also for probation and "approved" schools services, children's services and services for the blind,[3] but no specific estimates of these transfers are included in the Table.

Estimates for subventions include, in addition to grants already made through the Department of Social Welfare, the amount provided for scout and guide organizations through the Department of Education, an additional $250,000 for other youth organizations and small grants for children's services.

II SINGAPORE

Detailed accounts of the functions and operations of the Singapore Social Welfare Department are available in the Annual Reports of the Colony and of the Department.[4] We therefore include here only special tabulations and explanatory notes that underly our conclusions and recommendations in Chapter 7.

Government and Aided Institutions

In 1954 the Social Welfare Department was operating 18 nonresidential and nine residential institutions, with operating costs of slightly more than $1 million a year. In addition, it was making grants-in-aid of about $191,000 with respect to children and aged persons in 15 residential institutions operated by voluntary agencies. These operations are summarized in Table 7.

---

[3] In the case of the last, the transfer may be to the Malayan Association for the Blind if circumstances indicate that this will be more desirable than transfer to the State/Settlement departments, especially if the Association develops substantial voluntary financial support.

[4] See especially the *Annual Report of the Social Welfare Department for 1953*, by T. P. Cromwell, Singapore, 1954.

The facilities, governmental and voluntary, are in general insufficient to meet current needs.

Classification of Expenditures: 1954

Singapore's expenditures for social welfare have increased from $1 million in 1948 to $8 million in 1954 (Table 3, Chapter 7). A breakdown of

TABLE 7 Social Welfare Institutions, Government and Aided, 1954, Singapore

Type of Institution	Number of Institutions	Residents	Operating Costs	
			Total	Per Resident per Month
Government institutions				
Nonresidential				
Children's centers[1]	16	1,700	$270,370	$13
Creches[2]	2	100	31,900	27
Residential				
Children's homes, etc.[3] . . .	4	450	475,000	88
Old people's homes	2	270	180,000	56
Hostels (boys')	2	60	50,000	69
Mentally defectives' home .	1	20	40,000	167
			Government Grants	Private Expenditures
Aided voluntary institutions				
Homes and orphanages[4]	12	1,300	$130,800[5]	$450,000[6]
Crippled children's home[7]	1	30	23,800[5]	48,000[6]
Old people's home[8]	1	300	5,020	n.a.
Blind children's home and school[9]	1	40	31,000	n.a.

[1] Some also used increasingly as community centers for various activities.
[2] Day care centers.
[3] Includes a place of safety for girls, an "approved" school for boys, a girls' home and a boys' orphanage.
[4] Salvation Army Boys' Home, Overseas Chinese Creche (Home), etc.
[5] Grant-in-aid on a monthly per capita basis.
[6] Estimated.
[7] British Red Cross Society.
[8] Little Sisters of the Poor. Grant for electricity and water charges.
[9] Singapore Association for the Blind. Institution was to have been built in 1954. Annual grant estimated at $31,000 plus the salaries of two normal-trained school teachers (Department of Social Welfare establishment). Nothing actually spent in 1954. Government also provided $200,000 as a grant toward the capital costs.

SOURCE: Social Welfare Department.

the expenditures for 1954 is shown in Table 8. Over two-thirds went for public assistance allowances and their administration; all other activities, including residential institutions, community centers and "constructive" social services accounted for only 30%. Capital projects used only 1% of the total.

Subventions

Contributions to voluntary institutions and agencies in 1954 amounted to $326,300. Table 7 shows expenditures of $190,620 as grants to voluntary

TABLE 8   Expenditures, Social Welfare Department, 1954, Singapore

(Thousand $)

Activity or Type of Expenditure	PE[1]	OCAR[1]	OCSE[1]	PW (NR)[1]	Total Amount	Total %
Public assistance—total . .	156	5,097	86	—	5,339	70.0
Administration	156	—	—	—	156	2.0
P.a. and sickness allowances[2]	—	3,643	—	—	3,643	47.8
Tb. treatment allowances	—	1,454	—	—	1,454	19.1
Special allowances[3] . . .	—	—	86	—	86	1.1
Residential institutions . .	293	374	47	—	714	9.4
Community centers[4] . . .	257	132	2	—	391	5.1
Probation, etc.[5]	130	4	—	—	134	1.8
General administration . .	493	114	13	—	620	8.1
Research	36	20	—	—	56	0.7
Contributions[6]	—	288	—	—	288	3.8
Sub-total	1,365	6,029	148	—	7,542	98.9
Capital projects	—	—	—	80	80	1.1
Total from public funds	1,365	6,029	148	80	7,622	100.0
Trust funds[7]	—	108	—	—	108	
Total	1,365	6,137	148	80	7,730	

[1] PE: Personal Emoluments; OCAR: Other Charges, Annually Recurrent; OCSE: Other Charges, Special Expenditures; PW(NR): Public Works (Non-Recurrent).
[2] Public assistance, sickness and departmental institutions allowances.
[3] Special payments to victims of civil disasters (floods, fires, etc.).
[4] Children's social centers, creches and youth organizations.
[5] Juvenile court and probation services, women and girls' protection, children and young persons, counselling and advice services.
[6] Subventions to voluntary organizations and institutions.
[7] Silver Jubilee Fund ($108,181).
SOURCE: Social Welfare Department.

residential institutions (homes, orphanages, etc.). The Department also made the following contributions to voluntary agencies:

Singapore Anti-Tuberculosis Clinic $110,000
    For the free care of over 300 patients under the tuberculosis
    treatment allowance program ($28,000 for overhead ex-
    penses and $20 per patient per month)

Youth Organizations . . . . 22,680[5]
    Singapore Youth Council $15,000
    Boy Scouts 4,280
    Girl Guides 2,000
    Girls' Life Brigade 1,400

Aftercare Association 3,000
    For the aftercare of released prisoners and their families

These subventions through the Department of Social Welfare were supplemented in 1954 by grants of $45,000 to the Family Planning Association (through the Colonial Secretary's Office) and of $87,700 to other socio-medical organizations: St. Andrew's Mission Hospital, St. Andrew's Orthopaedic Hospital, Red Cross Society—hospital car service, and St. John's Ambulance Brigade (through the Medical Department).

Proposals for Capital Expenditures: 1954-60

Most of the Department's institutions and facilities have been converted to their present uses though built for other purposes. Those observed in our field studies ranged from meager and improvised social welfare centers to substantial children's homes and modern community centers. In addition to replacement and improvement of inadequate structures, the total number and capacity of departmental institutions should be rapidly expanded to meet current needs and the increased demand expected to result from growth and redistribution of population on the Island. The following list includes the priority projects proposed by the Department for the years 1954-60, amplified by our own estimates:

    Community centers and day nurseries (40)
    Hostels: girls' (3) and boys' (2)
    Children's home (1)
    Youth center (1)

[5] Exclusive of $40,000 from departmental funds used as additional ad hoc grants to various youth organizations.

Youth holiday camp (1)
Remand home (1)
"Approved" schools: junior (1), senior (1) and girls' (1)
Staff quarters for residential institutions.

The expansion of community centers and day nurseries, the largest item in the schedule, should presumably have priority. At least three, and if possible six, new ones should be developed in each of the next six or seven years.

TABLE 9   Estimates of Government Expenditures for Social Welfare, 1954-60, Singapore

(Thousand $)

Activity or Type of Expenditure	1954[1]	1955	1956	1957	1958	1959	1960
Public assistance—total . . .	5,085	6,338	8,955	10,215	12,055	13,375	14,325
Administration	180	288	455	465	555	675	775
General allowances[2] . . .	3,605	4,350	6,500	7,350	8,000	8,200	8,950
Tb allowances[3]	1,300	1,700	2,000	2,400	3,500	4,500	4,600
Residential institutions . . .	759	846	792	1,044	1,064	1,185	1,185
Community centers	420	515	700	848	1,035	1,193	1,322
Youth welfare	140	85	216	278	334	364	393
Probation	87	65	108	115	122	129	136
Women and girls' protection .	46	50	70	74	74	77	77
Children and young persons .	33	25	40	44	44	47	47
Counselling	45	35	57	71	74	74	84
Research	121	70	121	121	121	121	121
Contributions[4]	324	450	450	500	500	500	500
Special allowances[5]	110	—	—	—	—	—	—
General administration . . .	429	670	666	675	675	772	777
Subtotal	7,589	9,149	12,175	13,985	16,098	17,837	18,967
Capital projects[6]	711	980	1,077	1,467	1,457	1,267	982
Total	8,310	10,129	13,252	15,452	17,555	19,104	19,949

[1] Estimates. Excludes expenditures from Trust Funds.

[2] Public assistance and sickness allowances (aged persons, advanced tuberculous, widows and orphans, the permanently or temporarily disabled and the unemployed) and recommended treatment allowances for lepers and dependents.

[3] Tuberculosis treatment allowances.

[4] Subventions to voluntary organizations and institutions.

[5] Payments to victims of civil disasters (floods, fires, etc.).

[6] Includes permanent equipment (other charges, special expenditures).

SOURCE: Social Welfare Department and mission estimates.

The aggregate cost of these projects (at 1954 prices) is estimated to be slightly less than $8 million. It was distributed over the seven-year period in Table 9 after taking account of financial, community development, construction and staffing factors.

Estimates of Total Expenditures: 1954-60

The general policies followed in developing budgets for 1955-60 are presented in Chapter 7, Part III. Departmental estimates prepared for the mission took account of the outlook for social welfare service needs in the Colony, the development of institutions and the possibilities for recruitment and training of staff. These estimates were modified with respect to capital needs as shown above, and the resulting annually recurrent costs were added. Prospective public assistance costs (for allowances and administration) were expanded to include the funds needed to carry out our recommendations for (a) more adequate noninstitutional relief, (b) a larger increase in the number of general and old-age assistance cases than had been projected, (c) a considerable increase in tuberculosis treatment allowance cases as part of the recommended campaign against tuberculosis (see p. 621) and (d) provision of treatment allowances for lepers and their dependents as recommended with respect to control of leprosy (see p. 619). The estimates for other social welfare services were also adjusted to provide funds to carry out the mission's general recommendations. The results are summarized in Table 9.

The Present System

The Malayan dollar is legal tender not only in the Federation and Singapore, but in the Colonies of North Borneo and Sarawak and the State of Brunei as well. It also circulates unofficially in parts of Indonesia. Currency is issued and redeemed freely and exclusively in exchange for sterling, at the rate of two shillings and four pence sterling per dollar, by a currency board known as the Commissioners of Currency, Malaya and British Borneo.[1] The currency issue consists predominantly of notes, with a small proportion of token coin. Since banking habits are relatively well developed, bank deposits are more important than currency in the total money supply (see Table 1).

In accordance with the normal British colonial practice, the sterling received by the currency board in exchange for the issue of currency is held in London. Apart from a liquid working balance, it is invested in sterling securities (United Kingdom, Dominion and Colonial bonds, other than the bonds of the participating governments).[2] The board's dealings are in practice entirely with banks; it charges a small commission, which provides a margin within which the banks' buying and selling rates for exchange required in commercial transactions fluctuate according to the state of the market. Income from interest on investments and commission charges, after meeting the board's expenses, is in part credited to the Currency Fund sterling reserve as long as the latter is less than 110% of the currency issue, and in part distributed among the participating governments. Malayan currency is thus on a sterling exchange standard, with over 100% sterling backing for the currency issue; except for the revenue that accrues to the

[1] The Board has five members: the two Financial Secretaries of the Federation and Singapore, one officer appointed jointly by the Governors of the three Borneo territories, and two persons appointed jointly by the five participating governments.

[2] The legislation provides that it may also be invested in "such other securities as may from time to time be approved by the Secretary of State," but this provision has not yet been used. The possibility that some small part of the sterling reserves of dependent territories might be invested in locally issued securities has been recently recognized in principle, subject to the circumstances of individual territories, by authorities in the United Kingdom.

640

TABLE 1 Currency and Bank Deposits

(*Million $*)

End of Year	1948	1949	1950	1951	1952	1953
Form of holdings						
Notes	401	403	633	764	787	741
Coin	4	7	13	21	25	23
Total currency[1]	405	410	646	785	812	764
Demand deposits	581	565	865	1,054	989	857
Other deposits	81	106	155	185	223	250
Total bank deposits[2]	662	671	1,020	1,239	1,212	1,107
Distribution of holdings						
Private currency holdings[1] . . .	308	319	533	680	660	650
Private bank deposits	605	608	932	1,140	1,093	1,000
Total private money supply .	913	927	1,465	1,820	1,753	1,650
Bank currency holdings	97	91	113	105	152	114
Official bank deposits[3]	57	63	88	99	119	107
Total bank & official holdings	154	154	201	204	271	221
Total	1,067	1,081	1,666	2,024	2,024	1,871

[1] Including currency circulating outside Malaya, believed to be upwards of 10% of the total. Excluding prewar notes written off in 1951 and 1953 and silver coin demonetized in 1952.

[2] Excluding inter-bank deposits. Excluding also deposits with the Post Office Savings Banks ($66 million in 1948, rising to $148 million in 1953).

[3] Including a negligible proportion of notes and coins.

participating governments, the effect is exactly as if United Kingdom currency circulated in Malaya. This system, together with the exchange rate of 2/4d. sterling per dollar, is a continuation, with no modification of principle, of arrangements first instituted in the Straits Settlements in 1906.

As might be expected from Malaya's commercial history, commercial banking facilities are extensive and efficient. There are more than a score of banks with respectably-sized businesses in Malaya. These include the Exchange Banks with head offices in London and operations extending throughout the East, and other overseas banks, but there are also several important banks whose ownership and management is entirely local (Malayan Chinese) and whose share of the business is growing. Table 2

TABLE 2   Assets and Liabilities of Commercial Banks

(Million $)

End of Year	1948	1949	1950	1951	1952	1953
Assets						
Cash (Malayan currency)	97	91	113	105	152	114
Treasury bills (Malayan)	30	7	23	26	15	10
Other local investments	111	110	117	125	137	143
Local advances, etc.	259	336	461	451	484	437
Overseas assets (net)	209	189	363	613	520	491
Total	706	733	1,077	1,320	1,308	1,195
Liabilities						
Deposits	662	671	1,020	1,239	1,212	1,107
Other liabilities (net)	44	62	57	81	96	88
Total	706	733	1,077	1,320	1,308	1,195

shows the assets and liabilities of the Malayan banking system as a whole.

This Table, however, conceals major differences in balance sheet structure among the different types of banks. For instance, four or five overseas banks account for about two-thirds of the total deposits and for over 80% of the overseas assets, but for only about half of the local advances, etc.; their lending in Malaya tends to be restricted by the limited scope for business which they consider acceptable and within their legitimate field—chiefly the finance of overseas and internal trade and other working capital requirements of larger firms. Funds which on this basis cannot be used in Malaya are invested elsewhere (mainly in London) through their head offices. The typical local bank, on the other hand, although still concerned primarily with commodity finance, appears to maintain a much higher ratio of local liquid assets and to take a somewhat wider view of what constitutes acceptable business, and at the same time to be more limited by liquid reserve considerations in its total lending.

The Money Supply and the Balance of Payments

The main factors governing changes in the money supply and in the liquidity of the banking system and private business are found in the balance of payments. To describe the mechanism in its simplest terms: money comes into existence in the form of claims on banks in Malaya arising from the proceeds of exports, capital inflow and other receipts from abroad; payments and receipts within Malaya change the distribution of money holdings, without altering the total supply, but the purchase of imports, capital outflow, profit transfers and other payments abroad extinguish money holdings in Malaya. If this were the whole story, the entire money supply (both currency and bank deposits) would be backed by overseas assets, divided between the currency board and the banks in accordance with the division of money holdings between currency and bank deposits—these overseas assets of the monetary system being the cumulated difference between receipts and payments abroad. In addition, however, money comes into existence or is extinguished as the result of increases or decreases in the local noncash assets (advances, investments, etc.) of the banks. But this factor in the money supply is itself closely bound up with international trading conditions and the balance of payments, since bank lending tends to respond more or less automatically to the needs of trade and, in the case of the local banks, also to be influenced by liquid reserve considerations, which in turn are largely dominated by the balance of payments.

Only one major factor is capable of, and often likely to be, working strongly against the tide of the normal fluctuations in international receipts and payments: this is accumulation by the governments of revenue and loan proceeds in excess of their total spending. To the extent that this accumulation takes the form of an increase of official sterling balances in London—in effect, an outflow of capital from Malaya—both the total money supply and the liquidity of the Malayan banking system are *pro tanto* reduced; to the extent that it takes the form of the accumulation of official bank deposits in Malaya, the money supply in private hands, but not bank liquidity, is reduced. Official spending in excess of current revenue and loan proceeds has the opposite effect in each case.

The influences of these various factors in changing the money supply in recent years are illustrated in Table 3.

The Table shows that the increase of official balances, chiefly sterling balances, in the years 1949-52 and their reduction in 1953 played a substantial part in smoothing out the fluctuations in the money supply in the postwar years. Even so, total private money supply doubled between 1948 and 1951 (see Table 1). Over the following two years it fell by about 10%.

There are, however, clearly limits on the extent to which government can maintain a continuing level of expenditure in excess of revenue (in-

TABLE 3   Determination of Money Supply

(*Million $*)

	1949	1950	1951	1952	1953
Balance of payments on current account .	−122	+684	+714	−105	−244
Private capital inflow, errors and omissions	+105	−145	− 65	+ 15	+ 65
Official borrowing, etc. abroad	+ 68	+ 22	+ 48	+116	+ 63
Net receipts from abroad	+ 51	+561	+697	+ 26	−116
less increase in official sterling balances . .	− 63	−143	−304	− 86	+ 50
Increase in overseas assets of currency board and banks	− 12	+418	+393	− 60	− 66
Increase in local advances, investments etc. of banks	+ 53	+148	+ 1	+ 34	− 46
less increase in official bank deposits . . .	− 6	− 25	− 11	− 20	+ 12
Adjustments[1]	− 21	− 3	− 28	− 21	− 3
Increase in private money supply	+ 14	+538	+355	− 67	−103

[1] Deduction of undistributed profits of the currency board and of increase in miscellaneous "other net liabilities" of banks.

cluding external grants) and internal and external borrowing. Nor in the context of the Malayan economy and banking system is it to be expected that in circumstances of a continuing balance-of-payments deficit the level of commercial bank credit would be increased or even maintained. A persistent balance-of-payments deficit after allowance for external grants and new capital inflows can therefore be expected to lead to a persistent contraction of the Malayan money supply. This in turn must ultimately bring about a situation in which the balance-of-payments deficit is corrected. For the contraction of the money supply and the balance-of-payments deficit both reflect the same external fact—that Malayan spending is in total in excess of current receipts; as households, business firms and government authorities become less and less liquid, the balances out of which excess spending can be financed diminish, and it becomes harder to raise capital and credit. Hence, in the end, personal, business and government spending—including spending on imports and other payments abroad—must in the aggregate be pruned and the balance of payments brought into equilibrium.[3] In any case, of course, fluctuations in export receipts tend to be

[3] A similar chain of events, in the opposite direction, is set in motion if the original condition is one of balance-of-payments surplus.

followed by sympathetic movements in import purchases, profit transfers, remittances, etc., out of income dependent on exports, but there is no reason to expect these direct reactions to be of just the right magnitude to keep the balance of payments in line. It is the automatic mechanism of the monetary system, working in terms of liquidity rather than income, which guarantees that Malaya cannot be faced with anything resembling a balance-of-payments problem or crisis as such. What in other countries with a different monetary system might appear ultimately as a shortage of international exchange is felt directly in Malaya by declining public and private liquidity and a resulting shortage of money.

The Scope for Monetary Policy

In some stages of economic development there is much to be said for an automatic monetary system of the British colonial currency board type. When subsistence production is a very large part of economic activity; when the money sector of the economy is dominated by export and import trade and by externally-owned capital; when the banking system is chiefly a matter of the provision of local facilities by overseas banks; when indigenous enterprise is organized in small and flexible family units; when such issues as employment and wage levels for workers dependent essentially on wage earnings are relatively unimportant—in these circumstances the exchange stability and security of the currency board system offer great advantages, while both the need and the opportunity for any form of local monetary management are very limited. In large measure, all this was true of the Malayan economy in the decades before the war, together with the special feature that an important part of the Malayan working population was itself migratory, coming and going according to the available opportunities. Indeed, in a sense it might have been misleading to speak of "the Malayan economy" at all—beyond the Malay rubber and rice smallholdings and kampongs, Malaya in many respects was rather a geographical region where capital and labor belonging to other economies found it convenient to carry on certain specialized operations, within the British monetary as well as political framework.

The situation today is very different. Although many of the prewar economic features remain, Malaya—taking the Federation and Singapore together, as is inevitable in this context—is now a distinct national economy, with its own settled labor force, a wide and growing area of monetary transactions and of local capital and enterprise, an indigenous banking system at least as important as the facilities provided by overseas banks, and its own evolving political organs which must cope with Malayan economic problems from a Malayan viewpoint. Above all, Malaya must think of its future development and the employment of its rapidly growing population not in terms of outside merchant, mining and plantation capital arriving on a large scale to develop economic opportunities in Malaya, but primarily in terms of making the best use of domestic savings for the development of natural resources and of a modern domestic industry. This task requires a new emphasis on domestic financial facilities and monetary conditions to help channel savings into effective investment and promote a favorable internal climate for steady economic development.

Accordingly, we have recommended, in Chapter 9 of Part IV, the establishment of a Central Bank of Malaya to serve as the instrument for deliberate management of the money and credit situation. Some specific suggestions as to the constitution of a central bank are made below. First it is necessary to consider what scope there is for monetary management in the Malayan economy.

We repeat our comment in Chapter 9 that there is no magic in monetary independence which can provide resources for investment beyond the capital which flows from local savings (private and governmental) or which can be obtained from abroad. Mere credit expansion, on a scale which permits spending beyond those resources, can result only in progressive inflation, exchange crises and the destruction of confidence on the part of both local savers and overseas investors. Wise monetary management, on the other hand, can reasonably aim to promote conditions in which saving will be encouraged; to economize on the average amount of sterling balances which in the long run the currency board, banks and governments would otherwise keep on hand, and so to permit some additional local investment; to make possible full use of the labor and other resources available in the economy when something less than full use occurs entirely as the result of deficiencies of monetary demand; and to soften the impact of economic fluctuations, usually emanating from export markets, which, if too violent, result in business miscalculations and interrupted or wasted investment, jeopardize promising new industries, and involve periods of speculative boom alternating with periods of economic depression.

For Malaya, this last objective is probably the most important. Malaya's long history of wide economic fluctuations (made especially acute by dependence on rubber, tin and entrepot trade), and the associated tendency for credit and other capital flows to dry up just when most needed, seem to have contributed to a heavy premium being placed by local business on the advantages of keeping to a highly liquid assets position and a highly flexible form of business organization. This makes long-term capital hard to raise, distorts the structure of interest rates, favors commodity dealing as compared with productive activities requiring substantial fixed investment, and discourages the replacement of the small family business by operations on an efficient scale with modern equipment. As indicated in the main report, these features of the Malayan economy are major obstacles to successful economic development. The mere existence of a central bank, as lender of last resort, might well have an important influence on the prevailing attitudes towards liquidity and flexibility, beginning with the local banks themselves and spreading through the various channels of credit and capital.

Nevertheless, the scope for typical central bank action to smooth out economic fluctuations is still greatly restricted in Malaya, in particular by the continued relative importance of fluctuating export markets, which limits the range of application of internal policy, and by the narrowness of the local market for government securities, which makes open-market operations of the traditional central banking type of doubtful practicability. Similar problems have been faced by central banks in other countries, where it has been found that, although the internal impact of major fluctuations in export markets can by no means be eliminated, two types of action can make an important contribution to internal economic stability.

1. By close and continuing study of balance-of-payments trends and their effects on monetary and credit conditions, a central bank can give guidance to the government in the planning of revenue and expenditure policies so that the peaks and troughs of fluctuations arising from export markets can in some measure be narrowed. In the postwar years, as was noted above, official cash surpluses and deficits have had a substantial compensatory effect of this character, but the results achieved were probably in part accidental (stemming from the inadequacy of the existing technical and administrative organization to carry out expenditure projects as quickly as the revenue came in during the boom), and in part due to conservative financial housekeeping by the two governments, rather than a matter

of deliberate stabilizing policy for the economy as a whole. Compensatory government financial policy is of course not a matter necessarily requiring the existence of a central bank, but a central bank can exercise an important advisory and persuasive influence, and may in certain circumstances and within prudent limits make a compensatory policy feasible by some financing of temporary government deficits at the right time.

2. The central bank, if legally authorized to require the commercial banks to observe minimum reserve ratios or to hold frozen central bank deposits, can vary the ratios or the amounts of the frozen deposits from time to time in order to vary the credit base of the banking system. Other direct forms of central bank credit regulation are possible. The diversity of the assets structure of the different banks operating in Malaya demands very careful consideration of the precise form of control to be exercised, but there is no doubt that an appropriate formula or combination of formulae can be found. Such control is an important equipoise to the readiness of a central bank to provide financial facilities for the banks as their needs require through rediscounting, advances, etc.

Sterling Reserves and Safeguards

In connection with the effective conduct of monetary policy, it will be necessary in constituting a central bank to reach decisions concerning the extent to which the holding of overseas assets is to be concentrated in the bank and on safeguards for the convertibility of Malayan currency into sterling. On these and other matters subsequently discussed we do not feel able to make detailed and definite recommendations and our views are, therefore, presented in general terms and should be considered as subject to further detailed enquiry. We would suggest that as the first step toward the establishment of a central bank, the two governments should enlist the assistance of the United Kingdom monetary authorities or the International Monetary Fund in making a detailed enquiry into the problems of central banking in Malaya and in advising on the content of legislation constituting the bank and the method of operations which the central bank should follow.

The central bank would of course take over the assets, liabilities and functions of the currency board. We would also expect initially that the commercial banks would be required to establish deposits with the central bank equivalent to some proportion of their Malayan liabilities and this, in effect, would involve a transfer of some part of the external assets of the commercial banks to the central bank. Beyond this, central banks in other countries commonly have broad authority to acquire the overseas assets, which are the counterpart of domestic liabilities of commercial banks, in exchange for deposits with the central bank denominated in local currency. The actual exercise of such authority varies from country to country depending on (a) the degree of concentration of overseas assets which in the particular circumstances is deemed adequate for effective conduct of monetary policy (and for efficient supervision of exchange controls where the central bank acts as agent of the government in this respect), and (b) the extent to which an adequate centralization of external assets results in any case from commercial bank policies of transferring such assets to the central bank in exchange for deposits (in order, for example, to minimize the risk involved in holding uncovered liabilities in domestic currency in view of possible variations in the rate of exchange).

It will undoubtedly be found appropriate to confer similar broad authority on the Central Bank of Malaya. The policy to be followed in regard to the centralization of overseas assets which are the counterpart of domestic liabilities of the banking system should, however, be one of the subjects for the detailed enquiry which we recommend. We would expect that an extensive transfer of such assets, if found desirable, would be undertaken only gradually and that the corresponding deposits (or other form of assets) accumulated with the central bank would have reasonably equivalent earning power to the overseas assets transferred.

The central bank should be the banker of the two governments and manage their external assets as well as their domestic currency assets. This could involve the transfer of these official assets to the central bank in exchange for interest-bearing deposits (subject to statutory or contractual hindrances to such transfer). Preferably, however, the central bank should manage these assets as agents for the two governments and, except for working balances, should not include them in its balance sheet. In this way such pressure for expansionary policies as might arise from large government deposits would be avoided, while at the same time the management of official assets would provide some scope for security market operations (discussed below) without affecting the reserves of the central bank itself.

If only to avoid the damage to confidence from too sharp a break with the past, two fundamental conditions should be imposed on the central bank's operations.

1. The existing obligation of the currency board to redeem Malayan currency for sterling at the rate of 2/4d. per dollar should become a constitutional obligation of the central bank. Although this particular rate of exchange is not sacrosanct, and circumstances might conceivably arise in which a change would be desirable, the presumption of exchange stability and convertibility into sterling should be maintained. Any suspension of sterling convertibility or variation in the rate of exchange should be authorized only by unanimous decision of the two governments, on the recommendation of the central bank, and (so long as Malaya retains a dependent status) with the approval of the Secretary of State for the Colonies.

2. To ensure a constant readiness to meet this obligation, some form of sterling reserve requirement should be laid down for the central bank. The precise form of this requirement and the extent of the discretion to be allowed to the central bank in determining the amount of the sterling assets to be held against its aggregate liabilities (including the currency issue, commercial banks' deposits and official deposits) requires further and very careful study. Within the limits set, the central bank would be free to pursue its own monetary policy, but once the limit had been reached, the central bank's ability to lend (and so to create liabilities against itself, not backed by sterling assets) would cease, and it would in effect revert temporarily to the status of a currency board.

The stability and security of the currency board system does not depend on 100% sterling backing for the currency; it depends on sufficient sterling being available to redeem that part of the currency in respect of which claims for redemption might conceivably arise. This fact provides a margin within which a central bank may effectively operate without losing any of the practical advantages of the existing system. Essentially, then, we are suggesting that provision be made for a fiduciary issue within a "currency board" framework. While some part of the margin of exchange reserves so provided might then be used for local investment, we would envisage the primary purpose of the margin, not for a once-and-for-all expenditure of sterling on local investment, but rather as a sort of central bank stabilization fund to provide some scope for easing domestic financial adjustments to external fluctuations.

The Security Market and Banking Organization

In addition to handling the wider issues of monetary policy, a central bank can usefully perform certain other functions which are important to the healthy working of the economy. It should be able, for instance, gradually to foster a wider market for government securities, by standing ready to buy and sell on appropriate terms, within limits dictated by its reserves position, and by prudent management of the official assets previously discussed. In this way there may be brought into the market potential investors who are at present deterred by the extreme illiquidity of this class of asset. That this is not an unreasonable aim is shown by the very extensive dealing that already occurs in the shares of rubber, tin and other companies on the Singapore share market. The central bank should also act as agent for the two governments and other public authorities in floating new bond issues and, as a further measure to widen the market, should endeavor, in consultation with them, to ensure that securities of different maturities, from three-month Treasury bills upwards, are available in proper proportions to provide a suitable gradation of assets for inclusion in the portfolios of the commercial banks and other investors. In this connection, the relative advantages and disadvantages of empowering the central bank to issue securities on its own account might also be considered.

The central bank should, in addition, act as the agent of the two governments in the administration of exchange controls. It might also be responsible for a system of inspection of the affairs of the commercial banks, designed to protect the public against possible mismanagement and insolvencies. There is at present no provision of this kind in Malaya, beyond the general requirements of the company law, although in most countries it has been felt necessary to regulate the business of banking in the interests of the depositors. Should this function not be assigned to a central bank, it should be otherwise provided for by special statute. It may also be found advisable for the central bank to assist, in consultation with the commercial banks, in establishing and maintaining a reasonable schedule of charges for commercial bank services such as transfers of receipts and payments arising out of foreign transactions.

Constitution of a Central Bank

The constitution of a Central Bank of Malaya presents unique problems, for its authority must clearly cover both Singapore and the Federation and possibly the three Borneo territories as well. For present purposes the question of the association of those territories with the Federation and Singapore in a central bank may reasonably be left to one side, on the assumption that any solution worked out for Singapore and the Federation can readily be modified to provide for some form of participation or association of the three minor partners in the existing Malayan currency system, or that, alternatively, they would elect to have their own currency.

The mission envisages that the central bank's constitution would provide that:

(a) Appointment of the bank's Board would be made jointly by the two governments. The constitution should, however, ensure the bank the maximum practicable independence from political direction by either or both of the participating governments. This would not be inconsistent with and should not preclude the close working relations with the two governments which will be necessary for the determination of monetary and credit policy for the common economy. The maintenance of these relations would be furthered by the inclusion of the Financial Secretaries of the Federation and of Singapore as *ex officio* members of the Board.[4]

(b) The Board should consist of a Governor, the two Financial Secretaries, and not less than two other persons, including at least one representative of the banking community. Appointments should be made for fairly long periods (say five or seven years). While the Board would be responsible for the policy decisions, the Governor should have full authority for administration (including all staff appointments) and for the execution of policy.

(c) The bank's initial capital should be appropriated from the surplus assets of the existing Currency Fund with due regard for the right of the three Borneo territories and the extent of their participation (if any) in the central bank. Its profits, after due provision for reserves, should be distributed between the participating govern-

---

[4] If and when Ministers of Finance are appointed, the *ex officio* members of the Board should be the Permanent Heads of the two Treasuries rather than the Ministers.

ments according to an agreed formula, as with the profits of the currency board.

In the preceding discussion, we have indicated some of the important issues arising in connection with the establishment of a central bank and have also presented suggestions for consideration in constituting a central bank and in deciding on the powers and functions which it should exercise. In Chapter 9, Part IV, we have also indicated the further advantages of a central bank in developing experience in, and a sound approach to, monetary and credit problems during the present period of political transition and in serving as a focus for centralized analysis and as a source of expert advice concerning the common economic problems of the two territories. We have further pointed out the narrow limits within which there is likely to be scope for prudent monetary management, which places a particular premium on sound and expert direction of monetary policy if the full advantages possible within these narrow limits are to be achieved. For all these reasons we would again emphasize the importance of appointing a well-qualified and competent staff to the central bank and we urge that assistance in this matter, as well as in the detailed enquiry and guidance necessary to the establishment of the bank, should be sought from the United Kingdom monetary authorities or the International Monetary Fund.

STATISTICAL APPENDIX

A *CONSOLIDATED ACCOUNTS OF PUBLIC AUTHORITIES —FEDERATION OF MALAYA*

General Note

(1) These accounts are a consolidation of the accounts of the following authorities: Federation Government; State and Settlement Governments; Municipalities of George Town, Kuala Lumpur, and Malacca; Central Electricity Board, Malayan Railways, Penang Harbour Board; War Damage Commission, Custodian of Enemy Property (Federation), Custodian of Property (Singapore)—these all being treated as Federation authorities for the convenience of having all war damage and property transactions in the one place, in spite of their pan-Malayan character (the accounts are squared by appropriate adjustments in Federation liabilities to Singapore); Rubber Replanting Funds, Malayan Rubber Fund, Education Development Board Fund; Rural and Industrial Development Authority; Federation Supplies Department (food trading accounts); and Post Office Savings Bank (Federation).

(2) The accounts of the Penang Harbour Board, which are for financial years ending June 30th, have been incorporated as if they were for calendar years (i.e., 1948-49 becomes 1949, etc.). However, those of the Central Electricity Board, which are for financial years ending August 31st, have been roughly adjusted to a calendar year basis.

(3) Figures for 1954 are from the approved Estimates.

654

TABLE 1 (A)   Consolidated Accounts of Public Authorities, Federation
Revenue

(*Million $*)

	1949	1950	1951	1952	1953	1954
						(Budget Estimates)
Direct Taxes						
Income Tax and Estate Duty	41	49	129	224	160	113
Export Duties—Rubber .	33	97	219	116	61	54
—Tin . . .	39	52	77	70	52	39
—Other . .	5	6	7	6	6	5
Total	118	204	432	416	279	211
Indirect Taxes						
Import Duties	116	148	214	206	198	214
Excise, Stamp and Other Duties and Taxes	16	21	30	30	36	32
Local Government Rates .	6	7	8	9	9	10
Road Transport and Other Licenses	13	15	23	26	29	31
Total	151	191	275	271	272	287
Surplus of Commercial Undertakings						
Posts and Telecommunications	5	6	2	−1	2	2
Electricity Supply	1	3	4	5	7	9
Railways and Harbors . .	6	8	10	5	10	6
Water Supplies, etc. . . .	4	6	5	4	8	6
Total	16	23	21	13	27	23
Revenue from Property						
Rents & Royalties (etc.)						
Lands & Mines . . .	15	16	18	26	26	25
Other Rents	2	3	3	4	4	4
Net Interest Received (+) or Paid (−)	−2	−1	10	11	9	2
Total	15	18	31	41	39	31
Fees and Charges for Services, etc.						
Local Government	6	7	8	10	9	9
Education	1	1	2	2	2	2

TABLE 1(A)—continued

	1949	1950	1951	1952	1953	(Million $) 1954 (Budget Estimates)
Fees and Charges for Services, etc. (continued)						
Other Fees and Charges .	15	19	19	22	27	25
Miscellaneous Receipts . .	5	6	8	9	10	5
Total	27	33	37	43	48	41
Total: Ordinary Revenue . . .	327	469	796	784	665	593
U.K. Grants Colonial Development & Welfare Grants . . .	1	2	2	4	5	10
Other U. K. Contributions to Revenue	43	26	—	3	1	58
Total	44	28	2	7	6	68
Total: Revenue	371	497	798	791	671	661

Notes on Table 1 (A)

(1) "Export Duties" include the rubber and tin research cesses.

(2) "Local Government Rates" exclude education rates (included with education fees and charges, below).

(3) "Surplus of Commercial Undertakings" is the excess of sales revenue over current operating expenses, excluding any debt service or provision for depreciation. "Electricity Supply" includes the Electricity Department for the first eight months of 1949, thereafter it refers to the Central Electricity Board. "Railways and Harbours" refers to the Malayan Railways and the Penang Harbour Board. "Water Supplies, etc." includes various municipal commercial undertakings.

(4) "Net Interest Received or Paid" includes the receipt of interest on securities held in surplus funds, etc. and in sinking funds, and the receipt of currency profits; it also includes net interest received by the Savings Bank, Provident Fund, etc., after deducting interest due to depositors and contributors; interest paid on the public debt, etc. (including the debts of the Central Electricity Board, Penang Harbour Board, etc.) appears as a negative element.

(5) "Other U.K. Contributions to Revenue" exclude the War Damage gift, which is treated as a capital transaction "below the line" in Table 4 (A).

(6) Singapore contributions to Federation revenue (for joint services, etc.) have been excluded altogether, the corresponding expenditure being deducted in Table 2 (A). The transfer of $5 million from "prewar deposits" account to revenue in 1949 has also been excluded.

TABLE 2 (A)   Consolidated Accounts of Public Authorities, Federation
Expenditure

(*Million $*)

	1949	1950	1951	1952	1953	1954
						(Budget Estimates)
Recurrent Expenditure						
Economic Services						
Agriculture, Forestry, Fisheries, etc.	10	13	14	18	20	20
Mining & Geological Survey . .	1	2	2	4	3	4
Land Survey	3	3	5	6	6	6
Cooperative Development & RIDA	—	—	1	4	6	5
Maintenance etc. of Drainage and Irrigation Works	3	3	4	5	10	8
Maintenance, etc. of Roads . . .	17	17	16	21	26	27
Civil Aviation, Marine, Meteorological Services	3	3	3	7	7	5
Total	37	41	45	65	78	75
Social Services						
Education	26	29	49	67	78	95
Health	25	25	39	46	47	57
Social Welfare and Other	3	3	5	5	6	7
Total	54	57	93	118	131	159
Other Governmental Services						
Local Government	17	18	25	29	30	35
Defense, Police and Emergency .	82	101	217	287	296	250
Administrative and Miscellaneous	111	108	125	144	165	147
Total	210	227	367	460	491	432
Current Transfers						
Pensions, etc.	19	17	21	24	30	25
Sinking Fund Provisions	8	9	10	12	12	12
Total	27	26	31	36	42	37
Total Recurrent Expenditure	328	351	536	679	742	703

TABLE 2(A)—continued

(*Million $*)

	1949	1950	1951	1952	1953	1954
						(Budget Estimates)
Capital Expenditure						
Economic Services						
Drainage & Irrigation Projects . .	8	5	5	7	6	12
Agriculture, Forestry, Fisheries, etc.						
Other Projects	1	1	1	3	3	7
Roads and Civil Aviation	5	4	9	12	7	24
Total	14	10	15	22	16	43
Social Services						
Education	1	1	3	4	9	18
Health and Other	—	1	1	3	3	6
Total	1	2	4	7	12	24
Other Governmental Services						
Local Government	1	1	2	2	3	14
Defense, Police and Emergency .	7	9	24	35	16	33
Housing for Government Servants	2	4	3	21	21	25
Administration and Miscellaneous	7	4	8	6	2	14
Total	17	18	37	64	42	86
Commercial Undertakings						
Posts and Telecommunications . .	6	6	9	10	15	17
Electricity Supply	6	8	18	21	22	20
Railways and Harbors	19	16	17	23	20	26
Water Supplies, etc.	3	3	4	4	11	33
Food Supplies, etc. (Stocks) . . .	5	−4	7	16	18	—
Total	39	29	55	74	86	96
Total Capital Expenditure .	71	59	111	167	156	249
Total Recurrent and Capital						
Expenditure	399	410	647	846	898	952

Notes on Table 2 (A)

(1) "Agriculture, Forestry, Fisheries, etc." includes the expenditure of the rubber research cess.

(2) "Education" excludes in 1953 the transfer of $4 million to the Development Fund, and includes in 1954 expenditure made out of the Fund.

(3) Singapore contributions (for joint services, etc.) have been deducted from "Administrative and Miscellaneous" expenditure (since usually the actual object of the expenditure cannot be identified), except for the special 1949 grant of $4 million, which has been deducted from "Defense, Police and Emergency" expenditure.

(4) "Sinking Fund Provisions" represent the total accumulation of sinking funds, including estimated interest earnings as well as annual contributions.

(5) The distinction between "recurrent" and "capital" expenditure is necessarily somewhat arbitrary. Broadly, capital expenditure refers to the construction of new public works, roads, buildings, etc., and the installation of equipment of a fairly permanent value, whether from revenue or from loan funds. Many items classified as "special expenditure" in the accounts have been treated as "recurrent"—including generally expenditure on motor vehicles, and on office, education, and medical furniture and equipment. "Recurrent" expenditure shown under "Defense, Police and Emergency" includes a large but unknown element of capital expenditure on resettlement, the "capital" expenditure shown under this heading being confined chiefly to barracks and other buildings. On the other hand, in 1949 (when occupation damage was still being made good) much rehabilitation and replacement expenditure has been treated as capital expenditure. There is also some element of arbitrariness in the classification of expenditures under particular headings, arising from cases where it was difficult to tell from the published accounts the exact nature of a particular expenditure. This and the division made by the mission between "recurrent" and "capital" expenditure account for the minor differences between the expenditure shown here for "Social Services" and those shown in Chapter 7, which latter have been revised on the basis of more recent tabulations prepared by the particular departments concerned.

(6) Capital expenditure in 1949 is overstated by the inclusion of about $5 million representing certain Federation works charged to loan account in that year, but actually carried out from advances in 1948 or earlier. This discrepancy has been adjusted in the total by deducting $5 million from "Administrative and Miscellaneous" recurrent expenditure in 1949.

(7) "Housing for Government Servants" covers expenditure readily identifiable as such, but additional provision for housing, quarters, etc., is included under education, health, and other heads.

(8) "Agriculture, Forestry, Fisheries, etc.—Other Projects" includes the expenditure of RIDA on "fixed assets," but excludes the Authority's loans, which appear "below the line" in the miscellaneous residual of Table 4 (A), Part B. Provision of loan funds for the Housing Trust and the Federal and Colonial Building Society has also been excluded from capital expenditure, and included in Table 4 (A) as "Advances for Housing." Similarly, the purchase and sale of existing assets (land purchases, sale of locomotives to Thailand, etc.) has been left "below the line" in Table 4 (A).

(9) Net expenditure on food supplies is shown as "Capital Expenditure"—it represents mainly the net change in food stocks, but includes also trading losses (positive) or profits (negative). For 1949 the figure given is the net change in the paid purchase and food supply advance accounts shown in the Federation balance sheets, thereafter from the (unpublished) accounts of the Supplies Department. Net changes in "unallocated stores" advance account are also included under this head.

(10) Because of variations in the presentation of accounts from year to year, the classification of expenditure is not always consistent. In 1954, in particular, certain items previously shown under "Administrative and Miscellaneous" have been transferred to more specific heads.

TABLE 3 (A) Consolidated Accounts of Public Authorities, Federation Cash and Investments

(Million $)

End of Year	1948			1949			1950			1951			1952			1953		
	Ma-layan	Ster-ling	Total	Ma-layan	Ster-ling	Total	Ma-layan	Ster-ling	Total	Ma-layan	Ster-ling	Total	Ma-layan	Ster-ling	Total	Ma-layan	Ster-ling	Total
Cash																		
Federation Govt.	23	−75	−52	29	−19	10	48	53	101	61	61	122	65	88	153	62	2	64
Other	4	—	4	4	—	4	7	8	15	9	21	30	26	2	28	23	—	23
Total	27	−75	−48	33	−19	14	55	61	116	70	82	152	91	90	181	85	2	87
Sinking Fund Investments																		
Federation Govt.	—	36	36	—	43	43	—	51	51	—	60	60	—	71	71	—	82	82
Other	3	3	6	4	3	7	5	3	8	6	3	9	7	3	10	8	3	11
Total	3	39	42	4	46	50	5	54	59	6	63	69	7	74	81	8	85	93
Other Investments																		
Federation Govt.	24	88	112	24	50	74	24	82	106	24	276	300	24	295	319	24	250	274
Post Office Savings Bank	11	28	39	14	36	50	14	46	60	21	61	82	30	64	94	34	68	102
Other	4	27	31	4	29	33	4	29	33	4	31	35	9	24	33	68	24	92
Total	39	143	182	42	115	157	42	157	199	49	368	417	63	383	446	126	342	468

Total Cash and Investments

Sinking Funds (Govt. & Other)	3	39	42	4	46	50	5	54	59	6	63	69	7	74	81	8	85	93
Post Office Savings Bank	11	28	39	14	36	50	14	46	60	21	61	82	30	64	94	34	68	102
Federation Government	47	13	60	53	31	84	72	135	207	85	337	422	89	383	472	86	252	338
Other	8	27	35	8	29	37	11	37	48	13	52	65	35	26	61	91	24	115
Total	69	107	176	79	142	221	102	272	374	125	513	638	161	547	708	219	429	648

NOTES: (1) For authorities included, see General Note. Some very minor holdings have been neglected.

(2) Sterling cash consists of Joint Colonial Fund deposits (advances shown as negative). Malayan cash is chiefly deposits in Malayan banks, with small amounts of notes and coin.

(3) Investments are shown as at market value at the end of 1948, and at estimated net cost in respect of changes thereafter—i.e., annual changes represent the actual funds absorbed by the purchase, or released by the sale, of securities. The market value of all investments was some $20 million less than is here shown at the end of 1953.

(4) Federation Government cash includes cash held by State and Settlement treasuries.

(5) Federation Treasury Deposit Receipts and Treasury Bills held by the War Damage Commission (in 1950) and by the Provident Fund and Rubber Replanting Funds (in 1952 and 1953) have been treated as direct deposits with the Federation Government and so are not shown as investments in this Table [the corresponding securities are also excluded from the liabilities shown in Table 4(A)]. However, Federation Bonds (held by the Provident Fund and others) are included in investments held by "other" authorities.

(6) Malayan investments consist of securities denominated in Malayan dollars and issued by Malayan Governments and semi-government authorities, with the exception of a small amount of Perak River Hydro-Electric Co. shares held by the Federation Government. The latter's holding of Central Electricity Board shares is not included, since these shares represent in part merely a transfer of former Electricity Department assets to the Board, and in part expenditure of Federation loan funds already included in Table 2(A).

(7) Sterling investments consist of securities denominated in sterling and issued in London by U.K., Dominion and Colonial Governments, with the exception of a small amount of Ceylonese rupee securities.

TABLE 4 (A) Consolidated Accounts of Public Authorities, Federation Revenue, Expenditure, and Capital Transactions

(Million $)

	1949	1950	1951	1952	1953
A. *Revenue Balance*					
(1) *Revenue* [Table 1(A)]					
Ordinary Revenue	+327	+469	+796	+784	+665
U.K. Grants	+ 44	+ 28	+ 2	+ 7	+ 6
Total	+371	+497	+798	+791	+671
(2) *Expenditure* [Table 2(A)]					
Current Expenditure	−328	−351	−536	−679	−742
Capital Expenditure	− 71	− 59	−111	−167	−156
Total	−399	−410	−647	−846	−898
Revenue Balance	− 28	+ 87	+151	− 55	−227
B. *Funds Raised on Capital Account*					
(1) *War Damage Transactions*					
Sale of Enemy Property, etc. . . .	+ 9	+ 23	+ 16	+ 41	+ 6
U.K. War Damage Gift	—	—	+ 34	+ 68	+ 68
U.K. War Damage Loan (interest free)	—	—	—	—	+ 21
Repayment of Rehabilitation Loans					
(Tin Mines)	—	+ 3	+ 20	+ 29	+ 13
Less: Claims Paid	− 8	− 19	− 55	−144	−109
Total	+ 1	+ 7	+ 15	− 6	− 1
(2) *Rubber Replanting Funds*					
Cess Collected	—	—	+ 50	+ 65	+ 62
Less: Grants to Smallholders . . .	—	—	—	—	− 3
Less: Refunds to Estates	—	—	—	− 3	− 42
Total	—	—	+ 50	+ 62	+ 17
(3) *Employees' Provident Fund*					
Contributions (including Interest Due)	—	—	—	+ 19	+ 58
Less: Withdrawals	—	—	—	—	− 1
Total	—	—	—	+ 19	+ 57

TABLE 4(A)—continued

(Million $)

	1949	1950	1951	1952	1953
(4) *Borrowing in Malaya*					
Federation Local Bonds Issued . .	—	—	+ 15	+ 35	+ 83
Federation Treasury Bills Issued .	+ 2	+ 22	+ 4	− 41	+ 10
Post Office Savings Bank Deposits	+ 11	+ 10	+ 23	+ 12	+ 10
Current Account Liabilities to					
Singapore Govt.	− 18	− 9	− 16	− 6	+ 3
Total	− 5	+ 23	+ 26	—	+106
(5) *Borrowing Abroad*					
Federation Sterling Bonds Issued .	+ 68	—	—	+ 1	—
Liabilities for Food Purchases . .	—	+ 6	− 2	+ 37	− 39
Current Account Liabilities to U.K.	—	+ 11	+ 2	+ 1	—
Colonial Development Corp. Loans					
to C.E.B.	—	+ 5	+ 14	+ 9	+ 13
Total	+ 68	+ 22	+ 14	+ 48	− 26
(6) *Miscellaneous Transactions*					
Sale of Railway Assets	+ 6	+ 1	—	—	—
Less: Purchase of Land, etc. . . .	− 1	− 1	− 1	− 6	− 4
Less: Advances for Housing . . .	—	—	—	—	− 1
Other Miscellaneous Net Liabilities	− 4	+ 5	− 1	− 4	+ 7
Total	+ 1	+ 5	− 2	− 10	+ 2
(7) Sinking Fund Provisions (from					
Revenue)	+ 8	+ 9	+ 10	+ 12	+ 12
Total: Funds Raised on Capital					
Account	+ 73	+ 66	+113	+125	+167
C. *Total Balance of Revenue and Capital Account*					
Revenue Account	− 28	+ 87	+151	− 55	−227
Capital Account	+ 73	+ 66	+113	+125	+167
Total	+ 45	+153	+264	+ 70	− 60
D. *Increase in Cash and Investments* [Table 3(A)]					
Cash in Banks, etc. in Malaya	+ 6	+ 22	+ 15	+ 21	− 6
Malayan Investments	+ 4	+ 1	+ 8	+ 15	+ 64
Sterling Cash and Investments	+ 35	+130	+241	+ 34	−118
Total	+ 45	+153	+264	+ 70	− 60

Notes on Table 4 (A)

(1) Part A is a summary of Tables 1 (A) and 2 (A), showing the final balance of total revenue against total expenditure.

(2) Part B shows the transactions of various official funds and other capital transactions which have the character of "borrowing" or "lending" rather than that of "revenue" or "expenditure." Transactions placing funds at the disposal of public authorities are shown as positive, while those absorbing funds are shown as negative. Changes in "balances" (cash and investments) are excluded.

(3) Part C shows the total of Parts A and B—i.e., the net change in funds available from revenue, borrowing, etc., after meeting expenditure and capital transfers which absorb funds.

(4) Part D is derived from Table 3 (A), and shows how the net change in funds is reflected in the increase or decrease of the balances held in the form of cash and investments.

(5) The figures of War Damage claims paid include estimated payments of War Risk (Goods) Insurance claims. The figures of sale of enemy property etc., are obtained as a residual, necessary to match the published balance sheet changes elsewhere. This residual includes also, as an anomalous element, decreases in the funds held, outside the government balance sheet, by the War Risk (Goods) Insurance Fund. However, outside assets held by the War Damage Commission are included in the figures of cash and investments in Table 3 (A) and in Part D of Table 4 (A).

(6) As explained in the Notes on Table 3 (A), the figures of Federation borrowing exclude changes in Treasury Bills and Treasury Deposit Receipts held by the War Damage Commission, the Employees' Provident Fund, and the Rubber Replanting Funds, these being treated as if they were direct deposits with the Federation Government.

(7) The figures of "Current Account Liabilities to the Singapore Government" include Federation liabilities for the costs of "relief supplies" incurred before 1949 and owing either to the Colony Government itself or to the Joint Supply Board, which was largely financed by the Colony Government. Purely bookkeeping adjustments, arising out of revisions in the estimated costs to be borne by the Federation, have been eliminated from the figures. Liabilities to Singapore also include (as explained in the General Note) certain adjustments in respect of war damage transactions.

(8) "Liabilities for Food Purchases" are from the (unpublished) accounts of the Supplies Department.

(9) "Other Miscellaneous Net Liabilities" are residual figures, being the net balance of all transactions other than those separately shown in the Table. The annual movements are quite small.

TABLE 5 (A)   Consolidated Accounts of Public Authorities, Federation
Public Finance

[Summary, from Table 4 (A)]

(Million $)

	1949	1950	1951	1952	1953
A. *Revenue Balance*	− 28	+ 87	+151	− 55	−227
B. *Finance*					
(1) *Net Finance from Malayan Public & Banks*					
Net Local Bonds (issues *less* investments)	− 4	− 1	+ 7	+ 20	+ 19
Net Treasury Bills, etc. (issues *less* cash)	− 4	—	− 11	− 62	+ 16
Post Office Savings Bank Deposits	+ 11	+ 10	+ 23	+ 12	+ 10
Rubber Replanting Funds (net receipts)	—	—	+ 50	+ 62	+ 17
Employees' Provident Fund (net receipts)	—	—	—	+ 19	+ 57
War Damage: Property Sales & Loan Repayments	+ 9	+ 26	+ 36	+ 70	+ 19
Less Claims Paid	− 8	− 19	− 55	−144	−109
Miscellaneous Transactions	+ 1	+ 5	− 2	− 10	+ 2
Total	+ 5	+ 21	+ 48	− 33	+ 31
(2) *Net Finance from Abroad*					
U.K. War Damage Gift and Loan	—	—	+ 34	+ 68	+ 89
Other Borrowing Abroad	+ 68	+ 22	+ 14	+ 48	− 26
Less Increase in Sterling Cash & Investments	− 35	−130	−241	− 34	+118
Total	+ 33	−108	−193	+ 82	+181
(3) *Net Finance from Malayan Official Sources*					
Singapore Government	− 18	− 9	− 16	− 6	+ 3
Sinking Fund Provisions	+ 8	+ 9	+ 10	+ 12	+ 12
Total	− 10	—	− 6	+ 6	+ 15
Total: Net Finance	+ 28	− 87	−151	+ 55	+227

B CONSOLIDATED ACCOUNTS OF PUBLIC AUTHORITIES— COLONY OF SINGAPORE

General Note

(1) These accounts are a consolidation of the accounts of the following authorities: Colony Government; Singapore City Council; Singapore Improvement Trust; the Rural, Education and Hospital Boards; Singapore Harbour Board; and the Post Office Savings Bank (Singapore).

(2) The accounts of the Harbour Board, which are for financial years ending June 30th, have been incorporated as if they were for calendar years (i.e., 1948-49 becomes 1949, etc.).

(3) Figures for 1954 are from the approved Estimates.

TABLE 1 (B)   Consolidated Accounts of Public Authorities, Singapore
Revenue

(Million $)

	1949	1950	1951	1952	1953	1954 (Budget Estimates)
Direct Taxes						
Income Tax	30	27	51	73	103	70
Estate Duty	3	3	4	5	4	4
Total	33	30	55	78	107	74
Indirect Taxes						
Import Duties	40	44	58	62	64	62
Excise, Stamp and Other Duties and Taxes	10	12	18	19	19	19
Local Government Rates	8	9	11	13	17	18
Licenses	7	8	11	12	13	12
Total	65	73	98	106	113	111
Surplus of Commercial Undertakings						
Posts and Telecommunications . .	4	3	3	4	4	—
Electricity, Water and Gas Supplies	8	11	11	10	15	17
Harbour Board	4	6	11	11	9	9
Singapore Improvement Trust . .	1	1	1	—	—	2
Total	17	21	26	25	28	28

TABLE I (B)—continued

(*Million $*)

	1949	1950	1951	1952	1953	1954
						(Budget Estimates)
Revenue from Property						
Rents	4	4	4	5	5	4
Net Interest Received	1	1	6	6	6	4
Total	5	5	10	11	11	8
Fees and Charges for Services, etc.						
Local Government	6	7	9	11	11	15
Education	1	1	1	1	2	2
Other Fees and Charges	3	3	5	4	6	6
Miscellaneous Receipts	7	4	7	11	7	6
Total	17	15	22	27	26	29
Total: Ordinary Revenue	137	144	211	247	285	250
U.K. Colonial Development and Welfare Grants	—	—	1	—	1	10
Total: Revenue	137	144	212	247	286	260

Notes on Table 1 (B)

(1) Local Government rates are those of the City Council and Rural Board. The Education Board rate is included under "Fees and Charges for Services, etc." and the Improvement Rate is taken into account in the "surplus" of the Singapore Improvement Trust.

(2) "Surplus of Commercial Undertakings" is the excess of sales revenue, etc. over current operating expenses, excluding any debt service or financial provision for depreciation. In the case of the Singapore Improvement Trust (which for convenience has been treated as a commercial undertaking) revenue includes rents received and the proceeds of the Improvement Rate, but not Colony Government contributions.

(3) "Net Interest Received" combines into one account all the interest payments and receipts of all government authorities including the commercial undertakings. Interest payments and receipts between Singapore Government authorities thus cancel out. Included are the receipt of interest on securities held in surplus funds, etc., and in sinking funds, and the receipt of currency profits; also net interest received by the Savings Bank after deducting interest due to depositors. Interest paid on the public debt, etc. (including the debt of the City Council), appears as a negative element.

(4) Federation contributions to Colony revenue (for joint services, etc.) have been excluded altogether, the corresponding expenditure being deducted in Table 2 (B).

TABLE 2 (B)   Consolidated Accounts of Public Authorities, Singapore
Expenditure

(*Million $*)

	1949	1950	1951	1952	1953	1954
Recurrent Expenditure						(Budget
Economic Services						Estimates)
Agriculture, Fisheries, Lands,						
Survey, etc.	1	1	1	2	2	2
Civil Aviation, Marine, Meteorological						
Services, etc.	3	3	3	4	4	6
Total	4	4	4	6	6	8
Social Services						
Education	7	13	15	18	21	31
Health	11	10	16	19	22	26
Social Welfare and Other	1	2	3	4	6	7
Total	19	25	34	41	49	64
Other Governmental Services						
Local Government	19	20	24	27	29	33
Defense and Police	15	12	20	33	28	39
Administration and Miscellaneous	36	32	33	30	31	35
Total	70	64	77	90	88	107
Current Transfers						
Pensions, etc.	5	5	5	5	6	7
Sinking Fund Provisions	7	8	8	10	11	12
Total	12	13	13	15	17	19
Total: Recurrent Expenditure	105	106	128	152	160	198
Capital Expenditure						
Economic Services						
Agriculture, Fisheries, etc. . . .	—	—	—	—	—	3
Civil Aviation, etc.	1	1	1	8	8	13
Total	1	1	1	8	8	16

TABLE 2 (B)—continued

(Million $)

	1949	1950	1951	1952	1953	1954
						(Budget Estimates)
Social Services						
Education	—	3	3	3	3	8
Health and Other	1	1	1	3	4	11
Total	1	4	4	6	7	19
Other Governmental Services						
Local Government	4	4	4	5	4	9
Defense and Police	—	—	1	4	3	6
Housing for Government Servants	—	1	1	1	1	2
Administration and Miscellaneous	—	1	2	2	2	3
Total	4	6	8	12	10	20
Commercial Undertakings						
Posts and Telecommunications . .	1	1	—	1	1	4
Electricity, Water and Gas Supplies	9	14	26	38	43	49
Harbour Board	1	1	3	4	2	2
Singapore Improvement Trust . .	4	8	12	15	11	23
Food Supplies (Stocks)	—	—3	3	—	—3	—
Total	15	21	44	58	54	78
Total: Capital Expenditure . .	21	32	57	84	79	133
Total: Recurrent and Capital						
Expenditure	126	138	185	236	239	331

Notes on Table 2 (B)

(1) Federation contributions (for joint services, etc.) have been deducted from "Administrative and Miscellaneous" expenditure (since usually the actual object of the expenditure cannot be identified).

(2) The special grants of $4 million to the Federation in 1949 and $9 million to H.M.G. in 1952 are included in "Defense and Police" expenditure.

(3) "Sinking Fund Provisions" represent the total accumulation of sinking funds, including estimated interest earnings as well as annual contributions.

(4) The distinction between "recurrent" and "capital" expenditure is necessarily somewhat arbitrary. Broadly, capital expenditure refers to the construction of new public works, roads, buildings, etc., and the installation of equipment of a fairly permanent value, whether from revenue or from loan funds. Many items classified as "special expenditure" in the

accounts have been treated as "recurrent"—including, generally, expenditure on motor vehicles, and on office, education and medical furniture and equipment. There is also some element of arbitrariness in the classification of expenditures under particular headings, arising from cases where it was difficult to tell from the published accounts the exact nature of a particular expenditure. This and the division made by the mission between "recurrent" and "capital" expenditure account for the minor differences between the expenditure shown here for "Social Services" and those shown in Chapter 7, which latter have been revised on the basis of more recent tabulations prepared by the particular departments concerned.

(5) "Housing for Government Servants" covers expenditure readily identifiable as such, but additional provision for housing, quarters, etc., is included under education, health and other heads.

(6) Net expenditure on food supplies is shown as "Capital Expenditure"—it represents mainly the net change in food stocks, but includes also trading losses (positive) or profits (negative), since the figures are from the food account advances shown in the Colony Government's balance sheets.

(7) Purchase of land is generally excluded from expenditure [appearing "below the line" in Table 4 (B)], but some land purchases, associated with other forms of capital expenditure (e.g., aerodrome construction) remain in the expenditure figures.

(8) Because of variations in the presentation of accounts from year to year, the classification of expenditure is not always consistent.

TABLE 3 (B) Consolidated Accounts of Public Authorities, Singapore
Cash and Investments

(Million $)

| | End of Year | | | | | | | | | | | | | | | | | |
| | 1948 | | | 1949 | | | 1950 | | | 1951 | | | 1952 | | | 1953 | | |
	Ma-layan	Stg.	Total	Ma-layan	Stg.	Total	Ma-layan	Stg.	Total	Ma-layan	Stg.	Total	Ma-layan	Stg.	Total	Ma-layan	Stg.	Total
Cash																		
Colony Government	26	−14	12	23	8	31	22	12	34	13	1	14	16	5	21	10	29	39
Other	4	—	4	7	—	7	11	2	13	16	3	19	12	5	17	12	2	14
Total	30	−14	16	30	8	38	33	14	47	29	4	33	28	10	38	22	31	53
Sinking Fund Investments																		
Colony Government	—	22	22	—	27	27	—	32	32	—	37	37	—	42	42	—	47	47
Other	11	13	24	11	15	26	14	15	29	17	15	32	18	19	37	24	19	43
Total	11	35	46	11	42	53	14	47	61	17	52	69	18	61	79	24	66	90
Other Investments																		
Colony Government	1	59	60	1	65	66	1	65	66	11	120	131	14	154	168	19	187	206
Post Office Savings Bank	11	27	38	7	23	30	7	25	32	9	30	39	11	35	46	15	39	54
Other	21	19	40	20	16	36	14	16	30	14	24	38	18	22	40	22	27	49
Total	33	105	138	28	104	132	22	106	128	34	174	208	43	211	254	56	253	309

TABLE 3 (B)—continued

(Million $)

	1948			1949			1950			1951			1952			1953		
	Ma-layan	Stg.	Total	Ma-layan	Stg.	Total	Ma-layan	Stg.	Total	Ma-layan	Stg.	Total	Ma-layan	Stg.	Total	Ma-layan	Stg.	Total
Total Cash and Investments																		
Sinking Funds (Govt. & Other)	11	35	46	11	42	53	14	47	61	17	52	69	18	61	79	24	66	90
Post Office Savings Bank	11	27	38	7	23	30	7	25	32	9	30	39	11	35	46	15	39	54
Colony Government	27	45	72	24	73	97	23	77	100	24	121	145	30	159	189	29	216	245
Other	25	19	44	27	16	43	25	18	43	30	27	57	30	27	57	34	29	63
Total	74	126	200	69	154	223	69	167	236	80	230	310	89	282	371	102	350	452

Column group header: End of Year

NOTES: (1) For authorities included, see General Note. Some very minor holdings have been neglected.

(2) Sterling cash consists of Joint Colonial Fund deposits (advances shown as negative). Malayan cash is chiefly deposits in Malayan banks, with small amounts of notes and coin.

(3) Investments are shown as at market value at the end of 1948, and at estimated net cost in respect of changes thereafter—i.e., annual changes represent the actual funds absorbed by the purchase, or released by the sale, of securities. The market value of all investments was about $20 million less than is here shown at the end of 1953.

(4) Malayan investments consist of securities denominated in Malayan dollars and issued by Malayan Governments and semi-government authorities.

(5) Sterling investments consist of securities denominated in sterling and issued in London by U.K. Dominion and Colonial Governments, with the exception of a small amount of Indian rupee securities.

TABLE 4 (B) Consolidated Accounts of Public Authorities, Singapore Revenue, Expenditure, and Capital Transactions

(Million $)

	1949	1950	1951	1952	1953
A. *Revenue Balance*					
(1) *Revenue* [Table 1(B)]					
Ordinary Revenue	+137	+144	+211	+247	+285
U.K. Colonial Development &					
Welfare Grants	—	—	+ 1	—	+ 1
Total	+137	+144	+212	+247	+286
Less					
(2) *Expenditure* [Table 2(B)]					
Recurrent Expenditures	−105	−106	−128	−152	−160
Capital Expenditure	− 21	− 32	− 57	− 84	− 79
Total	−126	−138	−185	−236	−239
Total: Revenue Balance . . .	+ 11	+ 6	+ 27	+ 11	+ 47
B. *Net Funds Raised on Capital Account*					
(1) *Borrowing in Malaya*					
City Council Bonds	—	—	+ 24	+ 26	+ 27
Colony Treasury Bills	− 11	− 21	—	—	—
Post Office Savings Bank Deposits	− 8	+ 2	+ 7	+ 7	+ 7
Less: Current Account Advances to					
Federation Govt.	+ 18	+ 9	+ 16	+ 6	− 3
Total	− 1	− 10	+ 47	+ 39	+ 31
(2) *Miscellaneous Transactions*					
Land Transfers, etc.	− 1	− 1	− 1	− 7	− 9
Other Miscellaneous Net Liabilities	+ 7	+ 10	− 7	+ 8	—
Total	+ 6	+ 9	− 8	+ 1	− 9
(3) *Sinking Fund Provisions* (from Revenue)	+ 7	+ 8	+ 8	+ 10	+ 12
Total: Net Funds Raised on					
Capital Account	+ 12	+ 7	+ 47	+ 50	+ 34

TABLE 4 (B)—continued

(*Million $*)

	1949	1950	1951	1952	1953
C. *Total Balance, Revenue and Capital Account*					
Revenue Account	+ 11	+ 6	+ 27	+ 11	+ 47
Capital Account	+ 12	+ 7	+ 47	+ 50	+ 34
Total: Balance	+ 23	+ 13	+ 74	+ 61	+ 81
D. *Increase in Cash and Investments* [Table 3(B)]					
Cash in Banks, etc. in Malaya . .	—	+ 3	— 4	— 1	— 6
Malayan Investments	— 5	— 3	+ 15	+ 10	+ 19
Sterling Cash and Investments . .	+ 28	+ 13	+ 63	+ 52	+ 68
Total: Cash and Investments .	+ 23	+ 13	+ 74	+ 61	+ 81

Notes on Table 4 (B)

(1) Part A is a summary of Tables 1 (B) and 2 (B), showing the final balance of total revenue against total expenditure.

(2) Part B shows capital transactions which have the character of "borrowing" or "lending" rather than that of "revenue" or "expenditure." Transactions placing funds at the disposal of public authorities are shown as positive, while those absorbing funds are shown as negative. Changes in "balances" (cash and investments) are excluded.

(3) Part C shows the total of Parts A and B—i.e., the net change in funds available from revenue, borrowing, etc., after meeting expenditure and capital transfers which absorb funds.

(4) Part D is derived from Table 3 (B), and shows how the net change in funds is reflected in the increase or decrease of the balances held in the form of cash and investments.

(5) "Current Account Advances to the Federation Government" are partly estimated (owing to successive changes in the presentation of accounts) and include changes in debts owed by the Federation Government to the Joint Supply Board, which was largely financed by the Colony Government (in effect, the Joint Supply Board has been treated as part of the Colony Government). The figures have also been adjusted, as explained in the notes on the Consolidated Accounts for the Federation, so as to treat all war damage and related property sale transactions as Federation transactions.

(6) "Other Miscellaneous Net Liabilities" are residual figures, being the net balance of all transactions other than those separately shown in the Table. The annual movements are quite small.

TABLE 5 (B)   Consolidated Accounts of Public Authorities, Singapore
Public Finance

[Summary, from Table 4 (B)]

(*Million $*)

	1949	1950	1951	1952	1953
A. *Revenue Balance*	+11	+ 6	+27	+11	+47
B. *Finance*					
(1) *Net Finance from Malayan Public and Banks*					
Net Local Bonds (issues *less* investments)	+ 5	+ 3	+ 9	+16	+ 8
Net Treasury Bills, etc. (issues *less* cash)	−11	−24	+ 4	+ 1	+ 6
Post Office Savings Bank Deposits . . .	− 8	+ 2	+ 7	+ 7	+ 7
Miscellaneous Transactions	+ 6	+ 9	− 8	+ 1	− 9
Total	− 8	−10	+12	+25	+12
(2) *Net Finance from Abroad*					
· Sterling Cash & Investments [increase (−) decrease (+)]	−28	−13	−63	−52	−68
(3) *Net Finance from Malayan Official Sources*					
Federation Government	+18	+ 9	+16	+ 6	− 3
Sinking Fund Provisions	+ 7	+ 8	+ 8	+10	+12
Total	+25	+17	+24	+16	+ 9
Total: Net Finance	−11	− 6	−27	−11	−47

C *TABLES RELATING TO THE BALANCE OF PAYMENTS, CAPITAL FORMATION AND SAVING, AND THE NATIONAL INCOME OF MALAYA*

TABLE 6 Merchandise Trade, Malaya

(Million $)

	1949	1950	1951	1952	1953
Exports of Domestic Produce (f.o.b.)					
Rubber	558	1,522	2,279	1,277	898
Tin	241	412	506	470	351
Coconut products	49	74	85	48	58
Palm oil and kernels	42	37	45	49	37
Sawn timber	5	12	12	6	13
Canned pineapples	6	12	17	13	19
Arecanuts	2	6	7	6	6
Sago and tapioca	5	7	13	9	13
Iron ore	7	9	17	23	21
Scrap metal	5	3	12	17	14
All others	23	35	58	55	56
Total exports of domestic produce	943	2,129	3,051	1,973	1,486
Re-exports (f.o.b.)	779	1,887	3,025	1,946	1,534
Total merchandise exports (f.o.b.)	1,722	4,016	6,076	3,919	3,020
Imports for Domestic Consumption (c.i.f.)					
Rice	200	177	222	213	277
Other foodstuffs	315	388	538	566	516
Drink and tobacco	63	74	106	114	101
Petroleum products	78	77	120	171	170
Textile manufactures	169	221	355	211	135
Vehicles, machinery, iron and steel, etc.	181	219	432	458	337
All others	185	293	539	442	328
Total imports for domestic consumption (c.i.f.)	1,191	1,449	2,312	2,175	1,864
Imports for re-export (c.i.f.) . .	660	1,466	2,443	1,698	1,374
Total merchandise imports (c.i.f.)	1,851	2,915	4,755	3,873	3,238
Merchandise trade balance . . .	−129	+1,101	+1,321	+ 46	−218

NOTES: (a) Total exports and imports are as recorded by the Registrar of Malayan Statistics, including parcel post, ships' stores and bunkers.
(b) Commodity items and the division in total between domestic and entrepot trade depend on

the analyses and estimates explained in the Notes on Table 1, p. 129. It should be noted that the method employed to estimate entrepot trade has the effect that any changes in stocks of goods intended for re-export are reflected in the figures of exports of domestic produce or of imports for domestic consumption.

(c) Declared values of trade, as recorded, are in some cases subject to considerable possibilities of error.

TABLE 7 Balance of Payments, Malaya

(Million $)

	1949	1950	1951	1952	1953
A. *Current Account*					
(Net receipts from abroad shown +)					
(1) *Goods and Services*					
Exports of domestic produce (f.o.b.) . .	+ 943	+2,129	+3,051	+1,973	+1,486
Imports for domestic consumption (c.i.f.)	−1,191	−1,449	−2,312	−2,175	−1,864
Sub-total: Domestic trade	− 248	+ 680	+ 739	− 202	− 378
Re-exports	+ 779	+ 1887	+ 3025	+ 1946	+ 1534
Imports for re-export	− 660	− 1466	− 2443	− 1698	− 1374
Sub-total: Entrepot trade	+ 119	+ 421	+ 582	+ 248	+ 160
Expenditure in Malaya by H.M. Forces	+ 160	+ 220	+ 270	+ 260	+ 260
Other net receipts for goods and services	+ 5	+ 15	− 2	− 13	− 4
Sub-total: Other goods and services	+ 165	+ 235	+ 268	+ 247	+ 256
Total: Net receipts for goods and services +	36	+ 1336	+ 1589	+ 293	+. 38
(2) *Transfers*					
Family remittances abroad	− 50	− 100	− 200	− 200	− 200
Net profits, dividends, etc. payable abroad	− 150	− 590	− 700	− 220	− 120
Sub-total: Private transfers	− 210	− 690	− 900	− 420	− 320
Government pensions	− 9	− 10	− 11	− 12	− 13
Interest received on official sterling investments, etc.	+ 19	+ 23	+ 37	+ 40	+ 48
Interest paid on official external debt . .	− 2	− 3	− 4	− 4	− 4
U.K. grants in aid of revenue	+ 44	+ 28	+ 3	− 2	+ 7
Sub-total: Official transfers	+ 52	+ 38	+ 25	+ 22	+ 38
Total: Net transfer receipts	− 158	− 652	− 875	− 398	− 282
Total: Balance on Current Account .	− 122	+ 684	+ 714	− 105	− 244

TABLE 7—continued

(Million $)

	1949	1950	1951	1952	1953
B. *Capital Account*					
(Net receipts from abroad shown +)					
(1) *Identifiable Items*					
New public loans raised abroad	+ 68	+ 5	+ 14	+ 10	+ 13
Liabilities for official food purchases, etc.	—	+ 17	—	+ 38	— 39
U.K. War Damage gift and loan	—	—	+ 34	+ 68	+ 89
Sub-total: Official borrowing, etc. .	+ 68	+ 22	+ 48	+ 116	+ 63
Sterling balances					
Federation authorities	— 35	— 130	— 241	— 34	+ 118
Singapore authorities	— 28	— 13	— 63	— 52	— 68
Currency Board	— 8	— 244	— 143	— 33	+ 37
Commercial Banks	+ 20	— 174	— 250	+ 93	+ 29
Sub-total: Inflow of sterling balances .	— 51	— 561	— 697	— 26	+ 116
Total: Net receipts from identifiable items +	17	— 539	— 649	+ 90	+ 179
(2) *Private Capital Inflow, Errors and Omissions* +	105	— 145	— 65	+ 15	+ 65
Total: Balance on Capital Account .	+ 122	— 684	— 714	+ 105	+ 244

Notes on Table 7

(a) The figures in this Table, other than those available from official trade records, public accounts, etc., are unofficial estimates made by the mission, based on data supplied by the Registrar of Malayan Statistics and on other information. Many of the figures are no more than "informed guesses" and due caution should therefore be employed in using the Table.

(b) "Expenditure in Malaya by H.M. Forces" is local expenditure, excluding munitions, etc., which were not recorded as imports in the official trade returns.

(c) "Other net receipts for goods and services" includes, as positive items, estimates of freight earned by Malayan ships, earnings of Malayan seamen remitted to Malaya, expenditure in Malaya by overseas ships' crews, travellers and tourists, expenditure on repair, etc., by overseas ships, and expenditure on consulates, etc., by overseas governments; and as negative items, estimates of travel and tourist expenditure by Malayans abroad, film royalties, various overseas business expenses, such as the head office expenses of overseas firms operating in Malaya, and an adjustment for ships' stores and bunker fuel supplied to Malayan ships and recorded as exports (prior to 1953).

(d) "Family remittances abroad" are more or less token figures, based on incomplete exchange control data.

(e) "Net profits, dividends, etc. payable abroad" includes the *whole* of the estimated net profits earned in Malaya by nonresident companies and their subsidiaries (after payment of tax), any reinvestment of such profits appearing under capital account as "private capital inflow." Estimated dividends payable to nonresident shareholders in Malayan companies are also included, together with other types of income payable abroad, except government pensions. The estimates of profit levels, etc., and of the proportions payable abroad were based on information from various sources—price and cost data (especially for the rubber and tin industries), taxation statistics, published accounts, analysis of shareholdings in Malayan-incorporated companies, etc., but are subject to a wide margin of error. (See in particular Note (f) below.) Estimated deductions for Malayan taxes refer to the tax payments actually made in the calendar year shown; hence the very low figure for 1953 in part reflects the collection in that year of taxes due on the higher profits earned in 1951 and 1952.

(f) No attempt has been made to adjust the declared values of imports and exports, as officially recorded, for probable errors and omissions (e.g., smuggled opium, errors of valuation involved in barter trade with Indonesia, tendency for rubber exports to be declared at the current price of R.S.S. No. 1 rather than at the actual f.o.b. price received). In general, we could find no basis for making such adjustments in one direction or the other. However, there is reason to suspect a particularly substantial overvaluation of rubber exports in 1950 and 1951 (possibly resulting from the very sharp and unexpected peak in rubber prices at the end of 1950 and the beginning of 1951, much of which may have been lost to Malaya under forward contracts); if so, the error is partly offset in the balance of payments as a whole by a corresponding overestimate of profits payable abroad in 1950 and 1951, since our estimates of rubber company profits also reflect the declared values of rubber exports.

(g) "Interest received on official sterling investments, etc." includes interest on sterling securities held by the Federation and Colony Governments, Harbour Boards, Singapore City Council, Post Office Savings Banks, municipal authorities, etc. (sinking funds as well as surplus funds), and also includes interest received by the Currency Board. The latter figure is net, after deducting currency profits distributed to Sarawak, North Borneo and Brunei, and external expenses (costs of minting, etc.).

(h) Under capital account, "Official borrowing, etc." is all on behalf of Federation authorities and the figures are taken from the Consolidated Accounts of Public Authorities [Table 4 (A)].

(i) For "Inflow of sterling balances" see Table 8.

(j) "Private capital inflow, errors and omissions" is the residual of the whole Table. Apart from miscellaneous errors and omissions, it includes not only the reinvestment of profits earned in Malaya by overseas firms and the net inflow (or outflow resulting from other deliberate private capital movements, but also casual changes from year to year in the amount of private credit (nonbank) outstanding in the ordinary course of trade, with discrepancies resulting from the fact that the timing of "import" and "export," as recorded, does not correspond with the timing of "purchase" and "sale." Therefore, even if all the other items in the Table were complete and correct, the residual for any one year could not be taken to measure the amount of deliberate movement of private capital into or out of Malaya, although over a series of years it should give a guide to such movements.

(k) There is one further general qualification to the interpretation of the capital account transactions. The figures for "Inflow of sterling balances" include the changes in Currency Board sterling assets which are the counterpart of Malayan currency held in Sarawak, North Borneo and Brunei (officially part of the Malayan currency area) and also in Indonesian territories. To the extent that holdings of Malayan currency outside Malaya have increased—as they probably have in each of the years shown in the Table—the effect is to add to the sterling balances of the Currency Board. This element is then reflected in the residual "Private capital inflow, etc.," increasing the apparent inflow or reducing the apparent outflow. In effect, the acceptance outside Malaya of Malayan currency is treated as an element of private capital inflow—which, in a sense, it is. The amount involved cannot be estimated year by year, but over the period as a whole it probably totalled upwards of $50 million.

TABLE 8   Malayan Sterling Balances, 1949-1953

(Million $)

	End of Year					
	1948	1949	1950	1951	1952	1953
Federation Authorities	107	142	272	513	547	429
Singapore Authorities	126	154	167	230	282	350
Currency Board	460	468	712	855	888	851
Commercial Banks	209	189	363	613	520	491
Total	902	953	1,514	2,211	2,237	2,121

NOTES: (a) Holdings by Federation and Singapore authorities include securities, etc., held by the Post Office Savings Banks and in Sinking Funds, as well as those held in the surplus funds, etc., of government, semi-government, and municipal authorities. See Table 3(A) and 3(B) in the Federation and Singapore "Consolidated Public Accounts."

(b) Currency Board holdings include London deposits and sterling securities. As with those of the Federation and Singapore authorities, securities are shown as at market value at the end of 1948, and at estimated net cost in respect of changes thereafter—i.e., annual changes represent the actual funds absorbed by the purchase, or released by the sale, of securities. The market value of Currency Board securities was $24 million less at the end of 1953 than the figure here shown. The market value of all sterling securities held by Federation and Singapore authorities and the Currency Board was some $50 million less at the end of 1953 than the figure here shown.

(c) Commercial bank holdings comprise net "balances due from banks abroad" (after deducting "balances due to banks abroad") and "overseas investments," as published in official Malayan statistics. It is not known on what basis "overseas investments" are valued, but they are an insignificant proportion of the total, most of which represents balances due by Head Offices of banks with branches operating in Malaya. Small holdings of balances in currencies other than sterling are included.

TABLE 9 Accounts of Currency Board, Malaya and British North Borneo

(Million $)

A. *Current and Capital Transactions*

	1949	1950	1951	1952	1953
Interest and commissions received	+12	+14	+20	+23	+25
less expenses of printing notes, etc.	− 3	− 2	− 2	− 5	− 1
less currency profits distributed to Borneo territories	—	—	—	− 2	− 1
Net income retained in Malaya . . .	+ 9	+12	+18	+16	+23
less currency profits distributed to Federation .	− 3	− 4	−10	− 6	− 8
less currency profits distributed to Singapore . .	− 1	− 1	− 3	− 4	− 4
Undistributed surplus	+ 5	+ 7	+ 5	+ 6	+11
Currency issued	+ 3	+237	+138	+27	−48
Increase in sterling cash and investments	+ 8	+244	+143	+33	−37

B. *Total Liabilities and Assets*

	1948	1949	1950	1951	1952	1953
Notes and coin held by commercial banks	97	91	113	105	152	114
Other notes and coin outstanding . .	308	319	533	680	660	650
Total currency outstanding . . .	405	410	646	785	812	764
Undistributed surplus	55	58	66	70	76	87
Sterling cash & investments . . .	460	468	712	855	888	851

NOTES: (a) Although this Table is derived from the annual reports of the Currency Commissioners, the accounts here shown do not correspond with the Board's accounts. For consistency with other Tables, we have eliminated in all years the pre-invasion notes written off by the Board in 1951 and 1953, and also eliminated throughout both the silver coin (believed to have been mainly melted down in earlier years) which was demonetized at the end of 1952 and its bullion value which was treated as an asset in the Board's account prior to that date. Further, we show securities as at market value at the end of 1948, and at net cost in respect of changes thereafter—i.e., annual changes represent the actual funds absorbed by the purchase, or released by the sale, of securities. The market value of securities was $24 million less at the end of 1953 than the figure shown here. These adjustments of course have a substantial effect on the figures shown for "undistributed surplus."

(b) "Notes and coin held by commercial banks" are from the quarterly banking returns.

TABLE 10   Liabilities and Assets of Commercial Banks, Malaya

(Million $)

	End of Year					
	1948	1949	1950	1951	1952	1953
A. *Liabilities*						
Demand deposits	581	565	865	1,054	989	857
Other deposits	81	106	155	185	223	250
Other net liabilities.	44	62	57	81	96	88
Total (liabilities)	706	733	1,077	1,320	1,308	1,195
Public authority deposits	57	63	88	99	119	107
Other deposits, etc.	649	670	989	1,221	1,189	1,088
Total (liabilities)	706	733	1,077	1,320	1,308	1,195
B. *Assets*						
(Percentage of total assets or liabilities shown in parentheses)						
Cash (Malayan notes and coin)	97 (14%)	91 (12%)	113 (11%)	105 (8%)	152 (12%)	114 (9%)
Treasury bills (Malayan) . . .	30 (4%)	7 (1%)	23 (2%)	26 (2%)	15 (1%)	10 (1%)
Local liquid assets	127 (18%)	98 (13%)	136 (13%)	131 (10%)	167 (13%)	124 (10%)
Local investments	111 (16%)	110 (15%)	117 (11%)	125 (10%)	137 (10%)	143 (12%)
Local loans and advances	259 (37%)	336 (46%)	461 (42%)	451 (34%)	484 (37%)	437 (37%)
Total local assets	497 (71%)	544 (74%)	714 (66%)	707 (54%)	788 (60%)	704 (59%)
Investments abroad	16 (2%)	28 (4%)	21 (2%)	28 (2%)	35 (3%)	39 (3%)
Balances due from banks abroad (net) .	193 (27%)	161 (22%)	342 (32%)	585 (44%)	485 (37%)	452 (38%)
Total (assets)	706 (100%)	733 (100%)	1,077 (100%)	1,320 (100%)	1,308 (100%)	1,195 (100%)

NOTES: (a) These figures are from the quarterly banking returns (Registrar of Malayan Statistics). Monthly returns do not always agree with quarterly returns for the same items, but it is believed that this is now the better series.

(b) "Demand deposits" include "margin held and sundry deposits" ($22 million in 1953, not previously distinguished). "Other deposits" consist of "time deposits" and "savings accounts." "Other net liabilities" is a residual figure, covering items in transit and other discrepancies in the reporting of local interbank balances (not here shown), and including also shareholders' funds, etc., *less* bank premises and other assets not shown in the published figures.

(c) "Public authority deposits" are from the "Consolidated Accounts of Public Authorities" tables. They include a small amount of notes and coin, but for convenience are here treated as if they consisted wholly of bank deposits.

(d) "Local investments" consist mainly of Malayan Government and semi-government bonds, but may include some private shares or debentures. "Local loans and advances" include bills locally drawn and discounted. "Investments abroad" are entirely, or almost entirely, sterling securities. "Balances due from banks abroad" are net, after deducting a very much smaller amount of "balances due to banks abroad." Most of these balances are due to Head Offices.

TABLE 11   Gross Private Capital Formation, Malaya

(Million $)

	1949	1950	1951	1952	1953
Fixed Capital Formation					
Machinery, equipment, etc.	70	95	115	150	115
Commercial vehicles and vessels . . .	15	20	50	65	50
New buildings	50	60	80	110	100
Agricultural and mining rehabilitation and development (n.e.s.)	60	40	40	35	35
Rubber replanting	20	25	40	45	40
Total	215	240	325	405	340
Value of Physical Increase in Stocks					
Rubber	−15	+30	−60	+ 5	−10
Tin	+40	−85	+ 5	− 5	+ 5
Other	+45	−35	+20	+100	+30
Total	+70	−90	−35	+100	+25
Total: Gross Private Capital Formation	285	150	290	505	365

NOTES: (a) The figures for "Fixed Capital Formation" are based chiefly on unpublished estimates prepared by the Registrar of Malayan Statistics. The mission has rounded the Registrar's figures, and made certain adjustments which are noted below. The figures relating to investment in stocks are estimates made by the mission, as explained below.

(b) The capital formation here estimated is "gross" in the sense that no deductions have been made to cover the depreciation of assets and the replacement of old assets by new ones. However, the figures do not include the cost of parts for machines, etc., or other expenditure incurred for the normal repair and maintenance of capital equipment and buildings. Passenger motor cars (other than taxi cabs) and durable consumer goods generally are excluded.

(c) The Registrar's estimates for machinery, etc., relate to total capital formation, public and private. We have therefore excluded items such as telecommunications and railways equipment which are identifiable as wholly or mainly intended for public authority investment, and also deducted a proportion of certain public capital expenditures (especially on electricity supply) which we estimate to represent the cost of imported equipment for public purposes included in the Registrar's figures. Any remaining duplication should not be large. On the other hand, we have made an extra allowance for the installation costs of capital equipment.

(d) The mission has made a substantial addition to the Registrar's figures for new private buildings (which are based on returns from architects), in order to allow for the cost of attap and other rural dwellings, especially in the Federation, and other private building omitted from the architects' returns.

(e) "Agricultural and mining rehabilitation and development (n.e.s.)" includes the cost of clearing and planting new land for rubber and other crops, the value of the increase in livestock, new capital expenditure on mines other than equipment, etc., already allowed for, and (especially in 1949) costs of postwar rehabilitation measures on mines and plantations. To cover the latter, the mission has considerably increased the Registrar's estimate for 1949. Smaller additions have been made in all years for miscellaneous developmental expenditure not covered in the official figures.

(f) Figures for expenditure on rubber replanting are mission estimates, based on the official statistics of acres replanted and estimated costs of planting and upkeep per acre.

(g) The "value of physical increase in stocks" differs from "increase in the value of stocks" in

TABLE 11—continued

that it excludes any revaluation of a given quantum of goods in stock as a result of price fluctuations. Figures for rubber and tin are the annual changes in stocks, as officially reported, valued at the average price prevailing during the year. Other direct information is available only for a few unrepresentative commodities. The figures for "other" stocks are therefore very rough estimates, obtained by using the movement in bank loans and advances as a guide to the value of total stocks, making appropriate allowance for price fluctuations (from the official indices of the average values of imports and exports), and deducting the previous estimates for rubber and tin to arrive at the figures shown. The results appear to be reasonable in the light of the business history of the period.

TABLE 12 Private Capital Account, Malaya

(Million $)

	1949	1950	1951	1952	1953
A. *Sources of Funds*					
(1) War damage compensation receipts	+ 8	+ 19	+ 55	+144	+109
(2) Private capital inflow from abroad	+105	−145	− 65	+ 15	+ 65
(3) Gross private domestic saving . .	+162	+716	+804	+416	+266
Total	+275	+590	+794	+575	+440
B. *Uses of Funds*					
(1) Absorption by private capital formation					
Gross fixed capital formation . . .	+215	+240	+325	+405	+340
Value of physical increase in stocks	+ 70	− 90	− 35	+100	+ 25
Total	+285	+150	+290	+505	+365
(2) Absorption by public authorities					
Private purchases of public authority securities	+ 16	− 20	+ 9	− 6	+ 36
Deposits with Post Office Savings Banks	+ 3	+ 12	+ 30	+ 19	+ 17
Accumulation in Federation Employees' Provident Fund . .	—	—	—	+ 19	+ 57
Accumulation in Rubber Replanting Funds	—	—	+ 50	+ 62	+ 17
Purchase of enemy property, etc. .	+ 9	+ 23	+ 16	+ 41	+ 6
Repayment of Federation loans for rehabilitation of mines . . .	—	+ 3	+ 20	+ 29	+ 13
Miscellaneous transactions with public authorities	+ 7	+ 14	− 10	− 9	− 7
Total	+ 35	+ 32	+115	+155	+139
(3) Absorption by commercial banks and Currency Board					
Private holdings of notes & coin .	+ 11	+214	+147	− 20	− 10
Private deposits etc., with commercial banks	+ 21	+319	+232	− 32	−101
Less loans and advances by commercial banks	− 77	−125	+ 10	− 33	+ 47
Total	− 45	+408	+389	− 85	− 64
Total	+275	+590	+794	+575	+440

NOTES: (a) The distinction between "sources" and "uses" in this Table is made purely for expository convenience, since both "sources" and "uses" are sometimes negative.

(b) Figures in A(1) are from the tables of "Consolidated Accounts of Public Authorities." Those in A(2) are from Table 7 above, and include not only true private capital inflow but the net outcome of all errors and omissions in the balance-of-payments estimates. Figures in A(3)—"Gross private domestic saving"—are obtained as the residual of this Table. (The combined total of "Private capital inflow" and "Gross private domestic saving" is therefore a much more reliable estimate than either item on its own, since in the combined total errors and omissions in the balance-of-payments estimates cancel out; the only major remaining uncertainty is then the accuracy of the estimates of gross private capital formation, on which the combined total, as a residual, depends.) The figures for private saving are "gross" to the extent that the figures for private capital formation are gross (see Notes on Table 11). The saving is "domestic", in the sense that it excludes the undistributed net profits of overseas firms (any reinvestment of the latter in Malaya being counted as private capital inflow), but it does include the depreciation provisions of all firms operating in Malaya, whether "resident or not". It also includes the saving represented by the share of overseas firms in the Rubber Replanting Funds, since the payment of the replanting cess and the receipt of refunds have been allowed for in estimating net profits payable abroad.

(c) Figures in B(1) are from Table 11 above. Figures in B(2) are from the tables of "Consolidated Accounts of Public Authorities," except that commercial bank holdings of local securities have been deducted from public authority security issues (using the figures of "local investments" and "treasury bills" held by banks given in Table 10 above). Securities held by public authorities themselves are excluded. Figures in B(3) are from Tables 9 and 10 above. "Private holdings of notes and coin" are the annual changes in "Other notes and coin outstanding" from Table 9 (the small public authority holdings of notes and coin being neglected). "Private deposits etc., with commercial banks" are the annual changes in "Other deposits etc." from Table 10. "Loans and advances by commercial banks" are also the annual changes in the totals given in Table 10.

TABLE 13   Public and Private Gross Capital Formation
and Its Financing, Malaya

(Million $)

	1949	1950	1951	1952	1953
A. *Gross Capital Formation*					
(1) *Public capital expenditure*					
Federation authorities	+ 71	+ 59	+111	+167	+156
Singapore authorities	+ 21	+ 32	+ 57	+ 84	+ 79
Total	+ 92	+ 91	+168	+251	+235
(2) *Private capital expenditure*					
Fixed capital	+215	+240	+325	+405	+340
Stocks	+ 70	− 90	− 35	+100	+ 25
Total	+285	+150	+290	+505	+365
Total	+377	+241	+458	+756	+600
B. *Sources of Finance*					
(1) *Gross saving of public authorities*					
Excess of ordinary revenue over					
recurrent expenditure—					
Federation	− 1	+118	+260	+105	− 77
Singapore	+ 32	+ 38	+ 83	+ 95	+125
Sinking Fund provisions—Federation	+ 8	+ 9	+ 10	+ 12	+ 12
Singapore	+ 7	+ 8	+ 8	+ 10	+ 12
Undistributed surplus, Currency					
Board	+ 3	+ 8	+ 4	+ 6	+ 11
Total	+ 49	+181	+365	+228	+ 83
(2) *U.K. grants and public borrowing abroad*					
C.D. and W. grants—Federation .	+ 1	+ 2	+ 2	+ 4	+ 5
Singapore .	—	—	+ 1	—	+ 1
Other U.K. grants in aid of revenue					
(Federation)	+ 43	+ 26	—	+ 3	+ 1
U.K. War Damage gift and loan .	—	—	+ 34	+ 68	+ 89
New public loans raised abroad					
(Federation)	+ 68	+ 5	+ 14	+ 10	+ 13
Other liabilities abroad (Federation)	—	+ 17	—	+ 38	− 39
Total	+112	+ 50	+ 51	+123	+ 70

TABLE 13—continued

(*Million $*)

	1949	1950	1951	1952	1953
(3) *Sterling balances of public authorities and banks*					
Federation authorities	− 35	−130	−241	− 34	+118
Singapore authorities	− 28	− 13	− 63	− 52	− 68
Currency Board	− 8	−244	−143	− 33	+ 37
Commercial banks	+ 20	−174	−250	+ 93	+ 29
Total	− 51	−561	−697	− 26	+116
(4) *Gross private domestic saving and private capital inflow*					
Gross private domestic saving . .	+162	+716	+804	+416	+266
Private capital inflow	+105	−145	− 65	+ 15	+ 65
Total	+267	+271	+739	+431	+331
Total	+377	+241	+458	+756	+600

NOTES: (a) This Table is a rearrangement of figures already given in the "Consolidated Accounts of Public Authorities" and the preceding Tables.

(b) There is an apparent contrast between this Table and the preceding Table 12 in that here the absorption of funds in holdings of notes and bank deposits, and the provision of funds by bank advances, is not in evidence. But changes in the sterling balances of the Currency Board and banks, which do appear in the above Table, are necessarily equal and opposite to the figures of "Absorption of funds by commercial banks and Currency Board" which appeared in Table 12, when allowance is made for the undistributed surplus of the Currency Board and for public authority as well as private transactions with the banks.

TABLE 14   Gross National Income and Expenditure

(Million $)

	1949	1950	1951	1952	1953
A. Gross Expenditure and Product					
1. Public Authority Expenditure on Goods and Services	440	460	730	950	1,005
2. Gross Private Capital Formation	285	150	290	505	365
3. Personal Consumption Expenditure . . .	2,790	3,400	4,910	4,600	4,370
4. *Gross Domestic Expenditure*	3,515	4,010	5,930	6,055	5,740
5. Net Exports etc. of Goods and Services .	35	1,335	1,590	295	40
6. *Gross National Product* (at market price) .	3,550	5,345	7,520	6,350	5,780
B. Gross Income and Product					
1. Gross Resident National Income	3,185	4,500	6,465	5,780	5,305
2. Net Profits, Interest, etc., Payable Abroad	150	580	680	195	90
3. *Gross National Income*	3,335	5,080	7,145	5,975	5,395
4. Indirect Taxes	215	265	375	375	385
5. *Gross National Product* (at market price) .	3,550	5,345	7,520	6,350	5,780
C. Gross Income by Industrial Origin					
1. Rubber	420	1,400	2,025	1,080	715
2. Mining	250	295	480	440	325
3. Other Agriculture and Forestry	840	1,030	1,380	1,355	1,430
4. All Other Activities	1,825	2,355	3,260	3,100	2,925
5. *Gross National Income*	3,335	5,080	7,145	5,975	5,395
D. Gross Private Income and Saving					
1. Gross National Income	3,335	5,080	7,145	5,975	5,395
2. *less* Public Authority Component	−25	−40	−45	−45	−55
3. *Gross Private Income*	3,310	5,040	7,100	5,930	5,340
4. *less* Private Net Profits, Interest, etc. Payable Abroad.	−160	−590	−700	−220	−120
5. *less* Direct Taxes	−150	−235	−485	−495	−385
6. *Gross Disposable Private Income*	3,000	4,215	5,915	5,215	4,835
7. *less* Personal Consumption Expenditure and Family Remittances	−2,840	−3,500	−5,110	−4,800	−4,570
8. *Gross Private Domestic Saving*	160	715	805	415	265

Notes on Table 14

Part A: "Public Authority Expenditure on Goods and Services" (line 1) is the total of the recurrent and capital expenditure shown in the "Consolidated Accounts of Public Authorities" [Tables 2 (A) and 2 (B)], excluding pension payments and sinking fund provisions and after deducting revenue from "Fees and Charges for Services etc.". The $9 million special defense contribution by Singapore to H.M.G. in 1952 has also been excluded. (Here and elsewhere in this Table figures appearing in other tables have been rounded to the nearest $5 million.) "Gross Private Capital Formation" (line 2) is from Table 11 above. "Personal Consumption Expenditure" (line 3) is expenditure on goods and services (at market price) as estimated by the mission, in the light of data prepared by the Registrar of Malayan Statistics. The estimates were made along the lines of those given for 1947–49 in Chapter V of Benham: *The National Income of Malaya*. (Allowance was made for changes in stocks of consumption goods already included in "Gross Private Capital Formation.") "Gross Domestic Expenditure" (line 4) is the total of all expenditure on goods and services for consumption, capital formation, and government purposes in Malaya. The total production of goods and services in Malaya—"Gross National Product" at market price (line 6)—is arrived at by adding to this expenditure the amount of goods and services sold abroad and subtracting goods and services purchased abroad, the net adjustment being shown as "Net Exports etc. of Goods and Services" (line 5). These figures are from the balance of payments estimated in Table 7 above.

Part B: The starting point of the figures in Part B is the "Gross National Product" derived in Part A and here repeated (line 5). "Gross National Income" (line 3) differs from "Gross National Product" in that it excludes indirect taxes, which form part of the market price at which goods and services are sold but not part of the incomes earned in production. "Indirect Taxes" (line 4) are as shown in Table 1 (A) and 1 (B) of the "Consolidated Public Accounts." They include import and excise duties, licenses, and local rates, but exclude export duties, which on conventional definitions would be regarded as indirect taxes but which in the Malayan situation it seems best to treat as direct taxes (e.g., as a type of income tax, levied on gross receipts rather than on net income). "Net Profits, Interest, etc. Payable Abroad" (line 2) is from the balance-of-payments estimates in Table 7 above. Deducting this from "Gross National Income," "Gross Resident National Income" (line 1) is obtained. This is the total income accruing to Malayan residents, as distinct from the income produced by activities in Malaya. All the figures of income and product are "gross" in the sense that no deduction has been made for the depreciation of capital equipment, etc. Further, they differ from the figures which would appear in the books of Malayan enterprises in that they include only the value of the physical change in stocks of goods, without any element of revaluation of stocks as prices change.

Part C: The division of "Gross National Income" between the four industrial sectors shown is a very rough one, made by the mission to provide some indication of the orders of magnitude involved. The gross income shown consists in each case of the total estimated value of output, less estimated costs of production (materials, freight, etc.) incurred outside the industry in question—in other words, it is the sum of the wages, interest, rent, and gross profits earned in the industry. However, "industry" is so defined as to include dealing and processing as well as primary production—

e.g., the gross income shown for the rubber industry includes the incomes earned by the dealers in and processors of Malayan rubber as well as those earned on plantations and smallholdings.

Part D: The "Public Authority Component" (line 2), which is subtracted from "Gross National Income" (line 1) to arrive at "Gross Private Income" (line 3), consists of the income earned by public authority commercial undertakings, *plus* transfers to public authorities in the form of rents and royalties, *less* transfers to private income in the form of pensions etc., and net interest paid to Malayan residents. These figures are from the Tables of "Consolidated Public Accounts," adjusted for external pensions and interest as shown in Table 7 above. "Private Net Profits, Interest, etc. Payable Abroad" (subtracted in line 4) is also from Table 7 above; "Direct Taxes" (subtracted in line 5) consists of income tax and estate duty, from the "Consolidated Public Accounts." "Gross Disposable Private Income" (line 6) is then obtained, as the gross income remaining at the disposal of Malayan residents. This is employed partly for "Personal Consumption Expenditure and Family Remittances" (line 7)—the figures are as given in Part A, line 3, *plus* "family remittances abroad" from Table 7 above. The final remainder is "Gross Private Domestic Saving" (line 8), which except for rounding corresponds with the figures already given in Table 12 above.

INDEX

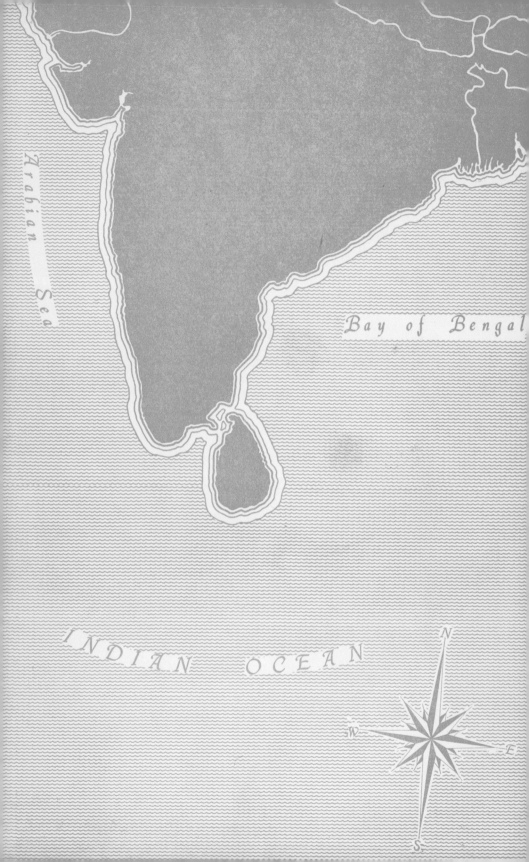